14 Days

W9-AXC-143

MODERN
British
DRAMAS

Edited by Harlan Hatcher

PROFESSOR OF ENGLISH, OHIO STATE UNIVERSITY

NEW YORK · MCMXLI

HARCOURT, BRACE AND COMPANY

PRINTED IN THE UNITED STATES OF AMERICA

CONTENTS

MODERN BRITISH DRAMA

MODERN British Drama has had many interesting moments, though it has never quite achieved a position of world leadership. When modern drama is mentioned the mind turns at once to Norway, Sweden, Russia, France, Germany, Central Europe, and America; it comes to England last of all. The British response to modern drama was reluctant and belated. British dramatists were hesitant about experimentation with new themes and new forms. Not one of the important currents or manifestations of modern drama originated in England or received any significant advancement at the hands of her playwrights or in her theatres.

British dramatists seemed strangely indisposed to come seriously and honestly to grips with life. Wilde was gay and artificial, specializing in intellectual comedy that often turned on a pun, or, as we now say, the wise-crack. Shaw, with all his intelligence and his wit, with all his style and range, succeeded largely by turning the method of Oscar Wilde upon more lively, topical, headline issues, usually of social import. Except for *Saint Joan, Androcles and the Lion,* and perhaps a few others, time has dealt harshly with the comedies of the brilliant Irish gadfly. Archer and Jones were excessively shy and irresolute in handling the potentially great themes of their plays. Barrie's contribution was his own kindly, Peter-Panish spirit. Even Pinero, Galsworthy, and Maugham, whose work best represents the English legacy in modern drama, kept well within the more ancient conventions of dramaturgy and the theatre.

Censorship may have had a subtle adverse effect upon the English dramatists. Less freedom has been allowed the London theatres than those in America or on the Continent. The playwrights and producers have made formal protests against the restrictions imposed upon them by the Government. In the earlier days of this century the Lord Chamberlain forbade Maeterlinck's *Monna Vanna;* Brieux's *Maternity,* and *The Three Daughters of M. Dupont;* Shaw's *Mrs. Warren's Profession;* Granville-Barker's *Waste;* Ibsen's *Ghosts;* and other plays. In more recent years *The Green Pastures,* which made theatrical history in America, and became one of the most cherished plays of our period, was solemnly banned in England. *Victoria Regina,* a huge success in New York and on tour in the United States, became a potent stimulant to the vogue of historical and biographical plays. It was denied to London audiences. *Desire Under the Elms,* one of O'Neill's greatest plays, admired and performed throughout the world, was kept under the Lord Chamberlain's ban for sixteen years, and could not be shown in London until the year 1940. British dramatists, generally conservative by temperament, have worked in an unfavorable, often in a hostile environment. It is not surprising that modern British drama, solid and substantial though it is, has always followed the advancing front at a conservative distance.

This is merely an observation on the fundamental character of modern British drama, not a derogatory criticism. Drama does not have to be experimental to be good. Despite the handicaps under which they have labored, the British have produced a number of distinguished plays and a few figures of world renown. Wilde may be artificial but he has grace, style, and beauty of language. Shaw was one of the most stinging and persuasive personalities in the English speaking world from the 1890's to the 1920's. He made talk exciting; he added to the world's small store of gaiety. As schoolmaster to one entire generation, he taught them to see the fallacies in the Victorian order, and to laugh at conventional shams. Archer, Jones, and Pinero were at least gifted and reputable transition figures. Galsworthy and Maugham were not given to experimentation, but in their respective manners they enriched and strengthened British drama and made it respected in Europe and America. These names alone give British drama a standing in the modern period.

The Irish drama was for a time more energetic, and it richly deserves the high praise it has received from all quarters. Any theatre that can number among its playwrights such figures as Lady Gregory, Lord Dunsany, Yeats, and Synge becomes naturally one of the important world centers of the drama. The first performances of the plays by these authors unleashed in audiences the fury of the Irish temper. The excitement has now grown quiescent. Following the cooling-off process, it is quite obvious that much of the world publicity given the Irish drama was occasioned less by the power or the newness of the plays themselves than by their riotous receptions. But the residue is a rich ore indeed. And although there has been a marked falling off in its general level of distinction, the Irish drama has been represented in recent years by St. John Ervine, Lennox Robinson, Sean O'Casey, and Paul Vincent Carroll—names that rank high at least in the company of their English contemporaries.

No recent dramatist in Britain has risen to the stature of Shaw, Galsworthy, and Maugham. No one has approached the standard set by O'Neill, or even Anderson, Sherwood, and Rice in America. Post-War drama in Britain has been interesting but not distinguished or engrossing. There has been a plethora of fairly competent playwrights who have kept the theatre open. They can usually be counted on to provide good entertainment for an evening. This is one legitimate function of the theatre, but it is the deeper and richer art of prying at life, of recreating and intensifying the stab and the thrust of the miracle of living, that lifts drama into significance.

Precisely this power is what we miss in the work of the score of English dramatists who come to mind in a catalogue of contemporary writers: John Drinkwater's biographical studies; John Van Druten's realistic plays, like *Young Woodley*, a study of a British school-boy; A. A. Milne's whimsical and engaging comedies, all bound up in harmless misunderstandings; Noel Coward's prolific outpouring of artificial pieces in a post-War adaptation of the Restoration mood; Halcott Glover's historical tragedies, biblical dramas, and realistic comedies; Harold Brighouse's and Stanley Houghton's studies of Midland middle and lower class characters; Clemence Dane's (Winifred Ashton) imaginative and poetic dramas like *Will Shakespeare*, and her realistic plays such as *A Bill of Divorcement* and *Granite;* Rudolph Besier's biographical plays; Clifford Bax's versatile productions in lyrical and thoughtful mood; James Bridie's studies of Edinburgh life and experiments in the phenomenon of time as in *The Sleeping Clergyman;* St. John Hankin, J. B. Priestley,

A. M. Shairp, R. C. Sheriff, Sutton Vane, Benn W. Levy—the list could go on and on like the rows of brick houses in a London suburb. These dramatists are all on an approximately equal level. No single figure towers over the scene to give it representation as Pinero, Galsworthy, and Maugham epitomized their respective eras.

A few individual plays have separated themselves from this mass by some unusual quality. This is especially true of Sutton Vane's *Outward Bound*, with its surprise disclosure that the ship is carrying a passenger list of the dead; of Rudolph Besier's *The Barretts of Wimpole Street*, with its dramatic handling of the conflict and the lyricism of the Browning's love affair; and of R. C. Sheriff's *Journey's End*, with its realistic presentation of the tragedy of war. Taken as a whole they do indicate the generally high level of the popular British theatre in the present day.

In a collection of thirty-one plays from the world at large, we pass over this vast output with some regret but with the comfort that in so doing we are not being blind or unjust. Perhaps a little more perspective may give major importance to some of these plays; perhaps also a few more years of growth may lift some of these playwrights into a position of distinction. The selections from British drama more or less dictate themselves. In this volume, however, appear three departures: Lord Dunsany's *If*, Monkhouse's *The Conquering Hero*, and the motion picture script of *The Informer*. The reasons are presented in the appropriate introductions.

SIR ARTHUR WING PINERO

SIR ARTHUR WING PINERO (1850–1934) served the English theatre for over fifty years, from 1877 to 1930, and produced on the average a play each year. A high percentage of them were successful on the stage. Few of them were, or were intended to be, anything more than good entertainment for an evening, but most of them pleased the customers. Any playwright who can entertain audiences continuously for a half-century in an English theatre may make at least a modest demand upon fame. And if he has any superiority of talent, the chances are at least fair that he may luckily hit off a play or two of distinction if not a masterpiece for the ages. Opinion on this point is not unanimous, but four of Pinero's fifty-two plays are easily outstanding both in the list of his works and in the not very notable bibliography of modern English plays: they are *The Second Mrs. Tanqueray* (1893), *Iris* (1901), *The Thunderbolt* (1908), and *Mid-Channel* (1909).

These plays were preceded by a long period of training on the stage and in writing for the theatre. *The Second Mrs. Tanqueray*, his first great critical success, was Pinero's twenty-seventh play. Those that preceded it are interesting solely from the point of view of Pinero's career and of the gloomy history of the English drama in the seventies and the eighties before Ibsen and the new theatre movement on the Continent crossed the Channel to reactivate it. Both serve to remind us that the modern movement in English drama is still recent enough to have been encom-passed by the active life of a man just dead.

Pinero was first of all a man of the theatre rather than a man of letters. His family was well placed and somewhat distinguished on both the Pinero and the Wing sides. He did not follow the fashionable pattern of public school and the university, but attended the London day schools, irregularly the evening classes at Birbeck Institute, and worked and studied with his solicitor father in his office at Lincoln's Inn Fields. His bent, however, was toward literature and the theatre. He wisely gave up the law and became an actor, apparently with a view toward trying his own hand at writing. The ambition was certainly not crushed by the prestige or the superlative merit of the plays then mounted on the English stage. When these vehicles were not ridiculous they were inconsequential. Any young man with talent, industry, and a little aptitude might hope to equal if not surpass the silly farces, the tricky adaptations from the French, and the sentimental sob-dramas that kept London and provincial theatres in operation.

Pinero had seven years of first-hand experience on the stage. He began by acting a minor part in Wilkie Collins's *The Woman in White* with the Wyndhams at the Theatre Royal in Edinburgh on June 22, 1874. His career included runs at Liverpool, Birmingham, and other provincial towns as well as in London, and a long association with Sir Henry Irving as character actor in his repertory of Shakespearean and modern plays. Pinero then gave up acting and turned full time to playwriting. At first he concocted farces and sentimental plays like those in fashion, no better and hardly worse than the general run of such trash. The cheap titles are an ominous give-away of the content of these pieces: *Two Can Play at That Game* (1877), *Daisy's Escape* (1879), *Hester's Mystery* (1880), *Girls and Boys* (1882), *The Hobby Horse* (1886), *Dandy Dick* (1887), *Sweet Lavender* (1888), et cetera. The only reason for not apologizing for listing plays of this order is that they show dramatically the poor estate of the English stage of the time; the man who was to be the foremost dramatist in England was turning out these pieces while Ibsen was writing the sensational series of plays from *A Doll's House* to *Hedda Gabler*. No wonder the Norwegian produced the effect of an explosion in the little isle.

These labors of Pinero were not a total loss. He learned the practical side of playmaking as seen by the actors who must get on and off the stage, and tell and act out a story in terms of drama and the theatre. Pinero mastered the technique. By the standards of his time, he was an expert stage carpenter who knew exactly how to knock together a piece that would play well. His plays might lack literary importance, but they gave satisfaction when spoken by a group of well-trained actors in the unreal atmosphere of a theatre where a not very intelligent group of people were gathered for diversion. Like a diligent professional man of the theatre, he had a fresh model ready for each new season. Such talent has an important place in a healthy theatre. The pretty good must not be prohibited because it is not a world-shattering masterpiece. The theatre can, without serious damage, use plays that never reach the literary distinction necessary to join the small anthology of great dramas that live in the library as well as in the exciting atmosphere created by a darkened theatre and a crowd of spectators.

We shall be under no critical illusions, then, about Sir Arthur and his plays. He was a good technician of the English stage, and he is historically one of its monumental institutions because he kept the theatres open. The plays that reward study are post-Ibsen. They show clearly how an intelligent but not original playwright kept pace with the advancing thought of his public, and how he geared the stage to the topics of the time. Pinero had in 1888 scored a financial hit with *Sweet Lavender*. It came at a lucky time, for it freed him from dependence just at the moment when the more serious plays on controversial problems were becoming acceptable to the torpid English mood. As Pinero himself rather pretentiously and somewhat inaccurately put it, he was thereafter able "to write great plays regardless of the predilections of the public."

The Second Mrs. Tanqueray produced a fair-sized sensation when the winsome Mrs. Patrick Campbell first played the fallen Paula at St. James's Theatre in London, May 27, 1893. It was so far in advance of the general run of English plays at the time that it is easy to understand why it has so often been cited as the beginning of modern drama in England. The structure of the play is a model within its own genre. The smooth, sharp, and crystal-clear exposition and character definition in the first act excites admiration. The routine suicide at the end is likewise manipulated with great skill. The flaws in construction, viewed from the perspective of a more diverse and richer technique, are quite obvious: the absence of a convincing motive for this pre-doomed marriage of Aubrey Tanqueray and Paula; the coincidental meeting in Paris of his innocent nineteen-year-old daughter with one of Paula's former lovers; and the return of this couple to Paula's house with the subsequent revelations, horrors, and suicide of Paula. Few plays, however, are devoid of weak links since the fundamental assumption of dramatic art itself is, from this point of view, artificial. The more serious objection to the play was the unconvincing effort at high seriousness in the theme itself. The problem is actually handled quite conventionally, in sharp contrast to the Ibsen, Strindberg, Hauptmann models. Later critics have summarized its theme in the aphorism: don't marry a woman with a past. It might be more accurate to say: at least, don't marry a woman with the disposition and the ill-manners of Paula Tanqueray. As Ashley Dukes wrote, Pinero "threw Paula to the Victorians, and made her fate a mock tragedy that satisfied the proprieties. . . . She is the Hedda Gabler of her shocking set."

Iris, Pinero's thirty-third play, and *The Thunderbolt*, his thirty-seventh, have about the same merits and defects as the best of the Pinero products. They are well-made, cut and fitted to the boards, with the carefully planned big scene, and a theme suited to the general level of audience interest in the early 1900's. Iris is a clinging, luxury-loving young widow who ends in the street because she weakly preferred her money to her young lover. When she lost her security, she preferred Maldonado's support without marriage to poverty; and finally through her compromise she lost both men in the big scene. *The Thunderbolt* is a study of the small minds and greedy souls of the Mortimore family as they prepare to divide the property of their late brother Edward who had died apparently intestate. They are eager to seize the estate and to exclude his illegitimate daughter Helen from a share. The "thunderbolt" is the discovery that all the property had been willed to Helen, who, in the end, deals generously with the harsh and petty family. Much of the interest derives from the contrast between the domineering attitude of the Mortimores before, and their wheedling subservience to Helen after the "thunderbolt." The play is written in Pinero's best manner, with humor, naturalness, and worldly wisdom.

Mid-Channel is Pinero's masterpiece in the serious vein, and the one most nearly universal in its theme. When he came to write it he had attained complete mastery of his technique and was at ease with the dramatic form. The suicide of Zoe Blundell is conventional, of course, in the Hedda Gabler manner. Preparation for it begins with a mention of suicide in the first minutes of the play, and continues to the final scene where attention is kept focused on the alluring balcony high above the street. Despite this careful build-up, however, the ending may now seem somewhat theatrical rather than natural. As Shaw once wisely said of Zoe's prototype, "Ibsen's suicides and catastrophies at last produced the cry of 'People don't do such things,' which he ridiculed through Judge Brack in Hedda Gabler. . . . But on the whole Brack was right. The tragedy of Hedda is not that she commits suicide but that she continues to live."

That is true of Zoe in normal experience, but on the other hand the dramatist has always been permitted to heighten his effects by telescoping time and events and sharpening up episodes like Nora's walk-out. And we must note that within the specific situation, within the confines and assumptions of this play and the prejudices, inadequacies, and unimaginativeness of the characters the catastrophe is fated and irrevocable. The study of the characters of Theodore and Zoe Blundell, and of the social atmosphere in which they lived, reveals movingly the reasons why they plunged into wreckage instead of coping intelligently and resolutely with their problem.

Though Pinero never achieved the subtle magic of literature, this play is competently written and enjoyable in the library. It was first performed in 1910 at St. James's Theatre in London with Irene Vanbrugh as Zoe. In New York Ethel Barrymore scored a triumph during a long run in the same part. *Mid-Channel* has been widely read and performed, and has taken a prominent place in the bibliography of the modern theatre.

MID–CHANNEL

CHARACTERS

THEODORE BLUNDELL

THE HONBLE. PETER MOTTRAM

LEONARD FERRIS

WARREN, *servant at Lancaster Gate*

COLE, *servant at the flat in Cavendish Square*

RIDEOUT, *Mr. Ferris's servant*

UPHOLSTERERS

ZOE BLUNDELL

MRS. PIERPOINT

ETHEL PIERPOINT

MRS. ANNERLY

LENA

The scene is laid in London. The events of the First Act take place on an afternoon in January. The rest of the action occurs on a day in the following June.

ACT I

A drawing-room, decorated and furnished in the French style. In the wall opposite the spectator there is a door, the upper part of which is glazed. A silk curtain hangs across the glazed panels, but above the curtain there is a view of the corridor beyond. The fireplace, where a bright fire is burning, is in the wall on the right. There is a door on the farther side of the fireplace, another on the nearer side. Both these doors are supposed to lead to a second drawing-room.

On either side of the fireplace there is an armchair, and on the farther side, standing out in the room, is a settee. Some illustrated papers of the popular sort are lying upon the armchair next to the settee. Behind the settee are an oblong table and a chair. In the middle of the room, on the left of the settee and facing the fire, is another armchair; and on the left of the armchair on the nearer side of the fireplace there is a fauteuil-stool. A writing-table, with a chair before it, stands on the left-hand side of the room, and among the objects on the writing-table are a hand-mirror

and some photographs in frames. Other pieces of furniture, of a more formal kind than those already specified, fill spaces against the walls. One of these, on the left of the glazed door, is a second settee.

The room is lighted only by the blaze of the fire, and the corridor also is in semi-darkness.

(Note: Throughout, "right" and "left" are the spectators' right and left, not the actor's.)

[*The corridor is suddenly lighted up. Then* WARREN *enters at the glazed door and switches on the light in the room. He is followed by* MRS. PIERPOINT, *a pleasant-looking, middle-aged lady, and by* ETHEL, *a pretty girl of five-and-twenty.*]

MRS. PIERPOINT (*to the servant*). You are sure Mrs. Blundell will be in soon?

WARREN. She said half-past four, ma'am.

MRS. PIERPOINT. It's that now, isn't it?

WARREN. Just upon, ma'am. (WARREN *withdraws, closing the door.*)

ETHEL. What beautiful rooms these are!

MRS. PIERPOINT. Money!

ETHEL. I always feel I'm in Paris when I'm here, in some smart house in the Champs-Elysées—not at Lancaster Gate. What *is* Mr. Blundell, Mother?

MRS. PIERPOINT. A stockbroker.

ETHEL. Stockbroker?

MRS. PIERPOINT. Blundell—something-or-other—and Mottram. He goes to the City every morning.

ETHEL. I know that. But I've never heard him, or Zoe, mention the Stock Exchange.

MRS. PIERPOINT (*sitting on the settee by the fire-place*). Prosperous stockbrokers and their wives—those who move in a decent set—*don't* mention the Stock Exchange.

ETHEL. Then that nice person, Mr. Mottram, is a stockbroker too?

MRS. PIERPOINT. Of course, dear. He's the "Mottram" of the firm.

ETHEL. And *he's* the son of a peer.

MRS. PIERPOINT. Peers' sons are common enough in the City nowadays—and peers, for that matter.

ETHEL (*moving to the fireplace and warming her hands*). Zoe is a doctor's daughter.

MRS. PIERPOINT. Has she given you leave to call her Zoe?

ETHEL. Yes, last week—asked me to. I'm so glad; I've taken such a liking to her.

MRS. PIERPOINT. She was a Miss Tucker. Her father practised in New Cavendish Street. He was a great gout man.

ETHEL. You *are* full of information, Mother.

MRS. PIERPOINT. Emma Lawton was giving me the whole history of the Blundells at lunch to-day. She has money, of her own.

ETHEL. Zoe?

MRS. PIERPOINT. Doctor Tucker left sixty or seventy thousand pounds, and she came in for it all. But they'd got on before then.

ETHEL. H'm! There are stockbrokers and stockbrokers, I suppose.

MRS. PIERPOINT. Straight and crooked, as in every other business or profession.

ETHEL. I do think, though, that a girl in Zoe's position might have chosen somebody slightly more refined than Mr. Blundell.

MRS. PIERPOINT. What's wrong with him? He's extremely amiable and inoffensive.

ETHEL. Amiable!

MRS. PIERPOINT. He strikes me as being so.

ETHEL. I don't call it particularly amiable or inoffensive in a husband to be as snappy with his wife as he is with Zoe.

MRS. PIERPOINT. Snappy?

ETHEL. Irritable—impatient.

MRS. PIERPOINT. Oh, I dare say there's an excellent understanding between them. They've been married a good many years.

ETHEL. Thirteen, she's told me.

MRS. PIERPOINT. Married people are allowed to be out of humor with each other occasionally.

ETHEL. A considerable allowance must be made for Mr. Blundell, I'm afraid.

MRS. PIERPOINT. You're prejudiced, Ethel. I've seen her just as snappy, as you term it, with him.

ETHEL. You can't blame her, if she's provoked.

MRS. PIERPOINT. Nor him, if he's provoked. The argument cuts both ways ——

ETHEL (*listening*). Sssh!

[ZOE, *a charming, animated, bright-eyed woman, wearing her hat and some costly furs, enters quickly at the glazed door.*]

ZOE. Delightful!

MRS. PIERPOINT (*rising*). Your servant insisted on our coming up.

ZOE (*shaking hands with* MRS. PIERPOINT). If he hadn't, I'd have wrung his neck. (*Kissing* ETHEL.) How are you, dear? (*Stripping off her gloves.*) The weather! Isn't it filthy! Do you remember what the sun's like? I had the blinds drawn all over the house at eleven o'clock this morning. What's the good of trying to make believe it's day? (*Taking off her coat.*) Do sit down. Ugh! Why is it that more people commit suicide in summer than in winter?

MRS. PIERPOINT (*resuming her seat on the settee by the fire*). Do they?

ETHEL (*sitting upon the fauteuil-stool*). Why, yes, Mother; what-do-you-call-them?—statistics—prove it.

ZOE (*throwing her coat and gloves upon the settee at the back and unpinning her hat*). You'll see, when I put an end to myself, it will be in the wintertime.

MRS. PIERPOINT. My dear!

ETHEL. Zoe!

MRS. PIERPOINT. If you are in this frame of mind, why don't you pack your trunks and fly?

ZOE. Fly?

ETHEL. Mother means cut it.

MRS. PIERPOINT. Ethel!

ZOE (*tossing her hat on to the settee and taking up the hand-mirror from the writing-table and adjusting her hair*). Don't scold her; she picks up her slang from me.

ETHEL. Evil communications——!

MRS. PIERPOINT. I mean, go abroad for a couple of months—Egypt——

ETHEL. Mother, how horrid of you! I should miss her terribly.

MRS. PIERPOINT. Cairo—Assouan——

ZOE (*looking into the hand-glass steadily*). That's funny. I have been thinking lately of "cutting it."

MRS. PIERPOINT. But I suppose it would have to be without your busy husband.

ZOE (*replacing the mirror*). Yes, it would be without Theo. (*Turning to* MRS. PIERPOINT *and* ETHEL *and rattling on again.*) Well! How have you been amusing yourselves? You wretches, you haven't been near me since Monday, either of you. Done anything—seen anything?

ETHEL. Nothing.

MRS. PIERPOINT (*to* ZOE). If *you're* under the weather, there's some excuse for me.

ZOE (*walking about restlessly*). Oh, but I will keep moving, though the heavens fall. I've been to the theater every night this week, and supped out afterward. They've opened such a ripping restaurant in Jermyn Street. (*Pausing.*) You haven't seen the new play at the St. Martin's, then?

MRS. PIERPOINT. No.

ETHEL. I want to, badly.

ZOE. I'll take you. We'll make up a party. (*Scribbling a memorandum at the writing-table.*) I'll tell Lenny Ferris to get seats.

ETHEL. Good business!

MRS. PIERPOINT. Ethel!

ZOE. It's all about children—kiddies. There are the sweetest little tots in it. Two especially—a tiny, round-eyed boy and a mite of a girl with straw-colored hair—you feel you must clamber on to the stage and hug them. You feel you *must!*

MRS. PIERPOINT. Aren't there any grown-ups?

ZOE (*dropping into the armchair facing the fire*). Oh, yes; they bore me.

ETHEL. I was reading the story to you, Mother——

ZOE. The story's no account—it's the kiddies. The man who wrote the thing must be awfully fond of children. I wonder whether he has any little 'uns. If he hasn't, it's of no consequence to him; he can imagine them. What a jolly gift! Fancy! To have the power of imagining children—bringing them to life! Just by shutting the door, and sitting down at your writing-table, and saying to your brain, "Now, then! I'm ready for them——!" (*Breaking off.*) Ring the bell, Ethel. (ETHEL *rises, and, going to the fireplace, rings the bell.*) Let's have tea.

MRS. PIERPOINT. I'm afraid we can't stay for tea. I've promised to be at old Miss Fremantle's at five o'clock. Ethel——

ETHEL. Yes, Mother?

MRS. PIERPOINT. Go downstairs for a few minutes. I want a little private conversation with Mrs. Blundell.

ETHEL (*surprised*). Private conversation!

MRS. PIERPOINT. If she won't think me too troublesome.

ZOE (*rising and opening the nearer door on the right—to* ETHEL). Come in here. There's a lovely fire. (*Disappearing.*) I'll switch the light on.

ETHEL (*following* ZOE—*at the door*). What is it about, Mother?

MRS. PIERPOINT (*rising*). Now, don't be inquisitive, Ethel.

ZOE (*from the adjoining room*). Come along!

[ETHEL *goes into the next room.* WARREN *enters at the glazed door.*]

MRS. PIERPOINT (*to* WARREN). Mrs. Blundell rang for tea.

WARREN. Very good, ma'am. (WARREN *withdraws as* ZOE *returns.*)

MRS. PIERPOINT. We shan't be heard?

ZOE (*closing the door*). No.

MRS. PIERPOINT. It's really most improper of me to bother you in this way.

ZOE (*advancing to* MRS. PIERPOINT). Can I be of any use to you?

MRS. PIERPOINT. Well, yes, you can. You can give me—what shall I call it?—a hint——

ZOE (*sitting on the fauteuil-stool*). A hint?

MRS. PIERPOINT. On a subject that concerns Ethel. (*Sitting in the chair facing the fire.*) We're quite new friends of yours, dear Mrs. Blundell—is it six weeks since we dined at the Darrells'?

ZOE. There or thereabouts.

MRS. PIERPOINT. A fortnight or so before Christmas, wasn't it? But my girl has formed a great attachment to you, and I fancy you are inclined to be interested in her.

ZOE. Rather! She and I are going to be tremendous pals.

MRS. PIERPOINT. That's splendid. Now, don't laugh at me for my extreme cautiousness, if you can help it.

ZOE. Cautiousness?

MRS. PIERPOINT. Tell me—as one woman to another—do you consider it advisable for Ethel to see much of Mr. Ferris?

ZOE. Advisable?

MRS. PIERPOINT. Oh, I've no doubt he's a highly respectable young man, as young men go—I'm not implying anything to the contrary——

ZOE. *Is* she seeing much of Mr. Ferris?

MRS. PIERPOINT. She meets him here.

ZOE. Ah, yes.

MRS. PIERPOINT. And he has suddenly taken to dropping in to tea with us pretty regularly; and twice this week—twice—he has sent her some magnificent flowers—magnificent.

ZOE. Dear old Lenny!

MRS. PIERPOINT. There's something in his manner, too—one can't describe it——

ZOE (*a little ruefully*). Ha! Ha, ha, ha!

MRS. PIERPOINT. I *am* amusing you.

ZOE. No, no. I beg your pardon. (*Rising and going to the fire.*) Somehow I've never pictured Lenny with a wife.

MRS. PIERPOINT. It may be only an excess of politeness on his part; there mayn't be the least foundation for my suspicions.

ZOE. I suppose every married woman believes that her bachelor chums will remain bachelors.

MRS. PIERPOINT. And pray, dear Mrs. Blundell, don't take me for a matchmaking mother. I've no desire to lose my girl yet awhile, I assure you. But I want to know, naturally—it's my duty to know—exactly who and what are the men who come into my drawing-room.

ZOE. Why, naturally.

MRS. PIERPOINT. And it occurred to me that, as we made Mr. Ferris's acquaintance in your house, you wouldn't object to giving me, as I put it, the merest hint——

ZOE. Ethel—what about her? Does she like him?

MRS. PIERPOINT. It's evident she doesn't dislike him. But she's not a girl who would be in a hurry to confide in anybody over a love affair, not even in her mother. True, there may be nothing to confide, in the present case. I repeat, I may be altogether mistaken. At the same time——

ZOE. You wish me to advise you as to whether Lenny Ferris should be encouraged.

MRS. PIERPOINT. Whether he should be cold-shouldered—I prefer that expression.

ZOE. Very well; I'll furnish you with his character, dear Mrs. Pierpoint, with pleasure.

[LEONARD FERRIS, *a fresh, boyish young man, enters at the glazed door, with the air of one who is at home.*]

LEONARD. Hallo!

ZOE (*just as carelessly*). Hallo, Len!

LEONARD (*shaking hands with* MRS. PIERPOINT). How d'ye do? How's Miss Ethel?

MRS. PIERPOINT (*inclining her head*). Thank you——

LEONARD (*rubbing his hands together*). Here's a day!

ZOE (*taking his hand*). Your hands are frozen.

LEONARD (*going to the fire*). I drove my car up here.

ZOE. You're crazy. (*Sitting on the settee by the fire.*) You never rang me up this morning, to ask if I was tired.

LEONARD. Wire was engaged. First-rate night, last night.

ZOE (*languidly*). The summit. Lenny——

LEONARD. Eh?

ZOE. Mrs. Pierpoint and I are talking secrets. Go into the next room for a seond.

LEONARD (*genially*). Shan't, if there isn't a fire.

ZOE. Of course there's a fire. Things ain't so bad in the City as all that.

LEONARD (*at the nearer door on the right*). Any tea?

ZOE. By and by. You'll find somebody in there you know.

LEONARD (*going into the room*). Who?

ZOE (*calling out*). Shut the door. (*The door is closed.*) Talk of the——!

MRS. PIERPOINT. Bless me, I hope not!

ZOE. No, I shouldn't turn him in there at this moment if he wasn't what he is —the dearest boy in the world— should I?

MRS. PIERPOINT. Boy——?

ZOE. He's thirty-two. A man of two-and-thirty *is* a boy to a woman of—to an old married woman. He's the simplest, wholesomest, best-natured fellow living. If you had him for a son-in-law, you'd be lucky.

MRS. PIERPOINT. It's a relief to me, at any rate——

ZOE. And I should lose one of my tame robins.

MRS. PIERPOINT. Tame robins?

ZOE (*rising and going over to the writing-table and taking up two of the photographs*). I always have his photo on my table—his and Peter Mottram's Peter Mottram is my husband's partner—you've met him here. I call them my tame robins. They come and eat crumbs off my windowsill. I've no end of tame robins—men chums—but these two are my specials. (*Replacing the photographs.*) Well! If Lenny ever goes, I shall have to promote Harry Estridge or Jim Mallandain or Cossy Rawlings.

MRS. PIERPOINT (*who has risen and followed* ZOE *to the writing-table*). But why should Mr. Ferris ever "go" completely?

ZOE (*smiling*). Oh, when a robin marries, Jenny doesn't share him with another wren. Not much!

[WARREN *enters at the glazed door with a female servant. They carry in the tea and lay it upon the table behind the settee by the fire.*]

ZOE (*after glancing at the servants—dropping her voice*). I'd better finish drawing up the prospectus, while I'm at it.

MRS. PIERPOINT. Prospectus?

ZOE. He's got two thousand a year. Both his people are dead. There's an aunt in the country who may leave him a bit extra; but she's a cantankerous old cat and, in my opinion, charity'll have every *sou*. Still, two thousand a year——

MRS. PIERPOINT. I oughtn't to hear any more. But you understand, don't you——?

ZOE. Perfectly. And he lives in a comfy little flat behind the Albert Hall and is mad on motor-cars. He's invented a wonderful wheel which is to give the knock to pneumatics. If anything will bring him to ruin, that will. (*Walking away toward the tea-table laughingly.*) There!

WARREN. Tea is served, ma'am.

MRS. PIERPOINT (*to* ZOE, *who returns to her*). I'm exceedingly obliged to you. You won't breathe a word to Ethel?

ZOE. Not a syllable. It would break my heart, but I hope it'll come off, for her sake.

MRS. PIERPOINT. She's a sweet, sensible child.

ZOE. And as for him, I'll tell you this for your comfort—I'm honestly certain that Lenny Ferris would be the sort of husband that lasts.

MRS. PIERPOINT. That lasts? What do you mean?

ZOE. Oh—never mind. (*Gaily.*) Tea! (*The servants have withdrawn. She runs across to the farther door at the right, opens it, and calls.*) Tea! (*Seating herself at the tea-table.*) Are you firm about going on?

MRS. PIERPOINT. It's Lizzie Fremantle's birthday. She's Ethel's godmother. (*To* ETHEL, *who enters with* LEONARD.) Are you ready, Ethel?

ETHEL (*to* MRS. PIERPOINT). Must we?

MRS. PIERPOINT. Now, my dear——!

ZOE (*to* LEONARD). Lenny, you've got to get tickets for the St. Martin's and take the whole crowd of us.

LEONARD (*with a wry face*). That kids' play again!

ZOE. Very well; Peter will do it.

LEONARD. No, no; right you are.

ZOE. I stand.

LEONARD. Rot!

ZOE. Then Peter has the job. (*To the ladies.*) We'll ask Peter Mottram to be one of us anyhow.

LEONARD. The supper's mine, then.

ZOE. Anything for peace. (*Shaking hands with* MRS. PIERPOINT, *who comes to her.*) Monday night?

MRS. PIERPOINT. You're a great deal too good.

[LEONARD *has opened the glazed door and is now in the corridor.* MRS. PIERPOINT *joins him.*]

LEONARD (*to* MRS. PIERPOINT, *as they disappear*). Got a vehicle?

MRS. PIERPOINT. My venerable four-wheeler—the oldest friend I have in London——

ETHEL (*to* ZOE, *who rises*). What did Mother have to say to you so mysteriously?

ZOE. Er—she wants me to consult Theo about something.

ETHEL. Her railway shares?

ZOE (*nodding*). H'm.

ETHEL (*satisfied*). Oh? Good-by.

ZOE. When are we to have a nice long jaw together—just you and I?

ETHEL. Mother won't let me out alone in these fogs.

ZOE. Fog or no fog, try and shunt her to-morrow.

ETHEL. I'll do my best.

ZOE. I'll be in all the morning. (*They turn their heads toward the door, listening.*) Lenny's whistling for you.

ETHEL. Mother——!

[*They kiss affectionately and* ETHEL *hurries away.* ZOE *resumes her seat at the tea-table and pours out tea. Presently* LEONARD *returns and, after closing the door, comes to her.*]

LEONARD (*cheerfully*). It's beginning to sleet now. 'Pon my soul——! (*She hands him a cup of tea in silence. He looks at her inquiringly.*) Anything wrong, Zoe?

ZOE (*with an air of indifference*). No.

LEONARD. Positive?

ZOE (*in the same tone, offering him a plate of bread and butter*). Quite.

LEONARD (*taking a slice*). Thought there'd been another row, perhaps.

ZOE (*putting the plate of bread and butter aside and taking up her cup and saucer*). Hell of a row last night.

LEONARD. Last night?

ZOE. This morning, rather.

LEONARD. When you came home?

ZOE (*sipping her tea*). After you and Peter brought me home.

LEONARD. What over?

ZOE. Nothing.

LEONARD (*drinking*). Must have been over something.

ZOE. Oh, some trifle—as usual.

LEONARD. Too bad of Theo—damned sight too bad.

ZOE. I dare say it was as much my fault as his.

LEONARD (*hotly*). It's a cursed shame!

ZOE. Drop it, Len. (*Handing him a dish of cakes.*) Cake?

LEONARD (*puting his empty cup down before her and taking a cake*). Tea.

ZOE (*pouring out another cup of tea for him*). First time you've drunk tea with me this week. Honored!

LEONARD. Sorry.

ZOE. M'yes—(*Giving him his tea.*)—Sorry that Mrs. Pierpoint and Ethel can't receive you this afternoon.

LEONARD (*after a pause, uncomfortably*). Mrs. Pierpoint been telling you anything about me?

ZOE. Mentioned that you frequently turn up in Sloane Street at teatime.

LEONARD. There's a man down that way who's frightfully gone on my wheel.

ZOE (*drinking*). Indeed?

LEONARD. My great difficulty, you know, is to get it on to the market.

ZOE. India-rubber people opposing you, I expect.

LEONARD. Tooth and nail.

ZOE (*nibbling a cake*). And the man who lives Sloane Street way——?

LEONARD. Very influential chap.

ZOE. Capitalist?

LEONARD. Millionaire.

ZOE. H'm! And when you're down Sloane Street way, do you take your flowers to Miss Pierpoint, or does your florist send them?

[*Again there is silence. He lays his cup down, leaves her side, and produces his cigarette case. Sticking a cigarette between his lips; he is about to close the case when she rises and takes a cigarette from it. She moves to the fireplace, lighting her cigarette with a match from a box attached to a gold chatelaine hanging from her waist. He seats himself in the chair facing the fire and lights his own cigarette.*]

LEONARD (*moodily*). I don't want to marry, Zoe.

ZOE. There's no reason why you shouldn't, if you feel disposed to; but you needn't be a sneak about it.

LEONARD. The aunt's pitching into me again like billy-oh. High time I settled down—high time I became a reputable member of society! I ask you, what the deuce have I ever done that's particularly disreputable? Then come two verses of Scripture——

ZOE (*advancing to him*). She hasn't ordered you to be underhanded with your best friends, I assume?

LEONARD. I'm not underhanded.

ZOE. Why this concealment, then?

LEONARD. There's no concealment; there's nothing to conceal; I give you my word there isn't. I—I haven't made up my mind one way or the other.

ZOE (*witheringly*). You're weighing the question!

LEONARD. Very well; I'm weighing it, if you like. (*Flinging the end of his match into the fireplace and jumping up.*) Confound it all! Mayn't a man send a basket or two of rotten flowers to a girl without having his special license bought for him by meddling people?

ZOE. Thank you.

LEONARD. I don't mean you, Zoe. You know I don't mean you. (*Pacing the room.*) Ethel—Miss Pierpoint—is a charming girl, but I'm no more in love with her than I am with my old hat.

ZOE. Then you oughtn't to pay her marked attention.

LEONARD. I'm not paying her marked attention. (ZOE *shrugs her shoulders.*) If Mrs. Pierpoint says I've been making love to her daughter——

ZOE. She has said nothing of the kind.

LEONARD (*sitting in the chair before the writing-table, in a huff*). That's all right. Pity she can't hold her tongue over trifles.

[*There is another pause. Then, partly kneeling upon the chair in the middle of the room, and resting her elbow on the back of it,* ZOE *softens.*]

ZOE (*making rings with her cigarette smoke*). Don't be wild, Len. I was only vexed with you for not consulting me. It would hurt my feelings dreadfully if you got engaged to anybody on the sly. Len——(*He turns to her, but with his head down.*) She *is* a charming girl. I'm not surprized at your being spoons on her. If I were a man, she's just the sort of girl *I'd* marry, if I were on the lookout for a wife.

LEONARD (*in a low voice*). Perhaps I *have* made myself a bit of an ass over her, Zoe. (*She laughs lightly. He raises his eyes.*) Zoe——

ZOE. Well?

LEONARD (*gazing at* ZOE). Do you know that she reminds me very often of you?

ZOE. She! I'm old enough to be her grandmother.

LEONARD. Oh, hang that! She's got hold of a lot of your odd little tricks—a lot of 'em.

ZOE. She's been with me a goodish deal lately.

LEONARD. That's it; and she has the most enormous admiration for you—enormous.

ZOE. She's a dear.

LEONARD (*gently hitting his knee with his fist*). I've thought of all that when I've been worrying it out in my mind.

ZOE. Thought of all what? 10

LEONARD. That you'd always be pals, you two—close pals.

ZOE. If she became Mrs. Lenny?

LEONARD (*nodding*). And so, if I did screw myself up to—to speaking to her, it wouldn't make the least difference to our friendship—yours and mine.

ZOE. No difference!

LEONARD. I should still be your tame 20 robin.

ZOE. Ah, no; don't make that mistake, Len.

LEONARD. Mistake?

ZOE (*shaking her head*). It never works. I've seen similar cases over and over again. There's any amount of gush at the start, between the young wife and the husband's women-pals; but the end is always the same.

LEONARD. The end?

ZOE. Gradually the wife draws the husband away. She manages it somehow. We have a gift for it. I did it myself when I married Theo.

LEONARD (*rising and walking about*). If I believed what you say, Zoe, I'd never size up a girl with a view to marrying as long as I live.

ZOE (*teasingly*). You're a vain creature. 40 I've plenty of other boys, Len, to fill your place.

LEONARD (*not heeding her*). If things were smoother with you and Theo, one mightn't hesitate half as much.

ZOE. There's Peter Mottram, Gus Hedmont, Harry Estridge, Claud Lowenstein——

LEONARD. As it is—Great Scott!—I'm a brute even to think of taking the risk.

ZOE. Cossy Rawlings, Jim Mallandain, Robby Relf——

LEONARD (*stopping in his walk*). Yes, but my friendship's more to you than the friendship of most of those other fellows, I should hope.

ZOE (*making a grimace at him*). Not a scrap.

LEONARD (*his brow darkening*). You told me once I was your favorite.

ZOE. My chaff; I've no favorite.

LEONARD (*laying the remains of his cigarette upon a little bronze tray on the writing-table*). Peter's a trump, and Harry Estridge and Rawlings are sound enough; but I often feel I'd like to knock young Lowenstein's teeth down his fat throat.

ZOE (*blowing her smoke in his direction as he comes to her and stands before her*). You get married and mind your own concerns.

LEONARD. Zoe, I hate to see men of that class buzzing around you.

ZOE (*mockingly*). Do you!

LEONARD. Look here! Whatever happens between you and Theo in the future, you'll never let anything or anybody drive you off the rails, will you?

ZOE (*frowning*). Len!

LEONARD. I couldn't stand it. (*Putting his hands upon her shoulders.*) I tell you straight, it 'ud break me. (*Passionately, his grip tightening.*) Zoe——!

[*She shakes herself free and backs away from him, confronting him with a flushed face.*]

ZOE (*quietly*). Don't be silly. (*Brushing her hair from her forehead.*) If ever you do that again, Len, I'll box your ears.

The HONBLE. PETER MOTTRAM, *a spruce, well-preserved man of fifty, enters at the glazed door.*]

PETER (*cheerily*). Good mornin'—or whatever it is.

ZOE (*dropping the end of her cigarette into the grate*). That you, Peter?

LEONARD (*surlily*). I'm just off.

PETER. Don't apologize.

LEONARD (*at the glazed door, to* PETER). See you later. (*He goes out.*)

PETER (*to* ZOE). What's the matter with the youth? 10

ZOE (*with a shrug*). Got the hump over something. (*Facing him.*) Tea?

PETER. No, thanks. (*Sitting in the chair in the middle of the room.*) And how are you to-day, my dear lady? (*She makes a wry mouth, sighs, and throws herself disconsolately upon the settee by the fire. He nods intelligently.*) Yes, sorry to hear you and old Theo have had another bad fall-out.

ZOE (*arranging a pillow for her head*). I guessed he'd carry it all to you.

PETER. Shockin'ly grieved, I am.

ZOE. *He* began this one.

PETER. By blowin' you up for goin' on the frisk every night.

ZOE. And I answered him back. I was dogweary. It was nearly one o'clock. He needn't have jumped upon me almost before I'd taken the key out of 30 the lock.

PETER (*demurely*). I also have been reproved, for aidin' and abettin'.

ZOE. Serves you jolly well right. Why didn't you and Lenny come in with me, you cowards? That might have saved a squabble. I begged you to have a whiskey.

PETER (*after a brief pause*). Zoe——

ZOE (*in a muffled voice, her head in the pil-* 40 *low*). Oh, be kind to me, Peter.

PETER. Why *do* you sally forth night after night?

ZOE. Because I must.

PETER. Must?

ZOE. I've got the fidgets.

PETER. I get the fidgets at times, in bed. D'ye know how I cure 'em?

ZOE. Of course I don't.

PETER. I lie perfectly stiff and still; I *make* myself lie perfectly still. I *won't* stir. I say to myself, "Peter, you *shan't* twist or turn." And I win.

ZOE. How easy it is to talk! I defy you to control yourself if you're shut up with a person who goads you to desperation.

PETER. Theo?

ZOE (*beating her pillow*). How *can* I stay at home and eat a long dinner, and spend an entire evening, alone with Theo? We're not entertaining just now; he says he's fed up with having people here.

PETER. Take him out with you.

ZOE. Then we quarrel before others. 20 That's too degrading. Oh, it's tiff, tiff, wrangle, jangle, outdoors *and* indoors with us!

PETER. You say things to Theo when you're angry, Zoe, that wound him to the quick.

ZOE (*satirically*). Really!

PETER. Really. You mayn't be aware of it; you scratch the poor old chap till he bleeds. 30

ZOE. Do you imagine he never says things to me that wound me to the quick?

PETER. He doesn't mean half of 'em.

ZOE. Neither do I.

PETER (*rising and going to the fire*). No; there's the crass foolishness of it all. (*In a tone of expostulation.*) My dear lady——

ZOE (*suddenly sitting upright*). We're on 40 each other's nerves, Peter. That's the plain truth, we're on each other's nerves.

PETER. Worryin' each other.

ZOE. Sick to death of each other! We shall have been married fourteen years on the thirtieth of next June. Isn't it appalling! He's getting so stodgy and pompous and flat-footed. He drives me mad with his elderly ways.

PETER (*soothingly*). Oh——!

ZOE. He's sick and tired of *me*, at any rate. My little jokes and pranks, that used to amuse him so—they annoy him now, scandalize him. He's con- 10 tinually finding fault with me—bullying me. That's all the notice he takes of me. As for my gowns or my hats—anything I put on—I might dress in sackcloth; he'd never observe it. (*Tearfully.*) Ah——! (*She searches for her handkerchief and fails to find it. PETER produces a folded handkerchief from his breast-pocket, shakes it out, and gives it to her. She wipes her eyes as she proceeds.*) 20 Sometimes, I own, I'm aggravating; but he forgets how useful I was to him in the old days, when we were climbing. Yes, *those* were the days— the first six or seven years of our marriage, when we were up north, in Fitzjohn's Avenue! (*Tossing PETER's handkerchief to him and getting to her feet.*) Oh! Oh, we were happy then, Peter! You didn't know us then, 30 when we were up north!

PETER (*wagging his head*). My dear lady, we were all happier when we were up north.

ZOE (*giving him a look of surprize as she paces the room on the left*). You!

PETER. I mean, in a previous stage of our careers.

ZOE. Ah, yes, yes.

PETER. That's the lesson of life, Mrs. 40 Zoe. We've all had our Fitzjohn's Avenue, in a sense. In other words, we've all been young and keen as mustard; with everythin' before us, instead of havin' most things behind us.

ZOE (*leaning on the back of the chair before the writing-table*). Oh, don't!

PETER (*thoughtfully*). D'ye know, I often wonder whether there's anythin' more depressin' than· to see the row of trophies standin' on the sideboard?

ZOE (*sitting at the writing-table and digging her fingers into her hair*). Be quiet, Peter!

PETER. That silver-gilt vase there! The old horse that gained it for you is lyin' in the paddock with a stone a'top of him, and you're usin' his hoof as an inkpot. Those goblets you won on the river, and the cup you helped yourself to on the links at Biarritz or St. Moritz—there's a little pile of ashes at the bottom of every one of 'em! So it is with life generally. You scoop in the prizes—and there are the pots on the sideboard to remind you that it ain't the *prizes* that count, but the pushin' and the strugglin' and th*r* cheerin'. Ah, they preach to us on Sundays about cherubim and seraphim! It's my firm hope and conviction that when we die and go to heaven we shall all find ourselves up north again—in Fitzjohn's Avenue! (*Coming to the chair in the middle of the room.*) Meanwhile, it's no good repinin'. (*Turning the chair toward her and sitting.*) The trophies *are* on the sideboard, dear lady, and they've got to be kep' clean and shiny. (*Gravely.*) Now, Zoe——(*She whimpers.*) Zoe, Zoe——(*She turns to him.*) Zoe, one ugly word passed between you and Theo last night——

ZOE. One——?

PETER. One ugly word that must never be repeated.

ZOE. What word?

[*The glazed door opens and WARREN appears carrying a teapot on a tray. He comes to the table and exchanges the teapot he is carrying for the one that is already there.*]

ZOE (*to the man*). Mr. Mottram won't have any tea, Warren.

WARREN (*removing the cups and saucers which have been used and putting them on to his tray*). No, ma'am; but Mr. Blundell's just come in, ma'am.

[WARREN *withdraws, closing the door.* ZOE *rises stifly, and gathers up her hat, coat, and gloves. Then she returns to* PETER, *who remains seated.*]

ZOE. What word was it?

PETER. Separation.

[THEODORE BLUNDELL, *a big, burly, but good-looking man, enters at the glazed door. He halts on entering and glances furtively at* ZOE, *as if expecting her to speak; but, without meeting his eyes, she passes him and leaves the room.*]

THEODORE (*with a shrug*). Ha! (PETER *looking over his shoulder, sees that he and* THEODORE *are alone.* THEODORE *seats himself at the tea-table and pours out his tea grimly.*) Lots o' good you seem to have done, Peter.

PETER. Haven't done much, I admit. Pity you came home quite so soon.

THEODORE. You left the office at half-past two.

PETER. She wasn't in when I first got here.

THEODORE (*taking a slice of bread and butter*). Anyhow, kind of you to offer to have a talk to her. (*Munching.*) Plenty of abuse of me, h'm?

PETER. She says you're on each other's nerves, Theo.

THEODORE. I'm afraid there's something in that.

PETER. And that you are growin' a bit heavy in hand, old man.

THEODORE (*drily*). Exceedingly sorry.

PETER (*after a pause*). Theo——

THEODORE. Hallo?

PETER. Shall I tell you what's at the bottom of it all?

THEODORE. Well?

PETER. She's got a feelin' that you're tired of her.

THEODORE (*gulping his tea*). If you knew how constantly I have that served up to me——!

PETER. Will you allow me to speak out?

THEODORE. Don't be so polite.

PETER. My belief is that, if you could avoid conveyin' that impression to Zoe, matters would improve considerably in this establishment.

THEODORE. Oh?

PETER. It's as easy as brushin' your hat. A little pettin'—a little sweetheartin'——

THEODORE. Yes?

PETER (*discouraged*). Well, those are my views, for what they're worth.

THEODORE (*pouring out another cup of tea*). My dear fellow, if you'd get married, and have thirteen or fourteen years of it, as I've had, your views would be worth more than they are.

PETER. Oh, that won't wash. (*Rising.*) When a man's sufferin' from gout in the toe, he doesn't stipulate that his M.D. shall be writhin' from the same ailment. No, very frequently, the outsider——

THEODORE. Good gracious, you're not going to remark that lookers-on see most of the game!

PETER. Words to that effect.

THEODORE. Ho! Why is it that, the moment a man's matrimonial affairs are in a tangle, every platitude in the language is chewed out at him? (*Leaning his head on his hands.*) If you've nothing fresher to say on the subject——!

PETER (*oracularly*). My dear chap, it's tryin' to say somethin' fresh on the subject of marriage that's responsible for a large share of the domestic un-happiness and discontent existin' at the present day. There's too much of this tryin' to say somethin' fresh on *every* subject, in my opinion.

THEODORE. Nobody can accuse *you*, Peter——

PETER. You take it from me, there are two institootions in this world that are never goin' to alter—men and women and the shape of chickens' eggs. Chickens' eggs are never goin' to be laid square; and men and women will continue to be mere men and women till the last contango.[1] (THEODORE *finishes his tea, rises, and comes to the fire.*) I'm referrin', of course, to real men and women. I don't inclood persons in petticoats with flat chests and no hips; nor individuals wearin' beards and trousers who dine on a basin of farinaceous food and a drink o' water out o' the filter. They belong to a distinct species. No; I mean the genuine article, like you and me and your missus—men and women with blood in their veins, and one-and-a-half per cent. of good, humanizin' alcohol in *that.*

THEODORE (*throwing a log on the fire*). What's the moral of your eloquent, but rather vague, discourse?

PETER (*at the chair in the middle of the room*). The moral? Oh, the moral is that men and women of the ordinary, regulation pattern must put up with the defects of each other's qualities. (*Turning the chair so that it faces* THEODORE *and again sitting in it.*) She complains that you don't admire her frocks and frills, Theo.

THEODORE (*groaning*). Oh!

PETER. Now, come! Where's the trou-

ble? There's my old mother—seventy-five in April! Whenever I'm at Stillwood, I make a reg'lar practice of complimentin' her on her rig-out. "By Jove, mater," I say, "you *are* a buck this mornin'!" Or evenin', as the case may be. I couldn't tell you what she's wearin', to save my life; but there's no harm done.

THEODORE. Yes, *you* do it; but your father doesn't do it, I'll be bound. (PETER *looks glum and is silent.*) It's too trivial! (*Producing his cigar case.*) A husband can't be everlastingly praising his wife's clothes. (*Offering a cigar to* PETER *which he declines.*) The absence of comment on my part is a sign that I'm satisfied with Zoe's appearance, surely.

PETER. She's one of the smartest women in London.

THEODORE (*irritably*). I know she is. I've told her so till I'm sick. (*Cutting and lighting a cigar.*) I've always been intensely proud of Zoe, as a matter of fact—intensely proud of her.

PETER. No more than her due.

THEODORE (*with increasing indignation*). Good God, how often, at a dinner-party, have I caught myself looking along the table and thinking she's the handsomest woman in the room! Tsch! It's a ridiculous thing to say
——

PETER. What?

THEODORE. I suppose no man has ever been "in love" with his wife for longer than I've been with mine.

PETER (*significantly*). Been.

THEODORE. And I have a very great affection for her still—or should have, if her behavior didn't check it.

PETER. If you showed your affection more plainly, wouldn't that check her behavior?

THEODORE (*leaving the fireplace and moving

[1] "Contango-day"—a Stock Exchange expression: the second day before settling day, i.e., the last day on which continuation of an account may be arranged.

about the room). Oh, my dear fellow, haven't you brains enough to see! We're middle-aged people, Zoe and I. I *am* middle-aged, and she's not far off it, poor girl. There must come a time on a journey when your pair of horses stop prancing and settle down to a trot.

PETER. How's that for a platitude!

THEODORE. I thought that worm-eaten illustration might appeal to you.

PETER. She keeps wonderfully young, Theo.

THEODORE. Isn't that a little to my credit? But Zoe's within three years of forty. You can't put the clock back.

PETER. A woman's as old as she looks——

THEODORE. And a man's as old as he feels! Another ancient wheeze!

PETER. And a *married* woman's as old as her husband *makes* her feel.

THEODORE. My dear Peter, I don't want Zoe to feel older than her years by a single hour. But I confess I do k her occasionally to feel as old *as* he years, and not to make herself dar nably absurd.

PETER. Absurd?

THEODORE. This infernal fooling about with th boys, for instance—the cause of last ight's flare-up—her "tame robins"—you're one——! (PETER *rises hastily and goes to the fire.*) Yes, you ought to be ashamed of yourself, for encouraging her.

PETER. Who's in fault? Because a man's wife has ceased to be attractive to him, it doesn't follow that she ain't attractive to others.

THEODORE (*contemptuously*). Attractive? The vanity of "attracting" a parcel of empty-headed young men! You're the patriarch of the group! (*Throwing himself into the chair just vacated by* PE-

TER.) The whole thing's undignified —raffish.

PETER (*extending a forefinger*). *You* contrive to be a trifle more sprightly at home, Theo——

THEODORE (*moving his head from side to side*). Oh, you will hammer away at that! I'm forty-six. My sprightly days are over.

PETER (*emphatically*). Humbug, old chap.

THEODORE. What's humbug?

PETER. Men are the biggest humbugs goin'—especially to themselves. And a man of your age or mine—and I'm four years your senior—is never a bigger humbug than when he's deloodin' himself with the notion that he's scrap-iron.

THEODORE. You're a gay old spark——

PETER. No, it's when the sun's workin' round to the west—it's when men are where we are now, that they're most liable to get into mischief.

THEODORE. Mischief? What are you driving at?

PETER. Nothin'. I'm simply layin' down a general principle.

THEODORE (*angrily*). Confound your general principles! Don't be an ass.

PETER (*coming to* THEODORE). That stoopid nonsense talked last night— early this mornin'—about livin' apart —who started it?

THEODORE. Zoe. I fancy it was Zoe— last night.

PETER. Oh, it wasn't the first time——?

THEODORE (*smoking with fierce puffs*). We had an awful scene—disgraceful. I felt inclined to rush out of the house then and there.

PETER. Why didn't you? You could have let yourself in again when she'd gone to by-by.

THEODORE (*sullenly*). No, that's not my style. If ever I do bang the front door, it'll be once and for all, my friend.

PETER (*shaking him*). Oh! Oh!

THEODORE. She's independent; she has her own income—you know—and I've told her I'd supplement it, if necessary. I've settled this house on her as it is; she'd be welcome to it, and every stick in it, worst come to the worst.

PETER. Theo!

THEODORE. And I'd go and live in a gar- 10 ret, in peace.

PETER. You're not considerin' such a step seriously?

THEODORE (*turning upon him roughly*). No, I'm not—not when I'm sitting here chatting quietly with you. Nor when she's rational and—and—and amenable, as she can be when she chooses. (*Clenching his hands.*) But when she's irritating me till I'm half beside myself, 20 I—I——

PETER. You——?

THEODORE (*looking up at* PETER). My God, Peter, you're a wise man, never to have taken it on!

PETER. Marriage?

THEODORE (*throwing his head back*). Oh, my dear fellow!

[*The glazed door opens and* ZOE *enters meekly. Her eyes are red, and a handker-* 30 *chief is crumpled up in her hand. She glances at the tea-table and comes to* THEO- DORE. PETER *retreats to the fire- place.*]

ZOE (*to* THEODORE, *in a piteous voice*). Have you—had your tea?

THEODORE (*frigidly*). I poured it out my- self.

[*After a moment's hesitation, she bends over him and gives him a kiss. Then she turns* 40 *away and, seating herself at the writing- table, proceeds to write a note. There is an awkward silence.*]

THEODORE (*breaking the silence, gruffly*). Er—Zo——

ZOE (*with a sniff, writing*). Yes?

THEODORE. What are you doing to- night?

ZOE. Jim Mallandain was going to take me to the Palace. I'm putting him off.

THEODORE. I'll dine you out and take you somewhere.

ZOE. No, I'd rather have a quiet evening at home, Theo—just you and me. (*Blowing her nose.*) I've ordered Mrs. Killick to send up an extra-nice din- ner.

THEODORE. Perhaps Peter——

ZOE (*stamping her foot*). No, I won't have him.

PETER. Besides, I'm booked.

ZOE (*petulantly*). I don't care whether you are or not. I want to dine alone with my husband. (*There is another pause, during which* ZOE *scratches away with her pen.*)

PETER (*clearing his throat*). Well, I'll be gettin' along. (THEODORE *rises.*) I say ——

THEODORE. H'm?

PETER. Why don't you and Zoe have a week or a fortnight in Paris? It 'ud do you both a heap of good.

THEODORE. Impossible. How can I?

PETER. Cert'nly you can. If anythin' im- portant crops up, Tom Slade or I will run over to you; or you could come back. (*Again there is a pause.* ZOE *stops writing.*) Do, old chap. (*Another pause.*) Won't you?

THEODORE (*without enthusiasm*). All right.

PETER. A fortnight? Nothin'll happen.

THEODORE (*nodding*). A fortnight.

[*Uttering a little chirp of delight,* ZOE *re- sumes writing.* PETER *goes to her as* THEO- DORE *moves away to the fireplace.*]

PETER (*to* ZOE). Good-by, ma'am. (*She gives him her left hand over her shoulder. He squeezes it and makes for the glazed door. There he appears to be struck by an idea. After a silence, he turns slowly, con-*

templates the pair for a moment with a puckered brow, and advances a step or two.)
Theo——

THEODORE *(who has picked up one of the illustrated papers and has seated himself upon the settee).* H'm?

PETER *(his hands in his pockets, rattling his keys).* About half-way between Dover and Calais—no, it's between Folkestone and Boulogne, ain't it?——

THEODORE *(examining the pictures).* What?

PETER. Of course! About half-way between Folkestone and Boulogne—mid-Channel—there's a shoal.

THEODORE *(turning a page of his paper).* What of it?

PETER. Le Colbart, the French sailormen call it—Le Colbart. *We* call it the Ridge. *(Coming forward.)* If you go by Folkestone and Boulogne, you'll pass over it.

THEODORE *(glancing at him suspiciously).* Thanks for the valuable information.

PETER. D'ye know, I've never encountered that blessed shoal without experiencin' a most unpleasant time?

ZOE *(addressing an envelope).* Oh, my dear Peter!

PETER. I've crossed on some of the finest days o' the year. The sun's been shinin', and outside the harbor the water's been as smooth as it's been *in*side. Everythin's looked as enticin' as could be; but as we've neared the Ridge—mid-Channel—I've begun to feel fidgety, restless, out o' sorts—hatin' myself and hatin' the man who's been sharin' my cabin with me. But the sensation hasn't lasted long.

ZOE *(sealing her letter).* Glad to hear it.

PETER. No; gradually the beastly motion has died down, and in a quarter of an hour or so I've found myself pacin' the deck again, arm-in-arm with the travelin'-companion I've been positively loathin' a few minutes earlier.

THEODORE *(gaping demonstratively).* Very interesting.

PETER. My dear pals, I remember the idea once occurrin' to me—I mentioned it to Charlie Westbrook at the time—there's a resemblance between *that* and marriage.

THEODORE *(shortly).* Ha! Thought that was coming.

[ZOE *turns in her chair, to listen to* PETER.]

PETER. Yes, and marriage, mark you, at its best and brightest. The happiest and luckiest of married couples have got to cross that wretched Ridge. However successful the first half of their journey may be, there's the rough-and-tumble of mid-Channel to negotiate. Some arrive there quicker than others, some later; it depends on wind and tide. But they *get* there; and a bad time it is, and must be—a time when travelin'-companions see nothin' but the spots on each other's yellow faces, and when innoomerable kind words and innoomerable kind acts are clean forgotten. (ZOE, *her letter in her hand, rises impulsively and comes to* PETER). But, as I tell you, it's soon over—*well* over, if only Mr. Jack and Mrs. Jill will understand the situation; if only they'll say to themselves, "We're on the Ridge; we're in mid-Channel; in another quarter of an hour the boat'll be steady again—as steady as when we stepped on to the gangway." *(To* THEODORE). Not offended, old man?

THEODORE *(uncomfortably).* Ha, ha, ha!

ZOE *(gently, giving her letter to* PETER). Tell Warren to give that to a messenger boy. *(To* THEODORE). Theo——! *(She puts her hands upon* PETER'S *shoulders and kisses him.)*

PETER *(chuckling).* Ha, ha! *(To* THEO-

DORE.) Division of profits. (*At the glazed door.*) When'll you be off?

THEODORE. Oh—one day next week.

PETER (*nodding*). To-morrow mornin', then. (*He goes out, closing the door.*)

ZOE. Dear old Peter!

THEODORE (*deep in his paper*). Peter's getting a bit of a bore, though.

ZOE (*mimicking* PETER, *as she wipes her eyes*). He's amusin'. (*Going to* THEODORE *and seating herself beside him.*) Theo——

THEODORE. H'm?

ZOE (*edging up to him*). Let's go by Folkestone and Boulogne—shall we?

THEODORE. *I* don't mind.

ZOE (*wistfully*). Let's go by Folkestone and Boulogne—and have done with it. (*Slipping her arm through his.*) Theo—last night—sorry. (*He nods and looks at another picture*). I take it all back—the things I said. I didn't mean them.

THEODORE. That's all right.

ZOE. And *you* didn't mean——?

THEODORE (*impatiently*). Of course I didn't.

ZOE (*giving herself a shake*). Ah! (*After a brief pause.*) Theo——

THEODORE. H'm?

ZOE (*taking the paper from him playfully*). Don't look at those improper young ladies. (*Coaxingly.*) Couldn't you manage to get away on Sunday?

THEODORE. Oh—I might.

ZOE. It's your treat to me, isn't it—and the beginning of better times? The *sooner* we begin——

THEODORE (*nodding*). You shall have it all your own way.

ZOE (*gleefully*). Sunday!

THEODORE. H'm.

ZOE. I'm dreadfully shabby. I've no new clothes. You don't object?

THEODORE (*distinctly*). Now, my dear Zo—my darling—understand this from me clearly. You are *never* shabby; you couldn't be shabby. As far as I am a judge, you are always dressed beautifully and—and—and in perfect taste.

ZOE. Beautifully!

THEODORE. If you were *not* well dressed, I should venture to call your attention to it.

ZOE. Silence is approval?

THEODORE. Absolutely. So don't expect me—a busy man—to be eternally praising your gowns and what not; because I cannot and will not do it.

ZOE. I won't—I won't. I know I'm inconsiderate—(*Stamping her foot.*) beastly inconsiderate. (*Excitedly.*) Write out a telegram now——

THEODORE. Telegram?

ZOE. To the hotel.

THEODORE. Yes, that 'ud be wise. (*He rises and goes over to the writing-table where, taking a sheet of note-paper, he sits and writes.*) We couldn't get an answer to a letter.

ZOE (*jumping up and walking about*). Jolly nice rooms, Theo!

THEODORE (*assentingly*). H'm, h'm.

ZOE (*humming*). Tra, la! ra, la! la, ra, la ——!

THEODORE (*in the throes of composition*). Sssh, sssh!

ZOE (*opening the illustrated paper*). Beg pardon.

THEODORE (*writing*). "——deux bonnes chambres à coucher—salle de bain—et salon——"

ZOE. There's Lena. Don't forget the maid.

THEODORE. Oh, they shove her anywhere.

ZOE (*imperatively*). No, no; I must have her handy. (*He writes.*) What hotel are we going to, Theo?

THEODORE (*writing*). "——aussi chambre pour servante même étage——"

ZOE. The Ritz?

THEODORE. Oh, blow the Ritz!

ZOE. We've always *been* comfortable at the Ritz.

THEODORE (*putting the finishing touches to his telegram*). Twenty francs a minute.

ZOE (*disappointed*). Where then? The Elysée Palace is too far out this weather. The Régina?

THEODORE (*reading*). "Pouvez-vous réserver pour Monsieur et Madame Blundell pour dimanche et nuits suivantes appartement composé deux bonnes chambres à coucher, salle de bain, et salon, aussi chambre pour servante même étage? Réponse télégraphique. Theodorus, London."

ZOE (*advancing*). Oh, Theo! Shall we try the new Meurice? The Langdales had a suite there that made them feel like Royalties.

THEODORE (*half-turning to her*). Gerald Duckfield was telling me of a capital little hotel where he and Bessie stayed—the Vendôme——

ZOE. Where's that?

THEODORE. In the Place Vendôme.

ZOE. The Ritz—the Bristol—the Rhin— they're the only hotels in the Place.

THEODORE. Oh, but this is in the part of the Place that runs down to the top of the Rue Castiglione.

ZOE. The *narrow* part!

THEODORE. Well, it isn't the broad part, certainly.

ZOE. The traffic of the Rue St. Honoré to help to send you to sleep!

THEODORE. No, no; there are double windows, Gerald says, to the best bedrooms. (*Turning to the writing-table.*) It 'ud be an experiment.

ZOE (*sitting in the chair in the middle of the room, with her back to him*). Yes, it would be an experiment.

THEODORE. Shall we risk it?

ZOE (*coldly*). By all means.

THEODORE (*writing*). "Directeur—Hôtel Vendôme."

ZOE (*tapping her feet upon the floor*). Ha!

THEODORE. H'm? "——Place Vendôme ——"

ZOE (*holding up the illustrated paper so that he may see, over her head, a risqué picture*). If you were taking this sort of woman with you, nothing 'ud be good enough for her.

THEODORE (*glancing at the picture, angrily*). Oh, don't be so coarse! (*There is a pause. He leans back in his chair, biting his pen. Suddenly she flings the illustrated paper away from her into the air. Throwing down his pen, he rises and paces the room.*) This promises well for an enjoyable fortnight in Paris!

ZOE (*rising and moving to the left*). Look here, old man! This trip was going to be *your* treat. Very well, that's off! I'll take *you* to Paris; *I'll* pay the expenses; and I won't stuff you up in a frowsy rabbit-hutch.

THEODORE (*coming forward on the right*). Don't insult me!

ZOE (*facing him*). Anyway, your treat or mine, I stay at no hotel in Paris that isn't top-hole.

THEODORE (*furiously*). Oh, stop your damned slang, for God's sake!

ZOE (*her eyes blazing*). What!

THEODORE (*sitting on the fauteuil-stool and rocking himself to and fro*). Oh! Oh!

ZOE. Stop my damned slang!

THEODORE (*his head in his hands*). Hold your tongue!

ZOE (*coming to him*). And how did I learn my damned slang, pray? (*He waves her from him.*) I learned it from the crew you surrounded me with when I condescended to marry you and went out of my world into yours.

THEODORE (*starting up*). Oh——! (*He goes to the bell and rings it continuously.*)

ZOE (*following him*). Yes, you were hugely tickled by it *then!* And so were *they*—the men you thought might be

serviceable to you; and who *were* serviceable to you, often through *me!*

THEODORE. Oh!

ZOE. Ha! And now that my tongue's
furred with it, and it isn't necessary to
attract the vulgar brutes any more,
you round on me and rag me! (*Pacing
the room on the left.*) Oh! Oh! If only
my dear old dad were alive! He'd
fuss over me and protect me. My fa- 10
ther was a gentleman. He warned me
I was chucking myself away!

THEODORE. Oh!

ZOE (*wildly*). Why do you keep on ringing that bell?

THEODORE (*in a loud voice*). I suppose I
can ring the bell if I like!

ZOE. You—you can go to the devil if you
like! (*She goes out at the glazed door. As
she disappears,* WARREN *passes her and
enters.*)

THEODORE (*crossing to the writing-table*).
Warren——

WARREN. Yessir?

THEODORE (*picking up the sheet of paper on
which he has written the message to the hotel*). Pack me a bag.

WARREN. Bag, sir?

THEODORE (*tearing the paper into small
pieces*). Yes; I'm not sleeping at home
to-night.

WARREN (*coming to the table and preparing
to remove the tea-things*). Very good, sir.

CURTAIN

ACT II

The same, but the disposition of some of the
furniture is changed. The settee on the right is
now placed with its back to the fireplace. At 20
the farther end of the settee are the oblong table and chair, and on the left of the table, facing the settee, is the chair which in the preced-
ing act stood in the middle of the room. An
armchair is at the nearer end of the settee; and
anoth— armchair and the fauteuil-stool stand
together, n . ur from the glazed door.

On the oblong table are a box of cigarettes,
matches, and an ash-tray.

The fireplace is banked with flowers, there 30
are flowers in vases upon the tables, and the
room is full of sunlight.

[*Two men—an upholsterer and his assistant
—are engaged in putting covers of gay
chintz upon the chairs and settees. The upholsterer is on his knees at the settee on the
right, the assistant is at the chair by the
writing-table.* LENA, ZOE'S *maid—a
bright, buxom woman—is arranging the
furniture in the middle of the room. Pres- 40
ently the assistant proceeds to collect the
brown paper and cord which litter the
floor.*]

UPHOLSTERER (*rising from his knees—to*
LENA). That's all right.

LENA (*coming to him*). And when are we
to have the pleasure of seeing *you*
again?

UPHOLSTERER. To-morrow.

LENA. What about next year, or the year
after! (*Producing her purse and giving him
a tip.*) In case I shouldn't live so long.

UPHOLSTERER. Thank you very much.
(*Moving away—quietly.*) William——

[*The assistant, laden with brown paper, advances, and* LENA *tips him.*]

ASSISTANT. Thank you, miss. Good morning, miss.

LENA. Good morning.

UPHOLSTERER (*at the glazed door*). Good
morning.

LENA (*tidying the furniture on the right*).
Good morning.

[*The men depart. Almost immediately, the
glazed door is reopened and* WARREN *appears showing in* LEONARD. LEONARD *is
gloved and is carrying a straw hat and a
walking-cane. He has lost his fresh, boyish
appearance and is sallow and lined.*]

LEONARD (*to* LENA). Good morning.

LENA (*familiarly*). Oh, good morning. (*To* WARREN.) I'll let Mrs. Blundell know. (*To* LEONARD, *as* WARREN *withdraws*.) She'll be down soon. Will you have a paper?

LEONARD. Thanks; seen 'em. How is she, Lena?

LENA. Middling. She's a little feverish, the doctor says. She must have caught a chill coming over. (LEONARD *nods*.) She would sit on deck, talking to Mr. Mallandain. We met him by accident on the platform as we were leaving Paris.

LEONARD (*nodding again*). She's told me.

LENA. She's to remain indoors again today and keep out o' draughts. (*Looking at a watch which she wears on her wrist and at the clock on the mantelpiece.*) What do you say the right time is?

LEONARD (*looking at his watch*). Quarter to twelve.

LENA (*going to the mantelpiece*). I'm to give her her med'cine an hour before meals. (*Moving the hands of the clock.*) Ha! They've all been playing tricks here while we've been away, clock-winder included.

LEONARD (*absently*). Indeed?

LENA. Servants, tradespeople, everybody! (*Unbuckling her bracelet.*) Because Mrs. Blundell is now on her own, I s'pose they fancy they can take advantage of her. (*Returning to* LEONARD). I'll teach 'em! (*"Timing" her watch.*) Think we're getting fairly straight?

LEONARD (*glancing idly at the room as he sits in the armchair near the glazed door*). Wonderfully.

LENA. Not bad, is it, considering we've been home only two days?

LEONARD (*placing his hat and cane upon the fauteuil-stool*). Capital.

LENA (*refastening her bracelet*). Ouf! The relief, after some of those foreign hotels!

LEONARD (*drawing off his gloves*). Tired of traveling, eh?

LENA. Don't ask me! I was saying to Mrs. Killick at breakfast—I've had enough of Italy to last me my life. Over four months of it, and without a courier! (*Going toward the glazed door*). That's a bit too stiff.

LEONARD. It is rather.

LENA (*halting by him and dropping her voice slightly*). Not that we wanted a courier when *you* came out to us. A splendid courier you were; I couldn't wish for a better.

LEONARD (*uncomfortably*). Ha, ha!

LENA (*laughing*). Do you remember our losing her hat-box at that wretched old Siena?

LEONARD. Yes—yes.

LENA. You woke 'em up there in grand style. Ha, ha! Your friend, the Italian policeman—the image in the feathers ——!

LEONARD. Ha, ha!

LENA. You did give him a dressing! (*Sobering herself.*) Yes, those three or four weeks you were with us were the pleasantest o' the lot, to my idea. (*Going.*) Well, good day. (*Stopping again.*) Oh, but I must show you this. (*Taking a ring from her finger.*) A present from her—last Saturday—one of the best shops in the Roo Royarl. (*Handing it to him.*) She went out and bought it herself.

LEONARD. Turquoise——

LENA. And diamonds.

LEONARD (*returning the ring*). Beautiful.

LENA. Wasn't it kind of her! I'm as vain as a peacock. (*Replacing the ring on her finger.*) But there, you've both been extremely good to me.

LEONARD. Not at all.

LENA. You have; you've spoilt me completely. (*At the door, speaking louder.*) Treacherous weather for June, isn't it?

LEONARD. Very.

LENA (*in the corridor*). Oh, here you are! Here's Mr. Ferris—I was just coming up to tell you——

[LEONARD *rises as* ZOE *appears in the corridor. She is dressed in an elegant robe of rich, soft material and carries a little bag in which are a few opened letters, her handkerchief, etc. She also is changed. Her face is wan and there are dark circles around her eyes.*]

ZOE. Ah? (*To* LEONARD, *formally, as she enters the room.*) Good morning.

LEONARD. Good morning.

ZOE. Lena, how charming the old chintz looks!

LENA (*who is lingering*). It's English!

ZOE (*laying her bag upon the oblong table*). If we could all be freshened up by the same process!

LENA (*her hand on the door-handle*). Don't forget you're to take your med'cine in three-quarters of an hour.

ZOE. Oh, bring me the filthy stuff when you like.

LENA (*in the corridor, closing the door*). Now, don't be naughty.

[*As the woman disappears,* LEONARD *walks over to* ZOE. *She puts out her hand to check him, and they stand for a moment or two watching the door and listening. Then she drops her hand and turns her face to him perfunctorily, and he kisses her as a matter of course.*]

ZOE. Your motor isn't outside?

LEONARD. No; I walked across the Park.

ZOE. That yellow car of yours is so conspicuous. (*Arranging a pillow on the settee.*) Sorry I wasn't visible yesterday.

LEONARD. You're better?

ZOE (*evasively.*) Oh, more or less decrepit. (*Sitting.*) What have you been doing with yourself?

LEONARD. Nothing much. (*Sitting in the armchair opposite to her.*) Except——

ZOE (*taking her bag from the table*). By-the-bye, I've had a note this morning from an old friend of yours.

LEONARD. Who?

ZOE (*producing a letter from the bag*). Ethel Pierpoint.

LEONARD (*inexpressively*). Oh? (*She extracts the letter from its envelope and tosses it across to him. He reads it silently, with a frown. She takes a cigarette from the box on the table.*) I thought you'd dropped her.

ZOE. I did, in a fashion. I stopped her letters by ceasing to answer them. (*Striking a match.*) I hated calling myself hers affectionately, knowing I'd been the cause of your slacking away from her.

LEONARD (*under his breath*). Pish!

ZOE (*lighting her cigarette*). *What* does she say?

LEONARD (*reading aloud*). "Dearest Zoe. Quite by chance I hear you are back at Lancaster Gate. Why do you still make no sign? I never wanted your friendship more than now—or the friendship of somebody who will give me good advice, or a sound shaking for being a fool. Please take pity on your troubled but ever devoted, Ethel Drayson Pierpoint." (*To* ZOE.) What does she mean by never wanting your friendship more than now? (ZOE *shakes her head. He continues to ponder over the letter.*) "—or the friendship of somebody who will give me good advice, or a sound shaking for being a fool."

ZOE (*smoking, thoughtfully*). When did you see the Pierpoints last?

LEONARD. About a month after you left London—just before I followed you. (*Returning the letter to her.*) I cooled off them gradually.

ZOE (*after a pause.*) She's a nice girl—Ethel.

LEONARD. Ye—es, she was nice enough.

[*There is a further pause. Then* ZOE *jumps up, as if to dismiss disagreeable reflections, and crosses to the writing-table. There she empties her bag of the letters it contains.*]

LEONARD (*gloomily*). Am I in the way?

ZOE (*fretfully*). Of course not. (*She sits at the writing-table and busies herself with re-* 10 *reading her letters and destroying some of them.* LEONARD *rises and takes a cigarette from the box.*) Poor Robby Relf has got neuritis.

LEONARD (*lighting his cigarette*). Zo——

ZOE. Eh?

LEONARD. I was going to tell you—I dined at the Carlton last night.

ZOE (*indifferently*). Oh?

LEONARD. With Cossy Rawlings. Guess 20 who was there.

ZOE (*becoming attentive*). Dun'no.

LEONARD. He didn't see me—he was at a table the other side of the room——

ZOE (*holding her breath*). Theodore?

LEONARD. Yes.

[*She throws the pieces of a letter into the wastepaper basket and leans back in her chair.*]

ZOE. How—how did he look?   30

LEONARD (*curling his lip*). I didn't study his appearance.

ZOE. He—he wasn't—by himself?

LEONARD. Hardly!

ZOE. That—that woman?

LEONARD (*nodding*). Same lady.

ZOE. Simply the two?

LEONARD (*sitting upon the settee on the right*). The two turtle doves.

[*After a brief silence, she pushes her letters* 40 *from her, rises, and moves about the room quietly but agitatedly.*]

ZOE. Who is this creature?

LEONARD (*impatiently*). I've told you—and Jim told you on Sunday.

ZOE. Hatherly—Annerly——?

LEONARD. Her husband was a Major Annerly—Frank Annerly. He divorced her over a man of the name of Bettison.

ZOE. Where's *he?*

LEONARD. He's dead. She's been through a good many hands since.

ZOE. Ho!

LEONARD. Fred Wishart was one—and Tod Arnold——

ZOE. She's quite young, isn't she?

LEONARD. Looks a baby.

ZOE. Ha!

LEONARD. I should put her at thirty.

ZOE. Pretty? They all are!

LEONARD. Passable.

ZOE (*behind the chair on the left of the oblong table*). Do you think she's—with him?

LEONARD. Not regularly. She's still living in Egerton Crescent, according to Cossy.

ZOE (*gripping the back of the chair*). She'll ruin him; she'll ruin him, Len.

LEONARD. Oh, I dare say there'll be a bit left, when she's done with him.

ZOE. There are other ways of dragging a man down besides through his pocket. Jim Mallandain says she's a vampire.

LEONARD. Why should you worry yourself——?

ZOE. I don't want him to come to grief. Why should I?

LEONARD. If he does, you've nothing to reproach yourself with.

ZOE (*giving him a swift look*). *What!*

LEONARD (*sullenly*). Oh, you know what I mean—nothing that occurred before he took himself off.

ZOE (*moving to the oblong table, with a long-drawn sigh*). Ah-h-h! (*Sitting, her elbows on the table, leaning her head on her hand.*) It will always be on my conscience that I drove him away.

LEONARD. You didn't drive him away.

ZOE. I did.

LEONARD. You were quite justified in doing it, anyhow. He made your life a burden to you.

ZOE. I might have been more patient with him; I might have waited.

LEONARD. Waited?

ZOE. Waited till we'd got through the middle period of our lives. (*Raising her head.*) Peter warned us, the very day we parted——

LEONARD (*sneeringly*). Peter! 10

ZOE. Mid-Channel! We should soon have reached the other side.

LEONARD. There's a limit to human endurance; you'd passed it.

ZOE (*staring before her*). It seems to me now, there wasn't so very much for me to put up with—not so very much. (*Rising and walking to the back of the settee on which* LEONARD *is sitting.*) There was a lot of good in him, really. After 20 all, he only needed managing, humoring——

LEONARD (*starting up and turning to her*). Upon my soul, Zoe! Ha! You're discovering no end of fine qualities in him suddenly!

ZOE (*bitterly*). Am I!

LEONARD. You hadn't a decent word for him when we were in Italy! Now he's perfect! 30

ZOE (*facing him*). No, he's not.

LEONARD (*satirically*). Sounds like it.

ZOE (*flaring up*). Neither he nor you! You can be just as unkind to me as he ever was.

LEONARD (*angrily*). I!

ZOE. Yes! And, with all his faults, he did try to take care of me—to keep me from harm! (*Her eyes ablaze.*) My God, what have *you* done! 40

[*They remain confronting one another for a moment without speaking. Then he turns away abruptly and picks up his hat and cane. She runs after him and clings to him.*]

ZOE. No, no; don't be hasty. I didn't mean it—I didn't mean it——

LEONARD (*endeavoring to free himself*). Let me go——

ZOE. Ah, no! I'm not well to-day——

LEONARD. I'll come back when you're better-tempered.

ZOE. I *am* better-tempered. Look! it's all over. (*Coaxing him to give up his hat and cane.*) Lenny—Lenny dear—Lenny —— (*Placing the hat and cane upon the writing-table, she takes her handkerchief from her bag and dries her eyes. He sits in the armchair near the glazed door sulkily.*) Ha, ha! Now you're beginning to see what sort of a time poor Theo had with me.

LEONARD. Oh, can't you leave off talking about him for a single second!

ZOE (*coming to him meekly*). I beg your pardon, dear.

LEONARD. You've got that fellow on the brain.

ZOE (*standing behind him*). You started it, by telling me of last night.

LEONARD. Why the deuce *shouldn't* I tell you of last night! Do sit down. (*She sits near him, upon the fauteuil-stool.*) I can't make you out, Zo. This woman's only what we've been waiting for. I've said all along he'd soon give you an opportunity of divorcing him. She completes your case for you.

ZOE (*dully*). Yes.

LEONARD (*grumbling*). You ought to be tremendously obliged to Jim for being the first to open your eyes—my eyes too—to what's going on. Instead of which, you're upset by it. And now, because *I've* seen Blundell and the lady together, I'm favored by hearing Mr. B. described as a model husband——

ZOE (*to silence him*). Ah——!

LEONARD (*changing his tone*). When do you interview your lawyers?

ZOE. I—I haven't written to them yet.

LEONARD. You were to do it after I left you on Monday.

ZOE. I—I've been feeling so cheap, Len.

LEONARD (*with a short laugh*). We shall be gray-haired before we're married, at this rate. (*She lays her hand on his appeasingly. He retains her hand.*) I believe you'll have to go through the form of trying to compel Blundell to return to you. Of course, he'll refuse. Meanwhile we must have the lady's house watched—or Blundell's flat. I shouldn't be surprised if he'd arrange that part of the business with you, to save trouble and expense. Drop a line to Maxwells to-day, will you?

ZOE (*obediently*). Yes.

LEONARD. Or ring them up. You'll be able to get out to-morrow—or one of them would wait on you.

ZOE. Yes.

LEONARD. That's right, old girlie. Kiss me. (*They kiss, quickly and cautiously, without ardor.*) Sorry.

ZOE (*turning to him and lowering her voice almost to a whisper*). Lenny——

LEONARD. What?

ZOE. Don't forget—Perugia.

LEONARD (*in an outburst*). Oh, yes—curse the place!—let's forget Perugia. I was off my head there. I behaved like a blackguard. You needn't be continually throwing it in my teeth.

ZOE. No, no; I'm not scolding you again. (*Gently.*) What I mean is—your breaking your word to me at Perugia —staying in the same hotel——

LEONARD. Well?

ZOE. If Theodore's solicitors got hold of that——

LEONARD (*rising and walking away*). Yes, but they won't get hold of it.

ZOE (*twisting herself around toward him*). You remember our meeting Claud Lowenstein at the railway station at Arezzo?

LEONARD. I explained to him that my being in the train with you was pure chance. I made that square.

ZOE. He was going on to Perugia—to the Brufani. (*Rising.*) He may have been suspicious—he may have ⸺ ⸺red ——

LEONARD. Even that little swine wouldn't tell tales.

ZOE (*coming to him*). Then there's Lena— they might pump Lena——

LEONARD. My dear girl, all this would be very terrible if Blundell wasn't as anxious to get rid of you as we are to get rid of him. No, you take my word for it—he won't defend. His game is to be free at any price.

ZOE. To marry again perhaps!

LEONARD. Probably.

ZOE (*clenching her hands*). Ah, no!

LEONARD (*his brow darkening again*). Doesn't *that* please you? There's no satisfying you, Zoe. (*She leaves him and paces the room distractedly.*) A minute ago you were frightened lest he should be ruined by Mrs. Annerly!

ZOE (*on the left*). I—I couldn't bear the idea of another woman being a better wife to him than I was! I couldn't bear it, Lenny!

LEONARD. Why, what concern would it be of yours——!

ZOE (*with a gesture, as the glazed door opens*). 'Ssh!

[WARREN *appears.*]

WARREN (*to* ZOE). I beg your pardon, ma'am—Mr. Mottram.

ZOE (*uttering a little, eager cry*). Ah!

WARREN. He'll call again, ma'am, if you're engaged.

ZOE. Did you say I—I'd anybody with me?

WARREN. No, ma'am.

ZOE (*after a slight pause—indicating the adjoining room*). Is that room still covered up?

WARREN. Yes, ma'am.

ZOE. Well—show him in there for the moment.

WARREN. Yes, ma'am. (*He withdraws, closing the door.*)

ZOE (*to* LEONARD, *in a low voice*). He'd better not find you here so early.

LEONARD (*also dropping his voice, testily*). Why need you bother yourself with old Peter this morning?

ZOE (*bringing* LEONARD *to her and caressing*). I haven't seen him since January. Don't look so cross. (*Caressing his cheek.*) Are you engaged to lunch anywhere?

LEONARD. No.

ZOE. Will you eat your lunch with me?

[*He nods. She takes a powder-puff from her bag and, looking into the hand-mirror, hurriedly removes the traces of her tears. While she is thus occupied,* LEONARD *listens at the nearer door on the right.*]

LEONARD (*leaving the door—in a whisper*). He's there.

[WARREN *appears.*]

WARREN (*to* ZOE). Mr. Mottram is in the next room, ma'am.

ZOE. Thank you.

[WARREN *withdraws.*]

ZOE (*to* LEONARD, *in a whisper, accompanying him to the glazed door*). Go into the Park and sit under the trees. Blow a kiss for me to all the kiddies. (*She watches him disappear down the corridor. Then, having closed the glazed door, she opens the farther door on the right.*) Peter!

PETER (*out of sight*). My dear lady!

ZOE (*going into the next room*). Why on earth have they put you into this dismal room! Come into the light. (*Returning with him, her arm tucked through his.*) Oh, my dear Peter—my dear Peter——!

PETER. Ah, yes, yes, yes! A nice way to serve a pal!

ZOE (*closing the door*). How did you——?

PETER. Jim Mallandain dropped in at the office this morning. (*They leave the door.*) He traveled with you from Paris on Sunday.

ZOE. I collided with him at the Gare du Nord.

PETER. And this is Wednesday!

ZOE (*withdrawing her arm*). I funked sending for you; that's a fact.

PETER. Funked it?

ZOE (*with the air of a child in disgrace*). Your letters to me have been awfully sweet, but I know you despise me for making a muck of things.

PETER (*protestingly*). Ah, Mrs. Zoe!

ZOE. And I'm rather a sick rabbit, Peter. (*Turning away.*) A sick rabbit has only one desire—to hide in its burrow. (*Facing him.*) My heart bounded when you were announced, though.

PETER (*following her*). You don't look very fit. Seen a doctor?

ZOE. I've let Lena call in Rashleigh, to humor her. (*Sitting on the settee on the right.*) And I've promised to swallow his pig-wash.

PETER. What's he say?

ZOE. Chill; but—(*Raising her eyes to his.*) —between ourselves?——

PETER. Honor.

ZOE (*with quivering lips*). Life, dear old chum!

PETER (*tenderly*). Ain't much in it?

ZOE. Damn little. (*Putting her hair back from her brow.*) Phew! Can't sleep, Peter.

PETER. Oh, lor'!

ZOE. I tumble into bed at twelve—one—two. I get an hour's stupor, from sheer fatigue, and then I'm wide awake—thinking! Then, dressing-gown and slippers and the cigarettes; and then it's to and fro, up and down—smoke—smoke—smoke—often till the servants start brushing the stairs. No game, eh?

PETER. How long has this——?

ZOE. It began at—(*Checking herself.*)—oh, a devil of a while. (*With a shiver.*) But I'm worse now I've set foot again in this house.

PETER (*eyeing her keenly*). Ghosts? (*Avoiding his gaze, she stretches out her hand toward the cigarette box. He pushes the box beyond her reach. She makes a grimace. There is a pause.*) Zoe—— 10

ZOE. Well?

PETER (*deliberately*). Why shouldn't you pick up the pieces?

"ᴋ up—the pieces?

PETER. ᴀ nd Theodore.

ZOE. Oh—ᴅᴏ.'t be—funny, Peter.

PETER. I'm not funny; I'm as serious as the clown at the circus. (*Another pause.*) Write to him—or give me a message to take to him. *See* him. 20

[*She gets to her feet and attempts to pass* PE-TER. *He detains her and she sinks back among her pillows.*]

ZOE. Ha, ha! You ridiculous man! (*Faintly.*) Pick up the pieces! As if that were possible!

PETER. Oh, the valuable family china is in a good many fragments, I admit. But there *are* the fragments, lyin' on the carpet. They can be collected, 30 fitted together.

ZOE (*with a sudden gesture of entreaty*). Ah, for God's sake, Peter——!

PETER. Why, I'm suggestin' nothin' unusual.

ZOE (*repeating her gesture*). Sssh!

PETER. Go into the homes of three-fifths of the married people you know—*I* know—and you'll find some imposin' specimens of porcelain that won't 40 bear inspectin' very narrowly.

ZOE (*waving the subject away*). Sssh, sssh!

PETER. Only yesterday afternoon I was callin' at a house in—never mind the district. I was wanderin' round the drawin'-room, lookin' at the *bric-à-brac*, and there, on a Louis Quatorze console-table, were as handsome a pair of old Chinese jars—genuine Mings—as ever I've met with. Such a sooperb glaze they've got, such depth o' color! They appear to be priceless, perfect, till you examine 'em closely; and then——! My dear Zoe, they're cracked; they've both had a nasty knock at some time or another; they're scarred shockin'ly with rivets and cᴇ ... ... Aᴀ ... whᴀᴇ ... was shᴇddᴀ' tears over 'em, in sailed madam, smilin' and holdin' out her hand to me—she'd been upstairs, rubbin' carmine on her lips——

ZOE (*in a murmur*). You horror!

PETER. How kind of me to call—and how wild Tom 'ud be at missin' me! To the casual observer, she's the happiest woman goin'; and Tom, who strolled in just as I was leavin', might be the most domesticated of husbands. You follow me? You grasp the poetic allegory? Those faulty old Mings are emblematic of the establishment they adorn. Mr. and Mrs. Tom fell out years ago; they turned against each other one fine day—in mid-Channel—and hadn't the sense to kiss and be friends on landin'; their lives are as damaged as those wounded crocks of theirs on the console-table. (*Persuasively.*) Well, but ain't it wiser to repair the broken china, rather than chuck the bits into the dust-bin? It's still showy and effective at a distance; and there are cases —rare, but they exist—where the mendin's been done so neatly that the flaws are almost imperceptible. (*Seating himself opposite* ZOE.) Zoe——

ZOE (*almost inaudibly*). Yes, Peter?

PETER (*leaning forward*). I believe yours is one of the cases—yours and Theodore's—where the mendin' would be exceptionally successful.

ZOE. What do you—what do you mean?

PETER. My dear, old Theo is as miserable over this affair as you are.

ZOE (*attempting a disdainful smile*). N-nonsense!

PETER. Oh, no, it ain't nonsense.

ZOE. W-what makes you think that?

PETER. Between ourselves?

ZOE (*a note of eagerness in her voice*). Honor.

PETER. He shows it in all manner o' ways. Neglects his business—ain't much good at it when he doesn't—is losin' his grip—looks confoundedly ill—*is* ill. Altogether he's a different man from the man he was, even when matters were at boilin' point here.

ZOE (*locking and unlocking her fingers*). Does he ever—speak of me?

PETER. Oh, lor', yes.

ZOE. N-not kindly?

PETER. Very. Very kindly.

ZOE (*after a silence, as if in pain*). Oh——! (*She rises, passes him, and goes to the other side of the room where she moves from one piece of furniture to another aimlessly.*) W-what's he say about me?

PETER (*not turning*). Frets about you— wonders how you're gettin' along— wonders as to the state of your finances—can't bear the idea of your bein' in the least pinched—wants to help you.

ZOE. He's extremely generous!

PETER. Theo? Never was anythin' else.

ZOE (*her eyes flashing*). His own expenses must be pretty considerable just now, too!

PETER (*pricking up his ears*). Must they? (*With great artlessness.*) Why?

ZOE. Oh, do you imagine I live with wool in my ears?

PETER (*over his shoulder*). Wool——?

ZOE. This woman he's continually with! (*PETER's face is still averted from ZOE. At*

this juncture his eyes open widely and his mouth shapes to a whistle.*) This—Mrs.— Mrs.—what's her name—Annerly! (*Pacing the room.*) A notorious woman —a woman without a shred of character—an any-man's-woman——!

PETER (*settling his features and turning his chair toward* ZOE—*in a tone of expostulation*). Oh!

ZOE. A baby-faced thing—seven years younger than I am! Precisely the class of goods a man of Theo's age flies at!

PETER. Oh—oh——!

ZOE. *They're* rather costly articles, aren't they?

PETER. My dear Mrs. Zoe——

ZOE. Oh, don't you pretend to be so innocent, Peter! You know jolly well he's all over the place with her. They were at Hurlingham together Saturday week.

PETER (*coolly*). I dessay.

ZOE. And they dine *tête-à-tête* at the Savoy, Ritz's, the Carlton——

PETER. Who supplies the information?

ZOE. They were at the Carlton last night.

PETER. Who's told you *that?*

ZOE. L—— (*She pulls herself up.*)

PETER (*curiously*). Who?

ZOE (*moistening her lips*). Oh, I—I first heard of it all from Jim Mallandain. He was full of it on board the boat on Sunday.

PETER. *Was* he! (*Rising lazily.*) A busy gentleman—Jim.

ZOE. It was Jim who met them at Hurlingham—had tea with 'em.

PETER (*curiously again*). But it can't be Jim who's blabbed about last night.

ZOE. Why?

PETER (*shrugging his shoulders*). He happened to mention this mornin' that he was with a party at Jules'.

ZOE (*confused*). N-no, it isn't from Jim I've got that. I——(*Throwing herself into the armchair near the glazed door.*) Oh, but really, it's a matter of supreme indifference to me, Peter, my dear boy, whom Theodore entertains at the Carlton, or whom he entertains at his flat——

PETER (*coming to her*). My dear Zoe——

ZOE (*laughing heartily*). Ha, ha, ha! His flat! I hear it's quite sumptuous. After his pathetic yearnings for peace and quiet in a garret, he sets up, within a month of our separating, in an enormous flat in Cavendish Square! I received that bit of news when I was in Florence. I—I was intensely amused. Oh, let him wallow in his precious flat——!

PETER (*argumentatively*). My dear lady——

ZOE (*her hand to her brow, exhausted*). Ah, drop it, Peter; drop it!

PETER. I ask you—a liberal-minded person—what 'ud become of friendship as an institootion if men and women couldn't be pals without havin' the—the—what-d'ye-call-it—the tongue of scandal wagged at 'em? The world 'ud be intolerable. It ain't all marmalade as it is; but if a fellow can't take the fresh air in the company of a female at Hurlingham, or give her a bite o' food at a restaurant——

ZOE (*her head against the back of her chair, her eyes closed*). Ah, la, la, la!

PETER. As for this—er—this Mrs. Annerly——(*He again purses his mouth and is evidently in a difficulty.*)

ZOE (*her eyes still shut*). Well?

PETER. It's true she chucked Annerly for another chap. I don't condone an act of that description—except that I knew Annerly, and if ever there was a dull dog——

ZOE. Was he duller than Theo?

PETER. Oh, go on with yer! And since then she's been a trifle—flighty—perhaps, now and again (*With a gulp.*), but to-day she might be your maiden aunt.

ZOE (*dreamily*). You humbug, Peter!

PETER (*sitting beside her, upon the fauteuil-stool*). Oh, I'm not maintainin' that we men always select our women pals from the right basket. I'm not sayin' that we don't make asses of ourselves occasionally, sometimes from sentiment, sometimes from vanity, sometimes from—various causes. But the same remark applies to you women over your men pals. (*Laying a hand on her arm.*) For instance—(*She opens her eyes.*)—for instance, here you are, throwin' stones at old Theo with regard to Alice Annerly. (*Significantly.*) My dear, there are a few panes o' glass in the house *you* live in, bear in mind.

[*She sits upright, looking at him.*]

ZOE. In the house—I——?

PETER (*gravely*). Mrs. Zoe, what you did when you were under your husband's protection is one thing; what you do now is another bag o' nuts entirely. And a woman situated as you are ought to be careful of retainin' a cub among her intimates.

ZOE. A cub?

PETER. Cub.

ZOE (*apprehensively*). To whom—are you alluding?

PETER. Lenny Ferris.

ZOE. L—enny?

PETER. It ain't an agreeable job, pitchin' into a fellow you've been on good terms with; but the fact remains—to put it mildly—that Master Lenny's a stoopid, blunderin' cub.

ZOE (*haughtily but palpitatingly*). He's nothing of the kind. What has he done that you should abuse him?

PETER. It's he who's told you that Theodore was at the Carlton last night, ain't it? (*She drops her eyes.*) Been here this mornin'?

ZOE (*raising her eyes, boldly*). Yes.

PETER. H'm! The sick rabbit doesn't hide in her burrow from everybody.

ZOE. H—how——?

PETER. I saw your lips make an L just now, before you could put the stopper on.

ZOE. Ha, ha! You ought to have been a 10 professional detective.

PETER (*scowling*). Ferris has kept out of my way lately, or I——

ZOE. If he *has* run in here for a moment —to ask whether I'm back—is there anything particularly cubbish in that?

PETER. It wasn't *that* I was referrin' to.

ZOE. N—no?

PETER. I was referrin' to his havin' the damned presumption to dance at- 20 tendance on you in Italy.

ZOE (*aghast*). I—Italy?

PETER. He was at Perugia while you were there.

ZOE. Oh—Perugia——

PETER (*with a shrug*). And other places, I assoom.

ZOE (*after a pause, pulling herself together*). H—ho! (*Mimicking* PETER.) And who supplies the information? (PETER 30 *waves the question from him.*) Lowenstein, by any chance—Claud Lowenstein? (PETER, *looking down his nose, is silent. She rises and walks away from him.*) The hound—the little hound!

PETER. Lowenstein came across you both at some railway station. He arrived at Perugia the day you left.

ZOE (*pacing the room on the right*). The contemptible little hound! 40

PETER. He put up at the Brufani too.

ZOE (*stopping in her walk—under her breath*). Ah!

PETER. Master Lenny might at least have had the common decency to quarter himself at another hotel.

ZOE. The—the Brufani is the most comfortable—the——(*A pause.*) I—I suppose it *was* thoughtless of Lenny.

PETER (*quietly*). Cub!

ZOE (*approaching* PETER). Does—Theodore—know?

PETER (*nodding*). Lowenstein went to him with it.

ZOE. Ha, ha! A busy gentleman—Claudy Lowenstein! (*Falteringly.*) It—it was all my fault, Peter. If—if anybody's to blame, I am. I—I wrote to the boy from Florence—complaining of feeling lonely——

PETER. That doesn't excuse him.

ZOE (*touching* PETER'S *shoulder with the tips of her fingers*). What—what does Theodore——?

PETER. He's savage.

ZOE. Savage?

PETER (*rising*). He'd like to punch Ferris's head—as I should.

ZOE (*in a low voice*). Savage——! (*Slowly.*) He—he's jealous, then? (*A shrug from* PETER. *Her eyes light up.*) Jealous! (*A pause.*) Peter—no man's jealous over a woman—unless he—unless he cares for her! (*Plucking at his sleeve.*) Peter!

PETER. You've heard me say old Theo's miserable—desperately wretched.

ZOE. He—he's grown fond of me again —fond of me——!

PETER. My dear, you and he have never left off bein' fond o' one another, actually. As I warned you, you've only been tossin' about, both of you, on a bit o' troubled water.

[*She stares at him for a moment with an expressionless face and then, as if stupefied, seats herself in the chair on the left of the oblong table.*]

PETER (*standing before her*). Well, at any rate, you'll let this Italian business be a lesson to you not to rush at conclusions respectin' other people. So, come

now; won't you try to patch it up?
I'll bet my noo hat, Theodore'll meet
you half-way. (*Urgently.*) Zoe!

ZOE (*locking and unlocking her fingers again*).
Peter——

PETER. Eh?

ZOE. Your Mr. and Mrs. Tom—the
world perhaps never heard of *their*
fall-out.

PETER. What o' that?

ZOE. Everybody is aware of the split between me and Theo.

PETER. Everybody! A handful! Besides,
n——in' is even a nine-days' wonder in
——e times. (*A pause.*) Will you do it?

ZOE (*suddenly, starting up and walking away
to the left*). Oh, no, no, no! I can't—I
can't!

PETER (*following her*). Can't?

ZOE (*helplessly*). I can't, Peter!

PETER (*taking her by the arms*). Oh——!

ZOE. I—I mean I—I'm sure it wouldn't
answer—I'm sure——

PETER. My dear girl——

ZOE (*piteously*). Ah, don't—don't! (*Escaping from him and crossing to the right.*)
Oh, leave me alone!

[WARREN *enters at the glazed door.*]

WARREN (*to* ZOE). Miss Pierpoint is
downstairs, ma'am.

ZOE (*seizing upon the interruption*). Ah,
yes!

WARREN. I'm to give you her love,
ma'am, and if it isn't convenient for
you to see her——

ZOE. It is—it *is*—quite convenient—
quite. (WARREN *withdraws, closing the
door.*) I'm awfully sorry, my dear
Peter, but this child wants to consult
me about something—something important. (*Giving him her hands.*) I must
kick you out. You don't feel hurt, do
you?

PETER (*ruefully*). Confound Miss Pierpoint! Zoe——

ZOE. What?

PETER. You'll think it over?

ZOE (*putting her hand to his lips*). Ah——!

PETER (*holding her hand*). No, no. Think
it over. Ask me to dine with you one
night next week.

ZOE. Monday—Tuesday——?

PETER. Monday.

ZOE (*artfully*). Ah, but I shall lay in a
chaperon for the occasion.

PETER. Rats! How can I talk to you before a chaperon?

ZOE. Ha, ha, ha, ha! (*She runs to the
glazed door, opens it, and, going into the
corridor, calls loudly and excitedly.*) Ethel
—Ethel—Ethel——! (ETHEL *appears
in the corridor and* ZOE *embraces her with
an excess of warmth.*) My dear Ethel!
My dear child! (*They kiss.*) What ages
since we've seen each other! (*Bringing
ETHEL *into the room.*) You know Mr.
Mottram?

ETHEL (*going to* PETER). Oh, yes.

PETER (*shaking hands with her*). How-d'ye-
do, Miss Pierpoint—and *au revoir.*

ETHEL (*as he moves toward the glazed door*).
I'm not driving you away?

PETER. I forgive you. (*He rejoins* ZOE, *who
is near the door.* ETHEL *lays her sunshade
upon the writing-table.*)

ZOE (*to* PETER). Monday night?

PETER. Monday night.

ZOE. Half-past eight.

PETER (*at the door, dropping his voice*). A
chaperon?

ZOE (*mockingly*). The proprieties!

PETER. You cat! (*He goes.*)

ZOE (*closing the door*). Ha, ha! (*She leans
wearily against the door for a moment and
again puts back her hair from her brow.
Her manner now becomes strained, artificial, distrait. She advances to* ETHEL.)
Now, then! (ETHEL *turns to her.*) Let
me have a good squint at you. How's
your dear mother?

ETHEL (*who is pale and sad-looking*).
Mother's flourishing. (*Leaving the*

writing-table.) You're not angry with me for rushing you at this hour?

ZOE. Isn't this our old hour for a chat?

ETHEL. We were at Madame Levine's yesterday—Mother and I—ordering frocks, and Camille, the skirt-maker, told us you were back. Zoe, how unkind you've been!

ZOE. Am I in your bad books?

ETHEL. Why have you treated us so horridly?

ZOE. Well, my dear child, the fact is— the fact is it suddenly dawned on me that perhaps your mother mightn't consider me any longer a suitable pal for her daughter.

ETHEL (*protestingly*). Oh!

ZOE. Heaps of folks, you know, haven't much use for single married women.

ETHEL. But we both showed you that our sympathies were on your side!

ZOE. Yes, we often sympathize with people we wouldn't touch with the end of a wet umbrella.

ETHEL (*coming close to* ZOE). So that's the reason you left off answering my letters!

ZOE. C-certainly.

ETHEL. And why we hear of your return through fat old Camille! (*Fingering a jewel at* ZOE's *neck.*) You've had a pleasant time abroad?

ZOE (*taking* ETHEL's *face between her hands, abruptly*). How thin your face is, Ethel!

ETHEL (*gazing at* ZOE). Your cheeks are not as round as they were.

ZOE (*leading* ETHEL *to the settee on the right*). I caught a rotten chill on board the boat and have been beastly seedy. (*Putting* ETHEL *on the settee.*) What's wrong with you? That's a dreary note I've had from you this morning.

ETHEL (*tracing a pattern on the floor with the point of her shoe*). Now I'm with you, I —I can't——

ZOE (*looking down upon her*). You want advice, you say.

ETHEL (*tremulously*). Yes.

ZOE. Or a good shaking.

ETHEL. I—I suppose I ought to be ashamed of myself for being so, but I —I'm very unhappy, Zoe.

ZOE. Unhappy?

ETHEL. It's no use my attempting to talk to Mother. Mother's a person who prides herself on her level-headedness. Anybody with a fixed income and a poor circulation can be level-headed! It only means you're fish-like. But you—you're warm-blooded and human——

ZOE. Well?

ETHEL. Z-Zoe——

ZOE. Yes?

ETHEL (*her eyes on the ground*). Did you ever suspect that there was anything between Mr. Ferris and me?

ZOE (*calmly, steadying herself*). Mr. Ferris —and you?

ETHEL. An attachment.

ZOE (*with affected astonishment*). My dear child!

ETHEL (*looking up*). Oh, don't keep on calling me "child"! I'm nearly six-and-twenty. (*Taking* ZOE's *hands.*) Didn't you ever guess?

ZOE. He—he always seemed delighted to meet you here.

ETHEL. He's one of your "boys"—hasn't he ever talked to you about me?

ZOE. Of course, frequently.

ETHEL. Never as if he were—in love with me?

ZOE (*withdrawing her hands*). I—I can't say that it—struck me——

ETHEL (*dejectedly*). You didn't know, perhaps, that at the beginning of the year—before you went away—he was a great deal in Sloane Street?

ZOE. Why, yes, he used to have tea with you and your mother sometimes, didn't he? (*Turning from* ETHEL.) How did I hear that?

ETHEL (*hanging her head*). Very often he came early in the afternoon—by arrangement with me—while Mother was resting.

ZOE (*with a hard laugh*). Ha, ha! Ethel!

ETHEL. Yes, worthy of a vulgar shop-girl, wasn't it?

ZOE (*sitting in the chair opposite* ETHEL). 10 He—he came early in the afternoon ——?

ETHEL. And we sat together, in the fire-light. I'm sure he loved me, Zoe—then.

ZOE (*breathing heavily*). And—and *you* ——?

ETHEL (*her elbows on her knees, hiding her face in her hands*). Oh, I'm a fool—an awful fool!   20

ZOE (*after a silence*). Did he ever—hint—at marriage? (ETHEL *nods, without uncovering her face.*) He did!

ETHEL (*raising her head*). Well, we got as far as agreeing that a small house in the country, near his aunt, would be an ideal state of existence. (*Mirthlessly.*) Ha, ha, ha! And there matters broke off.

ZOE. What—what——?

ETHEL. All of a sudden there was a change—a change in his manner toward me. He still called on us, but not so regularly; and by degrees his visits—ceased altogether. (*She passes her hand across her eyes angrily and, stamping her foot, rises and moves to the other side of the room.*) The last time I spoke to him was one morning in the Row. Mother and I were walking and 40 we came face to face with him. That was at the end of February. He was out of sorts, he said, and was going into Devonshire. I presume he went. (*Turning to* ZOE *who, with parted lips, is staring guiltily at the carpet.*) He's in

London now, though. I saw him about a fortnight ago, at the Opera. I was with the Ormerods, in their box; he was in the stalls. (*Touching* ZOE's *shoulder.*) Zoe——

ZOE. Yes?

ETHEL. He's so altered.

ZOE. Altered?

ETHEL. In his appearance. You recollect how boyish and fresh-looking he was?

ZOE. Y-yes.

ETHEL. All that's gone. He's become—oh, but I dare say you've seen him since you've been home?

ZOE. J-just for a minute or two.

ETHEL. You must have noticed——?

ZOE. N-now you mention it——

ETHEL. I watched him through the opera-glass several times during the evening. (*Simply.*) He looks like a lost soul.

ZOE. I—I've never—ha, ha!—I've never made the acquaintance of a lost—ha, ha!——

ETHEL (*after a pause*). Zoe, do you think anything has happened to Lenny Ferris?

ZOE. H-happened?

30 ETHEL. Anything bad.

ZOE. Bad?

ETHEL. Men's lives are constantly being wrecked by racing, or cards, or——(*Half turning from* ZOE.) Oh, I oughtn't to know about such things, but one doesn't live in the dark—he may have got mixed up with some woman of the wrong sort, mayn't he?

ZOE (*rising quickly and walking away to the left*). I—I really can't discuss topics of that kind with you, Ethel.

ETHEL (*wistfully*). No; but if he *is* in any scrape—any entanglement—and one could help him——

ZOE (*at the writing-table, taking up a bottle of salts—faintly*). Help him?

ETHEL. Save him——!

ZOE (*sniffing the salts*). How—how romantic you are!

ETHEL. Am I! (*Her elbows on the back of the armchair by the oblong table, timidly.*) Zoe, would it be possible—in your opinion—would it be possible for me to—to see him?

ZOE (*sitting in the chair at the writing-table*). See Mr. Ferris?

ETHEL (*plucking at the cover of the chair on which she is leaning*). Here—in your house—or elsewhere—see him and offer him my friendship—a sister's friendship? *You* could manage it.

ZOE. My—my dear!

ETHEL. Oh, yes, I'm lacking in dignity, aren't I—and self-respect! (*Coming forward.*) I've told myself that a thousand times. (*Warmly.*) But there 20 are quite enough dignified people in the world without me; and if I could influence Lenny, any one might have my dignity for twopence.

ZOE. Influence him——?

ETHEL. For his good. Oh, I don't want to boast, but I'm a straight, clean girl; and it may be that, at this particular moment of his life, the more he sees of women like you and me the better. 30 However, if you tell me the idea's improper, I'll accept it from you. (*Approaching* ZOE.) I'll take anything from you. (*Appealingly.*) But don't tell me that, if you can avoid it. Give me the opportunity, if you can, of showing him that I'm different from most girls—that I'm above petty, resentful feelings. (*Bending over* ZOE.) Zoe——

[LENA *enters at the further door on the right,* 40 *carrying a silver salver on which are a dose of medicine in a medicine-glass and a dish of sweetmeats.*]

LENA. Your med'cine! (*Closing the door.*) Good morning, Miss Pierpoint.

ETHEL. Ah, Lena!

ZOE (*to* ETHEL, *rising hastily*). Excuse me——

[LENA *advances and* ZOE *goes to her and, with a shaking hand, drinks the medicine.*]

LENA (*to* ZOE). Good gracious, how queer you look! (*To* ETHEL.) She's doing too much to-day, Miss Pierpoint. (*Going to* ETHEL.) Doctor Rashleigh says she's frightfully below par.

10 ETHEL (*picking up her sunshade*). What a shame of me! (*Running to* ZOE.) I won't stay another minute.

ZOE (*sitting on the settee on the right*). I *am* a little fatigued.

ETHEL. I ought to have seen it.

ZOE. I—I'll write to you. (*They kiss.*) My love to your mother.

ETHEL. And when you are well enough ——?

20 ZOE. I'll call upon her.

ETHEL (*to* LENA, *who precedes her into the corridor*). No, no; stop with Mrs. Blundell. I'm so sorry, Lena——

[LENA *and* ETHEL *talk together for a little while in undertones; then the girl disappears.* LENA *returns.*]

LENA (*shutting the door*). Silly chatterbox! (*Finding* ZOE *lying at full length upon the settee, her head buried in a pillow.*) Why do you tire yourself like this? Shall I fetch you some brandy?

ZOE. No.

LENA (*lowering her voice*). *He's* in the house again.

ZOE. Who?

LENA. Mr. Ferris.

ZOE (*raising herself*). Mr. Ferris!

LENA (*with a jerk of her head in the direction of the next room*). In there. (ZOE *sits upright.*) Warren's making himself beautiful and Clara answered the door. She thought you were by yourself and let him come up. (ZOE *gets to her feet.*) I was just bringing you your med'cine and met him. (ZOE *goes to the writing-table, takes up the hand-mirror, and puts her hair in order*.) Lucky I'd heard that Miss Pierpoint was here; he didn't want to see her! Another second——!

ZOE. That'll do. (*Calmly.*) Take care I'm not interrupted again.

LENA. Ah, now! Mayn't I get rid of him?

ZOE. No. (*Turning.*) Run away, please.

LENA. Oh, very good. (*Picking up the salver which she has placed upon a piece of furniture near the glazed door*.) You'll do exactly as you choose. (*In the corridor.*) I declare I'd rather look after a pack of un___ ___ildren any day in the week——

[*She closes the door.* ZOE *glances over her shoulder, to assure herself that the woman has left the room, and then, with a fierce light in her eyes, goes to the nearer door on the right and throws it open.*]

ZOE (*in a hard voice, speaking into the adjoining room*). I'm alone. (*She moves from the door as* LEONARD, *still carrying his hat and cane, enters.*)

LEONARD. By George, that was a narrow squeak! (*Closing the door.*) Whatever possessed you to be at home to the Pierpoint girl this morning?

ZOE (*coldly*). I didn't expect you back before lunch.

LEONARD (*putting his hat and cane on the chair at the nearer end of the settee on the right*). I was talking to a man at Victoria Gate and I saw Peter driving away in a taxi. (*Facing her.*) I got sick of the Park. (*Seeing that something is amiss.*) Hallo! (*A pause.*) Any one been running me down?

[*She advances to him and, drawing herself to her full height, regards him scornfully.*]

ZOE (*making a motion with her hands as if she would strike him*). You—you——! (*Dropping her hands to her side.*) Oh, cruel—cruel—(*Walking away from him.*) —cruel!

LEONARD. What's cruel? Who's cruel?

ZOE (*at the further end of the room, on the right*). Ah—ah——!

LEONARD (*moving to the left*). Oh, come! Let's have it out; let's have it out.

ZOE. Sssh! Don't raise your voice here.

LEONARD. Somebody's been talking against me. Ethel Pierpoint?

ZOE (*coming to the oblong table*). You've behaved abominably to this girl.

LEONARD. Ho, it *is* Miss Pierpoint!

ZOE. No, she hasn't spoken a word against you. But she's opened her heart to me.

LEONARD (*going to* ZOE). You've known ___ ___t me and Ethel.

ZOE. It's ___ How much have I known? I knew th___ y___ were sizing her up, as you express___ it, ___t I never surmised that you'd as g___od ___ proposed marriage to her.

LEONARD. I told you ___ months ago—admitted it—that I'd m___le myself a bit of an idiot over Ethel. I fancied you tumbled to the state o' thing___.

ZOE. Did you! Why, do you think—maniac as I was when you ___me through to me to Florence!—do y___u think I'd have allowed you to remain near me for five minutes if I'd known as much as I do now!

LEONARD. Look here, Zoe——

ZOE. Oh, you're a cruel fellow! You've been cruel to her and cruel to me. I believe you're capable of being cruel to any woman who comes your way. Still, *she's* the fortunate one. Her scratches'll heal; but I (*Sitting at the oblong table and hitting it with her fist.*) I loathe myself more than ever—more than ever!

LEONARD (*after a pause*). Zoe, I wish you'd try to be a little fair to me.

ZOE (*ironically*). Fair!

LEONARD. Perhaps I did go rather further with Ethel Pierpoint than I led you to understand.

ZOE. Oh——!

LEONARD. I own up. Yes, but what prospect was there, when I was thick with her, of your being free of Blundell? None. And what was I to you? Merely a pal of yours—one of your "tame robins"—one of a dozen; and I'd come to a loose end in my life. It was simply the fact that there *was* no prospect for me with you that drove me to consider whether I hadn't better settle down to a humdrum with a decent girl of the Ethel breed. Otherwise, do you imagine I'd have crossed the street to speak to another woman? (*Leaving* ZOE.) Oh, you might do me common justice! (*Hotly.*) If circumstances *have* made a cad of me, am I *all* black? Can't you find *any* good in me? (*Turning to her.*) What did I tell you at Perugia?

ZOE (*rising*). Ah, don't——!

LEONARD. That I'd been in love with you from the day I first met you—from the very moment Mrs. Hope-Cornish introduced me to you at Sandown! Well! Isn't there anything to my credit on that score? Didn't I keep my secret? For four years I kept it; though, with matters as they often were between you and Blundell, many a man might have thought you ripe grapes. (*Walking across to the right.*) Only once I was off my guard with you—when I laid hold of you and begged you, whatever happened, never to—never to——

ZOE (*leaning against the table, her back to him*). Ha, ha, ha!

LEONARD. Yes, and I meant it; as God hears me, I meant it. If anybody had told me that afternoon that it was I who—oh, hang! (*Sitting upon the settee.*) But what I want to impress upon you is that, if I were quite the low scoundrel you make me out to be, I shouldn't have gone through what I *have* gone through these past four years and more. Great Scot, it's been nothing but hell—hot hell—all the time! Four whole years of pretending I was just an ordinary friend of yours —hell! Four years of reasoning with myself—preaching to myself—hell! That awful month after Blundell left you—when you'd gone to Italy and I was in London—worse than hell! My chase after you—our little tour together—my struggle even then to play the correct game—and I *did* struggle—hell! And since then—hell! (*His elbows on his knees, digging his knuckles into his forehead.*) Hell all the time! Hell all the time!

[*There is a silence, and then, with a look of settled determination, she comes to him slowly and lays her hands upon his head.*]

ZOE. Poor boy! I'm sorry I blackguarded you. (*Sitting in the chair opposite to him and speaking in a steady, level voice.*) Len ——

LEONARD. Eh?

ZOE. Let's part.

LEONARD (*raising his head*). Part?

ZOE. Say good-by to each other. (*Meeting his eyes.*) Go back to that girl.

LEONARD. To Ethel!

ZOE. Take up with her again.

LEONARD. Oh, stop it, Zo.

ZOE. She's devoted to you; and she's sound right through, if ever a girl was. She's one of the best, Len.

LEONARD. Suppose she *is*——

ZOE. Be careful that she doesn't guess I've given her away. (*He rises impatiently. She rises with him and holds him by the lapels of his jacket.*) Tell her—she's sure to ask you—tell her that you haven't seen me since last Monday, nor had a line from me. Fake up some tale to account for your breaking off with her—you were in doubt whether you'd coin enough to marry on——

LEONARD (*who has become thoughtful*). Zoe——

ZOE. Yes?

LEONARD (*looking her full in the face*). Are you giving me the boot?

ZOE (*releasing him and returning his gaze firmly*). Yes; I am.

LEONARD (*after a pause*). Oh? (*Another pause.*) What's your motive?

ZOE. Motive?

LEONARD. What's behind all this?

ZOE (*simply*). I want you to be happy, Len—really and truly happy. I believe you'd stand a jolly good chance of being so with Ethel Pierpoint; never with me.

LEONARD. And *you?*

ZOE. I?

LEONARD. What's to become of *you?* What are your plans for yourself?

ZOE (*avoiding his eyes*). Oh, don't you—don't you worry about me.

LEONARD. Rot!

ZOE (*nervously*). Perhaps some day—when Theodore's tired of Mrs. Annerly—ha, ha!—stranger things have happened——

LEONARD. Rot, I say. (*She retreats a little.*) Do you think you can drum me out like this! (*Following her.*) Have you got some other——? (*He checks himself.*)

ZOE (*confronting him*). Some other——?

LEONARD. Oh, never mind.

ZOE. Out with it!

LEONARD. Some other fancy-man in tow?

ZOE. Ah! You brute! (*Hitting him in the chest.*) You brute! (*Throwing herself into the armchair near the glazed door.*) You coward! You coward!

[*There is a pause and then he slouches up to her.*]

LEONARD. I—I beg your pardon. I beg your pardon. (*He sits beside her, upon the fauteuil-stool.*) Knock my damned head off. Go on. Knock my damned head off.

ZOE (*panting*). Well—we won't part—on top of a row. (*Dashing a tear away.*) After all, why *should* you think better of me than that?

LEONARD (*penitently*). Zoe——

ZOE. Sssh! Listen. Putting Ethel Pierpoint out of the question, do you ever picture to yourself what our married life would be?

LEONARD. What it 'ud be?

ZOE. The marriage of a woman of seven—nearly eight—and thirty to a man of thirty-two! *I* do. I walk my bedroom half the night and act it all over to myself. And you've had the best of me, too; I'm not even a novelty to you. Why, of course you've realized what you've let yourself in for.

LEONARD. I take my oath——

ZOE. Sssh! When you're in front of your glass in the morning, what do you see there?

LEONARD. See?

ZOE. This girl has noticed the alteration in your looks. She took stock of you at the opera the other night.

LEONARD (*passing his hands over his face consciously*). Men can't go to hell, Zo, without getting a bit scorched.

ZOE (*imitating his action*). No, nor women either. (*Turning to him.*) But it's only quite lately that you've lost your bloom, Len.

LEONARD. Oh, naturally I've been horribly bothered about you—about both of us—since——

ZOE. Since your trip to Italy? (*He nods.*) Yes, and naturally you've told yourself, over and over again, the truth—since your trip to Italy.

LEONARD. Truth?

ZOE. The simple truth—that you've got

into a mess with a married woman
——

LEONARD. I—I——

ZOE. And that you must go through with it, at all costs.

LEONARD. I swear to you, Zoe——

ZOE (*touching his hand*). Oh, my dear boy, you haven't perhaps *said* these things to yourself, in so many words, but they're at the back of your brain just 10 the same. (*She rises and crosses to the fireplace and rings three times.*)

LEONARD (*rising*). What—what are you doing?

ZOE. Ringing for Lena, to tell her I'm not lunching downstairs.

LEONARD. By God, Zoe——!

ZOE (*imperiously*). Be quiet!

LEONARD (*shaking his fist at her*). You dare treat me in this way! You dare! 20

ZOE (*advancing*). Ah, I'm only hurting your pride a little; I'm only mortifying your vanity. You'll get over that in twenty-four hours.

LEONARD. Do you know what you *are;* do you know what you make yourself by this!

ZOE. Yes, what you made of me at Perugia, and at Siena, and at——! (*Suddenly, clinging to him.*) Lenny— 30 Lenny—kiss me——!

LEONARD (*pushing her from him*). Not I.

ZOE. Ah, yes. Don't let's part enemies. It's good-by. Lenny!

LEONARD. No.

ZOE (*struggling with him entreatingly*). Quick! It's for the last time. You'll never be alone with me again. (*Her arms tightly around him.*) It's for the last time. (*Kissing him passionately.*) Good 40 luck to you! Good luck to you! Good luck to you! (*She leaves him and sits at the writing-table where she makes a pretense of busying herself with her papers.*)

LEONARD (*glancing expectantly at the glazed door—between his teeth*). You—you ——!

[*Presently he goes to the chair on the right and snatches up his hat and cane.* LENA *enters at the glazed door.*]

LENA (*to* ZOE). Is it me you've rung for?

ZOE. Yes. (*Sharply.*) Wait.

[*There is a pause. Struck by* ZOE'S *tone, and the attitude of the pair,* LENA *looks inquisitively at* LEONARD *and* ZOE *out of the corners of her eyes, as if she guesses there has been a quarrel.* LEONARD *moves toward the door.*]

LEONARD (*to* ZOE). Good morning.

ZOE. Good morning.

LEONARD (*to* LENA, *as he passes her*). Good morning.

LENA. Good morning.

[*He departs and* LENA *quietly closes the door.*]

ZOE (*rising*). Lena——

LENA. Yes?

ZOE (*walking across to the settee on the right*). I'm not coming down to the dining-room. (*Sitting, feebly.*) Let me have a snack upstairs.

LENA. Very well.

ZOE. That's all.

[LENA *withdraws, almost on tiptoe, and* ZOE *instantly produces her handkerchief and cries into it softly. Then she gets to her feet and searches for the cigarette box. Still shaken by little sobs, she puts a cigarette between her lips and, as she does so, the expression of her face changes and her body stiffens.*]

ZOE (*under her breath*). Oh——! (*After a moment's resolution, she hurriedly dries her eyes and, going to the glazed door, opens it, and calls.*) Lena—Lena——!

LENA (*in the distance*). Yes?

[ZOE *returns to the oblong table and is lighting her cigarette when* LENA *reappears.*]

ZOE. Lena——

LENA. Well?

ZOE. I'll dress directly after lunch.

LENA (*coming to her, surprized*). Dress?

ZOE. Yes; I'm going out this afternoon.

LENA. Going out! Why, you must be crazy——!

CURTAIN

ACT III

A fine, spacious room, richly furnished and decorated. In the center of the wall at the back is the fireplace, and on the left of the fireplace is a door which when open reveals part of a dining-room. In the right-hand wall there is a bay-window hung with lace and other curtains. Facing the window, in the wall on the 10 *left, is a double door opening into the room from a corridor.*

On either side of the fireplace there is an armchair, and between the fireplace and the dining-room door stands a small table on which are a decanter of whisky, a syphon of soda-water, and two or three tumblers. A grand piano and a music-stool are in the right-hand corner of the room, and on the left of the piano is a settee. Some photographs are on the 20 *top of the piano. On the other side of the room there is a second settee with a table at the nearer end of it. An armchair stands by this table, another at the farther end of the settee. In the bay-window there is a writing-table with a writing-chair before it, and on the writing-table is a telephone-instrument. Other articles of furniture, some pieces of sculpture, and some handsome lamps on pedestals, fill spaces not provided for in this description.*

A scarf of mousseline de soie *and a pair of white gloves lie on the chair on the right of the fireplace.*

The fireless grate is hidden by a screen and, through the lace curtains, which are drawn over the window, a fierce sunlight is seen. The door at the back is slightly ajar.

[*The telephone bell rings and presently* THEODORE BLUNDELL *enters at the door at the* 40 *back, and goes to the writing-table. His step has become heavier, his shoulders are somewhat bent, and he looks a "bad color."*]

THEODORE (*at the telephone*). Halloo! . . . Yes? . . . I *am* Mr. Blundell. . . . Oh, is that you, Peter? . . . What? . . . Want to see me? . . . Anything wrong? . . . Where are you? . . . Where? . . . Café Royal? . . . Come along to me now, then? . . . Oh, I say! . . . Are you there? . . . (*Dropping his voice.*) I say! Mrs. A. is lunching with me. . . . Mrs. A.—Alice. . . . No, but I thought I'd tell you. . . . Good-by.

[*He is about to return to the dining-room when* MRS. ANNERLY *appears in the doorway at the back. She is a pretty, charmingly dressed creature with classical, immobile features and a simple, virginal air.*]

MRS. ANNERLY (*advancing*). I've told Cole we'll have coffee in this room. (*He nods and sits moodily upon the settee on the right. Resting her elbows on the back of the armchair at the further end of the settee on the left, she surveys her face in a tiny mirror which she carries, with some other trinkets, attached to a chain.*) Who's that you were talking to on the 'phone, boy, dear?

THEODORE (*who is smoking a big cigar*). Mottram.

MRS. ANNERLY. What's *he* want?

THEODORE. Wants to see me about something.

MRS. ANNERLY. Business?

THEODORE. Dun'no.

MRS. ANNERLY (*sweetly*). He doesn't like poor little me.

THEODORE (*indifferently*). Doesn't he?

MRS. ANNERLY. You know he doesn't. (*Arranging a curl.*) That's why you gave him the tip that I'm lunching here.

THEODORE. Ho! Listeners—*et cetera.*

MRS. ANNERLY. I couldn't help hearing you; positively I couldn't. (*Examining her teeth in the mirror.*) He's one of your wife's tame cats, isn't he?

THEODORE. He's a friend of hers—yes.

MRS. ANNERLY. *Just* a friend, and nothing else.

THEODORE (*angrily*). Now, look here, Alice——!

[COLE, *a man servant, enters from the dining-room with the coffee and liqueurs.* MRS. ANNERLY *takes a cup of coffee.*]

COLE (*to* MRS. ANNERLY). Brandy—Kümmel, ma'am?

MRS. ANNERLY. No, thanks.

THEODORE (*to* COLE, *who comes to him with the tray—irritably*). Leave it. (COLE *places the tray on the top of the piano and is returning to the dining-room.*) Cole—— 20

COLE. Yessir?

THEODORE. I'm expecting Mr. Mottram.

COLE. Very good, sir.

[*The man withdraws, closing the door.* THEODORE *rises and pours some brandy into a large liqueur-glass.*]

MRS. ANNERLY (*who has seated herself upon the settee on the left*). What's the matter with you to-day, boy, dear? You're as cross as two sticks. 30

THEODORE. Liver.

MRS. ANNERLY (*sipping her coffee*). I don't wonder.

THEODORE. Why?

MRS. ANNERLY. You're getting rather too fond of—(*Pointing to the brandy.*)—h'm, h'm.

THEODORE (*bluntly*). It's false.

MRS. ANNERLY (*with undisturbed complacency*). I've seen so much of that sort 40 o' thing in my time. (*He makes a movement, as if to put down his glass without drinking.*) Still, I must say you've every excuse.

THEODORE. Alice——

MRS. ANNERLY. What?

[*He gulps his brandy, puts the empty glass on the tray, and comes to her.*]

THEODORE (*standing before her*). Alice, will you oblige me by refraining from making any allusion to my wife, direct or indirect, in the future? It annoys me.

MRS. ANNERLY. Everything annoys you this afternoon.

10 THEODORE. You were at it last night, at the Carlton. And to-day, during lunch——

MRS. ANNERLY (*in an injured tone*). It was you who told me that that little Jew chap had met her careering about Italy with young what's-his-name. (*He sits in the armchair at the farther end of the settee and leans his head on his hand.*) Ah, but that was in your loving days —when you used to confide in me.

THEODORE. I was in a rage and said a great deal more than I thought.

MRS. ANNERLY. If you did, you needn't jump on me for trying to feel interested in you and your affairs.

THEODORE (*facing her*). At any rate, understand me clearly, Alice—and then drop the subject. (*Shortly.*) Mrs. Blundell and I are separated; she's gone one way, I another. There were faults on both sides, as usual, but I was mainly to blame. There's the thing in a nutshell.

MRS. ANNERLY. This isn't in the least your old story.

THEODORE. Never mind my old story. (*Extending a forefinger.*) *You* forget the old story, my girl, if you wish our acquaintance to continue—d'ye hear?

40 MRS. ANNERLY (*shaking herself*). You're a nasty savage.

THEODORE. As for that interfering cad, Lowenstein, it unfortunately happens that one of Mrs. Blundell's characteristics is a habit of disregarding *les convenances*—a habit which I didn't go the right way to check. It's probable that, before she's done, she won't leave herself with as much reputation as 'ud cover a sixpence. She's impulsive, reckless, a fool—but she's no worse. (*Eying the stump of his cigar fiercely.*) My wife's no worse. So, hands off, if you please, in my presence. Whatever reports are circulated to her discredit, the man who speaks 10 against her in my hearing is kicked for his pains; and the woman who does so, if she's under my roof, gets taken by the shoulders and shown the mat. (*Looking at her.*) *Comprenez?*

MRS. ANNERLY (*pouting*). I should be a juggins if I didn't. *Parfaitement*—in my very best French.

THEODORE (*rising and walking about*). That's settled, then. 20

MRS. ANNERLY (*after a pause, rising and depositing her cup upon the table on the left—thoughtfully*). Boy, dear——

THEODORE (*at the back*). Hey?

MRS. ANNERLY. It was regular cat-and-dog between you two at the end, wasn't it?

THEODORE (*breaking out again*). It's no concern of yours whether it was or was not. I've asked you——

MRS. ANNERLY (*crossing to the right, with a 30 shrug*). Oh——!

THEODORE. Yes, it *was*. (*Half-sitting upon the back of the settee on the left.*) I—I tired of her.

MRS. ANNERLY (*philosophically*). Ah, men *do* tire.

THEODORE. And she of me. We'd been married close upon fourteen years.

MRS. ANNERLY. Oh, well, come; that's a long while. 40

THEODORE (*as much to himself as to her*). Our wedding-day's on the thirtieth of this month. (*Hitting the back of the settee softly with his fist.*) We'd reached a time in our lives when—when we were in mid-Channel——

MRS. ANNERLY. Mid-Channel?

THEODORE (*rising*). Oh, you don't know anything about that.

[*There is a further silence. She sits upon the settee on the right, watching him as he moves about the room again.*]

MRS. ANNERLY. Here! (*Beckoning him with a motion of her head.*) Here! (*He goes to her. She looks up into his face.*) Why don't you marry *me*, Theo?

THEODORE (*staring at her*). Marry—you?

MRS. ANNERLY. You'd find me awfully easy to get on with.

THEODORE (*turning from her, quietly*). Oh ——!

MRS. ANNERLY. Wait; you might listen, anyhow. (*He turns to her.*) I am—awfully easy to get on with. And I'd be as strict as—as strict as a nun. Honest Injun! I treated Annerly pretty badly, but that's ancient history. I was only seventeen when I married Frank—too inexperienced for words. I've learned a lot since.

THEODORE (*bitterly*). Ha!

MRS. ANNERLY. Now, don't be satirical. (*Inviting him to sit by her side.*) Theo —— (*He sits beside her.*) I say—bar chaff—I wish you *would*.

THEODORE (*absently*). What? 30

MRS. ANNERLY. Marry me. Really I do. (*A note of wistfulness in her voice.*) I really do want to reestablish myself. My life, these past few years, has been frightfully unsatisfactory.

THEODORE (*touching her dress, sympathetically*). Ah!

MRS. ANNERLY. And I'm a lady, remember—giddy as I may have been. Put me in any society and I'm presentable, as far as manners go. I'd soon right myself, with your assistance. (*Slipping her arm through his.*) I suppose, under the circumstances, you couldn't divorce *her*, could you?

THEODORE. What d'ye mean?

MRS. ANNERLY. Your wife—over that Italian business.

THEODORE (*jumping up*). Damn!

MRS. ANNERLY. Oh, I beg your pardon; it slipped out. (*He walks away to the table at the back and begins to mix himself a whisky-and-soda.*) I'm dreadfully grieved; gospel, I am. (*Rising.*) Don't —don't, boy, dear. Do leave that stuff alone. (*He puts down the decanter and comes to the settee on the left.*) I can't do more than apologize.

THEODORE (*sitting*). Tsch! Hold your tongue.

MRS. ANNERLY (*sitting beside him*). No, but you could let *her* go for *you*, though; *that* could be fixed up. I'd even consent to be dragged into the case myself, if it would help matters forward; and goodness knows I've no ambition to appear in the divorce court again —I hate the hole. (*Coaxingly.*) You *will* consider it, won't you?

THEODORE. Consider *what?*

MRS. ANNERLY. Marrying me. Just say you'll consider it and I won't tease you any more to-day. You do owe me something, you know.

THEODORE. Owe you——?

MRS. ANNERLY. Well, you *have* compromised me by being seen about with me at different places lately; now, haven't you? (THEODORE *throws his head back and laughs boisterously.*) There's nothing to laugh at. Perhaps I haven't a shred of character left, in your estimation!

THEODORE. Ho, ho!

MRS. ANNERLY (*rising, piqued*). I presume you think I'm a person who'll accept a dinner at a restaurant from any man who holds up a finger to me!

THEODORE. Why, my dear girl, you were always bothering me to take you to the cook-shops.

MRS. ANNERLY. Bothering! (*Going to the chair on the right of the fireplace and gathering up her scarf.*) Oh, you're too rude!

THEODORE. I was perfectly content with our quiet little means here or in Egerton Crescent.

MRS. ANNERLY. Yes, and to bore me to tears!

THEODORE. Bore——?

MRS. ANNERLY (*winding her scarf around her shoulders.*) Bore, bore, bore!

THEODORE (*scowling*). Oh, I—I bored you, did I?

MRS. ANNERLY. Talking to me, as you used to, like a sentimental young fellow of five-and-twenty! Ridiculous! (*Picking up her gloves.*) I want a taxicab.

THEODORE (*rising*). Stop—stop——

MRS. ANNERLY. I've had quite sufficient of you for to-day.

THEODORE (*with a set jaw*). I'm glad you've brought matters to a head, Ally. I've something to propose to you.

MRS. ANNERLY (*pulling on a glove*). I've no desire to hear it.

THEODORE. Something that's been on my mind for—oh, a month or more.

MRS. ANNERLY. You can keep it to yourself. I'm not accustomed to being jeered at.

THEODORE (*slowly walking over to the right*). I'm sorry if I've hurt your feelings——

MRS. ANNERLY. It's the first time I've ever made advances to a man, and I assure you it'll be the last.

THEODORE. Ally——

MRS. ANNERLY (*moving toward the double door*). Cole will get me a taxi.

THEODORE (*authoritatively*). Come here; come here; come here.

MRS. ANNERLY (*halting behind the settee on the left, with a twist of her body*). I shall not.

THEODORE (*snapping his finger and thumb*).

Ally—(*She approaches him with assumed reluctance.*)—Ally—(*Deliberately.*)—what'll you take?

MRS. ANNERLY (*elevating her brows*). Take?

THEODORE. To put an end to this.

MRS. ANNERLY. An end!

THEODORE. To end your boredom—and mine; terminate our—friendship.

MRS. ANNERLY (*uncomfortably*). Oh, you—you needn't cut up as rough as all this.

THEODORE. Ah, no, no, no; I'm not angry. I'm in earnest, though. Come! What'll satisfy you? (*She curls her lip fretfully.*) A man of my years deserves to pay heavily at this game. What'll make you easy and comfortable for a bit? I'll be liberal with you, my dear, and—(*Offering his hand.*)—shake hands—(*She turns her shoulder to him.*) —shake hands—(*She gives him her hand sulkily.*)—and I—I'll ask you to forgive me——

MRS. ANNERLY (*withdrawing her hand*). Oh, for goodness' sake, don't let's have any more of *that*. (*Contemptuously.*) You elderlies always wind up in the same way.

[*He seats himself at the writing-table and, unlocking a drawer, produces his check-book.*]

THEODORE. Would a couple of thousand be of any service to you?

MRS. ANNERLY (*opening her eyes widely*). A couple of——!

THEODORE (*preparing to write*). I mean it.

MRS. ANNERLY (*breathlessly*). You don't! (*He writes.*) Why, of course it would. (*Melting completely.*) Oh, but it's too much; it is positively. I *couldn't*. And I've had such a lot out of you already. You *are* generous. (*Behind his chair.*) Fancy my being huffy with you just now! (*Bending over him and arresting his pen.*) Boy, dear——

THEODORE. Hey?

MRS. ANNERLY (*in a whisper*). Make it—

three—will you? (*He looks at her over his shoulder with a cynical smile. She retreats.*) Oh, well! One isn't young and attractive forever, you know.

[*He finishes writing the check and, having locked up his check-book methodically, rises and comes to her.*]

THEODORE (*giving her the check*). There you are.

MRS. ANNERLY (*examining it*). You—you've split the difference! You *are* kind. I didn't expect it in the least. (*Folding the check neatly and finding a place for it in her bosom.*) I *am* ashamed of myself for hinting so broadly. Thanks, a hundred times. (*Blinking at him.*) Shan't I miss you!

[COLE *enters at the double door followed by* PETER.]

COLE. Mr. Mottram.

THEODORE (*greeting* PETER *at the fireplace as* COLE *retires*). Hallo!

PETER. Hallo! (*Bowing to* MRS. ANNERLY.) How d'ye do?

MRS. ANNERLY (*who has moved over to the right—distantly*). How do you do?

THEODORE (*to* MRS. ANNERLY). By-the-bye, did you say you want a taxi-cab?

MRS. ANNERLY. If I'm not troubling you.

[THEODORE *goes out at the double door, closing it upon* PETER *and* MRS. ANNERLY. *There is a pause.* MRS. ANNERLY, *pulling on her second glove, looks out of the window;* PETER *whistles silently.*]

PETER (*after a while*). Fine afternoon.

MRS. ANNERLY. Delightful. (*After another pause, turning to him.*) Er—h'm—how do you think he's looking?

PETER. Blundell? Seen him looking better.

MRS. ANNERLY (*with a sigh*). Ah! (*In a mincing voice, approaching* PETER.) Mr. Mottram, will you excuse me for offering a suggestion?

PETER (*politely*). Fire away.

MRS. ANNERLY (*sweetly*). Why don't you

THEODORE. You—you meddlesome old buffer!

PETER (*chuckling*). Ha, ha!

THEODORE. How—how did she take it?

PETER. In a way that convinced me you've only to assure her that your old feelin's for her have returned, and in spite of everythin'——

THEODORE. Everything! Wait till she hears of sweet Alice.

PETER. *Wait!*

THEODORE (*looking at* PETER). Why, d'ye mean——?

PETER. Oh, yes; it's got to her.

THEODORE (*dully*). Already?

PETER. Jim Mallandain traveled with her from Paris on Sunday.

THEODORE. Did *he*——?

PETER. I suppose he thought it 'ud amuse her.

THEODORE. The skunk!

PETER. If it hadn't been Jim, it 'ud have been somebody else.

THEODORE (*thickly*). You're right; somebody had to be first.

PETER. However, I did my best for yer.

THEODORE. Denied it?

PETER. Warmly. I defended you and the young lady with all the eloquence I could command.

THEODORE. Zoe didn't believe you? (*A pause.*) She didn't believe you? (PETER *shrugs his shoulders.*) Of course she didn't. (*Passing* PETER *and walking about the room.*) What did she say? Hey? Oh, I can guess; you needn't tell me. What's everybody saying? Peter, I'd give half as much as I'm worth to wipe the Annerly incident off my slate. I would, on the nail. Just fancy! To reach my age—and to be of decent repute—and then to have your name linked with a brainless, mercenary little trull like Alice Annerly! Ha, ha! Glorious fun for 'em in the City, and at the club! *You* hear

it all. Confound you, can't you open your mouth! Ho! *Of course* Zoe sums it all up; she's cute enough when she chooses. (*Sitting upon the settee on the left and mopping his face and throat with his handkerchief.*) How did it end?

PETER. End?

THEODORE. Your chat with my missus.

PETER. It ended in my urgin' her to consider the matter—think it over. (*Coming to him.*) I'm dinin' with her next week. (*Sitting in the chair at the further end of the settee.*) If you'll authorize me to open negotiations with her on your behalf——

THEODORE. I—I approach her!

PETER. Cert'nly.

THEODORE (*twisting his handkerchief into a rope*). No—no——

PETER. Why not?

THEODORE. A couple o' months back I could have done it. Even as late as a fortnight ago—before I'd given myself away by showing myself in public with Alice—it might have been feasible. (*Between his teeth.*) But now— when I—when I've lost any remnant of claim I may have had—on her respect——!

PETER (*in his judicial manner*). My dear chap, here is a case——

THEODORE. Hell with you and your case! (*Jumping up and walking away to the right.*) I couldn't screw myself up to it; I—I couldn't humble myself to that extent. (*Moving about.*) Ho! How she'd grin! She's got a cruel sense o' humor, Peter—or had once. You see, I always posed to her as being a *strong*, rather cold-blooded man——

PETER. A favorite pose, that, of husbands.

THEODORE. It was more than a pose—I thought I *was* a strong man. And then—to crawl back to her—all over mud——! (*He halts in the middle of the room and, with a shaky hand, produces his cigar-case from his pocket and takes out a cigar.*)

PETER. I was about to remark, when you chipped in with your usual politeness —I was about to remark that this is a case where *two* persons have behaved more or less stoopidly.

THEODORE. Two——?

PETER. You more, she less.   10

THEODORE (*his brow darkening*). You— you're referring to——?

PETER. Er—Mrs. Zoe——

THEODORE (*cutting his cigar viciously*). With—Ferris.

PETER. Yes; and I think that the friend of both parties—the individual on whose shoulders the task of adjustin' matters would fall—(*Rising.*)—I think that that friend might manage 20 to impose a condition which 'ud be greatly to your advantage.

THEODORE. Condition?

PETER. No imputations to be made on either side.

THEODORE (*broodingly*). No—imputations——?

PETER. I—the party acceptin' the statement of the other party, and promisin' not to rake up anythin' that's oc- 30 curred durin' the past four months.

THEODORE. I—I understand.

PETER. It 'ud help to save your face for the moment, and the healin' hand of time might be trusted to do the rest.

THEODORE (*quietly*). Peter——

PETER. Hallo!

THEODORE. When I was at the house on Monday—my wife's house—half-past eleven in the morning——   40

PETER. Well?

THEODORE. There was a yellow car at the door.

PETER. Yaller car?

THEODORE. I couldn't get near, but— that fellow has a yellow car.

PETER. Has he?

THEODORE (*grimly*). Why, he's driven you in it.

PETER (*carelessly*). I'd forgotten.

THEODORE (*looking at* PETER). He's still hanging on to her skirts, hey?

PETER. He's an ill-bred, tactless cub. But he's got a nice 'ead of 'air and smells' o' soap; and that's the sort women love to have danglin' about after 'em.

THEODORE (*with an effort*). There— there's nothing in it, Peter, beyond that?

PETER (*waving his hand disdainfully*). Good God!

THEODORE. Oh, I know there isn't; I know there isn't. With all her faults, I know she's as straight as a die. (*Looking at* PETER *again.*) Did you touch on the subject with her?

PETER (*nodding*). I rubbed it in. I told her her conduct had been indiscreet to a degree. I thought it policy to rub it in.

THEODORE. Did she—offer any explanation?

PETER (*nodding*). Pure thoughtlessness.

THEODORE. And you felt that she was— speaking the truth?

PETER (*testily*). My dear Theodore——

THEODORE. You swear that? (*Suddenly, grasping the lapel of* PETER'S *coat.*) Damn it, man, *you* began talking about the thing——!

[COLE *enters at the double door carrying a note in the shape of a cocked hat.*]

THEODORE (*angrily*). What d'ye want?

COLE. I beg your pardon, sir.

THEODORE (*going to him*). Hey? (*He snatches the note from the man and, as he glances at the writing on it, his jaw drops.*)

COLE (*in a low voice*). An answer, sir?

THEODORE (*trying to unfold the note*). Messenger?

COLE. The lady herself, I think, sir.

[*There is a pause, and then* THEODORE *slowly gets the note open and reads it.*]

THEODORE (*to* COLE). Where——?

COLE. In the smoking room, sir.

THEODORE. Er—wait.

COLE. Yessir. (COLE *withdraws.*)

THEODORE (*to* PETER, *who has wandered away*). Peter——

[PETER *comes to him and* THEODORE *hands him the note.* PETER's *eyes bolt as he recog-* 10 *nizes the handwriting.*]

PETER (*reading the note*). "Will you see me?" Short—(*Examining both sides of the paper and then returning the note to* THEODORE.)—sweet.

THEODORE (*chewing his unlighted cigar*). This is your doing.

PETER (*beaming*). I flatter myself it must be. (*Laying a hand on* THEODORE's *shoulder.*) My dear Theo, this puts a 20 noo aspect on the affair—clears the air.

THEODORE. New aspect——?

PETER. She makes the first advances, dear kind soul as she is. (*A pause.*) Shall I—fetch her in?

THEODORE. Hold hard, hold hard; don't be in such a devil of a hurry. (*He leaves* PETER *and seats himself in a heap in the chair on the right of the fireplace.* 30 PETER *moves softly to the double door.*)

PETER (*his hand on the door-handle—to* THEODORE). *May* I?

[THEODORE *raises his head and nods.* PETER *goes out. As the door closes,* THEODORE *gets to his feet and flings his cigar into the grate. Then, hastily, he proceeds to put the room in order, closing the piano and beating out and rearranging the pillows on the settees. Finally, he comes upon* MRS. AN- 40 NERLY's *empty coffee cup, picks it up, and vanishes with it into the dining-room. After a little while, the double door opens and* PETER *returns. He glances around the room, looks surprized at not finding* THEO- DORE *and, with a motion of the head, in-*

vites ZOE *to enter. Presently she appears, beautifully dressed. She also looks around; and, passing* PETER, *she moves tremblingly to the fireplace. He closes the door and joins her.*]

PETER (*to* ZOE). You're a brick to do this.

ZOE (*almost inaudibly*). Am I?

PETER. You'll never regret it.

ZOE (*clutching* PETER's *arm*). He will be— kind to me?

PETER. As kind as you are to him.

ZOE (*drawing a deep breath*). Ah! (*She sits upon the settee on the right and her eyes roam about the room.*) What a ripping flat!

PETER (*disparagingly*). Oh, I dun'no.

ZOE (*with a wry mouth, plaintively*). He *has* been doing himself jolly well, in all conscience.

[*The dining-room door opens and* THEODORE *appears. He shuts the door and edges to- ward* PETER, *who leads him to* ZOE.]

PETER. My dear old pals——

[ZOE *gets to her feet and* THEODORE *awk- wardly holds out his hand to her.*]

THEODORE. How are you, Zoe?

ZOE. Fairly—thanks——

[*She hurriedly produces her handkerchief from a gold bag hanging from her wrist and moves away to the left. There she sits upon the settee, struggling to command herself.* PETER *gives* THEODORE's *arm a friendly grip and makes for the double door. As he passes behind the settee on which* ZOE *is seated, he stops to pat her shoulder.*]

ZOE (*in a whisper, seizing his hand*). Don't go, Peter; don't go.

[*He releases his hand, giving hers a reassuring squeeze, and goes to the door.*]

PETER (*at the door, to* THEODORE). I shall be in the City till six.

[*He departs. After a silence,* THEODORE *ap- proaches* ZOE. *They carefully avoid meet- ing each other's eyes.*]

THEODORE. It—it's very good of you, Zo, to—to hunt me up.

ZOE. I—I went first to Copthall Court. (*Wiping a tear from her cheek.*) I—I thought I should find you there.

THEODORE. I—I haven't been at all regular at the office lately. (*A pause. They look about the room in opposite directions.*) Er—Peter tells me he had a little talk with you this morning.

ZOE. Y-yes.

THEODORE. About our—being reconciled. 10

ZOE. Yes.

THEODORE. W-well? (*She puts her handkerchief away and takes from her bag a torn envelope with some inclosures. She gives it to him timidly and he extracts from the envelope a letter and a key.*) The—the damned cruel letter I left behind me— that evening—with my latch-key. (*She inclines her head.*) May I—destroy it?

[*She nods assent, and he tears up the envelope and letter and crams the pieces into his trouser-pocket.*]

THEODORE (*looking at the key*). The—the key——?

ZOE. It—it's yours again—if you like.

THEODORE. You—you're willing——? (*Again she inclines her head, and he puts the key into a pocket in his waistcoat and seats himself humbly in the chair at the 30 farther end of the settee.*) Thank'ee. (*After a pause.*) Zo——

ZOE. Yes?

THEODORE (*turning to her but not lifting his eyes*). Look here. I'm not going to— try to deceive you. I—I want you to understand exactly what you're offering to take back.

ZOE. Exactly——?

THEODORE. I gather from Peter that you 40 came over from Paris on Sunday in the company of Mr. Jim Mallandain.

ZOE. I picked him up by chance at the Gare du Nord.

THEODORE. And Mr. Jim whiled away the journey by—by gossiping to you

about me and—a woman of the name of Annerly?

ZOE. On the boat.

THEODORE. Quite so. (*A pause.*) When you mentioned the matter to Peter, he produced the whitewash bucket, didn't he?

ZOE. Slapped it on thick.

THEODORE (*looking at her from under his brows*). But you didn't——? (*She shakes her head.*) You're right; Peter's a liar. It's a true bill. I wish it wasn't; but it is.

ZOE (*after a pause, steadily*). Well?

THEODORE (*looking at her again*). Are you prepared to forgive me that too, then? (*She nods, but with compressed lips. He bows his head.*) Anyhow, I'm easier for making a clean breast of it.

ZOE. How—how did you—come to——?

THEODORE. Lower myself with this hussy? (*Looking up.*) Isn't it all of a piece? Isn't it the natural finish of the mistakes of the last year or so—the errors we've committed since we began kicking each other's shins? (*Quickly.*) Oh, I'm not reproaching you now for your share o' the transaction. It was my job—the husband's job—to be patient with you; to smooth you down gently, and to wait. But instead of doing that, I let my mind dwell on my own grievances; with the result that latterly the one being in the world I envied was the fellow who'd kept his liberty, or who'd had the pluck to knock off the shackles. (*Rising and walking about, gathering his thoughts as he proceeds.*) Well, I got my freedom at last, didn't I! And a nice mess I made of it. I started by taking a furnished lodging in St. James's Street—sky-high, quiet, *peaceful!* Ha! Hardly a fortnight was out before I had blue-devils and was groaning to myself at the very state of things I'd been longing for. Why should I be condemned, I said to myself—why should I be condemned to an infernal dull life while others around me were enjoying themselves like fighting-cocks! And just then this flat was offered to me as it stands; and in less than a month after I'd slammed the front door at Lancaster Gate I was giving a dinner-party here—a housewarming—(*Halting at the window, his back to* ZOE.)—a dinner-party to four-and-twenty people, and not all of 'em men.

ZOE (*in a low voice*). I heard of your setting up here while I was—in Florence —(*Clenching her hands.*)—in Florence.

THEODORE (*resuming his walk*). However, so far it was nothing but folly on my part—egregious folly. And so it continued till I—till I had the honor of being introduced to Mrs. Annerly at a supper at Jack Poncerot's. (*Eying* ZOE *askance.*) I won't give you the details of the pretty story; your imagination'll supply those—the heading o' the chapters, at any rate. Chapter One, Conceit—I had the besotted vanity to fancy she—she liked me and was genuinely sympathetic toward me; (*At the mantelpiece, looking down into the grate.*) and so on to Chapter the Last—the chapter with the inevitable title— Disgust—Loathing——!

ZOE (*thoughtfully*). You—you're sure you've reached the—the final chapter?

THEODORE (*turning to her*). Heavens, yes! (*Shaking himself.*) It's all over. I've paid her off—to-day, as it happens. I've been itching to do it; and I've done it. (*Sitting upon the settee on the right.*) Another month of her society, and I believe I'd have gone to the dogs completely (*His elbows on his knees, holding his head.*) Zo——

ZOE. Eh?

THEODORE. Peter says you're walking your room half the night and smoking your nerves raw.

ZOE. Does he? He needn't have repeated ——

THEODORE. Zo, I've been walking this horrible flat in the same way. *I* can't get to bed till I hear the rattle of the milk-carts. And *I'm* smoking too much —and—not only *that*——

ZOE (*looking at him for the first time*). Not only *what*?

THEODORE. Well, a man doesn't smoke till four or five o'clock in the morning on cocoa, does he?

[*There is a moment's silence, and then she rises and goes to him.*]

ZOE. Oh—Theo——!

THEODORE (*looking up at her*). So your liberty hasn't made you over happy, either, has it, old girl?

ZOE (*faintly*). No.

THEODORE. You've been thinking, too, of the good times we've had together, hey?

ZOE. Y-yes. (*He rises and places his hands upon her shoulders yearningly as if about to draw her to him. She shrinks from him with a startled look.*) Theo——

THEODORE (*dropping his hands*). What?

ZOE (*nervously*). There—there's one thing I—I want to say to you—before we— before we go further——

THEODORE (*feeling the rebuff*). H'm?

ZOE. As I've told you, I'm willing that you should return to Lancaster Gate. You may return as soon as you please; but——

THEODORE. But?

ZOE. It must be—simply as a companion, Theo; a friend.

THEODORE (*stiffly*). A friend?

ZOE (*with a slight shrug*). Not that we've been much else to each other these last few years—except enemies. Still ——

THEODORE (*frowning*). You wish to make it perfectly clear.

ZOE. Yes.

THEODORE (*after a pause, icily*). I beg your pardon. I was forgetting myself just now. Thanks for the reminder. (*Walking away from her.*) Oh, I know you can feel only the most utter contempt for me—wholesale contempt.

ZOE (*entreatingly*). Ah, no; don't take 10 that tone.

THEODORE. Stand the naughty boy in the corner; he's earned any amount of humiliation you choose to inflict.

ZOE. You shall never be humiliated by me, Theo.

THEODORE (*throwing himself upon the settee on the left*). Evidently!

ZOE (*turning away*). Oh, for God's sake, don't let's begin fighting again. (*Sit-* 20 *ting on the settee on the right.*) Don't let's do that.

THEODORE. Ha, ha! No, no; we won't squabble. Right you are; I accept the terms—*any* terms. (*Lying at full length upon his back on the settee.*) As you say, we've been little more than friends of late years—good friends or bad. (*Throwing one leg over the other.*) It's your laying down the law so emphati- 30 cally that riled me. Sorry I growled. (*There is silence between them. She watches him guiltily. Suddenly he changes the position of his legs.*) Zoe——

ZOE. Yes?

THEODORE (*gazing at the ceiling*). At the same time, I'm blessed if I wouldn't rather you wanted to tear my eyes out than that you should treat me in this lofty, condescending style— 40 scratch my face and tear my eyes out.

ZOE. Well, I—I don't, you see.

THEODORE (*smiling unpleasantly*). Alice Annerly's an extremely handsome creature, my dear, whatever else she may be.

ZOE. I'm—I'm sure of it.

THEODORE. Her photo's on the top of the piano.

ZOE (*restraining an impulse to glance over her shoulder*). I—I'm not curious.

THEODORE. Ho! You mayn't be aware of the fact, but I've paid you the compliment of resenting the deep devotion your pet poodle—Master Lenny Ferris—has been paying you recently. You might do me a similar honor. (*Meditatively.*) Master—blooming—Lenny——! (*Again there is a pause; and then, slowly, he turns upon his side so that he may face her.*) I say, that was a pretty disgraceful business—your trapesing about Italy with that fellow. (*Another pause.*) Hey?

ZOE (*holding her breath*). It *was*—unwise of me, I own.

THEODORE. Unwise! Peter and I were discussing it when your note was brought in.

ZOE (*moistening her lips*). Were you?

THEODORE (*harshly*). Yes, we were. (*Another pause.*) My God, I think it's *I* who ought to dictate what our domestic arrangements are to be in the future —not you! (*A pause. With a motion of the head, he invites her to come to him.*) Zoe—— (*A pause.*) Don't you hear me!

[*She hesitates; then she nerves herself and rises and, with a light step, crosses the room.*]

ZOE (*resting her arms on the back of the chair at the farther end of the settee on which he is lying*). Still the same dear old bully, I notice.

THEODORE. Sit down.

ZOE. Your gentle voice is quite audible where I am.

THEODORE (*putting his feet to the ground*). You sit down a minute.

ZOE. Puh! (*She sits haughtily.*)

THEODORE. Now, you look here, my

lady; I should like an account of that Italian affair from the word go.

ZOE. I'm not in the mood to furnish it.

THEODORE. Perhaps not; but I'm in the mood to receive it. (*A pause.*) When did he join you?

ZOE. He—he didn't join me; that's not the way to put it.

THEODORE. Put it any way you like. When was it?

ZOE. At the—end of February, I think.

THEODORE. You think! (*A pause.*) What made him go out to you?

ZOE. He knew I was awfully in the dumps——

THEODORE. Did he? How did he know that?

ZOE. He—guessed I must be.

THEODORE. Guessed!

ZOE. Well, I'd seen him before I went away. I *was* dreadfully depressed, Theo—dreadfully *désolée*. I never thought you'd bang out of the house as you did. I never meant, for a single moment——

THEODORE. Where were you when he turned up?

ZOE. I—I'd got to Florence. I'd been to Genoa and Pisa—I was drifting about——

THEODORE. Did he dream you were in Florence?

ZOE. Dream——?

THEODORE. He *must* have dreamt it.

ZOE. Oh, I see what you're driving at. He—he'd had a post-card from me——

THEODORE. *A* post-card!

ZOE (*feebly*). I—I don't mean *one*—you—you silly! I—I sent him a picture from each town—so I did to Peter——

THEODORE. Why don't you admit that you and Ferris were corresponding?

ZOE. I—I am admitting it. It's nothing to admit.

THEODORE. Isn't it? (*A pause.*) Well, he arrives in Florence——

ZOE. Don't worry me this afternoon, Theo——

THEODORE. How long was he with you in Florence?

ZOE. I'm seedy; I had quite a temperature yesterday. Lena called in Rashleigh——

THEODORE. How long was he with you in Florence?

ZOE. He wasn't "with" me.

THEODORE. How long?

ZOE. A week—eight days——

THEODORE. Same hotel?

ZOE. No, no, no!

THEODORE. And afterward——?

ZOE. I wanted to do a little tour of the quiet old places—Perugia—Siena——

THEODORE. So did *he*, hey?

ZOE. He tacked on. I saw no harm in it at the time.

THEODORE. At the time!

ZOE. Nor do I now.

THEODORE. It was coming from Perugia you fell up against Lowenstein.

ZOE. If you were a man you'd thrash that beast.

THEODORE. Lowenstein had the room at the hotel there—the Brufani—that Ferris had had.

ZOE (*protestingly*). Ah——!

THEODORE. In the same corridor as yours was.

ZOE. It was stupid—stupid—stupid of Lenny to let them carry his bag up to the Brufani. It was all done before—before it dawned on him——

THEODORE. Where were you moving on to when Lowenstein met you at Arezzo? (*A pause.*) Hey?

ZOE (*passing her hand across her brow, weakly*). Let me off to-day, Theo; my head's going like a clock. (*Getting to her feet.*) Take it up again another time.

(*She goes to the settee on the right and picks up her bag which she has left there. He rises and follows her, so that when she turns they come face to face. She steadies herself.*) Well, you turn it over in your mind about coming back to me. I don't want to put pressure on you; only I— I understood from Peter you were feeling kindly toward me again.

THEODORE (*quickly*). When did you see Ferris last?

ZOE. Oh, drop Ferris.

THEODORE. When?

ZOE. Oh—over two months ago—at the end of the little jaunt.

THEODORE. Not since? (*She looks at him vacantly and shakes her head.*) That's a lie. He was with you on Monday morning at half-past eleven. D'ye deny it?

ZOE. You—you're so jealous, one—one's afraid——

THEODORE (*with sudden, fierce earnestness*). Zoe——

ZOE (*helplessly*). I'm not going to remain here to be——

THEODORE. Give me your word nothing wrong's occurred between you and Ferris. (*A pause.*) I don't ask for your oath; I'll be satisfied with your word. (*A pause.*) Give me your word.

[*She sits upon the settee, her hands lying in her lap.*]

ZOE (*staring at him*). Theo—I've forgiven you; forgive me.

[*There is a silence and then, dumbfounded, he moves to the chair at the further end of the settee on the left and sits there.*]

THEODORE (*after a while*). Florence?

ZOE. No. Perugia—Siena—— (*Brokenly.*) It was in Florence I first lost my senses. I'd been pitying you, hating myself for the way I'd served you, and had been trying to concoct a letter to you. And then one arrived from *him,* telling me you'd taken this big flat and were having a splendid time. It made me furious; and when he came through to me, I was half beside myself. And then he planned out the little tour, and I said Yes to it. (*Wringing her hands.*) Why! Why did I fall in with it! I shall never know why—except that I was mad—blind mad——! (*Leaning back, her eyes closed.*) Get me a drop o' water.

[*He rouses himself and goes to the table on the left of the fireplace and half fills a tumbler with soda-water. Then he brings her the tumbler and holds it out to her.*]

THEODORE. Here——

ZOE (*opening her eyes and looking up at him beseechingly*). Be—merciful to me.

THEODORE (*peremptorily*). Take it.

ZOE (*barely touching the glass*). Don't— don't be hard on me, old man.

[*He thrusts the tumbler into her hand and she drinks.*]

THEODORE (*heavily*). I—I must have some advice about this—some advice.

ZOE. Advice? (*He goes to the writing-table, sits there, and places the telephone receiver to his ear.*) You—you won't do anything to disgrace me publicly, will you, Theo? (*He taps the arm of the instrument impatiently.*) You won't do anything spiteful? (*He rings again.*) You and I are both sinners, Theo; we've both gone a mucker.

THEODORE (*speaking into the telephone*). London Wall, one, three, double five, eight.

ZOE. That's Peter. *He* won't advise you to do anything spiteful. (*She rises painfully, puts the tumbler on the top of the piano, and walks about the room.*) What *can* you do? You can do nothing to hurt me; nor I you. We're both sinners.

THEODORE (*into the telephone*). Hallo! . . . Are you Blundell, Slade, and Mottram? . . . Is that Mr. Ewart?

. . . Mr. Blundell. . . . Mr. Mottram not back yet, I suppose? . . .

ZOE (*in a murmur*). Both—both gone a mucker.

THEODORE (*into the telephone*). . . . When he comes in, tell him I want to see him at once. . . . Cavendish Square . . . at once. . . . (*Replacing the receiver.*) Good-by.

ZOE (*on the left*). Peter—Peter won't let 10 you—be too rough on me.

THEODORE (*leaning his head on his hands*). Ho, ho! An eye-opener for Peter! But he's been a first-rate prophet all the same. (*In a muffled voice.*) Yes, Peter's been right all along the line, with his precious mid-Channel!

ZOE (*looking at him and speaking in low, measured tones*). Theo——(*He makes no response.*) Theo——(*Coming to him* 20 *slowly.*) I—I was thinking it over—beating it all out—driving into the city and back again. *Our* marriage was doomed long, long before we reached mid-Channel.

THEODORE (*absently, not stirring*). Oh?

ZOE. It was doomed nearly fourteen years ago.

THEODORE (*as before*). Oh?

ZOE. From the very beginning. 30

THEODORE (*raising his head*). What d'ye ——?

ZOE. It was doomed from the moment we agreed that we'd never be encumbered in our career with any—brats of children. (*He partly turns in his chair, to listen to her.*) I want you to remember that bargain, in judging me; and I want you to tell Peter of it.

THEODORE. Yes, it suits you to rake that 40 up now——

ZOE (*pressing her fingers to her temples*). If there had been "brats of children" at home, it would have made a different woman of me, Theo; such a different woman of me—and a different man

of you. But, no; everything in the earlier years of our marriage was sacrificed to coining money—to shoving our way through the crowd—to "getting on"; everything was sacrificed to that.

THEODORE (*angrily*). Oh——!

ZOE. And then, when we had succeeded —when we had *got* on—we had commenced to draw apart from each other; and there was the great, showy, empty house at Lancaster Gate for me to fret and pine in. (*He waves his arm scornfully.*) Oh, yes, we were happy in those climbing days— greedily, feverishly happy; but we didn't look to the time when we should need another interest in life to bind us together—the time when we'd got on in years as well as in position. (THEODORE *starts up.*) Ah, Theo, I believe we should have crossed that Ridge safely enough (*Laying her hands upon his breast.*) but for o' cursed, cursed selfishness——!

THEODORE (*shaking himself free*). Well, there's not the slightest use in talking about what might, or might not, have been. (*Passing her and pacing the room.*) One thing is absolutely certain—it's impossible for us ever to live under the same roof again under *any* conditions. That's out o' the question; I couldn't stoop to that.

ZOE (*leaning against the chair at the writing-table*). No, you draw the line at stooping to Mrs. Annerly.

THEODORE. Oh, don't keep on harping on that string. The cases are as far apart as the poles.

ZOE (*faintly*). Ha, ha!

THEODORE (*halting in the middle of the room and drumming upon his brow with his fingers*). Of course, we can make our separation a legal one; but that wouldn't give us release. And as long

as we're tied to one another—
(*Abruptly, looking at her.*) Zoe——

ZOE (*meekly*). Eh?

THEODORE. If I allowed you to divorce
me—made it easy for you—would
Ferris—would that scoundrel marry
you?

ZOE (*turning to him, blankly*). M-marry me?

THEODORE. Because—if it 'ud save you
from going utterly to the bad——   10

ZOE (*advancing a step or two*). No, no; I
wouldn't—I wouldn't marry Lenny.

THEODORE (*after a moment's pause, sharply*).
You wouldn't?

ZOE. No—no——

THEODORE (*coming close to her*). Why not?
(*She shrugs her shoulders confusedly.*)
Why not?

[*She wavers, then grasps his arm. Again he
shakes her off.*]

ZOE (*appealingly*). Oh, Theo, stick to me. 20
Don't throw me over. Wait—wait for
Peter. Theo, I've never ceased to be
fond of you——

THEODORE. Faugh!

ZOE. Not at the bottom of my heart. No,
nor you of me; there's the tragedy of it.
Peter says the same. (*Seizing his hand.*)
Take time; don't decide to-day——

THEODORE (*freeing his hand and looking at her* 30
piercingly). When did you see him last?

ZOE. H-him?

THEODORE. Ferris.

ZOE. This—this morning.

THEODORE. This morning!

ZOE. I—I confess—this morning. I—I
sent him away.

THEODORE. Sent him—away?

ZOE (*noddingly*). Yes—yes——

THEODORE (*slowly*). And so you rush off 40
to me—straight from the young gentleman——

ZOE. W-well?

THEODORE (*suddenly*). Why, damn you,
you've quarrelled!

ZOE. No——

THEODORE. He's chucked you——!

ZOE. No——

THEODORE. Had enough of you!

ZOE (*her eyes blazing*). That's not true!

THEODORE. Ho, ho! You bring me his
cast-off trash, do you——!

ZOE. It's a lie!

THEODORE. Mr. Lenny Ferris's leavings!

ZOE. It's a lie! He'd give his soul to
make me his wife.

THEODORE. Will he tell *me* that?

ZOE. Tell *you!*

THEODORE (*between his teeth*). If he
doesn't, I'll break every bone in his
carcase.

ZOE (*throwing her head up defiantly*). Of
course he'd tell you.

THEODORE (*walking away to the fireplace*).
He shall have a chance of doing it.

ZOE (*making for the door, wildly*). The
sooner the better!

THEODORE (*looking at his watch*). If Peter
were here——

ZOE (*behind the settee on the left, turning to
THEODORE*). Mind! I've your bond!
If Lenny promises to marry me,
you'll let me free myself from you?

THEODORE. I've said so.

ZOE (*missing her bag, which is again lying
upon the settee on the left, and pointing to
it*). Please——

[*He picks up the bag, and is about to take it to
her, when he remembers that he has the
latch-key in his pocket. He produces the key
and drops it into the bag.*]

THEODORE (*as he does so*). You'll want
this for your *new* husband.

ZOE. Thank God, I've done with the old
one! (*He tosses the bag to her in a fury
and she catches it.*) Ha, ha! (*At the door.*)
Ta, ta! (*She disappears.*)

THEODORE (*flourishing his hands*). Oh——
(*Going to the piano, he takes the decanter
of brandy and a glass from the tray and
fills the glass to the brim.*)

                              CURTAIN

ACT IV

A pretty, irregularly shaped room, simply but tastefully furnished. At the back, facing the spectator, are two double windows opening to the floor. These windows give on to a balcony which appears to continue its course outside the adjoining rooms both on the right and left. Beyond the balcony there is an open space and, in the distance, a view of the upper part of the Albert Hall and of other lofty buildings. On the left is the fireplace— 10 its grate empty, save for a few pots of flowers —and, nearer the spectator, there is a door opening from a corridor. Opposite this door is a door of like dimensions, admitting to a bedroom.

On either side of the fireplace and of the left-hand window there is an armchair; facing the fireplace there is a settee; and at the back of the settee are a small writing-table and writing-chair. A leathern tub for waste-paper 20 stands beside the writing-table. On the right of the room is a round table upon which tea is laid for three persons. Two chairs—one on the left, another at the farther side—and a settee on the right are drawn up close to this table. Elsewhere are a bookcase, a smoking-cabinet, and some odds and ends of furniture—the whole being characteristic of a room in a small flat occupied by a well-to-do, but not wealthy, young man. 30

Both the windows are open, and the glare of the afternoon sun is on the balcony and the opposite buildings.

[MRS. PIERPOINT, ETHEL, *and* LEONARD— *the ladies in their hats and gaily dressed— are seated at the round table.*]

LEONARD (*in the chair on the left of the table—handing a dish of cakes to* MRS. PIERPOINT). Do try one of these little cakes. 40

MRS. PIERPOINT (*in the chair at the farther side of the table*). I couldn't.

LEONARD. I bought them and carried 'em home myself.

MRS. PIERPOINT. You really must excuse me.

LEONARD (*pushing the dish toward* ETHEL, *who is on the settee facing him*). Buck up, Ethel.

ETHEL. Good-by to my dinner, then. (*Taking a cake and biting it as she speaks.*) May I, Mother?

MRS. PIERPOINT (*cheerfully*). Now, isn't that the modern young lady exactly! "May I, Mother!" And the cake is half-eaten before the poor mother can even nod her head.

ETHEL (*laughing*). Ha, ha!

MRS. PIERPOINT. "May I go out for a walk, Mother?" and the front door bangs on the very words! "May I do this?" "May I do that?" And a nice life the mother leads if she dares to say "No."

ETHEL. This sounds suspiciously like a sermon. (*To* LEONARD.) Lenny, sit up straight and be preached to. (*Pushing her cup to* MRS. PIERPOINT *who has the tea-tray before her.*) Another cup of tea, your reverence.

MRS. PIERPOINT. Ethel! How—how irreligious! (*Pouring out tea.*) Ah, but it's true, every syllable of it. And in nothing is this spirit of—what shall I describe it as?——

ETHEL. Go-as-you-pleasèdness.

MRS. PIERPOINT (*giving* ETHEL *her tea*). In nothing is this wilful, thoughtless spirit more plainly shown than in the way love-affairs are conducted at the present day.

ETHEL (*whistling slyly*). Phew!

MRS. PIERPOINT (*to* LEONARD). More tea, Leonard?

LEONARD. No, thanks.

MRS. PIERPOINT (*resignedly*). I *suppose* I must call you Leonard now?

ETHEL (*into her teacup*). What's the matter with "Lenny"?

MRS. PIERPOINT. I may be wrong, but I don't *think* that it was the fashion in my youth for a young lady suddenly to appear before her mother and to say, without a note of warning, "Mr. So-and-so is in the drawing-room and we wish to be engaged." Take the case of Ethel's papa—*there's* a case in point——

LEONARD. I certainly intended to speak 10 to you first, Mrs. Pierpoint.

ETHEL (*to* LEONARD). You fibber!

MRS. PIERPOINT. Ethel!

LEONARD. Well, I—what I mean is——

ETHEL. If you *had* done so, I'd never have looked at you again. Surely, if there is one thing which is a girl's own particular business, it is settling preliminaries with her best young man.

MRS. PIERPOINT. My dear! 20

ETHEL (*jumping up*). Anyhow, Mother, if you wanted to play the dragon, you shouldn't have been upstairs, sleeping off the effects of an exceedingly heavy lunch, when Lenny arrived this afternoon.

MRS. PIERPOINT. Fiddle, heavy lunch! A morsel of minced chicken——!

ETHEL. Ha, ha! (*Bending over* MRS. PIERPOINT.) And you don't mind, do you 30 —not actually—(*Kissing* MRS. PIERPOINT.)—as long as——?

MRS. PIERPOINT. As long as what?

ETHEL. As long as—Lenny's contented?

MRS. PIERPOINT (*shaking herself*). Oh, go away.

[*Laughingly,* ETHEL *wanders about inspecting the various objects in the room.*]

LEONARD (*to* MRS. PIERPOINT, *producing his cigarette-case*). Do you object? 40

MRS. PIERPOINT. Not in the least. Ethel's papa used to indulge, in moderation.

LEONARD (*to* ETHEL, *over his shoulder*). Cigarette, Ethel?

MRS. PIERPOINT. Ethel. I forbid it.

ETHEL (*putting on her gloves*). I would, but it makes me swimmy.

MRS. PIERPOINT (*to* ETHEL). How do *you* know?

ETHEL. I've smoked with Zoe Blundell.

MRS. PIERPOINT. This is news to *me*.

ETHEL. Zoe smokes like a chimney.

MRS. PIERPOINT (*to* LEONARD). By-the-bye, she's in London again.

LEONARD (*uncomfortably*). Yes—yes.

MRS. PIERPOINT. Ethel called on her this morning at Lancaster Gate.

LEONARD. Did she?

ETHEL (*to* LEONARD). I told you, Len.

LEONARD. Ah, yes.

MRS. PIERPOINT (*to* LEONARD). Have *you* seen her? I presume not.

LEONARD. Er—for a few minutes. I was in the neighborhood on—on Monday, and I noticed the blinds were up, and I—I just rang the bell to—to inquire.

MRS. PIERPOINT (*elevating her eyebrows*). She received you?

LEONARD. She—she happened to be in the hall.

MRS. PIERPOINT. I was going to *say*—a woman in her peculiar position ought hardly——

LEONARD. No, of course.

MRS. PIERPOINT. Looks ill, I understand?

ETHEL. Frightfully.

LEONARD. Does she?

MRS. PIERPOINT. I am afraid—I am very much afraid—that dear Mrs. Blundell was not *entirely* free from blame in her treatment of that big, rough husband of hers.

ETHEL (*at the left-hand window*). Rubbish, Mother!

MRS. PIERPOINT. Ethel, you are *too* disrespectful.

ETHEL. Sorry.

MRS. PIERPOINT. At the same time, she is an exceedingly attractive person—a trifle vulgar, poor soul, occasionally ——

ETHEL (*hotly*). Mother!

MRS. PIERPOINT (*to* LEONARD). But good-natured people frequently *are* vulgar—aren't they?

ETHEL (*going on to the balcony*). Oh——!

MRS. PIERPOINT (*to* LEONARD). You were quite a friend of hers before the sad split, weren't you—quite a friend?

LEONARD. Yes, I—I always found her a very decent sort. 10

ETHEL (*her hands upon the rail of the balustrade, calling*). Mother, do come and look at the tiny men and women.

MRS. PIERPOINT. Men and women——? (MRS. PIERPOINT *rises and goes to the window, whereupon* LEONARD *jumps up as if relieved by the interruption.*) You're soiling your gloves, Ethel.

ETHEL. Look down there. What tots!

MRS. PIERPOINT (*drawing back from the win-* 20 *dow*). Oh, my dear, I can't——

ETHEL. Do Mother.

MRS. PIERPOINT. You know I don't care for heights.

ETHEL. I'll steady you. (MRS. PIERPOINT *timidly ventures on to the balcony.* ETHEL *takes her arm.*) There's been a concert—or a meeting. (*Calling.*) Lenny——

[LEONARD *has walked away to the writing-table gloomily. He is about to join the la-* 30 *dies on the balcony when the door on the left opens and* RIDEOUT, *his servant, appears.*]

LEONARD (*to* RIDEOUT). Eh?

[*After glancing discreetly in the direction of the ladies on the balcony,* RIDEOUT *produces a visiting-card from behind his back.* LEONARD *goes to him and takes the card, and looks at it in astonishment.*]

RIDEOUT (*quietly*). There's some writing on it, sir. 40

LEONARD. I see. (*In a low voice.*) Where is she?

RIDEOUT. In my room, sir. I said you were engaged.

LEONARD (*uneasily*). You didn't tell her who's here.

RIDEOUT. No, sir; merely some friends to tea.

LEONARD. All right. I shan't be very long. (RIDEOUT *is going.*) Tss——!

RIDEOUT (*stopping*). Yessir?

LEONARD. Keep your door shut.

RIDEOUT. Yessir.

(RIDEOUT *withdraws.* LEONARD *crams the card into his waistcoat pocket and is again about to join the ladies when* MRS. PIERPOINT *comes back into the room.*]

MRS. PIERPOINT (*to* LEONARD). Thank you for showing us your charming little nest. Quite—quite delightful!

LEONARD (*standing by the round table*). Oh, for bachelor quarters——

MRS. PIERPOINT (*in the middle of the room*). There! I declare I often wonder what there is to tempt a bachelor to marry in these days.

LEONARD. You're not a bachelor, Mrs. Pierpoint.

MRS. PIERPOINT. No; that's true. That's perfectly true. But I've a distinct remembrance of the rooms Ethel's pap' lived in when *he* was a bachel ... (ETHEL *returns and goes to the firep ... e.*) They were in Keppel Stree ., and vastly different from these. (... rning to ETHEL.) Have I ever tol' you that poor papa lived in Kepp Street?

ETHEL (*demurely*). Yes, M ther.

MRS. PIERPOINT (*to* ET EL). And now, my dear, as we h ve to dine at half-past seven—(*To* LEONARD.)—what time does *Louise* begin?——

LEONARD. Oh, if we get there at nine

MRS. PIERPOINT. So kind of you to take us—and as Ethel must lie down on her bed for an hour if we want her to look her best—(*Pointing to the tea-table.*)—may I trouble you—my fan?

——

[LEONARD *searches for* MRS. PIERPOINT'S *fan among the tea things.*]

ETHEL (*kneeling upon the settee on the left, her elbows on the back of it, gazing into space*). Mother——

MRS. PIERPOINT. Eh? (*Receiving her fan from* LEONARD.) Thank you.

ETHEL (*slowly*). Mother—this is going to be an awfully happy night.

MRS. PIERPOINT. I'm sure I hope so, my darling. It won't be my fault if it isn't —(*Tapping* LEONARD's *shoulder with her* 10 *fan.*)—nor Leonard's.

ETHEL. Ah, no; I mean *the* night of one's life perhaps.

MRS. PIERPOINT. Oh, I trust we shall have many, many——

LEONARD. Rather!

ETHEL (*raising herself and gripping the back of the settee*). No, no; you don't understand, you gabies. In everybody's life there's one especial moment—— 20

MRS. PIERPOINT. Moment?

ETHEL. Hour—day—night; when all the world seems *yours*—as if it had been made for *you*, and when you can't help pitying other people—they seem so ordinary and insignificant. Well, I believe this is to be *my* evening.

MRS. PIERPOINT. One would imagine *I* had never given you *any* pleasure, to hear you talk. 30

ETHEL (*rising*). I say, Mother, don't make me lie down and lose consciousness when I get home. (*Going to* MRS. PIERPOINT *with extended arms.*) Ah ha! You duck——!

[*In advancing to* MRS. PIERPOINT, ETHEL *knocks over the waste-paper tub with her skirt and its contents are scattered on the floor.*]

ETHEL (*going down on her knees and replac-* 40 *ing the litter*). Sorry.

MRS. PIERPOINT (*to* ETHEL). You'll crease your skirt, Ethel.

LEONARD (*going to* ETHEL). Never mind that.

ETHEL. Oh, but if I do anything clumsy

at home——! (*Coming upon some fragments of a photograph.*) Oh——! (*Trying to fit the pieces together.*) Zoe!

LEONARD. Yes, I—I——

MRS. PIERPOINT (*who has moved to the fireplace*). Pray get off the floor, child.

ETHEL (*finding more pieces*). Why, you've been tearing up Zoe's photos.

LEONARD. They're old things.

ETHEL. *That* they're not. *This* one isn't, at all events. (*Examining one of the scraps closely.*) "—Firenze."

MRS. PIERPOINT. Ethel, we *must* be going.

LEONARD (*almost roughly*). Leave them alone, Ethel.

[*A little startled by his tone, she drops the pieces into the basket and he assists her to rise.*]

MRS. PIERPOINT (*opening the door on the left*). Come along at once, I insist.

[MRS. PIERPOINT *goes out.* ETHEL *is following her mother when she turns to* LEONARD *who is behind her.*]

ETHEL (*to* LEONARD, *with a smile*). Sorry I contradicted you.

[*They kiss hurriedly and* ETHEL *runs after her mother.* LEONARD *follows and closes the door. After a little while, the door is reopened, and* RIDEOUT *enters with* ZOE. ZOE *is dressed as when last seen.*]

RIDEOUT (*to* ZOE, *as she passes him*). Mr. Ferris has gone to the lift, ma'am. He won't be a minute.

ZOE (*going to the left-hand window, languidly*). All right.

RIDEOUT (*at the round table, putting the tea things together upon the tray*). Shall I make you some tea, ma'am?

ZOE (*looking out of the window, speaking in a dull voice*). No; I've had tea, in a teashop. (*Turning.*) Rideout——

RIDEOUT. Yes, ma'am?

ZOE. I should like to tidy myself, if I may; I've been walking about.

RIDEOUT (*going to the door on the right and opening it*). Cert'nly, ma'am. (*As* ZOE *approaches.*) The hot water flows cold for a few seconds, ma'am.

ZOE. Is there any scent?

RIDEOUT. There's some eau-de-cologne on the dressing-table, ma'am.

[*She disappears and* RIDEOUT *closes the door and continues his preparations for removing the tea things.* LEONARD *returns.*]

RIDEOUT (*answering a look of inquiry from* LEONARD). Mrs. Blundell's tidying herself, sir.

LEONARD. Oh, yes. (*Moving about the room, irritably.*) Won't she have some tea?

RIDEOUT. I did ask her, sir. She's had it.

LEONARD (*halting*). Did Mrs. Blundell— say anything, Rideout?

RIDEOUT (*folding the tablecloth*). Only that she wanted to see you just for ten minutes, sir, and that she thought she'd wait. And then she wrote on her card and told me to slip it into your hand if I got the opportunity.

LEONARD (*resuming his walk*). Yes, yes.

RIDEOUT (*after a pause*). What time'll you dress, sir?

LEONARD. Quarter to seven. I have to dine at half-past.

RIDEOUT. Which suit'll you wear, sir?

LEONARD (*considering*). Er—pink lining.

RIDEOUT. Theater, sir?

LEONARD. Opera. Two pairs o' gloves. (RIDEOUT *goes toward the door on the left, carrying the tea-tray.*) Tss——!

RIDEOUT. Yessir?

LEONARD. There's no necessity to put out my clothes yet a while.

RIDEOUT (*placing the tray upon a piece of furniture so that he can open the door*). No, sir.

LEONARD. I'll ring when you can come through.

RIDEOUT (*opening the door*). Yessir.

LEONARD. And I'm not at home to any-body else.

RIDEOUT (*taking up the tray*). No, sir. (*As the man is leaving the room,* LEONARD *comes to the door to close it.*) Thank you very much, sir.

[RIDEOUT *goes out and* LEONARD *shuts the door. As he turns from the door, his eyes fall upon the waste-paper tub. He snatches it up angrily.*]

LEONARD (*reopening the door and calling*). Rideout——

RIDEOUT (*out of sight*). Yessir? (RIDEOUT *presents himself at the door without the tray.*)

LEONARD (*shaking up the contents of the tub and then giving it to* RIDEOUT). Burn this waste paper.

RIDEOUT. Yessir.

[RIDEOUT *closes the door and* LEONARD *is again walking about the room when* ZOE, *carrying her hat, gloves, and bag, appears on the balcony outside the right-hand window. She enters and they look at one another for a moment without speaking.*]

LEONARD. Hallo, Zo!

ZOE. Hallo, Len!

LEONARD. This *is* a surprize.

ZOE (*putting her hat, gloves, and bag upon the round table—nervously*). Is it?

LEONARD. I thought you'd dropped my acquaintance for good and all.

ZOE. N-no, Len. Why should you think that?

LEONARD. Ha! Well, I bear the marks of the point of your shoe somewhere about me.

ZOE. Oh, you—you mustn't take me too seriously when I'm in one of my vile tempers. (*A pause.*) I—I'm not—keeping you——?

LEONARD. No, no.

ZOE (*turning the chair on the left of the round table so that it faces the writing-table*). May I sit down?

LEONARD. Do.

ZOE. I was here three-quarters of an hour ago, but the porter said you were out; so I went and got some tea.

(*Sitting.*) You've been entertaining, according to Rideout.

LEONARD (*turning the chair at the writing-table and sitting facing her*). A couple o' people turned up—old friends——

ZOE. You *are* a gay dog. (*Suddenly, staring at the writing-table.*) Why—where—where am *I*?

LEONARD. You?

ZOE. You always have a photograph of me, standing on your writing-table.

LEONARD. Oh—oh, it's——

ZOE (*remembering*). And there isn't one now—(*Glancing at the door on the right.*) —in your——!

LEONARD. The frames had got beastly shabby. Rideout's taken 'em to be done up.

ZOE (*flutteringly*). Honor? (*A pause.*) Honor?

LEONARD. If—if I say so——

ZOE. I beg your pardon. No, you wouldn't *out* my photos because of a—because of a little tiff, would you?

LEONARD. L-likely!

ZOE (*rising and going to him*). I'm sure you wouldn't, dear boy; I'm sure you wouldn't. (*Again there is a pause, during which she passes her hand over his shoulder caressingly.*) Len——

LEONARD. Eh?

ZOE (*standing behind him*). After that—stupid fall-out of ours this morning—what d'ye think I did?

LEONARD. Did?

ZOE. Ha, ha! I—I took it into my head to—to pay Theodore a visit.

LEONARD. Pay him a visit!

ZOE. It—it was one of my silly impulses —I was so upset at having offended you——

LEONARD. Did you see him?

ZOE. Y-yes.

LEONARD. And what had *he* to say for himself?

ZOE. Oh, I—I made such a mash of it, Len.

LEONARD. Mash——?

ZOE. Yes, I—I let him worm it out of me.

LEONARD. Worm it out of you?

ZOE. Worm it—all out——

LEONARD. Worm *what* out of you?

ZOE (*faintly*). P-Perugia——

[*There is a silence, and then* LEONARD *rises with an angry look.*]

ZOE (*holding the lapels of his coat*). Don't be savage with me, Len. It wasn't altogether my fault. He *had* heard of it from Claud Lowenstein. And it's of no consequence; none whatever. It's just as you said this morning—he *is* ready to make matters smooth for us.

LEONARD (*blankly*). Smooth—for us!

ZOE. Yes, to let *me* divorce *him*. He's promised—he's promised to do so, if you'll—only——

LEONARD (*his jaw dropping*). If *I*——?

ZOE. If you'll give him your word that you'll do the right thing by me.

LEONARD. The right thing——!

ZOE. Marry me. (*A pause.*) I—I suppose he—I suppose he'll demand to see you. Or perhaps he'll make Peter Mottram a go-between.

[*Again there is a silence, and then he walks away from her. She follows him with her eyes.*]

LEONARD (*thickly*). But you—you wished me good-by this morning—finished with me.

ZOE (*clenching her hands*). I know—I know! (*Coming to him.*) But he—he insulted me, Len—stung me. He flung it in my face that you—that you'd chucked me; that I was your cast-off, your leavings. I couldn't bear it from him; and I—I told him that you were all eagerness to make me your wife. (*A pause.*) Well! And so you were—this morning!

[*He sits in the chair on the left of the round table, his elbows on his knees, holding his head.*]

LEONARD. Zoe——

ZOE. W-what?

LEONARD. These people I've had to tea this afternoon—ladies—two ladies——

ZOE. Yes?

LEONARD. Mrs. Pierpoint was one of them—and—and——

ZOE. Mrs. Pierpoint——?

LEONARD (*raising his head and looking at her*). The other was—Ethel.

ZOE. Eth-el——!

LEONARD (*in a low voice*). You—you made me do it.

ZOE (*dazed*). I—I made you——! (*Drawing a deep breath.*) Oh-h-h! (*She turns from him slowly and seats herself in the chair at the writing-table.*) I—I'd forgotten Ethel.

LEONARD. Yes, you persuaded me to do it. (*A pause.*) Zo, you egged me on to do it.

ZOE (*quietly*). You—you did lose much time, did you?

LEONARD. I—I was furious when I left you—furious.

ZOE (*with an attempt at a smile*). Why, you—you must have bolted straight off to her.

LEONARD. I—I went to the club and had some food; and then I came back here and changed—and——

ZOE. Got rid of those photos!

LEONARD. I was furious—furious.

ZOE. And then you—you bustled off to Sloane Street! (*He rises and paces the room. After a while she pulls herself together.*) Oh, well, it—it can't be helped, old boy.

LEONARD (*agitatedly*). It *must* be helped; it *must* be helped. I must get out of it; I must get out of it. Somehow or other, I must get out of it.

ZOE. Get out of it?

LEONARD. The—the Pierpoints——!

ZOE. Oh, don't talk such utter rubbish; I'd kill myself sooner. (*He throws himself into the chair on the right of the left-hand window.*) No, I'm a rotter, Len, but I'm not as low as that. Oh, no, I'm not as low as all that. (*She rises and goes slowly to the round table and, in a listless way, pulls the pins out of her hat.*) I—I'll be toddling home now. (*Tracing a pattern on the crown of her hat with the hat-pins.*) Home——! (*Knitting her brows.*) I shall clear out of that—big—flashy—empty——! (*Putting on her hat.*) Ha, ha! I *have* made a mash of it, haven't I? My father always said I was a heedless, irresponsible little puss. (*With a puzzled look, her arms hanging at her side.*) There was a lot o' good in me, too—any amount o' good——! (*She is drawing on a glove when she turns her head in the direction of the door on the left. At the same moment, LEONARD, also looking at the door, gets to his feet.*)

ZOE (*listening*). What's that, dear?

[*He tiptoes to the door, opens it an inch or two, and puts his ear to the opening.*]

LEONARD (*carefully closing the door and turning to her*). Blundell.

ZOE (*under her breath*). Oh——!

LEONARD (*in a whisper*). Don't worry. I've told him out—— (*There is a pause. They stand looking at each other in silence, waiting. Suddenly LEONARD returns to the door and, without opening it, listens again.*) Curse the brute, he won't go!

[*He faces her irresolutely and, in a panic, she picks up her bag and her other glove and runs out at the door on the right. LEONARD is in the middle of the room when the door on the left is thrown open and THEODORE and PETER enter followed by RIDEOUT. THEODORE and PETER have their hats on.*]

RIDEOUT (*to* LEONARD). I—I beg your pardon, sir——

LEONARD (*to* RIDEOUT). All right.

THEODORE (*to* PETER, *with a hoarse laugh*). You give the man half a sovereign, Peter; that'll soothe his feelings.

PETER (*to* THEODORE, *sharply*). Sssh, sssh! Theo——!

[RIDEOUT *withdraws.*]

THEODORE (*advancing to* LEONARD). Ho! 10 Not at home, hey?

LEONARD (*facing him*). No, I'm not; not to *you.*

PETER. You be quiet, Ferris.

LEONARD (*to* THEODORE). What the devil do you mean by forcing your way into my place?

THEODORE (*raising a walking-cane which he carries*). You——!

[PETER *quickly puts himself between the two* 20 *men as* LEONARD *seizes the chair on the left of the round table.*]

PETER (*to* THEODORE, *endeavoring to get the walking-cane from him*). Give me that. (*To* LEONARD.) You keep a civil tongue in your head. (*To* THEODORE.) Give it me. (*Holding the cane.*) You know what you promised. Give it up. (THEODORE *resigns the cane to* PETER *and walks away to the fireplace where he* 30 *stands with his back to the others.* PETER *lays the cane upon the writing-table and then turns to* LEONARD.) You ought to be ashamed o' yourself. (*Lowering his voice.*) You see the man's laborin' under great excitement.

LEONARD (*sullenly*). I dare say a good many people in London are laboring under excitement. That's no reason why they should have the run of my 40 flat.

PETER (*coolly*). Will you oblige me by sittin' down and listenin' to me for a moment?

LEONARD. Any man who treats me courteously'll be treated courteously in return. (*Sitting in the chair on the left of the round table.*) I can do with *you*, Peter.

PETER. Can you? Then you'll be so kind as to drop addressin' me by my Christian name. (*Sitting in the chair at the writing-table.*) Ferris——

LEONARD (*curling his lip*). Yes, Mister Mottram?

PETER. Mrs. Blundell called upon her husband today—this afternoon, about three o'clock——

LEONARD (*with an assumption of ease*). Oh? Did she?

PETER. And made a communication to him—a communication of a very painful, very shockin' character. (*A pause.*) I presoom you don't require me—or Blundell—to enter into particklers?

LEONARD (*in a low voice*). Oh, for heaven's sake, no.

PETER. We may take it, without goin' further, that what Mrs. Blundell has stated is absolutely the truth?

LEONARD. Absolutely. (*A pause.* THEODORE *moves from the fireplace to the left-hand window and stands there staring at the prospect.*) One thing, though, she mayn't have stated as clearly as she might——

PETER. What's that?

LEONARD. That she—that she's an injured woman—badly dealt with by her husband, and worse by your humble servant; and——

PETER. And——?

LEONARD. And that both Blundell and I damn well deserve to be hanged.

[THEODORE *turns to* LEONARD *fiercely.*]

PETER (*to* THEODORE). Well! Have you any objection to *that*?

[THEODORE *draws himself up, as if to retort; then his body relaxes and he drops into the chair on the left of the window.*]

PETER (*to* LEONARD). Now, then! Attend to me.

JOHN GALSWORTHY

JOHN GALSWORTHY was almost equally eminent as a novelist and as a dramatist. At the time of Galsworthy's death early in 1933, Ford Madox Ford expressed the rather general opinion of the time that in years to come he would possibly be remembered for his plays. His plays have retained much of their vigor, They are frequently revived with success in London, New York, and elsewhere; and in their printed form they are a distinguished part of modern English literature. But Galsworthy the novelist seems, quite understandably, to have gained the ascendency, especially since the award to him of the Nobel Prize for Literature in November 1932. He had written no important play since *Escape* in 1926. On the other hand, Soames Forsyte continued to impress himself on an ever expanding public. Sir James Barrie expressed the prevailing opinion in his letter of congratulation to Galsworthy; he characterized the Forsytes as "the best-known abroad of all the families from this island," and added, "I am not sure that Soames could not legitimately protest against the Nobel prize going to Mr. Galsworthy instead of to himself. At any rate he has the nearest right to enter a claim, and I can see Mr. Galsworthy, with his famous sense of fairness, doubled up by the problem." In the public eye, the prize had gone to the creator of *The Forsyte Saga* rather than to the author of the brilliant and solid series of twenty-seven plays that appeared between 1906 and 1929.

Galsworthy, however, seems firmly placed in the development of the modern drama of his country and of the world. At least a half-dozen of his plays belong to the permanent treasury of the theatre; they are not thrown into shadow by the work of any of his contemporaries. Time has damaged them less than it has most of the plays of the same period written by the more flashy pen of G. B. Shaw. In fact Galsworthy's quiet and firmly constructed plays are the chief British answer to the charge that modern English drama is a form of art practised with distinction chiefly by Irishmen and Scotchmen.

Galsworthy made a deep impression upon his age simply by being the man he was. Barrie, using a current phrase, called him a "bar of gold." His unostentatious charities, from rescuing a needy man at his door to converting the $45,000 Nobel Prize into a trust fund for the benefit of the P.E.N. Club, were a mark of his character. His friends and acquaintances were unanimous in acclaiming his compassion, his sense of sportsmanship, and his unaffected humanitarianism.

Galsworthy was, in short, the perfect type of the cultivated English gentleman of the late Victorian-Edwardian era. His family was well-to-do. His Victorian father had much of the old Forsyte rock in his character. Galsworthy held him in such respect that, for nine long years, he and his cousin's wife Ada loved in secret rather than offend his convictions against divorce. Not until his father's death in 1904 did Galsworthy and Ada openly reveal their passion, so that her husband could divorce her, and they could be married. Traces of the effect of this internal struggle upon the gentlemanly Galsworthy may be seen throughout his early writings.

Galsworthy's life, from his birth in 1867 until he took up writing in a serious way about 1905, was rather representative of that of his class. The family had come from Wembury, Devonshire; Galsworthy was describing his own beginnings in the *Saga* when he took Soames down there to see the cradle of the Forsytes. He lived in beautiful country houses in the midst of the intimate English fields, woodlands, and downs. He went to Harrow where he was prominent in all capacities from madrigal singing and scholarship to track, football, and the broadjump. At New College, Oxford, he continued his accomplishments. He trained for the law, but that profession did not interest him. He traveled about the world. In 1893, he made the voyage from Adelaide to Cape Town on the famous sailing vessel, the *Torrens*, on which Joseph Conrad was first mate. The friendship between the two men begun during those days lasted warmly until Conrad's death in 1923.

In London, Galsworthy lived the life of a rich young gentleman about town. Once when he read a newspaper account of his early hardships before he became famous, Galsworthy laughed and told Ford that he had never had less than several thousands a year. He seemed to his friend Ford to be the Fortunate Youth. He lived in the right bachelor apartments, dressed with cultivated negligence, went to the best houses for tea and for dinner, sat in the proper stalls at the theatre, the proper boxes at the races, doing all the right things unobtrusively and with the English modesty that conveys the impression of having much to be modest about. On a visit to Ford's house, young Galsworthy ran the mile and a quarter from the station alongside the cart, in which Ford had driven over to meet him, talking all the while as a Forsyte would talk about adjoining properties, country families, and the East Kent Hounds. Such was the favored young Englishman who married Ada, and turned his full energies to literature and the drama in the early years of the twentieth century.

Galsworthy himself said, "Until I was twenty-seven years and eight months old it never occurred to me to write anything. And then it didn't occur to me; it occurred to one who was not then my wife." He wrote for eleven years "without making a penny, or any name to speak of." Then in 1906 came what was to be the first of *The Forsyte Saga*, *The Man of Property*, on which he had worked for three years. It was a success; "my name was made; my literary independence assured; and my income steadily swollen." But *The Man of Property* was only half the story for the remarkable season of 1906. On September 25th, his first play, *The Silver Box*, was produced at the Court Theatre. It caused "a strong and immediate sensation." In a single year Galsworthy had placed himself in the front rank both in the novel and the drama of England.

During the next twenty-three years Galsworthy averaged more than a play a season, and at the same time maintained his work on an exceptionally high level of distinction. He belonged to what may be called the second generation of modern drama. Most of the battles of the theatre were already fought and won by the time Galsworthy began to produce plays. A quarter of a century had passed since *A Doll's House* and *Ghosts* had startled a Victorian world. Fourteen years separated *The Silver Box* from Shaw's first play, *Widowers' Houses*. The plays of Brieux, like *The Three Daughters of M. Dupont* (1897), *The Red Robe* (1900), and *Damaged Goods* (1902), were losing their aura of daring, and could be read and produced without devastation to the audience. The age was prepared to accept the naturalists' approach to social questions, and willing to permit the theatre to present plays that exposed the maladjustments of social institutions. Galsworthy did not have to fight for this privilege, as Ibsen, Hauptmann, and Shaw had fought for it; he could and did assume it as a right no longer subject to question. His work was the justification for the revolutionary efforts of his predecessors.

All of Galsworthy's memorable plays had strong social implications that arose from his sense of fair play, his inherent kindliness, and his humanitarianism. He was pained by the sight of injustice and discrimination against the weak and the underprivileged. But his dramatic method was not that of the pamphleteer, as was essentially true of Brieux, Shaw, and such thesis dramatists. It was the approach of the artistic and restrained naturalist who attempts to give an accurate picture of life by cutting away the non-essentials. "I cannot help thinking," he once wrote, "that the artist's point of view is that of a bird hovering over a field, and seeing not one corner only but all four corners; and that when he comes to put the picture on the canvas he puts what lies behind as well as what leaps to the eye." The thesis is suggested by the play, and may be deduced from it; but it is not to be separated from the plot and the characters, as it may be, for example, in *Damaged Goods*.

Galsworthy, who has left many illuminating comments on his art, coined the phrase "a spire of meaning" to describe his concept of his own social dramas. "A drama must be shaped so as to have a spire of meaning. Every grouping of life and character has its inherent moral; and the business of the dramatist is so to pose the group as to bring that moral poignantly to the light of day." In shaping his plays, Galsworthy attempted, therefore, "to set before the public no cut-and-dried codes, but the phenomena of life and character, selected and combined, *but not distorted*, by the dramatist's outlook, set down without fear, favor, or prejudice, leaving the public to put down such poor moral as nature may afford. . . . Take care of character: action and dialogue will take care of themselves."

These pronouncements, taken from *Some Platitudes Concerning Drama*, provide a helpful approach to Galsworthy's plays. They have, all of them, a basic interest in some social problem; and the problem is elevated and dramatized with severe, yet sympathetic, naturalness in the twisted lives of characters who are overtaken by forces greater than themselves. These destructive forces, roughly the equivalent of the ancients' Fate, are generated by the nature of modern life, and the inflexible institutions set up to guard and preserve the system. The ponderous majesty of the law and the injustice of the machinery of justice are the themes most favored by Galsworthy for creating dramatic situations.

In *The Silver Box* the "spire of meaning" is that the law is lenient with the well-placed and influential, harsh and severe with the poor and the lowly. The wayward son of John Bartwick, a wealthy liberal M.P., and the unem-

ployed husband of the Bartwick's char-
woman, Jones, are both guilty of petty
theft. Bartwick gets off without difficulty because of his family position;
Jones is caught in the wheels of the law
and sent to prison. Jones shouts the thesis in his last speech as he is hustled off
to a month of hard labor: "Call this
justice? What about 'im? 'E got drunk!
'E took the purse—'e took the purse but
it's 'is *money* got 'im off—*Justice!*" Then
Galsworthy, with his often obvious
irony, has the magistrate rise from his
seat as Jones is shut away, and announce, "We will now adjourn for
lunch!" As this central thread of interest unravels, Galsworthy satirically
exposes the Bartwick household, its
standards and values, and makes of
Mrs. Jones an appealing, pathetic soul
who suffers because of the nature of the
society in which she lives.

Strife (1909) is a trenchant play in the
tradition of Hauptmann's *The Weavers.*
It is a study of the personalities involved
in a long and bitter dispute between the
directors and the workmen of a tin
plate works. David Roberts, the fiery
spokesman for labor, is singled out from
the workmen's committee; he is set off
against John Anthony, the equally
strong and obstinate representative of
British capital and its determination to
retain personal control of industry.
After a devastating, winter-long strike
with attendant miseries of starvation,
suffering, and business losses, the issues
are compromised, with the closing observation of Tench, the secretary, to
Harness of the Trade Union: "D' you
know, sir—these terms, they're the *very
same* we drew up together, you and I,
and put to both sides before the fight
began? All this—all this—and—and
what for?"

Strife stirred audiences profoundly

and was "received with acclamation."
Enthusiasm ran high. It was translated
and performed in many languages, and
is still regarded as one of the best of Galsworthy's plays for its structure, its dialogue, and its honest handling of a serious social problem complicated by human vanity and obstinacy. Joseph Conrad summed up its virtues when, in a
letter to Galsworthy, he praised its "intellectual honesty" and "the artistic
simplicity" of its method; and added,
"We have there human beings in their
littleness and their heroism presented to
us in a work of art with no didactic purpose but with a moral intention."

That is the sort of comment most
critics have found themselves making on
Galsworthy's plays. In *The Eldest Son*
(1909) the moral intention was, as in
The Silver Box, to show how the standard
of judgment is altered when the eldest
son of a wealthy family is guilty of the
same sin, in this case the seduction of a
housemaid—as one of the menservants.
In *The Pigeon* (1912) which Galsworthy
deliberately tried to make fantastical,
the theme was man's tendency to insti-
tutionalize everything and thus to become inhuman; but the author warned
that "the play, being satire and night-
marish, must not be too rigorously
scrutinized for definite meaning." In
The Fugitive (1913) he pictured a woman
who fled from her incompatible husband, lost the sympathy of her friends,
and committed suicide in the supper
room of a cheap house on Derby Day.

The Mob (1914) dramatized the process by which in time of war-hysteria the
honest individual who espouses a cause
that is counter to the mass view is attacked and killed by a mob. *The Skin
Game* (1920) showed how two jealous
and hostile families came into conflict,
bitterly fought each other over a trifle,

and how each paid the penalty of its folly in the end. *Loyalties* (1922) presented the English scene after the Armistice, and arranged the conflicts between individuals and various classes around the motive of loyalty to the group. Each was loyal, but loyalty alone was not enough. *Old English* (1924) was a splendid character study of old Sylvanus Heythorp, a sturdy and crotchety old gentleman who might have belonged to the tribe of Forsytes. *Escape* (1926) was another study in the ponderous movement of the law, through the agencies of courts and prisons, to inflict punishment out of all proportion to the crime and the motives behind it.

Such, in bare simplification, were the "spires of meaning" that arose from the Galsworthy plays. Their range and their thrust were limited, of course, but they were important when considered as a superstructure erected upon the foundation of character. In this general setting *Justice* becomes a focus for the singular dramatic qualities of John Galsworthy. It was presented at the Duke of York's Theatre on February 21, 1910, and it caused a sensation, especially the cell scene. Galsworthy had diligently and passionately prepared himself to write the play, and to create that terrible scene. He had visited various English prisons, including Dartmoor, Pentonville, Chelmsford, and Lewes Gaols. He had interviewed convicts, and studied the effects upon them of indiscriminate solitary confinement. He had talked with members of the Government about reforming this practice. He had written to the press on the subject. All this zealous concern lent weight and added dimension and emotional power to his portrait of Falder, the weak, honorably-motivated boy who broke the first rule of an acquisitive

society and was ground to death under the machinery of Justice.

Justice was an instrument for effecting prison reform, but Galsworthy was somewhat annoyed to find the public laying too great stress on what he considered a minor point in the total play. He was trying, he said, to show the "spirit of the whole process. . . . The play was in no sense conceived as an attack on any department of the administration of justice, but as a picture of the whole as it presents itself to a certain temperament." In this larger intent he succeeded admirably. An atmosphere of impending and pitiless disaster engulfs the play. It is all the more distressing because no single villain personified the evil force; it is the unseen and unassailable tyranny of the hard rules of society itself.

The play is tragedy in true, early twentieth-century style. Not the gods but the machinery of "justice," remote, unpersonalized, and baffling, sweep the pitiful Falder to annihilation. One is not even purged with pity and terror by this perverse concentration of the millstones on a boy who was himself moved by pity to commit a forgery. Our sympathy is powerless. Deep in our minds we know, too, that abolition of solitary confinement will have no real bearing on the fundamental problem. It goes beyond this surface to the nature of man himself and his devices for self-protection against his fears—as shown in the careful balance of the arguments for and against letting the traditional procedure take its course against Falder.

Justice is naturalism at its peak, and Galsworthy at his most typical. The structure is natural, yet dramatic. The dialogue is a masterful creation in considered style of the illusion of appropriate and accurately characterized diction. The characters are alive and individualized. The theme is kept under discipline, and the legal matters in restraint. Galsworthy tried to be just to both sides of his case. While maintaining his detachment and over-all view, he builds his theme to a powerful statement and climax. His almost classic simplicity and restraint, so characteristic of the man and his code, surround the play with an atmosphere of permanence. All these qualities, and more, distinguish *Justice* and the work of the dramatist as a whole. And because of these qualities, Galsworthy is the unquestioned English representative of the drama of social consciousness.

JUSTICE

CHARACTERS

JAMES HOW ⎫
WALTER HOW, *his son* ⎰ *solicitors*

ROBERT COKESON, *their managing clerk*

WILLIAM FALDER, *their junior clerk*

SWEEDLE, *their office-boy*

WISTER, *a detective*

COWLEY, *a cashier*

MR. JUSTICE FLOYD, *a judge*

HAROLD CLEAVER, *an old advocate*

HECTOR FROME, *a young advocate*

CAPTAIN DANSON, V.C., *a prison governor*

THE REV. HUGH MILLER, *a prison chaplain*

EDWARD CLEMENTS, *a prison doctor*

WOODER, *a chief warder*

MOANEY ⎫

CLIPTON ⎬ *convicts*

O'CLEARY ⎭

RUTH HONEYWILL, *a woman*

A NUMBER OF BARRISTERS, SOLICITORS, SPECTATORS, USHERS, REPORTERS, JURYMEN, WARDERS, AND PRISONERS

TIME: *The Present*

ACT I

The scene is the managing clerk's room, at the offices of JAMES and WALTER HOW, on a July morning. The room is old-fashioned, furnished with well-worn mahogany and leather, and lined with tin boxes and estate plans. It has three doors. Two of them are close together in the centre of a wall. One of these two doors leads to the outer office, which is only divided from the managing clerk's room by a partition of wood and clear glass; and when the door into this outer office is opened there can be seen the wide outer door leading out on to the stone stairway of the building. The other of these two centre doors leads to the junior clerk's room. The third door is that leading to the partners' room.

The managing clerk, COKESON, is sitting at his table adding up figures in a pass-book, and murmuring their numbers to himself. He is a man of sixty, wearing spectacles; rather short, with a bald head, and an honest, pug-dog face. He is dressed in a well-worn black frock-coat and pepper-and-salt trousers.

COKESON. And five's twelve, and three—fifteen, nineteen, twenty-three, thirty-two, forty-one—and carry four. (*He ticks the page, and goes on murmuring.*) Five, seven, twelve, seventeen, twenty-four and nine, thirty-three, thirteen and carry one.

[*He again makes a tick. The outer office door is opened, and* SWEEDLE, *the office-boy, appears, closing the door behind him. He is a pale youth of sixteen, with spiky hair.*]

COKESON (*with grumpy expectation*). And carry one.

SWEEDLE. There's a party wants to see Falder, Mr. Cokeson.

COKESON. Five, nine, sixteen, twenty-

75

one, twenty-nine—and carry two. Sent him to Morris's. What name?

SWEEDLE. Honeywill.

COKESON. What's his business?

SWEEDLE. It's a woman.

COKESON. A lady?

SWEEDLE. No, a person.

COKESON. Ask her in. Take this pass-book to Mr. James. (*He closes the pass-book.*)

SWEEDLE (*reopening the door.*) Will you come in, please?

[RUTH HONEYWILL *comes in. She is a tall woman, twenty-six years old, unpretentiously dressed, with black hair and eyes, and an ivory-white, clear-cut face. She stands very still, having a natural dignity of pose and gesture.*]

[SWEEDLE *goes out into the partners' room with the pass-book.*]

COKESON (*looking round at* RUTH). The young man's out. (*Suspiciously.*) State your business, please.

RUTH (*who speaks in a matter-of-fact voice, and with a slight West-Country accent*). It's a personal matter, sir.

COKESON. We don't allow private callers here. Will you leave a message?

RUTH. I'd rather see him, please. (*She narrows her dark eyes and gives him a hon-eyed look.*)

COKESON (*expanding*). It's all against the rules. Suppose I had *my* friends here to see me! It'd never do!

RUTH. No, sir.

COKESON (*a little taken aback*). Exactly! And here you are wanting to see a *junior* clerk!

RUTH. Yes, sir; I must see him.

COKESON (*turning full round to her with a sort of outraged interest*). But this is a lawyer's office. Go to his private address.

RUTH. He's not there.

COKESON (*uneasy*). Are you related to the party?

RUTH. No, sir.

COKESON (*in real embarrassment*). I don't know what to say. It's no affair of the office.

RUTH. But what am I to do?

COKESON. Dear me! I can't tell you that.

[SWEEDLE *comes back. He crosses to the outer office and passes through into it, with a quizzical look at* COKESON, *carefully leaving the door an inch or two open.*]

COKESON (*fortified by this look*). This won't do, you know, this won't do at all. Suppose one of the partners came in!

[*An incoherent knocking and chuckling is heard from the outer door of the outer office.*]

SWEEDLE (*putting his head in*). There's some children outside here.

RUTH. They're mine, please.

SWEEDLE. Shall I hold them in check?

RUTH. They're quite small, sir. (*She takes a step towards* COKESON.)

COKESON. You mustn't take up his time in office hours; we're a clerk short as it is.

RUTH. It's a matter of life and death.

COKESON (*again outraged*). Life and death!

SWEEDLE. Here *is* Falder.

[FALDER *has entered through the outer office. He is a pale, good-looking young man, with quick, rather scared eyes. He moves towards the door of the clerks' office, and stands there irresolute.*]

COKESON. Well, I'll give you a minute. It's not regular. (*Taking up a bundle of papers, he goes out into the partners' room.*)

RUTH (*in a low, hurried voice*). He's on the drink again, Will. He tried to cut my throat last night. I came out with the children before he was awake. I went round to you——

FALDER. I've changed my digs.

RUTH. Is it all ready for to-night?

FALDER. I've got the tickets. Meet me 11.45 at the booking office. For God's sake don't forget we're man and wife! (*Looking at her with tragic intensity.*) Ruth!

RUTH. You're not afraid of going, are you?

FALDER. Have you got your things, and the children's?

RUTH. Had to leave them, for fear of waking Honeywill, all but one bag. I can't go near home again.

FALDER (*wincing*). All that money gone for nothing. How much *must* you have? 10

RUTH. Six pounds—I could do with that, I think.

FALDER. Don't give away where we're going. (*As if to himself.*) When I get out there I mean to forget it all.

RUTH. If you're sorry, say so. I'd sooner he killed me than take you against your will.

FALDER (*with a queer smile*). We've got to go. I don't care; I'll have *you*. 20

RUTH. You've just to say; it's not too late.

FALDER. It *is* too late. Here's seven pounds. Booking office—11.45 to-night. If you weren't what you are to me, Ruth——!

RUTH. Kiss me!

[*They cling together passionately, then fly apart just as* COKESON *re-enters the room.* RUTH *turns and goes out through the outer* 30 *office.* COKESON *advances deliberately to his chair and seats himself.*]

COKESON. This isn't right, Falder.

FALDER. It shan't occur again, sir.

COKESON. It's an improper use of these premises.

FALDER. Yes, sir.

COKESON. You quite understand—the party was in some distress; and, having children with her, I allowed my 40 feelings——(*He opens a drawer and produces from it a tract.*) Just take this! "Purity in the Home." It's a well-written thing.

FALDER (*taking it, with a peculiar expression*). Thank you, sir.

COKESON. And look here, Falder, before Mr. Walter comes, have you finished up that cataloguing Davis had in hand before he left?

FALDER. I shall have done with it to-morrow, sir—for good.

COKESON. It's over a week since Davis went. Now it won't do, Falder. You're neglecting your work for private life. I shan't mention about the party having called, but——

FALDER (*passing into his room*). Thank you, sir.

[COKESON *stares at the door through which* FALDER *has gone out; then shakes his head, and is just settling down to write, when* WALTER HOW *comes in through the outer office. He is a rather refined-looking man of thirty-five, with a pleasant, almost apologetic voice.*]

WALTER. Good-morning, Cokeson.

COKESON. Morning, Mr. Walter.

WALTER. My father here?

COKESON (*always with a certain patronage as to a young man who might be doing better*). Mr. James has been here since eleven o'clock.

WALTER. I've been in to see the pictures, at the Guildhall.

COKESON (*looking at him as though this were exactly what was to be expected*). Have you now—ye-es. This lease of Boulter's—am I to send it to counsel?

WALTER. What does my father say?

COKESON. 'Aven't bothered him.

WALTER. Well, we can't be too careful.

COKESON. It's such a little thing—hardly worth the fees. I thought you'd do it yourself.

WALTER. Send it, please. I don't want the responsibility.

COKESON (*with an indescribable air of compassion*). Just as you like. This "right-of-way" case—we've got 'em on the deeds.

WALTER. I know; but the intention was

obviously to exclude that bit of common ground.

COKESON. We needn't worry about that. We're the *right* side of the law.

WALTER. I don't like it.

COKESON (*with an indulgent smile*). We shan't want to set ourselves up against the law. Your father wouldn't waste his time doing that.

[*As he speaks* JAMES HOW *comes in from the partners' room. He is a shortish man, with white side-whiskers, plentiful grey hair, shrewd eyes, and gold pince-nez.*]

JAMES. Morning, Walter.

WALTER. How are you, father?

COKESON (*looking down his nose at the papers in his hand as though deprecating their size*). I'll just take Boulter's lease in to young Falder to draft the instructions. (*He goes out into* FALDER's *room.*)

WALTER. About that right-of-way case?

JAMES. Oh, well, we must go forward there. I thought you told me yesterday the firm's balance was over four hundred.

WALTER. So it is.

JAMES (*holding out the pass-book to his son*). Three—five—one, no recent cheques. Just get me out the cheque-book.

[WALTER *goes to a cupboard, unlocks a drawer, and produces a cheque book.*]

JAMES. Tick the pounds in the counterfoils. Five, fifty-four, seven, five, twenty-eight, twenty, ninety, eleven, fifty-two, seventy-one. Tally?

WALTER (*nodding*). Can't understand. Made sure it was over four hundred.

JAMES. Give me the cheque-book. (*He takes the cheque-book and cons the counterfoils.*) What's this ninety?

WALTER. Who drew it?

JAMES. You.

WALTER (*taking the cheque-book*). July 7th? That's the day I went down to look over the Trenton Estate—last Friday week; I came back on the Tuesday,

you remember. But look here, father, it was *nine* I drew a cheque for. Five guineas to Smithers and my expenses. It just covered all but half a crown.

JAMES (*gravely*). Let's look at that ninety cheque. (*He sorts the cheque out from the bundle in the pocket of the pass-book.*) Seems all right. There's no nine here. This is bad. Who cashed that nine-pound cheque?

WALTER (*puzzled and pained*). Let's see! I was finishing Mrs. Reddy's will— only just had time; yes—I gave it to Cokeson.

JAMES. Look at that t y : that yours?

WALTER (*after consideration*). My *y's* curl back a little; this doesn't.

JAMES (*as* COKESON *re-enters from* FALDER's *room*). We must ask him. Just come here and carry your mind back a bit, Cokeson. D'you remember cashing a cheque for Mr. Walter last Friday week—the day he went to Trenton?

COKESON. Ye-es. Nine pounds.

JAMES. Look at this. (*Handing him the cheque.*)

COKESON. No! Nine pounds. My lunch was just coming in; and of course I *like* it hot; I gave the cheque to Davis to run round to the bank. He brought it back, all gold—you remember, Mr. Walter, you wanted some silver to pay your cab. (*With a certain contemptuous compassion.*) Here, let *me* see. You've got the wrong cheque. (*He takes cheque-book and pass-book from* WALTER.)

WALTER. Afraid not.

COKESON (*having seen for himself*). It's funny.

JAMES. You gave it to Davis, and Davis sailed for Australia on Monday. Looks black, Cokeson.

COKESON (*puzzled and upset*). Why this'd be a felony! No, no! there's some mistake.

JAMES. I hope so.

COKESON. There's never been anything of that sort in the office the twenty-nine years I've been here.

JAMES (*looking at cheque and counterfoil*). This is a very clever bit of work; a warning to you not to leave space after your figures, Walter.

WALTER (*vexed*). Yes, I know—I was in such a tearing hurry that afternoon.

COKESON (*suddenly*). This has upset me.

JAMES. The counterfoil altered too—very deliberate piece of swindling. What was Davis's ship?

WALTER. *City of Rangoon.*

JAMES. We ought to wire and have him arrested at Naples; he can't be there yet.

COKESON. His poor young wife. I liked the young man. Dear, oh dear! In this office!

WALTER. Shall I go to the bank and ask the cashier?

JAMES (*grimly*). Bring him round here. And ring up Scotland Yard.

WALTER. Really?

[*He goes out through the outer office.* JAMES *paces the room. He stops and looks at* COKESON, *who is disconsolately rubbing the knees of his trousers.*]

JAMES. Well, Cokeson! There's something in character, isn't there?

COKESON (*looking at him over his spectacles*). I don't quite take you, sir.

JAMES. Your story would sound d——d thin to any one who didn't know you.

COKESON. Ye-es! (*He laughs. Then with sudden gravity.*) I'm sorry for that young man. I feel it as if it was my own son, Mr. James.

JAMES. A nasty business!

COKESON. It unsettles you. All goes on regular, and then a thing like this happens. Shan't relish my lunch to-day.

JAMES. As bad as that, Cokeson?

COKESON. It makes you think. (*Confidentially.*) He must have had temptation.

JAMES. Not so fast. We haven't convicted him yet.

COKESON. I'd sooner have lost a month's salary than had this happen. (*He broods.*)

JAMES. I hope that fellow will hurry up.

COKESON (*keeping things pleasant for the cashier*). It isn't fifty yards, Mr. James. He won't be a minute.

JAMES. The idea of dishonesty about this office—it hits me hard, Cokeson. (*He goes towards the door of the partners' room.*)

SWEEDLE (*entering quietly, to* COKESON *in a low voice*). She's popped up again, sir —something she forgot to say to Falder.

COKESON (*roused from his abstraction*). Eh? Impossible. Send her away!

JAMES. What's that?

COKESON. Nothing, Mr. James. A private matter. Here, I'll come myself. (*He goes into the outer office as* JAMES *passes into the partners' room.*) Now, you really mustn't—we can't have anybody just now.

RUTH. Not for a minute, sir?

COKESON. Reely! Reely! I can't have it. If you want him, wait about; he'll be going out for his lunch directly.

RUTH. Yes, sir.

[WALTER, *entering with the cashier, passes* RUTH *as she leaves the outer office.*]

COKESON (*to the cashier, who resembles a sedentary dragoon.*) Good-morning. (*To* WALTER.) Your father's in there.

[WALTER *crosses and goes into the partners' room.*]

COKESON. It's a nahsty, unpleasant little matter, Mr. Cowley. I'm quite ashamed to have to trouble you.

COWLEY. I remember the cheque quite well. (*As if it were a liver.*) Seemed in perfect order.

COKESON. Sit down, won't you? I'm not a sensitive man, but a thing like this about the place—it's not nice. I like people to be open and jolly together.

COWLEY. Quite so.

COKESON (*buttonholing him, and glancing towards the partners' room*). Of course he's a young man. I've told him about it before now—leaving space after his figures, but he *will* do it. 10

COWLEY. I should remember the person's face—quite a youth.

COKESON. I don't think we shall be able to show him to you, as a matter of fact.

[JAMES *and* WALTER *have come back from the partners' room.*]

JAMES. Good-morning, Mr. Cowley. You've seen my son and myself, you've seen Mr. Cokeson, and you've 20 seen Sweedle, my office-boy. It was none of us, I take it.

[*The cashier shakes his head with a smile.*]

JAMES. Be so good as to sit there. Cokeson, engage Mr. Cowley in conversation, will you? (*He goes towards* FALDER's *room.*)

COKESON. Just a word, Mr. James.

JAMES. Well?

COKESON. You don't want to upset the 30 young man in there, do you? He's a nervous young feller.

JAMES. This must be thoroughly cleared up, Cokeson, for the sake of Falder's name, to say nothing of yours.

COKESON (*with some dignity*). That'll look after itself, sir. He's been upset once this morning; I don't want him startled again.

JAMES. It's a matter of form; but I can't 40 stand upon niceness over a thing like this—too serious. Just talk to Mr. Cowley. (*He opens the door of* FALDER's *room.*)

JAMES. Bring in the papers in Boulter's lease, will you, Falder?

COKESON (*bursting into voice*). Do you keep dogs?

[*The cashier, with his eyes fixed on the door, does not answer.*]

COKESON. You haven't such a thing as a bulldog pup you could spare me, I suppose?

[*At the look on the cashier's face his jaw drops, and he turns to see* FALDER *standing in the doorway, with his eyes fixed on* COWLEY, *like the eyes of a rabbit fastened on a snake.*]

FALDER (*advancing with the papers*). Here they are, sir!

JAMES (*taking them*). Thank you.

FALDER. Do you want me, sir?

JAMES. No, thanks!

[FALDER *turns and goes back into his own room. As he shuts the door* JAMES *gives the cashier an interrogative look, and the cashier nods.*]

JAMES. Sure? This isn't as we suspected.

COWLEY. Quite. He knew me. I suppose he can't slip out of that room?

COKESON (*gloomily*). There's only the window—a whole floor and a basement.

[*The door of* FALDER's *room is quietly opened, and* FALDER, *with his hat in his hand, moves towards the door of the outer office.*]

JAMES (*quietly*). Where are you going, Falder?

FALDER. To have my lunch, sir.

JAMES. Wait a few minutes, would you? I want to speak to you about this lease.

FALDER. Yes, sir. (*He goes back into his room.*)

COWLEY. If I'm wanted, I can swear that's the young man who cashed the cheque. It was the last cheque I handled that morning before my lunch. These are the numbers of the notes he had. (*He puts a slip of paper on the table; then, brushing his hat round.*) Good-morning!

JAMES. Good-morning, Mr. Cowley!

COWLEY (*to* COKESON). Good-morning.

COKESON (*with stupefaction*). Good-morning.

[*The cashier goes out through the outer office.* COKESON *sits down in his chair, as though it were the only place left in the morass of his feelings.*]

WALTER. What are you going to do?

JAMES. Have him in. Give me the cheque 10 and the counterfoil.

COKESON. I don't understand. I thought young Davis——

JAMES. We shall see.

WALTER. One moment, father: have you thought it out?

JAMES. Call him in!

COKESON (*rising with difficulty and opening* FALDER's *door; hoarsely*). Step in here a minute. 20

[FALDER *comes in.*]

FALDER (*impassively*). Yes, sir?

JAMES (*turning to him suddenly with the cheque held out*). You know this cheque, Falder?

FALDER. No, sir.

JAMES. Look at it. You cashed it last Friday week.

FALDER. Oh! yes, sir; that one—Davis gave it me. 30

JAMES. I know. And you gave Davis the cash?

FALDER. Yes, sir.

JAMES. When Davis gave you the cheque was it exactly like this?

FALDER. Yes, I think so, sir.

JAMES. You know that Mr. Walter drew that cheque for *nine* pounds?

FALDER. No, sir—ninety.

JAMES. Nine, Falder. 40

FALDER (*faintly*). I don't understand, sir.

JAMES. The suggestion, of course, is that the cheque was altered; whether by you or Davis is the question.

FALDER. I—I——

COKESON. Take your time, take your time.

FALDER (*regaining his impassivity*). Not by me, sir.

JAMES. The cheque was handed to Cokeson by Mr. Walter at one o'clock; we know that because Mr. Cokeson's lunch had just arrived.

COKESON. I couldn't leave it.

JAMES. Exactly; he therefore gave the cheque to Davis. It was cashed by you at 1.15. We know that because the cashier recollects it for the last cheque he handled before *his* lunch.

FALDER. Yes, sir, Davis gave it to me because some friends were giving him a farewell luncheon.

JAMES (*puzzled*). You accuse Davis, then?

FALDER. I don't know, sir—it's very funny.

[WALTER, *who has come close to his father, says something to him in a low voice.*]

JAMES. Davis was not here again after that Saturday, was he?

COKESON (*anxious to be of assistance to the young man, and seeing faint signs of their all being jolly once more*). No, he sailed on the Monday.

JAMES. Was he, Falder?

FALDER (*very faintly*). No, sir.

JAMES. Very well, then, how do you account for the fact that this nought was added to the nine in the counterfoil on or after *Tuesday?*

COKESON (*surprised*). How's that?

[FALDER *gives a sort of lurch; he tries to pull himself together, but he has gone all to pieces.*]

JAMES (*very grimly*). Out, I'm afraid, Cokeson. The cheque-book remained in Mr. Walter's pocket till he came back from Trenton on Tuesday morning. In the face of this, Falder, do you still deny that you altered both cheque and counterfoil?

FALDER. No, sir—no, Mr. How. I did it, sir; I did it.

COKESON (*succumbing to his feelings*). Dear, dear! what a thing to do!

FALDER. I wanted the money so badly, sir. I didn't know what I was doing.

COKESON. However such a thing could have come into your head!

FALDER (*grasping at the words*). I can't think, sir, really! It was just a minute of madness.

JAMES. A long minute, Falder. (*Tapping the counterfoil.*) Four days at least.

FALDER. Sir, I swear I didn't know what I'd done till afterwards, and then I hadn't the pluck. Oh! sir, look over it! I'll pay the money back—I will, I promise.

JAMES. Go into your room.

[FALDER, *with a swift imploring look, goes back into his room. There is silence.*]

JAMES. About as bad a case as there could be.

COKESON. To break the law like that—in here!

WALTER. What's to be done?

JAMES. Nothing for it. Prosecute.

WALTER. It's his first offence.

JAMES (*shaking his head*). I've grave doubts of that. Too neat a piece of swindling altogether.

COKESON. I shouldn't be surprised if he was tempted.

JAMES. Life's one long temptation, Cokeson.

COKESON. Ye-es, but I'm speaking of the flesh and the devil, Mr. James. There was a woman come to see him this morning.

WALTER. The woman we passed as we came in just now. Is it his wife?

COKESON. No, no relation. (*Restraining what in jollier circumstances would have been a wink.*) A married person, though.

WALTER. How do you know?

COKESON. Brought her children. (*Scandalised.*) There they were outside the office.

JAMES. A real bad egg.

WALTER. I should like to give him a chance.

JAMES. I can't forgive him for the sneaky way he went to work—counting on our suspecting young Davis if the matter came to light. It was the merest accident the cheque-book stayed in your pocket.

10 WALTER. It *must* have been the temptation of a moment. He hadn't time.

JAMES. A man doesn't succumb like that in a moment, if he's a clean mind and habits. He's rotten; got the eyes of a man who can't keep his hands off when there's money about.

WALTER (*dryly*). We hadn't noticed that before.

20 JAMES (*brushing the remark aside*). I've seen lots of those fellows in my time. No doing anything with them except to keep 'em out of harm's way. They've got a blind spot.

WALTER. It's penal servitude.

COKESON. They're *nahsty* places—prisons.

JAMES (*hesitating*). I don't see how it's possible to spare him. Out of the question to keep him in this office—
30 honesty's the *sine qua non*.

COKESON (*hypnotised*). Of course it *is*.

JAMES. Equally out of the question to send him out amongst people who've no knowledge of his character. One must think of society.

WALTER. But to brand him like this?

JAMES. If it had been a straightforward case I'd give him another chance. It's far from that. He has dissolute
40 habits.

COKESON. I didn't say that—extenuating circumstances.

JAMES. Same thing. He's gone to work in the most cold-blooded way to defraud his employers, and cast the blame on an innocent man. If that's not a case for the law to take its course, I don't know what is.

WALTER. For the sake of his future, though.

JAMES (*sarcastically*). According to you, no one would ever prosecute.

WALTER (*nettled*). I hate the idea of it.

COKESON. That's *rather ex parte*, Mr. Walter! We must have protection. 10

JAMES. This is degenerating into talk. (*He moves towards the partners' room.*)

WALTER. Put yourself in his place, father.

JAMES. You ask too much of me.

WALTER. We can't possibly tell the pressure there was on him.

JAMES. You may depend on it, my boy, if a man is going to do this sort of thing he'll do it, pressure or no 20 pressure; if he isn't nothing'll make him.

WALTER. He'll never do it again.

COKESON (*fatuously*). S'pose I were to have a talk with him. We don't want to be hard on the young man.

JAMES. That'll do, Cokeson. I've made up my mind. (*He passes into the partners' room.*)

COKESON (*after a doubtful moment*). We 30 must excuse your father. I don't want to go against your father; if he thinks it right.

WALTER. Confound it, Cokeson! Why don't you back me up? You know you feel——

COKESON (*on his dignity*). I really can't say what I feel.

WALTER. We shall regret it.

COKESON. He must have known what he 40 was doing.

WALTER (*bitterly*). "The quality of mercy is not strained."

COKESON (*looking at him askance*). Come, come, Mr. Walter. We must try and see it sensible.

SWEEDLE (*entering with a tray*). Your lunch, sir.

COKESON. Put it down!

[*While* SWEEDLE *is putting it down on* COKESON'S *table, the detective,* WISTER, *enters the outer office, and, finding no one there, comes to the inner doorway. He is a square, medium-sized man, clean-shaved, in a serviceable blue serge suit and strong boots.*]

WISTER (*to* WALTER). From Scotland Yard, sir. Detective-Sergeant Wister.

WALTER (*askance*). Very well! I'll speak to my father. (*He goes into the partners' room.* JAMES *enters.*)

JAMES. Morning! (*In answer to an appealing gesture from* COKESON). I'm sorry; I'd stop short of this if I felt I could. Open that door. (SWEEDLE, *wondering and scared, opens it.*) Come here, Mr. Falder.

[*As* FALDER *comes shrinkingly out, the detective, in obedience to a sign from* JAMES, *slips his hand out and grasps his arm.*]

FALDER (*recoiling*). Oh! no,—oh! no!

WISTER. Come, come, there's a good lad.

JAMES. I charge him with felony.

FALDER. Oh, sir! There's some one—I did it for her. Let me be till to-morrow.

[JAMES *motions with his hand. At that sign of hardness,* FALDER *becomes rigid. Then, turning, he goes out quietly in the detective's grip.* JAMES *follows, stiff and erect.* SWEEDLE, *rushing to the door with open mouth, pursues them through the outer office into the corridor. When they have all disappeared* COKESON *spins completely round and makes a rush for the outer office.*]

COKESON (*hoarsely*). Here, Here! What are we doing?

[*There is silence. He takes out his handkerchief and mops the sweat from his face. Going back blindly to his table, sits down, and stares blankly at his lunch.*]

THE CURTAIN FALLS

ACT II

A Court of Justice, on a foggy October afternoon—crowded with barristers, solicitors, reporters, ushers, and jurymen. Sitting in the large, solid dock is FALDER, *with a warder on either side of him, placed there for his safe custody, but seemingly indifferent to and unconscious of his presence.* FALDER *is sitting exactly opposite to the* JUDGE, *who, raised above the clamour of the court, also seems unconscious of and indifferent to everything.* 10 HAROLD CLEAVER, *the counsel for the Crown, is a dried, yellowish man, of more than middle age, in a wig worn almost to the colour of his face.* HECTOR FROME, *the counsel for the defence, is a young, tall man, clean-shaved, in a very white wig. Among the spectators, having already given their evidence, are* JAMES *and* WALTER HOW, *and* COWLEY, *the cashier.* WISTER, *the detective, is just leaving the witness-box.* 20

CLEAVER. That is the case for the Crown, me lud! (*Gathering his robes together, he sits down.*)

FROME (*rising and bowing to the* JUDGE). If it please your lordship and gentlemen of the jury. I am not going to dispute the fact that the prisoner altered this cheque, but I am going to put before you evidence as to the condition of his 30 mind, and to submit that you would not be justified in finding that he was responsible for his actions at the time. I am going to show you, in fact, that he did this in a moment of aberration, amounting to temporary insanity, caused by the violent distress under which he was labouring. Gentlemen, the prisoner is only twenty-three years old. I shall call before you a woman 40 from whom you will learn the events that led up to this act. You will hear from her own lips the tragic circumstances of her life, the still more tragic infatuation with which she has inspired the prisoner. This woman, gentlemen, has been leading a miserable existence with a husband who habitually ill-uses her, from whom she actually goes in terror of her life. I am not, of course, saying that it's either right or desirable for a young man to fall in love with a married woman, or that it's his business to rescue her from an ogre-like husband. I'm not saying anything of the sort. But we all know the power of the passion of love; and I would ask you to remember, gentlemen, in listening to her evidence, that, married to a drunken and violent husband, she has no power to get rid of him; for, as you know, another offence besides violence is necessary to enable a woman to obtain a divorce; and of this offence it does not appear that her husband is guilty.

JUDGE. Is this relevant, Mr. Frome?

FROME. My lord, I submit, extremely—I shall be able to show your lordship that directly.

JUDGE. Very well.

FROME. In these circumstances, what alternatives were left to her? She could either go on living with this drunkard, in terror of her life; or she could apply to the Court for a separation order. Well, gentlemen, my experience of such cases assures me that this would have given her very insufficient protection from the violence of such a man; and even if effectual would very likely have reduced her either to the workhouse or the streets—for it's not easy, as she is now finding, for an unskilled woman without means of livelihood to support herself and her children without resorting either to the

Poor Law or—to speak quite plainly —to the sale of her body.

JUDGE. You are ranging rather far, Mr. Frome.

FROME. I shall fire point-blank in a minute, my lord.

JUDGE. Let us hope so.

FROME. Now, gentlemen, mark—and this is what I have been leading up to —this woman will tell you, and the 10 prisoner will confirm her, that, confronted with such alternatives, she set her whole hopes on himself, knowing the feeling with which she had inspired him. She saw a way out of her misery by going with him to a new country, where they would both be unknown, and might pass as husband and wife. This was a desperate and, as my friend Mr. Cleaver will no 20 doubt call it, an immoral resolution; but, as a fact, the minds of both of them were constantly turned towards it. One wrong is no excuse for another, and those who are never likely to be faced by such a situation possibly have the right to hold up their hands—as to that I prefer to say nothing. But whatever view you take, gentlemen, of this part of the prison- 30 er's story—whatever opinion you form of the right of these two young people under such circumstances to take the law into their own hands— the fact remains that this young woman in her distress, and this young man, little more than a boy, who was so devotedly attached to her, did conceive this—if you like—reprehensible design of going away together. Now, 40 for that, of course, they required money, and—they had none. As to the actual events of the morning of July 7th, on which this cheque was altered, the events on which I rely to prove the defendant's irresponsibility —I shall allow those events to speak for themselves, through the lips of my witnesses. Robert Cokeson. (*He turns, looks round, takes up a sheet of paper, and waits.*)

[COKESON *is summoned into court, and goes into the witness-box, holding his hat before him. The oath is administered to him.*]

FROME. What is your name?

COKESON. Robert Cokeson.

FROME. Are you managing clerk to the firm of solicitors who employ the prisoner?

COKESON. Ye-es.

FROME. How long had the prisoner been in their employ?

COKESON. Two years. No, I'm wrong there—all but seventeen days.

FROME. Had you him under your eye all that time?

COKESON. Except Sundays and holidays.

FROME. Quite so. Let us hear, please, what you have to say about his general character during those two years.

COKESON (*confidentially to the jury, and as if a little surprised at being asked*). He was a nice, pleasant-spoken young man. I'd no fault to find with him—quite the contrary. It was a *great* surprise to me when he did a thing like that.

FROME. Did he ever give you reason to suspect his honesty?

COKESON. No! To have dishonesty in our office, that'd never do.

FROME. I'm sure the jury fully appreciate that, Mr. Cokeson.

COKESON. Every man of business knows that honesty's the sign qua non.

FROME. Do you give him a good character all round, or do you not?

COKESON (*turning to the* JUDGE). Certainly. We were all very jolly and pleasant together, until this happened. Quite upset me.

FROME. Now, coming to the morning of the 7th of July, the morning on which the cheque was altered. What have you to say about his demeanour that morning?

COKESON (*to the jury*). If you ask me, I don't think he was quite compos when he did it.

THE JUDGE (*sharply*). Are you suggesting that he was insane?

COKESON. Not compos.

THE JUDGE. A little more precision, please.

FROME (*smoothly*). Just tell us, Mr. Cokeson.

COKESON (*somewhat outraged*). Well, in my opinion—(*Looking at the* JUDGE.)—such as it is—he was jumpy at the time. The jury will understand my meaning.

FROME. Will you tell us how you came to that conclusion?

COKESON. Ye-es, I will. I have my lunch in from the restaurant, a chop and a potato—saves time. That day it happened to come just as Mr. Walter How handed me the cheque. Well, I like it hot; so I went into the clerks' office and I handed the cheque to Davis, the other clerk, and told him to get change. I noticed young Falder walking up and down. I said to him: "This is not the Zoological Gardens, Falder."

FROME. Do you remember what he answered?

COKESON. Ye-es: "I wish to God it were!" Struck me as funny.

FROME. Did you notice anything else peculiar?

COKESON. I did.

FROME. What was that?

COKESON. His collar was unbuttoned. Now, I like a young man to be neat. I said to him: "Your collar's unbuttoned."

FROME. And what did he answer?

COKESON. Stared at me. It wasn't nice.

THE JUDGE. Stared at you? Isn't that a very common practice?

COKESON. Ye-es, but it was the look in his eyes. I can't explain my meaning—it was funny.

FROME. Had you ever seen such a look in his eyes before?

COKESON. No. If I had I should have spoken to the partners. We can't have anything eccentric in our profession.

THE JUDGE. Did you speak to them on that occasion?

COKESON (*confidentially*). Well, I didn't like to trouble them about prime facey evidence.

FROME. But it made a very distinct impression on your mind?

COKESON. Ye-es. The clerk Davis could have told you the same.

FROME. Quite so. It's very unfortunate that we've not got him here. Now can you tell me of the morning on which the discovery of the forgery was made? That would be the 18th. Did anything happen that morning?

COKESON (*with his hand to his ear*). I'm a little deaf.

FROME. Was there anything in the course of that morning—I mean before the discovery—that caught your attention?

COKESON. Ye-es—a woman.

THE JUDGE. How is *this* relevant, Mr. Frome?

FROME. I am trying to establish the state of mind in which the prisoner committed this act, my lord.

THE JUDGE. I quite appreciate that. But this was long after the act.

FROME. Yes, my lord, but it contributes to my contention.

THE JUDGE. Well!

FROME. You say a woman. Do you mean that she came to the office?

COKESON. Ye-es.

FROME. What for?

COKESON. Asked to see young Falder; he was out at the moment.

FROME. Did you see her?

COKESON. I did.

FROME. Did she come alone?

COKESON (*confidentially*). Well, there you put me in a difficulty. I mustn't tell you what the office-boy told me.

FROME. Quite so, Mr. Cokeson, quite so ——

COKESON (*breaking in with an air of "You are young—leave it to me"*). But I think we can get round it. In answer to a question put to her by a third party the woman said to me: "They're mine, sir."

THE JUDGE. What are? What were?

COKESON. Her children. They were outside.

THE JUDGE. How do you know?

COKESON. Your lordship mustn't ask me that, or I shall have to tell you what I was told—and that'd never do.

THE JUDGE (*smiling*). The office-boy made a statement.

COKESON. Egg-zactly.

FROME. What I want to ask you, Mr. Cokeson, is this. In the course of her appeal to see Falder, did the woman say anything that you specially remember?

COKESON (*looking at him as if to encourage him to complete the sentence*). A leetle more, sir.

FROME. Or did she not?

COKESON. She did. I shouldn't like you to have led me to the answer.

FROME (*with an irritated smile*). Will you tell the jury what it was?

COKESON. "It's a matter of life and death."

FOREMAN OF THE JURY. Do you mean the woman said that?

COKESON (*nodding*). It's not the sort of thing you like to have said to you.

FROME (*a little impatiently*). Did Falder come in while she was there? (COKESON *nods*.) And she saw him, and went away?

COKESON. Ah! there I can't follow you. I didn't see her go.

FROME. Well, is she there now?

COKESON (*with an indulgent smile*). No!

FROME. Thank you, Mr. Cokeson. (*He sits down.*)

CLEAVER (*rising*). You say that on the morning of the forgery the prisoner was jumpy. Well, now, sir, what precisely do you mean by that word?

COKESON (*indulgently*). I *want* you to understand. Have you ever seen a dog that's lost its master? He was kind of everywhere at once with his eyes.

CLEAVER. Thank you; I was coming to his eyes. You called them "funny." What are we to understand by that? Strange, or what?

COKESON. Ye-es, funny.

CLEAVER (*sharply*). Yes, sir, but what may be funny to you may not be funny to me, or to the jury. Did they look frightened, or shy, ⌐ fierce, or what?

COKESON. You make it very hard for me. I give you the word, and you want me to give you another.

CLEAVER (*rapping his desk*). Does "funny" mean mad?

COKESON. Not mad, fun——

CLEAVER. Very well! Now you say he had his collar unbuttoned? Was it a hot day?

COKESON. Ye-es; I think it was.

CLEAVER. And did he button it when you called his attention to it?

COKESON. Ye-es, I think he did.

CLEAVER. Would you say that that denoted insanity?

[*He sits down.* COKESON, *who has opened his mouth to reply, is left gaping.*]

FROME (*rising hastily*). Have you ever caught him in that dishevelled state before?

COKESON. No! He was *always* clean and quiet.

FROME. That will do, thank you.

[COKESON *turns blandly to the* JUDGE, *as though to rebuke counsel for not remembering that the* JUDGE *might wish to have a chance; arriving at the conclusion that he is to be asked nothing further, he turns and descends from the box, and sits down next to* JAMES *and* WALTER.]

FROME. Ruth Honeywill.

[RUTH *comes into court, and takes her stand stoically in the witness-box. She is sworn.*]

FROME. What is your name, please?

RUTH. Ruth Honeywill.

FROME. How old are you?

RUTH. Twenty-six.

FROME. You are a married woman, living with your husband? A little louder.

RUTH. No, sir; not since July.

FROME. Have you any children?

RUTH. Yes, sir, two.

FROME. Are they living with you?

RUTH. Yes, sir.

FROME. You know the prisoner?

RUTH (*looking at him*). Yes.

FROME. What was the nature of your relations with him?

RUTH. We were friends.

THE JUDGE. Friends?

RUTH (*simply*). Lovers, sir.

THE JUDGE (*sharply*). In what sense do you use that word?

RUTH. We love each other.

THE JUDGE. Yes, but——

RUTH (*shaking her head*). No, your lordship—not yet.

THE JUDGE. Not yet! H'm! (*He looks from* RUTH *to* FALDER.) Well!

FROME. What is your husband?

RUTH. Traveller.

FROME. And what was the nature of your married life?

RUTH (*shaking her head*). It don't bear talking about.

FROME. Did he ill-treat you, or what?

RUTH. Ever since my first was born.

FROME. In what way?

RUTH. I'd rather not say. All sorts of ways.

THE JUDGE. I am afraid I must stop this, you know.

RUTH (*pointing to* FALDER). *He* offered to take me out of it, sir. We were going to South America.

FROME (*hastily*). Yes, quite—and what prevented you?

RUTH. I was outside his office when he was taken away. It nearly broke my heart.

FROME. You knew, then, that he had been arrested?

RUTH. Yes, sir. I called at his office afterwards, and (*Pointing to* COKESON.) that gentleman told me all about it.

FROME. Now, do you remember the morning of Friday, July 7th?

RUTH. Yes.

FROME. Why?

RUTH. My husband nearly strangled me that morning.

THE JUDGE. Nearly strangled you!

RUTH (*bowing her head*). Yes, my lord.

FROME. With his hands, or——?

RUTH. Yes, I just managed to get away from him. I went straight to my friend. It was eight o'clock.

THE JUDGE. In the morning? Your husband was not under the influence of liquor then?

RUTH. It wasn't always that.

FROME. In what condition were you?

RUTH. In very bad condition, sir. My dress was torn, and I was half choking.

FROME. Did you tell your friend what had happened?

RUTH. Yes. I wish I never had.

FROME. It upset him?

RUTH. Dreadfully.

FROME. Did he ever speak to you about a cheque?

RUTH. Never.

FROME. Did he ever give you any money?

RUTH. Yes.

FROME. When was that?

RUTH. On Saturday.

FROME. The 8th?

RUTH. To buy an outfit for me and the children, and get all ready to start.

FROME. Did that surprise you, or not?

RUTH. What, sir?

FROME. That he had money to give you.

RUTH. Yes, because on the morning when my husband nearly killed me my friend cried because he hadn't the money to get me away. He told me afterwards he'd come into a windfall.

FROME. And when did you last see him?

RUTH. The day he was taken away, sir. It was the day we were to have started.

FROME. Oh, yes, the morning of the arrest. Well, did you see him at all between the Friday and that morning? (RUTH *nods*.) What was his manner then?

RUTH. Dumb-like—sometimes he didn't seem able to say a word.

FROME. As if something unusual had happened to him?

RUTH. Yes.

FROME. Painful, or pleasant, or what?

RUTH. Like a fate hanging over him.

FROME (*hesitating*). Tell me, did you love the prisoner very much?

RUTH (*bowing her head*). Yes.

FROME. And had he a very great affection for you?

RUTH (*looking at* FALDER). Yes, sir.

FROME. Now, ma'am, do you or do you not think that your danger and un-happiness would seriously affect his balance, his control over his actions?

RUTH. Yes.

FROME. His reason, even?

RUTH. For a moment like, I think it would.

FROME. Was he very much upset that Friday morning, or was he fairly calm?

RUTH. Dreadfully upset. I could hardly bear to let him go from me.

FROME. Do you still love him?

RUTH (*with her eyes on* FALDER). He's ruined himself for me.

FROME. Thank you. (*He sits down.* RUTH *remains stoically upright in the witness-box.*)

CLEAVER (*in a considerate voice*). When you left him on the morning of Friday the 7th you would not say that he was out of his mind, I suppose?

RUTH. No, sir.

CLEAVER. Thank you; I've no further questions to ask you.

RUTH (*bending a little forward to the jury*). I would have done the same for him; I would indeed.

THE JUDGE. Please, please! You say your married life is an unhappy one? Faults on both sides?

RUTH. Only that I never bowed down to him. I don't see why I should, sir, not to a man like that.

THE JUDGE. You refused to obey him?

RUTH (*avoiding the question*). I've always studied him to keep things nice.

THE JUDGE. Until you met the prisoner—was that it?

RUTH. No; even after that.

THE JUDGE. I ask, you know, because you seem to me to glory in this affection of yours for the prisoner.

RUTH (*hesitating*). I—I do. It's the only thing in my life now.

THE JUDGE (*staring at her hard*). Well, step down, please.

[RUTH *looks at* FALDER, *then passes quietly down and takes her seat among the witnesses.*]

FROME. I call the prisoner, my lord.

[FALDER *leaves the dock; goes into the witness-box, and is duly sworn.*]

FROME. What is your name?

FALDER. William Falder.

FROME. And age?

FALDER. Twenty-three.

FROME. You are not married?

[FALDER *shakes his head.*]

FROME. How long have you known the last witness?

FALDER. Six months.

FROME. Is her account of the relationship 10 between you a correct one?

FALDER. Yes.

FROME. You became devotedly attached to her, however?

FALDER. Yes.

THE JUDGE. Though you knew she was a married woman?

FALDER. I couldn't help it, your lordship.

THE JUDGE. Couldn't help it?   20

FALDER. I didn't seem able to.

[*The* JUDGE *slightly shrugs his shoulders.*]

FROME. How did you come to know her?

FALDER. Through my married sister.

FROME. Did you know whether she was happy with her husband?

FALDER. It was trouble all the time.

FROME. You knew her husband?

FALDER. Only through her—he's a brute.

THE JUDGE. I can't allow indiscriminate 30 abuse of a person not present.

FROME (*bowing*). If your lordship pleases. (*To* FALDER.) You admit altering this cheque?

[FALDER *bows his head.*]

FROME. Carry your mind, please, to the morning of Friday, July the 7th, and tell the jury what happened.

FALDER (*turning to the jury*). I was having my breakfast when she came. Her 40 dress was all torn, and she was gasping and couldn't seem to get her breath at all; there were the marks of his fingers round her throat; her arm was bruised, and the blood had got into her eyes dreadfully. It frightened me,

and then when she told me, I felt—I felt—well—it was too much for me! (*Hardening suddenly.*) If you'd seen it, having the feelings for her that I had, you'd have felt the same, I know.

FROME. Yes?

FALDER. When she left me—because I had to go to the office—I was out of my senses for fear that he'd do it again, and thinking what I could do. I couldn't work—all the morning I was like that—simply couldn't fix my mind on anything. I couldn't think at all. I seemed to have to keep moving. When Davis—the other clerk—gave me the cheque—he said: "It'll do you good, Will, to have a run with this. You seem half off your chump this morning." Then when I had it in my hand—I don't know how it came, but it just flashed across me that if I put the t y and the nought there would be the money to get her away. It just came and went—I never thought of it again. Then Davis went out to his luncheon, and I don't really remember what I did till I'd pushed the cheque through to the cashier under the rail. I remember his saying "Gold or notes?" Then I suppose I knew what I'd done. Anyway, when I got outside I wanted to chuck myself under a 'bus; I wanted to throw the money away; but it seemed I was in for it, so I thought at any rate I'd save her. Of course the tickets I took for the passage and the little I gave her's been wasted, and all, except what I was obliged to spend myself, I've restored. I keep thinking over and over however it was I came to do it, and how I can't have it all again to do differently! (FALDER *is silent, twisting his hands before him.*)

FROME. How far is it from your office to the bank?

FALDER. Not more than fifty yards, sir.

FROME. From the time Davis went out to lunch to the time you cashed the cheque, how long do you say it must have been?

FALDER. It couldn't have been four minutes, sir, because I ran all the way.

FROME. During those four minutes you say you remember nothing?

FALDER. No, sir; only that I ran.

FROME. Not even adding the t y and the nought?

FALDER. No, sir. I don't really.

[FROME sits down, and CLEAVER rises.]

CLEAVER. But you remember running, do you?

FALDER. I was all out of breath when I got to the bank.

CLEAVER. And you don't remember altering the cheque?

FALDER (faintly). No, sir.

CLEAVER. Divested of the romantic glamour which my friend is casting over the case, is this anything but an ordinary forgery? Come.

FALDER. I was half frantic all that morning, sir.

CLEAVER. Now, now! You don't deny that the t y and the nought were so like the rest of the handwriting as to thoroughly deceive the cashier?

FALDER. It was an accident.

CLEAVER (cheerfully). Queer sort of accident, wasn't it? On which day did you alter the counterfoil?

FALDER (hanging his head). On the Wednesday morning.

CLEAVER. Was that an accident too?

FALDER (faintly). No.

CLEAVER. To do that you had to watch your opportunity, I suppose?

FALDER (almost inaudibly). Yes.

CLEAVER. You don't suggest that you were suffering under great excitement when you did that?

FALDER. I was haunted.

CLEAVER. With the fear of being found out?

FALDER (very low). Yes.

THE JUDGE. Didn't it occur to you that the only thing for you to do was to confess to your employers, and restore the money?

FALDER. I was afraid. (There is silence.)

CLEAVER. You desired, too, no doubt, to complete your design of taking this woman away?

FALDER. When I found I'd done a thing like that, to do it for nothing seemed so dreadful. I might just as well have chucked myself into the river.

CLEAVER. You knew that the clerk Davis was about to leave England—didn't it occur to you when you altered this cheque that suspicion would fall on him?

FALDER. It was all done in a moment. I thought of it afterwards.

CLEAVER. And that didn't lead you to avow what you'd done?

FALDER (sullenly). I meant to write when I got out there—I would have repaid the money.

THE JUDGE. But in the meantime your innocent fellow clerk might have been prosecuted.

FALDER. I knew he was a long way off, your lordship. I thought there'd be time. I didn't think they'd find it out so soon.

FROME. I might remind your lordship that as Mr. Walter How had the cheque-book in his pocket till after Davis had sailed, if the discovery had been made only one day later Falder himself would have left, and suspicion would have attached to him, and not to Davis, from the beginning.

THE JUDGE. The question is whether the prisoner knew that suspicion would light on himself, and not on Davis. (To FALDER sharply.) Did you know that Mr. Walter How had the cheque-book till after Davis had sailed?

FALDER. I—I—thought—he——

THE JUDGE. Now speak the truth—yes or no!

FALDER (*very low*). No, my lord. I had no means of knowing.

THE JUDGE. That disposes of your point, Mr. Frome.

[FROME *bows to the* JUDGE.]

CLEAVER. Has any aberration of this nature ever attacked you before?

FALDER (*faintly*). No, sir.

CLEAVER. You had recovered sufficiently to go back to your work that afternoon?

FALDER. Yes, I had to take the money back.

CLEAVER. You mean the *nine* pounds. Your wits were sufficiently keen for you to remember that? And you still persist in saying you don't remember altering this cheque. (*He sits down.*)

FALDER. If I hadn't been mad I should never have had the courage.

FROME (*rising*). Did you have your lunch before going back?

FALDER. I never ate a thing all day; and at night I couldn't sleep.

FROME. Now, as to the four minutes that elapsed between Davis's going out and your cashing the cheque: do you say that you recollect *nothing* during those four minutes?

FALDER (*after a moment*). I remember thinking of Mr. Cokeson's face.

FROME. Of Mr. Cokeson's face! Had that any connection with what you were doing?

FALDER. No, sir.

FROME. Was that in the office, before you ran out?

FALDER. Yes, and while I was running.

FROME. And that lasted till the cashier said: "Will you have gold or notes?"

FALDER. Yes, and then I seemed to come to myself—and it was too late.

FROME. Thank you. That closes the evidence for the defence, my lord.

[*The* JUDGE *nods, and* FALDER *goes back to his seat in the dock.*]

FROME (*gathering up notes*). If it please your lordship—Gentlemen of the Jury,—My friend in cross-examination has shown a disposition to sneer at the defence which has been set up in this case, and I am free to admit that nothing I can say will move you, if the evidence has not already convinced you that the prisoner committed this act in a moment when to all practical intents and purposes he was not responsible for his actions; a moment of such mental and moral vacuity, arising from the violent emotional agitation under which he had been suffering, as to amount to temporary madness. My friend has alluded to the "romantic glamour" with which I have sought to invest this case. Gentlemen, I have done nothing of the kind. I have merely shown you the background of "life"— that palpitating life which, believe me —whatever my friend may say—always lies behind the commission of a crime. Now gentlemen, we live in a highly civilized age, and the sight of brutal violence disturbs us in a very strange way, even when we have no personal interest in the matter. But when we see it inflicted on a woman whom we love—what then? Just think of what your own feelings would have been, each of you, at the prisoner's age; and then look at him. Well! he is hardly the comfortable, shall we say bucolic, person likely to contemplate with equanimity marks of gross violence on a woman to whom he was devotedly attached. Yes, gentlemen, look at him! He has not a strong face; but neither has he a vicious face. He is just the sort of man who would easily become the prey of his emotions. You have heard the description of his eyes. My friend may laugh at the word "funny"—*I* think it better describes the peculiar uncanny look of those who are strained to breaking-point than any other word which 10 could have been used. I don't pretend, mind you, that his mental irresponsibility was more than a flash of darkness, in which all sense of proportion became lost; but I do contend, that, just as a man who destroys himself at such a moment may be, and often is, absolved from the stigma attaching to the crime of self-murder, so he may, and frequently does, commit 20 other crimes while in this irresponsible condition, and that he may as justly be acquitted of criminal intent and treated as a patient. I admit that this is a plea which might well be abused. It is a matter for discretion. But here you have a case in which there is every reason to give the benefit of the doubt. You heard me ask the prisoner what he thought of during 30 those four fatal minutes. What was his answer? "I thought of Mr. Cokeson's face!" Gentlemen, no man could invent an answer like that; it is absolutely stamped with truth. You have seen the great affection (legitimate or not) existing between him and this woman, who came here to give evidence for him at the risk of her life. It is impossible for you to doubt his dis- 40 tress on the morning when he committed this act. We well know what terrible havoc such distress can make in weak and highly nervous people. It was all the work of a moment. The rest has followed, as death follows a stab to the heart, or water drops if you hold up a jug to empty it. Believe me, gentlemen, there is nothing more tragic in life than the utter impossibility of changing what you have done. Once this cheque was altered and presented, the work of four minutes—four mad minutes—the rest has been silence. But in those four minutes the boy before you has slipped through a door, hardly opened, into that great cage which never again quite lets a man go—the cage of the Law. His further acts, his failure to confess, the alteration of the counterfoil, his preparations for flight, are all evidence—not of deliberate and guilty intention when he committed the prime act from which these subsequent acts arose; no—they are merely evidence of the weak character which is clearly enough his misfortune. But is a man to be lost because he is bred and born with a weak character? Gentlemen, men like the prisoner are destroyed daily under our law for want of that human insight which sees them as they are, patients, and not criminals. If the prisoner be found guilty, and treated as though he were a criminal type, he will, as all experience shows, in all probability become one. I beg you not to return a verdict that may thrust him back into prison and brand him for ever. Gentlemen, Justice is a machine that, when some one has once given it the starting push, rolls on of itself. Is this young man to be ground to pieces under this machine for an act which at the worst was one of weakness? Is he to become a member of the luckless crews that man those dark, ill-starred ships called prisons? Is that to be his voyage—from which so few return? Or is he to have another chance, to be still looked on as one who has gone a little astray, but who will come back? I urge you, gentlemen, do not ruin this young man! For, as a result of those four minutes, ruin, utter and irretrievable, stares him in the face. He can be saved now. Imprison him as a criminal, and I affirm to you that he will be lost. He has neither the face nor the manner of one who can survive that terrible ordeal. Weigh in the scales his criminality and the suffering he has undergone. The latter is ten times heavier already. He has lain in prison under this charge for more than two months. Is he likely ever to forget that? Imagine the anguish of his mind during that time. He has had his punishment, gentlemen, you may depend. The rolling of the chariot-wheels of Justice over this boy began when it was decided to prosecute him. We are now already at the second stage. If you permit it to go on to the third I would not give— that for him. (*He holds up finger and thumb in the form of a circle, drops his hand, and sits down.*)

[*The jury stir, and consult each other's faces; then they turn towards the counsel for the Crown, who rises, and, fixing his eyes on a spot that seems to give him satisfaction, slides them every now and then towards the jury.*]

CLEAVER. May it please your lordship— (*Rising on his toes.*) Gentlemen of the Jury,—The facts in this case are not disputed, and the defence, if my friend will allow me to say so, is so thin that I don't propose to waste the time of the Court by taking you over the evidence. The plea is one of temporary insanity. Well, gentlemen, I daresay it is clearer to me than it is to you why this rather—what shall we call it?—bizarre defence has been set up.

The alternative would have been to plead guilty. Now, gentlemen, if the prisoner had pleaded guilty my friend would have had to rely on a simple appeal to his lordship. Instead of that, he has gone into the byways and hedges and found this—er—peculiar plea, which has enabled him to show you the proverbial woman, to put her in the box—to give, in fact, a romantic glow to this affair. I compliment my friend; I think it highly ingenious of him. By these means, he has—to a certain extent—got round the Law. He has brought the whole story of motive and stress out in court, at first hand, in a way that he would not otherwise have been able to do. But when you have once grasped that fact, gentlemen, you have grasped everything. (*With good-humoured contempt.*) For look at this plea of insanity; we can't put it lower than that. You have heard the woman. She has every reason to favour the prisoner, but what did she say? She said that the prisoner was *not* insane when she left him in the morning. If he were going out of his mind through distress, that was obviously the moment when insanity would have shown itself. You have heard the managing clerk, another witness for the defence. With some difficulty I elicited from him the admission that the prisoner, though jumpy (a word that he seemed to think you would understand, gentlemen, and I'm sure I hope you do), was *not* mad when the cheque was handed to Davis. I agree with my friend that it's unfortunate that we have not got Davis here, but the prisoner has told you the words with which Davis in turn handed him the cheque; he obviously, therefore, was *not* mad when he received it, or he would not have remembered those words. The cashier has told you that he was certainly in his senses when he cashed it. We have therefore the plea that a man who is sane at ten minutes past one, and sane at fifteen minutes past, may, for the purposes of avoiding the consequences of a crime, call himself insane between those points of time. Really, gentlemen, this is so 10 peculiar a proposition that I am not disposed to weary you with further argument. You will form your own opinion of its value. My friend has adopted this way of saying a great deal to you—and very eloquently— on the score of youth, temptation, and the like. I might point out, however, that the offence with which the prisoner is charged is one of the most 20 serious known to our law; and there are certain features in this case, such as the suspicion which he allowed to rest on his innocent fellow-clerk, and his relations with this married woman, which will render it difficult for you to attach too much importance to such pleading. I ask you, in short, gentlemen, for that verdict of guilty which, in the circumstances, I 30 regard you as, unfortunately, bound to record. (*Letting his eyes travel from the* JUDGE *and the jury to* FROME, *he sits down.*)

THE JUDGE (*bending a little towards the jury, and speaking in a business-like voice*). Gentlemen, you have heard the evidence, and the comments on it. My only business is to make clear to you the issues you have to try. The facts 40 are admitted, so far as the alteration of this cheque and counterfoil by the prisoner. The defence set up is that he was not in a responsible condition when he committed the crime. Well, you have heard the prisoner's story,

and the evidence of the other witnesses—so far as it bears on the point of insanity. If you think that what you have heard establishes the fact that the prisoner was insane at the time of the forgery, you will find him guilty, but insane. If, on the other hand, you conclude from what you have seen and heard that the prisoner was sane —and nothing short of insanity will count—you will find him guilty. In reviewing the testimony as to his mental condition you must bear in mind very carefully the evidence as to his demeanour and conduct both before and after the act of forgery— the evidence of the prisoner himself, of the woman, of the witness—er— Cokeson, and—er—of the cashier. And in regard to that I especially direct your attention to the prisoner's admission that the idea of adding the t y and the nought did come into his mind at the moment when the cheque was handed to him; and also to the alteration of the counterfoil, and to his subsequent conduct generally. The bearing of all this on the question of premeditation (and premeditation will imply sanity) is very obvious. You must not allow any considerations of age or temptation to weigh with you in the finding of your verdict. Before you can come to a verdict of guilty but insane you must be well and thoroughly convinced that the condition of his mind was such as would have qualified him at the moment for a lunatic asylum. (*He pauses; then, seeing that the jury are doubtful whether to retire or no, adds:*) You may retire, gentlemen, if you wish to do so.

[*The jury retire by a door behind the* JUDGE. *The* JUDGE *bends over his notes.* FALDER, *leaning from the dock, speaks excitedly to his solicitor, pointing down at* RUTH. *The solicitor in turn speaks to* FROME.]

FROME (*rising*). My lord. The prisoner is very anxious that I should ask you if your lordship would kindly request the reporters not to disclose the name of the woman witness in the Press reports of these proceedings. Your lordship will understand that the consequences might be extremely serious 10 to her.

THE JUDGE (*pointedly—with the suspicion of a smile*). Well, Mr. Frome, you deliberately took this course which involved bringing her here.

FROME (*with an ironic bow*). If your lordship thinks I could have brought out the full facts in any other way?

THE JUDGE. H'm! Well.

FROME. There is very real danger to her, 20 your lordship.

THE JUDGE. You see, I have to take your word for all that.

FROME. If your lordship would be so kind. I can assure your lordship that I am not exaggerating.

THE JUDGE. It goes very much against the grain with me that the name of a witness should ever be suppressed. (*With a glance at* FALDER, *who is grip-* 30 *ping and clasping his hands before him, and then at* RUTH, *who is sitting perfectly rigid with her eyes fixed on* FALDER.) I'll consider your application. It must depend. I have to remember that she may have come here to commit perjury on the prisoner's behalf.

FROME. Your lordship, I really——

THE JUDGE. Yes, yes—I don't suggest anything of the sort, Mr. Frome. 40 Leave it at that for the moment.

[*As he finishes speaking, the jury return, and file back into the box.*]

CLERK OF ASSIZE. Gentlemen, are you agreed on your verdict?

FOREMAN. We are.

CLERK OF ASSIZE. Is it Guilty, or Guilty but insane?

FOREMAN. Guilty.

[*The* JUDGE *nods; then, gathering up his notes, sits looking at* FALDER, *who stands motionless.*]

FROME (*rising*). If your lordship would allow me to address you in mitigation of sentence. I don't know if your lordship thinks I can add anything to what I have said to the jury on the score of the prisoner's youth, and the great stress under which he acted.

THE JUDGE. I don't think you can, Mr. Frome.

FROME. If your lordship says so—I do most earnestly beg your lordship to give the utmost weight to my plea. (*He sits down.*)

THE JUDGE (*to the* CLERK). Call upon him.

THE CLERK. Prisoner at the bar, you stand convicted of felony. Have you anything to say for yourself, why the Court should not give you judgment according to law?

[FALDER *shakes his head.*]

THE JUDGE. William Falder, you have been given fair trial and found guilty, in my opinion rightly found guilty, of forgery. (*He pauses; then, consulting his notes, goes on.*) The defence was set up that you were not responsible for your actions at the moment of committing this crime. There is no doubt, I think, that this was a device to bring out at first hand the nature of the temptation to which you succumbed. For throughout the trial your counsel was in reality making an appeal for mercy. The setting up of this defence of course enabled him to put in some evidence that might weigh in that direction. Whether he was well advised to do so is another matter. He claimed that you should be treated rather as a patient than as a criminal. And this plea of his, which in the end amounted to a passionate appeal, he based in effect on an indictment of the march of Justice, which he practically accused of confirming and completing the process of criminality. Now, in considering how far I should allow weight to his appeal, I have a number of factors to take into ac- 10 count. I have to consider on the one hand the grave nature of your offence, the deliberate way in which you subsequently altered the counterfoil, the danger you caused to an innocent man—and that, to my mind, is a very grave point—and finally I have to consider the necessity of deterring others from following your example. On the other hand, I have to bear in 20 mind that you are young, that you have hitherto borne a good character, that you were, if I am to believe your evidence and that of your witnesses, in a state of some emotional excitement when you committed this crime. I have every wish, consistently with my duty—not only to you, but to the community—to treat you with leniency. And this brings me to what are 30 the determining factors in my mind in my consideration of your case. You are a clerk in a lawyer's office—that is a very serious element in this case; there can be no possible excuse made for you on the ground that you were not fully conversant with the nature of the crime you were committing, and the penalties that attach to it. It is said, however, that you were car- 40 ried away by your emotions. The story has been told here to-day of your relations with this—er—Mrs. Honeywill; on that story both the defence and the plea for mercy were in effect based. Now what is that story? It is that you, a young man, and she, a young woman, unhappily married, had formed an attachment, which you both say—with what truth I am unable to gauge—had not yet resulted in immoral relations, but which you both admit was about to result in such relationship. Your counsel has made an attempt to palliate this, on the ground that the woman is in what he describes, I think, as "a hopeless position." As to that I can express no opinion. She is a married woman, and the fact is patent that you committed this crime with the view of furthering an immoral design. Now, however I might wish, I am not able to justify to my conscience a plea for mercy which has a basis inimical to morality. It is vitiated *ab initio*, and would, if successful, free you for the completion of this immoral project. Your counsel has made an attempt to trace your offence back to what he seems to suggest is a defect in the marriage law; he has made an attempt also to show that to punish you with further imprisonment would be unjust. I do not follow him in these flights. *The Law is what it is*—a majestic edifice, sheltering all of us, each stone of which rests on another. I am concerned only with its administration. The crime you have committed is a very serious one. I cannot feel it in accordance with my duty to Society to exercise the powers I have in your favour. You will go to penal servitude for three years.

[FALDER, *who throughout the* JUDGE'S *speech has looked at him steadily, lets his head fall forward on his breast.* RUTH *starts up from her seat as he is taken out by the warders. There is a bustle in court.*]

THE JUDGE (*speaking to the reporters*). Gentlemen of the Press, I think that the name of the female witness should not be reported.

[*The reporters bow their acquiescence.*]

THE JUDGE (*to* RUTH, *who is staring in the direction in which* FALDER *has disappeared*). Do you understand, your name will not be mentioned?

COKESON (*pulling her sleeve*). The judge is speaking to you.

[RUTH *turns, stares at the* JUDGE, *and turns away.*]

THE JUDGE. I shall sit rather late to-day. Call the next case.

CLERK OF ASSIZE (*to a warder*). Put up John Booley.

To cries of "Witnesses in the case of Booley":

THE CURTAIN FALLS

ACT III

SCENE I

A prison. A plainly furnished room, with two large barred windows, overlooking the prisoners' exercise yard, where men, in yellow clothes marked with arrows, and yellow brimless caps, are seen in single file at a distance of four yards from each other, walking rapidly on serpentine white lines marked on the concrete floor of the yard. Two warders in blue uniforms, with peaked caps and swords, are stationed amongst them. The room has distempered walls, a bookcase with numerous official-looking books, a cupboard between the windows, a plan of the prison on the wall, a writing-table covered with documents. It is Christmas Eve.

The GOVERNOR, *a neat, grave-looking man, with a trim, fair moustache, the eyes of a theorist, and grizzled hair, receding from the temples, is standing close to this writing-table looking at a sort of rough saw made out of a piece of metal. The hand in which he holds it is gloved, for two fingers are missing. The chief warder,* WOODER, *a tall, thin, military-looking man of sixty, with grey moustache and melancholy, monkey-like eyes, stands very upright two paces from him.*

THE GOVERNOR (*with a faint, abstracted smile*). Queer-looking affair, Mr. Wooder! Where did you find it?

WOODER. In his mattress, sir. Haven't come across such a thing for two years now.

THE GOVERNOR (*with curiosity*). Had he any set plan?

WOODER. He'd sawed his window-bar about that much. (*He holds up his thumb and finger a quarter of an inch apart.*)

THE GOVERNOR. I'll see him this afternoon. What's his name? Moaney! An old hand, I think?

WOODER. Yes, sir—fourth spell of penal. You'd think an old lag like him would have had more sense by now. (*With pitying contempt.*) Occupied his mind, he said. Breaking in and breaking out —that's all they think about.

THE GOVERNOR. Who's next him?

WOODER. O'Cleary, sir.

THE GOVERNOR. The Irishman.

WOODER. Next him again there's that young fellow, Falder—star class—and next him old Clipton.

THE GOVERNOR. Ah, yes! "The philosopher." I want to see him about his eyes.

WOODER. Curious thing, sir: they seem to know when there's one of these tries at escape going on. It makes them restive—there's a regular wave going through them just now.

THE GOVERNOR (*meditatively*). Odd things—those waves. (*Turning to look at the prisoners exercising.*) Seem quiet enough out here!

WOODER. That Irishman, O'Cleary, began banging on his door this morning.

Little thing like that's quite enough to upset the whole lot. They're just like dumb animals at times.

THE GOVERNOR. I've seen it with horses before thunder—it'll run right through cavalry lines.

[*The prison* CHAPLAIN *has entered. He is a dark-haired, ascetic man, in clerical undress, with a peculiarly steady, tight-lipped face and slow, cultured speech.*]

THE GOVERNOR (*holding up the saw*). Seen this, Miller?

THE CHAPLAIN. Useful-looking specimen.

THE GOVERNOR. Do for the Museum, eh! (*He goes to the cupboard and opens it, displaying to view a number of quaint ropes, hooks, and metal tools with labels tied on them.*) That'll do, thanks, Mr. Wooder.

WOODER (*saluting*). Thank you, sir. (*He goes out.*)

THE GOVERNOR. Account for the state of the men last day or two, Miller? Seems going through the whole place.

THE CHAPLAIN. No. I don't know of anything.

THE GOVERNOR. By the way, will you dine with us on Christmas Day?

THE CHAPLAIN. To-morrow. Thanks very much.

THE GOVERNOR. Worries me to feel the men discontented. (*Gazing at the saw.*) Have to punish this poor devil. Can't help liking a man who tries to escape. (*He places the saw in his pocket and locks the cupboard again.*)

THE CHAPLAIN. Extraordinary perverted will-power—some of them. Nothing to be done till it's broken.

THE GOVERNOR. And not much afterwards, I'm afraid. Ground too hard for golf?

[WOODER *comes in again.*]

WOODER. Visitor who's been seeing Q 3007 asks to speak to you, sir. I told him it wasn't usual.

THE GOVERNOR. What about?

WOODER. Shall I put him off, sir?

THE GOVERNOR (*resignedly*). No, no. Let's see him. Don't go, Miller.

[WOODER *motions to some one without, and as the visitor comes in withdraws. The visitor is* COKESON, *who is attired in a thick overcoat to the knees, woollen gloves, and carries a top hat.*]

COKESON. I'm sorry to trouble you. I've been talking to the young man.

THE GOVERNOR. We have a good many here.

COKESON. Name of Falder, forgery. (*Producing a card, and handing it to the* GOVERNOR.) Firm of James and Walter How. Well known in the law.

THE GOVERNOR (*receiving the card—with a faint smile*). What do you want to see me about, sir?

COKESON (*suddenly seeing the prisoners at exercise*). Why! what a sight!

THE GOVERNOR. Yes, we have that privilege from here; my office is being done up. (*Sitting down at his table.*) Now, please!

COKESON (*dragging his eyes with difficulty from the window*). I *wanted* to say a word to you; I shan't keep you long. (*Confidentially.*) Fact is, I oughtn't to be here by rights. His sister came to me—he's got no father and mother—and she was in some distress. "My husband won't let me go and see him," she said; "says he's disgraced the family. And his other sister," she said, "is an invalid." And she asked me to come. Well, I take an interest in him. He was our junior—I go to the same chapel—and I didn't like to refuse. And what I wanted to tell you was, he seems lonely here.

THE GOVERNOR. Not unnaturally.

COKESON. I'm afraid it'll prey on my mind. I see a lot of them about working together.

THE GOVERNOR. Those are local prisoners. The convicts serve their three months here in separate confinement, sir.

COKESON. But we don't want to be unreasonable. He's quite downhearted. I wanted to ask you to let him run about with the others.

THE GOVERNOR (*with faint amusement*). Ring the bell—would you, Miller? (*To* COKESON.) You'd like to hear what the doctor says about him, perhaps.

THE CHAPLAIN (*ringing the bell*). You are not accustomed to prisons, it would seem, sir.

COKESON. No. But it's a pitiful sight. He's quite a young fellow. I said to him: "Before a month's up," I said, "you'll be out and about with the others; it'll be a nice change for you." "A month!" he said—like that! "Come!" I said, "we mustn't exaggerate. What's a month? Why, it's nothing!" "A day," he said, "shut up in your cell thinking and brooding as I do, it's longer than a year outside. I can't help it," he said; "I try—but I'm built that way, Mr. Cokeson." And he held his hand up to his face. I could see the tears trickling through his fingers. It wasn't nice.

THE CHAPLAIN. He's a young man with large, rather peculiar eyes, isn't he? Not Church of England, I think?

COKESON. No.

THE CHAPLAIN. I know.

THE GOVERNOR (*to* WOODER, *who has come in*). Ask the doctor to be good enough to come here for a minute. (WOODER *salutes, and goes out.*) Let's see, he's not married?

COKESON. No. (*Confidentially.*) But there's a party he's very much attached to, not altogether com-il-fo. It's a sad story.

THE CHAPLAIN. If it wasn't for drink and women, sir, this prison might be closed.

COKESON (*looking at the* CHAPLAIN *over his spectacles*). Ye-es, but I wanted to tell you about that, special. He had hopes they'd have let her come and see him, but they haven't. Of course he asked me questions. I did my best, but I couldn't tell the poor young fellow a lie, with him in here—seemed like hitting him. But I'm afraid it's made him worse.

THE GOVERNOR. What was this news then?

COKESON. Like this. The woman had a nahsty, spiteful feller for a husband, and she'd left him. Fact is, she was going away with our young friend. It's not nice—but I've looked over it. Well, when he was put in here she said she'd earn her living apart, and wait for him to come out. That was a great consolation to him. But after a month she came to me—I *don't* know her personally—and she said: "I can't earn the children's living, let alone my own—I've got no friends. I'm obliged to keep out of everybody's way, else my husband'd get to know where I was. I'm very much reduced," she said. And she has lost flesh. "I'll have to go in the workhouse!" It's a painful story. I said to her: "No," I said, "not that! I've got a wife an' family, but sooner than you should do that I'll spare you a little myself." "Really," she said—she's a nice creature—"I don't like to take it from you. I think I'd better go back to my husband." Well, I know he's a nahsty, spiteful feller—drinks—but I didn't like to persuade her not to.

THE CHAPLAIN. Surely, no.

COKESON. Ye-es, but I'm sorry now; it's upset the poor young fellow dreadfully. And what I wanted to say was: He's got his three years to serve. I *want* things to be pleasant for him.

THE CHAPLAIN (*with a touch of impatience*). The law hardly shares your view, I'm afraid.

COKESON. But I can't help thinking that to shut him up there by himself'll turn him silly. And nobody wants that, I s'pose. I *don't* like to see a man cry.

THE CHAPLAIN. It's a very rare thing for them to give way like that.

COKESON (*looking at him—in a tone of sudden dogged hostility*). I keep dogs.

THE CHAPLAIN. Indeed?

COKESON. Ye-es. And I say this: I wouldn't shut one of them up all by himself, month after month, not if he'd bit me all over.

THE CHAPLAIN. Unfortunately, the criminal is not a dog; he has a sense of right and wrong.

COKESON. But that's not the way to make him feel it.

THE CHAPLAIN. Ah! there I'm afraid we must differ.

COKESON. It's the same with dogs. If you treat 'em with kindness they'll do anything for you; but to shut 'em up alone, it only makes 'em savage.

THE CHAPLAIN. Surely you should allow those who have had a little more experience than yourself to know what is best for prisoners.

COKESON (*doggedly*). I know this young feller, I've watched him for years. He's eurotic—got no stamina. His father died of consumption. I'm thinking of his future. If he's to be kept there shut up by himself, without a cat to keep him company, it'll do him harm. I said to him: "Where do you feel it?" "I can't tell you, Mr. Cokeson," he said, "but sometimes I could beat my head against the wall." It's not nice.

[*During this speech the* DOCTOR *has entered. He is a medium-sized, rather good-looking man, with a quick eye. He stands leaning against the window.*]

THE GOVERNOR. This gentleman thinks the separate is telling on Q 3007—Falder, young thin fellow, star class. What do you say, Doctor Clements?

THE DOCTOR. He doesn't like it, but it's not doing him any harm.

COKESON. But he's told me.

THE DOCTOR. Of course he'd say so, but we can always tell. He's lost no weight since he's been here.

COKESON. It's his state of mind I'm speaking of.

THE DOCTOR. His mind's all right so far. He's nervous, rather melancholy. I don't see signs of anything more. I'm watching him carefully.

COKESON (*nonplussed*). I'm glad to hear you say that.

THE CHAPLAIN (*more suavely*). It's just at this period that we are able to make some impression on them, sir. I am speaking from my special standpoint.

COKESON (*turning bewildered to the* GOVERNOR). I *don't* want to be unpleasant, but having given him this news, I do feel it's awkward.

THE GOVERNOR. I'll make a point of seeing him to-day.

COKESON. I'm much obliged to you. I thought perhaps seeing him every day you wouldn't notice it.

THE GOVERNOR (*rather sharply*). If any sign of injury to his health shows itself his case will be reported at once. That's fully provided for. (*He rises.*)

COKESON (*following his own thoughts*). Of course, what you don't see doesn't trouble you; but having seen him, I don't want to have him on my mind.

THE GOVERNOR. I think you may safely leave it to us, sir.

COKESON (*mollified and apologetic*). I thought you'd understand me. I'm a plain man—never set myself up against authority. (*Expanding to the* CHAPLAIN.) Nothing personal meant. *Good*-morning. (*As he goes out the three officials do not look at each other, but their faces wear peculiar expressions.*)

THE CHAPLAIN. Our friend seems to think that prison is a hospital.

COKESON (*returning suddenly with an apologetic air*). There's just one little thing. This woman—I suppose I mustn't ask you to let him see her. It'd be a rare treat for them both. He's thinking about her all the time. Of course she's not his wife. But he's quite safe in here. They're a pitiful couple. You couldn't make an exception?

THE GOVERNOR (*wearily*). As you say, my dear sir, I couldn't make an exception; he won't be allowed another visit of any sort till he goes to a convict prison.

COKESON. I see. (*Rather coldly.*) Sorry to have troubled you. (*He again goes out.*)

THE CHAPLAIN (*shrugging his shoulders*). The plain man indeed, poor fellow. Come and have some lunch, Clements? (*He and the* DOCTOR *go out talking.*)
[*The* GOVERNOR, *with a sigh, sits down at his table and takes up a pen.*]

THE CURTAIN FALLS

SCENE II

Part of the ground corridor of the prison. The walls are coloured with greenish distemper up to a stripe of deeper green about the height of a man's shoulder, and above this line are whitewashed. The floor is of blackened stones. Daylight is filtering through a heavily barred window at the end. The doors of four cells are visible. Each cell door has a little round peep-hole at the level of a man's eye, covered by a little round disc, which, raised upwards, affords a view of the cell. On the wall, close to each cell door, hangs a little square board with the prisoner's name, number, and record.

Overhead can be seen the iron structures of the first-floor and second-floor corridors.

The WARDER INSTRUCTOR, *a bearded man in blue uniform, with an apron, and some dangling keys, is just emerging from one of the cells.*

INSTRUCTOR (*speaking from the door into the cell*). I'll have another bit for you when that's finished.

O'CLEARY (*unseen—in an Irish voice*). Little doubt o' that, sirr.

INSTRUCTOR (*gossiping*). Well, you'd rather have it than nothing, I s'pose.

O'CLEARY. An' that's the blessed truth.
[*Sounds are heard of a cell door being closed and locked, and of approaching footsteps.*]

INSTRUCTOR (*in a sharp, changed voice*). Look alive over it! (*He shuts the cell door, and stands at attention.*)
[*The* GOVERNOR *comes walking down the corridor, followed by* WOODER.]

THE GOVERNOR. Anything to report?

INSTRUCTOR (*saluting*). Q 3007 (*He points to a cell.*) is behind with his work, sir. He'll lose marks to-day.
[*The* GOVERNOR *nods and passes on to the end cell. The* INSTRUCTOR *goes away.*]

THE GOVERNOR. This is our maker of saws, isn't it?

[*He takes the saw from his pocket as* WOODER *throws open the door of the cell. The convict* MOANEY *is seen lying on his bed, athwart the cell, with his cap on. He springs up and stands in the middle of the cell. He is a raw-boned fellow, about fifty-six years old, with outstanding bat's ears and fierce, staring, steel-coloured eyes.*]

WOODER. Cap off! (MOANEY *removes his cap.*) Out here!
[MOANEY *comes to the door.*]

THE GOVERNOR (*beckoning him out into the corridor, and holding up the saw—with the manner of an officer speaking to a private*). Anything to say about this, my man? (MOANY *is silent*.) Come!

MOANEY. It passed the time.

THE GOVERNOR (*pointing into the cell*). Not enough to do, eh?

MOANEY. It don't occupy your mind.

THE GOVERNOR (*tapping the saw*). You might find a better way than this.

MOANEY (*sullenly*). Well! What way? I must keep my hand in against the time I get out. What's the good of anything else to me at my time of life? (*With a gradual change to civility, as his tongue warms.*) Ye know that, sir. I'll be in again within a year or two, after I've done this lot. I don't want to disgrace meself when I'm out. *You've* got your pride keeping the prison smart; well, I've got mine. (*Seeing that the GOVERNOR is listening with interest, he goes on, pointing to the saw.*) I must be doin' a little o' this. It's no harm to any one. I was five weeks makin' that saw—a bit of all right it is, too; now I'll get cells, I suppose, or seven days' bread and water. You can't help it, sir, I know that—I quite put meself in your place.

THE GOVERNOR. Now, look here, Moaney, if I pass it over will you give me your word not to try it on again? Think! (*He goes into the cell, walks to the end of it, mounts the stool, and tries the window-bars.*)

THE GOVERNOR (*returning*). Well?

MOANEY (*who has been reflecting*). I've got another six weeks to do in here, alone. I can't do it and think o' nothing. I must have something to interest me. You've made me a sporting offer, sir, but I can't pass my word about it. I shouldn't like to deceive a gentleman. (*Pointing into the cell.*) Another four hours' steady work would have done it.

THE GOVERNOR. Yes, and what then? Caught, brought back, punishment. Five weeks' hard work to make this, and cells at the end of it, while they put a new bar to your window. Is it worth it, Moaney?

MOANEY (*with a sort of fierceness*). Yes, it is.

THE GOVERNOR (*putting his hand to his brow*). Oh, well! Two days' cells—bread and water.

MOANEY. Thank 'e, sir. (*He turns quickly like an animal and slips into his cell.*)

[*The GOVERNOR looks after him and shakes his head as WOODER closes and locks the cell door.*]

THE GOVERNOR. Open Clipton's cell.

[WOODER *opens the door of* CLIPTON's *cell.* CLIPTON *is sitting on a stool just inside the door, at work on a pair of trousers. He is a small, thick, oldish man, with an almost shaven head, and smouldering little dark eyes behind smoked spectacles. He gets up and stands motionless in the doorway, peering at his visitors.*]

THE GOVERNOR (*beckoning*). Come out here a minute, Clipton.

[CLIPTON, *with a sort of dreadful quietness, comes into the corridor, the needle and thread in his hand. The GOVERNOR signs to WOODER, who goes into the cell and inspects it carefully.*]

THE GOVERNOR. How are your eyes?

CLIPTON. I don't complain of them. I don't see the sun here. (*He makes a stealthy movement, protruding his neck a little.*) There's just one thing, Mr. Governor, as you're speaking to me. I wish you'd ask the cove next door here to keep a bit quieter.

THE GOVERNOR. What's the matter? I don't want any tales, Clipton.

CLIPTON. He keeps me awake. I don't know who he is. (*With contempt.*) One of this *star* class, I expect. Oughtn't to be here with *us*.

THE GOVERNOR (*quietly*). Quite right,

Clipton. He'll be moved when there's a cell vacant.

CLIPTON. He knocks about like a wild beast in the early morning. I'm not used to it—stops me getting my sleep out. In the evening too. It's not fair, Mr. Governor, as you're speaking to me. Sleep's the comfort I've got here; I'm entitled to take it out full.

[WOODER *comes out of the cell, and instantly, as though extinguished,* CLIPTON *moves with stealthy suddenness back into his cell.*]

WOODER. All right, sir.

[*The* GOVERNOR *nods. The door is closed and locked.*]

THE GOVERNOR. Which is the man who banged on his door this morning?

WOODER (*going toward* O'CLEARY'S *cell*). This one, sir; O'Cleary. (*He lifts the disc and glances through the peep-hole.*)

THE GOVERNOR. Open.

[WOODER *throws open the door.* O'CLEARY, *who is seated at a little table by the door as if listening, springs up and stands at attention just inside the doorway. He is a broad-faced, middle-aged man, with a wide, thin, flexible mouth, and little holes under his high cheek-bones.*]

THE GOVERNOR. Where's the joke, O'Cleary?

O'CLEARY. The joke, your honour? I've not seen one for a long time.

THE GOVERNOR. Banging on your door?

O'CLEARY. Oh! that!

THE GOVERNOR. It's womanish.

O'CLEARY. An' it's that I'm becoming this two months past.

THE GOVERNOR. Anything to complain of?

O'CLEARY. No, sirr.

THE GOVERNOR. You're an old hand; you ought to know better.

O'CLEARY. Yes, I've been through it all.

THE GOVERNOR. You've got a youngster next door; you'll upset him.

O'CLEARY. It cam' over me, your honour.

I can't always be the same steady man.

THE GOVERNOR. Work all right?

O'CLEARY (*taking up a rush mat he is making*). Oh! I can do it on me head. It's the miserablest stuff—don't take the brains of a mouse. (*Working his mouth.*) It's here I feel it—the want of a little noise—a terrible little wud ease me.

THE GOVERNOR. You know as well as I do that if you were out in the shops you wouldn't be allowed to talk.

O'CLEARY (*with a look of profound meaning*). Not with my mouth.

THE GOVERNOR. Well, then?

O'CLEARY. But it's the great conversation I'd have.

THE GOVERNOR (*with a smile*). Well, no more conversation on your door.

O'CLEARY. No, sirr, I wud not have the little wit to repeat meself.

THE GOVERNOR (*turning*). Good-night.

O'CLEARY. Good-night, your honour.

[*He turns into his cell. The* GOVERNOR *shuts the door.*]

THE GOVERNOR (*looking at the record card*). Can't help liking the poor blackguard.

WOODER. He's an amiable man, sir.

THE GOVERNOR (*pointing down the corridor*). Ask the doctor to come here, Mr. Wooder.

[WOODER *salutes and goes away down the corridor. The* GOVERNOR *goes to the door of* FALDER'S *cell. He raises his uninjured hand to uncover the peep-hole; but, without uncovering it, shakes his head and drops his hand; then, after scrutinising the record board, he opens the cell door.* FALDER, *who is standing against it, lurches forward.*]

THE GOVERNOR (*beckoning him out*). Now tell me: can't you settle down, Falder?

FALDER (*in a breathless voice*). Yes, sir.

THE GOVERNOR. You know what I mean? It's no good running your head against a stone wall, is it?

FALDER. No, sir.

THE GOVERNOR. Well, come.

FALDER. I try, sir.

THE GOVERNOR. Can't you sleep?

FALDER. Very little. Between two o'clock and getting up's the worst time.

THE GOVERNOR. How's that?

FALDER (*his lips twitch with a sort of smile*). I don't know, sir. I was always nervous. (*Suddenly voluble.*) Everything seems to get such a size then. I feel I'll never get out as long as I live.

THE GOVERNOR. That's morbid, my lad. Pull yourself together.

FALDER (*with an equally sudden dogged resentment*). Yes—I've got to——

THE GOVERNOR. Think of all these other fellows?

FALDER. They're used to it.

THE GOVERNOR. They all had to go through it once for the first time, just as you're doing now.

FALDER. Yes, sir, I shall get to be like them in time, I suppose.

THE GOVERNOR (*rather taken aback*). H'm! Well! That rests with you. Now come. Set your mind to it, like a good fellow. You're still quite young. A man can make himself what he likes.

FALDER (*wistfully*). Yes, sir.

THE GOVERNOR. Take a good hold of yourself. Do you read?

FALDER. I don't take the words in. (*Hanging his head.*) I know it's no good; but I can't help thinking of what's going on outside. In my cell I can't see out at all. It's thick glass, sir.

THE GOVERNOR. You've had a visitor. Bad news?

FALDER. Yes.

THE GOVERNOR. You mustn't think about it.

FALDER (*looking back at his cell*). How can I help it, sir? (*He suddenly becomes motionless as WOODER and the DOCTOR approach. The GOVERNOR motions to him to go back into his cell.*)

FALDER (*quick and low*). I'm quite right in my head, sir. (*He goes back into his cell.*)

THE GOVERNOR (*to the DOCTOR*). Just go in and see him, Clements.

[*The DOCTOR goes into the cell. The GOVERNOR pushes the door to, nearly closing it, and walks towards the window.*]

WOODER (*following*). Sorry you should be troubled like this, sir. Very contented lot of men, on the whole.

THE GOVERNOR (*shortly*). You think so?

WOODER. Yes, sir. It's Christmas doing it, in my opinion.

THE GOVERNOR (*to himself*). Queer, that!

WOODER. Beg pardon, sir?

THE GOVERNOR. Christmas! (*He turns towards the window, leaving WOODER looking at him with a sort of pained anxiety.*)

WOODER (*suddenly*). Do you think we make show enough, sir? If you'd like us to have more holly?

THE GOVERNOR. Not at all, Mr. Wooder.

WOODER. Very good, sir.

[*The DOCTOR has come out of FALDER's cell, and the GOVERNOR beckons to him.*]

THE GOVERNOR. Well?

THE DOCTOR. I can't make anything much of him. He's nervous, of course.

THE GOVERNOR. Is there any sort of case to report? Quite frankly, Doctor.

THE DOCTOR. Well, I don't think the separate's doing him any good; but then I could say the same of a lot of them—they'd get on better in the shops, there's no doubt.

THE GOVERNOR. You mean you'd have to recommend others?

THE DOCTOR. A dozen at least. It's on his nerves. There's nothing tangible. That fellow there (*Pointing to O'CLEARY's cell.*) for instance—feels it just as much, in his way. If I once get away from physical facts—I shan't know where I am. Conscientiously, sir, I don't know how to differentiate him. He hasn't lost weight. Nothing wrong with his eyes. His pulse is good. Talks all right.

THE GOVERNOR. It doesn't amount to melancholia?

THE DOCTOR (*shaking his head*). I can report on him if you like; but if I do I ought to report on others.

THE GOVERNOR. I see. (*Looking towards* FALDER'S *cell*.) The poor devil must 10 just stick it then. (*As he says this he looks absently at* WOODER.)

WOODER. Beg pardon, sir?

[*For answer the* GOVERNOR *stares at him, turns on his heel, and walks away. There is a sound as of beating on metal.*]

THE GOVERNOR (*stopping*). Mr. Wooder?

WOODER. Banging on his door, sir. I thought we should have more of that. (*He hurries forward, passing the* GOVER- 20 NOR, *who follows closely.*)

THE CURTAIN FALLS

SCENE III

FALDER'S *cell, a whitewashed space thirteen feet broad by seven deep, and nine feet high, with a rounded ceiling. The floor is of shiny blackened bricks. The barred window of opaque glass, with a ventilator, is high up in the middle of the end wall. In the middle of the opposite end wall is the narrow door. In a corner are the mattress and bedding rolled up (two blankets, two sheets, and a coverlet). Above them is a quarter-circular wooden shelf, on which is a Bible and several little devotional books, piled in a symmetrical pyramid; there are also a black hair-brush, tooth-brush, and a bit of soap. In another corner is the wooden frame of a bed, standing on end. There is a dark ventilator under the window, and another over the door.* FALDER'S *work (a shirt to which he is putting buttonholes) is hung to a nail on the wall over a small wooden table, on which the novel "Lorna Doone" lies open. Low down in the* corner by the door is a thick glass screen, about a foot square, covering the gas-jet let into the wall. There is also a wooden stool, and a pair of shoes beneath it. Three bright round tins are set under the window.*

In fast-failing daylight, FALDER, *in his stockings, is seen standing motionless, with his head inclined towards the door, listening. He moves a little closer to the door, his stock-inged feet making no noise. He stops at the door. He is trying harder and harder to hear something, any little thing that is going on outside. He springs suddenly upright—as if at a sound—and remains perfectly motionless. Then, with a heavy sigh, he moves to his work, and stands looking at it, with his head down; he does a stitch or two, having the air of a man so lost in sadness that each stitch is, as it were, a coming to life. Then turning abruptly, he begins pacing the cell, moving his head, like an animal pacing its cage. He stops again at the door, listens, and, placing the palms of his hands against it with his fingers spread out, leans his forehead against the iron. Turning from it, presently, he moves slowly back towards the window, tracing his way with his finger along the top line of the distemper that runs round the wall. He stops under the window, and, picking up the lid of one of the tins, peers into it. It has grown very nearly dark. Suddenly the lid falls out of his hand with a clatter—the only sound that has broken the silence—and he stands staring intently at the wall where the stuff of the shirt is hanging rather white in the darkness—he seems to be seeing somebody or something there. There is a sharp tap and click; the cell light behind the glass screen has been turned up. The cell is brightly lighted.* FALDER *is seen gasping for breath.*

A sound from far away, as of distant, dull beating on thick metal, is suddenly audible. FALDER *shrinks back, not able to bear this sudden clamour. But the sound grows, as though some great tumbril were rolling towards the cell. And gradually it seems to hyp-*

*notise him. He begins creeping inch by inch
nearer to the door. The banging sound, travelling from cell to cell, draws closer and closer;*
FALDER'S *hands are seen moving as if his
spirit had already joined in this beating, and
the sound swells till it seems to have entered
the very cell. He suddenly raises his clenched
fists. Panting violently, he flings himself at his
door, and beats on it.*

THE CURTAIN FALLS

ACT IV

The scene is again COKESON'S *room, at a
few minutes to ten of a March morning, two
years later. The doors are all open.* SWEEDLE,
*now blessed with a sprouting moustache, is
getting the offices ready. He arranges papers
on* COKESON'S *table; then goes to a covered
washstand, raises the lid, and looks at himself in the mirror. While he is gazing his fill*
RUTH HONEYWILL *comes in through the
outer office and stands in the doorway. There* 10
*seems a kind of exultation and excitement be-
hind her habitual impassivity.*

SWEEDLE (*suddenly seeing her, and dropping
the lid of the washstand with a bang*).
Hello! It's you!

RUTH. Yes.

SWEEDLE. There's only me here! They
don't waste their time hurrying down
in the morning. Why, it must be two 20
years since we had the pleasure of seeing you. (*Nervously.*) What have you
been doing with yourself?

RUTH (*sardonically*). Living.

SWEEDLE (*impressed*). If you want to see
him (*He points to* COKESON'S *chair.*) he'll
be here directly—never misses—not
much. (*Delicately.*) I hope our friend's
back from the country. His time's
been up these three months, if I re- 30
member. (RUTH *nods.*) I was awful
sorry about that. The governor made
a mistake—if you ask me.

RUTH. He did.

SWEEDLE. He ought to have given him a
chanst. And, *I* say, the judge ought to
ha' let him go after that. They've forgot what human nature's like.

Whereas *we* know. (RUTH *gives him a
honeyed smile.*)

SWEEDLE. They come down on you like
a cartload of bricks, flatten you out,
and when you don't swell up again
they complain of it. I know 'em—
seen a lot of that sort of thing in my
time. (*He shakes his head in the plenitude
of wisdom.*) Why, only the other day
the governor——

[*But* COKESON *has come in through the outer
office; brisk with east wind, and decidedly
greyer.*]

COKESON (*drawing off his coat and gloves*).
Why! it's you! (*Then motioning*
SWEEDLE *out, and closing the door.*)
Quite a stranger! Must be two years.
D'you want to see me? I can give you
a minute. Sit down! Family well?

RUTH. Yes. I'm not living where I was.

COKESON (*eyeing her askance*). I hope
things are more comfortable at home.

RUTH. I couldn't stay with Honeywill,
after all.

COKESON. You haven't done anything
rash, I hope. I should be sorry if you'd
done anything rash.

RUTH. I've kept the children with me.

COKESON (*beginning to feel that things are
not so jolly as he had hoped*). Well, I'm
glad to have seen you. You've not
heard from the young man, I suppose, since he came out?

RUTH. Yes, I ran across him yesterday.

COKESON. I hope he's well.

RUTH (*with sudden fierceness*). He can't get
anything to do. It's dreadful to see
him. He's just skin and bone.

COKESON (*with genuine concern*). Dear me! I'm sorry to hear that. (*On his guard again.*) Didn't they find him a place when his time was up?

RUTH. He was only there three weeks. It got out.

COKESON. I'm sure I don't know what I can do for you. I don't like to be snubby.

RUTH. I can't bear his being like that.   10

COKESON (*scanning her not unprosperous figure*). I know his relations aren't very forthy about him. Perhaps *you* can do something for him, till he finds his feet.

RUTH. Not now. I could have—but not *now*.

COKESON. I don't understand.

RUTH (*proudly*). I've seen him again— that's all over.   20

COKESON (*staring at her—disturbed*). I'm a family man—I don't want to hear anything unpleasant. Excuse me— I'm very busy.

RUTH. I'd have gone home to my people in the country long ago, but they've never got over me marrying Honeywill. I never was waywise, Mr. Cokeson, but I'm proud. I was only a girl, you see, when I married him. I thought   30 the world of him, of course . . . he used to come travelling to our farm.

COKESON (*regretfully*). I did hope you'd have got on better, after you saw me.

RUTH. He used me worse than ever. He couldn't break my nerve, but I lost my health; and then he began knocking the children about. . . . I couldn't stand that. I wouldn't go back now, if he were dying.   40

COKESON (*who has risen and is shifting about as though dodging a stream of lava*). We mustn't be violent, must we?

RUTH (*smouldering*). A man that can't behave better than that——(*There is silence.*)

COKESON (*fascinated in spite of himself*). Then there you were! And what did you do then?

RUTH (*with a shrug*). Tried the same as when I left him before . . . making skirts . . . cheap things. It was the best I could get, but I never made more than ten shillings a week, buying my own cotton and working all day; I hardly ever got to bed till past twelve. I kept at it for nine months. (*Fiercely.*) Well, I'm not fit for that; I wasn't made for it. I'd rather die.

COKESON. My dear woman! We mustn't talk like that.

RUTH. It was starvation for the children too—after what they'd always had. I soon got not to care. I used to be too tired. (*She is silent.*)

COKESON (*with fearful curiosity*). Why, what happened then?

RUTH (*with a laugh*). My employer happened then—he's happened ever since.

COKESON. Dear! Oh dear! I never came across a thing like this.

RUTH (*dully*). He's treated me all right. But I've done with that. (*Suddenly her lips begin to quiver, and she hides them with the back of her hand.*) I never thought I'd see *him* again, you see. It was just a chance I met him by Hyde Park. We went in there and sat down, and he told me all about himself. Oh! Mr. Cokeson, give him another chance.

COKESON (*greatly disturbed*). Then you've both lost your livings! What a horrible position!

RUTH. If he could only get here—where there's nothing to find out about him!

COKESON. We can't have anything derogative to the firm.

RUTH. I've no one else to go to.

COKESON. I'll speak to the partners, but I don't think they'll take him, under the circumstances. I don't really.

RUTH. He came with me; he's down there in the street. (*She points to the window.*)

COKESON (*on his dignity*). He shouldn't have done that until he's sent for. (*Then softening at the look on her face.*) We've got a vacancy, as it happens, but I can't promise anything.

RUTH. It would be the saving of him.

COKESON. Well, I'll do what I can, but 10 I'm not sanguine. Now tell him that I don't want him till I see how things are. Leave your address? (*Repeating her.*) 83 Mullingar Street? (*He notes it on blotting-paper.*) Good-morning.

RUTH. Thank you. (*She moves towards the door, turns as if to speak, but does not, and goes away.*)

COKESON (*wiping his head and forehead with a large white cotton handkerchief*). What a 20 business! (*Then looking amongst his papers, he sounds his bell.* SWEEDLE answers it.*)

COKESON. Was that young Richards coming here to-day after the clerk's place?

SWEEDLE. Yes.

COKESON. Well, keep him in the air; I don't want to see him yet.

SWEEDLE. What shall I tell him, sir? 30

COKESON (*with asperity*). Invent something. Use your brains. Don't stump him off altogether.

SWEEDLE. Shall I tell him that we've got illness, sir?

COKESON. No! Nothing untrue. Say I'm not here to-day.

SWEEDLE. Yes, sir. Keep him hankering?

COKESON. Exactly. And look here. You remember Falder? I may be having 40 him round to see me. Now, treat him like you'd have him treat you in a similar position.

SWEEDLE. I naturally should do.

COKESON. That's right. When a man's down never hit 'im. 'Tisn't necessary.

Give him a hand up. That's a metaphor I recommend to you in life. It's sound policy.

SWEEDLE. Do you think the governors will take him on again, sir?

COKESON. Can't say anything about that. (*At the sound of some one having entered the outer office.*) Who's there?

SWEEDLE (*going to the door and looking*). It's Falder, sir.

COKESON (*vexed*). Dear me! That's very naughty of her. Tell him to call again. I don't want——

[*He breaks off as* FALDER *comes in.* FALDER *is thin, pale, older, his eyes have grown more restless. His clothes are very worn and loose.* SWEEDLE, *nodding cheerfully, withdraws.*]

COKESON. Glad to see you. You're rather previous. (*Trying to keep things pleasant.*) Shake hands! She's striking while the iron's hot. (*He wipes his forehead.*) I don't blame her. She's anxious.

[FALDER *timidly takes* COKESON's *hand and glances towards the partners' door.*]

COKESON. No—not yet! Sit down! (FALDER *sits in the chair at the side of* COKESON's *table, on which he places his cap.*) Now you are here I'd like you to give me a little account of yourself. (*Looking at him over his spectacles.*) How's your health?

FALDER. I'm alive, Mr. Cokeson.

COKESON (*preoccupied*). I'm glad to hear that. About this matter. I don't like doing anything out of the ordinary; it's not my habit. I'm a plain man, and I want everything smooth and straight. But I promised your friend to speak to the partners, and I always keep my word.

FALDER. I just want a chance, Mr. Cokeson. I've paid for that job a thousand times and more. I have, sir. No one knows. They say I weighed more when I came out than when I went in. They couldn't weigh me here (*He touches his head.*) or here. (*He touches his heart, and gives a sort of laugh.*) Till last night I'd have thought there was nothing in here at all.

COKESON (*concerned*). You've not got heart disease?

FALDER. Oh! they passed me sound enough.

COKESON. But they got you a place, didn't they?

FALDER. Yes; very good people, knew all about it—very kind to me. I thought I was going to get on first rate. But one day, all of a sudden, the other clerks got wind of it. . . . I couldn't stick it, Mr. Cokeson, I couldn't, sir.

COKESON. Easy, my dear fellow, easy!

FALDER. I had one small job after that, but it didn't last.

COKESON. How was that?

FALDER. It's no good deceiving you, Mr. Cokeson. The fact is, I seem to be struggling against a thing that's all round me. I can't explain it: it's as if I was in a net; as fast as I cut it here, it grows up there. I didn't act as I ought to have, about references; but what are you to do? You must have them. And that made me afraid, and I left. In fact, I'm—I'm afraid all the time now. (*He bows his head and leans dejectedly silent over the table.*)

COKESON. I feel for you—I do really. Aren't your sisters going to do anything for you?

FALDER. One's in consumption. And the other——

COKESON. Ye . . . es. She told me her husband wasn't quite pleased with you.

FALDER. When I went there—they were at supper—my sister wanted to give me a kiss—I know. But he just looked at her, and said: "What have you come for?" Well, I pocketed my pride and I said: "Aren't you going to give me your hand, Jim? Cis is, I know," I said. "Look here!" he said, "that's all very well, but we'd better come to an understanding. I've been expecting you, and I've made up my mind. I'll give you fifteen pounds to go to Canada with." "I see," I said—"good riddance! No, thanks; keep your fifteen pounds." Friendship's a queer thing when you've been where I have.

COKESON. I understand. Will you take the fifteen pound from me? (*Flustered, as* FALDER *regards him with a queer smile.*) Quite without prejudice; I meant it kindly.

FALDER. I'm not allowed to leave the country.

COKESON. Oh! ye . . . es—ticket-of-leave? You aren't looking the thing.

FALDER. I've slept in the Park three nights this week. The dawns aren't all poetry there. But meeting her—I feel a different man this morning. I've often thought the being fond of her's the best thing about me; it's sacred, somehow—and yet it did for me. That's queer, isn't it?

COKESON. I'm sure we're all very sorry for you.

FALDER. That's what I've found, Mr. Cokeson. Awfully sorry for me. (*With quiet bitterness.*) But it doesn't do to associate with criminals!

COKESON. Come, come, it's no use calling yourself names. That never did a man any good. Put a face on it.

FALDER. It's easy enough to put a face on it, sir, when you're independent. Try it when you're down like me. They talk about giving you your deserts. Well, I think I've had just a bit over.

COKESON (*eyeing him askance over his spectacles*). I hope they haven't made a Socialist of you.

[FALDER *is suddenly still, as if brooding over his past self; he utters a peculiar laugh.*]

COKESON. You must give them credit for the best intentions. Really you must. Nobody wishes you harm, I'm sure.

FALDER. I believe that, Mr. Cokeson. Nobody wishes you harm, but they down you all the same. This feeling ——(*He stares round him, as though at something closing in.*) It's crushing me. (*With sudden impersonality.*) I know it is.

COKESON (*horribly disturbed*). There's nothing there! We must try and take it quiet. I'm sure I've often had you in my prayers. Now leave it to me. I'll use my gumption and take 'em when they're jolly. (*As he speaks the two partners come in.*)

COKESON (*rather disconcerted, but trying to put them all at ease*). I didn't expect you quite so soon. I've just been having a talk with this young man. I think you'll remember him.

JAMES (*with a grave, keen look*). Quite well. How are you, Falder?

WALTER (*holding out his hand almost timidly*). Very glad to see you again, Falder.

FALDER (*who has recovered his self-control, takes the hand*). Thank you, sir.

COKESON. Just a word, Mr. James. (*To* FALDER, *pointing to the clerks' office.*) You might go in there a minute. You know your way. Our junior won't be coming this morning. His wife's just had a little family.

[FALDER *goes uncertainly out into the clerks' office.*]

COKESON (*confidentially*). I'm bound to tell you all about it. He's quite penitent. But there's a prejudice against him. And you're not seeing him to advantage this morning; he's under-nourished. It's very trying to go without your dinner.

JAMES. Is that so, Cokeson?

COKESON. I wanted to ask you. He's had his lesson. Now *we* know all about him, and we want a clerk. There is a young fellow applying, but I'm keeping him in the air.

JAMES. A gaol-bird in the office, Cokeson? I don't see it.

WALTER. "The rolling of the chariot-wheels of Justice!" I've never got that out of my head.

JAMES. I've nothing to reproach myself with in this affair. What's he been doing since he came out?

COKESON. He's had one or two places, but he hasn't kept them. He's sensitive—quite natural. Seems to fancy everybody's down on him.

JAMES. Bad sign. Don't like the fellow—never did from the first. "Weak character" 's written all over him.

WALTER. I think we owe him a leg up.

JAMES. He brought it all on himself.

WALTER. The doctrine of full responsibility doesn't quite hold in these days.

JAMES (*rather grimly*). You'll find it safer to hold it for all that, my boy.

WALTER. For oneself, yes—not for other people, thanks.

JAMES. Well! I don't want to be hard.

COKESON. I'm glad to hear you say that. He seems to see something (*Spreading his arms.*) round him. 'Tisn't healthy.

JAMES. What about that woman he was mixed up with? I saw some one uncommonly like her outside as we came in.

COKESON. *That!* Well, I can't keep anything from you. He has met her.

JAMES. Is she with her husband?

COKESON. No.

JAMES. Falder living with her, I suppose?

COKESON (*desperately trying to retain the new-found jollity*). I don't know that of my own knowledge. 'Tisn't my business.

JAMES. It's *our* business, if we're going to engage him, Cokeson.

COKESON (*reluctantly*). I ought to tell you, perhaps. I've had the party here this morning.

JAMES. I thought so. (*To* WALTER.) No, my dear boy, it won't do. Too shady altogether!

COKESON. The two things together make it very awkward for you—I see that.   10

WALTER (*tentatively*). I don't quite know what we have to do with his private life.

JAMES. No, no! He must make a clean sheet of it, or he can't come here.

WALTER. Poor devil!

COKESON. Will you have him in? (*And as* JAMES *nods*.) I think I can get him to see reason.

JAMES (*grimly*). You can leave that to   20 me, Cokeson.

WALTER (*to* JAMES, *in a low voice, while* COKESON *is summoning* FALDER). His whole future may depend on what we do, dad.

[FALDER *comes in. He has pulled himself together, and presents a steady front.*]

JAMES. Now look here, Falder. My son and I want to give you another chance; but there are two things I   30 must say to you. In the first place: It's no good coming here as a victim. If you've any notion that you've been unjustly treated—get rid of it. You can't play fast and loose with morality and hope to go scot-free. If Society didn't take care of itself, nobody would—the sooner you realise that the better.

FALDER. Yes, sir; but—may I say some-   40 thing?

JAMES. Well?

FALDER. I had a lot of time to think it over in prison. (*He stops.*)

COKESON (*encouraging him*). I'm sure you did.

FALDER. There were all sorts there. And what I mean, sir, is, that if we'd been treated differently the first time, and put under somebody that could look after us a bit, and not put in prison, not a quarter of us would ever have got there.

JAMES (*shaking his head*). I'm afraid I've very grave doubts of that, Falder.

FALDER (*with a gleam of malice*). Yes, sir, so I found.

JAMES. My good fellow, don't forget that you began it.

FALDER. I never wanted to do wrong.

JAMES. Perhaps not. But you did.

FALDER (*with all the bitterness of his past suffering*). It's knocked me out of time. (*Pulling himself up.*) That is, I mean, I'm not what I was.

JAMES. This isn't encouraging for us, Falder.

COKESON. He's putting it awkwardly, Mr. James.

FALDER (*throwing over his caution from the intensity of his feeling*). I mean it, Mr. Cokeson.

JAMES. Now, lay aside all those thoughts, Falder, and look to the future.

FALDER (*almost eagerly*). Yes, sir, but you don't understand what prison is. It's here it gets you. (*He grips his chest.*)

COKESON (*in a whisper to* JAMES). I told you he wanted nourishment.

WALTER. Yes, but, my dear fellow, that'll pass away. Time's merciful.

FALDER (*with his face twitching*). I hope so, sir.

JAMES (*much more gently*). Now, my boy, what you've got to do is to put all the past behind you and build yourself up a steady reputation. And that brings me to the second thing. This woman you were mixed up with— you must give us your word, you know, to have done with that. There's no chance of your keeping straight if you're going to begin your future with such a relationship.

FALDER (*looking from one to the other with a hunted expression*). But sir . . . but sir . . . it's the one thing I looked forward to all that time. And she too . . . I couldn't find her before last night.

[*During this and what follows* COKESON *becomes more and more uneasy.*]

JAMES. This is painful, Falder. But you must see for yourself that it's impossible for a firm like this to close its eyes to everything. Give us this proof of your resolve to keep straight, and you can come back—not otherwise.

FALDER (*after staring at* JAMES, *suddenly stiffens himself*). I couldn't give her up. I couldn't! Oh, sir! I'm all she's got to look to. And I'm sure she's all I've got.

JAMES. I'm very sorry, Falder, but I must be firm. It's for the benefit of you both in the long run. No good can come of this connection. It was the cause of all your disaster.

FALDER. But sir, it means—having gone through all that—getting broken up —my nerves are in an awful state— for nothing. I did it for her.

JAMES. Come! If she's anything of a woman she'll see it for herself. She won't want to drag you down further. If there were a prospect of your being able to marry her—it might be another thing.

FALDER. It's not my fault, sir, that she couldn't get rid of him—she would have if she could. That's been the whole trouble from the beginning. (*Looking suddenly at* WALTER.) . . . If anybody would help her! It's only money wanted now, I'm sure.

COKESON (*breaking in, as* WALTER *hesitates, and is about to speak*). I don't think we need consider that—it's rather far-fetched.

FALDER (*to* WALTER, *appealing*). He must have given her full cause since; she could prove that he drove her to leave him.

WALTER. I'm inclined to do what you say, Falder, if it can be managed.

FALDER. Oh, sir! (*He goes to the window and looks down into the street.*)

COKESON (*hurriedly*). You don't take me, Mr. Walter. I have my reasons.

FALDER (*from the window*). She's down there, sir. Will you see her? I can beckon to her from here.

[WALTER *hesitates, and looks from* COKESON *to* JAMES.]

JAMES (*with a sharp nod*). Yes, let her come.

[FALDER *beckons from the window.*]

COKESON (*in a low fluster to* JAMES *and* WALTER). No, Mr. James. She's not been quite what she ought to ha' been, while this young man's been away. She's lost her chance. We can't consult how to swindle the Law.

[FALDER *has come from the window. The three men look at him in a sort of awed silence.*]

FALDER (*with instinctive apprehension of some change—looking from one to the other*). There's been nothing between us, sir, to prevent it. . . . What I said at the trial was true. And last night we only just sat in the Park.

[SWEEDLE *comes in from the outer office.*]

COKESON. What is it?

SWEEDLE. Mrs. Honeywill. (*There is silence.*)

JAMES. Show her in.

[RUTH *comes slowly in, and stands stoically with* FALDER *on one side and the three men on the other. No one speaks.* COKESON *turns to his table, bending over his papers as though the burden of the situation were forcing him back into his accustomed groove.*]

JAMES (*sharply*). Shut the door there. (SWEEDLE *shuts the door.*) We've asked you to come up because there are certain facts to be faced in this matter. I understand you have only just met Falder again.

RUTH. Yes—only yesterday.

JAMES. He's told us about himself, and we're very sorry for him. I've promised to take him back here if he'll make a fresh start. (*Looking steadily at* RUTH.) This is a matter that requires courage, ma'am.

[RUTH, *who is looking at* FALDER, *begins to twist her hands in front of her as though prescient of disaster.*]

FALDER. Mr. Walter How is good enough to say that he'll help us to get you a divorce.

[RUTH *flashes a startled glance at* JAMES *and* WALTER.]

JAMES. I don't think that's practicable, Falder.

FALDER. But, sir——!

JAMES (*steadily*). Now, Mrs. Honeywill. You're fond of him.

RUTH. Yes, sir; I love him. (*She looks miserably at* FALDER.)

JAMES. Then you don't want to stand in his way, do you?

RUTH (*in a faint voice*). I could take care of him.

JAMES. The best way you can take care of him will be to give him up.

FALDER. Nothing shall make me give you up. You can get a divorce. There's been nothing between us, has there?

RUTH (*mournfully shaking her head—without looking at him*). No.

FALDER. We'll keep apart till it's over, sir; if you'll only help us—we promise.

JAMES (*to* RUTH). You see the thing plainly, don't you? You see what I mean?

RUTH (*just above a whisper*). Yes.

COKESON (*to himself*). There's a dear woman.

JAMES. The situation is impossible.

RUTH. Must I, sir?

JAMES (*forcing himself to look at her*). I put it to you, ma'am. His future is in your hands.

RUTH (*miserably*). I want to do the best for him.

JAMES (*a little huskily*). That's right, that's right!

FALDER. I don't understand. You're not going to give me up—after all this? There's something——(*Starting forward to* JAMES.) Sir, I swear solemnly there's been nothing between us.

JAMES. I believe you, Falder. Come, my lad, be as plucky as she is.

FALDER. Just now you were going to help us. (*He stares at* RUTH, *who is standing absolutely still; his face and hands twitch and quiver as the truth dawns on him.*) What is it? You've not been ——

WALTER. Father!

JAMES (*hurriedly*). There, there! That'll do, that'll do! I'll give you your chance, Falder. Don't let me know what you do with yourselves, that's all.

FALDER (*as if he has not heard*). Ruth?

[RUTH *looks at him; and* FALDER *covers his face with his hands. There is silence.*]

COKESON (*suddenly*). There's some one out there. (*To* RUTH.) Go in here. You'll feel better by yourself for a minute.

[*He points to the clerks' room and moves towards the outer office.* FALDER *does not move.* RUTH *puts out her hand timidly. He shrinks back from the touch. She turns and goes miserably into the clerks' room. With a brusque movement he follows, seizing her by the shoulder just inside the doorway.* COKESON *shuts the door.*]

JAMES (*pointing to the outer office*). Get rid of that, whoever it is.

SWEEDLE (*opening the office door, in a scared voice*). Detective-Sergeant Wister.

[*The detective enters, and closes the door behind him.*]

WISTER. Sorry to disturb you, sir. A clerk you had here, two years and a half ago. I arrested him in this room.

JAMES. What about him?

WISTER. I thought perhaps I might get his whereabouts from you. (*There is an awkward silence.*)

COKESON (*pleasantly, coming to the rescue*). We're not responsible for his movements; you know that.

JAMES. What do you want with him?

WISTER. He's failed to report himself this last four weeks.

WALTER. How d'you mean?

WISTER. Ticket-of-leave won't be up for another six months, sir.

WALTER. Has he to keep in touch with the police till then?

WISTER. We're bound to know where he sleeps every night. I dare say we shouldn't interfere, sir, even though he hasn't reported himself. But we've just heard there's a serious matter of obtaining employment with a forged reference. What with the two things together—we must have him.

[*Again there is silence.* WALTER *and* COKESON *steal glances at* JAMES, *who stands staring steadily at the detective.*]

COKESON (*expansively*). We're very busy at the moment. If you could make it convenient to call again we might be able to tell you then.

JAMES (*decisively*). I'm a servant of the Law, but I dislike peaching. In fact, I can't do such a thing. If you want him you must find him without us. (*As he speaks his eye falls on* FALDER'S *cap, still lying on the table, and his face contracts.*)

WISTER (*noting the gesture—quietly*). Very good, sir. I ought to warn you that, having broken the terms of his licence, he's still a convict, and sheltering a convict——

JAMES. I shelter no one. But you mustn't come here and ask questions which it's not my business to answer.

WISTER (*dryly*). I won't trouble you further then, gentlemen.

COKESON. I'm sorry we couldn't give you the information. You quite understand, don't you? Good-morning!

[WISTER *turns to go, but instead of going to the door of the outer office he goes to the door of the clerks' room.*]

COKESON. The other door . . . the other door!

[WISTER *opens the clerks' door.* RUTH'S *voice is heard:* "Oh, do!" *and* FALDER'S: "*I can't!*" *There is a little pause; then, with sharp fright,* RUTH *says:* "Who's that?" WISTER *has gone in.*]

[*The three men look aghast at the door.*]

WISTER (*from within*). Keep back, please!

[*He comes swiftly out with his arm twisted in* FALDER'S. *The latter gives a white, staring look at the three men.*]

WALTER. Let him go this time, for God's sake!

WISTER. I couldn't take the responsibility, sir.

FALDER (*with a queer, desperate laugh*). Good! (*Flinging a look back at* RUTH, *he throws up his head, and goes out through the outer office, half dragging* WISTER *after him.*)

WALTER (*with despair*). That finishes him. It'll go on for ever now.

[SWEEDLE *can be seen staring through the outer door. There are sounds of footsteps descending the stone stairs; suddenly a dull thud, a faint* "My God!" *in* WISTER'S *voice.*]

JAMES. What's that?

[SWEEDLE *dashes forward. The door swings to behind him. There is dead silence.*]

WALTER (*starting forward to the inner room*). The woman—she's fainting! (*He and* COKESON *support the fainting* RUTH *from the doorway of the clerks' room.*)

COKESON (*distracted*). Here, my dear! There, there!

WALTER. Have you any brandy?

COKESON. I've got sherry.

WALTER. Get it, then. Quick! (*He places* RUTH *in a chair—which* JAMES *has dragged forward.*)

COKESON (*with sherry*). Here! It's good strong sherry.

[*They try to force the sherry between her lips. There is the sound of feet, and they stop to listen. The outer door is reopened—*WISTER *and* SWEEDLE *are seen carrying some burden.*]

JAMES (*hurrying forward*). What is it?

[*They lay the burden down in the outer office, out of sight, and all but* RUTH *cluster round it, speaking in hushed voices.*]

WISTER. He jumped—neck's broken.

WALTER. Good God!

WISTER. He must have been mad to think he could give me the slip like that. And what was it—just a few months!

WALTER (*bitterly*). Was that all?

JAMES. What a desperate thing! (*Then, in a voice unlike his own.*) Run for a doctor—you! (SWEEDLE *rushes from the outer office.*) An ambulance!

[WISTER *goes out. On* RUTH'S *face an expression of fear and horror has been seen growing, as if she dared not turn towards the voices. She now rises and steals towards them.*]

WALTER (*turning suddenly*). Look!

[*The three men shrink back out of her way, one by one, into* COKESON'S *room.* RUTH *drops on her knees by the body.*]

10 RUTH (*in a whisper*). What is it? He's not breathing. (*She crouches over him.*) My dear! My pretty!

[*In the outer office doorway the figures of men are seen standing.*]

RUTH (*leaping to her feet*). No, no! No, no! He's dead!

[*The figures of the men shrink back.*]

COKESON (*stealing forward. In a hoarse voice*). There, there, poor dear woman!

20 [*At the sound behind her* RUTH *faces round at him.*]

COKESON. No one'll touch him now! Never again! He's safe with gentle Jesus!

[RUTH *stands as though turned to stone in the doorway staring at* COKESON, *who, bending humbly before her, holds out his hand as one would to a lost dog.*]

THE CURTAIN FALLS

W. SOMERSET MAUGHAM

W SOMERSET MAUGHAM, like his col-
league and fellow countryman
John Galsworthy, won almost equal distinction in both fiction and drama. As a
dramatist, Galsworthy was serious-
minded; his plays were weighted to the
point of tragedy with protest against injustice and social evils. And as a person,
Galsworthy was the sum and substance
of the solid, conservative Englishman.
Maugham, on the contrary, wrote primarily to entertain, albeit on an intellectual level, and felt no call to reform
the world. He wrote gay, ironical comedies. And he personifies, not the insular
Englishman, but the genuine cosmopolite, the sophisticated man of the world.

As if these characteristics were being
predetermined by his destiny, Maugham
was born not in England but in Paris in
1874, just seven years after Galsworthy.
He has written a sprightly account of
his father and mother as "Beauty and
the Beast" in his indispensable professional autobiography, *The Summing Up*
—a book that combines the facts about
himself which he finds important, or
cares to lay before the reader, with a discourse on his theory and practice of
writing fiction and drama. It is remarkable for its wit and modesty as well as
for its wisdom and insight. His father,
possibly drawn "by some such restless-
ness for the unknown as has consumed
his son," took up residence in Paris as
solicitor to the British Embassy. Like his
son, he was a great traveler. In middle
life he married a beautiful English girl
half his age who was also living in Paris.
She died of consumption in 1882 when
Maugham was eight years old. His
father died two years later. Knowing
more French than English, Maugham
was then sent to England as the ward of
an uncle, the vicar of Whitstable in
Kent.

This change in his life was the beginning of a bleak and melancholy period
that lasted many years. Maugham
wrote in the opening paragraph of *The
Summing Up:* "Fact and fiction are so
intermingled in my work that now, looking back on it, I can hardly distinguish
one from the other." We may assume
that the early portions of his masterpiece, *Of Human Bondage*, drew heavily
upon his first years in England, and,
with due allowance for its fiction, that it
is sufficiently accurate to be taken as a
personal record of his life with his uncle
and his experiences at King's School,
Canterbury. He attended the school irregularly because of ill-health. He was
happy for the excuse to break out of the
bondage and go to southern France to
recuperate. The pleasure of the inter-
lude dislocated him still further in the
school. In 1891 he withdrew entirely
and went to Heidelberg, Germany, for a
year of study. He returned to England,
attempted a clerkship as an accountant
for six weeks, and then entered St.
Thomas's Hospital for medical training
in the autumn of 1892. He liked having
his own lodgings, but found the curricu-
lum dull. He preferred reading and
writing. The Hospital was on the edge
of the Lambeth slums where the young
medical student saw life in the raw. In
those three years, he said, he must have

witnessed "pretty well every emotion of which man is capable."

It is significant that this spectacle appealed to Maugham's "dramatic instinct," to the novelist in him rather than to the physician. Like Anton Chekhov, he preferred letters to medicine. He had been trained to look upon sick, warped, uneducated people as a scientist would look; he had gained an insight into human nature; and he had learned to work directly from life using living models—a practice which he has followed throughout his career. His first professional step after graduation was not to set up as a doctor but to publish a realistic novel about the environs of St. Thomas's, *Liza of Lambeth* (1897). Then he traveled in Spain, and lived again in Paris, in Montparnasse, writing all the while. His publications, though interesting, were not very successful. He had long been attracted to the theatre and playwriting. The economy of dramatic form, its compression, its demands upon dialogue, and the prizes it offered to the successful, all appealed to Maugham. He first tried his hand in 1902 with a one act play, *Schiffbrüchig*, produced in Berlin in German. In 1903 the London Stage Society gave two performances of his *Man of Honor*, with little advancement to his fame or fortune. The lean, apprentice years continued until 1908, when Maugham completely captured the public. He scored the unprecedented triumph of having four plays running in London at the same time: *Lady Frederick, Jack Straw, Mrs. Dot*, and *The Explorer*.

Maugham's fortune was now made. He wrote more than a score of plays in the next two decades. They were all expertly contrived, never dull or pretentious or too disturbing, and just far enough in advance of the times to intrigue the fancy. They pleased an age that had learned to patronize the Victorians. Maugham's career since 1908 has been that of the cosmopolite, the world traveler, and world celebrity. His life has been filled with exciting episodes, notably his service with the Medical Corps in the First World War; his activities in Russia after the collapse of the monarchy, in his Majesty's secret service; his harrowing escape from France to England in the summer of 1940; and his return to the United States in the autumn of that year. The entire record, down to the Second World War, has been transmuted into his long list of plays, novels, and short-stories: "In one way and another I have used in my writings whatever has happened to me in the course of my life."

As a dramatist Maugham is happily and firmly placed in the great tradition of English comedy. The tradition is long and joyous. The unabated popularity of Congreve and Wycherley, of Goldsmith and Sheridan, and of Oscar Wilde is proof that this type of comedy, faultily labeled "artificial," as Maugham has noted, is linked with a native bias in the English temper. This comedy, he writes, "treats with indulgent cynicism the humours, follies, and vices of the world of fashion. It is urbane, sentimental at times, for that is in the English character, and a trifle unreal. It does not preach: sometimes it draws a moral, but with a shrug of the shoulders as if to invite you to lay no too great stress on it." Maugham's own sensational conquest of the London stage is added evidence of these truths. And his singular genius for representing with suave detachment or amused indulgence the blunderings of the race not only gave him undisputed rule for a quarter of a century over English comedy, but enriched the theatre on the continent and in America.

Thanks to Maugham's *The Summing Up* and to his various essays and prefaces, we have his own word for the theory of play writing which he has followed. He has always aimed not to instruct but to please. He is mildly impatient with the professors and the solemn people who take plays and the theatre too seriously. The fixed and unalterable conditions for the performance of a play in a theatre make the art of playwriting a minor one. Heavy-duty thinking is not only out of place, it is impossible. The audience is about as important in the performance as the actors and the script. But it is heterogeneous, running the scale of intelligence from the *Times's* dramatic critic to the vacuous shopgirl. The thought level at which this mixed crowd may be fused into the unit necessary to give success to the play is not very high. "One man's thought is another man's truism." Intellectually, therefore, says Maugham, the theatre is always about thirty years behind the times. If you plan to write plays for production, "a lofty purpose will not serve you so well as a competent technique."

Maugham takes an ironic pleasure in that word "competent" since certain heavy-footed critics began to use it inaccurately and in a depreciatory sense as a label for his skill. But Maugham knows, and says, that a lofty purpose will not save a play from failure when, as so often happens, the theme doesn't interest, the characterization is poor, the construction is unsound, and the dialogue is verbose and heavy. The dramatist ought to be intelligent, if possible, but ideas, as such, new or old, are no concern of his. His aim is to entice and to please an audience.

Ever since that phenomenal season of 1908, Maugham has quite consistently pleased audiences with his plays. In his own inimitable manner, if the author will forgive the slander, he has also instructed. He has not felt called upon to tamper with standard specifications for dramatic craftsmanship. He has perfected his own technique within the comfortable frame of the great tradition without feeling shut in. He has made disciplined use of his "very high spirits, a facility for amusing dialogue, an eye for a comic situation, and a flippant gaiety." His rule is as simple as it is effective: "Stick to the point and whenever you can, cut."

Maugham has held on to the point, and has evidently cut until his plays have attained his ideal of maximum concentration. The concentration often takes the form of a brilliant epigram faultlessly timed to point the scene or to end an episode in wry, intellectual laughter. In *The Constant Wife*, Constance has subtly helped on with the central viewpoint of the play by observing to her mother that John "has all the solid qualities that make a man a good husband; an agreeable temper, a sense of humor and an entire indifference to petty extravagance." Then she finished it off with the aphorism: "It's not the seven deadly virtues in life that make a man a good husband, but the three hundred pleasing amiabilities."

Maugham's best plays have a core of sound humanity and a "go" to them that give them vitality even in the library and independently of changing fashions. *Our Betters* (1917), *The Circle* (1921), *The Constant Wife* (1927), and *The Bread-Winner* (1930) are now among the classic comedies of the modern theatre. *Our Betters* was a biting satire on the Anglo-American society set—a vitriolic modernization of the old Henry James situation in Restoration style. A New York heiress has married an English title and become Lady George Grayson. Around her are gathered the idle noblemen of the realm, and some noblewomen of English and American origin, whose morals and manners prove so outrageous to Lady Grayson's American sister that she flees from a marriage with one of them back home to her own American sweetheart. *The Circle* presented Lady Kitty and Lord Porteous as they now are some thirty years after their passionate romance when she deserted her husband and eloped with Porteous, all for love. Their grim and horrible example fails to deter Lady Kitty's daughter-in-law from trying out the same experiment by deserting her husband Arnold and going away with her romantic lover, Edward Luton. Maugham drops the story at that point, leaving only the title to suggest the outcome. *The Bread-Winner* details the revolt of the badgered husband and father, Charles Battle, and how he asserted himself against the demands of the young generation and regained his freedom. Maugham was reticent about commenting on this play. "Of *The Bread-Winner*," he wrote, "I have no more to say than that in London it amused audiences for the greater part of a year, but in New York ran for no more than a fortnight."

The Constant Wife is one of the best of Maugham's comedies. It so merrily hits off the era of the 1920's with its exaggerated concern over problems of marriage, sex, and individual freedom that it ran in New York, with Ethel Barrymore as Constance and C. Aubrey Smith as John, for 233 performances, and in Chicago for 121 performances. It is the natural end point of the long series of plays that began with *A Doll's House*, and included Pinero's *Mid-Channel*, Shaw's *Candida*, Houghton's *Hindle Wake* and a thousand others. Maugham is too much the man of the world to treat the theme with a long face. He boldly announced that in the present age of emancipation "jealousy was no longer a theme for tragedy, but only for comedy." In *The Constant Wife* Maugham simply assumes this attitude without arguing about it, and skilfully contrives to put the defense of conventional attitudes into the mouths of the spinster sister and the Victorian-minded bachelor Bernard, while the emancipated Constance and her mother, who in traditional drama would weep over their wrongs, carry on the propaganda war against their own sex. Under Maugham's crisp and precise style, and with his gay spirit, his tolerant detachment, and his knowledge of women (where Shaw's ignorance, for example, is abysmal), the hackneyed triangle is given fresh life, and the little sermon has been preached so unobtrusively that it hardly appears to contradict the author's announced intention merely to please.

THE CONSTANT WIFE

CHARACTERS

CONSTANCE

JOHN MIDDLETON, F.R.C.S.

BERNARD KERSAL

MRS. CULVER

MARIE-LOUISE

MARTHA

BARBARA

MORTIMER DURHAM

BENTLEY

The action of the play takes place in John's house in Harley Street.

ACT I

CONSTANCE'S *drawing-room. It is a room furnished with singularly good taste.* CONSTANCE *has a gift for decoration and has made this room of hers both beautiful and comfortable.*

It is afternoon.

MRS. CULVER *is seated alone. She is an elderly lady with a pleasant face and she is dressed in walking costume. The door is opened and* BENTLEY *the butler introduces* MARTHA CULVER. *This is her daughter and a fine young woman.*

BENTLEY. Miss Culver. (*He goes out.*)

MARTHA (*with astonishment*). Mother.

MRS. CULVER (*very calmly*). Yes, darling.

MARTHA. You're the last person I expected to find here. You never told me you were coming to see Constance.

MRS. CULVER (*good-humouredly*). I didn't intend to till I saw in your beady eye that *you* meant to. I thought I'd just as soon be here first.

MARTHA. Bentley says she's out.

MRS. CULVER. Yes. . . . Are you going to wait?

MARTHA. Certainly.

MRS. CULVER. Then I will, too.

MARTHA. That'll be very nice.

MRS. CULVER. Your words are cordial, but your tone is slightly frigid, my dear.

MARTHA. I don't know what you mean by that, mother.

MRS. CULVER. My dear, we've known one another a great many years, haven't we? More than we always find it convenient to mention.

MARTHA. Not at all. I'm thirty-two. I'm not in the least ashamed of my age. Constance is thirty-six.

MRS. CULVER. And yet we still think it worth while to be a trifle disingenuous with one another. Our sex takes a natural pleasure in dissimulation.

MARTHA. I don't think anyone can accuse me of not being frank.

MRS. CULVER. Frankness of course is the pose of the moment. It is often a very effective screen for one's thoughts.

MARTHA. I think you're being faintly disagreeable to me, mother.

MRS. CULVER. I, on the other hand, think you're inclined to be decidedly foolish.

MARTHA. Because I want to tell Constance something she ought to know?

MRS. CULVER. Ah, I *was* right then. And it's to tell her that you've broken an engagement, and left three wretched people to play cut-throat.

MARTHA. It is.

MRS. CULVER. And may I ask why you think Constance ought to know?

MARTHA. Why? Why? Why? That's one of those questions that really don't need answering.

MRS. CULVER. I've always noticed that the questions that really don't need answering are the most difficult to answer.

MARTHA. It isn't at all difficult to answer. She ought to know the truth because it's the truth.

MRS. CULVER. Of course truth is an excellent thing, but before one tells it one should be quite sure that one does so for the advantage of the person who hears it rather than for one's own self-satisfaction.

MARTHA. Mother, Constance is a very unhappy person.

MRS. CULVER. Nonsense. She eats well, sleeps well, dresses well, and she's losing weight. No woman can be unhappy in those circumstances.

MARTHA. Of course if you won't understand it's no use my trying to make you. You're a darling, but you're the most unnatural mother. Your attitude simply amazes me.

[*The door opens and* BENTLEY *ushers in* MRS. FAWCETT. MRS. FAWCETT *is a trim, business-like woman of forty.*]

BENTLEY. Mrs. Fawcett.

MRS. CULVER. Oh, Barbara, how very nice to see you.

BARBARA (*going up to her and kissing her*). Bentley told me you were here and Constance was out. What are you doing?

MRS. CULVER. Bickering.

BARBARA. What about?

MRS. CULVER. Constance.

MARTHA. I'm glad you've come, Barbara. . . . Did you know that John was having an affair with Marie-Louise?

BARBARA. I hate giving a straight answer to a straight question.

MARTHA. I suppose everyone knows but us. How long have you known? They say it's been going on for months. I can't think how it is we've only just heard it.

MRS. CULVER (*ironically*). It speaks very well for human nature that with the masses of dear friends we have it's only today that one of them broke the news to us.

BARBARA. Perhaps the dear friend only heard it this morning.

MARTHA. At first I refused to believe it.

MRS. CULVER. Only quite, quite at first, darling. You surrendered to the evidence with an outraged alacrity that took my breath away.

MARTHA. Of course I put two and two together. After the first shock I understood everything. I'm only astonished that it never occurred to me before.

BARBARA. Are you very much upset, Mrs. Culver?

MRS. CULVER. Not a bit. I was brought up by a very strict mother to believe that men were naturally wicked. I am seldom surprised at what they do and never upset.

MARTHA. Mother has been simply maddening. She treats it as though it didn't matter a row of pins.

MRS. CULVER. Constance and John have been married for fifteen years. John is a very agreeable man. I've sometimes wondered whether he was any more faithful to his wife than most husbands, but as it was really no concern of mine I didn't let my mind dwell on it.

MARTHA. Is Constance your daughter or is she not your daughter?

MRS. CULVER. You certainly have a passion for straight questions, my dear. The answer is yes.

MARTHA. And are you prepared to sit there quietly and let her husband grossly deceive her with her most intimate friend?

MRS. CULVER. So long as she doesn't know I can't see that she's any the worse. Marie-Louise is a nice little thing, silly of course, but that's what men like, and if John is going to deceive Constance it's much better that it should be with someone we all know.

MARTHA (*to* BARBARA). Did you ever hear a respectable woman—and mother is respectable. . . .

MRS. CULVER (*interrupting*). Oh, quite.

MARTHA. Talk like that?

BARBARA. You think that something ought to be done about it?

MARTHA. I am determined that something shall be done about it.

MRS. CULVER. Well, my dear, I'm determined that there's at least one thing you shan't do and that is to tell Constance.

BARBARA (*a trifle startled*). Is that what you want to do?

MARTHA. Somebody ought to tell her. If mother won't I must.

BARBARA. I'm extremely fond of Constance. Of course I've known what was going on for a long time and I've been dreadfully worried.

MARTHA. John has put her into an odious position. No man has the right to humiliate his wife as he has humiliated Constance. He's made her perfectly ridiculous.

MRS. CULVER. If women were ridiculous because their husbands are unfaithful to them, there would surely be a great deal more merriment in the world than there is.

BARBARA (*delighted to have a good gossip*). You know they were lunching together today?

MARTHA. We hadn't heard that. But they were dining together the night before last.

MRS. CULVER (*brightly*). We know what they had to eat for dinner. Do you know what they had to eat for luncheon?

MARTHA. Mother.

MRS. CULVER. Well, I thought she seemed rather uppish about the lunch.

MARTHA. You have no sense of decency, mother.

MRS. CULVER. Oh, my dear, don't talk to me about decency. Decency died with dear Queen Victoria.

BARBARA (*to* MRS. CULVER). But you can't approve of John having an open and flagrant intrigue with Constance's greatest friend.

MRS. CULVER. It may be that with advancing years my arteries have hardened. I am unable to attach any great importance to the philanderings of men. I think it's their nature. John is a very hard-working surgeon. If he likes to lunch and dine with a pretty woman now and then I don't think he's much to blame. It must be very tiresome to have three meals a day with the same woman for seven days a week. I'm a little bored myself at seeing Martha opposite me at the dinner-table. And men can't stand boredom as well as women.

MARTHA. I'm sure I'm very much obliged to you, mother.

BARBARA (*significantly*). But they're not only lunching and dining together.

MRS. CULVER. You fear the worst, my dear?

BARBARA (*with solemnity*). I know the worst.

MRS. CULVER. I always think that's such a comfort. With closed doors and no one listening to us, so long as a man is kind and civil to his wife do you blame him very much if he strays occasionally from the narrow path of virtue?

MARTHA. Do you mean to say that you attach no importance to husbands and wives keeping their marriage vows?

MRS. CULVER. I think wives should.

BARBARA. But that's grossly unfair. Why should *they* any more than men?

MRS. CULVER. Because on the whole they like it. We ascribe a great deal of merit to ourselves because we're faithful to our husbands. I don't believe we deserve it for a minute. We're naturally faithful creatures and we're faithful because we have no particular inclination to be anything else.

BARBARA. I wonder.

MRS. CULVER. My dear, you are a widow and perfectly free. Have you really had any great desire to do anything that the world might say you shouldn't?

BARBARA. I have my business. When you work hard eight hours a day you don't much want to be bothered with love. In the evening the tired business woman wants to go to a musical comedy or play cards. She doesn't want to be worried with adoring males.

MARTHA. By the way, how is your business?

BARBARA. Growing by leaps and bounds. As a matter of fact I came here today to ask Constance if she would like to come in with me.

MRS. CULVER. Why should she? John earns plenty of money.

BARBARA. Well, I thought if things came to a crisis she might like to know that her independence was assured.

MRS. CULVER. Oh, you want them to come to a crisis, too?

BARBARA. No, of course I don't. But, you know, they can't go on like this. It's a miracle that Constance hasn't heard yet. She's bound to find out soon.

MRS. CULVER. I suppose it's inevitable.

MARTHA. I hope she'll find out as quickly as possible. I still think it's mother's duty to tell her.

MRS. CULVER. Which I have no intention of doing.

MARTHA. And if mother won't I think I ought.

MRS. CULVER. Which I have no intention of permitting.

MARTHA. He's humiliated her beyond endurance. Her position is intolerable. I have no words to express my opinion of Marie-Louise, and the first time I see her I shall tell her exactly what I think of her. She's a horrid, ungrateful, mean and contemptible little cat.

BARBARA. Anyhow, I think it would be a comfort to Constance to know that if anything happened she has me to turn to.

MRS. CULVER. But John would make her a handsome allowance. He's a very generous man.

MARTHA (*indignantly*). Do you think Constance would accept it?

BARBARA. Martha's quite right, Mrs. Culver. No woman in those circumstances would take a penny of his money.

MRS. CULVER. That's what she'd say. But she'd take care that her lawyer made the best arrangement he could.

Few men know with what ingenuity we women can combine the disinterested gesture with a practical eye for the main chance.

BARBARA. Aren't you rather cynical, Mrs. Culver?

MRS. CULVER. I hope not. But when women are alone together I don't see why they shouldn't tell the truth now and then. It's a rest from the weary 10 round of pretending to be something that we quite well know we're not.

MARTHA (stiffly). I'm not aware that I've ever pretended to be anything I wasn't.

MRS. CULVER. I dare say not, my dear. But I've always thought you were a little stupid. You take after your poor father. Constance and I have the brains of the family.

[CONSTANCE comes into the room. She is a handsome woman of six and thirty. She has been out and wears a hat.]

BARBARA (eagerly). Constance.

CONSTANCE. I'm so sorry I wasn't in. How nice of you all to wait. How are you, mother darling? (She kisses them one after another.)

MARTHA. What have you been doing all day, Constance?

CONSTANCE. Oh, I've been shopping with Marie-Louise. She's just coming up.

BARBARA (with dismay). Is she here?

CONSTANCE. Yes. She's telephoning.

MARTHA (ironically). You and Marie-Louise are quite inseparable.

CONSTANCE. I like her. She amuses me.

MARTHA. Were you lunching together?

CONSTANCE. No, she was lunching with a beau.

MARTHA (with a glance at MRS. CULVER). Oh, really. (Breezily.) John always comes home to luncheon, doesn't he?

CONSTANCE (with great frankness). When he doesn't have to be at the hospital too early.

MARTHA. Was he lunching with you to-day?

CONSTANCE. No. He was engaged.

MARTHA. Where?

CONSTANCE. Good heavens, I don't know. When you've been married as long as I have you never ask your husband where he's going.

MARTHA. I don't know why not.

10 CONSTANCE (smiling). Because he might take it into his head to ask you.

MRS. CULVER. And also because if you're a wise woman you have confidence in your husband.

CONSTANCE. John has never given me a moment's uneasiness yet.

MARTHA. You're lucky.

CONSTANCE (with her tongue in her cheek). Or wise.

20 [MARIE-LOUISE appears. She is a very pretty little thing, beautifully dressed, of the clinging, large-eyed type.]

MARIE-LOUISE. Oh, I didn't know there was a party.

MRS. CULVER. Martha and I are just going.

CONSTANCE. You know my mother, Marie-Louise.

MARIE-LOUISE. Of course I do.

30 CONSTANCE. She's a very nice mother.

MRS. CULVER. With her head screwed on the right way and very active for her years. (MARIE-LOUISE kisses BARBARA and MARTHA.)

MARIE-LOUISE. How do you do.

MARTHA (looking at her dress). That's new, isn't it, Marie-Louise?

MARIE-LOUISE. Yes, I've never had it on before.

40 MARTHA. Oh, did you put it on because you were lunching with a beau?

MARIE-LOUISE. What makes you think I was lunching with a beau?

MARTHA. Constance told me so.

CONSTANCE. It was only a guess on my part. (To MARIE-LOUISE.) When we

MARTHA. met I noticed that your eyes were shining and you had that pleased, young look a woman always gets when some one has been telling her she's the most adorable thing in the world.

MARTHA. Tell us who it was, Marie-Louise.

CONSTANCE. Do nothing of the kind, Marie-Louise. Keep it a secret and give us something to gossip about.

BARBARA. How is your husband, dear?

MARIE-LOUISE. Oh, he's very well. I've just been telephoning to him.

BARBARA. I never saw anyone adore his wife so obviously as he adores you.

MARIE-LOUISE. Yes, he's sweet, isn't he?

BARBARA. But doesn't it make you a little nervous sometimes? It must be nerve-racking to be obliged to live up to such profound devotion. It would be a dreadful shock if he ever found out that you were not everything he thought you.

CONSTANCE (charmingly). But Marie-Louise is everything he thinks her.

MARIE-LOUISE. And even if I weren't I think it would require more than the evidence of his eyes to persuade him.

CONSTANCE. Listen. There's John. (She goes to the door and calls.) John! John!

JOHN (downstairs). Hulloa.

CONSTANCE. Are you coming up? Marie-Louise is here.

JOHN. Yes, I'm just coming.

CONSTANCE. He's been operating all the afternoon. I expect he's tired out.

MARTHA (with a look at MARIE-LOUISE). I dare say he only had a sandwich for luncheon.

[JOHN comes in. He is a tall, spare man of about forty.]

JOHN. Good Lord, I never saw such a lot of people. How is my mother-in-law?

MRS. CULVER. Mother-in-lawish.

JOHN (kissing her—to BARBARA). You know, I only married Constance because her mother wouldn't have me.

MRS. CULVER. I was too young at the time to marry a boy twenty years younger than myself.

CONSTANCE. It hasn't prevented you from flirting outrageously with the creature ever since. It's lucky I'm not a jealous woman.

JOHN. What have you been doing all day, darling?

CONSTANCE. I've been shopping with Marie-Louise.

JOHN (shaking hands with MARIE-LOUISE). Oh, how do you do? Did you lunch together?

MARTHA. No, she lunched with a beau.

JOHN. I wish it had been me. (To MARIE-LOUISE.) What have you been doing with yourself lately? We haven't seen you for ages.

MARIE-LOUISE. You're never about. Constance and I almost live in one another's pockets.

JOHN. How's that rich husband of yours?

MARIE-LOUISE. I've just been speaking to him. Isn't it a bore, he's got to go down to Birmingham for the night.

CONSTANCE. You'd better come and dine with us.

MARIE-LOUISE. Oh, it's awfully nice of you. But I'm tired out. I shall just go to bed and have an egg.

JOHN. I was just going to tell you, Constance. I shan't be in this evening. I've got an acute appendix to do.

CONSTANCE. Oh, what a nuisance.

MARTHA. You've got a wonderful profession, John. If you ever want to do anything or go anywhere you've only got to say you've got an operation and no one can prove it's a lie.

CONSTANCE. Oh, my dear, you mustn't put suspicions into my innocent head. It would never occur to John to be so deceitful. (To JOHN.) Would it?

JOHN. I think I'd have to go an awful long way before I managed to deceive you, darling.

CONSTANCE (*with a little smile*). Sometimes I think you're right.

MARIE-LOUISE. I do like to see a husband and wife so devoted to one another as you and John. You've been married fifteen years, haven't you?

JOHN. Yes. And it doesn't seem a day too 10 much.

MARIE-LOUISE. Well, I must be running along. I'm late already. Good-bye, darling. Good-bye, Mrs. Culver.

CONSTANCE. Good-bye, darling. We've had such a nice afternoon.

MARIE-LOUISE (*giving her hand to* JOHN). Good-bye.

JOHN. Oh, I'll come downstairs with you.

MARTHA. I was just going, Marie-Louise. 20 I'll come with you.

MARIE-LOUISE (*with presence of mind*). John, I wonder if you'd mind looking at my knee for a minute. It's been rather painful for the last day or two.

JOHN. Of course not. Come into my consulting-room. These knee-caps are troublesome things when you once get them out of order.

MARTHA (*firmly*). I'll wait for you. You 30 won't be long, will you? We might share a taxi.

MARIE-LOUISE. I've got my car.

MARTHA. Oh, how nice! You can give me a lift then.

MARIE-LOUISE. Of course. I shall be delighted.

[JOHN *opens the door for* MARIE-LOUISE. *She goes out and he follows her.* CONSTANCE *has watched this little scene coolly, but* 40 *with an alert mind.*]

MARTHA. What is the matter with her knee?

CONSTANCE. It slips.

MARTHA. What happens then?

CONSTANCE. She slips too.

MARTHA. Are you never jealous of these women who come and see John in his consulting-room?

CONSTANCE. He always has a nurse within call in case they should attempt to take liberties with him.

MARTHA (*amiably*). Is the nurse there now?

CONSTANCE. And anyway I can't help thinking that the sort of woman who wants to be made love to in a consulting-room with a lively odour of antiseptics is the sort of woman who wears horrid undies. I could never bring myself to be jealous of her.

MARTHA. Marie-Louise gave me two of her chemises to copy only the other day.

CONSTANCE. Oh, did she give you the cerise one with the Irish lace insertions? I thought that sweet. I've copied that.

BARBARA. It's true that Marie-Louise is very pretty.

CONSTANCE. Marie-Louise is a darling. But she and John have known each other far too long. John likes her of course, but he says she has no brain.

MARTHA. Men don't always say what they think.

CONSTANCE. Fortunately, or we shouldn't always know what they feel.

MARTHA. Don't you think John has any secrets from you?

CONSTANCE. I'm sure of it. But of course a good wife always pretends not to know the little things her husband wishes to keep hidden from her. That is an elementary rule in matrimonial etiquette.

MARTHA. Don't forget that men were deceivers ever.

CONSTANCE. My dear, you talk like a confirmed spinster. What woman was ever deceived that didn't want to be? Do you really think that men are mysterious? They're children. Why, my dear, John at forty isn't nearly so grown up as Helen at fourteen.

BARBARA. How is your girl, Constance?

CONSTANCE. Oh, she's very well. She loves boarding-school, you know. They're like little boys, men. Sometimes of course they're rather naughty and you have to pretend to be angry with them. They attach so much importance to such entirely unimportant things that it's really touching. And they're so helpless. Have you never nursed a man when he's ill? It wrings your heart. It's just like a dog or a horse. They haven't got the sense to come in out of the rain, poor darlings. They have all the charming qualities that accompany general incompetence. They're sweet and good and silly and tiresome and selfish. You can't help liking them, they're so ingenuous and so simple. They have no complexity or finesse. I think they're sweet, but it's absurd to take them seriously. You're a wise woman, mother. What do you think?

MRS. CULVER. I think you're not in love with your husband.

CONSTANCE. What nonsense.

[JOHN comes in.]

JOHN. Marie-Louise is waiting for you, Martha. I've just put a little bandage round her knee.

CONSTANCE. I hope you weren't rough.

MARTHA (to CONSTANCE). Good-bye, dear. Are you coming, mother?

MRS. CULVER. Not just yet.

MARTHA. Good-bye, Barbara.

[MARTHA and JOHN go out.]

BARBARA. Constance, I've got a suggestion to make to you. You know that my business has been growing by leaps and bounds and I simply cannot get along alone any more. I was wondering if you'd like to come in with me.

CONSTANCE. Oh, my dear, I'm not a business woman.

BARBARA. You've got marvellous taste and you have ideas. You could do all the decorating and I'd confine myself to buying and selling furniture.

CONSTANCE. But I've got no capital.

BARBARA. I've got all the capital I want. I must have help and I know no one more suitable than you. We'd go fifty-fifty and I think I can promise that you'd make a thousand to fifteen hundred a year.

CONSTANCE. I've been an idle woman so long. I think I'd find it dreadfully hard to work eight hours a day.

BARBARA. Won't you think it over? It's very interesting, you know. You're naturally energetic. Don't you get bored with doing nothing all the time?

CONSTANCE. I don't think John would like it. After all, it would look as though he couldn't afford to support me.

BARBARA. Oh, not nowadays, surely. There's no reason why a woman shouldn't have a career just as much as a man.

CONSTANCE. I think my career is looking after John—running a house for him, entertaining his friends and making him happy and comfortable.

BARBARA. Don't you think it rather a mistake to put all your eggs in one basket? Supposing that career failed you?

CONSTANCE. Why should it?

BARBARA. Of course I hope it won't. But men, you know, are fluctuating and various. Independence is a very good thing, and a woman who stands on her own feet financially can look upon the future with a good deal of confidence.

CONSTANCE. It's sweet of you, but so long as John and I are happy together I think I should be a fool to do anything that would vex him.

BARBARA. Of course I'm in no immediate hurry. One never knows what the future will bring forth. I want you to know that if you change your mind the job is open to you. I don't think I shall ever find any one so competent as you. You have only to say the word.

CONSTANCE. Oh, Barbara, you are kind to me. It's a splendid offer and I'm ever so grateful to you. Don't think me horrid if I say I hope I shall never need to accept it.

BARBARA. Of course not. Good-bye, darling.

CONSTANCE. Good-bye, dear.

[*They kiss, and* BARBARA *goes out.* CONSTANCE *rings the bell.*]

MRS. CULVER. Are you quite happy, dear?

CONSTANCE. Oh, quite. Don't I look it?

MRS. CULVER. I'm bound to say you do. So far as I can judge by the look of you I should say you haven't a trouble in the world.

CONSTANCE. You'd be wrong. My cook has given notice and she makes the best meringues I've ever eaten.

MRS. CULVER. I like John.

CONSTANCE. So do I. He has all the solid qualities that make a man a good husband: an agreeable temper, a sense of humour and an entire indifference to petty extravagance.

MRS. CULVER. How right you are, darling, to realize that those are the solid qualities.

CONSTANCE. It's not the seven deadly virtues that make a man a good husband: but the three hundred pleasing amiabilities.

MRS. CULVER. Of course one has to compromise in life. One has to make the best of things. One mustn't expect too much from people. If one wants to be happy in one's own way one must let others be happy in theirs. If one can't get this, that and the other the wise thing is to make up one's mind to do without it. The great thing is not to let vanity warp one's reasonable point of view.

CONSTANCE. Mother, Mother, pull yourself together.

MRS. CULVER. Everybody's so clever nowadays. They see everything but the obvious. I've discovered that I only have to say it quite simply in order to be thought a most original and amusing old lady.

CONSTANCE. Spare me, darling.

MRS. CULVER (*affectionately*). If at any time anything went wrong with you, you would tell your mother, wouldn't you?

CONSTANCE. Of course.

MRS. CULVER. I hate the thought that you might be unhappy and let a foolish pride prevent you from letting me console and advise you.

CONSTANCE (*with feeling*). It wouldn't, Mother dear.

MRS. CULVER. I had rather an odd experience the other day. A little friend of mine came to see me and told me that her husband was neglecting her. I asked her why she told me and not her own mother. She said that her mother had never wanted her to marry and it would mortify her now to have to say that she had made a mistake.

CONSTANCE. Oh, well, John never neglects me, mother.

MRS. CULVER. Of course I gave her a good talking to. She didn't get much sympathy from me.

CONSTANCE (*with a smile*). That was very unkind, wasn't it?

MRS. CULVER. I have my own ideas about

marriage. If a man neglects his wife it's her own fault, and if he's systematically unfaithful to her in nine cases out of ten she only has herself to blame.

CONSTANCE (*ringing the bell*). Systematically is a grim word.

MRS. CULVER. No sensible woman attaches importance to an occasional slip. Time and chance are responsible for that.

CONSTANCE. And shall we say, masculine vanity?

MRS. CULVER. I told my little friend that if her husband was unfaithful to her it was because he found other women more attractive. Why should she be angry with him for that? Her business was to be more attractive than they.

CONSTANCE. You are not what they call a feminist, mother, are you?

MRS. CULVER. After all, what is fidelity?

CONSTANCE. Mother, do you mind if I open the window?

MRS. CULVER. It is open.

CONSTANCE. In that case do you mind if I shut it? I feel that when a woman of your age asks such a question I should make some sort of symbolic gesture.

MRS. CULVER. Don't be ridiculous. Of course I believe in fidelity for women. I suppose no one has ever questioned the desirability of that. But men are different. Women should remember that they have their homes and their name and position and their family, and they should learn to close their eyes when it's possible they may see something they are not meant to.

[*The* BUTLER *comes in.*]

BENTLEY. Did you ring, madam?

CONSTANCE. Yes. I am expecting Mr. Bernard Kersal. I'm not at home to anybody else.

BENTLEY. Very good, madam.

CONSTANCE. Is Mr. Middleton in?

BENTLEY. Yes, madam. He's in the consulting-room.

CONSTANCE. Very well.

[*The* BUTLER *goes out.*]

MRS. CULVER. Is that a polite way of telling me that I had better take myself off?

CONSTANCE. Of course not. On the contrary I particularly want you to stay.

MRS. CULVER. Who is this mysterious gentleman?

CONSTANCE. Mother. Bernard.

MRS. CULVER. That says nothing to me at all. Not Saint Bernard, darling?

CONSTANCE. Pull yourself together, my pet. You must remember Bernard Kersal. He proposed to me.

MRS. CULVER. Oh, my dear, you cannot expect me to remember the names of all the young men who proposed to you.

CONSTANCE. Yes, but he proposed more than any of the others.

MRS. CULVER. Why?

CONSTANCE. I suppose because I refused him. I can't think of any other reason.

MRS. CULVER. He made no impression on me.

CONSTANCE. I don't suppose he tried to.

MRS. CULVER. What did he look like?

CONSTANCE. He was tall.

MRS. CULVER. They were all tall.

CONSTANCE. He had brown hair and brown eyes.

MRS. CULVER. They all had brown hair and brown eyes.

CONSTANCE. He danced divinely.

MRS. CULVER. They all danced divinely.

CONSTANCE. I very nearly married him, you know.

MRS. CULVER. Why didn't you?

CONSTANCE. I think he was a trifle too much inclined to lie down on the floor and let me walk over him.

MRS. CULVER. In short he had no sense of humour.

CONSTANCE. I was quite certain that he loved me, and I was never absolutely sure that John did.

MRS. CULVER. Well, you're sure now, dear, aren't you?

CONSTANCE. Oh, yes. John adores me.

MRS. CULVER. And what's this young man coming for today?

CONSTANCE. He's not such a very young man any more. He was twenty-nine then and so he must be nearly forty-five now.

MRS. CULVER. He isn't still in love with you?

CONSTANCE. I shouldn't think so. Do you think it possible after fifteen years? It's surely very unlikely. Don't look at me like that, mother. I don't like it.

MRS. CULVER. Don't talk stuff and nonsense to me, child. Of course you know if he's in love with you or not.

CONSTANCE. But I haven't seen him since I married John. You see he lives in Japan. He's a merchant or something in Kobe. He was here during the war on leave. But that was when I was so dreadfully ill and I didn't see him.

MRS. CULVER. Oh! Why's he here now then? Have you been corresponding with him?

CONSTANCE. No. One can't write letters to any one one never sees for fifteen years. He always sends me flowers on my birthday.

MRS. CULVER. That's rather sweet of him.

CONSTANCE. And the other day I had a letter from him saying he was in England and would like to see me. So I asked him to come today.

MRS. CULVER. I wondered why you were so smart.

CONSTANCE. Of course he may be terribly changed. Men go off so dreadfully, don't they? He may be bald and fat now.

MRS. CULVER. He may be married.

CONSTANCE. Oh, if he were I don't think he'd want to come and see me, would he?

MRS. CULVER. I see you're under the impression that he's still in love with you.

CONSTANCE. Oh, I'm not.

MRS. CULVER. Then why are you so nervous?

CONSTANCE. It's only natural that I shouldn't want him to think me old and haggard. He adored me, mother. I suppose he still thinks of me as I was then. It wouldn't be very nice if his face fell about a yard and a half when he came into the room.

MRS. CULVER. I think I'd much better leave you to face the ordeal alone.

CONSTANCE. Oh, no, mother, you must stay. I particularly want you. You see, he may be awful and I may wish I'd never seen him again. It 'll be so much easier if you're here. I may not want to be alone with him at all.

MRS. CULVER. Oh.

CONSTANCE (*with a twinkle in her eye*). On the other hand I may.

MRS. CULVER. It seems to me you're putting me in a slightly embarrassing situation.

CONSTANCE. Now listen. If I think he's awful we'll just talk about the weather and the crops for a few minutes and then we'll have an ominous pause and stare at him. That always makes a man feel a perfect fool and the moment a man feels a fool he gets up and goes.

MRS. CULVER. Sometimes they don't know how to, poor dears, and the earth will never open and swallow them up.

CONSTANCE. On the other hand if I think he looks rather nice I shall just take out my handkerchief and carelessly place it on the piano.

MRS. CULVER. Why?

CONSTANCE. Darling, in order that you may rise to your aged feet and say, well, you really must be running along.

MRS. CULVER. Yes, I know that, but why should you carelessly place your handkerchief on the piano?

CONSTANCE. Because I am a creature of impulse. I shall have an impulse to place my handkerchief on the piano.

MRS. CULVER. Oh, very well. But I always mistrust impulses.

[BENTLEY *enters and announces* BERNARD KERSAL. *He is a tall good-looking man, sunburned and of healthy appearance. He is evidently very fit and he carries his forty-five years well.*]

BENTLEY. Mr. Kersal.

CONSTANCE. How do you do? Do you remember my mother?

BERNARD (*shaking hands with her*). I'm sure she doesn't remember me.

[CONSTANCE *takes a small handkerchief out of her bag.*]

MRS. CULVER. That is the soft answer that turneth away wrath.

CONSTANCE. It's rather late for tea, isn't it? Would you like a drink? (*As she says this she goes towards the bell and places her handkerchief on the piano.*)

BERNARD. No, thanks. I've just this moment had one.

CONSTANCE. To brace you for seeing me?

BERNARD. I was nervous.

CONSTANCE. Have I changed as much as you expected?

BERNARD. Oh, that's not what I was nervous about.

MRS. CULVER. Is it really fifteen years since you saw Constance?

BERNARD. Yes. I didn't see her when I was last in England. When I got demobbed I had to go out to Japan again and get my business together. I haven't had a chance to come home before.

[CONSTANCE *has been giving her mother significant looks, but her mother does not notice them.* CONSTANCE *takes a second handkerchief out of her bag and when the opportunity arises places it neatly on the piano beside the first one.*]

MRS. CULVER. And are you home for long?

BERNARD. A year.

MRS. CULVER. Have you brought your wife with you?

BERNARD. I'm not married.

MRS. CULVER. Oh, Constance said you were married to a Japanese lady.

CONSTANCE. Nonsense, mother. I never said anything of the sort.

MRS. CULVER. Oh, perhaps I was thinking of Julia Linton. She married an Egyptian pasha. I believe she's very happy. At all events he hasn't killed her yet.

BERNARD. How is your husband?

CONSTANCE. He's very well. I dare say he'll be in presently.

BERNARD. Haven't you got a little sister? I suppose she's out now?

MRS. CULVER. He means Martha. She's come out and gone in again.

CONSTANCE. She was not so very much younger than me, you know. She's thirty-two now. (MRS. CULVER *has taken no notice of the handkerchiefs and in desperation* CONSTANCE *takes a third from her bag and places it beside the other two.*)

MRS. CULVER. Do you like the East, Mr. Kersal?

BERNARD. One has a pretty good time there, you know.

[*Now* MRS. CULVER *catches sight of the three handkerchiefs and starts.*]

MRS. CULVER. I wonder what the time is.

CONSTANCE. It's late, Mother. Are you dining out tonight? I suppose you want to have a lie-down before you dress for dinner.

MRS. CULVER. I hope I shall see you again, Mr. Kersal.

BERNARD. Thank you very much.

[CONSTANCE *accompanies her to the door.*]

MRS. CULVER. Good-bye, darling. (*In a whisper.*) I couldn't remember if the handkerchiefs meant go or stay.

CONSTANCE. You had only to use your eyes. You can see at a glance that he is the kind of man one would naturally 10 want to have a heart-to-heart talk with after fifteen years.

MRS. CULVER. You only confused me by putting more and more handkerchiefs on the piano.

CONSTANCE. For goodness' sake go, Mother. (*Aloud.*) Good-bye, my sweet. I'm sorry you've got to run away so soon.

MRS. CULVER. Good-bye. (*She goes out 20 and* CONSTANCE *comes back into the room.*)

CONSTANCE. Did you think it very rude of us to whisper? Mother has a passion for secrets.

BERNARD. Of course not.

CONSTANCE. Now let's sit down and make ourselves comfortable. Let me look at you. You haven't changed much. You're a little thinner and perhaps a little more lined. Men are so 30 lucky, if they have any character they grow better-looking as they grow older. Do you know I'm thirty-six now?

BERNARD. What does that matter?

CONSTANCE. Shall I tell you something? When you wrote and suggested coming here I was delighted at the thought of seeing you again and wrote at once making a date. And then I was panic-stricken. I would have 40 given almost anything not to have sent that letter. And all today I've had such a horrible feeling at the pit of my stomach. Didn't you see my knees wobble when you came into the room?

BERNARD. In God's name, why?

CONSTANCE. Oh, my dear, I think you must be a little stupid. I should be a perfect fool if I didn't know that when I was a girl I was very pretty. It's rather a pang when you are forced to the conclusion that you're not quite so pretty as you were. People don't tell one. One tries to hide it from oneself. Anyhow I thought I'd rather know the worst. That's one of the reasons I asked you to come.

BERNARD. Whatever I thought you can hardly imagine that I should be deliberately rude.

CONSTANCE. Of course not. But I watched your face. I was afraid I'd see there: By God, how she's gone off.

BERNARD. And did you?

CONSTANCE. You were rather shy when you came in. You weren't thinking of me.

BERNARD. It's quite true, fifteen years ago you were a pretty girl. Now you're lovely. You're ten times more beautiful than you were then.

CONSTANCE. It's nice of you to say so.

BERNARD. Don't you believe it?

CONSTANCE. I think you do. And I confess that's sufficiently gratifying. Now tell me, why aren't you married? It's time you did, you know, or it 'll be too late. You'll have a very lonely old age if you don't.

BERNARD. I never wanted to marry anyone but you.

CONSTANCE. Oh, come, you're not going to tell me that you've never been in love since you were in love with me?

BERNARD. No, I've been in love half a dozen times, but when it came to the point I found I still loved you best.

CONSTANCE. I like you for saying that. I shouldn't have believed it if you'd said you'd never loved anybody else and I should have been vexed with you for thinking me such a fool as to believe it.

BERNARD. You see, it was you I loved in the others. One because she had hair like yours and another because her smile reminded me of your smile.

CONSTANCE. I hate to think that I've made you unhappy.

BERNARD. But you haven't. I've had a very good time; I've enjoyed my 10 work; I've made a bit of money and I've had a lot of fun. I don't blame you for having married John instead of me.

CONSTANCE. Do you remember John?

BERNARD. Of course I do. He was a very nice fellow. I dare say he's made you a better husband than I should have. I've had my ups and downs. I'm very irritable sometimes. John's been able 20 to give you everything you wanted. You were much safer with him. By the way, I suppose I can still call you Constance.

CONSTANCE. Of course. Why not? Do you know, I think you have a very nice nature, Bernard.

BERNARD. Are you happy with John?

CONSTANCE. Oh, very. I don't say that he has never given me a moment's 30 uneasiness. He did once, but I took hold of myself and saw that I mustn't be silly. I'm very glad I did. I think I can quite honestly say that ours has been a very happy and successful marriage.

BERNARD. I'm awfully glad to hear that. Do you think it's cheek to ask if John loves you?

CONSTANCE. I'm sure he loves me.   40

BERNARD. And do you love him?

CONSTANCE. Very much.

BERNARD. May I make you a short speech?

CONSTANCE. If I may interrupt at suitable moments.

BERNARD. I hope you're going to let me see a great deal of you during this year I've got at home.

CONSTANCE. I want to see a great deal of you.

BERNARD. There's just one thing I want to get off my chest and then I needn't refer to it again. I am just as madly in love with you as I was when I asked you to marry me fifteen years ago. I think I shall remain in love with you all my life. I'm too old a dog to learn new tricks. But I want you to know that you needn't have the smallest fear that I shall make a nuisance of myself. I should think it an awfully caddish thing to try to come between you and John. I suppose we all want to be happy, but I don't believe the best way of being that is to try to upset other people's happiness.

CONSTANCE. That's not such a very long speech after all. At a public dinner they would hardly even call it a few remarks.

BERNARD. All I ask for is your friendship and if in return I care to give you my love I don't see that it's any one's business but my own.

CONSTANCE. I don't think it is. I think 30 I can be a very good friend, Bernard.

[*The door opens and* JOHN *comes in.*]

JOHN. Oh, I'm sorry. I didn't know you were engaged.

CONSTANCE. I'm not. Come in. This is Bernard Kersal.

JOHN. How do you do?

BERNARD. I'm afraid you don't remember me.

JOHN. If you ask me point-blank I think it's safer to confess I don't.

CONSTANCE. Don't be so silly, John. He used to come to mother's.

JOHN. Before we were married, d'you mean?

CONSTANCE. Yes. You spent several week-ends with us together.

JOHN. My dear, that was fifteen years ago. I'm awfully sorry not to remember you, but I'm delighted to see you now.

CONSTANCE. He's just come back from Japan.

JOHN. Oh, well, I hope we shall see you again. I'm just going along to the club 10 to have a rubber before dinner, darling. (*To* BERNARD.) Why don't you dine here with Constance? I've got an acute appendix and she'll be all alone, poor darling.

BERNARD. Oh, that's awfully kind of you.

CONSTANCE. It would be a friendly act. Are you free?

BERNARD. Always to do a friendly act.

CONSTANCE. Very well. I shall expect you at eight-fifteen.

ACT II

The scene is the same. A fortnight has passed.

MARTHA in walking costume and a hat is looking at an illustrated paper.

BENTLEY comes in.

BENTLEY. Mr. Kersal is here, Miss.

MARTHA. Oh! Ask him if he won't come up.

BENTLEY. Very good, Miss. (*He goes out and in a moment comes in again to announce* BERNARD, *and then goes.*) Mr. Kersal.

MARTHA. Constance is dressing. She won't be very long.

BERNARD. Oh, I see. Well, there's no violent hurry.

MARTHA. You're taking her to Ranelagh, aren't you?

BERNARD. That was the idea. I know some of the fellows who are playing today.

MARTHA. Are you having a good time in London?

BERNARD. Marvellous. When a man's lived in the East as long as I have, he's apt to feel rather out of it when he comes home. But Constance and John have been ripping to me.

MARTHA. Do you like John?

BERNARD. Yes. He's been awfully kind.

MARTHA. Do you know, I remember you quite well.

BERNARD. Oh, you can't. You were a kid when I used to come down and stay with your mother.

MARTHA. I was sixteen. Do you imagine I wasn't thrilled to the marrow by Constance's young men?

20 BERNARD. There were a good many of them. I should have thought your marrow got callous.

MARTHA. But you were one of the serious ones. I always thought you terribly romantic.

BERNARD. I was terribly romantic. I think it's becoming in the young.

MARTHA. I don't think it's unbecoming in the not quite as young.

30 BERNARD. Don't think I'm romantic now. I make a considerable income and I'm putting on weight. The price of silk has ousted love's young dream in my manly bosom.

MARTHA. You're an unconscionable liar.

BERNARD. To which I can only retort that you're excessively rude.

MARTHA. You were madly in love with Constance in those days, weren't 40 you?

BERNARD. You know, it's so long ago I forget.

MARTHA. I advised her to marry you rather than John.

BERNARD. Why?

MARTHA. Well, for one thing you lived in Japan. I would have married any one who would take me there.

BERNARD. I live there still.

MARTHA. Oh, I don't want to marry you.

BERNARD. I couldn't help suspecting that.

MARTHA. I could never really quite understand what she saw in John.

BERNARD. I suppose she loved him.

MARTHA. I wonder if she ever regrets that she married John rather than you.

BERNARD. Well, don't. She's perfectly satisfied with John and wouldn't change him for anything in the world.

MARTHA. It's exasperating, isn't it?

BERNARD. I don't think so. It must make it much more comfortable for a husband and wife to be content with one another.

MARTHA. You're in love with her still, aren't you?

BERNARD. Not a bit.

MARTHA. Upon my soul, you've got a nerve. Why, you donkey, you're giving it away all the time. Do you know what you look like when she's in the room? Have you any idea how your eyes change when they rest on her? When you speak her name it sounds as though you were kissing it.

BERNARD. I thought you were an odious child when you were sixteen, Martha, and now that you're thirty-two I think you're a horrible woman.

MARTHA. I'm not really. But I'm very fond of Constance and I'm inclined to be rather fond of you.

BERNARD. Don't you think you could show your attachment by minding your own business?

MARTHA. Why does it make you angry because I've told you that no one can see you with Constance for five minutes without knowing that you adore her?

BERNARD. My dear, I'm here for one year. I want to be happy. I don't want to give trouble or cause trouble. I value my friendship with Constance and I hate the idea that anything should interfere with it.

MARTHA. Hasn't it occurred to you that she may want more than your friendship?

BERNARD. No, it has not.

MARTHA. You need not jump down my throat.

BERNARD. Constance is perfectly happy with her husband. You must think me a damned swine if you think I'm going to butt in and try to smash up a perfectly wonderful union.

MARTHA. But, you poor fool, don't you know that John has been notoriously unfaithful to Constance for ages?

BERNARD. I don't believe it.

MARTHA. Ask any one you like. Mother knows it. Barbara Fawcett knows it. Every one knows it but Constance.

BERNARD. That certainly isn't true. Mrs. Durham told me when I met her at dinner two or three days ago that John and Constance were the most devoted couple she'd ever known.

MARTHA. Did Marie-Louise tell you that?

BERNARD. She did.

[MARTHA begins to laugh. She can hardly restrain herself.]

MARTHA. The nerve. Marie-Louise. Oh, my poor Bernard. Marie-Louise is John's mistress.

BERNARD. Marie-Louise is Constance's greatest friend.

MARTHA. Yes.

BERNARD. If this is a pack of lies I swear I'll damned well wring your neck.

MARTHA. All right.

BERNARD. That was a silly thing to say. I'm sorry.

MARTHA. Oh, I don't mind. I like a man to be violent. I think you're just the sort of man Constance needs.

BERNARD. What the devil do you mean by that?

MARTHA. It can't go on. Constance is being made perfectly ridiculous. Her position is monstrous. I thought she ought to be told and as every one else seemed to shirk the job I was prepared to do it myself. My mother was so disagreeable about it, I've had to promise not to say a word.

BERNARD. You're not under the delusion that I'm going to tell her?

MARTHA. No, I don't really think it would come very well from you. But things can't go on. She's bound to find out. All I want you to do is to . . . well, stand by.

BERNARD. But Marie-Louise has got a husband. What about him?

MARTHA. His only ambition in life is to make a million. He's the sort of fool who thinks a woman loves him just because he loves her. Marie-Louise can turn him round her little finger.

BERNARD. Has Constance never suspected?

MARTHA. Never. You've only got to look at her. Really, her self-confidence sometimes is positively maddening.

BERNARD. I wonder if it wouldn't be better that she never did find out. She's so happy. She's entirely carefree. You've only got to look at that open brow and those frank, trustful eyes.

MARTHA. I thought you loved her.

BERNARD. Enough to want her happiness above all things.

MARTHA. You *are* forty-five, aren't you? I forgot that for a moment.

BERNARD. Dear Martha. You have such an attractive way of putting things.

[CONSTANCE'S *voice on the stairs is heard calling:* "Bentley, Bentley."]

MARTHA. Oh, there's Constance. I can't imagine where mother is. I think I'll go into the brown room and write a letter.

[*Bernard takes no notice of what she says nor does he make any movement when she goes out. A moment later* CONSTANCE *comes in.*]

CONSTANCE. Have I kept you waiting?

BERNARD. It doesn't matter.

CONSTANCE. Hulloa! What's up?

BERNARD. With me? Nothing. Why?

CONSTANCE. You look all funny. Why are your eyes suddenly opaque?

BERNARD. I didn't know they were.

CONSTANCE. Are you trying to hide something from me?

BERNARD. Of course not.

CONSTANCE. Have you had bad news from Japan?

BERNARD. No. Far from it. Silk is booming.

CONSTANCE. Then you're going to tell me that you've just got engaged to a village maiden.

BERNARD. No, I'm not.

CONSTANCE. I hate people who keep secrets from me.

BERNARD. I have no secrets from you.

CONSTANCE. Do you think I don't know your face by now?

BERNARD. You'll make me vain. I would never have ventured to think that you took the trouble to look twice at my ugly face.

CONSTANCE (*with sudden suspicion*). Wasn't Martha here when you came? She hasn't gone, has she?

BERNARD. She's waiting for her mother. She's gone into another room to write letters.

CONSTANCE. Did you see her?

BERNARD (*trying to be very casual*). Yes.

We had a little chat about the weather.

CONSTANCE (*immediately grasping what has happened*). Oh——Don't you think we ought to be starting?

BERNARD. There's plenty of time. It's no good getting there too early.

CONSTANCE. Then I'll take off my hat.

BERNARD. And it's jolly here, isn't it? I love your room.

CONSTANCE. Do you think it's a success? I did it myself. Barbara Fawcett wants me to go into the decorating business. She's in it, you know, and she's making quite a lot of money.

BERNARD (*smiling to hide his anxiety in asking the question*). Aren't you happy at home?

CONSTANCE (*breezily*). I don't think it necessarily means one's unhappy at 20 home because one wants an occupation. One may very easily grow tired of going to parties all the time. But as a matter of fact I refused Barbara's offer.

BERNARD (*insisting*). You are happy, aren't you?

CONSTANCE. Very.

BERNARD. You've made *me* very happy during this last fortnight. I feel as 30 though I'd never been away. You've been awfully kind to me.

CONSTANCE. I'm very glad you think so. I don't know that I've done anything very much for you.

BERNARD. Yes, you have. You've let me see you.

CONSTANCE. I let the policeman at the corner do that, you know.

BERNARD. You mustn't think that be- 40 cause I take care only to talk to you of quite casual things I don't still love you with all my heart.

CONSTANCE (*quite coolly*). We agreed when first you came back that your feelings were entirely your business.

BERNARD. Do you mind my loving you?

CONSTANCE. Oughtn't we all to love one another?

BERNARD. Don't tease me.

CONSTANCE. My dear, I can't help being pleased and flattered and rather touched. It is rather wonderful that any one should care for me. . . .

BERNARD (*interrupting*). So much?

CONSTANCE. After so many years.

BERNARD. If any one had asked me fifteen years ago if I could love you more than I loved you then I should have said it was impossible. I love you ten times more than I ever loved you before.

CONSTANCE (*going on with her own speech*). But I don't in the least want you to make love to me now.

BERNARD. I know. I'm not going to. I know you far too well.

CONSTANCE (*amused and a trifle taken aback*). I don't quite know what you've been doing for the last five minutes.

BERNARD. I was merely stating a few plain facts.

CONSTANCE. Oh, I beg your pardon. I thought it was something quite different. I'm afraid you might mistake my meaning if I said I'm quite curious to see how you *do* make love.

BERNARD (*good-humouredly*). I have a notion that you're laughing at me.

CONSTANCE. In the hope of teaching you to laugh at yourself.

BERNARD. I've been very good during the last fortnight, haven't I?

CONSTANCE. Yes, I kept on saying to myself: I wonder if a pat of butter really would melt in his mouth.

BERNARD. Well, for just a minute I'm going to let myself go.

CONSTANCE. I wouldn't if I were you.

BERNARD. Yes, but you're not. I want to tell you just once that I worship the ground you tread on. There's never been any one in the world for me but you.

CONSTANCE. Oh, nonsense. There have been half a dozen. We are seven.

BERNARD. They were all you. I love you with all my heart. I admire you more than any woman I've ever met. I respect you. I'm an awful fool when it comes to the point. I don't know how to say all I've got in my heart without feeling like a perfect ass. I love you. I want you to know that if ever you're in trouble I should look upon it as the greatest possible happiness to be allowed to help you.

CONSTANCE. That's very kind of you. I don't see why I should be in any trouble.

BERNARD. Always and in all circumstances you can count on me absolutely. I will do anything in the world for you. If ever you want me you have only to give me a sign. I should be proud and happy to give my life for you.

CONSTANCE. It's sweet of you to say so.

BERNARD. Don't you believe it?

CONSTANCE (*with a charming smile*). Yes.

BERNARD. I should like to think that it meant—oh, not very much, but just a little to you.

CONSTANCE (*almost shaken*). It means a great deal. I thank you.

BERNARD. Now we won't say anything more about it.

CONSTANCE (*recovering her accustomed coolness*). But why did you think it necessary to say all this just now?

BERNARD. I wanted to get it off my chest.

CONSTANCE. Oh, really.

BERNARD. You're not angry with me?

CONSTANCE. Oh, Bernard, I'm not that kind of a fool at all. . . . It's a pity that Martha doesn't marry.

BERNARD. Don't think that I'm going to marry her.

CONSTANCE. I don't. I merely thought that a husband would be a pleasant and useful occupation for her. She's quite a nice girl, you know. A liar, of course, but otherwise all right.

BERNARD. Oh?

CONSTANCE. Yes, a terrible liar, even for a woman. . . . Shall we start now? It's no good getting there when the polo is over.

BERNARD. All right. Let's start.

CONSTANCE. I'll put my hat on again. By the way, you haven't had a taxi waiting all this time, have you?

BERNARD. No, I've got a car. I thought I'd like to drive you down myself.

CONSTANCE. Open or shut?

BERNARD. Open.

CONSTANCE. Oh, my dear, then I must get another hat. A broad brim like this is such a bore in an open car.

BERNARD. Oh, I am sorry.

CONSTANCE. It doesn't matter a bit. I shall only be a minute. And why on earth shouldn't one be comfortable if one can?

[*She goes out. In a moment* BENTLEY *shows in* MARIE-LOUISE.]

MARIE-LOUISE. Oh, how do you do. (*To* BENTLEY.) Will you tell Mr. Middleton at once?

BENTLEY. Yes, madam. (*Exit* BENTLEY.)

MARIE-LOUISE (*rather flustered*). I particularly wanted to see John for a minute and there are patients waiting to see him, so I asked Bentley if he couldn't come here.

BERNARD. I'll take myself off.

MARIE-LOUISE. I'm awfully sorry, but it's rather urgent. John hates to be disturbed like this.

BERNARD. I'll go into the next room.

MARIE-LOUISE. Are you waiting for Constance?

BERNARD. Yes, I'm taking her to Ranelagh. She's changing her hat.

MARIE-LOUISE. I see. Bentley told me she
was upstairs. Good-bye. I shall only
be a minute. (BERNARD *goes into the
adjoining room just as* JOHN *comes in.*) Oh,
John, I'm sorry to drag you away
from your patients.

JOHN. There's nothing urgent. They can
wait for a few minutes. (BERNARD *has* 10
closed the door behind him, and JOHN's *tone
changes. They speak now in a low voice and
quickly.*) Is anything the matter?

MARIE-LOUISE. Mortimer.

JOHN. What about Mortimer?

MARIE-LOUISE. I'm convinced he suspects.

JOHN. Why?

MARIE-LOUISE. He was so funny last
night. He came into my room to say 20
good-night to me. He sat on my bed.
He was chatting nicely and he was
asking what I'd been doing with myself all the evening. . . .

JOHN. Presumably you didn't tell him.

MARIE-LOUISE. No, I said I'd been dining
here. And suddenly he got up and just
said good-night and went out. His
voice was so strange that I couldn't
help looking at him. He was as red as 30
a turkey cock.

JOHN. Is that all?

MARIE-LOUISE. He never came in to say
good-morning to me before he went
to the City.

JOHN. He may have been in a hurry.

MARIE-LOUISE. He's never in too much of
a hurry for that.

JOHN. I think you're making a mountain
of a mole heap. 40

MARIE-LOUISE. Don't be stupid, John.
Can't you see I'm as nervous as a cat?

JOHN. I can. But I'm trying to persuade
you there's nothing to be nervous
about.

MARIE-LOUISE. What fools men are. They
never will see that it's the small things
that matter. I tell you I'm frightened
out of my wits.

JOHN. You know there's a devil of a distance between suspicion and proof.

MARIE-LOUISE. Oh, I don't think he
could prove anything. But he can
make himself awfully unpleasant.
Supposing he put ideas in Constance's
head?

JOHN. She'd never believe him.

MARIE-LOUISE. If the worst came to worst
I could manage Mortimer. He's awfully in love with me. That always
gives one such an advantage over a
man.

JOHN. Of course you can twist Mortimer
round your little finger.

MARIE-LOUISE. I should die of shame if
Constance knew. After all, she's my
greatest friend and I'm absolutely devoted to her.

JOHN. Constance is a peach. Of course I
don't believe there's anything in this
at all, but if there were, I'd be in favour of making a clean breast of it to
Constance.

MARIE-LOUISE. Never!

JOHN. I expect she'd kick up a row. Any
woman would. But she'd do anything
in the world to help us out.

MARIE-LOUISE. A lot you know about
women. She'd help you out, I dare
say. But she'd stamp on me with both
feet. That's only human nature.

JOHN. Not Constance's.

MARIE-LOUISE. Upon my word, it's lucky
I'm fairly sure of you, John, or the
way you talk of Constance would
really make me jealous.

JOHN. Thank God you can smile. You're
getting your nerve back.

MARIE-LOUISE. It's been a comfort to talk
it over. It doesn't seem so bad now.

JOHN. I'm sure you've got nothing to be
frightened about.

MARIE-LOUISE. I dare say it was only my fancy. It was a stupid risk to take all the same.

JOHN. Perhaps. Why did you look so devilish pretty?

MARIE-LOUISE. Oughtn't you to be getting back to your wretched patients?

JOHN. I suppose so. Will you stop and see Constance?

MARIE-LOUISE. I may as well. It would look rather odd if I went away without saying how d'you do to her.

JOHN (*going*). I'll leave you then. And don't worry.

MARIE-LOUISE. I won't. I dare say it was only a guilty conscience. I'll go and have my hair washed.

[*As* JOHN *is about to go,* MARTHA *comes in followed by* BERNARD.]

MARTHA (*with an almost exaggerated cordiality*). I had no idea you were here, Marie-Louise.

MARIE-LOUISE. It's not very important.

MARTHA. I was just writing letters, waiting for mother, and Bernard's only just told me.

MARIE-LOUISE. I wanted to see John about something.

MARTHA. I hope you haven't got anything the matter with you, darling.

MARIE-LOUISE. No. Mortimer's been looking rather run-down lately and I want John to persuade him to take a holiday.

MARTHA. Oh, I should have thought he'd be more likely to take a physician's advice than a surgeon's in a thing like that.

MARIE-LOUISE. He's got a tremendous belief in John, you know.

MARTHA. In which I'm sure he's justified. John is so very reliable.

JOHN. What can I do for you, Martha? If you'd like me to cut out an appendix or a few tonsils I shall be happy to oblige you.

MARTHA. My dear John, you've only left me the barest necessities of existence as it is. I don't think I could manage with anything less than I have.

JOHN. My dear, as long as a woman has a leg to stand on she need not despair of exciting her surgeon's sympathy and interest.

[CONSTANCE *comes in with* MRS. CULVER.]

MARIE-LOUISE (*kissing her*). Darling.

CONSTANCE. How is your knee, still slipping?

MARIE-LOUISE. It always gives me more or less trouble, you know.

CONSTANCE. Yes, of course. I think you're very patient. In your place I should be furious with John. Of course I would never dream of consulting him if I had anything the matter with me.

MRS. CULVER. I'm sorry I've been so long, Martha. Have you been very impatient?

MARTHA. No, I've been passing the time very pleasantly.

MRS. CULVER. For others, darling, or only for yourself?

CONSTANCE. I met mother on the stairs and she came up with me while I changed my hat. Bernard is taking me down to Ranelagh.

JOHN. Oh, that 'll be jolly.

BERNARD. We shall be dreadfully late.

CONSTANCE. Does it matter?

BERNARD. No.

[Bently comes in with a card on a small *salver and takes it to* CONSTANCE. *She looks at the card and hesitates.*]

CONSTANCE. How very odd.

JOHN. What's the matter, Constance?

CONSTANCE. Nothing. (*For an instant she reflects.*) Is he downstairs?

BENTLEY. Yes, madam.

CONSTANCE. I don't know why he should send up a card. Show him up.

BENTLEY. Very good, madam. (*Exit* BENTLEY.)

JOHN. Who is it, Constance?

CONSTANCE. Come and sit down, Marie-Louise.

MARIE-LOUISE. I must go and so must you.

CONSTANCE. There's plenty of time. Do you like this hat?

MARIE-LOUISE. Yes. I think it's sweet.

CONSTANCE. What are *you* doing here, John? Haven't you got any patients today?

JOHN. Yes, there are two or three waiting. I'm just going down. As a matter of fact I thought I deserved a cigarette. (*He puts his hand to his hip pocket.*) Hang, I've mislaid my cigarette-case. You haven't seen it about, Constance?

CONSTANCE. No, I haven't.

JOHN. I looked for it everywhere this morning. I can't think where I left it. I must ring up the nursing-home and ask if I left it there.

CONSTANCE. I hope you haven't lost it.

JOHN. Oh, no. I'm sure I haven't. I've just put it somewhere.

[*The door opens and* BENTLEY *announces the visitor.*]

BENTLEY. Mr. Mortimer Durham.

MARIE-LOUISE (*startled out of her wits*). Oh!

CONSTANCE (*quickly, seizing her wrist*). Sit still, you fool

[MORTIMER DURHAM *comes in. He is a stoutish biggish man of about forty, with a red face and an irascible manner. At the moment he is a prey to violent emotion.* BENTLEY *goes out.*]

CONSTANCE. Hulloa, Mortimer. What are you doing in these parts at this hour? Why on earth did you send up a card?

[*He stops and looks around.*]

MARIE-LOUISE. What is the matter, Mortimer?

MORTIMER (*to* CONSTANCE, *with difficulty restraining his fury*). I thought you might like to know that your husband is my wife's lover.

MARIE-LOUISE. Morty!

CONSTANCE (*keeping a firm hand on* MARIE-LOUISE *and very coolly to* MORTIMER). Oh? What makes you think that?

MORTIMER (*taking a gold cigarette-case out of his pocket*). Do you recognize this? I found it under my wife's pillow last night.

CONSTANCE. Oh, I am relieved. I couldn't make out where I'd left it. (*Taking it from him.*) Thank you so much.

MORTIMER (*angrily*). It's not yours.

CONSTANCE. Indeed it is. I was sitting on Marie-Louise's bed and I must have slipped it under the pillow without thinking.

MORTIMER. It has John's initials on it.

CONSTANCE. I know. It was presented to him by a grateful patient and I thought it much too nice for him, so I just took it.

MORTIMER. What sort of fool do you take me for, Constance?

CONSTANCE. My dear Morty, why should I say it was my cigarette-case if it wasn't?

MORTIMER. They had dinner together.

CONSTANCE. My poor Morty, I know that. You were going to a City banquet or something, and Marie-Louise rang up and asked if she might come and take pot-luck with us.

MORTIMER. Do you mean to say she dined here?

CONSTANCE. Isn't that what she told you?

MORTIMER. Yes.

CONSTANCE. It's quite easy to prove. If you won't take my word for it we can ring for the butler, and you can ask him yourself. . . . Ring the bell, John, will you?

MORTIMER (*uneasily*). No, don't do that. If you give me your word, of course I must take it.

CONSTANCE. That's very kind of you. I'm grateful to you for not exposing me to the humiliation of making my butler corroborate my statement.

MORTIMER. If Marie-Louise was dining here why were you sitting on her bed?

CONSTANCE. John had to go out and do an operation, and Marie-Louise wanted to show me the things she'd got from Paris, so I walked round to 10 your house. It was a lovely night. You remember that, don't you?

MORTIMER. Damn it, I've got more important things to do than look at the night.

CONSTANCE. We tried them all on and then we were rather tired, so Marie-Louise got into bed and I sat down and we talked.

MORTIMER. If you were tired why didn't 20 you go home and go to bed.

CONSTANCE. John had promised to come round and fetch me.

MORTIMER. And did he? At what time did he come?

JOHN. I couldn't manage it. The operation took much longer than I expected. It was one of those cases where when you once start cutting you really don't know where to stop. You 30 know the sort of thing, don't you, Mortimer?

MORTIMER. No, I don't. How the devil should I?

CONSTANCE. All that is neither here nor there. This is a terrible accusation you've made against John and Marie-Louise and I'm very much upset. But I will remain perfectly calm till I've heard everything. Now let me have 40 your proofs.

MORTIMER. My proofs? What d'you mean? The cigarette-case. When I found the cigarette-case I naturally put two and two together.

CONSTANCE (*with her eyes flashing*). I quite understand, but why did you make them five?

MORTIMER (*emphatically, in order not to show that he is wavering*). It isn't possible that I should have made a mistake.

CONSTANCE. Even the richest of us may err. I remember when Mr. Pierpont Morgan died, he was found to own seven million dollars of worthless securities.

MORTIMER (*uneasily*). You don't know what a shock it was, Constance. I had the most implicit confidence in Marie-Louise. I was knocked endways. I've been brooding over it ever since till I was afraid I should go mad.

CONSTANCE. And do you mean to say that you've come here and made a fearful scene just because you found my cigarette-case in Marie-Louise's room? I can't believe it. You're a man of the world and a business man. You're extremely intelligent. Surely you have something to go upon. You must be holding something back. Don't be afraid of hurting my feelings. You've said so much now that I must insist on your saying everything. I want the truth and the whole truth.

[*There is a pause.* MORTIMER *looks from* MARIE-LOUISE, *who is quietly weeping, to* CONSTANCE, *with the utmost bewilderment.*]

MORTIMER. I'm afraid I've made a damned fool of myself.

CONSTANCE. I'm afraid you have.

MORTIMER. I'm awfully sorry, Constance. I beg your pardon.

CONSTANCE. Oh, don't bother about me. You've exposed me to the most bitter humiliation. You've sown seeds of distrust between me and John which can never be . . . (*She looks for a word.*)

MRS. CULVER (*supplying it*). Fertilized.

CONSTANCE (*ignoring it*). Uprooted. But

I don't matter. It's Marie-Louise's pardon you must beg.

MORTIMER (*humbly*). Marie-Louise.

MARIE-LOUISE. Don't touch me. Don't come near me.

MORTIMER (*to* CONSTANCE, *miserably*). You know what jealousy is.

CONSTANCE. Certainly not. I think it's a most ugly and despicable vice.

MORTIMER (*to* MARIE-LOUISE). Marie-Louise, I'm sorry. Won't you forgive me?

MARIE-LOUISE. You've insulted me before all my friends. You know how devotedly I love Constance. You might have accused me of having an affair with anyone else—but not John.

CONSTANCE. Not her greatest friend's husband. The milkman or the dustman if you like, but not her greatest friend's husband.

MORTIMER. I've been a perfect swine. I don't know what came over me. I really wasn't responsible for my actions.

MARIE-LOUISE. I've loved you all these years. No one has ever loved you as I've loved you. Oh, it's cruel, cruel.

MORTIMER. Come away, darling. I can't say here what I want to say.

MARIE-LOUISE. No, no, no.

CONSTANCE (*putting her hand on his arm, gently*). I think you'd better leave her here for a little while, Morty. I'll talk to her when you've gone. She's naturally upset. A sensitive little thing like that.

MORTIMER. We're dining with the Vancouvers at 8.15.

CONSTANCE. For eight-thirty. I promise I'll send her home in good time to dress.

MORTIMER. She'll give me another chance?

CONSTANCE. Yes, yes.

MORTIMER. I'd do anything in the world for her. (CONSTANCE *puts her fingers to her lips and then points significantly to the pearl chain she is wearing. For a second* MORTIMER *does not understand, but as soon as her notion dawns on him he gives a pleased nod.*) You're the cleverest woman in the world. (*As he goes out he stops and holds out his hand to* JOHN.) Will you shake hands with me, old man? I made a mistake and I'm man enough to acknowledge it.

JOHN (*very cordially*). Not at all, old boy. I quite agree that it did look fishy, the cigarette-case. If I'd dreamt that Constance was going to leave an expensive thing like that lying about all over the place, I'm hanged if I'd have let her pinch it.

MORTIMER. You don't know what a weight it is off my mind. I felt a hundred when I came here, and now I feel like a two-year-old.

[*He goes out. The moment the door is closed behind him there is a general change in every attitude. The tension disappears and there is a feeling of relief.*]

JOHN. Constance, you're a brick. I shall never forget this. Never, so long as I live. And by George, what presence of mind you showed. I went hot and cold all over, and you never batted an eye-lash.

CONSTANCE. By the way, here is your cigarette-case. You'd better have a ring made and hang it on your key-chain.

JOHN. No, no. Keep it. I'm too old to take these risks.

CONSTANCE. By the way, did anyone see you go into Morty's house last night?

JOHN. No, we let ourselves in with Marie-Louise's latch key.

CONSTANCE. That's all right then. If Mortimer asks the servants they can tell him nothing. I had to take that chance.

MARIE-LOUISE (*with a little gesture of ashamed dismay*). Oh, Constance, what must you think of me?

CONSTANCE. I? Exactly the same as I thought before. I think you're sweet, Marie-Louise.

MARIE-LOUISE. You have every right to be angry with me.

CONSTANCE. Perhaps, but not the inclination.

MARIE-LOUISE. Oh, it's not true. I've treated you shamefully. You've made me feel such a pig. And you had your chance to get back on me and you didn't take it. I'm so ashamed.

CONSTANCE (*amused*). Because you've been having an affair with John, or because you've been found out?

MARIE-LOUISE. Oh, Constance, don't be heartless. Say anything you like, curse me, stamp on me, but don't smile at me. I'm in a terrible position.

CONSTANCE. And you want me to make a scene. I know and I sympathize. (*Very calmly.*) But the fact is that Mortimer told me nothing I didn't know before.

MARIE-LOUISE (*aghast*). Do you mean to say that you've known all along?

CONSTANCE. All along, darling. I've been spending the last six months in a desperate effort to prevent my friends and relations from telling me your ghastly secret. It's been very difficult sometimes. Often mother's profound understanding of life, Martha's passion for truth at any price, and Barbara's silent sympathy, have almost worn me down. But until today the t's were not definitely crossed nor the i's distinctly dotted, and I was able to ignore the facts that were staring at me—rather rudely, I must say—in the face.

MARIE-LOUISE. But why, why? It's not human. Why didn't you do anything?

CONSTANCE. That, darling, is my affair.

MARIE-LOUISE (*thinking she understands*). Oh, I see.

CONSTANCE (*rather tartly*). No, you don't. I have always been absolutely faithful to John. I have not winked at your intrigue in order to cover my own.

MARIE-LOUISE (*beginning to be a little put out*). I almost think you've been laughing at me up your sleeve all the time.

CONSTANCE (*good-humouredly*). Oh, my dear, you mustn't be offended just because I've taken away from you the satisfaction of thinking that you have been deceiving me all these months. I should hate you to think me capable of an intentional meanness.

MARIE-LOUISE. My head's going round and round.

CONSTANCE. Such a pretty head, too. Why don't you go and lie down? You want to look your best if you're dining with the Vancouvers.

MARIE-LOUISE. I wonder where Mortimer is?

CONSTANCE. You know that pearl necklace you showed me the other day and you said that Mortimer thought it cost a lot of money—well, he's gone to Cartier's to buy it for you.

MARIE-LOUISE (*excitedly*). Oh, Constance, do you think he has?

CONSTANCE. I think all men are born with the knowledge that when they have wounded a woman's soul—and our souls are easily wounded—the only cure is a trifling, but expensive jewel.

MARIE-LOUISE. Do you think he'll have the sense to bring it home with him so that I can wear it tonight?

CONSTANCE. Oh, my dear, don't be such a fool as to accept it with alacrity. Remember that Mortimer has grievously insulted you, he's made the most shocking accusation that a man can make against his wife, he's trampled on your love and now he's destroyed your trust in him.

MARIE-LOUISE. Oh, how right you are, Constance.

CONSTANCE. Surely I need not tell you what to do. Refuse to speak to him, but never let him get a word of defence in edgeways. Cry enough to make him feel what a brute he is, but not enough to make your eyes swell. Say you'll leave him and run sobbing to the door, but take care to let him stop you before you open it. Repeat yourself. Say the same thing over and over again—it wears them down—and if he answers you take no notice, but just say it again. And at last when you've reduced him to desperation, when his head is aching as though it would split, when he's sweating at every pore, when he's harassed and miserable and haggard and broken—then consent as an unmerited favour, as a sign of your forgiving temper and the sweetness of your nature, to accept, no, don't consent, *deign* to accept the pearl necklace for which the wretch has just paid ten thousand pounds. 30

MARIE-LOUISE (*with peculiar satisfaction*). Twelve, darling.

CONSTANCE. And don't thank him. That wouldn't be playing the game. Let him thank *you* for the favour you do him in allowing him to make you a paltry gift. Have you got your car here?

MARIE-LOUISE. No, I was in such a state when I came I took a taxi.

CONSTANCE. John, do take Marie-Louise 40 down and put her in a taxi.

JOHN. All right.

MARIE-LOUISE. No, not John. I couldn't. After all, I have some delicacy.

CONSTANCE. Oh, have you? Well, let Bernard go.

BERNARD. I shall be pleased.

CONSTANCE (*to* BERNARD). But come back, won't you?

BERNARD. Certainly.

MARIE-LOUISE (*kissing* CONSTANCE). This has been a lesson to me, darling. I'm not a fool, Constance. I can learn.

CONSTANCE. At least prudence, I hope.

[MARIE-LOUISE *goes out followed by* BERNARD KERSAL.]

JOHN. How did you guess that Marie-Louise had said she was dining here?

CONSTANCE. She's too crafty a woman to invent a new lie when an old one will serve.

JOHN. It would have been awkward if Mortimer had insisted on asking Bentley if it was true.

CONSTANCE. I knew he wouldn't dare. It's only if a man's a gentleman that he won't hesitate to do an ungentlemanly thing. Mortimer is on the boundary line and it makes him careful.

MARTHA (*significantly*). Don't you imagine your patients are growing a trifle restless, John?

JOHN. I like to keep them waiting. They grow more and more nervous as the minutes pass and when I recommend an operation that will cost them two hundred and fifty pounds they are too shaken to protest.

MARTHA (*pursing her lips*). I can't imagine you'll very much like to hear what I'm determined to say to Constance.

JOHN. It's because I shrewdly suspect that you have some very unpleasant things to say about me that I am prepared reluctantly to neglect the call of duty and listen to you with my own ears.

CONSTANCE. She's been exercising miracles of restraint for the last three months, John. I think she has a right to let herself go now.

JOHN. If she's suffering from suppressed desires she's come to the wrong establishment. She ought to go to a psycho-analyst.

MARTHA. I've only got one thing to say, John, and I'm perfectly willing that you should hear it. (*To* CONSTANCE.) I don't know what your reasons were for shielding that abominable woman. I can only suppose you wanted to avoid more scandal than was necessary. . . .

MRS. CULVER (*interrupting*). Before you go any further, my dear, you must let me put my word in. (*To* CONSTANCE.) My dear child, I beg you not to decide anything in a hurry. We must all think things over. First of all you must listen to what John has to say for himself.

MARTHA. What can he have to say for himself?

CONSTANCE (*ironically*). What indeed?

JOHN. Not the right thing anyway. I've seen too much of married life. . . .

CONSTANCE (*interrupting, with a smile*). Let us be just. Other people's rather than your own.

JOHN (*going on*). To imagine that even the Archangel Gabriel could say the right thing.

CONSTANCE. I've no reason, however, to suppose that the Archangel Gabriel could ever find himself in such a predicament.

JOHN. I'm for it and I'm prepared to take what's coming to me.

CONSTANCE (*to the world in general*). No man could say handsomer than that.

JOHN. I'm expecting you to make a scene, Constance. It's your right and your privilege. I'm willing to bear it. Give me hell. I deserve it. Drag me up and down the room by the hair of the head. Kick me in the face. Stamp on me. I'll grovel. I'll eat the dust. My name is mud. Mud.

CONSTANCE. My poor John, what is there to make a scene about?

JOHN. I know how badly I've treated you. I had a wife who was good, loving and faithful, devoted to my interests, a perfect mother and an excellent housekeeper. A woman ten times too good for me. If I'd had the smallest spark of decency I couldn't have treated you like this. I haven't a word to say for myself.

MARTHA (*interrupting him*). You've humiliated her to all her friends.

JOHN. I've behaved neither like a gentleman nor a sportsman.

MARTHA. Your conduct is inexcusable.

JOHN. I haven't a leg to stand on.

MARTHA. Even if you didn't love her, you might have treated her with respect.

JOHN. I've been as heartless as a crocodile and as unscrupulous as a typhoid bacillus.

CONSTANCE. Between you, of course, you're leaving me very little to say.

MARTHA. There *is* nothing to say. You're quite right. This is the sort of occasion when it's beneath a woman's dignity to make a scene. It just shows how little John knows women to think that you could demean yourself to vulgar abuse. (*To* JOHN.) I suppose you'll have the decency to put no obstacle in the way of Constance's getting her freedom.

MRS. CULVER. Oh, Constance, you're not going to divorce him?

MARTHA. Mother, you're so weak. How can she go on living with a man for whom she has no respect? What would her life be with this creature whom she can only mistrust and despise? Besides, you have to think of their child. How can Constance allow her daughter to be contaminated by the society of a person of this character?

CONSTANCE. John has always been an excellent father. Let us give the devil his due.

MRS. CULVER. Don't be too hard, darling. I can understand that at the moment you feel bitter, but it would be very sad if you let your bitterness warp your judgment.

CONSTANCE. I don't feel in the least bitter. I wish I looked as sweet as I feel.

MRS. CULVER. You can't deceive a mother, my dear. I know the angry resentment that you feel. Under the unfortunate circumstances it's only too natural.

CONSTANCE. When I look into my heart I can't find a trace of resentment, except perhaps for John's being so stupid as to let himself be found out.

JOHN. Let me say this in justification for myself, Constance. I did my little best to prevent it. Angels could do no more.

CONSTANCE. And angels presumably have not the pernicious habit of smoking straight-cut cigarettes.

JOHN. When you once get the taste for them, you prefer them to gippies.

MRS. CULVER. Don't be cynical, darling. That is the worst way to ease an aching heart. Come to your mother's arms, my dear, and let us have a good cry together. And then you'll feel better.

CONSTANCE. It's sweet of you, mother, but honestly I couldn't squeeze a tear out of my eyes if my life depended on it.

MRS. CULVER. And don't be too hard. Of course John is to blame. I admit that. He's been very, very naughty. But men are weak and women are so unscrupulous. I'm sure he's sorry for all the pain he's caused you.

MARTHA. What puzzles me is that you didn't do something the moment you discovered that John was having an affair.

CONSTANCE. To tell you the truth, I thought it no business of mine.

MARTHA (*indignantly*). Aren't you his wife?

CONSTANCE. John and I are very lucky people. Our marriage has been ideal.

MARTHA. How can you say that?

CONSTANCE. For five years we adored each other. That's much longer than most people do. Our honeymoon lasted five years and then we had a most extraordinary stroke of luck: we ceased to be in love with one another simultaneously.

JOHN. I protest, Constance. I've never ceased to be absolutely devoted to you.

CONSTANCE. I never said you had, darling. I'm convinced of it. I've never ceased to be devoted to you. We've shared one another's interests, we've loved to be together, I've exulted in your success and you've trembled in my illness. We've laughed at the same jokes and sighed over the same worries. I don't know any couple that's been bound together by a more genuine affection. But honestly, for the last ten years have you been in love with me?

JOHN. You can't expect a man who's been married for fifteen years. . . .

CONSTANCE. My dear, I'm not asking for excuses. I'm only asking for a plain answer.

JOHN. In the long run I enjoy your society much more than anybody else's. There's no one I like so much as you. You're the prettiest woman I've ever known and I shall say the same when you're a hundred.

CONSTANCE. But does your heart leap into your mouth when you hear my footstep on the stairs, and when I come into the room, is your first impulse to catch me in your manly arms? I haven't noticed it.

JOHN. I don't want to make a fool of myself.

CONSTANCE. Then I think you've answered my question. You're no more in love with me than I am with you.

JOHN. You never said a word of this before.

CONSTANCE. I think most married couples tell one another far too much. There are some things that two people may know very well, but which it's much more tactful for them to pretend they don't.

JOHN. How did you find out?

CONSTANCE. I'll tell you. One night as we were dancing together, all at once 20 I noticed that we weren't keeping such good step as we generally did. It was because my mind was wandering. I was thinking how it would suit me to do my hair like a woman who was dancing alongside of us. Then I looked at you and I saw you were thinking what pretty legs she'd got. I suddenly realized that you weren't in love with me any more and at the 30 same moment I realized that it was a relief, because I wasn't in love with you.

JOHN. I must say it never occurred to me for a moment.

CONSTANCE. I know. A man thinks it quite natural that he should fall out of love with a woman, but it never strikes him for a moment that a woman can do anything so unnatural 40 as to fall out of love with him. Don't be upset at that, darling, that is one of the charming limitations of your sex.

MARTHA. Do you mean mother and me to understand that since then John

has been having one affair after another and you haven't turned a hair?

CONSTANCE. Since this is the first time he's been found out, let us give him the benefit of the doubt and hope that till now he has never strayed from the strict and narrow path. You're not angry with me, John?

JOHN. No, darling, not angry. But I *am* 10 a little taken aback. I think you've been making rather a damned fool of me. It never struck me that your feelings for me had changed so much. You can't expect me to like it.

CONSTANCE. Oh, come now, you must be reasonable. You surely wouldn't wish me to have languished for all these years in a hopeless passion for you when you had nothing to give me in return but friendship and affection. Think what a bore it is to have someone in love with you whom you're not in love with.

JOHN. I can't conceive of your ever being a bore, Constance.

CONSTANCE (*kissing her hand to him*). Don't you realize that we must thank our lucky stars? We are the favoured of the gods. I shall never forget those five years of exquisite happiness you gave me when I loved you, and I shall never cease to be grateful to you, not because you loved me, but because you inspired me with love. Our love never degenerated into weariness. Because we ceased loving one another at the very same moment we never had to put up with quarrels and reproaches, recriminations and all the other paraphernalia of a passion that has ceased on one side and is still alive and eager on the other. Our love was like a cross-word puzzle in which we both hit upon the last word at the same moment. That is why our lives since have been so happy; that is why ours is a perfect marriage.

MARTHA. Do you mean to say that it meant nothing to you when you found out that John was carrying on with Marie-Louise?

CONSTANCE. Human nature is very imperfect. I'm afraid I must admit that at the first moment I was vexed. But only at the first moment. Then I re- flected that it was most unreasonable to be angry with John for giving to another something that I had no use for. That would be too much like a dog in the manger. And then I was fond enough of John to be willing that he should be happy in his own way. And if he was going to indulge in an intrigue . . . isn't that the proper phrase, John?

JOHN. I have not yet made up my mind whether it really is an indulgence.

CONSTANCE. Then it was much better that the object of his affections should be so intimate a friend of mine that I could keep a maternal eye on him.

JOHN. Really, Constance.

CONSTANCE. Marie-Louise is very pretty so that my self-esteem was not offended, and so rich that it was certain John would have no reason to squander money on her to the inconvenience of myself. She's not clever enough to acquire any ascendancy over him, and so long as I kept his heart I was quite willing that she should have his senses. If you wanted to deceive me, John, I couldn't have chosen anyone with whom I would more willingly be deceived than Marie-Louise.

JOHN. I don't gather that you have been very grossly deceived, darling. You have such penetration that when you look at me I feel as though I were shiv-ering without a stitch of clothing on.

MRS. CULVER. I don't approve of your attitude, Constance. In my day when a young wife discovered that her husband had been deceiving her, she burst into a flood of tears and went to stay with her mother for three weeks, not returning to her husband till he had been brought to a proper state of abjection and repentance.

MARTHA. Are we to understand, then, that you are not going to divorce John?

CONSTANCE. You know, I can never see why a woman should give up a comfortable home, a considerable part of her income and the advantage of having a man about to do all the tiresome and disagreeable things for her, because he has been unfaithful to her. She's merely cutting off her nose to spite her face.

MARTHA. I am at a loss for words. I cannot conceive how a woman of any spirit can sit down and allow her husband to make a perfect damned fool of her.

CONSTANCE. You've been very stupid, my poor John. In the ordinary affairs of life stupidity is much more tiresome than wickedness. You can mend the vicious, but what in Heaven's name are you to do with the foolish?

JOHN. I've been a fool, Constance. I know it, but I'm capable of learning by experience, so I can't be a damned fool.

CONSTANCE. You mean that in the future you'll be more careful to cover your tracks?

MRS. CULVER. Oh, no, Constance, he means that this has been a lesson to him, and that in the future you'll have no cause for complaint.

CONSTANCE. I've always been given to understand that men only abandon their vices when advancing years have made them a burden rather than a pleasure. John, I'm happy to say, is still in the flower of his age. I suppose you give yourself another fifteen years, John, don't you?

JOHN. Really, Constance, I don't know what you mean. The things you say sometimes are positively embarrassing.

CONSTANCE. I think at all events we may take it that Marie-Louise will have more than one successor.

JOHN. Constance, I give you my word of honour. . . .

CONSTANCE (interrupting). That is the only gift you can make for which I can find no use. You see, so long as I was able to pretend a blissful ignorance of your goings-on we could all be perfectly happy. You were enjoying yourself and I received a lot of sympathy as the outraged wife. But now I do see that the position is very difficult. You have put me in a position that is neither elegant nor dignified.

JOHN. I'm awfully sorry, Constance.

MARTHA. You're going to leave him?

CONSTANCE. No, I'm not going to leave him. John, you remember that Barbara offered to take me into her business? I refused. Well, I've changed my mind and I'm going to accept.

JOHN. But why? I don't see your point.

CONSTANCE. I'm not prepared any more to be entirely dependent upon you, John.

JOHN. But, my dear, everything I earn is at your disposal. It's a pleasure for me to provide for your wants. Heaven knows, they're not very great.

CONSTANCE. I know. Come, John, I've been very reasonable, haven't I? Don't try and thwart me when I want to do something on which I've set my heart.

[There is an instant's pause.]

JOHN. I don't understand. But if you put it like that, I haven't a word to say. Of course, you must do exactly as you wish.

CONSTANCE. That's a dear. Now go back to your patients or else I shall have to keep you as well as myself.

JOHN. Will you give me a kiss?

CONSTANCE. Why not?

JOHN (kissing her). It's peace between us?

CONSTANCE. Peace and good-will. (JOHN goes out.) He is rather sweet, isn't he?

MRS. CULVER. What have you got on your mind, Constance?

CONSTANCE. I, mother? (Teasing her.) What do you suspect?

MRS. CULVER. I don't like the look of you.

CONSTANCE. I'm sorry for that. Most people find me far from plain.

MRS. CULVER. You've got some deviltry in mind, but for the life of me I can't guess it.

MARTHA. I can't see what you expect to get out of working with Barbara.

CONSTANCE. Between a thousand and fifteen hundred a year, I believe.

MARTHA. I wasn't thinking of the money, and you know it.

CONSTANCE. I'm tired of being the modern wife.

MARTHA. What do you mean by the modern wife?

CONSTANCE. A prostitute who doesn't deliver the goods.

MRS. CULVER. My dear, what would your father say if he heard you say such things?

CONSTANCE. Darling, need we conjecture the remarks of a gentleman who's been dead for five and twenty years? Had he any gift for repartee?

MRS. CULVER. None whatever. He was good, but he was stupid. That is why the gods loved him and he died young.

[BERNARD KERSAL opens the door and looks in.]

BERNARD. May I come in?

CONSTANCE. Oh, there you are. I wondered what had become of you.

BERNARD. When Marie-Louise saw my car at the door she asked me to drive her. I couldn't very well refuse.

CONSTANCE. So you took her home.

BERNARD. No, she said she was in such a state she must have her hair washed. I drove her to a place in Bond Street. 10

CONSTANCE. And what did she say to you?

BERNARD. She said, I don't know what you must think of me.

CONSTANCE. That is what most women say to a man when his opinion doesn't matter two straws to them. And what did you answer?

BERNARD. Well, I said, I prefer not to offer an opinion on a matter which is 20 no business of mine.

CONSTANCE. Dear Bernard, one of the things I like most in you is that you always remain so perfectly in character. If the heavens fell you would still remain the perfect English gentleman.

BERNARD. I thought it the most tactful thing to say.

CONSTANCE. Well, mother, I won't de- 30 tain you any longer. I know that you and Martha have a thousand things to do.

MRS. CULVER. I'm glad you reminded me. Come, Martha. Good-bye, darling. Good-bye, Mr. Kersal.

BERNARD. Good-bye.

CONSTANCE (to MARTHA). Good-bye, dear. Thank you for all your sympathy. You've been a great help in 40 my hour of need.

MARTHA. I don't understand and it's no good saying I do.

CONSTANCE. Bless you. (MRS. CULVER and MARTHA go out. BERNARD closes the door after them.) Shall we be very late?

BERNARD. So late that it doesn't matter if we're a little later. I have something important to say to you.

CONSTANCE (teasing him a little). Important to me or important to you?

BERNARD. I can't tell you how distressed I was at that terrible scene.

CONSTANCE. Oh, didn't you think it had its lighter moments?

BERNARD. It's only this afternoon I 10 learned the truth, and then I never imagined for a moment that you knew it, too. I can't tell you how brave I think it of you to have borne all this torture with a smiling face. If I admired you before, I admire you ten times more now.

CONSTANCE. You're very sweet, Bernard.

BERNARD. My heart bleeds when I think of what you've gone through.

CONSTANCE. It's not a very good plan to 20 take other people's misfortunes too much to heart.

BERNARD. Hardly an hour ago I told you that if ever you wanted me I was only too anxious to do anything in the world for you. I little thought then that the time would come so soon. There's no reason now why I shouldn't tell you of the love that consumes me. Oh, Constance, come to me. You know that if things were as I thought they were between you and John nothing would have induced me to say a word. But now he has no longer any claims on you. He doesn't love you. Why should you go on wasting your life with a man who is capable of exposing you to all this humiliation? You know how long and 40 tenderly I've loved you. You can trust yourself to me. I'll give my whole life to making you forget the anguish you've endured. Will you marry me, Constance?

CONSTANCE. My dear, John may have

behaved very badly, but he's still my husband.

BERNARD. Only in name. You've done everything in your power to save a scandal and now if you ask him to let himself be divorced he's bound to consent.

CONSTANCE. Do you really think John has behaved so very badly to me?

BERNARD (*astonished*). You don't mean to say that you have any doubts in your mind about his relationship with Marie-Louise?

CONSTANCE. None.

BERNARD. Then what in God's name do you mean?

CONSTANCE. My dear Bernard, have you ever considered what marriage is among well-to-do people? In the working classes a woman cooks her husband's dinner, washes for him and darns his socks. She looks after the children and makes their clothes. She gives good value for the money she costs. But what is a wife in our class? Her house is managed by servants, nurses look after her children, if she has resigned herself to having any, and as soon as they are old enough she packs them off to school. Let us face it, she is no more than the mistress of a man of whose desire she has taken advantage to insist on a legal ceremony that will prevent him from discarding her when his desire has ceased.

BERNARD. She's also his companion and his helpmate.

CONSTANCE. My dear, any sensible man would sooner play bridge at his club than with his wife, and he'd always rather play golf with a man than with a woman. A paid secretary is a far better helpmate than a loving spouse. When all is said and done, the modern wife is nothing but a parasite.

BERNARD. I don't agree with you.

CONSTANCE. You see, my poor friend, you are in love and your judgment is confused.

BERNARD. I don't understand what you mean.

CONSTANCE. John gives me board and lodging, money for my clothes and my amusements, a car to drive in and a certain position in the world. He's bound to do all that because fifteen years ago he was madly in love with me, and he undertook it; though, if you'd asked him, he would certainly have acknowledged that nothing is so fleeting as that particular form of madness called love. It was either very generous of him or very imprudent. Don't you think it would be rather shabby of me to take advantage now of his generosity or his want of foresight?

BERNARD. In what way?

CONSTANCE. He paid a very high price for something that he couldn't get cheaper. He no longer wants that. Why should I resent it? I know as well as anybody else that desire is fleeting. It comes and goes and no man can understand why. The only thing that's certain is that when it's gone it's gone forever. So long as John continues to provide for me what right have I to complain that he is unfaithful to me? He bought a toy, and if he no longer wants to play with it, why should he? He paid for it.

BERNARD. That might be all right if a man had only to think about himself. What about the woman?

CONSTANCE. I don't think you need waste too much sympathy on her. Like ninety-nine girls out of a hundred, when I married I looked upon it as the only easy, honourable and lucrative calling open to me. When the average woman who has been married for fifteen years discovers her husband's infidelity it is not her heart that is wounded but her vanity. If she had any sense, she would regard it merely as one of the necessary inconveniences of an otherwise pleasant profession.

BERNARD. Then the long and short of it is that you don't love me.

CONSTANCE. You think that my principles are all moonshine?

BERNARD. I don't think they would have much influence if you were as crazy about me as I am about you. Do you still love John?

CONSTANCE. I'm very fond of him, he makes me laugh, and we get on together like a house on fire, but I'm not in love with him.

BERNARD. And is that enough for you? Isn't the future sometimes a trifle desolate? Don't you want love?

[*A pause. She gives him a long reflective look.*]

CONSTANCE (*charmingly*). If I did I should come to you for it, Bernard.

BERNARD. Constance, what do you mean? Is it possible that you could ever care for me? Oh, my darling, I worship the ground you tread on. (*He seizes her in his arms and kisses her passionately.*)

CONSTANCE (*releasing herself*). Oh, my dear, don't be so sudden. I should despise myself entirely if I were unfaithful to John so long as I am entirely dependent on him.

BERNARD. But if you love me?

CONSTANCE. I never said I did. But even if I did, so long as John provides me with all the necessities of existence I wouldn't be unfaithful. It all comes down to the economic situation. He has bought my fidelity and I should be worse than a harlot if I took the price he paid and did not deliver the goods.

BERNARD. Do you mean to say there's no hope for me at all?

CONSTANCE. The only hope before you at the moment is to start for Ranelagh before the game is over.

BERNARD. Do you still want to go?

CONSTANCE. Yes.

BERNARD. Very well. (*With a burst of passion.*) I love you.

CONSTANCE. Then go down and start up the car, put a spot of oil in the radiator or something, and I'll join you in a minute. I want to telephone.

BERNARD. Very well.

[*He goes out.* CONSTANCE *takes up the telephone.*]

CONSTANCE. Mayfair 2646 . . . Barbara? It's Constance. That offer you made me a fortnight ago—is it still open? Well, I want to accept it . . . No, no, nothing has happened. John is very well. He's always sweet, you know. It's only that I want to earn my own living. When can I start? The sooner the better.

ACT III

The scene is still the same. A year has passed. It is afternoon.

CONSTANCE *is seated at a desk writing letters. The* BUTLER *shows in* BARBARA FAWCETT *and* MARTHA.

BENTLEY. Mrs. Fawcett and Miss Culver.

CONSTANCE. Oh! Sit down, I'm just finishing a note.

BARBARA. We met on the doorstep.

MARTHA. I thought I'd just look round and see if there was anything I could do to help you before you start.

CONSTANCE. That's very nice of you, Martha. I really don't think there is.

I'm packed and ready, and for once I don't believe I've forgotten one of the things I shan't want.

BARBARA. I felt I must run in to say good-bye to you.

CONSTANCE. Now, my dear, you mustn't neglect your work the moment my back is turned.

BARBARA. Well, it's partly the work that's brought me. An order has just come in for a new house and they want an Italian room.

CONSTANCE. I don't like that look in your beady eye, Barbara.

BARBARA. Well, it struck me that as you're going to Italy you might go round the shops and buy any nice pieces that you can find.

CONSTANCE. Perish the thought. I've worked like a dog for a year and last night at six o'clock I downed tools. I stripped off my grimy overalls, wrung the sweat from my honest brow and scrubbed my horny hands. You said I could take six weeks' holiday.

BARBARA. I admit that you've thoroughly earned it.

CONSTANCE. When I closed the shop-door behind me, I ceased to be a British working-man and resumed the position of a perfect English lady.

MARTHA. I never saw you in such spirits.

CONSTANCE. Something accomplished, something done. But what I was coming to was this: for the next six weeks I refuse to give a moment's thought to bath-rooms or wall-papers, kitchen sinks, scullery floors, curtains, cushions and refrigerators.

BARBARA. I wasn't asking you to. I only wanted you to get some of that painted Italian furniture and a few mirrors.

CONSTANCE. No, I've worked hard and I've enjoyed my work, and now I'm going to enjoy a perfect holiday.

BARBARA. Oh, well, have it your own way.

MARTHA. Constance dear, I think there's something you ought to know.

CONSTANCE. I should have thought you had discovered by now that I generally know the things I ought to know.

MARTHA. You'll never guess whom I saw in Bond Street this morning.

CONSTANCE. Yes, I shall. Marie-Louise.

MARTHA. Oh!

CONSTANCE. I'm sorry to disappoint you, darling. She rang me up an hour ago.

MARTHA. But I thought she wasn't coming back for another month. She was going to stay away a year.

CONSTANCE. She arrived last night and I'm expecting her every minute.

MARTHA. Here?

CONSTANCE. Yes. She said she simply must run in and see me before I left.

MARTHA. I wonder what she wants.

CONSTANCE. Perhaps to pass the time of day. I think it's rather sweet of her, considering how busy she must be on getting back after so long.

BARBARA. She's been all over the place, hasn't she?

CONSTANCE. Yes, she's been in Malaya; Mortimer has interests there, you know, and in China, and now they've just come from India.

MARTHA. I often wondered if it was at your suggestion that they set off on that long tour immediately after that unfortunate scene.

CONSTANCE. Which, you must confess, no one enjoyed more than you, darling.

BARBARA. It was certainly the most sensible thing they could do.

MARTHA. Of course you know your own business best, darling, but don't you think it's a little unfortunate that you should be going away for six weeks just as she comes back?

CONSTANCE. We working-women have to take our holidays when we can.

BARBARA. Surely John has had his lesson. He's not going to make a fool of himself a second time.

MARTHA. Do you think he has really got over his infatuation, Constance?

CONSTANCE. I don't know at all. But here he is, you'd better ask him.

[*As she says these words,* JOHN *enters.*]

JOHN. Ask him what?

MARTHA (*not at all at a loss*). I was just wondering what you'd do with yourself during Constance's absence.

JOHN. I've got a lot of work, you know, and I shall go to the club a good deal.

MARTHA. It seems a pity that you weren't able to arrange things so that you and Constance should take your holidays together.

BARBARA. Don't blame me for that. I was quite willing to make my arrangements to suit Constance.

CONSTANCE. You see, I wanted to go to Italy and the only places John likes on the Continent are those in which it's only by an effort of the imagination that you can tell you're not in England.

MARTHA. What about Helen?

CONSTANCE. We've taken a house at Henley for August. John can play golf and go on the river, and I shall be able to come up to town every day to look after the business.

BARBARA. Well, dear, I'll leave you. I hope you'll have a wonderful holiday. You've deserved it. Do you know, I think I'm a very clever woman, John, to have persuaded Constance to work. She's been absolutely invaluable to me.

JOHN. I never liked the idea and I'm not going to say I did.

BARBARA. Haven't you forgiven me yet?

JOHN. She insisted on it and I had to make the best of a bad job.

BARBARA. Good-bye.

CONSTANCE (*Kissing her*). Good-bye, dear. Take care of yourself.

MARTHA. I'll come with you, Barbara. Mother said she'd look in for a minute to say good-bye to you.

CONSTANCE. Oh, all right. Good-bye. (*She kisses the two and accompanies them to the door. They go out.*)

JOHN. I say, Constance, I thought you had to go now because Barbara couldn't possibly get away.

CONSTANCE. Did I say that?

JOHN. Certainly.

CONSTANCE. Oh!

JOHN. If I'd dreamt that you could just as easily take your holiday when I take mine . . .

CONSTANCE (*interrupting*). Don't you think it's a mistake for husbands and wives to take their holidays together? The only reason one takes a holiday is for rest and change and recreation. Do you think a man really gets that when he goes away with his wife?

JOHN. It depends on the wife.

CONSTANCE. I know nothing more depressing than the sight of all those couples in a hotel dining-room, one little couple to one little table, sitting opposite to one another without a word to say.

JOHN. Oh, nonsense. You often see couples who are very jolly and cheerful.

CONSTANCE. Yes, I know, but look closely at the lady's wedding-ring and you'll see that it rests uneasily on the hand it adorns.

JOHN. We always get on like a house on fire and when I slipped a wedding-ring on your finger a bishop supervised the process. You're not going to tell me that I bore *you*.

CONSTANCE. On the contrary, you tickle me to death. It's that unhappy modesty of mine: I was afraid that you could have too much of my society. I thought it would refresh you if I left you to your own devices for a few weeks.

JOHN. If you go on pulling my leg so persistently I shall be permanently deformed.

CONSTANCE. Anyhow, it's too late now. My bags are packed, my farewells made, and nothing bores people so much as to see you tomorrow when they've made up their minds to get on without you for a month.

JOHN. H'm. Eyewash. . . . Look here, Constance, there's something I want to say to you.

CONSTANCE. Yes?

JOHN. Do you know that Marie-Louise has come back?

CONSTANCE. Yes. She said she'd try and look in to say how do you do before I started. It'll be nice to see her again after so long.

JOHN. I want you to do something for me, Constance.

CONSTANCE. What is it?

JOHN. Well, you've been a perfect brick to me, and hang it all, I can't take advantage of your good nature. I must do the square thing.

CONSTANCE. I'm afraid I don't quite understand.

JOHN. I haven't seen Marie-Louise since that day when Mortimer came here and made such a fool of himself. She's been away for nearly a year and taking all things into consideration I think it would be a mistake to resume the relations that we were on then.

CONSTANCE. What makes you think she wishes to?

JOHN. The fact that she rang you up the moment she arrived looks ominous to me.

CONSTANCE. Ominous? You know some women can't see a telephone without taking the receiver off and then, when the operator says, Number, please, they have to say something. I dare say ours was the first that occurred to Marie-Louise.

JOHN. It's no good blinking the fact that Marie-Louise was madly in love with me.

CONSTANCE. Well, we can neither of us blame her for that.

JOHN. I don't want to be unkind, but after all, circumstances have forced a break upon us and I think we had better look upon it as permanent.

CONSTANCE. Of course you must please yourself.

JOHN. I'm not thinking of myself, Constance. I'm thinking partly of course of Marie-Louise's good, but, I confess, chiefly of you. I could never look you in the face again if everything between Marie-Louise and me were not definitely finished.

CONSTANCE. I should hate you to lose so harmless and inexpensive a pleasure.

JOHN. Of course it'll be painful, but if one's made up one's mind to do a thing I think it's much better to do it quickly.

CONSTANCE. I think you're quite right. I'll tell you what I'll do, as soon as Marie-Louise comes I'll make an excuse and leave you alone with her.

JOHN. That wasn't exactly my idea.

CONSTANCE. Oh?

JOHN. It's the kind of thing that a woman can do so much better than a man. It struck me that it would come better from you than from me.

CONSTANCE. Oh, did it?

JOHN. It's a little awkward for me, but it would be quite easy for you to say—

well, you know the sort of thing, that you have your self-respect to think of, and to cut a long story short, she must either give me up or you'll raise hell.

CONSTANCE. But you know what a soft heart I have. If she bursts into tears and says she can't live without you I shall feel so sorry for her that I shall say, Well, damn it all, keep him.

JOHN. You wouldn't do me a dirty trick like that, Constance.

CONSTANCE. You know that your happiness is my chief interest in life.

JOHN (after a moment's hesitation). Constance, I will be perfectly frank with you. I'm fed up with Marie-Louise.

CONSTANCE. Darling, why didn't you say that at once?

JOHN. Be a sport, Constance. You know that's not the kind of thing one can say to a woman.

CONSTANCE. I admit it's not the kind of thing she's apt to take very well.

JOHN. Women are funny. When they're tired of you they tell you so without a moment's hesitation and if you don't like it you can lump it. But if you're tired of them you're a brute and a beast and boiling oil's too good for you.

CONSTANCE. Very well, leave it to me. I'll do it.

JOHN. You're a perfect brick. But you'll let her down gently, won't you? I wouldn't hurt her feelings for the world. She's a nice little thing, Constance.

CONSTANCE. Sweet.

JOHN. And it's hard luck on her.

CONSTANCE. Rotten.

JOHN. Make her understand that I'm more sinned against than sinning. I don't want her to think too badly of me.

CONSTANCE. Of course not.

JOHN. But be quite sure it's definite.

CONSTANCE. Leave it to me.

JOHN. You're a ripper, Constance. By George, no man could want a better wife.

[The BUTLER introduces MARIE-LOUISE.]

BUTLER. Mrs. Durham.

[The two women embrace warmly.]

MARIE-LOUISE. Darling, how perfectly divine to see you again. It's too, too wonderful.

CONSTANCE. My dear, how well you're looking. Are those the new pearls?

MARIE-LOUISE. Aren't they sweet? But Mortimer bought me the most heavenly emeralds when we were in India. Oh, John, how are you?

JOHN. Oh, I'm all right, thanks.

MARIE-LOUISE. Aren't you a little fatter than when I saw you last?

JOHN. Certainly not.

MARIE-LOUISE. I've lost pounds (To CONSTANCE.) I'm so glad I caught you. I should have been so disappointed to miss you. (To JOHN.) Where are you going?

JOHN. Nowhere. Constance is going alone.

MARIE-LOUISE. Is she? How perfectly divine. I suppose you can't get away. Are you making pots of money?

JOHN. I get along. Will you forgive me if I leave you? I've got to be off.

MARIE-LOUISE. Of course. You're always busy, aren't you?

JOHN. Good-bye.

MARIE-LOUISE. I hope we shall see something of you while Constance is away.

JOHN. Thank you very much.

MARIE-LOUISE. Mortimer's golf has improved. He'd love to play with you.

JOHN. Oh, yes, I should love it. (He goes out.)

MARIE-LOUISE. I did so hope to find you alone. Constance, I've got heaps and heaps to tell you. Isn't it tactful of John to leave us? First of all I want to tell you how splendidly everything has turned out. You know you were quite right. I'm so glad I took your advice and made Mortimer take me away for a year.

CONSTANCE. Mortimer is no fool.

MARIE-LOUISE. Oh, no, for a man he's really quite clever. I gave him hell, you know, for ever having suspected me, and at last he was just eating out of my hand. But I could see he wasn't quite sure of me. You know what men are—when they once get an idea in their heads it's dreadfully difficult for them to get it out again. But the journey was an inspiration; I was absolutely angelic all the time, and he made a lot of money, so everything in the garden was rosy.

CONSTANCE. I'm very glad.

MARIE-LOUISE. I owe it all to you, Constance. I made Mortimer buy you a perfectly divine star sapphire in Ceylon. I told him he owed you some sort of reparation for the insult he'd put upon you. It cost a hundred and twenty pounds, darling, and we're taking it to Cartier's to have it set.

CONSTANCE. How thrilling.

MARIE-LOUISE. You mustn't think I'm ungrateful. Now listen, Constance, I want to tell you at once that you needn't distress yourself about me and John.

CONSTANCE. I never did.

MARIE-LOUISE. I know I behaved like a little beast, but I never thought you'd find out. If I had, well, you know me well enough to be positive that nothing would have induced me to have anything to do with him.

CONSTANCE. You're very kind.

MARIE-LOUISE. I want you to do something for me, Constance. Will you?

CONSTANCE. I'm always eager to oblige a friend.

MARIE-LOUISE. Well, you know what John is. Of course he's a dear and all that kind of thing, but the thing's over and it's best that he should realize it at once.

CONSTANCE. Over?

MARIE-LOUISE. Of course I know he's head over heels in love with me still. I saw that the moment I came into the room. One can't blame him for that, can one?

CONSTANCE. Men do find you fascinating.

MARIE-LOUISE. But one has to think of oneself sometimes in this world. He must see that it could never be the same after we discovered that you knew all about it.

CONSTANCE. I kept it from you as long as I could.

MARIE-LOUISE. One couldn't help feeling then that you were rather making fools of us. It seemed to take the romance away, if you see what I mean.

CONSTANCE. Dimly.

MARIE-LOUISE. You know, I wouldn't hurt John's feelings for the world, but it's no good beating about the bush and I'm quite determined to have the thing finished and done with before you go.

CONSTANCE. This is very sudden. I'm afraid it'll be an awful shock to John.

MARIE-LOUISE. I've quite made up my mind.

CONSTANCE. There isn't much time for a very long and moving scene, but I'll see if John is in still. Could you manage it in ten minutes?

MARIE-LOUISE. Oh, but _I_ can't see him. I want you to tell him.

CONSTANCE. Me!

MARIE-LOUISE. You know him so well, you know just the sort of things to say to him. It's not very nice telling a man who adores you that you don't care for him in that way any more. It's so much easier for a third party.

CONSTANCE. Do you really think so?

MARIE-LOUISE. I'm positive of it. You see, you can say that for your sake I've made up my mind that from now on we can be nothing but friends. You've been so wonderful to both of us, it would be dreadful if we didn't play the game now. Say that I shall always think of him tenderly and that he's the only man I've ever really loved, but that we must part.

CONSTANCE. But if he insists on seeing you?

MARIE-LOUISE. It's no good, Constance, I can't see him. I shall only cry and get my eyes all bunged up. You will do it for me, darling. Please.

CONSTANCE. I will.

MARIE-LOUISE. I got the most divine evening frock in pale green satin on my way through Paris, and it would look too sweet on you. Would you like me to give it to you? I've only worn it once.

CONSTANCE. Now tell me the real reason why you're so determined to get rid of John without a moment's delay.

[MARIE-LOUISE *looks at her and gives a little roguish smile.*]

MARIE-LOUISE. Swear you won't tell.

CONSTANCE. On my honour.

MARIE-LOUISE. Well, my dear, we met a perfectly divine young man in India. He was A.D.C. to one of the governors and he came home on the same boat with us. He simply adores me.

CONSTANCE. And of course you adore him.

MARIE-LOUISE. My dear, I'm absolutely mad about him. I don't know what's going to happen.

CONSTANCE. I think we can both give a pretty shrewd guess.

MARIE-LOUISE. It's simply awful to have a temperament like mine. Of course you can't understand, you're cold.

CONSTANCE (*very calmly*). You're an immoral little beast, Marie-Louise.

MARIE-LOUISE. Oh, I'm not. I have affairs—but I'm not promiscuous.

CONSTANCE. I should respect you more if you were an honest prostitute. She at least does what she does to earn her bread and butter. You take everything from your husband and give him nothing that he pays for. You are no better than a vulgar cheat.

MARIE-LOUISE (*surprised and really hurt*). Constance, how can you say such things to me? I think it's terribly unkind of you. I thought you liked me.

CONSTANCE. I do. I think you a liar, a humbug and a parasite, but I like you.

MARIE-LOUISE. You can't if you think such dreadful things about me.

CONSTANCE. I do. You're good-tempered and generous and sometimes amusing. I even have a certain affection for you.

MARIE-LOUISE (*smiling*). I don't believe you mean a word you say. You know how devoted I am to you.

CONSTANCE. I take people as they are and I dare say that in another twenty years you'll be the pink of propriety.

MARIE-LOUISE. Darling, I knew you didn't mean it, but you will have your little joke.

CONSTANCE. Now run along, darling, and I'll break the news to John.

MARIE-LOUISE. Well, good-bye, and be gentle with him. There is no reason why we shouldn't spare him as much as possible. (*She turns to go and at the door—stops.*) Of course I've often wondered why with your looks you don't have more success than you do. I know now.

CONSTANCE. Tell me.

MARIE-LOUISE. You see—you're a humourist and that always puts men off. (*She goes out. In a moment the door is cautiously opened and* JOHN *puts his head in.*)

JOHN. Has she gone?

CONSTANCE. Come in. A fine night and all's well.

JOHN (*entering*). I heard the door bang. You broke it to her?

CONSTANCE. I broke it.

JOHN. Was she awfully upset?

CONSTANCE. Of course it was a shock, but she kept a stiff upper lip.

JOHN. Did she cry?

CONSTANCE. No. Not exactly. To tell you the truth I think she was stunned by the blow. But of course when she gets home and realizes the full extent of her loss, she'll cry like anything. 20

JOHN. I hate to see a woman cry.

CONSTANCE. It is painful, isn't it? But of course it's a relief to the nerves.

JOHN. I think you're rather cool about it, Constance. I am not feeling any too comfortable. I shouldn't like her to think I'd treated her badly.

CONSTANCE. I think she quite understands that you're doing it for my sake. She knows that you have still a 30 very great regard for her.

JOHN. But you made it quite definite, didn't you?

CONSTANCE. Oh, quite.

JOHN. I'm really very much obliged to you, Constance.

CONSTANCE. Not at all.

JOHN. At all events I'm glad to think that you'll be able to set out on your holiday with a perfectly easy mind. 40 By the way, do you want any money? I'll write you a cheque at once.

CONSTANCE. Oh, no, thank you. I've got plenty. I've earned fourteen hundred pounds during this year that I've been working.

JOHN. Have you, by Jove! That's a very considerable sum.

CONSTANCE. I'm taking two hundred of it for my holiday. I've spent two hundred on my clothes and on odds and ends and the remaining thousand I've paid into your account this morning for my board and lodging during the last twelve months.

10 JOHN. Nonsense, darling. I won't hear of such a thing. I don't want you to pay for your board and lodging.

CONSTANCE. I insist.

JOHN. Don't you love me any more?

CONSTANCE. What has that to do with it? Oh, you think a woman can only love a man if he keeps her. Isn't that rating your powers of fascination too modestly? What about your charm and good humour?

JOHN. Don't be absurd, Constance. I can perfectly well afford to support you in your proper station. To offer me a thousand pounds for your board and lodging is almost insulting.

CONSTANCE. Don't you think it's the kind of insult you could bring yourself to swallow? One can do a lot of amusing things with a thousand pounds.

30 JOHN. I wouldn't dream of taking it. I never liked the idea of your going into business. I thought you had quite enough to do looking after the house and so forth.

CONSTANCE. Have you been less comfortable since I began working?

JOHN. No, I can't say I have.

CONSTANCE. You can take my word for it, a lot of incompetent women talk a great deal of nonsense about housekeeping. If you know your job and have good servants it can be done in ten minutes a day.

JOHN. Anyhow, you wanted to work and I yielded. I thought in point of fact it would be a very pleasant occupation for you, but heaven knows I wasn't expecting to profit financially by it.

CONSTANCE. No, I'm sure you weren't.

JOHN. Constance, I could never help thinking that your determination had something to do with Marie-Louise.

[*There is a moment's pause and when* CON-STANCE *speaks it is not without serious-* 10 *ness.*]

CONSTANCE. Haven't you wondered why I never reproached you for your affair with Marie-Louise?

JOHN. Yes. I could only ascribe it to your unfathomable goodness.

CONSTANCE. You were wrong. I felt I hadn't the right to reproach you.

JOHN. What do you mean, Constance? You had every right. We behaved 20 like a couple of swine. I may be a dirty dog, but, thank God, I know I'm a dirty dog.

CONSTANCE. You no longer desired me. How could I blame you for that? But if you didn't desire me, what use was I to you? You've seen how small a share I take in providing you with the comfort of a well-ordered home.

JOHN. You were the mother of my child. 30

CONSTANCE. Let us not exaggerate the importance of that, John. I per-formed a natural and healthy func-tion of my sex. And all the tiresome part of looking after the child when she was born I placed in the hands of much more competent persons. Let us face it, I was only a parasite in your house. You had entered into legal obligations that prevented you 40 from turning me adrift, but I owe you a debt of gratitude for never letting me see by word or gesture that I was no more than a costly and at times inconvenient ornament.

JOHN. I never looked upon you as an inconvenient ornament. And I don't know what you mean by being a parasite. Have I ever in any way suggested that I grudged a penny that I spent on you?

CONSTANCE (*with mock amazement*). Do you mean to say that I ascribed to your beautiful manners what was only due to your stupidity? Are you as great a fool as the average man who falls for the average woman's stupen-dous bluff that just because he's mar-ried her he must provide for her wants and her luxuries, sacrifice his pleas-ures and comfort and convenience, and that he must look upon it as a privilege that she allows him to be her slave and bondman? Come, come, John, pull yourself together. You're a hundred years behind the times. Now that women have broken down the walls of the harem they must take the rough-and-tumble of the street.

JOHN. You forget all sorts of things. Don't you think a man may have gratitude to a woman for the love he has had for her in the past?

CONSTANCE. I think gratitude is often very strong in men so long as it demands from them no particular sacrifices.

JOHN. Well, it's a curious way of look-ing at things, but obviously I have reason to be thankful for it. But after all you knew what was going on long before it came out. What happened then that made you make up your mind to go into business?

CONSTANCE. I am naturally a lazy woman. So long as appearances were saved I was prepared to take all I could get and give nothing in return. I was a parasite, but I knew it. But when we reached a situation where only your politeness or your lack of intelligence prevented you from throwing the fact in my teeth, I changed my mind. I thought that I should very much like to be in a position where, if I felt inclined to, I could tell you, with calm and courtesy, but with determination— to go to hell.

JOHN. And are you in that position now?

CONSTANCE. Precisely. I owe you nothing. I am able to keep myself. For the last year I have paid my way. There is only one freedom that is really important and that is economic freedom, for in the long run the man who pays the piper calls the tune. Well, I have that freedom, and upon my soul it's the most enjoyable sensation I can remember since I ate my first strawberry ice.

JOHN. You know, I would sooner you had made me scenes for a month on end like any ordinary woman and nagged my life out than that you should harbor this cold rancour against me.

CONSTANCE. My poor darling, what are you talking about? Have you known me for fifteen years and do you think me capable of the commonness of insincerity? I harbour no rancour. Why, my dear, I'm devoted to you.

JOHN. Do you mean to tell me that you've done all this without any intention of making me feel a perfect cad?

CONSTANCE. On my honour. If I look in my heart I can only find in it affection for you and the most kindly and charitable feelings. Don't you believe me?

[*He looks at her for a moment and then makes a little gesture of bewilderment.*]

JOHN. Yes, oddly enough, I do. You are a remarkable woman, Constance.

CONSTANCE. I know, but keep it to yourself. You don't want to give a dog a bad name.

JOHN (*with an affectionate smile*). I wish I could get away. I don't half like the idea of your travelling by yourself.

CONSTANCE. Oh, but I'm not. Didn't I tell you?

JOHN. No.

CONSTANCE. I meant to. I'm going with Bernard.

JOHN. Oh! You never said so. Who else?

CONSTANCE. Nobody.

JOHN. Oh! (*He is rather taken aback at the news.*) Isn't that rather odd?

CONSTANCE. No. Why?

JOHN (*not knowing at all how to take it*). Well, it's not usual for a young woman to take a six weeks' holiday with a man who can hardly be described as old enough to be her father.

CONSTANCE. Bernard's just about the same age as you.

JOHN. Don't you think it'll make people gossip a bit?

CONSTANCE. I haven't gone out of my way to spread the news. In fact, now I come to think of it, I haven't told anyone but you, and you, I am sure, will be discreet.

[JOHN *suddenly feels that his collar is a little too tight for him, and with his fingers he tries to loosen it.*]

JOHN. You're pretty certain to be seen by someone who knows you and they're bound to talk.

CONSTANCE. Oh, I don't think so. You see we're motoring all the way and we neither of us care for frequented places. One of the advantages of having really nice friends like ours is that you can always be certain of finding them at the fashionable resorts at the very moment when everybody you know is there.

JOHN. Of course I am not so silly as to think that because a man and a woman go away together it is necessary to believe the worst about them, but you can't deny that it is rather unconventional. I wouldn't for a moment suggest that there'll be anything between you, but it's inevitable that ordinary persons should think there was. 10

CONSTANCE (*as cool as a cucumber*). I've always thought that ordinary persons had more sense than the clever ones are ready to credit them with.

JOHN (*deliberately*). What on earth do you mean?

CONSTANCE. Why, of course we're going as man and wife, John.

JOHN. Don't be a fool, Constance. You don't know what you're talking about. 20 That's not funny at all.

CONSTANCE. But, my poor John, whom do you take us for? Am I so unattractive that what I'm telling you is incredible? Why else should I go with Bernard? If I merely wanted a companion I'd go with a woman. We could have headaches together and have our hair washed at the same place and copy one another's night- 30 dresses. A woman's a much better travelling companion than a man.

JOHN. I may be very stupid, but I don't seem to be able to understand what you're saying. Do you really mean me to believe that Bernard Kersal is your lover?

CONSTANCE. Certainly not.

JOHN. Then what *are* you talking about?

CONSTANCE. My dear, I can't put it any 40 plainer. I'm going away for six weeks' holiday and Bernard has very kindly offered to come with me.

JOHN. And where do I come in?

CONSTANCE. You don't come in. You stay at home and look after your patients.

JOHN (*trying his best to control himself*). I flatter myself I'm a sensible man. I'm not going to fly into a passion. Many men would stamp and rave or break the furniture. I have no intention of being melodramatic, but you must allow me to say that what you've just told me is very surprising.

CONSTANCE. Just for a moment, perhaps, but I'm sure you have only to familiarize yourself with the notion in order to become reconciled to it.

JOHN. I'm doubtful whether I shall have time to do that, for I feel uncommonly as though I were about to have an apoplectic stroke.

CONSTANCE. Undo your collar then. Now I come to look at you I confess that you are more than usually red in the face.

JOHN. What makes you think that I am going to allow you to go?

CONSTANCE (*good-humouredly*). Chiefly the fact that you can't prevent me.

JOHN. I can't bring myself to believe that you mean what you say. I don't know what ever put such an idea into your head.

CONSTANCE (*casually*). I thought a change might do me good.

JOHN. Nonsense.

CONSTANCE. Why? You did. Don't you remember? You were getting rather flat and stale. Then you had an affair with Marie-Louise and you were quite another man. Gay and amusing, full of life, and much more agreeable to live with. The moral effect on you was quite remarkable.

JOHN. It's different for a man than for a woman.

CONSTANCE. Are you thinking of the possible consequences? We have long passed the Victorian Era when asterisks were followed after a certain interval by a baby.

JOHN. That never occurred to me. What I meant was that if a man's unfaithful to his wife she's an object of sympathy, whereas if a woman's unfaithful to her husband he's merely an object of ridicule.

CONSTANCE. That is one of those conventional prejudices that sensible people must strive to ignore.

JOHN. Do you expect me to sit still and let this man take my wife away from under my very nose? I wonder you don't ask me to shake hands with him and wish him good luck.

CONSTANCE. That's just what I am going to do. He's coming here in a few minutes to say good-bye to you.

JOHN. I shall knock him down.

CONSTANCE. I wouldn't take any risks in your place. He's pretty hefty and I'm under the impression that he's very nippy with his left.

JOHN. I shall have great pleasure in telling him exactly what I think of him.

CONSTANCE. Why? Have you forgotten that I was charming to Marie-Louise? We were the best of friends. She never bought a hat without asking me to go and help her choose it.

JOHN. I have red blood in my veins.

CONSTANCE. I'm more concerned at the moment with the grey matter in your brain.

JOHN. Is he in love with you?

CONSTANCE. Madly. Didn't you know?

JOHN. I? How should I?

CONSTANCE. He's been here a great deal during the last year. Were you under the impression that he only came to see you?

JOHN. I never paid any attention to him. I thought him rather dull.

CONSTANCE. He is rather dull. But he's very sweet.

JOHN. What sort of a man is it who eats a fellow's food and drinks his wine and then makes love to his wife behind his back?

CONSTANCE. A man very like you, John, I should say.

JOHN. Not at all. Mortimer is the sort of man who was born to be made a fool of.

CONSTANCE. None of us know for certain the designs of Providence.

JOHN. I see you're bent on driving me to desperation. I shall break something in a minute.

CONSTANCE. There's that blue-and-white bowl that your Uncle Henry gave us as a wedding present. Break that, it's only a modern imitation.

[He takes the bowl and hurls it on the floor so that it is shattered.]

JOHN. There.

CONSTANCE. Do you feel better?

JOHN. Not a bit.

CONSTANCE. It's a pity you broke it then. You might have given it away as a wedding present to one of your colleagues at the hospital.

[The BUTLER shows in MRS. CULVER.]

BENTLEY. Mrs. Culver.

CONSTANCE. Oh, mother, how sweet of you to come. I was so hoping I'd see you before I left.

MRS. CULVER. Oh, you've had an accident.

CONSTANCE. No, John's in a temper and he thought it would relieve him if he broke something.

MRS. CULVER. Nonsense, John's never in a temper.

JOHN. That's what you think, Mrs. Culver. Yes, I am in a temper. I'm in a filthy temper. Are you a party to this plan of Constance's?

CONSTANCE. No, mother doesn't know.

JOHN. Can't you do something to stop it? You have some influence over her.

You must see that the thing's preposterous.

MRS. CULVER. My dear boy, I haven't the ghost of an idea what you're talking about.

JOHN. She's going to Italy with Bernard Kersal. Alone.

MRS. CULVER (*with a stare*). It's not true; how d'you know?

JOHN. She's just told me so, as bold as brass, out of a blue sky. She mentioned it in the course of conversation as if she were saying, Darling, your coat wants brushing.

MRS. CULVER. Is it true, Constance?

CONSTANCE. Quite.

MRS. CULVER. But haven't you been getting on with John? I always thought you two were as happy as the day is long.

JOHN. So did I. We've never had the shadow of a quarrel. We've always got on.

MRS. CULVER. Don't you love John any more, darling?

CONSTANCE. Yes, I'm devoted to him.

JOHN. How can you be devoted to a man when you're going to do him the greatest injury that a woman can do to a man?

CONSTANCE. Don't be idiotic, John. I'm going to do you no more injury than you did me a year ago.

JOHN (*striding up to her, thinking quite erroneously that he sees light*). Are you doing this in order to pay me out for Marie-Louise?

CONSTANCE. Don't be such a fool, John. Nothing is further from my thoughts.

MRS. CULVER. The circumstances are entirely different. It was very naughty of John to deceive you, but he's sorry for what he did and he's been punished for it. It was all very dreadful and caused us a great deal of pain. But a man's a man and you expect that kind of thing from him. There are excuses for him. There are none for a woman. Men are naturally polygamous and sensible women have always made allowances for their occasional lapse from a condition which modern civilization has forced on them. Women are monogamous. They do not naturally desire more than one man and that is why the common sense of the world has heaped obloquy upon them when they have overstepped the natural limitations of their sex.

CONSTANCE (*smiling*). It seems rather hard that what is sauce for the gander shouldn't also be sauce for the goose.

MRS. CULVER. We all know that unchastity has no moral effect on men. They can be perfectly promiscuous and remain upright, industrious and reliable. It's quite different with women. It ruins their character. They become untruthful and dissipated, lazy, shiftless and dishonest. That is why the experience of ten thousand years has demanded chastity in women. Because it has learnt that this virtue is the key to all others.

CONSTANCE. They were dishonest because they were giving away something that wasn't theirs to give. They had sold themselves for board, lodging and protection. They were chattels. They were dependent on their husbands and when they were unfaithful to them they were liars and thieves. I'm not dependent on John. I am economically independent and therefore I claim my sexual independence. I have this afternoon paid into John's account one thousand pounds for my year's keep.

JOHN. I refuse to take it.

CONSTANCE. Well, you'll damned well have to.

MRS. CULVER. There's no object in losing your temper.

CONSTANCE. I have mine under perfect control.

JOHN. If you think what they call free love is fun you're mistaken. Believe me, it's the most overrated amusement that was ever invented.

CONSTANCE. In that case, I wonder why people continue to indulge in it.

JOHN. I ought to know what I'm talking about, hang it all. It has all the inconveniences of marriage and none of its advantages. I assure you, my dear, the game is not worth the candle.

CONSTANCE. You may be right, but you know how hard it is to profit by anybody's experience. I think I'd like to see for myself.

MRS. CULVER. Are you in love with Bernard?

CONSTANCE. To tell you the truth I haven't quite made up my mind. How does one know if one's in love?

MRS. CULVER. My dear, I only know one test. Could you use his tooth-brush?

CONSTANCE. No.

MRS. CULVER. Then you're not in love with him.

CONSTANCE. He's adored me for fifteen years. There's something in that long devotion which gives me a funny little feeling in my heart. I should like to do something to show him that I'm not ungrateful. You see, in six weeks he goes back to Japan. There is no chance of his coming to England again for seven years. I'm thirty-six now and he adores me; in seven years I shall be forty-three. A woman of forty-three is often charming, but it's seldom that a man of fifty-five is crazy about her. I came to the conclusion that it must be now or never and so I asked him if he'd like me to spend these last six weeks

with him in Italy. When I wave my handkerchief to him as the ship that takes him sails out of the harbour at Naples I hope that he will feel that all those years of unselfish love have been well worth the while.

JOHN. Six weeks. Do you intend to leave him at the end of six weeks?

CONSTANCE. Oh, yes, of course. It's because I'm putting a limit to our love that I think it may achieve the perfection of something that is beautiful and transitory. Why, John, what is it that makes a rose so lovely but that its petals fall as soon as it is full blown?

JOHN. It's all come as such a shock and a surprise that I hardly know what to say. You've got me at a complete disadvantage.

[MRS. CULVER, *who has been standing at the window, gives a little cry.*]

CONSTANCE. What is it?

MRS. CULVER. Here is Bernard. He's just driven up to the door.

JOHN. Do you expect me to receive him as if I were blissfully unconscious of your plans?

CONSTANCE. It would be more comfortable. It would be stupid to make a scene and it wouldn't prevent my going on this little jaunt with him.

JOHN. I have my dignity to think of.

CONSTANCE. One often preserves that best by putting it in one's pocket. It would be kind of you, John, to treat him just as pleasantly as I treated Marie-Louise when I knew she was your mistress.

JOHN. Does he know that I know?

CONSTANCE. Of course not. He's a little conventional, you know, and he couldn't happily deceive a friend if he thought there was no deception.

MRS. CULVER. Constance, is there nothing I can say to make you reconsider your decision?

CONSTANCE. Nothing, darling.

MRS. CULVER. Then I may just as well save my breath. I'll slip away before he comes.

CONSTANCE. Oh, all right. Good-bye, Mother. I'll send you a lot of picture post-cards.

MRS. CULVER. I don't approve of you, Constance, and I can't pretend that I do. No good will come of it. Men were meant by nature to be wicked and delightful and deceive their wives, and women were meant to be virtuous and forgiving and to suffer verbosely. That was ordained from all eternity and none of your new-fangled notions can alter the decrees of Providence.

[*The* BUTLER *enters, followed by* BERNARD.]

BENTLEY. Mr. Kersal.

MRS. CULVER. How do you do, Bernard, and good-bye. I'm just going.

BERNARD. Oh, I'm sorry. Good-bye.

[*She goes out.*]

CONSTANCE (*to* BERNARD). How d'you do? Just one moment. (*To the* BUTLER.) Oh, Bentley, get my things downstairs and put them in a taxi, will you?

BENTLEY. Very good, madam.

BERNARD. Are you just starting? It's lucky I came when I did. I should have hated to miss you.

CONSTANCE. And let me know when the taxi's here.

BENTLEY. Yes, madam.

CONSTANCE. Now I can attend to you.

[*The* BUTLER *goes out.*]

BERNARD. Are you looking forward to your holiday?

CONSTANCE. Immensely. I've never gone on a jaunt like this before, and I'm really quite excited.

BERNARD. You're going alone, aren't you?

CONSTANCE. Oh, yes, quite alone.

BERNARD. It's rotten for you not to be able to get away, old man.

JOHN. Rotten.

BERNARD. I suppose these are the penalties of greatness. I can quite understand that you have to think of your patients first.

JOHN. Quite.

CONSTANCE. Of course John doesn't very much care for Italy.

BERNARD. Oh, are you going to Italy? I thought you said Spain.

JOHN. No, she always said Italy.

BERNARD. Oh, well, that's hardly your mark, is it, old boy? Though I believe there are some sporting links on the Lake of Como.

JOHN. Are there?

BERNARD. I suppose there's no chance of your being anywhere near Naples towards the end of July?

CONSTANCE. I don't really know. My plans are quite vague.

BERNARD. I was only asking because I'm sailing from Naples. It would be fun if we met there.

JOHN. Great fun.

CONSTANCE. I hope you'll see a lot of John while I'm away. I'm afraid he'll be a trifle lonely, poor darling. Why don't you dine together one day next week?

BERNARD. I'm terribly sorry, but you know I'm going away.

CONSTANCE. Oh, are you? I thought you were going to stay in London till you had to start for Japan.

BERNARD. I meant to, but my doctor has ordered me to go and do a cure.

JOHN. What sort of a cure?

BERNARD. Oh, just a cure. He says I want bucking up.

JOHN. Oh, does he? What's the name of your doctor?

BERNARD. No one you ever heard of. A man I used to know in the war.

JOHN. Oh!

BERNARD. So I'm afraid this is good-bye. Of course, it's a wrench leaving London, especially as I don't expect to be in Europe again for some years, but I always think it rather silly not to take a man's advice when you've asked for it.

JOHN. More especially when he's charged you three guineas.

CONSTANCE. I'm sorry. I was counting on you to keep John out of mischief during my absence.

BERNARD. I'm not sure if I could guarantee to do that. But we might have done a few theatres together and had a game of golf or two.

CONSTANCE. It would have been jolly, wouldn't it, John?

JOHN. Very jolly.

[*The* BUTLER *comes in.*]

BENTLEY. The taxi's waiting, madam.

CONSTANCE. Thank you.

[*The* BUTLER *goes out.*]

BERNARD. I'll take myself off. In case I don't see you again I'd like to thank you now for all your kindness to me during the year I've spent in London.

CONSTANCE. It's been very nice to see you.

BERNARD. You and John have been most awfully good to me. I never imagined I was going to have such a wonderful time.

CONSTANCE. We shall miss you terribly. It's been a great comfort to John to think that there was someone to take me out when he had to be away on one of his operations. Hasn't it, darling?

JOHN. Yes, darling.

CONSTANCE. When he knew I was with you he never worried. Did you, darling?

JOHN. No, darling.

BERNARD. I'm awfully glad if I've been able to make myself useful. Don't forget me entirely, will you?

CONSTANCE. We're not likely to do that, are we, darling?

JOHN. No, darling.

BERNARD. And if you ever have a moment to spare you will write to me, won't you? You don't know how much it means to us exiles.

CONSTANCE. Of course we will. We'll both write. Won't we, darling?

JOHN. Yes, darling.

CONSTANCE. John writes such a good letter. So chatty, you know, and amusing.

BERNARD. That's a promise. Well, good-bye, old boy. Have a good time.

JOHN. Thanks, old bean.

BERNARD. Good-bye, Constance. There's so much I want to say to you that I don't know where to begin.

JOHN. I don't want to hurry you, but the taxi is just ticking its head off.

BERNARD. John is so matter-of-fact. Well, I'll say nothing then but God bless you.

CONSTANCE. Au revoir.

BERNARD. If you do go to Naples you will let me know, won't you? If you send a line to my club, it'll be forwarded at once.

CONSTANCE. Oh, all right.

BERNARD. Good-bye.

[*He gives them both a friendly nod and goes out.* CONSTANCE *begins to giggle and soon is seized with uncontrollable laughter.*]

JOHN. Will you kindly tell me what there is to laugh at? If you think it amuses me to stand here like patience on a monument and have my leg pulled you're mistaken. What did you mean by all that balderdash about meeting you by chance in Naples?

CONSTANCE. He was throwing you off the scent.

JOHN. The man's a drivelling idiot.

CONSTANCE. D'you think so? I thought he was rather ingenious. Considering he hasn't had very much practice in this sort of thing I thought he did very well.

JOHN. Of course if you're determined to find him a pattern of perfection it's useless for me to attempt to argue. But honestly, speaking without prejudice for or against, I'm sorry to think of you throwing yourself away on a man like that.

CONSTANCE. Perhaps it's natural that a man and his wife should differ in their estimate of her prospective lover.

JOHN. You're not going to tell me he's better-looking than I am.

CONSTANCE. No. You have always been my ideal of manly beauty.

JOHN. He's no better dressed than I am.

CONSTANCE. He could hardly expect to be. He goes to the same tailor.

JOHN. I don't think you can honestly say he's more amusing than I am.

CONSTANCE. No, I honestly can't.

JOHN. Then in Heaven's name why do you want to go away with him?

CONSTANCE. Shall I tell you? Once more before it's too late I want to feel about me the arms of a man who adores the ground I walk on. I want to see his face light up when I enter the room. I want to feel the pressure of his hand when we look at the moon together and the pleasantly tickling sensation when his arm tremulously steals around my waist. I want to let my hand fall on his shoulder and feel his lips softly touch my hair.

JOHN. The operation is automatically impossible, the poor devil would get such a crick in the neck he wouldn't know what to do.

CONSTANCE. I want to walk along country lanes holding hands and I want to be called by absurd pet names. I want to talk baby-talk by the hour together.

JOHN. Oh, God.

CONSTANCE. I want to know that I'm eloquent and witty when I'm dead silent. For ten years I've been very happy in your affection, John, we've been the best and dearest friends, but now just for a little while I hanker for something else. Do you grudge it me? I want to be loved.

JOHN. But, my dear, I'll love you. I've been a brute, I've neglected you, it's not too late and you're the only woman I've ever really cared for. I'll chuck everything and we'll go away together.

CONSTANCE. The prospect does not thrill me.

JOHN. Come, darling, have a heart. I gave up Marie-Louise. Surely you can give up Bernard.

CONSTANCE. But you gave up Marie-Louise to please yourself, not to please me.

JOHN. Don't be a little beast, Constance. Come away with me. We'll have such a lark.

CONSTANCE. Oh, my poor John, I didn't work so hard to gain my economic independence in order to go on a honeymoon with my own husband.

JOHN. Do you think I can't be a lover as well as a husband?

CONSTANCE. My dear, no one can make yesterday's cold mutton into tomorrow's lamb cutlets.

JOHN. You know what you're doing. I was determined in future to be a model husband and you're driving me right into the arms of Marie-Louise. I give you my word of honour that the moment you leave this house I shall drive straight to her door.

CONSTANCE. I should hate you to have a fruitless journey. I'm afraid you won't find her at home. She has a new young man and she says he's too divine.

JOHN. What!

CONSTANCE. He's the A.D.C. of a Colonial Governor. She came here today to ask me to break the news to you that henceforth everything was over between you.

JOHN. I hope you told her first that I was firmly resolved to terminate a connection that could only cause you pain.

CONSTANCE. I couldn't. She was in such a blooming hurry to give me her message.

JOHN. Really, Constance, for your own pride I should have thought you wouldn't like her to make a perfect fool of me. Any other woman would have said, What a strange coincidence. Why it's only half an hour since John told me he had made up his mind never to see you again. But of course you don't care two straws for me any more, that's quite evident.

CONSTANCE. Oh, don't be unjust, darling. I shall always care for you. I may be unfaithful, but I am constant. I always think that's my most endearing quality.

[*The* BUTLER *opens the door.*]

JOHN (*irritably*). What is it?

BENTLEY. I thought madam had forgotten that the taxi was at the door.

JOHN. Go to hell.

BENTLEY. Very good, sir.

[*He goes out.*]

CONSTANCE. I don't see why you should be rude to him. Bernard will pay the taxi. Anyhow I must go now or he'll begin to think I'm not coming. Good-bye, darling. I hope you'll get on all right in my absence. Just give the cook her head and you'll have no trouble. Won't you say good-bye to me?

JOHN. Go to the devil.

CONSTANCE. All right. I shall be back in six weeks.

JOHN. Back? Where?

CONSTANCE. Here.

JOHN. Here? Here? Do you think I'm going to take you back?

CONSTANCE. I don't see why not. When you've had time to reflect you'll realize that you have no reason to blame me. After all, I'm taking from you nothing that you want.

JOHN. Are you aware that I can divorce you for this?

CONSTANCE. Quite. But I married very prudently. I took the precaution to marry a gentleman and I know that you could never bring yourself to divorce me for doing no more than you did yourself.

JOHN. I wouldn't divorce you. I wouldn't expose my worst enemy to the risk of marrying a woman who's capable of treating her husband as you're treating me.

CONSTANCE (*at the door*). Well, then, shall I come back?

JOHN (*after a moment's hesitation*). You are the most maddening, wilful, capricious, wrong-headed, delightful and enchanting woman man was ever cursed with having for a wife. Yes, damn you, come back.

[*She lightly kisses her hand to him and slips out, slamming the door behind her.*]

ALLAN MONKHOUSE

ENGLAND HAD NO organization in the modern theatre comparable in distinction to the Moscow Art, the Abbey Theatre, or even Antoine's Théâtre Libre. But there was at all times a small group devotedly interested in the new forms of drama and their staging. J. T. Grein, Miss Horniman, and others founded the Independent Theatre in London in 1891, and for nearly a decade defended its productions of Ibsen and the moderns, including the first plays of a rising young Irish hot-head, G. B. Shaw. The London Stage Society was founded in 1899, but its purpose was primarily to evade the Victorian censorship of the Lord Chamberlain by giving private performances, usually on Sunday evening, of the advanced plays. England did excel, however, in her repertory theatres in the provincial towns. These active organizations in Manchester, Birmingham, Liverpool, and other cities infused so much new life into the theatre that the English dramatic critic Graham Sutton called the period from 1900 to 1914 the "Repertory Age."

Manchester was the most productive center outside London. The city was big and wealthy, with men of commerce eager to add culture to mercantile prosperity. Its journal, the Manchester Guardian, was held in esteem throughout the Empire. The Guardian's dramatic criticisms were respected everywhere. Miss Annie Elizabeth Fredericka Horniman (1861–1937), who had financed the Abbey Theatre, who had arranged for its London appearances and English tours, and who had for fifteen years been a most generous friend of modern drama, took over the old Midland Theatre in Manchester in the autumn of 1907 and founded a repertory theatre. The following spring she acquired the Gaiety Theatre and rapidly made it famous both for its productions of the established contemporary dramatists and for its discovery and development of new dramatic talent. A Manchester school of playwrights soon was flourishing in this Midlands manufacturing town. It was recruited from among the young men in the offices and warehouses who were prompted to literary creation by the opportunities and the excitement of a progressive and alert non-commercial theatre in their midst.

Several of these Manchester playwrights became famous. Stanley Houghton, a young lawyer of the city, made a name in modern English drama with his *Hindle Wakes* (1912). Harold Brighouse was established as a playwright with his short piece, *The Price of Coal* (1909), and with his graceful plays, *Lonesome-like* and *Spring in Bloomsbury*, both in 1911. Others, like Basil Dean and Charles McEvoy, contributed many interesting if less successful plays under the same aegis. To this group also belongs the work of the distinguished dramatic critic of the Manchester Guardian, novelist and man of letters, Allan Monkhouse.

Monkhouse was born in 1858 at Barnard Castle in Durham. Like other Lancashire men he had strong feelings for his county, but the sterner business of living took him to Manchester. He was educated there in the private schools. He was not a university man. He entered the cotton trade and worked from early manhood to middle age in the warehouses and offices of Manchester. He had a natural gift for writing which he cultivated and brought to a high degree of distinction. He wrote essays, stories, sketches, and novels. In 1902 he joined the editorial staff of the Manchester Guardian for which he wrote dramatic criticisms and some of his most memorable stories. He remained with this journal for thirty years.

Monkhouse entered the theatre under the guidance of Miss Horniman. Her endowed, semi-private Gaiety Theatre afforded beginning playwrights a stage for short, apprentice pieces to be used as curtain raisers, or to be grouped with several others into an evening's entertainment, just as the Abbey Theatre provided a stage for Synge's one act plays. These busy young Manchester men got their first training and developed their technical skill in this admirable theatrical school. Monkhouse made his first appearance with a rather promising one act play called *Reaping the Whirlwind*, which Miss Horniman produced in 1908. With this encouragement the author began to write plays at frequent intervals. His fame rose gradually to its high peak in 1924 when *The Conquering Hero* went far beyond the repertory class into a significant place in international contemporary drama. Monkhouse wrote in all a score of plays, including the one act pieces. He lived at Stockport, Cheshire, and died there in 1938 at the moment when his play about war was reasserting its importance and its timelessness.

The first plays of Monkhouse, *Reaping the Whirlwind, Resentment, The Stricklands*, and *The Hayling Family* were brought together in 1913 as *Four Tragedies*. These plays have perished with time and repertory, and Mr. Graham Sutton has composed an epitaph for them. "These are all somewhat dry and 'literary,'—not highbrow, in what the word connotes of affectation, but the work of a young man who has not yet gained the knack of making his folk talk much otherwise than he would talk himself: that is, the knack of *character* in dialogue."

Neither have the early full-length plays held up well. They seem now to belong to an inconsequential era of outmoded themes, interests, and sterile technique. The best of them are *Mary Broome* (1912) and *The Education of Mr. Suffrage* (1913). Both dealt with repertory theatre competence with the then fashionable theme of exposing the too arty, or fake artist, the hangers-on of the movements; and the conflict between the successful business fathers of the late Victorian era and their more artistic, sophisticated, and emancipated sons and daughters who patronize them. Monkhouse had enough understanding of the virtues of these fathers and enough malice for the shams of the children to give bite to the characters and pace and cleverness to the dialogue.

Monkhouse's versatility, however, is shown by such diverse plays as *The Grand Cham's Diamond* (1918) and *First Blood* (1924). The first is a one act play somewhat in the manner of Lord Dunsany. The famous diamond suddenly hurtles through a window in Mrs. Perkins's lower middle-class house in suburban London and sets off a train of romantic escape and character portrayal before it is finally returned to its owner. The romance is over, but poor

Mrs. Perkins sums it all up in the tag line, "Well, I'ad my bit o' fun for onct." *First Blood* ventured with some success into the post-War concern over the capitalist-labor disputes and the evolving ideology separating the two interests.

Three of Monkhouse's earlier plays have more interest for us because of their foreshadowing of *The Conquering Hero*. They were published as *War Plays, 1916: Shamed Life, Night Watches*, and *The Choice*. *The Choice* states Monkhouse's approach to the problem of war as it affects the young men who make the sacrifices and do the fighting. The hero loathes the thought of war, but goes off to fight in South Africa because of the pressure exerted upon him by his patriotic sweetheart. He was at heart peaceful to the point of cowardice, and was shot down by his commanding officer when at a critical moment his courage failed him.

This situation is elevated with reflection and emotion in *The Conquering Hero*, presented with success in London in 1923. It is probably the best war play produced in England; and it is Monkhouse's masterpiece. The literature about the World War had gone through its romantic phase and its glorification of the holy mission to rescue Belgium and end all wars. It had entered upon its debunking period of passionate revolt against the blood, the filth, the maddening meaninglessness of this continuous slaughtering. Toller's *Transfiguration* had been written. Anti-war plays of great power were to come: realistic dramas like Anderson and Stallings' *What Price Glory?* in 1924; Sherriff's *Journey's End* in 1928; and Wolf's *Sailors of Cattaro* in 1934; expressionistic and imaginative dramas like Nichols and Browne's *Wings Over Europe* in 1929; Chlumberg's *Miracle At*

Verdun in 1930; and Irwin Shaw's *Bury the Dead* in 1936; thoughtful plays like Sklar and Maltz's *Peace on Earth* in 1933; and Sherwood's *Idiot's Delight* in 1936, and *There Shall Be No Night* in 1940. Regardless of date and nationality these plays all have in common an intense loathing for the unspeakable process of war.

All the disillusion of modern thinking men with war as an instrument of national policy for bringing about changes or reform is concentrated in the quiet irony of Monkhouse's title, *The Conquering Hero*. The World War was unheroic. As in all wars there was no victory, only defeat for victors and vanquished alike. Those who joined up as volunteers in the first years of the war actually went under the duress of all the concentrated pressures that society can impose upon a young man. *The Conquering Hero* was written in the period of calm self-searching following the treaty of Versailles. It presents in the person of Christopher Rokeby, and to a lesser extent his brother Stephen, the dilemma of "those who hated war and went to war," as Monkhouse put it in the dedicatory lines. Two acts are given to the problem of Chris's enlistment, one short shattering act to the War, and a fourth to the consequences. The last two follow inevitably from the penetrating analysis in the first two.

Monkhouse builds his case around a young artist who respects mankind and man's achievements in civilization. He is too young—like all the boys who are put into war service—to have accomplished much, but he has belief and promise. (Sherwood took a more obvious example when he sent a Finnish Nobel prize-winning scientist to death behind a sandbag at the hands of an ignorant Russian peasant in *There Shall Be No Night*.) But Chris is not just a callow and egotistical boy when he says, "It isn't only Frank we want; it's the idea of Frank. Now I can give you that. . . . The world doesn't exist without me—I speak for the lot of us— wars are not worth fighting but for me." But the world comes along with another of its wars, and reduces all men to the lowest common level of combatants. Only one thing is any longer valuable: Soldiers. It is the tragedy of life, and the source of the brooding pathos of this play, that Christopher Rokeby finds that, rebel as he will, even he cannot escape or resist the blind force that sends men to war generation after generation. Without illusions, with clear knowledge of what they are facing, with repugnance for the entire process, they give up their private lives and the work that sustains them and perform their "duty"—the potential Edison, Einstein, Milton, and Beethoven side by side with the farm boy and the garage mechanic. This is the tragedy in which we are caught, the tragedy of Monkhouse's play.

The importance of *The Conquering Hero* was recognized by the reviewers and critics of the season 1923–1924. Martin Armstrong wrote in the *Spectator:* "We are shown, with remarkable insight and truth, the conflict between the humane, unrevengeful, and jealously personal attitude of the man who has fought, and the blood-thirsty, mock-heroic chauvinism of many stay-at-homes. Nowhere have I seen the intelligent fighting-man's attitude so penetratingly presented." Allardyce Nicoll praised its "concentrated passion" which "gives nobility and dignity to the treatment." And Graham Sutton, writing in 1924, concluded an essay on Monkhouse with these portentous words: "Let us have done with the stage-magnate's foolish fiction that such plays are out of date. Let us rather produce and ponder them with sharpened wits, instead of living in security as Chris Rokeby had lived . . . as you and I had lived and are preparing to live again. If not, be sure the next war will come without consulting us; and then it will be for us as it was for them, too late."

THE CONQUERING HERO

CHARACTERS

COLONEL ROKEBY

CHRISTOPHER ROKEBY ⎫
STEPHEN ROKEBY ⎭ *his sons*

MARGARET IREDALE, *his daughter*

CAPTAIN FRANCIS IREDALE

HELEN THORBURN

SIR JOHN ROMER

LADY ROMER

DAKIN

MEGSON

A PRUSSIAN OFFICER

AN OLD FOOTMAN

GERMAN SOLDIERS

ACT I

The hall of COLONEL ROKEBY'S *house, which is some 30 miles from London. It is twilight on a day in late summer, and it grows darker as the scene progresses.* CHRISTOPHER *and* STEPHEN ROKEBY, MARGARET *and* FRANCIS IREDALE *and* HELEN THORBURN *sit round an empty fireplace. Their voices are heard, but faces and forms are indistinguishable. The debris of tea is on a table behind them, but the detail of the room* 10 *is not revealed till the lights are turned up presently. It is a pleasant, comfortable room of an ordinary type. There is a door at the back leading to an outside hall or entrance, and windows looking directly upon the garden at one side. Other doors to left and right from the hall.*

MARGARET. What about lights? Let's turn up the lights.

HELEN. Oh, no! Margaret, let us cower in the dark a little longer.

MARGARET. We've got to face things at last.

HELEN. I know. You ought to be a soldier, Margaret.

IREDALE. Any reflection on me?

CHRIS. No, it's not on you, Frank. It's on the degenerate sons of the family. And as Stephen's a parson, he doesn't count.

STEPHEN. Why don't I count?

CHRIS. Well, you can't say it's wrong to be a parson. Even Margaret won't go as far as that.

MARGARET. I've never said it's wrong to be what you are. I only said I'm sorry for Father.

HELEN. What is Chris?

CHRIS. Listen to that!

HELEN. I didn't mean to be nasty, Chris, really. But you want defining, somehow.

CHRIS. Yes, it's going to be a definite world now. Drilling and marching and shooting. You're an able-bodied soldier or you're nothing.

20 HELEN. Chris is bitter about his novel. What will happen to it now?

CHRIS. Who cares?—except me.

MARGARET. You drilled at school, didn't you? Of course you did.

CHRIS. I never hated anything so much. Drilling's the dullest thing in the world. It's the speed of the slowest; it's the game of the stupidest.

THE CONQUERING HERO: Reprinted by permission of James B. Pinker & Son Ltd.

HELEN. Then why were you so good at it? Stephen said you were.

CHRIS. Because I'm clever enough not to be too clever.

HELEN. Well!

STEPHEN. He's speaking the truth.

MARGARET. We all know that Chris is clever. That's why it's such a pity that he does nothing.

IREDALE. Margaret——

MARGARET. I think of Father. I think of what he wanted. And now—now—he'd go if they'd let him. He's sixty-five.

STEPHEN. Well, the fool of the family went into the Church. That's all right.

MARGARET. I don't blame you, Stephen.

CHRIS. You'll never learn that it takes all kinds to make a world. Now, here's Frank——

MARGARET. Don't speak of Frank.

CHRIS. Why not?

MARGARET. You're not worthy to button his boots.

IREDALE. Oh! Deuce take it, Margaret.

MARGARET. For you to be contemptuous of him!

CHRIS. Contemptuous? Of Frank? Am I, Stephen?

STEPHEN. I don't know.

CHRIS. He stands for my idea of the soldier. And it is an idea. But there's room for others. Soldiering isn't the only thing.

HELEN. It is now.

CHRIS. Do you say that, Helen?

HELEN. P'raps I shouldn't.—You make me say it.

CHRIS. But I stand for something too.

MARGARET. What good is it, now? Who wants your novel? Or your pretty little stories? He's writing a play.

CHRIS. They are not pretty.

MARGARET. What does it matter? What does the world want? What does England want?

CHRIS. Yes. When the pipe bursts you send for the plumber. And the plumber's the most important person in the world. What's the good of being amusing or charming, or wise or virtuous? Are you a plumber? Why aren't you a plumber?

MARGARET. You can't understand a man like Frank.

CHRIS. I think I do. He's not just a machine of destruction to me—no, nor of saving us from destruction. Yes, and the plumber may be a charming man, but all you want is that he should plumb. So do I, for the moment.

HELEN. This is the moment.

CHRIS. Don't you see—don't you see—the point is that some of us have to keep the eternal going.

HELEN. Why you?

CHRIS. Because I'm an artist. It's my work—my duty, if you like. It isn't only Frank we want; it's the idea of Frank. Now, I can give you that.

MARGARET. This is rubbish. You are exasperating, Chris. You are out of place. You're not serious enough now.

HELEN. The world has left you behind.

CHRIS. The world doesn't exist without me—I speak for the lot of us—wars are not worth fighting but for me.

HELEN. And you're safe at home all the time.

CHRIS. Safe from bullets, not from insults.

HELEN. I didn't mean to be unkind.

CHRIS. Turn on Stephen a bit. You can't say he isn't serious.

IREDALE. Poor old Stephen's turn.

CHRIS. Stephen interests me. Stephen's rather big.

HELEN. He's kept so quiet. We don't know what he thinks.

CHRIS. Ah! You think Stephen's just

official—blessing the banners for the holy war and so on.

[*The door at the back opens and* DAKIN *stands silhouetted against the light outside. He will be seen presently as a grave and impassive type of footman who does all his work imperturbably.*]

DAKIN. Shall I turn on the lights, madam?

MARGARET. Presently, Dakin.—We'll do it when we want it.

[*He comes forward to the tea-table and takes the tray, etc. As he retires he stumbles over a stool and recovers himself.*]

DAKIN. I beg your pardon, madam.

MARGARET. You understand that Sir John and Lady Romer will be here with the Colonel directly. Captain Iredale will want the car again at half-past ten. Tell Bromley so as soon as they arrive, and see that he has his meal comfortably. We will dine as soon as they come.

DAKIN. Yes, madam. (DAKIN *goes out.*)

CHRIS. Good—the soldier's wife. Brief —to the point. You remind me of Mrs. O'Dowd in "Vanity Fair," though.

MARGARET (*passionately*). Oh, yes! It's a fine joke for you, and I may never see Frank again.

HELEN. Oh! Margaret. Don't mind him.

CHRIS (*rises*). You are unjust to me. Frank! Why! Mrs. O'Dowd was heroical.

IREDALE. It's all right, old boy. By Jove! I thought Dakin was going to spill the lot.

CHRIS (*sits again*). It's his first stumble. I never saw him make a mistake or turn a hair before. It's like the portents in "Julius Caesar."

IREDALE. He'd make a fine soldier.

CHRIS. Dakin! Dakin a soldier! Why! he's footman incarnate. He's got his vocation. This war will pass over Dakin like vapours over a rock. He can't be moved, can't be touched. Thank Heaven for Dakin. He makes one feel safer. He's an institution.

STEPHEN (*rising and making for the door*). It must be nine o'clock.

MARGARET. No dressing.

CHRIS. Stephen's escaping.

STEPHEN (*pausing at the door*). Escaping?

CHRIS. Have it out with them. Get it off your mind.

MARGARET. What is it?

CHRIS. Stephen on the war.

[*They wait for* STEPHEN *to speak. He comes forward slowly.*]

STEPHEN. Yes, I've been funking it.

MARGARET. Oh! Don't back Chris!

CHRIS. It's nothing to do with me.

HELEN. What about the war, Stephen?

STEPHEN. Perhaps it won't come.

MARGARET. You know it will. It's here.

STEPHEN. Well, you know, Margaret, I'm a parson.

MARGARET. It's a righteous war.

STEPHEN. No.

MARGARET. If ever there was one it's a righteous war.

STEPHEN. There's no righteous war.

MARGARET. Oh! It's too late in the day to talk like this.

HELEN. But, Stephen, what can we do if we're attacked?

STEPHEN. What would Christ have done?

IREDALE. Look here, old chap! It can't be Christian to let yourselves be annihilated and a worse lot take your place.

STEPHEN. You can't kill the spirit.

IREDALE. Are we to let the Germans walk right over us?

STEPHEN. I may be wrong. It's hard to see it so.

HELEN. You are wrong.

STEPHEN. Then Christ is wrong, too.

HELEN. You haven't to be literal. It's the spirit——

STEPHEN. He was perfectly explicit. Every word He said applies precisely now.

MARGARET. He said so many things.

IREDALE. Do you want us to lay down our arms?

STEPHEN. Of course, I know you won't, Frank.

CHRIS. You want a bit of logic on your side, Stephen. You're very fine and simple, but that's what you want. Without that your Christianity won't stand the strain.

STEPHEN. Can you help me, Chris?

MARGARET. Don't listen to him.

CHRIS. It's arguable that if we disbanded army and navy and said "Come in" to everybody we should take no harm.

MARGARET. Nonsense!

HELEN. You can't believe that.

CHRIS. I don't say I believe it. I say it's arguable.

MARGARET. Arguable by lunatics.

CHRIS. Christianity was a sort of lunacy when it started. It would be extremely interesting to see it tried again. Just think of it—if we should discover that Christ was the man of common sense after all!

HELEN. Is this helping you, Stephen?

STEPHEN. I'm not sure. I must think about it.

MARGARET. Stephen, Father will be here directly. You'll do nothing—you'll say nothing?

STEPHEN. All my instincts are cowardly.

CHRIS. But he has a passion—can't you see—can't you people see how fine Stephen is?

HELEN. Why have you never spoken of this before?

STEPHEN. Yes. Why, indeed? Haven't we all changed in a week? Haven't we searched ourselves?

HELEN. The war has awakened us, then.

It's not an evil. It'll help us, it'll save us.

STEPHEN. Then we must keep faith with ourselves.

MARGARET. What will you do?

STEPHEN. I suppose I shall continue to preach the gospel.

MARGARET. What gospel? There's only one gospel now for a man.

CHRIS. Margaret's good, too. She's a pure type.

HELEN. This dilettante stuff of Chris is hateful.

CHRIS. Well, I'm being faithful to myself, so I suppose I'm hateful.

HELEN. It isn't the time for you.

CHRIS. Is that my fault?

MARGARET. You can efface yourself. You can go into a corner and suck your thumb. Your day's over.

HELEN. What's the good now of your little refinements and graces?

CHRIS. Not one shall be lost.

MARGARET. We've wasted too much time. It's drill now for those who can't fight at once. Every man will be wanted.

CHRIS. Well, the old men and the boys must carry on literature and the arts.

HELEN. And a few stay-at-homes.

MARGARET. And cowards.

CHRIS. Do you think the world's books, for instance, have been written by cowards?

MARGARET. It doesn't matter.

CHRIS. No. But let me tell you this: no race, no sect, no kind has ever stood for its faith as we have for ours. Self-sacrifice! The only sort worth having is when you won't sacrifice yourself. Anything but that. When you've let the baser parts go there's nothing so austere. You ask me to give it all up, as though I were a child with a toy.

MARGARET. You are. All this is no more than a toy now.

CHRIS. All the art, all the thought, all the aspiration of the ages!

HELEN. Are you all that?

CHRIS. You think I'm negligible, but I'm not.

MARGARET. You think yourself too good to be shot.

CHRIS (after a pause). Yes, Margaret. 10 It's true. I do feel that.

MARGARET. Too clever, too important, too superior.

CHRIS. Yes, I suppose that's true. And we've no quarrel with these people.

MARGARET. We? Who are we?

CHRIS. Oh!—the artists, first and last. English or German, they're my comrades.

IREDALE. But, look here, old chap, if we 20 don't beat the Germans you'll go under with the rest.

CHRIS. Quite right, Frank.

MARGARET. Answer him.

CHRIS. I beg your pardon, Frank. I didn't quite hear what you said.

IREDALE. What I mean t'say is this: if we're beaten you're beaten too.

CHRIS. The Germans can't beat me.

IREDALE. Would you let them run over 30 us then?

CHRIS. You're a soldier. You must do what's good to you—your duty or whatever you call it. Leave me alone.

IREDALE. Hardly sportsmanlike, old chap.

MARGARET. It's shocking; it's abominable.

HELEN. He's angry. He doesn't mean it. 40

CHRIS. Yes, you'll goad me into something rash. It's going to be a bad time for me.

MARGARET. Hark! They're coming. They're here. (Sounds of arrival are heard.) Chris, if you talk to Father as you have done to us I'll never forgive you.

CHRIS. Don't provoke me then.

[The door is opened by DAKIN, and COLONEL ROKEBY enters with SIR JOHN and LADY ROMER. They are hurried and excited, and have still coats and wraps on, which they remove during the scene. DAKIN turns on the electric light and goes out. IREDALE'S sword in its scabbard is conspicuous on a chair. The group about the fireplace changes and disperses as the others enter. The greetings are spread casually over the next few minutes. The COLONEL advances, brandishing a newspaper. He is a fine type of the old soldier as IREDALE is of the young. SIR JOHN and LADY ROMER are of the world.]

STEPHEN (eagerly). Good news?

COL. ROKEBY. The best! We shall be at war with Germany by midnight.

[STEPHEN turns away and stands looking into the fireplace. As the others crowd round the COLONEL and the ROMERS, eager to see the printed news, CHRIS approaches STEPHEN and stands by him.]

STEPHEN (in a low voice to CHRIS). Untold suffering. Misery and desolation.

[Scraps of excited comment are heard as the paper is passed or dragged from hand to hand and ultimately laid on the sword. A burst of laughter from HELEN.]

CHRIS (to STEPHEN as he looks round at them). Are they sincere? Are they really joyful? What are they thinking?

COL. ROKEBY (coming forward with IREDALE, whom he holds affectionately by the arm). Yes, I called at the War Office. Couldn't see anyone. The excitement's terrific. One or two old friends. I gave in my name, of course. Damn it, Frank, why didn't it come earlier? I'm too old for the trenches. I envy you. Ah! Chris, my boy,—Stephen—this is great news. I wish—I wish—well, what about dinner?

We're hungry. (*To the* ROMERS.) Now then, John—Janet. Champagne to-night.

MARGARET. Dinner in ten minutes. No dressing.

COL. ROKEBY. I wish we were all dressed like Frank. (*He clasps* IREDALE *on the shoulder.*) Khaki's the only wear now. What time d'you go, Frank?

ROMER. I hear that Kitchener——

LADY ROMER. Margaret, is he all ready?

MARGARET. Yes, Aunt Janet.

COL. ROKEBY. I was at the War Office this afternoon. Smell of powder, by Gad! I'll get some sort of job, you'll see. Drilling!

LADY ROMER. Your father's like a boy again, Chris.

CHRIS. Splendid! Yes, it's a great thing for him.

HELEN. It *is* splendid, isn't it, Chris?

CHRIS. Of course it is.

COL. ROKEBY. What? What? Oh, nonsense! But Chris, my boy, what are you going to do? You've been through your drill. You'd make a soldier in a week. I believe I can get you a commission.

CHRIS. Thanks, Father.

ROMER. They say there'll be an Expeditionary Force in France within a fortnight.

LADY ROMER. We ought to have a million ready.

ROMER. I hear that Kitchener——

LADY ROMER. Chris had better give in his name at once. There'll be thousands applying.

COL. ROKEBY (*rather timidly*). Shall I speak to Mainwaring, Chris? It's too late to-night. I could send him a wire in the morning. He's busy, but he'd do anything he could.

CHRIS. I think not, Father.

SIR JOHN. Well, what's your notion?

CHRIS. About what?

LADY ROMER. What are you going to do?

CHRIS. I thought of just getting on with my work.

LADY ROMER. What work?

CHRIS. You think I'm an idler?

LADY ROMER. Oh! You mean—but surely——

MARGARET. Chris prefers to remain safely at home.

CHRIS. I wonder if I *am* cowardly. You make me angry and confused, Margaret.

MARGARET. Oh! take your chance, Chris. Don't refuse.

CHRIS (*looks at* HELEN, *who had made a movement, an exclamation*). It isn't quite fair.

HELEN. Don't make your mind up against it.

CHRIS. I never make my mind up.

HELEN. That's what's so dreadful.

IREDALE. But, old chap, if you go out you must make up your mind. You can't decide to chuck it and go home.

CHRIS. My body would have to go through with it. My mind would be in perpetual revolt.

MARGARET. He's a talker. He's made of words.

COL. ROKEBY (*who has followed the discussion anxiously*). No—no. Chris must do what he thinks right.

MARGARET. He must do what *is* right.

COL. ROKEBY. He sees something that I don't see. I don't understand you, my boy, and I daresay you're wiser than I am. I don't want to compel you—to bully you——

CHRIS. I know, sir. You're a trump.

MARGARET. Oh! thank God for Frank! (*She bursts into tears and lays her head on* IREDALE'S *shoulder.*)

IREDALE. Steady! Steady!

MARGARET. I swore I wouldn't. It's his fault. If only Stephen—if one of them ——

LADY ROMER. Margaret should have been the boy.

SIR JOHN. Well, at any rate, Stephen can get all the young men in his flock to enlist. The parsons now will have a great chance to help.

LADY ROMER. Could he get a chaplaincy to the troops?

CHRIS. Poor Stephen!

COL. ROKEBY (*anxiously*). It's a bad busi-10 ness, Stephen, but we've got to go through with it.

STEPHEN (*comes forward and pauses for a moment before speaking*). I'm horribly sorry, sir. I'm as bad as Chris.

COL. ROKEBY. Of course, of course, my boy. I understand——

MARGARET. Don't listen to them. They don't belong here.

SIR JOHN. What's Stephen's point? 20

STEPHEN. It's useless, but I do protest against this war—your delight in it, your levity.

COL. ROKEBY. Levity!

MARGARET. Protest then and be done. Father, what more news?

COL. ROKEBY. But, Stephen——

STEPHEN. What insolence it is—I don't speak to you, sir—to assume that a minister of Christ cares nothing for 30 Christ's word.

LADY ROMER. But, surely everybody—all the bishops—are agreed that——Ah! your mother was an eccentric woman. I beg your pardon, Henry.

CHRIS. Be warned, Stephen. The bishops are against you.

COL. ROKEBY. I do my best to be a Christian, Stephen. If Christ is against this war——(*He makes a gesture of dismis-*40 *sal.*)

CHRIS. That's it, sir. We must all do our best—not somebody else's best.

LADY ROMER. Well, Stephen, you must just keep quiet and you'll do no harm.

STEPHEN. I'm afraid I can't keep quiet.

MARGARET. Why, what will you do?

CHRIS. Stephen's a whole hogger. And he's got his pulpit.

MARGARET. What!

LADY ROMER. But surely——

STEPHEN. I must make my protest. I can't be silent.

LADY ROMER. Henry, I pity you.

COL. ROKEBY. My sons must do what they believe to be right.

CHRIS. You're beautiful about it, sir. I shall have to come to your side yet.

COL. ROKEBY. Ah! if you could——

[CHRIS *looks at him wistfully and turns away.*]

MARGARET. They don't matter. Father, Uncle John, you haven't told us whom you've seen. What's happening? Have you any idea where Frank will go?

COL. ROKEBY. No, they're keeping it all very dark. They're alive, though. I think they know what they're about.

SIR JOHN. This Radical Government has its chance now.

MARGARET. But we've no army.

COL. ROKEBY. Let them keep things going and we shall have. India, Canada, all over. They'll flock in. And we shall raise a million men here in six months.

CHRIS. Conscription?

MARGARET. You'll all be dragged in.

CHRIS. It's the end of freedom then?

MARGARET. Freedom! It's a fight for freedom. Can't you see that? Are you a fool? It's so simple.

SIR JOHN. What is your point, Chris? There may be a certain amount of logic in Stephen's position though, mind you,—but you've never set up for being a religious man. We'd no option. Grey's a peace man. Germany would have it, I tell you——

MARGARET. He's willing to be a German's slave.

CHRIS. We're all slaves to something.

SIR JOHN. It's an end of us. It's an end of the English race if we lose this war.

CHRIS. Perhaps. Then have no war.

HELEN. Why do we listen to him? He's decadent. He lives in a little circle. They talk big—among themselves. Great things are done, and they say smart things about them. The men of the nation will die in the trenches and they'll be at home writing sarcastic, witty things. They'll be keeping up the standard—the standard of diction —of words.

CHRIS (*after a short pause*). Yes, you hurt me. You hurt me considerably. Well done, Helen. That was awfully clever. She got at me, Stephen, didn't she? I wish my convictions *were* convictions. I'm not a politician. I don't understand these things you're talking about. I'm quietly at work—the work that matters more to me than anything in life—and you come buzzing round with your war—there's nothing in the world but war. Yes, there is.

MARGARET. Another of his poses.

IREDALE. Look here, old man, the point is—if they beat us we're done.

CHRIS. I'm not done.

HELEN. A slave.

CHRIS. No. Suppose the worst. Suppose they beat us—overrun our country. It's possible. Face the facts.

COL. ROKEBY. They cannot beat us if we're true to ourselves.

MARGARET. If the cowards will fight.

CHRIS. Forgive me, Father. Don't run into cowardly evasions. Yes, cowardly. You all know that we may be beaten. It's been a long peace with preparations—preparations for war. And who knows whether these infernal Germans aren't far ahead of us? How can you possibly tell? Every modern war has found one side efficient and the other not. How do we know which side it is this time? We may be beaten in a month.

SIR JOHN. The man who says so is a traitor.

CHRIS. The man who won't face this is a coward.

IREDALE. D'you mean to say our navy's no good?

CHRIS. Frank, Frank, don't misunderstand. I hope we're all right. If there are many like you, we are. Don't think I want you to be beaten.

HELEN. And what's the good of all this?

CHRIS. I've more faith in the nation than you have. Let them beat us. It would be horrible, of course. D'you think I shouldn't feel it. It's my trade to feel. It's my trade to look for the truth, to face things, to reveal them.

SIR JOHN. But not to serve your country.

CHRIS. Yes. In my own way.

COL. ROKEBY. You puzzle us, my boy. There's only one kind of service that matters now.

HELEN. Under the Germans there would still be a publishing season.

CHRIS. How clever Helen is! She can make me ludicrous. She can make my thought come out small and mean and me an ignoble fool. It's her sympathy, it's because she understands me. Margaret can't touch me like that.

HELEN. I want you to be fine—to be noble.

CHRIS. If that ghastly accident comes— if they invade us and subdue us and govern us—d'you think I and my kind will be conquered? It would all be a hideous irrelevance. They may trample on us or kill us, but they can't enslave our minds. We'll go on living —some of us. I've my faith too, and it isn't just in guns—England! I can think of England too. Humiliation and defeat may be our salvation.

STEPHEN. God may have it so.

COL. ROKEBY. It's impious, Stephen. I've heard enough.

MARGARET. Too much. Leave them together.

CHRIS. I've a brother still. Stephen has courage. We've not always hit it off, Stephen, but we're groping out to one another now. I'll come and hear you preach.

MARGARET. We're wasting time. Dinner in ten minutes. Aunt, you're in the blue room. Come on.

[*She and* LADY ROMER *go out,* STEPHEN *follows.* IREDALE *goes toward the door and pauses before* CHRIS.]

IREDALE. I'd give a good deal, old chap, to see your point.

CHRIS. Frank, you don't know how much I like you and admire you.

IREDALE. Then, why do you try to take the shine out of the thing like this?

CHRIS. Go in and win. God bless you. Heaven help you. Rule Britannia. I mean it, I mean it, Frank.

IREDALE. D'you know what you mean?

CHRIS. Perhaps not.

IREDALE. I do know what I mean.

CHRIS. You beat me there.

IREDALE. We've been friends in a way.

CHRIS. Yes, yes, Frank.

IREDALE. Well——(*He stares at* CHRIS, *and then looks round at the others in a puzzled way.*) Damned if I can understand him.

[*He goes out. The others have been listening.* COL. ROKEBY *and* ROMER *move together towards the door.* COL. ROKEBY *pauses before* CHRIS *very much as* IREDALE *did.*]

COL. ROKEBY. Yes, Chris, I wish we could be all together in this. Don't let us stress any differences. I mean—I wonder—of course, there's the Terri-

torials. I wonder if you'd like to join —home defence, you know.

CHRIS. I'll think of it, sir.

ROMER. They'll be called out. You can't decline to go.

COL. ROKEBY. Chris is not a coward, John.

ROMER. I can't make out what he is.

COL. ROKEBY (*goes towards the door and comes back*). You might write us something inspiring, Chris. Poetry, you know. I think Rudyard Kipling has done real service. We can't all be in the trenches. Just give us a hand somewhere.

CHRIS. Do you know what I'd like? I wish you could just take a birch-rod to me and make me do what you want. I wish I was a boy serving under you—fighting. I should be happy.

ROMER. Well, I'm like Frank. I'm damned if I see what you're driving at. (*He takes* COL. ROKEBY'S *arm and impels him from the room. The* COLONEL *glances back as he goes.* HELEN *starts up to follow them.*)

CHRIS. A moment, Helen.

HELEN (*hesitating by the door*). What's the good?

CHRIS. You'd like to think afterwards that you gave me every chance.

HELEN. I shall try not to think of you.

CHRIS. Pardon me—then we've broken? It's off?

HELEN. Yes.

CHRIS. What are your terms?

HELEN. Terms?

CHRIS. What must I do to be saved?

HELEN. You mean?——

CHRIS. If I go to the wars you'll marry me?

HELEN. What's the good of talking about it?

CHRIS. You would? Or have I dished myself already?

HELEN. Would you go?

CHRIS. I don't say that.

HELEN. Oh! how exasperating you are! How you talk! You torture me. You care nothing for me.

CHRIS. It seems that we must torture one another. All the time I've been listening for what you would say. You've just been trying to sting me and hurt me. The others speak, and I hear them, and answer, but I can't think 10 because you're bursting to speak again. And what you say is nothing. It's just following them. Let me hear you now. Talk to me. Give me a bit of your mind.

HELEN. You know it.

CHRIS. I thought I did. You could sympathise with me. You could understand me. But you've just got into the stream with the others. You parrot af- 20 ter them. By God! it's a baseness to leave me. You're cowardly. Margaret's all right; that's her line. But you!

HELEN. What is it, Chris? What do you want?

CHRIS. What do I want?

HELEN. Really, I don't know.

CHRIS. I've to put it so that twelve jurymen would understand?

HELEN. I want to understand. 30

CHRIS. I suppose I want to possess my own soul.

HELEN. How can you if a shell bursts on the roof? We're all together.

CHRIS. Yes—yes. That's it. Call for the plumber. Let's all be plumbers.

HELEN. Oh! I'm different from you. I've fancied myself aloof and superior to it all, and I've thought how fine to be apart. I've wanted to be like you, and 40 have a corner of my own in the world. And now I see that all the great things must be felt and suffered together. Frank and Margaret are a part of me —and your father. How can you desert your father? You talk of your own

individual soul. A traitor may have that.

CHRIS. What is a traitor?

HELEN. Simple people know.

CHRIS. Yes. Those that we call traitors may be the heroes—the men of conscience and ideals. It's my work to look into men's souls. It's truth I want, not this blatant simplicity. We are to be all one way now. What a time! The day of the cheap patriot has come.

HELEN. Not so cheap if he gives his life.

CHRIS. Ah! Frank's a hero. I delight in him. I love him. He doesn't know how much.

HELEN. I like to hear you say that.

CHRIS. He is kinder to me than you are. Did you see just now how he refrained from cursing me? I thought it was coming. I dreaded it. Yes, but he doubted; he was just.

HELEN. And I am not?

CHRIS. Oh! I'm an egoist, no doubt. I revolt against anything so big as this. I hate to be swept away. And yet I think I might love it. It's useless to talk to you. You've become simple. We want all to be to a pattern now or we shall be stoned. Don't you see, Helen, that the only thing that makes life worth while is to be ready to go off at a tangent anywhere? Not to be compelled—to be free.

HELEN. It's freedom we fight for.

CHRIS. Oh, yes! I know.

HELEN. And freedom for others.

CHRIS. I daresay.

HELEN. I want you to read something.

CHRIS. Read? Now?

HELEN. Yes. (*She looks hastily among some illustrated papers and selects one. She indicates a place and he takes it from her.*) They quote it here.

CHRIS (*reads*). "On the refusal of aid be-

tween nations"—Rossetti's sonnet. (*He looks at her and begins to read.*) "Not that the earth is changing, O my God!
Not that the seasons totter in their walk,"—
Yes, it's splendid. I'm glad you showed me that.

HELEN. You'll go if the poets lead?

CHRIS. There are German poets too.

HELEN. But you're not a German.

[CHRIS *turns over the pages of the paper and pauses.*]

HELEN. What are you looking at? (*He shows her.*) The Kaiser! Take it away.

CHRIS. He looks the part. Yes, you can see that he's a fine fellow.

HELEN. You make me hate you.

CHRIS (*staring at the picture*). Rather a stupid man—but exalted. There's a sort of nobility about him.

HELEN. Oh! I hate you.

CHRIS. And yet you'd have me like that. Here's your ideal. Here's the concentrated essence of the patriot. Here's my country, right or wrong.

HELEN (*snatches the paper from him and dashes it to the ground. Then her anger fades away and she looks at him sorrowfully*). I never thought it would end like this.

CHRIS. End? End?

HELEN. We are thousands of miles apart.

CHRIS. Because we know one another a little better.

HELEN. Good-bye.

CHRIS. Good-bye, Helen.

[DAKIN *appears at the door.*]

DAKIN. I beg your pardon, madam. Dinner is served.

HELEN. Thank you. (DAKIN *withdraws.*)

CHRIS. Well, the ritual of life will go on. I cling to Dakin. There's one thing the war can't touch.

HELEN. You have the lackeys on your side.

CHRIS (*sadly*). We must be magnanimous to one another now.

[*He follows her out, and the stage is empty for a few moments.* DAKIN *appears and strides forward, looking about him. He snatches up the newspaper which* COLONEL ROKEBY *brought and shakes it out; he concentrates upon it. Standing at the front of the stage he is young, eager, excited. He lowers the paper and stares into vacancy. He throws it down, and is hurrying out when he sees the sword. He stops, takes it up, and slowly draws it from its sheath. He holds it out, gazing along the blade, as the curtain falls.*]

ACT II

The same scene a month or two later. It is a morning in late September. In the latter part of the act a military band can be heard occasionally in the distance playing popular and martial airs. A desk has been brought into the hall and stands to the left of the spectator but well away from the wall. Anyone sitting at it faces the door to the right through which, as the scene opens, COLONEL ROKEBY, *in khaki, emerges, walks briskly to the desk, and sits down. He is followed by* SIR JOHN ROMER, *who is carrying his hat in his hand.*

ROMER. Anything I can do to help you, my dear fellow—only too glad. Now let me do something or I shall feel I'm in the way. It was Janet's idea to come down. She wanted to see how you're getting on, and she wouldn't let me wire.

COL. ROKEBY. Where is she?

ROMER. We met Margaret at the post office as we came through the village—they'll be here presently.

COL. ROKEBY. Well, John, I'm as busy as I can be.

ROMER. Best thing for you.

COL. ROKEBY. I'm drilling all the men for miles round—all kinds. And I get 'em to enlist wholesale—those that can. I'm in touch with Mainwaring, you know.

ROMER. Fine, I wish we had more like you.

COL. ROKEBY. Don't say that. There isn't a man in the service but's as keen as I am. And the nation's roused. It's tremendous, John. (*He stands up.*) I'm proud of 'em. It's given me fresh life.

ROMER. What's Chris doing?

COL. ROKEBY (*he sits again, but does not betray any emotion*). Chris? Oh! nothing particular.

ROMER. And Stephen?

COL. ROKEBY. Poor Stephen! He's a plucky beggar, John. He stood up in his pulpit here and preached against the war. You heard that?

ROMER. You're too easy, Henry.

COL. ROKEBY. Well, I like a fellow with pluck and conscience. Dreadful to-do, of course. Nearly had a riot in church. Then the vicar sacked him. Quite right, too.

ROMER. He's here?

COL. ROKEBY. For the present. Yes.

ROMER. And Chris goes on writing stories and such like?

COL. ROKEBY. He's very restless. Poor lad, I wish I could help him.

ROMER. Now, it's not good enough, Henry. You know it isn't.

COL. ROKEBY. I can't understand him.

ROMER. No, and you're as soft to him as if he was a well-behaved baby.

COL. ROKEBY. I suppose you think I ought to curse him and kick him out.

ROMER. Yes, I do.

COL. ROKEBY. But he's very unhappy.

ROMER. So he ought to be.

COL. ROKEBY. I'm a plain soldier, John, and I see my own duty. He knows all that I know and more. He's different from me. I can't drag him or drive him. He sees things that I don't see. When I talk to him he's my master.

ROMER. You're too humble.

COL. ROKEBY. I can't bully him. It's impossible to explain to you, John, how I feel to Chris. I'm altogether his inferior.

ROMER. What nonsense! You're worth ten of him.

COL. ROKEBY. Don't think he's a coward. He's not that. But things are different now from what they were when we were young. Oh! I'm miserable about it, of course.

ROMER. It doesn't matter what he is if he acts like a coward. But I don't come here to worry you, Henry. Let me help you. Give me something to do.

COL. ROKEBY. Helen's helping me—Helen Thorburn.

ROMER. She's here?

COL. ROKEBY. She came to be with Margaret when we heard about Frank.

ROMER. Any more news?

COL. ROKEBY. No; they've got him in Germany somewhere, I suppose. You know, it hurts Margaret's pride —his being a prisoner. One doesn't like to hear of all these prisoners, Henry. I know, I know. Modern warfare's different. When they're surrounded it's no use trying to fight it out. Frank's as brave as a lion. Well, John, you'll excuse me. It's a big day for me. We've recruiting going on here to-day. Just down the lane—by the post office. We're going to do a record. We bring 'em up in motors. It's like an election, and we'll poll our last man. Will you wait here? I'll be back directly.

ROMER. Give me a bit of clerking or

something. I want to think I'm helping.

COL. ROKEBY. Here! copy this list. I shall
want a copy. Follow me over there if
you like. But I must be off now.

[*He claps* ROMER *on the back and hurries out.*
ROMER *is settling to his work when* CHRIS
and STEPHEN *lounge in, from different di-*
rections. Seeing one another, they stop.]

CHRIS. Damn you, Stephen! I wish you'd 10
keep out of my way.

STEPHEN. I shan't be in it long.

CHRIS. What?

ROMER (*looking up*). You're a nice pair.

CHRIS. Hullo! Who's this?

STEPHEN. You, Uncle John?

ROMER. Doing a bit of work for your
father. His sons might do that at
least.

CHRIS. Come, come, Uncle John, you're 20
only playing at it. Don't let's have
any nagging. Call down the wrath
of God and be done.

ROMER. You know what I think of you.

CHRIS. It must be jolly always to know
what you think.

ROMER. No parish duties, Stephen?

CHRIS. He's got nothing to do but avoid
half bricks. Stephen's dished himself.
If it wasn't for my father he might be 30
another martyr Stephen. But they
only throw small stones here.

ROMER. Yes, I've heard of that. You're a
fine pair of sons for such a father.

CHRIS. Let's grant that I'm a bad case,
but leave Stephen alone. D'you think
it's fun to do what he's doing?

ROMER. Well, I'm not going to argue
with you. If you two are remaining
here I'll be off to join your father. 40

STEPHEN. That's severe, uncle.

ROMER. I don't mind that. (*He goes.*)

CHRIS. The way they lump us together is
so stupid. Only two kinds in the
world. The man who goes to the war
and the man who doesn't. I'm tired of

seeing you hanging about. Two's too
many.

STEPHEN. I'm off.

CHRIS. What! Where to?

STEPHEN. France.

CHRIS. You are? What to do? It's got
hold of you? Are you going to stand
between the hosts and raise a cross?

STEPHEN. The Red Cross.

CHRIS. What d'you mean?

STEPHEN. I've got a job as ambulance
man. What do they call it?—Orderly.
I can't stay here.

CHRIS. You're deserting me.

STEPHEN. You said two's too many.

CHRIS. Yes, but one's too few. Great
Heavens! It's got hold of Stephen.

STEPHEN. How—got hold of me? What?

CHRIS. The war!

STEPHEN. I hate the war.

CHRIS. But it's got you. You can't resist.

STEPHEN. I want to help.

CHRIS. Oh! I know. You think it's that,
but it's the war you want. It's the
neighing steed and the shrill trump.
It's the call. It's to follow where the
men are going. You won't kill anybody, of course. Nobody wants to kill.
It's a compelling force. It's the great
adventure. You can't escape it. Be
honest; it's the war.

STEPHEN. Chris, are you right?

CHRIS. Perhaps not. You're a good man.
You're an honest man.

STEPHEN. I've felt something of what
you say. I'm not bloodless. And yet
I've wanted to serve Christ. I wish I
could talk to you, Chris. I haven't a
friend. Not one but Him. And now
they want to take Him from me. He
was a man, you know; saying things
clearly and meaning them. Now,
Christianity has to conform to common sense. It's rational and liberal,
and there's quite a nice infusion of
Christ in it. You understand. You're

a good brother. You say strange, heartening things to me, but you're not my friend. You can see with me, but you're outside it all. Am I running away like a coward? Ought I to stay?

CHRIS. I'd like to be your comrade, Stephen. I'd like to be a simple warrior such as the old man. Anything but myself. You know, there's some- 10 thing too angelic in the way he leaves us alone. I try to fancy that he's reproaching us in his mind, but he isn't. He's horribly cut up, but there's no reproach in him. He isn't cunning enough to see that it's the way to get us.

STEPHEN. What are you going to do?

[HELEN enters.]

HELEN. Where's the Colonel? (*She crosses* 20 *to the desk and takes up paper*.) Who's been bothering here?

CHRIS. Please, it's not me.

STEPHEN. Sir John.

HELEN. Oh! I thought perhaps——

CHRIS. That we were making ourselves useful? No. (*She makes to go*.) But, Helen, stay and chat with us a bit. Pity the poor lost souls.

HELEN (*dryly*). What shall we talk about? 30

CHRIS. Stephen. He's going to the war.

HELEN. Stephen!

STEPHEN. Ambulance. I've got a Red Cross job.

CHRIS. But he'll smell the powder. He'll see and hear. See and hear! The senses weren't given for war. Blasts that split the drum of your ear! Sights that make your eyes a curse!

HELEN. What do you know of war? 40

CHRIS. As much as the correspondents faking up their stories from gossip in the towns. And here I am reading their wretched stuff and re-reading it down to the most petty, futile paragraph. I read the rubbish and scorn it.

I can't do my work. I go to and fro like an uneasy spirit.

HELEN. Do you read the letters home?

CHRIS. Yes, and I could write them. They're what we expect; they're a kind of literary convention. You read a story in the paper one day, and a week afterwards some poor wounded devil tells the same story. He had to tell something because his friends clamoured for experiences. They must all have their tales to tell.

HELEN. Don't—don't speak of them so.

CHRIS. I've said no harm of them. I have not. You wait to catch me—you patriots. I will not confuse my values. I haven't two ways of looking at things. You want me to look at these Germans as a patriot. I don't know how. I can only look at them as a man. You say they're savages, and if it is so it's extremely interesting. Of course as a man I'm horrified when I hear of their atrocities—that is, when I believe in them. But if we discovered that the Germans were all cannibals it would be very interesting indeed. (STEPHEN *is going*.) Hullo! Stephen, don't go—poor Stephen's had too much of this kind of thing. Stay and protect me from her, Stephen.

[STEPHEN *shakes his head and goes out*.]

HELEN. You are facetious.

CHRIS. Yes. Why? Why does one play the fool so? I was speaking seriously, and then, as you say, I became facetious. Between you and me it's intensely serious—nearly tragical. Yes, Helen. And I can only relieve myself by this clumsy facetiousness. One gets talking. We ought to be kinder, tenderer.

HELEN. We made a compact, didn't we, to be magnanimous with one another? But I can think of nothing but the war.

CHRIS. The war! The war! How to escape from it! There's only one way.

HELEN. What's that?

CHRIS. I know something of war. I've read Tolstoy and Stephen Crane. The psychology of it. And there's a ghastly Russian who piles up the corpses and gives you stenches and putrefaction. They say the shells overhead make a noise like ripping calico —homely if you're a draper. War is cold and heat, hunger and thirst, an awful exhaustion, a hideous ennui, skulking, shrieking, chatter and chaff and silence. There's a tremendous menace over it. That gives it dignity. Life would be no good without death.

HELEN. It's no good if you won't brave death.

CHRIS. We have to brave it sooner or later.

HELEN. Sooner, then.

CHRIS. Honour before life. Ah, yes! And there was no refusal of aid between nations. Look at Belgium. Where is Belgium?

HELEN. It's a light for all the ages.

CHRIS. You'll think it awfully base of me, Helen, but I keep wondering whether if I had been a Belgian and knew what was coming I wouldn't have said, "Walk through" when the Germans came.

HELEN. Yes, it's base.

CHRIS. And yet when you think and think and earnestly desire to do what's right, not what's easy——

HELEN. Easy!

CHRIS. You pray if you're a praying man, you humble yourself anyway: you try after the best in you and to forget what others would applaud. You may make a mistake, but is it base?

HELEN. The Belgians are glorious.

CHRIS. Yes. I feel that. So are we glo-rious. It's that one begins to doubt glory. Where's Stephen? He understands this. I want to talk to him.

HELEN. Stephen doesn't count now.

CHRIS. You must be wrong if you think Stephen doesn't count. He's simply a Christian. And that's tremendously interesting now when Christianity is just making itself agreeable to everybody.

HELEN. I don't know what you mean. I'm a Christian.

CHRIS. Then you must think of two things—of Christ and of the poor. Are these what you go to war for?

HELEN. I haven't patience—I haven't time——

CHRIS. No. Forgive me. I drift to and fro. I've always thought we make too much of human lives. Belgium! The poets are with you—with us. Do you know, Helen, I can't write a line of any sort? This war has taken hold of me. I might as well be there.

HELEN. That's the escape from it you meant?

CHRIS. I want to escape from myself. Ah! but what if I found myself! Could I do it! Could I face it? I wonder—I wonder——By God! I'm missing something.

HELEN. Chris, I'm going.

CHRIS. To the war?

HELEN. To train first. In three months or so I may be ready. Lady Wyfold will give me a place in her hospital. She's setting up somewhere in France.

CHRIS. You, too? The world's going to the war.

HELEN. All but you.

CHRIS. How strange it would be if I were wounded, in hospital, and looked up to see you!

HELEN. How could you be wounded?

CHRIS. Imagine it.

HELEN. You're better at that than I am.

If you don't go to the war you can't be wounded.

CHRIS. In a play, in a novel, it happens so. If you're a nurse and I'm a soldier it's sure to happen so—in the novel. But all these things belong to us through our imagination. I am a wounded soldier, I open my eyes and there's my sweetheart.

HELEN. I might imagine my part in it but not yours.

CHRIS. Another man there?

HELEN. No—no. I didn't mean that.

CHRIS. What did you mean? You are there. Who's the wounded man?

HELEN. How could it be you?

CHRIS. I may play with the idea surely. It's my trade to play with ideas. It's better than going to the war. We shouldn't meet if we both went there. But now we've the spirit of it. Do you see what we artists are for? We give you the spirit.

HELEN. Oh, write your story! Go and play!

CHRIS. Why not? If only I could! Isn't it better than shooting a few German peasants?

HELEN. I'm weary of it.

CHRIS. Yes—yes. We keep repeating ourselves. That's the nuisance. Repetitions—nagging. You attack me with supreme eloquence—good, magnificent. You go on doing it, and it's merely nagging. A bursting shell is terrific, appalling. Go on with it all day and it's nagging.

HELEN. I've really got something to do. Excuse me.

CHRIS. But what am I to do? How must I pass the time? (*He pursues her to the door.*)

HELEN. Lady Romer and Margaret will be here directly.

CHRIS. Oh Heavens! (*She goes out. A moment afterwards* DAKIN *enters.*)

DAKIN. I beg your pardon, sir. I thought the Colonel was here.

CHRIS. I think he went across to the recruiting place.

DAKIN. Do you think I might follow him, sir? I was intending to ask his permission to go there.

CHRIS. To go where?

DAKIN. To the recruiting station, sir.

CHRIS. For what purpose?

DAKIN. The fact is, sir, that I have made up my mind to enlist.

CHRIS. You!

DAKIN. You are surprised at that, sir?

CHRIS. I didn't think you were that kind.

DAKIN. It's every kind now, sir.

CHRIS. Not quite, Dakin. I haven't gone yet.

DAKIN. No, sir.

CHRIS. What do you think of me?

DAKIN. Sir!

CHRIS. Come! What do you think of me?

DAKIN. It is not for me to think anything about you, sir.

CHRIS. That won't do. Speak up like a man. You are a man now. You've seen me hanging about the place doing nothing, and others are going to the war—you are going to the war. What do you think of it?

DAKIN. I do not think of it, sir.

CHRIS. But you servants talk about us, surely. You know all about our affairs. You don't keep that respectful face in your own quarters.

DAKIN. I am not in my own quarters now.

CHRIS. That's better. Well?

DAKIN. I have nothing to say, sir.

CHRIS. Am I the talk of the kitchen?

DAKIN. Is that quite fair, sir?

CHRIS. No, and it's damned undignified. I beg your pardon for swearing. Dakin, why are you going to enlist? You're comfortable here?

DAKIN. Not in my mind.

CHRIS. Why not? How does it work? Tell me something about it.

DAKIN. Well, I think—I see all the good men going one way. I must go too.

CHRIS. Then it's not you yourself? You wouldn't go alone? If you were strong enough to resist——

DAKIN. It's my country calling me, sir.

CHRIS. That's just a catchword. I want to know what you think—what's at the back of your own mind.

DAKIN. We've got to beat the Germans, sir.

CHRIS. Yes, yes. Dakin, are you a better man than I?

DAKIN. Sir!

CHRIS. I wonder if you're stronger? Who's got the pluck? The tenacity? Let's wrestle. See if you can throw me. (CHRIS *thrusts back chairs to make a space. He takes his coat off and throws it on the floor.*) Off with your coat. Ju-jitsu, catch-as-catch-can, anything.

DAKIN (*horrified*). It's impossible, sir. I cannot do it.

CHRIS. I want to try my manhood. Come on.

DAKIN. I cannot, I cannot, indeed.

CHRIS. Damn you. Come on. I shall strike you if you don't.

DAKIN. It's not fair. I couldn't put forth my strength against you.

CHRIS. But I beg you to. As a comrade—as a friend. We are two young men together. You're my equal now. Nay, you're the better—in the mind—in the mind. Come, Dakin, honour me so far.

DAKIN. I would if I could—but I can't.

CHRIS. Why not?

DAKIN. You said—friend.

CHRIS. I meant it.

DAKIN. You can't change that all in a moment.

CHRIS. But if we fought in the trenches, side by side?

DAKIN. You'd be an officer.

CHRIS. I don't know that. But the same wind would blow on us, and the bullets wouldn't choose. Well, go and enlist.

DAKIN (*going*). Perhaps, sir, you would mention to the Colonel if you see him that I have gone across—but he was aware of my intention, and approved of it.

CHRIS. Stop! Do you know what you're doing?

DAKIN. I do not understand you, sir.

CHRIS. Listen! What's that?

DAKIN. I believe a band is playing at the recruiting station, sir.

CHRIS. Yes, the band is playing and the flags are flying, and you think that's war. You agree to the terms, you make the bargain. But it's a swindle. Look forward, and there you are in a wet ditch with a bullet in your head, your eyes, your belly. Did you agree to that?

DAKIN. I take my chance with the rest.

CHRIS. Lying there in your agony with no friend near you but death, does it seem a good bargain that you made when the band was playing?

DAKIN. You'd make a poor recruiting sergeant, sir.

CHRIS. Don't you think people should know what they are doing?

DAKIN (*sternly*). I think you are talking like a coward, sir.

CHRIS. There are several kinds of cowards. One will not look at the thing, another looks and goes back.

DAKIN. We must do the best we can.

CHRIS (*seated and following his own thoughts*). Good luck to you!

[*As* DAKIN *stands near the door looking at him,* MARGARET *and* LADY ROMER *enter dressed in outdoor things.* ROMER *follows them.* DAKIN *stands by the door and goes out when they have entered.*]

MARGARET. Whatever are you doing without your coat?

CHRIS. How are you, Aunt Janet? Will you still shake hands with me? Ah! you used to kiss me.

LADY ROMER. How are you, Chris? (*They shake hands.*) Kisses are for good boys. Well, you've got your coat off. Are you going to fight?

CHRIS. I forgot it. (*He puts on his coat.*) I wanted Dakin to wrestle.

MARGARET. Dakin!

CHRIS. He's gone to enlist. I wanted to have a bout with him.

ROMER. But, my boy——

CHRIS. Oh! we needn't go into it. The interest of it was really psychological. Now that's something in this war's favour. It breaks the surfaces. I got to know more about Dakin in ten minutes than I've known in five years. Quite an interesting fellow.

LADY ROMER. Where's Stephen?

ROMER. He was here just now.

CHRIS. He's off to the war, too. Stephen's going, Dakin's going, and Helen's going.

LADY ROMER. Stephen going!

MARGARET. The Red Cross.

CHRIS. He told you before he told me?

MARGARET. Helen's going to train as a nurse.

CHRIS. Poor Stephen thinks it's all up with the Churches. He's going to start Christianity again with just the handful that believe in it.

LADY ROMER. You're incorrigible.

CHRIS. By the by, Aunt Janet, I heard an amusing thing about the war. You remember Harriby—the exquisite Harriby? He's fairly in it, you know. His wife sends him out a clean pocket-handkerchief every week. One.

ROMER. Dakin, by Jove——

CHRIS. Yes, he seemed less likely than me, didn't he?

LADY ROMER. Well, Dakin has served you; now you'll let him defend you.

CHRIS. As cutting as ever, isn't she? Does it occur to any of you that I've been wonderfully goodnatured over all this?

LADY ROMER (*turning away from him*). Margaret, John had an idea about trying to hear about Frank. He's writing to a man in Germany through Stockholm. I hope they won't open his letter and think he's a spy. This man should be able to get to know something. He's—what, John?

ROMER. I'll tell Margaret all about it. (ROMER *strays out.*)

CHRIS. Margaret, would you like to hear that Frank's wounded?

MARGARET. Why do you ask me that?

CHRIS. Because you are unjust to him in your thoughts. He's a prisoner. It's ignominious to be a prisoner. You're a Roman mother. Has he his wounds in front?

MARGARET. I know he couldn't help it. I do not doubt him. Modern war's different.

CHRIS. I think nobody cared more for Frank than I did. No man, Margaret. I don't know why We hadn't much to say to one another. But I couldn't bear this war if it wasn't for Frank. It's thinking of him that will make me——Look here, Margaret (*He approaches her and handles her dress thoughtfully.*)—if—suppose—it's hard to think of him—but if once—just once—he faltered—if, for a moment, he became human and the pressure was too great. A gallant soldier—yes. Always. But there's a breaking point.

MARGARET. What do you mean?

CHRIS. If he came to you and said, "I wasn't just made of steel as you thought. It was more than I could bear. I—well—I ran away"?

MARGARET (*breaking away from him*). You shall not insult him. You are a coward with a coward's thoughts.

CHRIS. You daren't face that.

LADY ROMER. You have no right to say such things.

CHRIS. No. But I'm sensitive about Frank. I see her going about and nursing resentments. She would always have him where the winds are blowing and the flags flying! Yes, and the blood flowing. For Margaret there are only two things—glory and the grave.

LADY ROMER. Margaret is a soldier's daughter and a soldier's wife.

CHRIS. I know. She's a woman too.

MARGARET. Do you want me to doubt him?

CHRIS. I want you to see that the world's not made of iron.

MARGARET. You'd have him fall to your level.

CHRIS. If he did——

LADY ROMER. We've had enough of this.

CHRIS. But these things interest me. I must do something. How can you love a stiff figure that never goes wrong?

MARGARET. You try to torture me.

CHRIS. No—no. I think I want to help you. I am resentful too. She's too military, isn't she, Aunt Janet? Margaret and I were once great friends. (MARGARET *turns away.* HELEN, COLONEL ROKEBY *and* SIR JOHN ROMER *come in. Greetings between* LADY ROMER *and* HELEN *and* ROKEBY.)

LADY ROMER. Well, Henry, I'm glad they've found you something to do. Why! Helen, I hear you're going to a hospital?

HELEN. Yes, Lady Romer.

[STEPHEN *enters slowly, and is greeted by* LADY ROMER.]

LADY ROMER. And Stephen, too——

CHRIS. Another unquiet spirit at rest.

COL. ROKEBY. We met Dakin as we were coming in——

CHRIS. Ah! that reminds me——(*He goes out hastily.*)

LADY ROMER. Is it true that Dakin has enlisted?

COL. ROKEBY. He's on the way now. He spoke to me about it the other day.

LADY ROMER. Wonderful!

ROMER. How are your men coming in, Henry?

COL. ROKEBY. My own men? On the estate? Excellent. These agricultural labourers are hard to move, though.

STEPHEN. They're planted in the earth.

LADY ROMER. Well, Stephen, I'm glad to hear you've found some work to do.

STEPHEN. Thank you.

LADY ROMER. I'm sure it will be congenial to you.

STEPHEN (*with a short laugh*). Congenial? You think I like to see people in pain?

ROMER. Come, come, Stephen. That's not what it means.

HELEN. It's natural for Stephen to look after people in distress.

STEPHEN. I might find something of that nearer home.

HELEN. Well, Sir John, haven't you any gossip for us?

ROMER. Gossip, my dear?

HELEN. Even gossip's big now. But what's happening?

LADY ROMER. When do you set off, Stephen?

STEPHEN. If I go——

MARGARET. If!

COL. ROKEBY. But, my boy, I thought ——

STEPHEN. Yes, I suppose I shall go. But I've been unsettled. Chris—I've been thinking about it.

HELEN. Chris?

STEPHEN. Can it be true that I want to go?

MARGARET. What has Chris said to you?

STEPHEN. It's true that this war has an awful, compelling power. We're all very much alike. Yes, it was Chris who made me see that when I thought I was just doing right there was something else.

MARGARET. It's shameful of him.

HELEN. What did he say?

STEPHEN. Here am I pretending that it's a call to me as a Christian, and now I 10 know that I want to be in the battle, I want the excitement of it. I'm not thinking of Christ at all. Yes, sometimes, but I cheat myself.

ROMER. And all the better. We honour you for it.

STEPHEN. Honour!

COL. ROKEBY. Do what's right, my boy. Don't think about it too much.

HELEN. Yes, Stephen, that's it. 20

STEPHEN. You are right, sir, but till one gets something to do there's nothing but thinking, thinking.

MARGARET. You must avoid Chris like poison.

STEPHEN. No. We need him. We all need him.

MARGARET. Kitchener needs him.

STEPHEN. I don't think you know how much Chris is wanted now. I wish he 30 could speak and preach and write so that we should understand better.

ROMER. Nonsense! By the by, Henry ——

HELEN. What do you mean?

STEPHEN. You don't listen to what Chris says now, but he talks to me. You see this war and all the incidents of it like a foolish play—a melodrama. Yes, these story-tellers and play-writers 40 have falsified things to you.

LADY ROMER. But he's one himself.

STEPHEN. That's it. He's one. You don't make distinctions.

HELEN. Explain, Stephen. We don't understand.

STEPHEN. We accept all that happens just like those silly incidents in the play. The man's a traitor or he is not. Here are fiends torturing children; to the devil with them. There's a boy taking twenty prisoners and driving them before him with a pea-shooter. Your heroes have no qualms; your generals are confident. It's melodrama. There are seventy million people opposed to you, and it satisfies you to say that they are wrong. Simply wrong, nay—that they're all criminals.

HELEN. They are criminals.

LADY ROMER. It might be Chris talking.

STEPHEN. Yes, Chris infects me. I know that. His scepticism. No, it's his noble candour. His beautiful sincerity. I mustn't listen to Chris. I'm a stiff, rigid figure, and it's my only safety. My religion? Why! it's shaking and quivering. There are times when I see it impossible—opposed to common sense. Of course it's absurd to let these damned Germans trample over us. I see that. I'm not a fool. Yet it's blasphemy. Blasphemy! Whichever way I turn. I denounced the war, and I thought it was honest and courageous. I think it was to stifle my doubts. I can't be honest like Chris.

HELEN. We must close our minds against him.

STEPHEN. I don't say whether Chris does right or not. He sees and he makes me see.

HELEN. It's not the time to see.

STEPHEN. That's boldly said, Helen. It's not the time to be just, to be honest, to know yourself.

ROMER. Well, well—don't let's go into that.

STEPHEN. No. Don't let us go into anything.

LADY ROMER. Now, Stephen, don't get

vexed with us. We're just ordinary people seeing things in an ordinary way. You and Chris are very wonderful, I'm sure. You make yourselves miserable and everybody else. You do nothing but talk, and when we've beaten the Germans you'll go on talking. You'll want us to coddle them and be Christian to them and so on. We won't.

ROMER. That is to say——

LADY ROMER. No, John. Don't make any concessions to them. It's really all Chris's fault.

STEPHEN. You won't even allow me a will of my own.

LADY ROMER. Chris is the villain of the piece.

MARGARET. Yes, and we go on tolerating him. Father, you should turn him out of the house.

COL. ROKEBY. No.

HELEN (*to* MARGARET). Don't make it too hard for your father.

ROMER. Well now—to change the subject——

[CHRIS's *voice is heard outside before he enters rapidly and gaily.*]

CHRIS. Helen! Helen! Where are you? I've enlisted. Helen! St. George, Richmond, and Victory! A thousand hearts are great within my bosom. Ah! you're all here. Helen! I've enlisted. Margaret! (*He goes to his father, and they join hands.*) I've done it, sir.

COL. ROKEBY. Thank God! Thank you, my boy.

CHRIS. We're a united family. The incredible has happened. Ah! but Stephen—Stephen, have I deserted you? Remember, you went first. You didn't enlist, but it was the same thing.

LADY ROMER. But have you enlisted?

ROMER. Why? We could have got you a commission.

MARGARET. You've not had time. When did you do it?

CHRIS. Now, this moment, I've run all the way. What a relief! Helen, I'm happy.

HELEN. You make me happy.

COL. ROKEBY. It's magnificent, my boy, but we must get you a commission.

CHRIS. No, let me go the whole hog.

MARGARET. But you were here ten minutes ago—talking.

CHRIS. Talking. Yes. I've started doing now. You see? I can talk just as you do. It's quite easy to go over to the other side. That is, if you're a simple and sincere person, as I am. Everybody's right. I've changed.

MARGARET. He's fooling us.

HELEN. No, Margaret.

ROMER. Do you mean to say you've just been out and enlisted now?

CHRIS. I do.

ROMER. Wonderful!

CHRIS. I did it to get away from the war, I think. It's the only way. And I'm a romantic. And my father was always calling to me—and Frank too. I should never have gone for you, Helen. Oh! and there was Dakin. And a thousand other things that I don't remember.

HELEN. Dakin!

CHRIS. Dakin intrigued me. It was a queer notion I had that, after all, he was a better man than I.

STEPHEN. It was pride, then?

CHRIS. It was many things. I was extremely curious about Dakin. You'll hardly believe it, but I followed him. I wanted to see him enlist. I hadn't made up my mind about anything. And then—yonder—I came on those fellows waiting their turn. They were standing in a queue—Dobson, Pettigrew, that sturdy little fellow at the forge, some I didn't know. They were not very formidable to look at. The might of Germany wouldn't think much of them. Dakin fell in at the back, and that—somehow—affected me. They all looked so humble and faithful. They seemed to be gazing at something a long way off and not thinking of themselves at all. And then it came upon me that there had 10 never been anything in the world like this, that in all my life nothing had ever mattered so much, that I should never be happy again if I held back now. You don't blame me, Stephen?

STEPHEN. No.

LADY ROMER. Blame you! You're a hero.

MARGARET. Frank must know.

CHRIS. Yes. It's jolly to think of Frank knowing. I think I must go over to 20 Germany to tell him. I'd like to go and rescue him, as you do in a boy's game.

COL. ROKEBY. Remember, this isn't a boy's game.

CHRIS. I've got that all right at the back of my mind, Father.

ROMER. You've passed the doctor?

CHRIS. Oh! that's all right, but I've passed nothing. D'you know, I didn't 30 behave very nicely. I shoved in before all those fellows who were waiting. I wanted to get it done. I wanted to commit myself. They were rather surprised to see me when I got inside. I'm afraid I made the thing a bit spectacular. I ought to have lined up behind Dakin. But there—it's my last burst of aristocratic privilege. The doctor? I'm to see him this after- 40 noon. It's only Warburton. I'd punch his damned head if he talked of not passing me. Excuse me, Aunt Janet, but I must swear now I'm a trooper.

LADY ROMER. It does me good to hear you.

CHRIS. Don't begrudge me my bit of limelight, Stephen.

STEPHEN. I can't help being glad.

CHRIS. And have I done right?

STEPHEN. You've followed your instincts. You've done what you must.

CHRIS. Instincts? Yes, but——Ah! don't let's argue. I'm like a hesitating Ritualist that's joined the Mother Church. No more doubts. No more hesitations. Not in public.

ROMER. The next thing is to get you a commission.

COL. ROKEBY. I'll write to Mainwaring at once.

CHRIS. No, no. I tell you I'm going the whole hog.

ROMER. You don't know what it is.

COL. ROKEBY. I think you hardly realise, my boy——

CHRIS. I must do it my own way.

MARGARET. You make it a personal matter. You must do what's best for the country.

CHRIS. That's very much to the point, but I should make a very poor General.

MARGARET. You take it too lightly.

HELEN. No, Margaret, he doesn't.

ROMER. Some of those Tommies you know—well——

CHRIS. These are trifles. I'm ready to descend into Hell.

HELEN. You said you were happy.

CHRIS. Yes. And how gloriously happy I must be to forget about Hell.

HELEN. You're too serious and you're not serious enough.

CHRIS. That's the way with us.

[DAKIN enters with a telegram on a tray.]

DAKIN. A telegram, sir (to COL. ROKEBY).

CHRIS. Hullo! Dakin! Got it over? Seen the doctor?

DAKIN. I have not yet, sir——

[CHRIS intercepts him, clutches him, and the tray and telegram fall to the ground.]

CHRIS. Come on! We're equals now. I must have a tussle with you.

DAKIN. Impossible, sir. I cannot, indeed. I beg of you—really, sir—take care, take care—oh, hang it all!—confound you—damn——(*They wrestle together, and* CHRIS *is thrown. He gets up laughing.* MARGARET *has picked up the telegram and tries to get* COL. ROKEBY'S *attention.*)

CHRIS. Two out of three. It wasn't fair for you to say "damn." It made me laugh.

DAKIN. I beg pardon, I'm sure. I'm extremely sorry. It slipped out, somehow.

CHRIS. Of course it did. All sorts of things will slip out now. Now then—Ready?

DAKIN (*picking up the tray*). I really cannot, sir.

MARGARET. Stop this fooling, Chris. Father, the telegram. (COL. ROKEBY *takes it.* DAKIN *goes out.*)

CHRIS. I'll have it out with you, mind.

LADY ROMER. Well, I don't know what to make of you.

ROMER. Not very dignified, my boy.

CHRIS. Hadn't I better get my dignity down a peg or two?

[MARGARET *stands beside* COL. ROKEBY *as he opens the telegram. He looks at it for some time with a perfectly impassive face after having instinctively turned it away from her. She snatches it from her.*]

ROMER. What's this, Henry?

[*They all stand looking at* MARGARET. CHRIS *goes to her, puts his arm round her shoulders, and looks at the telegram.*]

CHRIS. Died of wounds.

[MARGARET *offers the telegram vaguely.* ROMER *takes it, and the others crowd round to read. The* COLONEL *stands as if at attention.* CHRIS *and* MARGARET *stand together, his arm still about her.*]

MARGARET (*to* CHRIS). You shall avenge him.

CHRIS (*breaking from her*). No, no, no. How can you say that?

[LADY ROMER *and* HELEN *approach* MARGARET.]

HELEN. Come, Margaret.

LADY ROMER. Come, my dear.

MARGARET. Avenge him! Avenge him, Chris.

CHRIS. How can you talk these abominable stupidities now?

HELEN. Hush! Hush!

CHRIS. Follow him, die with him, if you like. What has revenge got to do with him? Ah! it's a great thing, this war. It's taken Frank.

MARGARET. You were wrong, you see.

CHRIS. Wrong?

MARGARET. You thought he was a coward. You doubted him.

CHRIS. See how proud she is!

MARGARET. Haven't I cause? Who can be prouder than I to-day?

CHRIS. Margaret, you shall be proud of me, too.

[*She goes out as the Curtain falls.*]

ACT III

A barn in the North of France. There is a door in the middle of the wall facing the spectator, and to the left of it and above the level of a man's head a small window. A little to the left of the middle of the stage are two wooden boxes, a large and a small one, in such relation that they can be used as stool and desk. There are several heaps of straw round the walls, but no other furniture. When the curtain rises the stage is almost completely dark, and even the objects enumerated above cannot be discerned until the door opens. From time to time there are slight illuminations at the window, and distant boomings are heard;

then two or three rifle shots in middle distance.
Exclamations and a little scuffling are heard
outside. The door opens, and two men are
thrust into the barn. Behind them and by the
light of a lantern are seen several German
soldiers. The two prisoners, for this is what
they are, are CHRIS *and another English sol-*
dier. CHRIS *wears a tattered German overcoat,*
and both are dirty, dishevelled and exhausted.
They shamble and stumble forward, foul the 10
boxes, and sink down presently towards the
right on the straw.

A GERMAN SOLDIER. Wenn Sie entfliehen
versuchen, werden Sie geschossen.
Verstehe?—Vat you call shot—Hein?

CHRIS. I say—something to eat—bread
—das brod.

ENGLISH SOLDIER. Water.

CHRIS. Das Wasser. Not much to ask. 20

GERMAN SOLDIER (*closing the door as he goes*
out). Halt die Maule!

CHRIS (*after a silence*). Who are you?

ENGLISH SOLDIER. Haven't a card with
me.

CHRIS. I beg your pardon. My name's
Rokeby. I'm a corporal in the 3rd
Wessex.

ENGLISH SOLDIER. Oh!

CHRIS. You? 30

ENGLISH SOLDIER. The Belters. My name
is Megson. Gentleman ranker.

CHRIS. Oh! Well, we're in a damned
awkward mess, Mr. Megson.

MEGSON. We're safer here than we were
outside.

CHRIS. Perhaps. We've lost our liberty.

MEGSON. I don't think much of the sort
of liberty I've had these last few days.

CHRIS. Think of your ideals, Mr. Meg- 40
son.

MEGSON. Ideals! I wish I'd never come.

CHRIS. But what foul brutes you and I
are now without 'em! What filth and
misery and terror and humiliation

MEGSON. Speak for yourself.

CHRIS. Oh! You keeping the public
school spirit quite intact, Mr. Megson?

MEGSON. It was a high-class private
school I went to.

CHRIS. Really? Gymnasium, bracing situation, home from home?

MEGSON. Certainly.

CHRIS. Modern languages?

MEGSON. Here! what d'y' mean?

CHRIS. You'll have a chance to rub up
your German.

MEGSON. D'y say you're a corp'ral?

CHRIS. I am.

MEGSON. You're a gentleman, too, aren't
you?

CHRIS. Mr. Megson, you have your
ideals still.

MEGSON. What d'y' mean?

CHRIS. Blood's the thing.

MEGSON. Blood?

CHRIS. A gentleman should have good
blood in him.

MEGSON. What are you talking about?

CHRIS. About blood. Family, you know.
When a man's lying in the trenches
with a gash in him it must be a comfort to know it's good blood he's shedding.

MEGSON. Are y' a bit light-headed?
You're not wounded?

CHRIS. Only in the spirit, Mr. Megson.
And I'm hungry.

MEGSON. Why, what's the matter?

CHRIS. Oh! my dear fellow, I'm talking
like a fool. Let's be friends. We're suffering the last humiliation together.
We're prisoners. And what's gone before? I was a lost dog in a world of
enemies. You find out things about
yourself—not nice things. I say, Megson, can you keep your form? Do you
care whether you're a gentleman or
not? I admire you. Honestly, I do.

MEGSON. What have you been doing?

CHRIS. Much the same as you, I daresay. I've marched and marched. I've fought and I've run away. I've been brave—excited, at least—and I've been afraid—dreadfully, horribly afraid. I've admitted to myself things that no man has a right to admit. I've been cruel and vindictive, and I've shed silly, sentimental tears. Oh! the dirt and the confusion and the noise! 10 Megson, did you ever bayonet a man? Ugh! He nearly got me. What a relief! And yet I knew I should never be happy again.

MEGSON. It has to be done.

CHRIS. As you say, it has to be done. The man who's squeamish is a fool. And yet how are you to keep human?

MEGSON. You say a great deal too much.

CHRIS. No doubt. For instance?

MEGSON. Keep things dark, man. Make the best of it.

CHRIS. No, Megson. It's no use keeping things dark. Let the sun shine on them —let it illuminate—what's that?

MEGSON What?

CHRIS. What are you doing? Are you eating?

MEGSON. No. That is——What d'you 30 mean?

CHRIS. I heard your jaws going. You've got something. Damn it, man, share out.

MEGSON. I'd a crust. What's that to you? Mind y'r own business.

CHRIS. You hound! You sneak! Give me my share.

MEGSON. You're a nice one to talk. You admit you've been a coward.

CHRIS. I'm not a coward when I'm starving. Come! Throw me a bit and I won't ask what you keep.

MEGSON. I've none to spare. Keep off.

CHRIS (crawling to him). Where's your throat?

[*They struggle together on the ground, grunting and exclaiming.*]

MEGSON. You blackguard! You're murdering me.

CHRIS. Sneak!

[*The door of the barn opens, and a Prussian officer enters, followed by several soldiers, one of whom carries a lantern.*]

THE PRUSSIAN. Ach! Herr Je! What are you Englishmen doing? (*He speaks English correctly in a foreign way. They rise discomfited.*)

THE PRUSSIAN. Why did you fight?

CHRIS. We were wrestling to keep ourselves warm.

THE PRUSSIAN. Ach! Very likely. Geben Sie hier das Licht. (*He takes the lantern and holds it up to examine them*). Where did you get that coat?

20 CHRIS. I must apologise. I was freezing. I found it.

THE PRUSSIAN. You stole it?

CHRIS. He was dead.

THE PRUSSIAN. Indeed! What is your regiment?

CHRIS. The 3rd Wessex infantry.

THE PRUSSIAN. Ach! You are in General Rigby's division?

CHRIS. Yes.

30 THE PRUSSIAN. And how did you get apart from your regiment? You were appointed to spy? What?

CHRIS. Spy! No, no. We were scattered. I was lost. I've been wandering about.

THE PRUSSIAN. Take off that coat. (CHRIS *takes it off, and it drops to the ground.*) A corporal. You are a man of intelligence—what? One suitable to be sent on a little mission?

40 CHRIS. I have not been sent on any mission.

THE PRUSSIAN (*turns the lantern on MEGSON*). Another lost sheep?

MEGSON. My name is Megson. I belong to what we call the Belters.

THE PRUSSIAN. Belters? What's that? (*He*

turns the lantern on to MEGSON'S *shoulder strap.*) Ach! (*He returns to* CHRIS, *then puts down the lantern on the larger box and sits down on the other.*) Nehme jenen Mann hinaus. Alles hinaus und mache die Thüre zu. (*The soldier and* MEGSON *go out, and the door is shut.*) Now, sir, a word with you. You are not what is called a common soldier.

CHRIS. I enlisted like anybody else.

THE PRUSSIAN. General Rigby's division. He is wounded—what?

CHRIS. I've not heard that.

THE PRUSSIAN. Let me see. He is operating with——What is the division on his left?

CHRIS. On his left?

THE PRUSSIAN. Exactly.

CHRIS. But ought I to tell you that?

THE PRUSSIAN. Why not? 20

CHRIS. Pardon me, sir, but as a fellow soldier——

THE PRUSSIAN. What!

CHRIS. We are both soldiers. You are an officer, of course——

THE PRUSSIAN. You have the impudence to speak to me as to an equal? On your knees.

CHRIS. But——

THE PRUSSIAN (*drawing a revolver*). On 30 your knees.

CHRIS (*collapses suddenly and kneels*). You might have spared me that.

THE PRUSSIAN. What did you say is the division on General Rigby's left? And remember I know something. You had better not make a mistake.

CHRIS. My father is a colonel in the British Army. I am a gentleman. I appeal to you—— 40

THE PRUSSIAN. Stand up! (CHRIS *stands up.*) Two paces back, please. (*He takes them.*) You make a mistake. I only ask for information such as any prisoner lets out in gossip. A matter of curiosity. I have one or two little wagers

with comrades. Your answers may decide them. Now!

CHRIS. For God's sake, don't press me.

THE PRUSSIAN. Are you tired of your life?

CHRIS. No, no. Stop! You are a German officer and a gentleman. You don't shoot prisoners.

THE PRUSSIAN. You are not an ordinary prisoner. You are a spy.

CHRIS. I am not indeed. I assure you on my honour——

THE PRUSSIAN. Let us not talk of honour. You are caught here behind our lines and wearing our uniform. (*He points to the coat on the floor.*)

CHRIS. But I was cold, I was freezing, and the coat was there. And, besides, here's my uniform underneath. I've lost my cap. I can't talk German. How could I be a spy?

THE PRUSSIAN. I did not say you were an efficient one.

CHRIS. You have humiliated me enough.

THE PRUSSIAN. Perhaps you will now answer my questions.

CHRIS. I can't know anything that would be of value to you.

THE PRUSSIAN. You may speak freely, then.

CHRIS. But think of me! Think what it means to me!

THE PRUSSIAN. You are a pawn in the game.

CHRIS. We are here alone. Save me!

THE PRUSSIAN. Save you?

CHRIS. You see what a coward I am. I might do what you ask. It would be terrible. Don't you see that? Can you bear it? You! What are you made of?

THE PRUSSIAN. We are not sentimentalists. A shivering fool will not turn me from my purpose.

CHRIS. It would be murder.

THE PRUSSIAN. You cannot murder a spy.

CHRIS. You know I'm not a spy.

THE PRUSSIAN. What does it matter? A carcase is a carcase.

CHRIS. I entreat you to spare me. Anything but that. I'll kneel again. I'll lick your boots. Don't make me— don't make me——

THE PRUSSIAN. Come, come!

CHRIS. But it's monstrous. It's shameful. You can't treat a man like that.

THE PRUSSIAN (*raps on the box with the butt of the revolver*). Your time is up.

CHRIS. Shoot, you devil.

THE PRUSSIAN (*after a pause*). So!

CHRIS. Quickly, quickly.

THE PRUSSIAN (*thoughtfully*). Very interesting. Perhaps you'll change your mind.

CHRIS. No. I'm at the bottom now.

THE PRUSSIAN. Your fear has gone?

CHRIS. I can't stand. (*He staggers towards the wall at the right and falls on the straw.*)

THE PRUSSIAN. Very curious. (*He takes out a cigar and lights it.*) By the by, I shall not shoot you. (*He smokes in silence for a time. Two or three shots are heard in the distance. He starts up and makes for the door as it is opened by a German soldier.*) Was ist's?

THE SOLDIER. Sie Kommen.

[*Confused exclamations outside are heard. They rush out. The lantern is left burning.* 30

More shots are fired. Shouts die away. The shots become more distant. MEGSON *enters cautiously.*]

MEGSON (*whispering*). Hullo! Are you there? (*He takes the lantern and finds* CHRIS *lying in the straw with his face to the wall.*) I say, there's a chance to be off. Are you hurt? What's up?

CHRIS (*slowly sitting up*). Who are you?

MEGSON. You know. Megson.

CHRIS. You were here just now, weren't you? It seems a long time ago.

MEGSON. What's happened to you?

CHRIS. Dreadful, dreadful things. I've been seeing ghosts.

MEGSON. I thought you were light-headed. Come on. I think our chaps are attacking away on the right there. We may get to them.

CHRIS. I'm as weak as water.

MEGSON (*spying round with the lantern, he picks up something*). Here's that bit of bread. I say, I've been sorry about that. I was thinking about it outside there. You see—well, I can't explain.

CHRIS. Thank you. (*He takes the bread and breaks it in two.*) Here—halves.

MEGSON. No, no. Take the lot. (CHRIS *bursts into sobs.*) I say! I say!

CURTAIN

ACT IV

The hall at COLONEL ROKEBY'S *again. Many months have passed. The disposition of the furniture is very much what it was in the first act.* SIR JOHN *and* LADY ROMER, *in motor coats, etc., enter from outside, followed by an old footman and then by* CHRIS. *He is muffled, and his face is hardly seen. A bent, shambling figure, he passes across the hall at once and goes out to the right.*

FOOTMAN (*staring after him*). I beg your pardon, Sir John—who is that? Where is he going?

ROMER. That is Mr. Christopher, of course.

FOOTMAN. Mr. Christopher?

LADY ROMER. He has gone to his room. You may ask him presently if he wants anything. (SIR JOHN *says a word to her apart.*) No; just leave him alone for the present.

FOOTMAN. I'm afraid, my lady, that they'll all be disappointed.

LADY ROMER. You mean the Colonel and Mrs. Iredale? Well, they'll be back directly, I suppose.

FOOTMAN. Yes, my lady, and Miss Thorburn too. But all the people thought he was coming by the train. Quite a crowd went to meet him.

ROMER. A crowd?

FOOTMAN. Yes, Sir John, and a band.

ROMER. A band!

LADY ROMER. Good heavens!

FOOTMAN. We're all very much excited about his coming home.

LADY ROMER. What an escape!

ROMER. You see—what is your name?

FOOTMAN. Perkins, sir.

ROMER. You see, Perkins, Mr. Christopher wishes to be quiet. He is a good deal shaken and wants rest.

FOOTMAN. Is he wounded, sir?

ROMER. I don't know that he's wounded —but——

LADY ROMER. Oh! the hardships, the privations of that terrible war, Perkins! Illness kills more than wounds.

FOOTMAN. It's been dreadful, my lady.

LADY ROMER. So you'll understand that Mr. Christopher wants to be very quiet and—no fuss, you know. He doesn't want to be talked about.

FOOTMAN. Quite so, my lady.

[HELEN and MARGARET enter.]

MARGARET. Oh! here you are. Where's Chris?

HELEN. How have we missed you? When did you come?

MARGARET. Where's Chris?

LADY ROMER. He's gone to his room. Tired. We decided to come in the car.

MARGARET. Well, but——

ROMER. Chris decided.

HELEN. How is he?

LADY ROMER. Oh! well, you know—— (*Taking off her coat.*) Just take these things, Perkins.

FOOTMAN. Yes, my lady. (*He gathers various wraps and goes out.*)

MARGARET. It makes rather a mess of the preparations.

LADY ROMER. Where's your father?

MARGARET. He stopped to send a wire. He'll be here directly. But there's a band and a triumphal arch. I suppose you missed it all. You came by the low road?

LADY ROMER. Yes.

MARGARET. Is anything wrong?

ROMER. Not exactly wrong, but it's hardly a case for triumphal arches.

LADY ROMER. The poor boy is very much changed.

HELEN. In what way?

LADY ROMER. Oh! don't misunderstand me. There's nothing really wrong with him—except that everything is wrong. But you must judge for yourselves. I may be giving you quite a wrong idea.

MARGARET. Do you say he wouldn't come by the train?

LADY ROMER. I think he must have scented that band.

MARGARET. Father was disappointed. He would have gone to Dover—— Oh! here he is.

[*The* COLONEL *enters rather briskly. He is not in khaki now, but ordinary country clothes. He is older and greyer.*]

COL. ROKEBY. I heard you'd come. Where's Chris? Well, Janet, how are you? I envy you the first greeting of him. Hah! John. But why didn't you keep to the arrangement? Where's Chris?

LADY ROMER. Better go and fetch him, John.

ROMER. Yes. He's a bit run down, you know, Henry.

MARGARET. Do let's see him.

ROMER. All right in a few days, of course. (*He goes out.*)

MARGARET. What is it? He's not hurt?

LADY ROMER. He went straight off to bed last night. And he hardly spoke on the way down.

COL. ROKEBY. Did he tell you anything about his—adventures?

LADY ROMER. Nothing. Dreadfully reticent, poor boy. He's washed out, Henry. He wants a good rest and feeding up. And you must get his mind away from it all. Helen, you must look after him.

HELEN. Will he let me?

LADY ROMER. Oh, my dear, don't wait till he asks you.

[ROMER *enters, looking back for* CHRIS, *who follows slowly.* CHRIS *is dressed in dark civilian clothes. He is pallid, shrunken, a little bent, prematurely aged. As a rule he speaks rather listlessly, but he is shaken by gusts of nervous excitement. He hangs back a little, and* ROMER *urges him on.* HELEN *is nearest to the door, and he passes her hurriedly with averted eyes. He sees his father, and advances to him.* COLONEL ROKEBY *stands looking at him, and then steps forward to meet him.*]

CHRIS (*in rather a high-pitched, protesting voice*). I did my best, sir.

COL. ROKEBY. Yes, yes, I know. Welcome, my boy. Well done. (*He takes* CHRIS *into his arms.* CHRIS *yields for a moment and then repulses him.*)

CHRIS. None of that. I can't stand that. (*He turns away greatly agitated and encounters* HELEN. *He recovers and speaks casually, shaking hands with her and* MARGARET.) How d'you do, Helen? Hullo! Margaret.

COL. ROKEBY. Well, my boy, you don't look first-rate.

CHRIS. Uncle John was kind enough— his motor. Hope you don't mind.

COL. ROKEBY. Yes, yes. All right. But the people were disappointed.

MARGARET. They had prepared a reception for you.

CHRIS. Horrible. Horrible. What's that?

[*The distant strains of "See the Conquering Hero comes" are heard.*]

MARGARET. It's the band. They've found you out.

CHRIS. But it's impossible. It's indecent. Don't they know that Stephen's dead? He is dead? Someone told me so.

MARGARET. Yes, Chris.

[*The band is a little nearer.*]

CHRIS. Let them play a funeral march, then. The best men have gone. But I wanted to see Stephen. I wanted to talk to him about all this. What did he say? Are there any letters?

HELEN. Your father has some.

CHRIS. Oh! but he would have talked to me. Stephen dead! Why! that's intolerable. (*The old Footman enters.*) Who's that? Where's Dakin?

COL. ROKEBY. Dakin was killed in action.

CHRIS. Dakin! (*He laughs incredulously; the laugh dies down quickly.*) Dakin, dead, Stephen dead, Frank dead. How strange it is that I should be alive! Am I alive? I've been looking in the glass. What does it matter?

THE FOOTMAN. If you please, sir, the people are all over the lawn. I think they want to see Mr. Christopher.

CHRIS. See me! Impossible. No, no.

MARGARET. Why shouldn't you show yourself?

COL. ROKEBY. Yes. Come out with me. Perkins, tell them we're coming.

THE FOOTMAN. Yes, sir. (*He goes out.*)

CHRIS. No, no. I couldn't do that. That's absurd. Isn't it, Helen? Of course you don't understand.

MARGARET. Chris, you've done nothing to be ashamed of?

HELEN. Margaret!

COL. ROKEBY. You must not say that, Margaret.

CHRIS. Ashamed?

MARGARET. What is wrong?

CHRIS. Oh! you have these romantic notions.

MARGARET. What do you mean?

COL. ROKEBY. He will tell us his adventures presently.

CHRIS. My adventures? But it's all different from what you think. Don't make me pretend to be what I am not. You know, sir, what war is.

COL. ROKEBY. You remember that I have never been in action.

CHRIS. How strange that is! Then you don't know—you don't know yourself? Ah, but you're different from me. Forgive me, sir. You're a soldier. You're a hero.

MARGARET. Are you not?

CHRIS. One ebbs and flows. To and fro, to and fro.

HELEN. Speak plainly. We can forgive.

CHRIS (*haughtily*). What have you to forgive?

COL. ROKEBY. Come, Chris! you must go for a moment. I'll go with you. Just for a moment. Stand up. Look your best.

CHRIS. Oh! but I can't. I'm not a hero. I hate it all. I'm a miserable, drifting man. And yet why not? Nobody knows me but myself. Don't you fear, Margaret. There's nothing against me. I can make a case for the heroical with anyone. In my heart? In my soul? Oh! never mind.

COL. ROKEBY. Will you come? Must I explain that you're not well?

[*Shouts outside are heard.*]

CHRIS (*fascinated and hesitating*). Shall I? I'm as good as the rest. And I had dreams of this once. No, no, sir; it's stupid and impossible.

HELEN. Don't let him go.

[*Another shout outside.*]

CHRIS. Yes, I'll take the call, as the actors say. Come on, sir. I did my best. You can't do more.

[*He goes out with* COLONEL ROKEBY. *There is a shout of greeting.* ROMER *follows the others out. The three women stare at each other.*]

MARGARET. What's happened to him?

LADY ROMER. Helen, if you love him, you may help him now.

HELEN. I loved him. I'm afraid of him now, I think. Oh, no! that can't be.

MARGARET. You must make him tell you everything.

HELEN. How can I do that? And it's not the things that happened he cares about. It's what he thinks and feels.

MARGARET. He must tell you what he has done or not done.

HELEN. What is it you suspect?

MARGARET. Some horrible cowardice.

HELEN. No, no.

LADY ROMER. Nonsense, Margaret.

MARGARET. We must know.

[COL. ROKEBY *and* CHRIS *return. The band strikes up again, and its sound grows fainter as the people march away.*]

COL. ROKEBY. There! Soon over. That's better. I wish you could have said a few words, too.

CHRIS. What an absurdity! What folly! Why did I go? I'm sorry, sir, but this isn't in my line.

MARGARET. Now tell us what you've been doing. Sit down and talk.

COL. ROKEBY. Of course we want to know, but give the poor lad time to rest.

MARGARET. Why have you not written? Where have you been?

CHRIS. Margaret, you're a Grand Inquisitor.

MARGARET. When you went away you told me I should be proud of you. Well?

CHRIS. I remember. I remember.

MARGARET. Well?

CHRIS. What does it matter? It's not really important—except to myself.

LADY ROMER. Chris, you talk so strangely you make us all afraid. You know

Margaret—you know what it means to her. And your father—think of him.

CHRIS. What a curious, ironical thing it is—he's never been in action.

MARGARET. He is a brave soldier, nevertheless.

COL. ROKEBY. Chris does not doubt me.

CHRIS. No, no, sir. Not for a moment. You and Frank——

COL. ROKEBY. And you, my boy? 10

CHRIS. I have not disgraced you, sir. (*There is visible relief. He sits down and continues in a low voice, though he must know that the others hear him.*) Now why did I say that? I had to say it.

MARGARET. But it's true?

CHRIS. Yes, I suppose so. I don't know. Yes, yes. But I'm speaking your language, not my own.

HELEN. Oh! Chris. Don't torture us. 20

CHRIS. Father, I think on the whole I came out pretty well. Of course I had my moments of funk like most people. I was complimented once or twice. I ought to have got my commission, but I was in hospital so long. Nerves, breakdown—that sort of thing. Quite common. It doesn't always mean funk. I got lost and had a horrible time wandering about. 30 Don't ask me to talk about that. Not that. May I blot out a few hours, a few minutes? I was very low. To become a sergeant isn't so bad. No, I haven't disgraced you.

MARGARET. Oh! Chris, I'm so glad.

COL. ROKEBY. You must tell us all about it.

CHRIS. Ask me any questions you like?

ROMER. Did you see anything of these 40 atrocities?

CHRIS. Atrocities? It's all atrocities.

ROMER. Well, but I mean—you know what I mean.

CHRIS. You trouble yourselves about such trifles.

ROMER. Trifles!

LADY ROMER. Did you fraternise with the Germans on Christmas Day?

CHRIS (*wearily*). What does it matter? I beg your pardon, Aunt, but you ask such funny questions.

HELEN. Why are they funny?

CHRIS. You'll be wanting me to give a lecture on the war with magic lantern.

LADY ROMER. And why not?

CHRIS. Jolly fellows in the trenches singing the National Anthem. Quite true, they did. Trifles.

MARGARET. And what is not a trifle?

CHRIS. How could I tell you? It's what a man carries in his heart. The Germans? I had impulses of affection for them. Decent folk. But it's no use charging with the bayonet unless you become a wild beast. I like the way they write about it in the newspapers. Nice, hearty sport. Oh, hell! Oh, hell!

COL. ROKEBY. Well, my boy, you're glad to get home.

CHRIS (*he looks round at them all, and to their consternation begins to sob. He recovers himself*). Devil take it. That's what I'm like now.

COL. ROKEBY. It'll pass off. It'll be all right.

CHRIS. The sort of thing to keep out of the newspapers.

[LADY ROMER *nods to her husband, and they go out together quietly.*]

MARGARET. Chris, I will be proud of you if you'll let me.

CHRIS. Thanks, Margaret.

COL. ROKEBY. Just settle down here, my boy, and have a quiet nap. You'll be all right then.

CHRIS. Good idea.

[MARGARET *and* COL. ROKEBY *go out, and* HELEN *is following, when she pauses and then comes back to* CHRIS, *who is lying back in an easy chair. He looks at her without moving.*]

HELEN. I think you've done nobly—beautifully. It was harder for you than for others. Oh, Chris! (*She holds out her hands as she stands before him.*)

CHRIS (*he moves uneasily in his chair but does not rise*). Thank you very much, Helen.

HELEN (*discomfited*). You are dreadfully knocked up, I'm afraid.

CHRIS. Yes, I don't seem to have much life left in me.

HELEN. You must tell me all about it some day. I want to know all you've thought and done.

CHRIS. Do you, Helen?

HELEN. Yes, I'm not afraid. I want to share it all with you. The bad and the good.

CHRIS. Oh! but how can I? How can I? Our language—words—are made for peace. I can't tell you about war.

HELEN. You're not sincere.

CHRIS. No. We're all shamming and posing. Sincere! We must keep decent. The stoics, you know—the stoics were rather a canny lot. They never talked in their sleep.

HELEN. Chris! what have you done?

CHRIS (*sharply*). There's nothing against me. I'm telling you the truth. That is to say—it's the truth as far as the world has any business with it. Of course if we're going into the awful things that might have been—what right have you to pry into my mind? Oh, Helen! I've suffered the agonies of death.

HELEN. Chris—you weren't wounded?

CHRIS. My skin's whole, and it's the skin that counts. You treat us all alike. The world's justice. Of course a few poor devils are cashiered and publicly disgraced. They may be no worse than the rest. But we come home to brass bands, and there are secrets in our hearts. We're different; every man is different, but you give us the same tune. The brass band is ridiculous now. It was right when we went out. We were heroes then; we'd taken the plunge and we were all alike. I think I was never so happy as when I first marched to it.

HELEN. You are a hero now.

CHRIS. That's my business.

HELEN. You make me miserable.

CHRIS. Oh! I'm sorry, Helen. I tell you I've behaved like a hero—several times. Yes, and I've been in hell—cowed—degraded—brutish. These are only words. I've got things that I can't share. I must be alone now. And what I've seen. Horrible! Horrible! Good lads, my comrades—beside me—shattered—crying out to me——(*He puts up his hands before his face and is shaken by sobs.*) We come back to glowing welcomes, to take up the old, pleasant life again. No.

HELEN (*after a pause*). There's your work?

CHRIS. What work?

HELEN. Your writing.

CHRIS. Yes, yes. Certainly. Some day, I suppose. (*He rises.*)

HELEN. There is something else, Chris—surely.

CHRIS (*he looks at her in fear*). You mean——

HELEN. There's me.

CHRIS (*muttering*). Thank you, thank you, Helen. (*He turns away.*) Just let me think a moment.

HELEN. Think!

CHRIS. You're very kind. You're very generous. We might make a mistake.

HELEN. Chris, my dear—if we love one another——

CHRIS. I want rest. I want warmth. I

want food. The blood has gone out of my body.

HELEN. Oh! my poor boy!

CHRIS. I'm changed; I'm weak and broken. I want to be alone. You're immaculate.

HELEN. It's only that I've not been tried.

CHRIS. Yes, you're generous. If you had been—if you had been—if I could have picked you from the gutter—a prostitute from the streets——Forgive me.

HELEN. Chris! we have done wrong. We should not have let you go.

CHRIS. You mustn't judge things by their results. It was right to go. I have no regrets. How could I stay while Frank and Stephen and all the rest were dying there? How could I see my father every day? And deep down in me—yes, deep—I'm an Englishman—all the old voices and the old tunes were calling.

HELEN. In time, Chris—in time, all may be well.

CHRIS. Yes, the world's broken, but it will mend. I'm broken, and I suppose I shall mend. I can see things when I don't feel them. I can see that you're beautiful and generous.

HELEN. Some day—some day——

CHRIS. No, Helen. You must look for a better man.

HELEN. There isn't a better.

CHRIS. Yes; the great man isn't crushed by war, not even by what I've gone through. If I'd been stronger—if I'd been better—— It's very hard on men like me. This war is very hard on men like me.

HELEN. I've been blind.

[COLONEL ROKEBY *enters*.]

COL. ROKEBY. Now, you've talked to him long enough. Let him have his rest.

[HELEN *goes out sadly*.]

CHRIS. Good idea, sir. A sleep will refresh me.

COL. ROKEBY. Yes. Chris, it is a strange thing, isn't it, that I've never had any fighting? It's not for want of trying. I envy you.

CHRIS (*puts his arm round his father's neck*). You're an old innocent, you know!

COL. ROKEBY. What!

CHRIS. We've both done our best, Daddy. (*He begins to cry, and his father leads him to the arm-chair*.)

COL. ROKEBY. You want rest, my boy—rest.

[CHRIS *sinks into the chair and lies back in it, staring before him. His father hesitates and then goes quietly out*.]

CURTAIN

J. M. SYNGE

THE NAME OF Edmund John Milling-ton Synge is inseparably linked with that of the Abbey Theatre, Dublin; and both with the most delicately wrought plays and the most turbulent receptions to be found in all the history of contemporary drama. One is often hard put to it to decide whether the action was more dramatic behind or before the footlights, whether the aroused audiences or the actors themselves gave the more sensational performances. The Abbey Theatre has known few dull seasons; it developed at least one major dramatist.

In the quickened days when Antoine was making news in Paris and the Free Theatre in Berlin was making Hauptmann's work known, when Stanislavsky and Nemirovitch-Dantchenko were laying plans for the Moscow Art Theatre, William Butler Yeats and Lady Gregory spent a wet autumn afternoon discussing plays and the pity of the fact that Ireland had no theatre where works such as those of Yeats and his friend Edward Martyn, Lady Gregory's neighbor, could be given. They talked on and on, and before the end of that afternoon in 1898 they had made a plan to get money, take a Dublin theatre, and give Martyn's *Heather Field* and Yeats's *The Countess Cathleen*. A few days later they drew up a letter which, quite unconsciously on their part, in a sense began the theatrical phase of the "Celtic Movement." It read:

"We propose to have performed in Dublin, in the spring of every year certain Celtic and Irish plays, which whatever be their degree of excellence will be written with a high ambition, and so to build up a Celtic and Irish school of dramatic literature. We hope to find in Ireland an uncorrupted and imaginative audience trained to listen by its passion for oratory, and believe that our desire to bring upon the stage the deeper thoughts and emotions of Ireland will ensure for us a tolerant welcome, and that freedom to experiment which is not found in theatres of England, and without which no new movement in art or literature can succeed. We will show that Ireland is not the home of buffoonery and of easy sentiment, as it has been represented, but the home of an ancient idealism. We are confident of the support of all Irish people, who are weary of misrepresentation, in carrying out a work that is outside all the political questions that divide us."

After a great deal of effort and much cutting of red tape, the plays were performed by English actors on May 8, 1899, at the Ancient Concert Rooms—with hooting and booing from the gallery by young men of the Catholic University who had come to protest the "insult to their faith" which, they said, will implied by the line after Cathleen's death, "God looks on the intention, not the deed." But the movement was launched, and the disturbance served only to publicize it.

A fair sized library has already been written about this Irish renaissance, the enthusiasm with which men and women of all talents and genius engaged in it, and the swift growth of the experiment. It passed by gradual though quite distinct stages involving many different people, from the short-lived Irish Literary Theatre (as the Yeats, Martyn, Lady Gregory group was called) to the Irish National Theatre Society; and then, through the zeal of Yeats, W. G. and Frank Fay, and others, and through the generosity of Miss Annie Horniman, the Abbey Theatre itself was founded in 1904. This theatre, as W. G. Fay, insists, "was first and foremost a theatrical, not a literary movement," and the only direct connexion between it and the Irish Literary Theatre, which was dead before the Abbey was conceived, "was the purely personal one that Mr. Yeats was actively associated with both." The Fays were convinced that Irish plays required Irish actors to give them a complete performance, and they proceeded to prove their convictions. The result was the now celebrated company of Abbey players, which for naturalness and simplicity of action, rhythm, and group effects, and for beauty of diction are not surpassed even by the Moscow Art Theatre.

In the midst of this intense activity the genius of J. M. Synge began to stir. In October, 1903, in the Molesworth Hall, the Fays put on a one act play *In the Shadow of the Glen*, with W. G. Fay as the Tramp, by this unknown and untried author. In this dramatization of a tale current among the peasants on the West Coast of Ireland, a Tramp arrives one damp night at old Dan Burke's cottage at the head of a glen. Dan is lying dead under a sheet in the room. Nora, his young wife, welcomes the Tramp, then takes her shawl and goes to find young farmer Michael Dara. While she is away, Dan draws down the sheet and comes to life to tell the Tramp of his plot to test this couple. Then he plays

dead again as Nora and Michael come in, and he hears Nora say that she married him for "a bit of a farm, and cows on it, and sheep on the back hills" and that "I do be thinking in the long nights it was a big fool I was that time, Michael Dara . . ." Dan jumps up from his bier, orders Nora to leave, and when the simple Michael hangs back, Nora gathers a few things into her shawl, and goes off with the Tramp: "you've a fine bit of talk, stranger, and it's with yourself I'll go. . . . What is it you'll have now but a black life, Daniel Burke, and it's not long I'm telling you, till you'll be lying again under that sheet, and you dead surely."

The play, says W. G. Fay, was Synge's "first effort, but it showed little sign of the 'prentice hand. It was a peasant play, but oh, how different from any of our other peasant pieces! It was the first of the modern Irish realistic plays. From beginning to end there was not a syllable of sentiment. The dialect used was entirely strange to us, which was hardly surprising seeing that Synge had invented it himself. His device was the simple enough one of translating practically word for word from Gaelic." Fay soon mastered the difficulties of the dialogue, "got at how the speeches were built up, and could say any of the lines exactly in the way he [Synge] wanted" with a balance and a lilt. Thus had come together a literary movement, a theatrical company, and one of the great modern dramatists.

If Synge's first play showed "little sign of the 'prentice hand," the reason may be found in the story of his life and career down to that October in 1903. He was born on April 16, 1871, at Rathfarnham, a Dublin suburb. His family was of superior stock, with several men of distinction in the church, in scholarship, and in art scattered through the lineage. His lawyer father, John Hatch Synge, died when John Millington was not yet a year old, leaving a modest income for the support of his family who moved to Rathgar, a less expensive suburb of Dublin. Synge was educated in Dublin, in part by private tutor. He took his degree at Trinity College in 1893 where he proved himself an unusual linguist, and gained proficiency in music. Following his graduation he went to Germany for a year to study music, but after wandering about Darmstadt, Coblentz, and other towns, he gave up the idea of a career in music for a life of letters. Paris was the center of life for literary men, especially for the Irish who found the Latin Quarter more hospitable in those days than the pubs of Sackville Street, Dublin. With an income of forty pounds a year from Ireland, Synge established himself on the Left Bank, often did his own cooking to save expense, studied French literature, and practised writing with the intention of becoming a literary critic.

Here Synge lived, suffered from ill health, studied, and wrote for some five years, broken at intervals by visits to Ireland and brief journeys out from Paris. But in the midst of all the colorful life of the Paris of the nineties, Synge was quiet, modest, poor, and not at all colorful or Bohemian. Certainly there was little about this big, swarthy, soft-spoken Irishman, this exile from turbulent Ireland studying Racine and writing aesthetic pieces in the French capital, to suggest that in a few years he should become the foremost interpreter of the peasants of his native islands.

It was William Butler Yeats who persuaded Synge to get out of this literary cul-de-sac into a full-blooded milieu worthy of his dormant genius. Yeats found him in Paris in March 1898 at the moment when his own eagerness was high and youthful and the Celtic renaissance was in the air. He was blunt in telling Synge that his future lay not in Paris but in Ireland. He advised him to cut loose and go back to the primitive earth with its unspoiled peasant folk and its undamaged speech. Synge left his Paris attic for the Aran Isles off the west coast of Ireland. It was a historic decision, and few odysseys have brought back richer treasure. Synge himself left a lyrical record of his life there in the long essay "The Aran Islands." These islands received handsome pictorial treatment a few years ago in the international prize-winning motion picture *Man of Aran*. This sojourn was the beginning of many years of travel among the people of Aran and close, sympathetic study of their speech, customs, legends, and folklore. Synge himself said that when he was writing *In the Shadow of the Glen*, "I got more aid than any learning could have given me from a chink in the floor of the old Wicklow house where I was staying, that let me hear what was being said by the servant girls in the kitchen."

The music of these voices and the timeless tales of age, death, sorrow, and the sea fell forcibly on Synge's ear made sensitive and acute by long absence. He was essentially a poet who was abnormally alert to the melancholy beauty of this speech—"fully flavored as a nut or apple," he said—and a dramatist who could capture its music and create the atmosphere of the sea and the sky, of the rocky earth and dangerous coast, and the meaning of the lives of the men and women who walked the strand and sailed the sea.

Lady Gregory has left a pleasing sketch of Synge from those days when he was storing up wisdom and understanding among the islanders for his future plays. She had first seen him in the north island of Aran where she was also staying, gathering folk-lore, and hearing the talk of "the fishers and sea-weed gatherers." Neither spoke; each looked upon the other as an intruder. But Yeats spoke highly of Synge to Lady Gregory as "really a most excellent man. . . . He works very hard and is learning Breton; he will be a very useful scholar." She asked him to Coole and they became friends. "I said of him in a letter: 'One never has to rearrange one's mind to talk to him.' He was quite direct, sincere, and simple, not only a good listener but too good a one, not speaking much in general society. His fellow guests at Coole always liked him, and he was pleasant and genial with them, though once, when he had come straight from life on a wild coast, he confessed that a somewhat warlike English lady in the house was 'Civilization in its most violent form.' . . . He told me that the people of the play he was writing often seemed the real people among whom he lived, and I think his dreamy look came from this."

With his spirit nurtured and stimulated by his leisurely, wandering life through the interesting parts of Ireland, with his ear sharpened by folk-tales in native speech, and with his pen skilled by the essays he turned out for various papers from the autumn of 1898 on through several years, Synge was ready in 1903 to write plays for the new group of actors to produce. The success of *In the Shadow of the Glen*, despite the usual hissing on the opening night, encouraged both. The following February the Irish National Theatre Society performed Synge's *Riders to the Sea*, which Fay called "the most perfect one-act

play that has come out of the Irish Theatre whether at the Molesworth Hall or the Abbey. It has all the austere strength of a Greek tragedy. From beginning to end there is not a superfluous word. It never fails to make the audience accept its inevitableness, and it plays just as well with actors that are not Irish." Synge had got the basic incident of this play during one of his periods on the Aran Islands when a body was washed ashore just as he describes that of Michael in his poetic drama. With flawless precision he has caught and interpreted the sorrowing heart of old Maurya as for the sixth time she faces the cruelty of the sea in the death of her sons. "They're all gone now, and there isn't anything more the sea can do to me. . . . "

In the few years that remained of the tragically short life of Synge he wrote four more plays. *The Tinker's Wedding* (published in 1909) was an excursion into comedy, bordering on farce, in the difficult two act length. The play was not a success, but it has many high spirited passages as it exploits the two tinkers and their views of marriage. In his preface to the play, Synge wrote of humor as one of the things which "nourish the imagination," and declared that in the greater part of Ireland "the whole people, from the tinkers to the clergy, have still a life, and view of life, that are rich and genial and humorous. I do not think that these country people, who have so much humor themselves, will mind being laughed at without malice, as the people in every country have been laughed at in their own comedies." The play was not produced until after Synge's death.

The Well of the Saints, Synge's first full-length play and one of his most perfect in structure despite the difficult long speeches, was produced at the newly founded Abbey Theatre on February 4, 1905, with W. G. Fay as Martin Doul, the blind beggar. Martin and his blind wife Mary see the world and each other as beautiful in their mind's eye. A saintly wandering friar with the gift of healing restores sight to their eyes, but the blessing carried with it the curse of disillusionment. In the end they lose their sight again and return to their rapturous imagination of the world they no longer see. And Martin says, in refusing to allow another miracle by the Saint, "if it's a right some of you have to be working and sweating the like of Timmy the smith, and a right some of you have to be fasting and praying and talking holy talk the like of yourself, I'm thinking it's a good right ourselves have to be sitting blind, hearing a soft wind turning round the little leaves of the spring and feeling the sun, and we not tormenting our souls with the sight of the gray days, and the holy men, and the dirty feet is trampling the world."

Deirdre of the Sorrows, upon which Synge was working in the last months of his life in convalescence in Germany and in a Dublin hospital where he died on March 24, 1909, was left in incomplete form, though nearly finished. Making use of the same gifts of language, poetic feeling, and understanding of the heart which are so evident in the other plays, Synge created his own version of the ancient Irish legend of Deirdre, making of her a living Irish woman contemplating love and death and the inevitable impermanence of life.

Synge's most famous play, however, is *The Playboy of the Western World*. It was presented by W. G. Fay at the Abbey Theatre on Saturday, January 26, 1907, amid the most riotous uproar ever to accompany an opening night.

Fay himself played the part of Christy Mahon. He had anticipated trouble with the sensitive and unsophisticated audience of the time when he first saw Synge's script. He was certain that the audience would consider the play an attack and would retaliate. There was also some rough language in the play, including the words "bloody" and "shift" both of which were shocking and inflammatory to an Irish audience of pre-War days. Synge would not alter his play, however, and Fay went on with the production. Many accounts of the riot have been written by eye-witnesses. Fay reports that the first act went splendidly, and the second opened with laughter. Then Widow Quin came on stage, the line about "all bloody fools" was spoken, the word "shift" was uttered, and the audience was turned "into a veritable mob of howling devils." During the last act the house was in an uproar, and the curtain fell on a riot. The players gave other performances amid continuous riots and fist fights, but not until well into the first week could the audience hear the play. Overnight Synge was famous, and *The Playboy* was launched on its phenomenal career, followed by a train of controversy that reached to New York, Boston, and Philadelphia. Even in recent years Irish-American societies have tried to restrain the Abbey Players from presenting this comedy.

For the most part, however, these storms have died away, and are interesting now only as documentation for the tremendous excitement that accompanied the rise of the contemporary theatre. *The Playboy* was founded on an actual incident, as Synge himself tells us in *The Aran Islands*. An old man, the oldest on the island, was fond of telling him anecdotes "of things that have happened here in his lifetime. He often tells me about a Connaught man who killed his father with the blow of a spade when he was in a passion, and then fled to this island and threw himself on the mercy of some of the natives with whom he was said to be related. They hid him in a hole—which the old man has shown me —and kept him safe for weeks, though the police came and searched for him, and he could hear their boots grinding on the stone— over his head. In spite of reward which was offered, the island was incorruptible, and after much trouble the man was safely shipped to America.

"This impulse to protect the criminal is universal in the west. . . . If a man has killed his father, and is already sick and broken with remorse, they can see no reason why he should be dragged away and killed by the law. . . . They ask, 'Would any one kill his father if he was able to help it?' "

And in the preface to *The Playboy*, Synge explains: ". . . I have used one or two words only that I have not heard among the people of Ireland, or spoken in my own nursery before I could read the newspapers. . . . Anyone who has lived in real intimacy with the Irish peasantry will know that the wildest sayings and ideas in this play are tame indeed, compared with the fancies one may hear in any little hillside cabin in Geesala, or Carraroe, or Dingle Bay."

Synge succeeded in compressing this aspect of Irish life into a play. Its spirit is exuberant; its dialogue quick and racy and enriched with all the color that Synge had gathered from the Irish earth itself; its structure masterly; and its feeling for character of the highest order. *The Playboy* is universally regarded in critical circles as one of the great comedies of our time by one of the great dramatists of the modern world.

THE PLAYBOY OF THE WESTERN WORLD

CHARACTERS

CHRISTOPHER MAHON

OLD MAHON, *his father, a squatter*

MICHAEL JAMES FLAHERTY, *called* MICHAEL JAMES, *a publican*

MARGARET FLAHERTY, *called* PEGEEN MIKE, *his daughter*

WIDOW QUIN, *a woman of about thirty*

SHAWN KEOGH, *her cousin, a young farmer*

PHILLY CULLEN *and* JIMMY FARRELL, *small farmers*

SARA TANSEY, SUSAN BRADY, *and* HONOR BLAKE, *village girls*

A BELLMAN

SOME PEASANTS

The action takes place near a village, on a wild coast of Mayo. The first Act passes on an evening of autumn, the other two Acts on the following day.

ACT I

A country public-house or shebeen, very rough and untidy. There is a sort of counter on the right with shelves, holding many bottles and jugs, just seen above it. Empty barrels stand near the counter. At back, a little to left of counter, there is a door into the open air, then, more to the left, there is a settle with shelves above it, with more jugs, and a table beneath a window. At the left there is a large open fire-place, with turf fire, and a small door into inner room. PEGEEN, *a wild-looking but fine girl, of about twenty, is writing at table. She is dressed in the usual peasant dress.*

PEGEEN (*slowly as she writes*). Six yards of stuff for to make a yellow gown. A pair of lace boots with lengthy heels on them and brassy eyes. A hat is suited for a wedding-day. A fine tooth comb. To be sent with three barrels of porter in Jimmy Farrell's creel cart on the evening of the coming Fair to Mister Michael James Flaherty. With the best compliments of this season. Margaret Flaherty.

SHAWN KEOGH (*a fat and fair young man comes in as she signs, looks round awkwardly, when he sees she is alone*). Where's himself?

PEGEEN (*without looking at him*). He's coming. (*She directs the letter.*) To Mister Sheamus Mulroy, Wine and Spirit Dealer, Castlebar.

SHAWN (*uneasily*). I didn't see him on the road.

PEGEEN. How would you see him (*Licks stamp and puts it on letter.*) and it dark night this half hour gone by?

SHAWN (*turning towards the door again*). I stood a while outside wondering would I have a right to pass on or to walk in and see you, Pegeen Mike (*Comes to fire.*), and I could hear the cows breathing, and sighing in the stillness of the air, and not a step moving any place from this gate to the bridge.

PEGEEN (*putting letter in envelope*). It's above at the cross-roads he is, meeting Philly Cullen; and a couple more are going along with him to Kate Cassidy's wake.

SHAWN (*looking at her blankly*). And he's going that length in the dark night?

PEGEEN (*impatiently*). He is surely, and leaving me lonesome on the scruff of the hill. (*She gets up and puts envelope on dresser, then winds clock.*) Isn't it long the nights are now, Shawn Keogh, to be leaving a poor girl with her own 10 self counting the hours to the dawn of day?

SHAWN (*with awkward humour*). If it is, when we're wedded in a short while you'll have no call to complain, for I've little will to be walking off to wakes or weddings in the darkness of the night.

PEGEEN (*with rather scornful good humour*). You're making mighty certain, Sha- 20 neen, that I'll wed you now.

SHAWN. Aren't we after making a good bargain, the way we're only waiting these days on Father Reilly's dispensation from the bishops, or the Court of Rome.

PEGEEN (*looking at him teasingly, washing up at dresser*). It's a wonder, Shaneen, the Holy Father'd be taking notice of the likes of you; for if I was him I 30 wouldn't bother with this place where you'll meet none but Red Linahan, has a squint in his eye, and Patcheen is lame in his heel, or the mad Mulrannies were driven from California and they lost in their wits. We're a queer lot these times to go troubling the Holy Father on his sacred seat.

SHAWN (*scandalized*). If we are, we're as good this place as another, maybe, 40 and as good these times as we were for ever.

PEGEEN (*with scorn*). As good, is it? Where now will you meet the like of Daneen Sullivan knocked the eye from a peeler, or Marcus Quin, God

rest him, got six months for maiming ewes, and he a great warrant to tell stories of holy Ireland till he'd have the old women shedding down tears about their feet. Where will you find the like of them, I'm saying?

SHAWN (*timidly*). If you don't, it's a good job, maybe; for (*With peculiar emphasis on the words.*) Father Reilly has small conceit to have that kind walking around and talking to the girls.

PEGEEN (*impatiently, throwing water from basin out of the door*). Stop tormenting me with Father Reilly (*Imitating his voice.*) when I'm asking only what way I'll pass these twelve hours of dark, and not take my death with the fear. (*Looking out of door.*)

SHAWN (*timidly*). Would I fetch you the Widow Quin, maybe?

PEGEEN. Is it the like of that murderer? You'll not, surely.

SHAWN (*going to her, soothingly*). Then I'm thinking himself will stop along with you when he sees you taking on, for it'll be a long night-time with great darkness, and I'm after feeling a kind of fellow above in the furzy ditch, groaning wicked like a maddening dog, the way it's good cause you have, maybe, to be fearing now.

PEGEEN (*turning on him sharply*). What's that? Is it a man you seen?

SHAWN (*retreating*). I couldn't see him at all; but I heard him groaning out, and breaking his heart. It should have been a young man from his words speaking.

PEGEEN (*going after him*). And you never went near to see was he hurted or what ailed him at all?

SHAWN. I did not, Pegeen Mike. It was a dark, lonesome place to be hearing the like of him.

PEGEEN. Well, you're a daring fellow, and if they find his corpse stretched above in the dews of dawn, what'll you say then to the peelers, or the Justice of the Peace?

SHAWN (*thunderstruck*). I wasn't thinking of that. For the love of God, Pegeen Mike, don't let on I was speaking of him. Don't tell your father and the men is coming above; for if they heard that story, they'd have great blabbing this night at the wake.   10

PEGEEN. I'll maybe tell them, and I'll maybe not.

SHAWN. They are coming at the door. Will you whisht, I'm saying?

PEGEEN. Whisht yourself.

[*She goes behind counter.* MICHAEL JAMES, *fat jovial publican, comes in followed by* PHILLY CULLEN, *who is thin and mistrusting, and* JIMMY FARRELL, *who is fat and amorous, about forty-five.*]   20

MEN (*together*). God bless you. The blessing of God on this place.

PEGEEN. God bless you kindly.

MICHAEL (*to men who go to the counter*). Sit down now, and take your rest. (*Crosses to* SHAWN *at the fire.*) And how is it you are, Shawn Keogh? Are you coming over the sands to Kate Cassidy's wake?

SHAWN. I am not, Michael James. I'm 30 going home the short cut to my bed.

PEGEEN (*speaking across the counter*). He's right too, and have you no shame, Michael James, to be quitting off for the whole night, and leaving myself lonesome in the shop?

MICHAEL (*good-humouredly*). Isn't it the same whether I go for the whole night or a part only? and I'm thinking it's a queer daughter you are if you'd have 40 me crossing backward through the Stooks of the Dead Women, with a drop taken.

PEGEEN. If I am a queer daughter, it's a queer father'd be leaving me lonesome these twelve hours of dark, and

I piling the turf with the dogs barking, and the calves mooing, and my own teeth rattling with the fear.

JIMMY (*flatteringly*). What is there to hurt you, and you a fine, hardy girl would knock the head of any two men in the place?

PEGEEN (*working herself up*). Isn't there the harvest boys with their tongues red for drink, and the ten tinkers is camped in the east glen, and the thousand militia—bad cess to them!—walking idle through the land. There's lots surely to hurt me, and I won't stop alone in it, let himself do what he will.

MICHAEL. If you're that afeard, let Shawn Keogh stop along with you. It's the will of God, I'm thinking, himself should be seeing to you now.

[*They all turn on* SHAWN.]

SHAWN (*in horrified confusion*). I would and welcome, Michael James, but I'm afeard of Father Reilly; and what at all would the Holy Father and the Cardinals of Rome be saying if they heard I did the like of that?

MICHAEL (*with contempt*). God help you! Can't you sit in by the hearth with the light lit and herself beyond in the room? You'll do that surely, for I've heard tell there's a queer fellow above, going mad or getting his death, maybe, in the gripe of the ditch, so she'd be safer this night with a person here.

SHAWN (*with plaintive despair*). I'm afeard of Father Reilly, I'm saying. Let you not be tempting me, and we near married itself.

PHILLY (*with cold contempt*). Lock him in the west room. He'll stay then and have no sin to be telling to the priest.

MICHAEL (*to* SHAWN, *getting between him and the door*). Go up now.

SHAWN (*at the top of his voice*). Don't stop

me, Michael James. Let me out of the door, I'm saying, for the love of the Almighty God. Let me out. (*Trying to dodge past him.*) Let me out of it, and may God grant you His indulgence in the hour of need.

MICHAEL (*loudly*). Stop your noising, and sit down by the hearth. (*Gives him a push and goes to counter laughing.*)

SHAWN (*turning back, wringing his hands*). Oh, Father Reilly and the saints of God, where will I hide myself to-day? Oh, St. Joseph and St. Patrick and St. Brigid, and St. James, have mercy on me now! (SHAWN *turns round, sees door clear, and makes a rush for it.*)

MICHAEL (*catching him by the coat-tail*). You'd be going, is it?

SHAWN (*screaming*). Leave me go, Michael James, leave me go, you old Pagan, leave me go, or I'll get the curse of the priests on you, and of the scarlet-coated bishops of the courts of Rome. (*With a sudden movement he pulls himself out of his coat, and disappears out of the door, leaving his coat in* MICHAEL'S *hands.*)

MICHAEL (*turning round, and holding up coat*). Well, there's the coat of a Christian man. Oh, there's sainted glory this day in the lonesome west; an by the will of God I've got you a decent man, Pegeen, you'll have no call to be spying after if you've a score of young girls, maybe, weeding in your fields.

PEGEEN (*taking up the defence of her property*). What right have you to be making game of a poor fellow for minding the priest, when it's your own the fault is, not paying a penny pot-boy to stand along with me and give me courage in the doing of my work? (*She snaps the coat away from him, and goes behind counter with it.*)

MICHAEL (*taken aback*). Where would I get a pot-boy? Would you have me send the bellman screaming in the streets of Castlebar?

SHAWN (*opening the door a chink and putting in his head, in a small voice*). Michael James!

MICHAEL (*imitating him*). What ails you?

SHAWN. The queer dying fellow's beyond looking over the ditch. He's come up, I'm thinking, stealing your hens. (*Looks over his shoulder.*) God help me, he's following me now (*He runs into room.*), and if he's heard what I said, he'll be having my life, and I going home lonesome in the darkness of the night.

[*For a perceptible moment they watch the door with curiosity. Some one coughs outside. Then* CHRISTY MAHON, *a slight young man, comes in very tired and frightened and dirty.*]

CHRISTY (*in a small voice*). God save all here!

MEN. God save you kindly.

CHRISTY (*going to the counter*). I'd trouble you for a glass of porter, woman of the house. (*He puts down coin.*)

PEGEEN (*serving him*). You're one of the tinkers, young fellow, is beyond camped in the glen?

CHRISTY. I am not; but I'm destroyed walking.

MICHAEL (*patronizingly*). Let you come up then to the fire. You're looking famished with the cold.

CHRISTY. God reward you. (*He takes up his glass and goes a little way across to the left, then stops and looks about him.*) Is it often the police do be coming into this place, master of the house?

MICHAEL. If you'd come in better hours, you'd have seen "Licensed for the sale of Beer and Spirits, to be consumed on the premises," written in white letters above the door, and what would the polis want spying on me, and not a decent house within four miles, the way every living Christian is a bona fide, saving one widow alone?

CHRISTY (*with relief*). It's a safe house, so. (*He goes over to the fire, sighing and moaning. Then he sits down, putting his glass beside him and begins gnawing a turnip, too miserable to feel the others staring at him with curiosity.*)

MICHAEL (*going after him*). Is it yourself is fearing the polis? You're wanting, maybe?

CHRISTY. There's many wanting.

MICHAEL. Many surely, with the broken harvest and the ended wars. (*He picks up some stockings, etc., that are near the fire, and carries them away furtively.*) It should be larceny, I'm thinking?

CHRISTY, (*dolefully*). I had it in my mind 20 it was a different word and a bigger.

PEGEEN. There's a queer lad. Were you never slapped in school, young fellow, that you don't know the name of your deed?

CHRISTY (*bashfully*). I'm slow at learning, a middling scholar only.

MICHAEL. If you're a dunce itself, you'd have a right to know that larceny's 30 robbing and stealing. Is it for the like of that you're wanting?

CHRISTY (*with a flash of family pride*). And I the son of a strong farmer (*With a sudden qualm.*), God rest his soul, could have bought up the whole of your old house a while since, from the butt of his tailpocket, and not have missed the weight of it gone.

MICHAEL (*impressed*). If it's not stealing, 40 it's maybe something big.

CHRISTY (*flattered*). Aye; it's maybe something big.

JIMMY. He's a wicked-looking young fellow. Maybe he followed after a young woman on a lonesome night.

CHRISTY (*shocked*). Oh, the saints forbid, mister; I was all times a decent lad.

PHILLY (*turning on* JIMMY). You're a silly man, Jimmy Farrell. He said his father was a farmer a while since, and there's himself now in a poor state. Maybe the land was grabbed from him, and he did what any decent man would do.

10 MICHAEL (*to* CHRISTY, *mysteriously*). Was it bailiffs?

CHRISTY. The divil a one.

MICHAEL. Agents?

CHRISTY. The divil a one.

MICHAEL. Landlords?

CHRISTY (*peevishly*). Ah, not at all, I'm saying. You'd see the like of them stories on any little paper of a Munster town. But I'm not calling to mind any person, gentle, simple, judge or jury, did the like of me.

[*They all draw nearer with delighted curiosity.*]

PHILLY. Well, that lad's a puzzle-the-world.

JIMMY. He'd beat Dan Davies' circus, or the holy missioners making sermons on the villainy of man. Try him again, Philly.

30 PHILLY. Did you strike golden guineas out of solder, young fellow, or shilling coins itself?

CHRISTY. I did not, mister, not sixpence nor a farthing coin.

JIMMY. Did you marry three wives maybe? I'm told there's a sprinkling have done that among the holy Luthers of the preaching north.

CHRISTY (*shyly*). I never married with 40 one, let alone with a couple or three.

PHILLY. Maybe he went fighting for the Boers, the like of the man beyond, was judged to be hanged, quartered and drawn. Were you off east, young fellow, fighting bloody wars for Kruger and the freedom of the Boers?

CHRISTY. I never left my own parish till Tuesday was a week.

PEGEEN (*coming from counter*). He's done nothing, so. (*To* CHRISTY.) If you didn't commit murder or a bad, nasty thing, or false coining, or robbery, or butchery, or the like of them, there isn't anything that would be worth your troubling for to run from now. You did nothing at all.

CHRISTY (*his feelings hurt*). That's an unkindly thing to be saying to a poor orphaned traveller, has a prison behind him, and hanging before, and hell's gap gaping below.

PEGEEN (*with a sign to the men to be quiet*). You're only saying it. You did nothing at all. A soft lad the like of you wouldn't slit the windpipe of a screeching sow.

CHRISTY (*offended*). You're not speaking the truth.

PEGEEN (*in mock rage*). Not speaking the truth, is it? Would you have me knock the head of you with the butt of the broom?

CHRISTY (*twisting round on her with a sharp cry of horror*). Don't strike me. I killed my poor father, Tuesday was a week, for doing the like of that.

PEGEEN (*with blank amazement*). Is it killed your father?

CHRISTY (*subsiding*). With the help of God I did surely, and that the Holy Immaculate Mother may intercede for his soul.

PHILLY (*retreating with* JIMMY). There's a daring fellow.

JIMMY. Oh, glory be to God!

MICHAEL (*with great respect.*) That was a hanging crime, mister honey. You should have had good reason for doing the like of that.

CHRISTY (*in a very reasonable tone*). He was a dirty man, God forgive him, and he getting old and crusty, the way I couldn't put up with him at all.

PEGEEN. And you shot him dead?

CHRISTY (*shaking his head*). I never used weapons. I've no license, and I'm a law-fearing man.

MICHAEL. It was with a hilted knife maybe? I'm told, in the big world it's bloody knives they use.

CHRISTY (*loudly, scandalized*). Do you take me for a slaughter-boy?

PEGEEN. You never hanged him, the way Jimmy Farrell hanged his dog from the license, and had it screeching and wriggling three hours at the butt of a string, and himself swearing it was a dead dog, and the peelers swearing it had life?

CHRISTY. I did not then. I just riz the loy and let fall the edge of it on the ridge of his skull, and he went down at my feet like an empty sack, and never let a grunt or groan from him at all.

MICHAEL (*making a sign to* PEGEEN *to fill* CHRISTY'S *glass*). And what way weren't you hanged, mister? Did you bury him then?

CHRISTY (*considering*). Aye. I buried him then. Wasn't I digging spuds in the field?

MICHAEL. And the peelers never followed after you the eleven days that you're out?

CHRISTY (*shaking his head*). Never a one of them, and I walking forward facing hog, dog, or divil on the highway of the road.

PHILLY (*nodding wisely*). It's only with a common week-day kind of a murderer them lads would be trusting their carcase, and that man should be a great terror when his temper's roused.

MICHAEL. He should then. (*To* CHRISTY.) And where was it, mister honey, that you did the deed?

CHRISTY (*looking at him with suspicion*). Oh, a distant place, master of the house, a windy corner of high, distant hills.

PHILLY (*nodding with approval*). He's a close man, and he's right, surely.

PEGEEN. That'd be a lad with the sense of Solomon to have for a pot-boy, Michael James, if it's the truth you're seeking one at all.

PHILLY. The peelers is fearing him, and if you'd that lad in the house there isn't one of them would come smelling around if the dogs itself were lapping poteen from the dung-pit of the yard.

JIMMY. Bravery's a treasure in a lonesome place, and a lad would kill his father, I'm thinking, would face a foxy divil with a pitchpike on the flags of hell.

PEGEEN. It's the truth they're saying, and if I'd that lad in the house, I wouldn't be fearing the loosèd kharki cut-throats, or the walking dead.

CHRISTY (*swelling with surprise and triumph*). Well, glory be to God!

MICHAEL (*with deference*). Would you think well to stop here and be pot-boy, mister honey, if we gave you good wages, and didn't destroy you with the weight of work?

SHAWN (*coming forward uneasily*). That'd be a queer kind to bring into a decent quiet household with the like of Pegeen Mike.

PEGEEN (*very sharply*). Will you whisht? Who's speaking to you?

SHAWN (*retreating*). A bloody-handed murderer the like of . . .

PEGEEN (*snapping at him*). Whisht I am saying; we'll take no fooling from your like at all. (*To* CHRISTY *with a honeyed voice.*) And you, young fellow, you'd have a right to stop, I'm thinking, for we'd do our all and utmost to content your needs.

CHRISTY (*overcome with wonder*). And I'd be safe in this place from the searching law?

MICHAEL. You would, surely. If they're not fearing you, itself, the peelers in this place is decent droughty poor fellows, wouldn't touch a cur dog and not give warning in the dead of night.

10 PEGEEN (*very kindly and persuasively*). Let you stop a short while anyhow. Aren't you destroyed walking with your feet in bleeding blisters, and your whole skin needing washing like a Wicklow sheep.

CHRISTY (*looking round with satisfaction*). It's a nice room, and if it's not humbugging me you are, I'm thinking that I'll surely stay.

20 JIMMY (*jumps up*). Now, by the grace of God, herself will be safe this night, with a man killed his father holding danger from the door, and let you come on, Michael James, or they'll have the best stuff drunk at the wake.

MICHAEL (*going to the door with men*). And begging your pardon, mister, what name will we call you, for we'd like to know?

30 CHRISTY. Christopher Mahon.

MICHAEL. Well, God bless you, Christy, and a good rest till we meet again when the sun'll be rising to the noon of day.

CHRISTY. God bless you all.

MEN. God bless you.

[*They go out except* SHAWN, *who lingers at door.*]

SHAWN (*to* PEGEEN). Are you wanting me 40 to stop along with you and keep you from harm?

PEGEEN (*gruffly*). Didn't you say you were fearing Father Reilly?

SHAWN. There'd be no harm staying now, I'm thinking, and himself in it too.

PEGEEN. You wouldn't stay when there was need for you, and let you step off nimble this time when there's none.

SHAWN. Didn't I say it was Father Reilly . . .

PEGEEN. Go on, then, to Father Reilly (*In a jeering tone.*), and let him put you in the holy brotherhoods, and leave that lad to me.

SHAWN. If I meet the Widow Quin . . . 10

PEGEEN. Go on, I'm saying, and don't be waking this place with your noise. (*She hustles him out and bolts the door.*) That lad would wear the spirits from the saints of peace. (*Bustles about, then takes off her apron and pins it up in the window as a blind.* CHRISTY *watching her timidly. Then she comes to him and speaks with bland good-humour.*) Let you stretch out now by the fire, young fellow. 20 You should be destroyed travelling.

CHRISTY (*shyly again, drawing off his boots*). I'm tired, surely, walking wild eleven days, and waking fearful in the night. (*He holds up one of his feet, feeling his blisters, and looking at them with compassion.*)

PEGEEN (*standing beside him, watching him with delight*). You should have had great people in your family, I'm 30 thinking, with the little, small feet you have, and you with a kind of a quality name, the like of what you'd find on the great powers and potentates of France and Spain.

CHRISTY (*with pride*). We were great surely, with wide and windy acres of rich Munster land.

PEGEEN. Wasn't I telling you, and you a fine, handsome young fellow with a 40 noble brow?

CHRISTY (*with a flash of delighted surprise*). Is it me?

PEGEEN. Aye. Did you never hear that from the young girls where you come from in the west or south?

CHRISTY (*with venom*). I did not then. Oh, they're bloody liars in the naked parish where I grew a man.

PEGEEN. If they are itself, you've heard it these days, I'm thinking, and you walking the world telling out your story to young girls or old.

CHRISTY. I've told my story no place till this night, Pegeen Mike, and it's foolish I was here, maybe, to be talking free, but you're decent people, I'm thinking, and yourself a kindly woman, the way I wasn't fearing you at all.

PEGEEN (*filling a sack with straw*). You've said the like of that, maybe, in every cot and cabin where you've met a young girl on your way.

CHRISTY (*going over to her, gradually raising his voice*). I've said it nowhere till this night, I'm telling you, for I've seen none the like of you the eleven long days I am walking the world, looking over a low ditch or a high ditch on my north or my south, into stony scattered fields, or scribes of bog, where you'd see young, limber girls, and fine prancing women making laughter with the men.

PEGEEN. If you weren't destroyed travelling, you'd have as much talk and streeleen, I'm thinking, as Owen Roe O'Sullivan or the poets of the Dingle Bay, and I've heard all times it's the poets are your like, fine fiery fellows with great rages when their temper's roused.

CHRISTY (*drawing a little nearer to her*). You've a power of rings, God bless you, and would there be any offence if I was asking are you single now?

PEGEEN. What would I want wedding so young?

CHRISTY (*with relief*). We're alike, so.

PEGEEN (*she puts sack on settle and beats it up*). I never killed my father. I'd be afeard to do that, except I was the like of yourself with blind rages tearing me within, for I'm thinking you should have had great tussling when the end was come.

CHRISTY (*expanding with delight at the first confidential talk he has ever had with a woman*). We had not then. It was a hard woman was come over the hill, and if he was always a crusty kind 10 when he'd a hard woman setting him on, not the divil himself or his four fathers could put up with him at all.

PEGEEN (*with curiosity*). And isn't it a great wonder that one wasn't fearing you?

CHRISTY (*very confidentially*). Up to the day I killed my father, there wasn't a person in Ireland knew the kind I was, and I there drinking, waking, 20 eating, sleeping, a quiet, simple poor fellow with no man giving me heed.

PEGEEN (*getting a quilt out of the cupboard and putting it on the sack*). It was the girls were giving you heed maybe, and I'm thinking it's most conceit you'd have to be gaming with their like.

CHRISTY (*shaking his head, with simplicity*). Not the girls itself, and I won't tell 30 you a lie. There wasn't anyone heeding me in that place saving only the dumb beasts of the field. (*He sits down at fire.*)

PEGEEN (*with disappointment*). And I thinking you should have been living the like of a king of Norway or the Eastern world. (*She comes and sits beside him after placing bread and mug of milk on the table.*)   40

CHRISTY (*laughing piteously*). The like of a king, is it? And I after toiling, moiling, digging, dodging from the dawn till dusk with never a sight of joy or sport saving only when I'd be abroad in the dark night poaching rabbits on hills, for I was a devil to poach, God forgive me (*Very naïvely.*), and I near got six months for going with a dung fork and stabbing a fish.

PEGEEN. And it's that you'd call sport, is it, to be abroad in the darkness with yourself alone?

CHRISTY. I did, God help me, and there I'd be as happy as the sunshine of St. Martin's Day, watching the light passing the north or the patches of fog, till I'd hear a rabbit starting to screech and I'd go running in the furze. Then when I'd my full share I'd come walking down where you'd see the ducks and geese stretched sleeping on the highway of the road, and before I'd pass the dunghill, I'd hear himself snoring out, a loud lonesome snore he'd be making all times, the while he was sleeping, and he a man 'd be raging all times, the while he was waking, like a gaudy officer you'd hear cursing and damning and swearing oaths.

PEGEEN. Providence and Mercy, spare us all!

CHRISTY. It's that you'd say surely if you seen him and he after drinking for weeks, rising up in the red dawn, or before it maybe, and going out into the yard as naked as an ash tree in the moon of May, and shying clods against the visage of the stars till he'd put the fear of death into the banbhs and the screeching sows.

PEGEEN. I'd be well-nigh afeard of that lad myself, I'm thinking. And there was no one in it but the two of you alone?

CHRISTY. The divil a one, though he'd sons and daughters walking all great states and territories of the world, and not a one of them, to this day, but would say their seven curses on him, and they rousing up to let a cough or sneeze, maybe, in the deadness of the night.

PEGEEN (*nodding her head*). Well, you should have been a queer lot. I never cursed my father the like of that, though I'm twenty and more years of age.

CHRISTY. Then you'd have cursed mine, I'm telling you, and he a man never gave peace to any, saving when he'd 10 get two months or three, or be locked in the asylums for battering peelers or assaulting men (*With depression.*) the way it was a bitter life he led me till I did up a Tuesday and halve his skull.

PEGEEN (*putting her hand on his shoulder*). Well, you'll have peace in this place, Christy Mahon, and none to trouble you, and it's near time a fine lad like 20 you should have your good share of the earth.

CHRISTY. It's time surely, and I a seemly fellow with great strength in me and bravery of . . .

[*Someone knocks.*]

CHRISTY (*clinging to* PEGEEN). Oh, glory! it's late for knocking, and this last while I'm in terror of the peelers, and the walking dead.

[*Knocking again.*]

PEGEEN. Who's there?

VOICE (*outside*). Me.

PEGEEN. Who's me?

VOICE. The Widow Quin.

PEGEEN (*jumping up and giving him the bread and milk*). Go on now with your supper, and let on to be sleepy, for if she found you were such a warrant to talk, she'd be stringing gabble till the 40 dawn of day. [*He takes bread and sits shyly with his back to the door.*]

PEGEEN (*opening door, with temper*). What ails you, or what is it you're wanting at this hour of the night?

WIDOW QUIN (*coming in a step and peering at* CHRISTY). I'm after meeting Shawn Keogh and Father Reilly below, who told me of your curiosity man, and they fearing by this time he was maybe roaring, romping on your hands with drink.

PEGEEN (*pointing to* CHRISTY). Look now is he roaring, and he stretched away drowsy with his supper and his mug of milk. Walk down and tell that to Father Reilly and to Shaneen Keogh.

WIDOW QUIN (*coming forward*). I'll not see them again, for I've their word to lead that lad forward for to lodge with me.

PEGEEN (*in blank amazement*). This night, is it?

WIDOW QUIN (*going over*). This night. "It isn't fitting," says the priesteen, "to have his likeness lodging with an orphaned girl." (*To* CHRISTY.) God save you, mister!

CHRISTY (*shyly*). God save you kindly.

WIDOW QUIN (*looking at him with half-amazed curiosity*). Well, aren't you a little smiling fellow? It should have been great and bitter torments did rouse your spirits to a deed of blood.

CHRISTY (*doubtfully*). It should, maybe.

WIDOW QUIN. It's more than "maybe" I'm saying, and it'd soften my heart to see you sitting so simple with your cup and cake, and you fitter to be saying your catechism than slaying your da.

PEGEEN (*at counter, washing glasses*). There's talking when any'd see he's fit to be holding his head high with the wonders of the world. Walk on from this, for I'll not have him tormented and he destroyed travelling since Tuesday was a week.

WIDOW QUIN (*peaceably*). We'll be walking surely when his supper's done, and you'll find we're great company, young fellow, when it's of the like of you and me you'd hear the penny poets singing in an August Fair.

CHRISTY (*innocently*). Did you kill your father?

PEGEEN (*contemptuously*). She did not. She hit himself with a worn pick, and the rusted poison did corrode his blood the way he never overed it, and died after. That was a sneaky kind of murder did win small glory with the boys itself.

[*She crosses to* CHRISTY'S *left.*]

WIDOW QUIN (*with good-humour*). If it didn't, maybe all knows a widow woman has buried her children and destroyed her man is a wiser comrade for a young lad than a girl, the like of you, who'd go helter-skeltering after any man would let you a wink upon the road.

PEGEEN (*breaking out into wild rage*). And you'll say that, Widow Quin, and you gasping with the rage you had racing the hill beyond to look on his face.

WIDOW QUIN (*laughing derisively*). Me, is it? Well, Father Reilly has cuteness to divide you now. (*She pulls* CHRISTY *up.*) There's great temptation in a man did slay his da, and we'd best be going, young fellow; so rise up and come with me.

PEGEEN (*seizing his arm*). He'll not stir. He's pot-boy in this place, and I'll not have him stolen off and kidnabbed while himself's abroad.

WIDOW QUIN. It'd be a crazy pot-boy'd lodge him in the shebeen where he works by day, so you'd have a right to come on, young fellow, till you see my little houseen, a perch off on the rising hill.

PEGEEN. Wait till morning, Christy Mahon. Wait till you lay eyes on her leaky thatch is growing more pasture for her buck goat than her square of fields, and she without a tramp itself to keep in order her place at all.

WIDOW QUIN. When you see me contriving in my little gardens, Christy Mahon, you'll swear the Lord God formed me to be living lone, and that there isn't my match in Mayo for thatching, or mowing, or shearing a sheep.

PEGEEN (*with noisy scorn*). It's true the Lord God formed you to contrive indeed. Doesn't the world know you reared a black lamb at your own breast, so that the Lord Bishop of Connaught felt the elements of a Christian, and he eating it after in a kidney stew? Doesn't the world know you've been seen shaving the foxy skipper from France for a threepenny bit and a sop of grass tobacco would wring the liver from a mountain goat you'd meet leaping the hills?

WIDOW QUIN (*with amusement*). Do you hear her now, young fellow? Do you hear the way she'll be rating at your own self when a week is by?

PEGEEN (*to* CHRISTY). Don't heed her. Tell her to go into her pigsty and not plague us here.

WIDOW QUIN. I'm going; but he'll come with me.

PEGEEN (*shaking him*). Are you dumb, young fellow?

CHRISTY (*timidly, to* WIDOW QUIN). God increase you; but I'm pot-boy in this place, and it's here I'd liefer stay.

PEGEEN (*triumphantly*). Now you have heard him, and go on from this.

WIDOW QUIN (*looking round the room*). It's lonesome this hour crossing the hill, and if he won't come along with me, I'd have a right maybe to stop this night with yourselves. Let me stretch out on the settle, Pegeen Mike; and himself can lie by the hearth.

PEGEEN (*short and fiercely*). Faith, I won't. Quit off or I will send you now.

WIDOW QUIN (*gathering her shawl up*). Well, it's a terror to be aged a score. (*To* CHRISTY.) God bless you now, young fellow, and let you be wary, or there's right torment will await you here if you go romancing with her like, and she waiting only, as they bade me say, on a sheepskin parchment to be wed with Shawn Keogh of Killakeen.

CHRISTY (*going to* PEGEEN *as she bolts the door*). What's that she's after saying?

PEGEEN. Lies and blather, you've no call to mind. Well, isn't Shawn Keogh an impudent fellow to send up spying on me? Wait till I lay hands on him. Let him wait, I'm saying.

CHRISTY. And you're not wedding him at all?

PEGEEN. I wouldn't wed him if a bishop came walking for to join us here.

CHRISTY. That God in glory may be thanked for that.

PEGEEN. There's your bed now. I've put a quilt upon you I'm after quilting a while since with my own two hands, and you'd best stretch out now for your sleep, and may God give you a good rest till I call you in the morning when the cocks will crow.

CHRISTY (*as she goes to inner room*). May God and Mary and St. Patrick bless you and reward you, for your kindly talk. (*She shuts the door behind her. He settles his bed slowly, feeling the quilt with immense satisfaction.*) Well, it's a clean bed and soft with it, and it's great luck and company I've won me in the end of time—two fine women fighting for the likes of me—till I'm thinking this night wasn't I a foolish fellow not to kill my father in the years gone by.

CURTAIN

ACT II

Scene, as before. Brilliant morning light. CHRISTY, *looking bright and cheerful, is cleaning a girl's boots.*

CHRISTY (*to himself, counting jugs on dresser*). Half a hundred beyond. Ten there. A score that's above. Eighty jugs. Six cups and a broken one. Two plates. A power of glasses. Bottles, a school-master'd be hard set to count, and enough in them, I'm thinking, to drunken all the wealth and wisdom of the County Clare. (*He puts down the boot carefully.*) There's her boots now, nice and decent for her evening use, and isn't it grand brushes she has? (*He puts them down and goes by degrees to the looking-glass.*) Well, this'd be a fine place to be my whole life talking out with swearing Christians, in place of my old dogs and cat, and I stalking around, smoking my pipe and drinking my fill, and never a day's work but drawing a cork an odd time, or wiping a glass, or rinsing out a shiny tumbler for a decent man. (*He takes the looking-glass from the wall and puts it on the back of a chair; then sits down in front of it and begins washing his face.*) Didn't I know rightly I was handsome, though it was the divil's own mirror we had beyond, would twist a squint across an angel's brow; and I'll be growing fine from this day, the way I'll have a soft lovely skin on me and won't be the like of the clumsy young fellows do be ploughing all times in the earth and dung. (*He starts.*) Is she coming again? (*He looks out.*) Stranger girls. God help me, where'll I hide myself away and my long neck naked to the world? (*He looks out.*) I'd best go to the room maybe till I'm dressed again.

[*He gathers up his coat and the looking-glass, and runs into the inner room. The door is pushed open, and* SUSAN BRADY *looks in, and knocks on door.*]

SUSAN. There's nobody in it.

[*Knocks again.*]   10

NELLY (*pushing her in and following her, with* HONOR BLAKE *and* SARA TANSEY). It'd be early for them both to be out walking the hill.

SUSAN. I'm thinking Shawn Keogh was making game of us and there's no such man in it at all.

HONOR (*pointing to straw and quilt*). Look at that. He's been sleeping there in the night. Well, it'll be a hard case if 20 he's gone off now, the way we'll never set our eyes on a man killed his father, and we after rising early and destroying ourselves running fast on the hill.

NELLY. Are you thinking them's his boots?

SARA (*taking them up*). If they are, there should be his father's track on them. Did you never read in the papers the way murdered men do bleed and 30 drip?

SUSAN. Is that blood there, Sara Tansey?

SARA (*smelling it*). That's bog water, I'm thinking, but it's his own they are surely, for I never seen the like of them for whity mud, and red mud, and turf on them, and the fine sands of the sea. That man's been walking, I'm telling you. (*She goes down right, putting on one of his boots.*)   40

SUSAN (*going to window*). Maybe he's stolen off to Belmullet with the boots of Michael James, and you'd have a right so to follow after him, Sara Tansey, and you the one yoked the ass cart and drove ten miles to set your eyes on the man bit the yellow lady's nostril on the northern shore. (*She looks out.*)

SARA (*running to window with one boot on*). Don't be talking, and we fooled to-day. (*Putting on other boot.*) There's a pair do fit me well, and I'll be keeping them for walking to the priest, when you'd be ashamed this place, going up winter and summer with nothing worth while to confess at all.

HONOR (*who has been listening at the door*). Whisht! there's someone inside the room. (*She pushes door a chink open.*) It's a man.

[SARA *kicks off boots and puts them where they were. They all stand in a line looking through chink.*]

SARA. I'll call him. Mister! Mister! (*He puts in his head.*) Is Pegeen within?

CHRISTY (*coming in as meek as a mouse, with the looking-glass held behind his back*). She's above on the cnuceen, seeking the nanny goats, the way she'd have a sup of goat's milk for to colour my tea.

SARA. And asking your pardon, is it you's the man killed his father?

CHRISTY (*sidling toward the nail where the glass was hanging*). I am, God help me!

SARA (*taking eggs she has brought*). Then my thousand welcomes to you, and I've run up with a brace of duck's eggs for your food to-day. Pegeen's ducks is no use, but these are the real rich sort. Hold out your hand and you'll see it's no lie I'm telling you.

CHRISTY (*coming forward shyly, and holding out his left hand*). They're a great and weighty size.

SUSAN. And I run up with a pat of butter, for it'd be a poor thing to have you eating your spuds dry, and you after running a great way since you did destroy your da.

CHRISTY. Thank you kindly.

HONOR. And I brought you a little cut of cake, for you should have a thin stomach on you, and you that length walking the world.

NELLY. And I brought you a little laying pullet—boiled and all she is—was crushed at the fall of night by the curate's car. Feel the fat of that breast, mister.

CHRISTY. It's bursting, surely. (*He feels it with the back of his hand, in which he holds the presents.*)

SARA. Will you pinch it? Is your right hand too sacred for to use at all? (*She slips round behind him.*) It's a glass he has. Well, I never seen to this day a man with a looking-glass held to his back. Them that kills their fathers is a vain lot surely.

[*Girls giggle.*]

CHRISTY (*smiling innocently and piling presents on glass*). I'm very thankful to you all to-day . . .

WIDOW QUIN (*coming in quickly, at door*). Sara Tansey, Susan Brady, Honor Blake! What in glory has you here at this hour of day?

GIRLS (*giggling*). That's the man killed his father.

WIDOW QUIN (*coming to them*). I know well it's the man; and I'm after putting him down in the sports below for racing, leaping, pitching, and the Lord knows what.

SARA (*exuberantly*). That's right, Widow Quin. I'll bet my dowry that he'll lick the world.

WIDOW QUIN. If you will, you'd have a right to have him fresh and nourished in place of nursing a feast. (*Taking presents.*) Are you fasting or fed, young fellow?

CHRISTY. Fasting, if you please.

WIDOW QUIN (*loudly*). Well, you're the lot. Stir up now and give him his breakfast. (*To* CHRISTY.) Come here to me (*She puts him on bench beside her while the girls make tea and get his breakfast.*) and let you tell us your story before Pegeen will come, in place of grinning your ears off like the moon of May.

CHRISTY (*beginning to be pleased*). It's a long story; you'd be destroyed listening.

WIDOW QUIN. Don't be letting on to be shy, a fine, gamey, treacherous lad the like of you. Was it in your house beyond you cracked his skull?

CHRISTY (*shy but flattered*). It was not. We were digging spuds in his cold, sloping, stony, divil's patch of a field.

WIDOW QUIN. And you went asking money of him, or making talk of getting a wife would drive him from his farm?

CHRISTY. I did not, then; but there I was, digging and digging, and "You squinting idiot," says he, "let you walk down now and tell the priest you'll wed the Widow Casey in a score of days."

WIDOW QUIN. And what kind was she?

CHRISTY (*with horror*). A walking terror from beyond the hills, and she two score and five years, and two hundredweights and five pounds in the weighing scales, with a limping leg on her, and a blinded eye, and she a woman of noted misbehaviour with the old and young.

GIRLS (*clustering round him, serving him*). Glory be.

WIDOW QUIN. And what did he want driving you to wed with her? (*She takes a bit of the chicken.*)

CHRISTY (*eating with growing satisfaction*). He was letting on I was wanting a protector from the harshness of the world, and he without a thought the whole while but how he'd have her hut to live in and her gold to drink.

WIDOW QUIN. There's maybe worse than a dry hearth and a widow woman and your glass at night. So you hit him then?

CHRISTY (*getting almost excited*). I did not. "I won't wed her," says I, "when all know she did suckle me for six weeks when I came into the world, and she a hag this day with a tongue on her has the crows and seabirds scattered, 10 the way they wouldn't cast a shadow on her garden with the dread of her curse."

WIDOW QUIN (*teasingly*). That one should be right company.

SARA (*eagerly*). Don't mind her. Did you kill him then?

CHRISTY. "She's too good for the like of you," says he, "and go on now or I'll flatten you out like a crawling beast 20 has passed under a dray." "You will not if I can help it," says I. "Go on," says he, "or I'll have the divil making garters of your limbs to-night." "You will not if I can help it," says I. (*He sits up, brandishing his mug.*)

SARA. You were right surely.

CHRISTY (*impressively*). With that the sun came out between the cloud and the 30 hill, and it shining green in my face. "God have mercy on your soul," says he, lifting a scythe; "or on your own," says I, raising the loy.

SUSAN. That's a grand story.

HONOR. He tells it lovely.

CHRISTY (*flattered and confident, waving bone*). He gave a drive with the scythe, and I gave a lep to the east. Then I turned around with my back 40 to the north, and I hit a blow on the ridge of his skull, laid him stretched out, and he split to the knob of his gullet. (*He raises the chicken bone to his Adam's apple.*)

GIRLS (*together*). Well, you're a marvel!

Oh, God bless you! You're the lad surely!

SUSAN. I'm thinking the Lord God sent him this road to make a second husband to the Widow Quin, and she with a great yearning to be wedded, though all dread her here. Lift him on her knee, Sara Tansey.

WIDOW QUIN. Don't tease him.

SARA (*going over to dresser and counter very quickly, and getting two glasses and porter*). You're heroes surely, and let you drink a supeen with your arms linked like the outlandish lovers in the sailor's song. (*She links their arms and gives them the glasses.*) There now. Drink a health to the wonders of the western world, the pirates, preachers, poteen-makers, with the jobbing jockies; parching peelers, and the juries fill their stomachs selling judgments of the English law. (*Brandishing the bottle.*)

WIDOW QUIN. That's a right toast, Sara Tansey. Now Christy.

[*They drink with their arms linked, he drinking with his left hand, she with her right. As they are drinking, PEGEEN MIKE comes in with a milk can and stands aghast. They all spring away from CHRISTY. He goes down left. WIDOW QUIN remains seated.*]

PEGEEN (*angrily, to SARA*). What is it you're wanting?

SARA (*twisting her apron*). An ounce of tobacco.

PEGEEN. Have you tuppence?

SARA. I've forgotten my purse.

PEGEEN. Then you'd best be getting it and not fooling us here. (*To the WIDOW QUIN, with more elaborate scorn.*) And what is it you're wanting, Widow Quin?

WIDOW QUIN (*insolently*). A penn'orth of starch.

PEGEEN (*breaking out*). And you without

a white shift or a shirt in your whole family since the drying of the flood. I've no starch for the like of you, and let you walk on now to Killamuck.

WIDOW QUIN (*turning to* CHRISTY, *as she goes out with the girls*). Well, you're mighty huffy this day, Pegeen Mike, and, you young fellow, let you not forget the sports and racing when the noon is by.

[*They go out.*]

PEGEEN (*imperiously*). Fling out that rubbish and put them cups away. (CHRISTY *tidies away in great haste.*) Shove in the bench by the wall. (*He does so.*) And hang that glass on the nail. What disturbed it at all?

CHRISTY (*very meekly*). I was making myself decent only, and this a fine country for young lovely girls.   20

PEGEEN (*sharply*). Whisht your talking of girls. (*Goes to counter—right.*)

CHRISTY. Wouldn't any wish to be decent in a place . . .

PEGEEN. Whisht I'm saying.

CHRISTY (*looks at her face for a moment with great misgivings, then as a last effort, takes up a loy, and goes towards her, with feigned assurance*). It was with a loy the like of that I killed my father.   30

PEGEEN (*still sharply*). You've told me that story six times since the dawn of day.

CHRISTY (*reproachfully*). It's a queer thing you wouldn't care to be hearing it and them girls after walking four miles to be listening to me now.

PEGEEN (*turning round astonished*). Four miles.

CHRISTY (*apologetically*). Didn't himself 40 say there were only four bona fides living in the place?

PEGEEN. It's bona fides by the road they are, but that lot came over the river lepping the stones. It's not three perches when you go like that, and I

was down this morning looking on the papers the post-boy does have in his bag. (*With meaning and emphasis.*) For there was great news this day, Christopher Mahon. (*She goes into room left.*)

CHRISTY (*suspiciously*). Is it news of my murder?

PEGEEN (*inside*). Murder, indeed.

CHRISTY (*loudly*). A murdered da?   10

PEGEEN (*coming in again and crossing right*). There was not, but a story filled half a page of the hanging of a man. Ah, that should be a fearful end, young fellow, and it worst of all for a man who destroyed his da, for the like of him would get small mercies, and when it's dead he is, they'd put him in a narrow grave, with cheap sacking wrapping him round, and pour down quick-lime on his head, the way you'd see a woman pouring any frish-frash from a cup.

CHRISTY (*very miserably*). Oh, God help me. Are you thinking I'm safe? You were saying at the fall of night, I was shut of jeopardy and I here with yourselves.

PEGEEN (*severely*). You'll be shut of jeopardy no place if you go talking with a pack of wild girls the like of them do be walking abroad with the peelers, talking whispers at the fall of night.

CHRISTY (*with terror*). And you're thinking they'd tell?

PEGEEN (*with mock sympathy*). Who knows, God help you.

CHRISTY (*loudly*). What joy would they have to bring hanging to the likes of me?

PEGEEN. It's queer joys they have, and who knows the thing they'd do, if it'd make the green stones cry itself to think of you swaying and swiggling at the butt of a rope, and you with a fine, stout neck, God bless you! the way you'd be a half an hour, in great anguish, getting your death.

CHRISTY (*getting his boots and putting them on*). If there's that terror of them, it'd be best, maybe, I went on wandering like Esau or Cain and Abel on the sides of Neifin or the Erris plain.

PEGEEN (*beginning to play with him*). It would, maybe, for I've heard the Circuit Judges this place is a heartless crew.

CHRISTY (*bitterly*). It's more than Judges this place is a heartless crew. (*Looking up at her.*) And isn't it a poor thing to be starting again and I a lonesome fellow will be looking out on women and girls the way the needy fallen spirits do be looking on the Lord?

PEGEEN. What call have you to be that lonesome when there's poor girls walking Mayo in their thousands now?

CHRISTY (*grimly*). It's well you know what call I have. It's well you know it's a lonesome thing to be passing small towns with the lights shining sideways when the night is down, or going in strange places with a dog noising before you and a dog noising behind, or drawn to the cities where you'd hear a voice kissing and talking deep love in every shadow of the ditch, and you passing on with an empty, hungry stomach failing from your heart.

PEGEEN. I'm thinking you're an odd man, Christy Mahon. The oddest walking fellow I ever set my eyes on to this hour to-day.

CHRISTY. What would any be but odd men and they living lonesome in the world?

PEGEEN. I'm not odd, and I'm my whole life with my father only.

CHRISTY (*with infinite admiration*). How would a lovely handsome woman the like of you be lonesome when all men should be thronging around to hear the sweetness of your voice, and the little infant children should be pestering your steps I'm thinking, and you walking the roads.

PEGEEN. I'm hard set to know what way a coaxing fellow the like of yourself should be lonesome either.

CHRISTY. Coaxing?

PEGEEN. Would you have me think a man never talked with the girls would have the words you've spoken to-day? It's only letting on you are to be lonesome, the way you'd get around me now.

CHRISTY. I wish to God I was letting on; but I was lonesome all times, and born lonesome, I'm thinking, as the moon of dawn. (*Going to door.*)

PEGEEN (*puzzled by his talk*). Well, it's a story I'm not understanding at all why you'd be worse than another, Christy Mahon, and you a fine lad with the great savagery to destroy your da.

CHRISTY. It's little I'm understanding myself, saving only that my heart's scalded this day, and I going off stretching out the earth between us, the way I'll not be waking near you another dawn of the year till the two of us do arise to hope or judgment with the saints of God, and now I'd best be going with my wattle in my hand, for hanging is a poor thing (*Turning to go.*), and it's little welcome only is left me in this house to-day.

PEGEEN (*sharply*). Christy! (*He turns round.*) Come here to me. (*He goes towards her.*) Lay down that switch and throw some sods on the fire. You're pot-boy in this place, and I'll not have you mitch off from us now.

CHRISTY. You were saying I'd be hanged if I stay.

PEGEEN (*quite kindly at last*). I'm after going down and reading the fearful crimes of Ireland for two weeks or three, and there wasn't a word of your murder. (*Getting up and going over to the counter.*) They've likely not found the body. You're safe so with ourselves.

CHRISTY (*astonished, slowly*). It's making game of me you were (*Following her with fearful joy.*), and I can stay so, working at your side, and I not lonesome from this mortal day.

PEGEEN. What's to hinder you from staying, except the widow woman or the young girls would inveigle you off?

CHRISTY (*with rapture*). And I'll have your words from this day filling my ears, and that look is come upon you meeting my two eyes, and I watching you loafing around in the warm sun, or rinsing your ankles when the night is come.

PEGEEN (*kindly, but a little embarrassed*). I'm thinking you'll be a loyal young lad to have working around, and if you vexed me a while since with your leaguing with the girls, I wouldn't give a thraneen for a lad hadn't a mighty spirit in him and a gamey heart.

[SHAWN KEOGH *runs in carrying a cleeve on his back, followed by the* WIDOW QUIN.]

SHAWN (*to* PEGEEN). I was passing below, and I seen your mountainy sheep eating cabbages in Jimmy's field. Run up or they'll be bursting surely.

PEGEEN. Oh, God mend them! (*She puts a shawl over her head and runs out.*)

CHRISTY (*looking from one to the other. Still in high spirits*). I'd best go to her aid maybe. I'm handy with ewes.

WIDOW QUIN (*closing the door*). She can do that much, and there is Shaneen has long speeches for to tell you now. (*She sits down with an amused smile.*)

SHAWN (*taking something from his pocket and offering it to* CHRISTY). Do you see that, mister?

CHRISTY (*looking at it*). The half of a ticket to the Western States!

SHAWN (*trembling with anxiety*). I'll give it to you and my new hat (*Pulling it out of hamper.*); and my breeches with the double seat (*Pulling it off.*); and my new coat is woven from the blackest shearings for three miles around (*Giving him the coat.*); I'll give you the whole of them, and my blessing, and the blessing of Father Reilly itself, maybe, if you'll quit from this and leave us in the peace we had till last night at the fall of dark.

CHRISTY (*with a new arrogance*). And for what is it you're wanting to get shut of me?

SHAWN (*looking to the* WIDOW *for help*). I'm a poor scholar with middling faculties to coin a lie, so I'll tell you the truth, Christy Mahon. I'm wedding with Pegeen beyond, and I don't think well of having a clever fearless man the like of you dwelling in her house.

CHRISTY (*almost pugnaciously*). And you'd be using bribery for to banish me?

SHAWN (*in an imploring voice*). Let you not take it badly, mister honey, isn't beyond the best place for you where you'll have golden chains and shiny coats and you riding upon hunters with the ladies of the land. (*He makes an eager sign to the* WIDOW QUIN *to come to help him.*)

WIDOW QUIN (*coming over*). It's true for him, and you'd best quit off and not have that poor girl setting her mind on you, for there's Shaneen thinks she wouldn't suit you though all is saying that she'll wed you now.

[CHRISTY *beams with delight.*]

SHAWN (*in terrified earnest*). She wouldn't

suit you, and she with the divil's own temper the way you'd be strangling one another in a score of days. (*He makes the movement of strangling with his hands.*) It's the like of me only that she's fit for, a quiet simple fellow wouldn't raise a hand upon her if she scratched itself.

WIDOW QUIN (*putting* SHAWN'S *hat on* CHRISTY). Fit them clothes on you anyhow, young fellow, and he'd maybe loan them to you for the sports. (*Pushing him towards inner door.*) Fit them on and you can give your answer when you have them tried.

CHRISTY (*beaming, delighted with the clothes*). I will then. I'd like herself to see me in them tweeds and hat. (*He goes into room and shuts the door.*)

SHAWN (*in great anxiety*). He'd like herself to see them. He'll not leave us, Widow Quin. He's a score of divils in him the way it's well nigh certain he will wed Pegeen.

WIDOW QUIN (*jeeringly*). It's true all girls are fond of courage and do hate the like of you.

SHAWN (*walking about in desperation*). Oh, Widow Quin, what'll I be doing now? I'd inform again him, but he'd burst from Kilmainham and he'd be sure and certain to destroy me. If I wasn't so God-fearing, I'd near have courage to come behind him and run a pike into his side. Oh, it's a hard case to be an orphan and not to have your father that you're used to, and you'd easy kill and make yourself a hero in the sight of all. (*Coming up to her.*) Oh, Widow Quin, will you find me some contrivance when I've promised you a ewe?

WIDOW QUIN. A ewe's a small thing, but what would you give me if I did wed him and did save you so?

SHAWN (*with astonishment*). You?

WIDOW QUIN. Aye. Would you give me the red cow you have and the mountainy ram, and the right of way across your rye path, and a load of dung at Michaelmas, and turbary upon the western hill?

SHAWN (*radiant with hope*). I would surely, and I'd give you the wedding-ring I have, and the loan of a new suit, the way you'd have him decent on the wedding-day. I'd give you two kids for your dinner, and a gallon of poteen, and I'd call the piper on the long car to your wedding from Crossmolina or from Ballina. I'd give you . . .

WIDOW QUIN. That'll do so, and let you whisht, for he's coming now again.

[CHRISTY *comes in very natty in the new clothes.* WIDOW QUIN *goes to him admiringly.*]

WIDOW QUIN. If you seen yourself now, I'm thinking you'd be too proud to speak to us at all, and it'd be a pity surely to have your like sailing from Mayo to the Western World.

CHRISTY (*as proud as a peacock*). I'm not going. If this is a poor place itself, I'll make myself contented to be lodging here.

[WIDOW QUIN *makes a sign to* SHAWN *to leave them.*]

SHAWN. Well, I'm going measuring the race-course while the tide is low, so I'll leave you the garments and my blessing for the sports to-day. God bless you!

[*He wriggles out.*]

WIDOW QUIN (*admiring* CHRISTY). Well, you're mighty spruce, young fellow. Sit down now while you're quiet till you talk with me.

CHRISTY (*swaggering*). I'm going abroad on the hillside for to seek Pegeen.

WIDOW QUIN. You'll have time and plenty for to seek Pegeen, and you heard me saying at the fall of night the two of us should be great company.

CHRISTY. From this out I'll have no want of company when all sorts is bringing me their food and clothing (*He swaggers to the door, tightening his belt.*), the way they'd set their eyes upon a gallant orphan cleft his father with one blow to the breeches belt. (*He opens door, then staggers back.*) Saints of glory! Holy angels from the throne of light!

WIDOW QUIN (*going over*). What ails you?

CHRISTY. It's the walking spirit of my murdered da?

WIDOW QUIN (*looking out*). Is it that tramper?

CHRISTY (*wildly*). Where'll I hide my poor body from that ghost of hell?

[*The door is pushed open, and* OLD MAHON *appears on threshold.* CHRISTY *darts in behind door.*]

WIDOW QUIN (*in great amusement*). God save you, my poor man.

MAHON (*gruffly*). Did you see a young lad passing this way in the early morning or the fall of night?

WIDOW QUIN. You're a queer kind to walk in not saluting at all.

MAHON. Did you see the young lad?

WIDOW QUIN (*stiffly*). What kind was he?

MAHON. An ugly young streeler with a murderous gob on him, and a little switch in his hand. I met a tramper seen him coming this way at the fall of night.

WIDOW QUIN. There's harvest hundreds do be passing these days for the Sligo boat. For what is it you're wanting him, my poor man?

MAHON. I want to destroy him for breaking the head on me with the clout of a loy. (*He takes off a big hat, and shows his head in a mass of bandages and plaster, with some pride.*) It was he did that, and amn't I a great wonder to think

I've traced him ten days with that rent in my crown?

WIDOW QUIN (*taking his head in both hands and examining it with extreme delight*). That was a great blow. And who hit you? A robber maybe?

MAHON. It was my own son hit me, and he the divil a robber, or anything else, but a diry, stuttering lout.

WIDOW QUIN (*letting go his skull and wiping her hands in her apron*). You'd best be wary of a mortified scalp, I think they call it, lepping around with that wound in the splendour of the sun. It was a bad blow surely, and you should have vexed him fearful to make him strike that gash in his da.

MAHON. Is it me?

WIDOW QUIN (*amusing herself*). Aye. And isn't it a great shame when the old and hardened do torment the young?

MAHON (*raging*). Torment him is it? And I after holding out with the patience of a martyred saint till there's nothing but destruction on, and I'm driven out in my old age with none to aid me.

WIDOW QUIN (*greatly amused*). It's a sacred wonder the way that wickedness will spoil a man.

MAHON. My wickedness, is it? Amn't I after saying it is himself has me destroyed, and he a liar on walls, a talker of folly, a man you'd see stretched the half of the day in the brown ferns with his belly to the sun.

WIDOW QUIN. Not working at all?

MAHON. The divil a work, or if he did itself, you'd see him raising up a haystack like the stalk of a rush, or driving our last cow till he broke her leg at the hip, and when he wasn't at that he'd be fooling over little birds he had —finches and felts—or making mugs at his own self in the bit of a glass we had hung on the wall.

WIDOW QUIN (*looking at* CHRISTY). What

way was he so foolish? It was running wild after the girls may be?

MAHON (*with a shout of derision*). Running wild, is it? If he seen a red petticoat coming swinging over the hill, he'd be off to hide in the sticks, and you'd see him shooting out his sheep's eyes between the little twigs and the leaves, and his two ears rising like a hare looking out through a gap. Girls, indeed! 10

WIDOW QUIN. It was drink maybe?

MAHON. And he a poor fellow would get drunk on the smell of a pint. He'd a queer rotten stomach, I'm telling you, and when I gave him three pulls from my pipe a while since, he was taken with contortions till I had to send him in the ass cart to the females' nurse.

WIDOW QUIN (*clasping her hands*). Well, I never till this day heard tell of a man the like of that! 20

MAHON. I'd take a mighty oath you didn't surely, and wasn't he the laughing joke of every female woman where four baronies meet, the way the girls would stop their weeding if they seen him coming the road to let a roar at him, and call him the looney of Mahon's. 30

WIDOW QUIN. I'd give the world and all to see the like of him. What kind was he?

MAHON. A small low fellow.

WIDOW QUIN. And dark?

MAHON. Dark and dirty.

WIDOW QUIN (*considering*). I'm thinking I seen him.

MAHON (*eagerly*). An ugly young blackguard. 40

WIDOW QUIN. A hideous, fearful villain, and the spit of you.

MAHON. What way is he fled?

WIDOW QUIN. Gone over the hills to catch a coasting steamer to the north or south.

MAHON. Could I pull up on him now?

WIDOW QUIN. If you'll cross the sands below where the tide is out, you'll be in it as soon as himself, for he had to go round ten miles by the top of the bay. (*She points to the door.*) Strike down by the head beyond and then follow on the roadway to the north and east.

[MAHON *goes abruptly.*]

WIDOW QUIN (*shouting after him*). Let you give him a good vengeance when you come up with him, but don't put yourself in the power of the law, for it'd be a poor thing to see a judge in his black cap reading out his sentence on a civil warrior the like of you. (*She swings the door to and looks at* CHRISTY, *who is cowering in terror, for a moment, then she bursts into a laugh.*) Well, you're the walking Playboy of the Western World, and that's the poor man you had divided to his breeches belt.

CHRISTY (*looking out: then, to her*). What'll Pegeen say when she hears that story? What'll she be saying to me now?

WIDOW QUIN. She'll knock the head of you, I'm thinking, and drive you from the door. God help her to be taking you for a wonder, and you a little schemer making up the story you destroyed your da.

CHRISTY (*turning to the door, nearly speechless with rage, half to himself*). To be letting on he was dead, and coming back to his life, and following after me like an old weazel tracing a rat, and coming in here laying desolation between my own self and the fine women of Ireland, and he a kind of carcase that you'd fling upon the sea . . .

WIDOW QUIN (*more soberly*). There's talking for a man's one only son.

CHRISTY (*breaking out*). His one son, is it? May I meet him with one tooth and it aching, and one eye to be seeing seven and seventy divils in the twists of the road, and one old timber leg on him to limp into the scalding grave. (*Looking out.*) There he is now crossing the strands, and that the Lord God would send a high wave to wash him from the world.

WIDOW QUIN (*scandalized*). Have you no shame? (*Putting her hand on his shoulder and turning him round.*) What ails you? Near crying, is it?

CHRISTY (*in despair and grief*). Amn't I after seeing the love-light of the star of knowledge shining from her brow, and hearing words would put you thinking on the holy Brigid speaking to the infant saints, and now she'll be turning again, and speaking hard words to me, like an old woman with a spavindy ass she'd have, urging on a hill.

WIDOW QUIN. There's poetry talk for a girl you'd see itching and scratching, and she with a stale stink of poteen on her from selling in the shop.

CHRISTY (*impatiently*). It's her like is fitted to be handling merchandise in the heavens above, and what'll I be doing now, I ask you, and I a kind of wonder was jilted by the heavens when a day was by.

[*There is a distant noise of girls' voices. WIDOW QUIN looks from window and comes to him, hurriedly.*]

WIDOW QUIN. You'll be doing like myself, I'm thinking, when I did destroy my man, for I'm above many's the day, odd times in great spirits, abroad in the sunshine, darning a stocking or stitching a shift; and odd times again looking out on the schooners, hookers, trawlers is sailing the sea, and I thinking on the gallant hairy fellows are drifting beyond, and myself long years living alone.

CHRISTY (*interested*). You're like me, so.

WIDOW QUIN. I am your like, and it's for that I'm taking a fancy to you, and I with my little houseen above where there'd be myself to tend you, and none to ask were you a murderer or what at all.

CHRISTY. And what would I be doing if I left Pegeen?

WIDOW QUIN. I've nice jobs you could be doing, gathering shells to make a whitewash for our hut within, building up a little goose-house, or stretching a new skin on an old curragh I have, and if my hut is far from all sides, it's there you'll meet the wisest old men, I tell you, at the corner of my wheel, and it's there yourself and me will have great times whispering and hugging. . . .

VOICES (*outside, calling far away*). Christy! Christy Mahon! Christy!

CHRISTY. Is it Pegeen Mike?

WIDOW QUIN. It's the young girls, I'm thinking, coming to bring you to the sports below, and what is it you'll have me to tell them now?

CHRISTY. Aid me for to win Pegeen. It's herself only that I'm seeking now. (WIDOW QUIN *gets up and goes to window.*) Aid me for to win her, and I'll be asking God to stretch a hand to you in the hour of death, and lead you short cuts through the Meadows of Ease, and up the floor of Heaven to the Footstool of the Virgin's Son.

WIDOW QUIN. There's praying.

VOICES (*nearer*). Christy! Christy Mahon!

CHRISTY (*with agitation*). They're coming. Will you swear to aid and save me for the love of Christ?

WIDOW QUIN (*looks at him for a moment*). If I aid you, will you swear to give me a right of way I want, and a mountainy ram, and a load of dung at Michaelmas, the time that you'll be master here?

CHRISTY. I will, by the elements and stars of night.

WIDOW QUIN. Then we'll not say a word of the old fellow, the way Pegeen won't know your story till the end of time.

CHRISTY. And if he chances to return again?

WIDOW QUIN. We'll swear he's a maniac and not your da. I could take an oath I seen him raving on the sands to-day. [Girls run in.]

SUSAN. Come on to the sports below. Pegeen says you're to come.

SARA TANSEY. The lepping's beginning, and we've a jockey's suit to fit upon you for the mule race on the sands below.

HONOR. Come on, will you?

CHRISTY. I will then if Pegeen's beyond.

SARA TANSEY. She's in the boreen making game of Shaneen Keogh.

CHRISTY. Then I'll be going to her now. (He runs out followed by the girls.)

WIDOW QUIN. Well, if the worst comes in the end of all, it'll be great game to see there's none to pity him but a widow woman, the like of me, has buried her children and destroyed her man. (She goes out.)

CURTAIN

ACT III

Scene, as before. Later in the day. JIMMY comes in, slightly drunk.

JIMMY (calls). Pegeen! (Crosses to inner door.) Pegeen Mike! (Comes back again into the room.) Pegeen! (PHILLY comes in in the same state.) (To PHILLY.) Did you see herself?

PHILLY. I did not; but I sent Shawn Keogh with the ass cart for to bear him home. (Trying cupboards which are locked.) Well, isn't he a nasty man to get into such staggers at a morning wake? and isn't herself the divil's daughter for locking, and she so fussy after that young gaffer, you might take your death with drought and none to heed you?

JIMMY. It's little wonder she'd be fussy, and he after bringing bankrupt ruin on the roulette man, and the trick-o'-the-loop man, and breaking the nose of the cockshot-man, and winning all in the sports below, racing, lepping, dancing, and the Lord knows what! He's right luck, I'm telling you.

PHILLY. If he has, he'll be rightly hobbled yet, and he not able to say ten words without making a brag of the way he killed his father, and the great blow he hit with the loy.

JIMMY. A man can't hang by his own informing, and his father should be rotten by now.

[OLD MAHON passes window slowly.]

PHILLY. Supposing a man's digging spuds in that field with a long spade, and supposing he flings up the two halves of that skull, what'll be said then in the papers and the courts of law?

JIMMY. They'd say it was an old Dane, maybe, was drowned in the flood. (OLD MAHON comes in and sits down near door listening.) Did you never hear tell of the skulls they have in the city of Dublin, ranged out like blue jugs in a cabin of Connaught?

PHILLY. And you believe that?

JIMMY (pugnaciously). Didn't a lad see them and he after coming from harvesting in the Liverpool boat? "They have them there," says he, "making a show of the great people there was one time walking the world. White skulls and black skulls and yellow skulls, and some with full teeth, and some haven't only but one."

PHILLY. It was no lie, maybe, for when I was a young lad there was a grave-yard beyond the house with the rem-nants of a man who had thighs as long as your arm. He was a horrid man, I'm telling you, and there was many a 10 fine Sunday I'd put him together for fun, and he with shiny bones, you wouldn't meet the like of these days in the cities of the world.

MAHON (*getting up*). You wouldn't, is it? Lay your eyes on that skull, and tell me where and when there was an-other the like of it, is splintered only from the blow of a loy.

PHILLY. Glory be to God! And who hit 20 you at all?

MAHON (*triumphantly*). It was my own son hit me. Would you believe that?

JIMMY. Well, there's wonders hidden in the heart of man!

PHILLY (*suspiciously*). And what way was it done?

MAHON (*wandering about the room*). I'm after walking hundreds and long scores of miles, winning clean beds 30 and the fill of my belly four times in the day, and I doing nothing but tell-ing stories of that naked truth. (*He comes to them a little aggressively*.) Give me a supeen and I'll tell you now.

[WIDOW QUIN *comes in and stands aghast behind him. He is facing* JIMMY *and* PHILLY, *who are on the left.*]

JIMMY. Ask herself beyond. She's the stuff hidden in her shawl. 40

WIDOW QUIN (*coming to* MAHON *quickly*). You here, is it? You didn't go far at all?

MAHON. I seen the coasting steamer passing, and I got a drought upon me and a cramping leg, so I said, "The divil go along with him," and turned again. (*Looking under her shawl*.) And let you give me a supeen, for I'm de-stroyed travelling since Tuesday was a week.

WIDOW QUIN (*getting a glass, in a cajoling tone*). Sit down then by the fire and take your ease for a space. You've a right to be destroyed indeed, with your walking, and fighting, and fac-ing the sun. (*Giving him poteen from a stone jar she has brought in*.) There now is a drink for you, and may it be to your happiness and length of life.

MAHON (*taking glass greedily and sitting down by fire*). God increase you!

WIDOW QUIN (*taking men to the right stealthily*). Do you know what? That man's raving from his wound to-day, for I met him a while since telling a rambling tale of a tinker had him de-troyed. Then he heard of Christy's deed, and he up and says it was his son had cracked his skull. O isn't madness a fright, for he'll go killing someone yet, and he thinking it's the man has struck him so?

JIMMY (*entirely convinced*). It's a fright, surely. I knew a party was kicked in the head by a red mare, and he went killing horses a great while, till he eat the insides of a clock and died after.

PHILLY (*with suspicion*). Did he see Christy?

WIDOW QUIN. He didn't. (*With a warning gesture*.) Let you not be putting him in mind of him, or you'll be likely sum-moned if there's murder done. (*Look-ing round at* MAHON.) Whisht! He's lis-tening. Wait now till you hear me taking him easy and unravelling all. (*She goes to* MAHON.) And what way are you feeling, mister? Are you in contentment now?

MAHON (*slightly emotional from his drink*). I'm poorly only, for it's a hard story the way I'm left to-day, when it was I did tend him from his hour of birth, and he a dunce never reached his second book, the way he'd come from school, many's the day, with his legs lamed under him, and he blackened with his beatings like a tinker's ass. It's a hard story, I'm saying, the way some do have their next and nighest raising up a hand of murder on them, 10 and some is lonesome getting their death with lamentation in the dead of night.

WIDOW QUIN (*not knowing what to say*). To hear you talking so quiet, who'd know you were the same fellow we seen pass to-day?

MAHON. I'm the same surely. The wrack and ruin of three score years; and it's a terror to live that length, I tell you, 20 and to have your sons going to the dogs against you, and you wore out scolding them, and skelping them, and God knows what.

PHILLY (*to* JIMMY). He's not raving. (*To* WIDOW QUIN.) Will you ask him what kind was his son?

WIDOW QUIN (*to* MAHON, *with a peculiar look*). Was your son that hit you a lad of one year and a score maybe, a great 30 hand at racing and lepping and licking the world?

MAHON (*turning on her with a roar of rage*). Didn't you hear me say he was the fool of men, the way from this out he'll know the orphan's lot with old and young making game of him and they swearing, raging, kicking at him like a mangy cur.

[*A great burst of cheering outside, some way* 40 *off.*]

MAHON (*putting his hands to his ears*). What in the name of God do they want roaring below?

WIDOW QUIN (*with the shade of a smile*). They're cheering a young lad, the

champion Playboy of the Western World.

[*More cheering.*]

MAHON (*going to window*). It'd split my heart to hear them, and I with pulses in my brain-pan for a week gone by. Is it racing they are?

JIMMY (*looking from door*). It is then. They are mounting him for the mule race will be run upon the sands. That's the playboy on the winkered mule.

MAHON (*puzzled*). That lad, is it? If you said it was a fool he was, I'd have laid a mighty oath he was the likeness of my wandering son. (*Uneasily, putting his hand to his head.*) Faith, I'm thinking I'll go walking for to view the race.

WIDOW QUIN (*stopping him, sharply*). You will not. You'd best take the road to Belmullet, and not be dilly-dallying in this place where there isn't a spot you could sleep.

PHILLY (*coming forward*). Don't mind her. Mount there on the bench and you'll have a view of the whole. They're hurrying before the tide will rise, and it'd be near over if you went down the pathway through the crags below.

MAHON (*mounts on bench*, WIDOW QUIN *beside him*). That's a right view again the edge of the sea. They're coming now from the point. He's leading. Who is he at all?

WIDOW QUIN. He's the champion of the world, I tell you, and there isn't a hop'orth isn't falling lucky to his hands to-day.

PHILLY (*looking out, interested in the race*). Look at that. They're passing him now.

JIMMY. He'll win it yet.

PHILLY. Take your time, Jimmy Farrell. It's too soon to say.

WIDOW QUIN (*shouting*). Watch him taking the gate. There's riding.

JIMMY (*cheering*). More power to the young lad!

MAHON. He's passing the third.

JIMMY. He'll lick them yet!

WIDOW QUIN. He'd lick them if he was running races with a score itself.

MAHON. Look at the mule he has, kicking the stars.

WIDOW QUIN. There was a lep! (*Catching hold of* MAHON *in her excitement*.) He's fallen! He's mounted again! Faith, he's passing them all!

JIMMY. Look at him skelping her!

PHILLY. And the mountain girls hooshing him on!

JIMMY. It's the last turn! The post's cleared for them now!

MAHON. Look at the narrow place. He'll be into the bogs! (*With a yell*.) Good rider! He's through it again!

JIMMY. He neck and neck!

MAHON. Good boy to him! Flames, but he's in!

[*Great cheering, in which all join.*]

MAHON (*with hesitation*). What's that? They're raising him up. They're coming this way. (*With a roar of rage and astonishment*.) It's Christy! by the stars of God! I'd know his way of spitting and he astride the moon. (*He jumps down and makes for the door, but* WIDOW QUIN *catches him and pulls him back*.)

WIDOW QUIN. Stay quiet, will you. That's not your son. (*To* JIMMY.) Stop him, or you'll get a month for the abetting of manslaughter and be fined as well.

JIMMY. I'll hold him.

MAHON (*struggling*). Let me out! Let me out, the lot of you! till I have my vengeance on his head to-day.

WIDOW QUIN (*shaking him, vehemently*). That's not your son. That's a man is going to make a marriage with the daughter of this house, a place with fine trade, with a license, and with poteen too.

MAHON (*amazed*). That man marrying a decent and a moneyed girl! Is it mad yous are? Is it in a crazy-house for females that I'm landed now?

WIDOW QUIN. It's mad yourself is with the blow upon your head. That lad is the wonder of the Western World.

MAHON. I seen it's my son.

WIDOW QUIN. You seen that you're mad. (*Cheering outside*.) Do you hear them cheering him in the zig-zags of the road? Aren't you after saying that your son's a fool, and how would they be cheering a true idiot born?

MAHON (*getting distressed*). It's maybe out of reason that that man's himself. (*Cheering again*.) There's none surely will go cheering him. Oh, I'm raving with a madness that would fright the world! (*He sits down with his hand to his head*.) There was one time I seen ten scarlet divils letting on they'd cork my spirit in a gallon can; and one time I seen rats as big as badgers sucking the life blood from the butt of my lug; but I never till this day confused that dribbling idiot with a likely man. I'm destroyed surely.

WIDOW QUIN. And who'd wonder when it's your brain-pan that is gaping now?

MAHON. Then the blight of the sacred drought upon myself and him, for I never went mad to this day, and I not three weeks with the Limerick girls drinking myself silly, and parlatic from the dusk to dawn. (*To* WIDOW QUIN, *suddenly*.) Is my visage astray?

WIDOW QUIN. It is then. You're a sniggering maniac, a child could see.

MAHON (*getting up more cheerfully*). Then I'd best be going to the union beyond, and there'll be a welcome before me, I tell you (*With great pride*.), and I a terrible and fearful case, the way that there I was one time, screeching in a straitened waistcoat, with seven doctors writing out my sayings in a printed book. Would you believe that?

WIDOW QUIN. If you're a wonder itself, you'd best be hasty, for them lads caught a maniac one time and pelted the poor creature till he ran out, raving and foaming, and was drowned in the sea.

MAHON (*with philosophy*). It's true mankind is the divil when your head's astray. Let me out now and I'll slip down the boreen, and not see them so.

WIDOW QUIN (*showing him out*). That's it. Run to the right, and not a one will see.

[*He runs off.*]

PHILLY (*wisely*). You're at some gaming, Widow Quin; but I'll walk after him and give him his dinner and a time to rest, and I'll see then if he's raving or as sane as you.

WIDOW QUIN (*annoyed*). If you go near that lad, let you be wary of your head, I'm saying. Didn't you hear him telling he was crazed at times?

PHILLY. I heard him telling a power; and I'm thinking we'll have right sport, before night will fall. (*He goes out.*)

JIMMY. Well, Philly's a conceited and foolish man. How could that madman have his senses and his brain-pan slit? I'll go after them and see him turn on Philly now.

[*He goes;* WIDOW QUIN *hides poteen behind counter. Then hubbub outside.*]

VOICES. There you are! Good jumper! Grand lepper! Darlint boy! He's the racer! Bear him on, will you!

[CHRISTY *comes in, in Jockey's dress, with* PEGEEN MIKE, SARA, *and other girls, and men.*]

PEGEEN (*to crowd*). Go on now and don't destroy him and he drenching with sweat. Go along, I'm saying, and

have your tug-of-warring till he's dried his skin.

CROWD. Here's his prizes! A bagpipes! A fiddle was played by a poet in the years gone by! A flat and three-thorned blackthorn would lick the scholars out of Dublin town!

CHRISTY (*taking prizes from the men*). Thank you kindly, the lot of you. But you'd say it was little only I did this day if you'd seen me a while since striking my one single blow.

TOWN CRIER (*outside, ringing a bell*). Take notice, last event of this day! Tug-of-warring on the green below! Come on, the lot of you! Great achievements for all Mayo men!

PEGEEN. Go on, and leave him for to rest and dry. Go on, I tell you, for he'll do no more. (*She hustles crowd out;* WIDOW QUIN *following them.*)

MEN (*going*). Come on then. Good luck for the while!

PEGEEN (*radiantly, wiping his face with her shawl*). Well, you're the lad, and you'll have great times from this out when you could win that wealth of prizes, and you sweating in the heat of noon!

CHRISTY (*looking at her with delight*). I'll have great times if I win the crowning prize I'm seeking now, and that's your promise that you'll wed me in a fortnight, when our banns is called.

PEGEEN (*backing away from him*). You've right daring to go ask me that, when all knows you'll be starting to some girl in your own townland, when your father's rotten in four months, or five.

CHRISTY (*indignantly*). Starting from you, is it? (*He follows her.*) I will not, then, and when the airs is warming in four months, or five, it's then yourself and me should be pacing Neifin in the dews of night, the times sweet smells do be rising, and you'd see a little shiny new moon, maybe, sinking on the hills.

PEGEEN (*looking at him playfully*). And it's that kind of a poacher's love you'd make, Christy Mahon, on the sides of Neifin, when the night is down?

CHRISTY. It's little you'll think if my love's a poacher's, or an earl's itself, when you'll feel my two hands 10 stretched around you, and I squeezing kisses on your puckered lips, till I'd feel a kind of pity for the Lord God is all ages sitting lonesome in his golden chair.

PEGEEN. That'll be right fun, Christy Mahon, and any girl would walk her heart out before she'd meet a young man was your like for eloquence, or talk, at all.

CHRISTY (*encouraged*). Let you wait, to hear me talking, till we're astray in Erris, when Good Friday's by, drinking a sup from a well, and making mighty kisses with our wetted mouths, or gaming in a gap or sunshine, with yourself stretched back unto your necklace, in the flowers of the earth.

PEGEEN (*in a lower voice, moved by his tone*). I'd be nice so, is it? 30

CHRISTY (*with rapture*). If the mitred bishops seen you that time, they'd be the like of the holy prophets, I'm thinking, do be straining the bars of Paradise to lay eyes on the Lady Helen of Troy, and she abroad, pacing back and forward, with a nosegay in her golden shawl.

PEGEEN (*with real tenderness*). And what is it I have, Christy Mahon, to make me 40 fitting entertainment for the like of you, that has such poet's talking, and such bravery of heart?

CHRISTY (*in a low voice*). Isn't there the light of seven heavens in your heart alone, the way you'll be an angel's lamp to me from this out, and I abroad in the darkness, spearing salmons in the Owen, or the Carrowmore?

PEGEEN. If I was your wife, I'd be along with you those nights, Christy Mahon, the way you'd see I was a great hand at coaxing bailiffs, or coining funny nick-names for the stars of night.

CHRISTY. You, is it? Taking your death in the hailstones, or in the fogs of dawn.

PEGEEN. Yourself and me would shelter easy in a narrow bush (*With a qualm of dread.*), but we're only talking, maybe, for this would be a poor, thatched place to hold a fine lad is the like of you.

CHRISTY (*putting his arm round her*). If I wasn't a good Christian, it's on my naked knees I'd be saying my prayers and paters to every jackstraw you have roofing your head, and every stony pebble is paving the laneway to your door.

PEGEEN (*radiantly*). If that's the truth, I'll be burning candles from this out to the miracles of God that have brought you from the south to-day, and I, with my gowns bought ready, the way that I can wed you, and not wait at all.

CHRISTY. It's miracles, and that's the truth. Me there toiling a long while, and walking a long while, not knowing at all I was drawing all times nearer to this holy day.

PEGEEN. And myself, a girl, was tempted often to go sailing the seas till I'd marry a Jew-man, with ten kegs of gold, and I not knowing at all there was the like of you drawing nearer, like the stars of God.

CHRISTY. And to think I'm long years hearing women talking that talk, to

all bloody fools, and this the first time
I've heard the like of your voice talking sweetly for my own delight.

PEGEEN. And to think it's me is talking
sweetly, Christy Mahon, and I the
fright of seven townlands for my biting tongue. Well, the heart's a wonder; and, I'm thinking, there won't
be our like in Mayo, for gallant lovers,
from this hour, to-day. (*Drunken sing-* 10
ing is heard outside.) There's my father
coming from the wake, and when he's
had his sleep we'll tell him, for he's
peaceful then. (*They separate.*)

MICHAEL (*singing outside*).
    The jailor and the turnkey
        They quickly ran us down,
    And brought us back as prisoners
        Once more to Cavan town.
(*He comes in supported by* SHAWN.)
    There we lay bewailing
        All in a prison bound. . . .
(*He sees* CHRISTY. *Goes and shakes him
drunkenly by the hand, while* PEGEEN *and*
SHAWN *talk on the left.*)

MICHAEL (*to* CHRISTY). The blessing of
God and the holy angels on your
head, young fellow. I hear tell you're
after winning all in the sports below;
and wasn't it a shame I didn't bear 30
you along with me to Kate Cassidy's
wake, a fine, stout lad, the like of you,
for you'd never see the match of it for
flows of drink, the way when we sunk
her bones at noonday in her narrow
grave, there were five men, aye, and
six men, stretched out retching
speechless on the holy stones.

CHRISTY (*uneasily, watching* PEGEEN). Is
that the truth?   40

MICHAEL. It is then, and aren't you a
louty schemer to go burying your poor
father unbeknownst when you'd a
right to throw him on the crupper of a
Kerry mule and drive him westwards,
like holy Joseph in the days gone by,

the way we could have given him a
decent burial, and not have him rot-
ting beyond, and not a Christian
drinking a smart drop to the glory of
his soul?

CHRISTY (*gruffly*). It's well enough he's
lying, for the likes of him.

MICHAEL (*slapping him on the back*). Well,
aren't you a hardened slayer? It'll be
a poor thing for the household man
where you go sniffing for a female
wife; and (*Pointing to* SHAWN.) look
beyond at that shy and decent Christian I have chosen for my daughter's
hand, and I after getting the gilded
dispensation this day for to wed them
now.

CHRISTY. And you'll be wedding them
this day, is it?

MICHAEL (*drawing himself up*). Aye. Are
you thinking, if I'm drunk itself, I'd
leave my daughter living single with a
little frisky rascal is the like of you?

PEGEEN (*breaking away from* SHAWN). Is it
the truth the dispensation's come?

MICHAEL (*triumphantly*). Father Reilly's
after reading it in gallous Latin, and
"It's come in the nick of time," says
he; "so I'll wed them in a hurry,
dreading that young gaffer who'd
capsize the stars."

PEGEEN (*fiercely*). He's missed his nick of
time, for it's that lad, Christy Mahon,
that I'm wedding now.

MICHAEL (*loudly with horror*). You'd be
making him a son to me, and he wet
and crusted with his father's blood?

PEGEEN. Aye. Wouldn't it be a bitter
thing for a girl to go marrying the like
of Shaneen, and he a middling kind of
a scarecrow, with no savagery or fine
words in him at all?

MICHAEL (*gasping and sinking on a chair*).
Oh, aren't you a heathen daughter to
go shaking the fat of my heart, and I
swamped and drownded with the

weight of drink? Would you have them turning on me the way that I'd be roaring to the dawn of day with the wind upon my heart? Have you not a word to aid me, Shaneen? Are you not jealous at all?

SHAWN (*in great misery*). I'd be afeard to be jealous of a man did slay his da.

PEGEEN. Well, it'd be a poor thing to go marrying your like. I'm seeing there's a world of peril for an orphan girl, and isn't it a great blessing I didn't wed you, before himself came walking from the west or south?

SHAWN. It's a queer story you'd go picking a dirty tramp up from the highways of the world.

PEGEEN (*playfully*). And you think you're a likely beau to go straying along with, the shiny Sundays of the opening year, when it's sooner on a bullock's liver you'd put a poor girl thinking than on the lily or the rose?

SHAWN. And have you no mind of my weight of passion, and the holy dispensation, and the drift of heifers I am giving, and the golden ring?

PEGEEN. I'm thinking you're too fine for the like of me, Shawn Keogh of Killakeen, and let you go off till you'd find a radiant lady with droves of bullocks on the plains of Meath, and herself bedizened in the diamond jewelleries of Pharaoh's ma. That'd be your match, Shaneen. So God save you now! (*She retreats behind* CHRISTY.)

SHAWN. Won't you hear me telling you . . . ?

CHRISTY (*with ferocity*). Take yourself from this, young fellow, or I'll maybe add a murder to my deeds to-day.

MICHAEL (*springing up with a shriek*). Murder is it? Is it mad yous are? Would you go making murder in this place, and it piled with poteen for our drink to-night? Go on to the foreshore if it's fighting you want, where the rising tide will wash all traces from the memory of man. (*Pushing* SHAWN *towards* CHRISTY.)

SHAWN (*shaking himself free, and getting behind* MICHAEL). I'll not fight him, Michael James. I'd liefer live a bachelor, simmering in passions to the end of time, than face a lepping savage the like of him has descended from the Lord knows where. Strike him yourself, Michael James, or you'll lose my drift of heifers and my blue bull from Sneem.

MICHAEL. Is it me fight him, when it's father-slaying he's bred to now? (*Pushing* SHAWN.) Go on you fool and fight him now.

SHAWN (*coming forward a little*). Will I strike him with my hand?

MICHAEL. Take the loy is on your western side.

SHAWN. I'd be afeard of the gallows if I struck him with that.

CHRISTY (*taking up the loy*). Then I'll make you face the gallows or quit off from this.

[SHAWN *flies out of the door.*]

CHRISTY. Well, fine weather be after him (*Going to* MICHAEL, *coaxingly.*), and I'm thinking you wouldn't wish to have that quaking blackguard in your house at all. Let you give us your blessing and hear her swear her faith to me, for I'm mounted on the springtide of the stars of luck, the way it'll be good for any to have me in the house.

PEGEEN (*at the other side of* MICHAEL). Bless us now, for I swear to God I'll wed him, and I'll not renege.

MICHAEL (*standing up in the center, holding on to both of them*). It's the will of God, I'm thinking, that all should win an easy or a cruel end, and it's the will of God that all should rear up lengthy families for the nurture of the earth.

What's a single man, I ask you, eating a bit in one house and drinking a sup in another, and he with no place of his own, like an old braying jackass strayed upon the rocks? (*To* CHRISTY.) It's many would be in dread to bring your like into their house for to end them, maybe, with a sudden end; but I'm a decent man of Ireland, and I liefer face the grave untimely and I seeing a score of grandsons growing up little gallant swearers by the name of God, than go peopling my bedside with puny weeds the like of what you'd breed, I'm thinking, out of Shaneen Keogh. (*He joins their hands.*) A daring fellow is the jewel of the world, and a man did split his father's middle with a single clout, should have the bravery of ten, so may God and Mary and St. Patrick bless you, and increase you from this mortal day.

CHRISTY *and* PEGEEN. Amen, O Lord!

[*Hubbub outside.*]

[OLD MAHON *rushes in, followed by all the crowd, and* WIDOW QUIN. *He makes a rush at* CHRISTY, *knocks him down, and begins to beat him.*]

PEGEEN (*dragging back his arm*). Stop that, will you. Who are you at all?

MAHON. His father, God forgive me!

PEGEEN (*drawing back*). Is it rose from the dead?

MAHON. Do you think I look so easy quenched with the tap of a loy? (*Beats* CHRISTY *again.*)

PEGEEN (*glaring at* CHRISTY). And it's lies you told, letting on you had him slitted, and you nothing at all.

CHRISTY (*catching* MAHON'S *stick*). He's not my father. He's a raving maniac would scare the world. (*Pointing to* WIDOW QUIN.) Herself knows it is true.

CROWD. You're fooling Pegeen! The Widow Quin seen him this day, and you likely knew! You're a liar!

CHRISTY (*dumbfounded*). It's himself was a liar, lying stretched out with an open head on him, letting on he was dead.

MAHON. Weren't you off racing the hills before I got my breath with the start I had seeing you turn on me at all?

PEGEEN. And to think of the coaxing glory we had given him, and he after doing nothing but hitting a soft blow and chasing northward in a sweat of fear. Quit off from this.

CHRISTY (*piteously*). You've seen my doings this day, and let you save me from the old man; for why would you be in such a scorch of haste to spur me to destruction now?

PEGEEN. It's there your treachery is spurring me, till I'm hard set to think you're the one I'm after lacing in my heart-strings half-an-hour gone by. (*To* MAHON.) Take him on from this, for I think bad the world should see me raging for a Munster liar, and the fool of men.

MAHON. Rise up now to retribution, and come on with me.

CROWD (*jeeringly*). There's the playboy! There's the lad thought he'd rule the roost in Mayo. Slate him now, mister.

CHRISTY (*getting up in shy terror*). What is it drives you to torment me here, when I'd asked the thunders of the might of God to blast me if I ever did hurt to any saving only that one single blow.

MAHON (*loudly*). If you didn't, you're a poor good-for-nothing, and isn't it by the like of you the sins of the whole world are committed?

CHRISTY (*raising his hands*). In the name of the Almighty God. . . .

MAHON. Leave troubling the Lord God. Would you have him sending down droughts, and fevers, and the old hen and the cholera morbus?

CHRISTY (to WIDOW QUIN). Will you come between us and protect me now?

WIDOW QUIN. I've tried a lot, God help me, and my share is done.

CHRISTY (looking round in desperation). And I must go back into my torment is it, or run off like a vagabond straying through the Unions with the dusts of August making mudstains in the gullet of my throat, or the winds of March blowing on me till I'd take an oath I felt them making whistles of my ribs within?

SARA. Ask Pegeen to aid you. Her like does often change.

CHRISTY. I will not then, for there's torment in the splendour of her like, and she a girl any moon of midnight would take pride to meet, facing southwards on the heaths of Keel. But what did I want crawling forward to scorch my understanding at her flaming brow?

PEGEEN (to MAHON, vehemently, fearing she will break into tears). Take him on from this or I'll set the young lads to destroy him here.

MAHON (going to him, shaking his stick). Come on now if you wouldn't have the company to see you skelped.

PEGEEN (half laughing, through her tears). That's it, now the world will see him pandied, and he an ugly liar was playing off the hero, and the fright of men.

CHRISTY (to MAHON, very sharply). Leave me go!

CROWD. That's it. Now Christy. If them two set fighting, it will lick the world.

MAHON (making a grab at CHRISTY). Come here to me.

CHRISTY (more threateningly). Leave me go, I'm saying.

MAHON. I will maybe, when your legs is limping, and your back is blue.

CROWD. Keep it up, the two of you. I'll back the old one. Now the playboy.

CHRISTY (in low and intense voice). Shut your yelling, for if you're after making a mighty man of me this day by the power of a lie, you're setting me now to think if it's a poor thing to be lonesome, it's worse maybe to go mixing with the fools of earth.

[MAHON makes a movement towards him.]

CHRISTY (almost shouting). Keep off . . . lest I do show a blow unto the lot of you would set the guardian angels winking in the clouds above. (He swings round with a sudden rapid movement and picks up a loy.)

CROWD (half frightened, half amused). He's going mad! Mind yourselves! Run from the idiot!

CHRISTY. If I am an idiot, I'm after hearing my voice this day saying words would raise the topknot on a poet in a merchant's town. I've won your racing, and your lepping, and . . .

MAHON. Shut your gullet and come on with me.

CHRISTY. I'm going, but I'll stretch you first.

[He runs at OLD MAHON with the loy, chases him out of the door, followed by crowd and WIDOW QUIN. There is a great noise outside, then a yell, and dead silence for a moment. CHRISTY comes in, half dazed, and goes to fire.]

WIDOW QUIN (coming in, hurriedly, and going to him). They're turning again you. Come on, or you'll be hanged, indeed.

CHRISTY. I'm thinking, from this out, Pegeen'll be giving me praises the same as in the hours gone by.

WIDOW QUIN (impatiently). Come by the back-door. I'd think bad to have you stifled on the gallows tree.

CHRISTY (indignantly). I will not, then. What good'd be my life-time, if I left Pegeen?

WIDOW QUIN. Come on, and you'll be no worse than you were last night; and you with a double murder this time to be telling to the girls.

CHRISTY. I'll not leave Pegeen Mike.

WIDOW QUIN (*impatiently*). Isn't there the match of her in every parish public, from Binghamstown unto the plain of Meath? Come on, I tell you, and I'll find you finer sweethearts at each waning moon.

CHRISTY. It's Pegeen I'm seeking only, and what'd I care if you brought me a drift of chosen females, standing in their shifts itself, maybe, from this place to the Eastern World?

SARA (*runs in, pulling off one of her petticoats*). They're going to hang him. (*Holding out petticoat and shawl.*) Fit these upon him, and let him run off to the east.

WIDOW QUIN. He's raving now; but we'll fit them on him, and I'll take him, in the ferry, to the Achill boat.

CHRISTY (*struggling feebly*). Leave me go, will you? when I'm thinking of my luck to-day, for she will wed me surely, and I a proven hero in the end of all.

[*They try to fasten petticoat round him.*]

WIDOW QUIN. Take his left hand, and we'll pull him now. Come on, young fellow.

CHRISTY (*suddenly starting up*). You'll be taking me from her? You're jealous, is it, of her wedding me? Go on from this. (*He snatches up a stool, and threatens them with it.*)

WIDOW QUIN (*going*). It's in the madhouse they should put him, not in jail, at all. We'll go by the back-door, to call the doctor, and we'll save him so.

[*She goes out, with* SARA, *through inner room. Men crowd in the doorway.* CHRISTY *sits down again by the fire.*]

MICHAEL (*in a terrified whisper*). Is the old lad killed surely?

PHILLY. I'm after feeling the last gasps quitting his heart.

[*They peer in at* CHRISTY.]

MICHAEL (*with a rope*). Look at the way he is. Twist a hangman's knot on it, and slip it over his head, while he's not minding at all.

PHILLY. Let you take it, Shaneen. You're the soberest of all that's here.

SHAWN. Is it me to go near him, and he the wickedest and worst with me? Let you take it, Pegeen Mike.

PEGEEN. Come on, so. (*She goes forward with the others, and they drop the double hitch over his head.*)

CHRISTY. What ails you?

SHAWN (*triumphantly, as they pull the rope tight on his arms*). Come on to the peelers, till they stretch you now.

CHRISTY. Me!

MICHAEL. If we took pity on you, the Lord God would, maybe, bring us ruin from the law to-day, so you'd best come easy, for hanging is an easy and a speedy end.

CHRISTY. I'll not stir. (*To* PEGEEN.) And what is it you'll say to me, and I after doing it this time in the face of all?

PEGEEN. I'll say, a strange man is a marvel, with his mighty talk; but what's a squabble in your back-yard, and the blow of a loy, have taught me that there's a great gap between a gallous story and a dirty deed. (*To* MEN.) Take him on from this, or the lot of us will be likely put on trial for his deed to-day.

CHRISTY (*with horror in his voice*). And it's yourself will send me off, to have a horny-fingered hangman hitching his bloody slip-knots at the butt of my ear.

MEN (*pulling rope*). Come on, will you?

[*He is pulled down on the floor.*]

CHRISTY (*twisting his legs round the table*). Cut the rope, Pegeen, and I'll quit the lot of you, and live from this out, like the madmen of Keel, eating muck and green weeds, on the faces of the cliffs.

PEGEEN. And leave us to hang, is it, for a saucy liar, the like of you? (*To* MEN.) Take him on, out from this.

SHAWN. Pull a twist on his neck, and squeeze him so.

PHILLY. Twist yourself. Sure he cannot hurt you, if you keep your distance from his teeth alone.

SHAWN. I'm afeard of him. (*To* PEGEEN.) Lift a lighted sod, will you, and scorch his leg.

PEGEEN (*blowing the fire, with a bellows*). Leave go now, young fellow, or I'll scorch your shins.

CHRISTY. You're blowing for to torture me. (*His voice rising and growing stronger.*) That's your kind, is it? Then let the lot of you be wary, for, if I've to face the gallows, I'll have a gay march down, I tell you, and shed the blood of some of you before I die.

SHAWN (*in terror*). Keep a good hold, Philly. Be wary, for the love of God. For I'm thinking he would liefest wreak his pains on me.

CHRISTY (*almost gaily*). If I do lay my hands on you, it's the way you'll be at the fall of night, hanging as a scarecrow for the fowls of hell. Ah, you'll have a gallous jaunt I'm saying, coaching out through Limbo with my father's ghost.

SHAWN (*to* PEGEEN). Make haste, will you? Oh, isn't he a holy terror, and isn't it true for Father Reilly, that all drink's a curse that has the lot of you so shaky and uncertain now?

CHRISTY. If I can wring a neck among you, I'll have a royal judgment looking on the trembling jury in the courts of law. And won't there be crying out in Mayo the day I'm stretched upon the rope with ladies in their silks and satins snivelling in their lacy kerchiefs, and they rhyming songs and ballads on the terror of my fate? (*He squirms round on the floor and bites* SHAWN's *leg.*)

SHAWN (*shrieking*). My leg's bit on me. He's the like of a mad dog, I'm thinking, the way that I will surely die.

CHRISTY (*delighted with himself*). You will then, the way you can shake out hell's flags of welcome for my coming in two weeks or three, for I'm thinking Satan hasn't many have killed their da in Kerry, and in Mayo too.

[OLD MAHON *comes in behind on all fours and looks on unnoticed.*]

MEN (*to* PEGEEN). Bring the sod, will you?

PEGEEN (*coming over*). God help him so. (*Burns his leg.*)

CHRISTY (*kicking and screaming*). O, glory be to God! (*He kicks loose from the table, and they all drag him towards the door.*)

JIMMY (*seeing* OLD MAHON). Will you look what's come in?

[*They all drop* CHRISTY *and run left.*]

CHRISTY (*scrambling on his knees face to face with* OLD MAHON). Are you coming to be killed a third time, or what ails you now?

MAHON. For what is it they have you tied?

CHRISTY. They're taking me to the peelers to have me hanged for slaying you.

MICHAEL (*apologetically*). It is the will of God that all should guard their little cabins from the treachery of law, and what would my daughter be doing if I was ruined or was hanged itself?

MAHON (*grimly, loosening* CHRISTY). It's little I care if you put a bag on her back, and went picking cockles till the hour of death; but my son and myself will be going our own way, and we'll have great times from this out telling stories of the villainy of Mayo, and the fools is here. (*To* CHRISTY, *who is freed.*) Come on now.

CHRISTY. Go with you, is it? I will then, like a gallant captain with his heathen slave. Go on now and I'll see you from this day stewing my oatmeal and washing my spuds, for I'm master of all fights from now. (*Pushing* MAHON.) Go on, I'm saying.

MAHON. Is it me?

CHRISTY. Not a word out of you. Go on from this.

MAHON (*walking out and looking back at* CHRISTY *over his shoulder*). Glory be to God! (*With a broad smile.*) I am crazy again! (*Goes.*)

CHRISTY. Ten thousand blessings upon all that's here, for you've turned me a likely gaffer in the end of all, the way I'll go romancing through a romping lifetime from this hour to the dawning of the judgment day. (*He goes out.*)

MICHAEL. By the will of God, we'll have peace now for our drinks. Will you draw the porter, Pegeen?

SHAWN (*going up to her*). It's a miracle Father Reilly can wed us in the end of all, and we'll have none to trouble us when his vicious bite is healed.

PEGEEN (*hitting him a box on the ear*). Quit my sight. (*Putting her shawl over her head and breaking out into wild lamentations.*) Oh my grief, I've lost him surely. I've lost the only Playboy of the Western World.

CURTAIN

LORD DUNSANY

ONE OF THE most singular personalities, of many turned up by the Irish Renaissance and its revival of wonder, was Lord Dunsany, Edward John Moreton Drax Plunkett before he became the eighteenth baron of his line in 1899 at the family estate in County Meath in east Ireland. He was born on July 24, 1878. He attended Cheam School and Eton, and then went on to Sandhurst to prepare for an army career. Even in these early school days the odd dichotomy of his nature was clearly evident. Though he had a passion for cricket, hunting, and soldiering, he also had a sensitive poet's heart and an "imagination as elfish as moonlight mist." He read Grimm and Andersen. At Cheam, he said, "I was given a lot of the Bible to read. This turned my thoughts eastward. For years no style seemed to me natural but that of the Bible and I feared that I never would become a writer when I saw that other people did not use it." Also at Cheam he first learned Greek. The grandeur of that literature and the appeal of its beautiful and forsaken gods affected him much as they did John Keats. "This mood," he wrote, "never quite left me."

A giant out-of-doors man standing six feet four, he entered the army from Sandhurst, and saw active service with the Coldstream Guards in the South African war. He was a Captain in the Royal Inniskilling Fusiliers during the World War, where he was wounded, and where he complained that "our trenches were only six feet deep." Though remaining spiritually close to the traditions that cluster about his castle and his fifteenth century title, he has traveled in all parts of the world, and has been a frequent and familiar visitor to America. In 1940, at the age of sixty-two he ventured into a new field by becoming Byron Professor of English Literature at the University of Athens. Yet in the midst of this extraordinarily varied and active life, he has written rather steadily during the twentieth century. His first book, a collection of prose pieces, was published in 1905 and called *The Gods of Pegana*. Several volumes of such essays, sketches, tales, and short stories followed this book at two-year intervals down to the World War. The titles themselves suggest how closely even this part of Lord Dunsany's work is linked with the Celtic imagination of old Irish poetry and its modern revival: *Time and the Gods* (1906); *The Sword of Welleran* (1908); *A Dreamer's Tales* (1910); *The Book of Wonder* (1912). This tenuous subject matter, however, is conveyed in limpid prose that is at once imaginative and vividly realistic.

The irrepressible and ebullient William Butler Yeats, who had persuaded Lady Gregory to inaugurate production of new Irish plays, who had sought out and inspired John M. Synge, who was so active in his own writing and lecturing and in stirring up Irish genius that he became the acknowledged leader of the Irish movement—this man at whose touch genius sprang into action, exerted his peculiar power on Lord Dunsany and urged him to write plays. Yeats had Lord Dunsany's first play, *The Glittering Gate*, produced at the Abbey Theatre in

253

1909. That very short one act play set in "a lonely place" at the present time, with two persons Jim and Bill, lately burglars and both dead, as the only actors, depended for its effect upon its surprise ending. For the Glittering Gate is Heaven's own doorway, and when the awed Bill and Jim push it open they find behind it nothing but "empty night and stars." As Bill staggers and gazes into this "revealed Nothing in which far stars go wandering," he gasps in astonishment: "Stars. Blooming great stars. There ain't no Heaven, Jim." And Jim answers, "That's like them. That's very like them. Yes, they'd do that!" as the curtain falls, and "the laughter still howls on."

The Glittering Gate, with its lightness of touch, its air of complete reality in a wholly imaginative and fantastic setting, its sure sense of character and speech, its deft workmanship, and the teasing quality of its speculation at once playful and serious, defined at the outset the rare nature of Lord Dunsany's gift to the Irish movement and to contemporary drama at large.

Since 1909 Lord Dunsany has devised nearly two score plays, most of them in the short form especially well adapted to the slender episodes or concentrated moods which all these Irish writers seem to find most congenial. Like other dramatists who felt themselves identified with a distinct movement, he has written critical articles in explanation of his approach to his craft—an activity, we must bear in mind, that has been engaged in by Lord Dunsany in the spirit of an enthusiastic amateur. His most revealing and most characteristic views were set down in an essay which he called "Romance and the Modern Stage" (1911). It was written at the outset of his career as a playwright.

An age is unsound when its drama deserts romance which, in Lord Dunsany's opinion, is inseparable from life. He declared that "all we need to obtain romantic drama is for the dramatist to find any age and any country where life is not too thickly veiled and cloaked with puzzles and conventions, in fact to find a people that is not in the agonies of self-consciousness." Synge found such folk in the Aran Islands and lived among them with notebook in hand, but Lord Dunsany found it "simpler to imagine such a people, as it saves the trouble of reading to find a romantic age, or the trouble of making a journey to lands where there is no press."

In these archly expressed views we have the clue to the dramatic writings of Lord Dunsany. They are all imaginative, a few of them are sportive in mood, and most of them are set in Lord Dunsany's own private world of fancy which is intriguing in itself and at the same time sets in bold relief the truth about the world of reality in which we live. Lord Dunsany has called this realm of his own ingenious mythology the Edge of the World or the Lands of Wonder; here are cities like Sardathion and Zericon; and hither go the three thieves with the Lewis Carroll names of Slith and Sippy and Slorg in search of the Golden Box. Gently ironic surprise brings us back from this land with the fall of the curtain. The pleasure has been in the escape, not in the homily. In a letter to Mrs. Emma Garnett Boyd, Lord Dunsany was unequivocal on this point. "I will say first that in my plays I tell very simple stories—so simple that sometimes people of this complex age, being brought up in intricacies, even fail to understand them. . . . I am not trying to teach anybody anything. I merely set out to make a work of art out of a simple theme, and God knows we want works of art in this age of corrugated iron. How many people hold the error that Shakespeare was of the schoolroom! Whereas he was of the playground, as all artists are."

These short plays of Lord Dunsany's, then, are artistic little episodes, moods, and parables. They began, he said, "with anything, or with next to nothing," then got under way and rushed on without interrupting the mood, and were finished "in a sitting or two." *The Gods of the Mountain* (1911) is entirely typical of a dozen in the same genre. The Gods are seven jade idols drowsily sitting in their mountains at Marma cross-legged with "their right elbows resting on their left hands, the right forefinger pointing upward," while the calling of the seven beggars languishes. The beggars decide to impersonate the gods, and return to the city in the guise of men to reap profit. But the real gods pursue them in vengeance; the beggars are turned into stone, and the skeptical citizens "abase themselves, foreheads to the floor," as they say, "They have turned to stone because we have doubted them. They were the true gods." Throughout the play are lines of wisdom in Lord Dunsany's best style, as when Agmar says: "In our ancient calling a man may sit at one street corner for fifty years doing the one thing, and yet a day may come when it is well for him to rise up and do another thing while the timorous man starves."

A Night at an Inn (1916) shows the same power of invention, the sense of awe, and the same theme of just revenge, in a little more spookish atmosphere. It tells of the three English thieves who stole the ruby eye of an oriental idol; how they lured forth and slew the priests one by one; and how, just as they began to feel secure, the idol himself came in, picked up the ruby eye, and strode away before the horrified witnesses, drawing after him to their doom the thieves themselves. And thus run the Lord Dunsany plays: *The Golden Doom* (1912); *The Silk Hat* (1913); *The Tents of the Arabs* (1914); *The Prince of Stamboul* (1918); *The Laughter of the Gods* (1919); etc.

If (1921) is Lord Dunsany's one full evening-length play, and it has had a notable success. Though he seems most at home in the shorter form, in *If* he makes the most of his wider opportunities and sustains the drama of the idea and the situation at high pitch to the final curtain. Though it develops in the land of dream and fantasy, it is rooted in everyday life of modern London with its railroad stations, suburban houses and flower gardens, and audiences have found the combination very satisfactory. Allardyce Nicoll called *If* Lord Dunsany's greatest triumph; and William Beebe, who wrote an introduction to the printed play, found the "dull main street of life" leavened "with the crystal of Ali"; and the play a "relief from the eternal straight line or triangle drama, which can develop or end only happily or unhappily, to a play which begins in a spirit of comedy, develops mysteriously, and ends satisfactorily."

Lord Dunsany's *If* is naturally linked with Barrie's famous play on destiny and the second chance, *Dear Brutus* (1917). Both deal with the eternal puzzle of the road not taken, and the question whether accident or fate rules our lives, whether our character is our destiny. The gentle Barrie seems to think we would do no better with the second chance, or if we had taken the other road. And he made Purdie say that it is not accident that shapes our lives. "It's not Fate, Joanna. Fate is something outside us. What really plays the dickens with us is something in ourselves. Something that makes us go on doing the same sort of fool things, however many chances we get." Lord Dunsany holds otherwise. Chance plays a part, and character is not fate. The minute's difference between catching and missing a train may alter a life completely, and character does not drive on to its preappointed end regardless of circumstances.

Pursuing these reflections, not too doggedly of course, Lord Dunsany invented John Beal, the undistinguished London citizen who was separated from adventure and high romance by the single act of missing a train. Using the dream technique, and compelling the suspension of our disbelief with his dramatic art and Ali's crystal, he takes John Beal back to the railroad station, puts him on the train he missed, and shows him as he might have been. A moment, an accident, a flip of a coin makes all the difference. Character alone is not Destiny.

This play with its extraordinary combination of realism, romance, and speculation, and its high-spirited tale of adventure, was enthusiastically received by Londoners when it opened at the Ambassador's Theatre in June, 1921. It had a long run there. It was not so successful in America when it was produced in New York at the Little Theatre on October 25, 1927. It ran for twenty-seven performances. This marked difference in response between the two cities has been demonstrated time and again; plays successful in America often fall flat in London, and some of the greatest London hits have failed dismally in the New York theatres.

Fortunately *If* is a play to be read as well as to be seen. It is the expression of Lord Dunsany's belief that the realism of the poets "who see the whole of life's journey" is a higher truth than a realism that sees only "how man equips himself with morals, and money, and custom for the journey; but knows not where the journey leads nor why man wants to go." What we need, he thinks, is the kind of drama that "will build new worlds for the fancy, for the spirit as much as the body sometimes needs a change of scene."

IF

CHARACTERS

JOHN BEAL

MARY BEAL

LIZA

ALI

BILL ⎫
BERT ⎭ *two railway porters*

THE MAN IN THE CORNER

MIRALDA CLEMENT

HAFIZ EL ALCOLAHN

DAOUD

ARCHIE BEAL

BAZZALOL ⎫
THOOTHOOBABA ⎭ *two Nubian door-keepers*

BEN HUSSEIN, *Lord of the Pass*

ZABNOOL ⎫
SHABEESH ⎭ *two conjurers*

OMAR, *a singer*

ZAGBOOLA, *mother of Hafiz*

THE SHEIK OF THE BISHAREENS

Notables, soldiers, Bishareens, dancers, etc.

ACT I

SCENE 1

A small railway station near London.
Time: Ten years ago.

BERT. 'Ow goes it, Bill?

BILL. Goes it? 'Ow d'yer think it goes?

BERT. I don't know, Bill. 'Ow is it?

BILL. Bloody.

BERT. Why? What's wrong?

BILL. Wrong? Nothing ain't wrong.

BERT. What's up then?

BILL. Nothing ain't right.

BERT. Why, wot's the worry?

BILL. Wot's the worry? They don't give you better wages nor a dog, and then they thinks they can talk at yer and talk at yer, and say wot they likes, like.

BERT. Why? You been on the carpet. Bill? 20

BILL. Ain't I! Proper.

BERT. Why, wot about, Bill?

BILL. Wot about? I'll tell yer. Just coz I let a lidy get into a train. That's wot about. Said I ought to 'ave stopped 'er. Thought the train was moving. Thought it was dangerous. Thought I tried to murder 'er, I suppose.

BERT. Wot? The other day?

BILL. Yes.

BERT. Tuesday?

BILL. Yes. 10

BERT. Why. The one that dropped her bag?

BILL. Yes. Drops 'er bag. Writes to the company. They writes back she shouldn't 'ave got in. She writes back she should. Then they gets on to me. Any more of it and I'll . . .

BERT. I wouldn't, Bill; don't you.

BILL. I will.

BERT. Don't you, Bill. You've got your family to consider.

BILL. Well, anyway, I won't let any more of them passengers go jumping

IF: Reprinted by permission of G. P. Putnam's Sons, New York and London.

into trains any more, not when they're moving, I won't. When the train gets in, doors shut. That's the rule. And they'll 'ave to abide by it.

BERT. Well, I wouldn't stop one, not if . . .

BILL. I don't care. They ain't going to 'ave me on the mat again and talk all that stuff to me. No, if someone 'as to suffer . . . 'Ere she is. . . .

[*Noise of approaching train heard.*]

BERT. Ay, that's her.

BILL. And shut goes the door.

[*Enter* JOHN BEAL.]

BERT. Wait a moment, Bill.

BILL. Not if he's . . . Not if he was *ever* so.

JOHN (*preparing to pass*). Good morning. . . .

BILL. Can't come through. Too late.

JOHN. Too late? Why, the train's only just in.

BILL. Don't care. It's the rule.

JOHN. O, nonsense. (*He carries on.*)

BILL. It's too late. I tell you you can't come.

JOHN. But that's absurd. I want to catch my train.

BILL. It's too late.

BERT. Let him go, Bill.

BILL. I'm blowed if I let him go.

JOHN. I want to catch my train.

[JOHN *is stopped by* BILL *and pushed back by the face.* JOHN *advances towards* BILL *looking like fighting. The train has gone.*]

BILL. Only doing my duty.

[JOHN *stops and reflects at this, deciding it isn't good enough. He shrugs his shoulders, turns round and goes away.*]

JOHN. I shouldn't be surprised if I didn't get even with you one of these days, you . . . and some way you won't expect.

CURTAIN

SCENE 2

Yesterday evening.

[*Curtain rises on* JOHN *and* MARY *in their suburban home.*]

JOHN. I say, dear. Don't you think we ought to plant an acacia?

MARY. An acacia, what's that, John?

JOHN. O, it's one of those trees that they have.

MARY. But why, John?

JOHN. Well, you see the house is called The Acacias, and it seems rather silly not to have at least one.

MARY. O, I don't think that matters. Lots of places are called lots of things. Everyone does.

JOHN. Yes, but it might help the post-man.

MARY. O, no, it wouldn't, dear. He wouldn't know an acacia if he saw it any more than I should.

JOHN. Quite right, Mary, you're always right. What a clever head you've got!

MARY. Have I, John? We'll plant an acacia if you like. I'll ask about it at the grocer's.

JOHN. You can't get one there.

MARY. No, but he's sure to know where it can be got.

JOHN. Where do they grow, Mary?

MARY. I don't know, John; but I am sure they do, somewhere.

JOHN. Somehow I wish sometimes, I almost wish I could have gone abroad for a week or so to places like where acacias grow naturally.

MARY. O, would you really, John?

JOHN. No, not really. But I just think of it sometimes.

MARY. Where would you have gone?

JOHN. O, I don't know. The East or some such place. I've often heard people speak of it, and somehow it seemed so . . .

MARY. The East, John? Not the East. I don't think the East somehow is quite respectable.

JOHN. O well, it's all right, I never went, and never shall go now. It doesn't matter.

MARY (*the photographs catching her eye*). O, John, I meant to tell you. Such a dreadful thing happened.

JOHN. What, Mary? 10

MARY. Well, Liza was dusting the photographs, and when she came to Jane's she says she hadn't really begun to dust it, only looked at it, and it fell down, and that bit of glass is broken right out of it.

JOHN. Ask her not to look at it so hard another time.

MARY. O, what do you mean, John?

JOHN. Well, that's how she broke it; she 20 said so, and as I know you believe in Liza . . .

MARY. Well, I can't think she'd tell a lie, John.

JOHN. No, of course not. But she mustn't look so hard another time.

MARY. And it's poor little Jane's photograph. She will feel it so.

JOHN. O, that's all right, we'll get it mended. 30

MARY. Still, it's a dreadful thing to have happened.

JOHN. We'll get it mended, and if Jane is unhappy about it she can have Alice's frame. Alice is too young to notice it.

MARY. She isn't, John. She'd notice it quick.

JOHN. Well, George, then.

MARY (*looking at photo thoughtfully*). Well, perhaps George might give up his 40 frame.

JOHN. Yes, tell Liza to change it. Why not make her do it now?

MARY. Not to-day, John. Not on a Sunday. She shall do it to-morrow by the time you get back from the office.

JOHN. All right. It might have been worse.

MARY. It's bad enough. I wish it hadn't happened.

JOHN. It might have been worse. It might have been Aunt Martha.

MARY. I'd sooner it had been her than poor little Jane.

JOHN. If it had been Aunt Martha's photograph she'd have walked in next day and seen it for certain; I know Aunt Martha. Then there'd have been trouble.

MARY. But, John, how could she have known?

JOHN. I don't know, but she would have; it's a kind of devilish sense she has.

MARY. John!

JOHN. What's the matter?

MARY. John! What a dreadful word you used. And on a Sunday too! Really!

JOHN. O, I'm sorry. It slipped out somehow. I'm very sorry.

[*Enter* LIZA.]

LIZA. There's a gentleman to see you, sir, which isn't, properly speaking, a gentleman at all. Not what I should call one, that is, like.

MARY. Not a gentleman! Good gracious, Liza! Whatever do you mean?

LIZA. He's black.

MARY. Black?

JOHN (*reassuring*). O . . . yes, that would be Ali. A queer old customer, Mary; perfectly harmless. Our firm gets hundreds of carpets through him; and then one day . . .

MARY. But what is he doing here, John?

JOHN. Well, one day he turned up in London; broke, he said; and wanted the firm to give him a little cash. Well, old Briggs was for giving him ten shillings. But I said "here's a man that's helped us in making thousands of pounds. Let's give him fifty."

MARY. Fifty pounds!

JOHN. Yes, it seems a lot; but it seemed only fair. Ten shillings would have been an insult to the old fellow, and he'd have taken it as such. You don't know what he'd have done.

MARY. Well, he doesn't want more?

JOHN. No, I expect he's come to thank me. He seemed pretty keen on getting some cash. Badly broke, you see. Don't know what he was doing in London. Never can tell with these fellows. East is East, and there's an end of it.

MARY. How did he trace you here?

JOHN. O, got the address at the office. Briggs and Cater won't let theirs be known. Not got such a smart little house, I expect.

MARY. I don't like letting people in that you don't know where they come from.

JOHN. O, he comes from the East.

MARY. Yes, I—I know. But the East doesn't seem quite to count, somehow, as the proper sort of place to come from, does it, dear?

JOHN. No.

MARY. It's not like Sydenham or Bromley, some place you can put your finger on.

JOHN. Perhaps just for once, I don't think there's any harm in him.

MARY. Well, just for once. But we can't make a practice of it. And you don't want to be thinking of business on a Sunday, your only day off.

JOHN. O, it isn't business, you know. He only wants to say thank you.

MARY. I hope he won't say it in some queer Eastern way. You don't know what these people . . .

JOHN. O, no. Show him up, Liza.

LIZA. As you like, mum. (*Exit.*)

MARY. And you gave him fifty pounds?

JOHN. Well, old Briggs agreed to it. So I suppose that's what he got. Cater paid him.

MARY. It seems a lot of money. But I think, as the man is actually coming up the stairs, I'm glad he's got something to be grateful for.

[*Enter* ALI, *shown in by* LIZA.]

ALI. Protector of the Just.

JOHN. O, er—yes. Good evening.

ALI. My soul was parched and you bathed it in rivers of gold.

JOHN. O, ah, yes.

ALI. Wherefore the name Briggs, Cater, and Beal shall be magnified and called blessed.

JOHN. Ha, yes. Very good of you.

ALI (*advancing, handing trinket*). Protector of the Just, my offering.

JOHN. Your offering?

ALI. Hush. It is beyond price. I am not bidden to sell it. I was in my extremity, but I was not bidden to sell it. It is a token of gratitude, a gift, as it came to me.

JOHN. As it came to you?

ALI. Yes, it was given me.

JOHN. I see. Then you had given somebody what you call rivers of gold?

ALI. Not gold; it was in Sahara.

JOHN. O, and what do you give in the Sahara instead of gold?

ALI. Water.

JOHN. I see. You got it for a glass of water, like.

ALI. Even so.

JOHN. And—and what happened?

MARY. I wouldn't take his only crystal, dear. It's a nice little thing, but (*To* ALI.), but you think a lot of it, don't you?

ALI. Even so.

JOHN. But look here, what does it do?

ALI. Much.

JOHN. Well, what?

ALI. He that taketh this crystal, so, in his hand, at night, and wishes, saying "At a certain hour let it be"; the hour comes and he will go back eight, ten, even twelve years if he will, into the past, and do a thing again, or act otherwise than he did. The day passes; the ten years are accomplished once again; he is here once more; but he is what he might have become had he done that one thing otherwise.

MARY. John!

JOHN. I—I don't understand.

ALI. To-night you wish. All to-morrow 10 you live the last ten years; a new way, master, a new way, how you please. To-morrow night you are here, what those years have made you.

JOHN. By Jove!

MARY. Have nothing to do with it, John.

JOHN. All right, Mary, I'm not going to. But, do you mean one could go back ten years? 20

ALI. Even so.

JOHN. Well, it seems odd, but I'll take your word for it. But look here, you can't live ten years in a day, you know.

ALI. My master has power over time.

MARY. John, don't have anything to do with him.

JOHN. All right, Mary. But who is your master?

ALI. He is carved of one piece of jade, a god in the greenest mountains. The years are his dreams. This crystal is his treasure. Guard it safely, for his power is in this more than in all the peaks of his native hills. See what I give you, master.

JOHN. Well, really, it's very good of you.

MARY. Good night, Mr. Ali. We are very much obliged for your kind offer, 40 which we are so sorry we can't avail ourselves of.

JOHN. One moment, Mary. Do you mean that I can go back ten years, and live till—till now again, and only be away a day?

ALI. Start early, and you will be here before midnight.

JOHN. Would eight o'clock do!

ALI. You could be back by eleven that evening.

JOHN. I don't quite see how ten years could go in a single day.

ALI. They will go as dreams go.

JOHN. Even so, it seems rather unusual, doesn't it?

ALI. Time is the slave of my master.

MARY. John!

JOHN. All right, Mary. (*In a lower voice.*) I'm only trying to see what he'll say.

MARY. All right, John, only . . .

ALI. Is there no step that you would wish untrodden, nor stride that you would make where once you faltered?

JOHN. I say, why don't you use it yourself?

ALI. I? I am afraid of the past. But you Engleesh, and the great firm of Briggs, Cater, and Beal; you are afraid of nothing.

JOHN. Ha, ha. Well—I wouldn't go quite as far as that, but—well, give me the crystal.

MARY. Don't take it, John! Don't take it.

JOHN. Why, Mary? It won't hurt me.

30 MARY. If it can do all that—if it can do all that . . .

JOHN. Well?

MARY. Why, you might never have met me.

JOHN. Never have met you? I never thought of that.

MARY. Leave the past alone, John.

JOHN. All right, Mary. I needn't use it. But I want to hear about it, it's so odd, it's so what-you-might-call queer; I don't think I ever—— (*To* ALI.) You mean if I work hard for ten years, which will only be all to-morrow, I may be Governor of the Bank of England to-morrow night.

ALI. Even so.

MARY. O, don't do it, John.

JOHN. But you said—I'll be back here before midnight to-morrow.

ALI. It is so.

JOHN. But the Governor of the Bank of England would live in the City, and he'd have a much bigger house anyway. He wouldn't live in Lewisham.

ALI. The crystal will bring you to this house when the hour is accomplished, even to-morrow night. If you be the great banker, you will perhaps come to chastise one of your slaves who will dwell in this house. If you be head of Briggs and Cater you will come to give an edict to one of your firm. Perchance this street will be yours and you will come to show your power unto it. *But you will come.*

JOHN. And if the house is not mine?

MARY. John! John! Don't.

ALI. *Still* you will come.

JOHN. Shall I remember?

ALI. No.

JOHN. If I want to do anything different to what I did, how shall I remember when I get back there?

MARY. Don't. Don't do anything different, John.

JOHN. All right.

ALI. Choose just before the hour of the step you desire to change. Memory lingers a little at first, and fades away slowly.

JOHN. Five minutes?

ALI. Even ten.

JOHN. Then I can change one thing. After that I forget.

ALI. Even so. One thing. And the rest follows.

JOHN. Well, it's very good of you to make me this nice present, I'm sure.

ALI. Sell it not. Give it, as I gave it, if the heart impels. So shall it come back one day to the hills that are brighter than grass, made richer by the grati-tude of many men. And my master shall smile thereat and the vale shall be glad.

JOHN. It's very good of you, I'm sure.

MARY. I don't like it, John. I don't like tampering with what's gone.

ALI. My master's power is in your hands. Farewell. (*Exit.*)

JOHN. I say, he's gone.

MARY. O, he's a dreadful man.

JOHN. I never really meant to take it.

MARY. O, John, I wish you hadn't.

JOHN. Why? I'm not going to use it.

MARY. Not going to use it, John?

JOHN. No, no. Not if you don't want me to.

MARY. O, I'm so glad.

JOHN. And besides, I don't want things different. I've got fond of this little house. And Briggs is a good old sort, you know. Cater's a bit of an ass, but there's no harm in him. In fact, I'm contented, Mary. I wouldn't even change Aunt Martha now. (*Points at frowning framed photograph centrally hung.*) You remember when she first came and you said "Where shall we hang her?" I said the cellar. You said we couldn't. So she had to go there. But I wouldn't change her now. I suppose there are old watch-dogs like her in every family. I wouldn't change anything.

MARY. O, John, wouldn't you really?

JOHN. No, I'm contented. Grim old soul, I wouldn't even change Aunt Martha.

MARY. I'm glad of that, John. I was frightened. I couldn't bear to tamper with the past. You don't know what it is, it's what's gone. But if it really isn't gone at all, if it can be dug up like that, why you don't know what mightn't happen! I don't mind the future, but if the past can come back like that. . . . O, don't, don't, John.

Don't think of it. It isn't canny. There's the children, John.

JOHN. Yes, yes, that's all right. It's only a little ornament. I won't use it. And I tell you I'm content. (*Happily.*) It's no use to me.

MARY. I'm so glad you're content, John. Are you really? Is there nothing that you'd have had different? I sometimes thought you'd rather that Jane had been a boy.

JOHN. Not a bit of it. Well, I may have at the time, but Arthur's good enough for me.

MARY. I'm so glad. And there's nothing you ever regret at all?

JOHN. Nothing. And you? Is there nothing you regret, Mary?

MARY. Me? O, no. I still think that sofa would have been better green, but you would have it red.

JOHN. Yes, so I would. No, there's nothing I regret.

MARY. I don't suppose there's many men can say that.

JOHN. No, I don't suppose they can. They're not all married to you. I don't suppose many of them can.

[MARY *smiles.*]

MARY. I should think that very few could say that they regretted nothing . . . very few in the whole world.

JOHN. Well, I won't say nothing.

MARY. What is it you regret, John?

JOHN. Well, there is one thing.

MARY. And what is that?

JOHN. One thing has rankled a bit.

MARY. Yes, John?

JOHN. O, it's nothing, it's nothing worth mentioning. But it rankled for years.

MARY. What was it, John?

JOHN. O, it seems silly to mention it. It was nothing.

MARY. But what?

JOHN. O, well, if you want to know, it was once when I missed a train. I don't mind missing a train, but it was the way the porter pushed me out of the way. He pushed me by the face. I couldn't hit back, because, well, you know what lawyers make of it; I might have been ruined. So it just rankled. It was years ago before we married.

MARY. Pushed you by the face. Good gracious!

JOHN. Yes, I'd like to have caught that train in spite of him. I sometimes think of it still. Silly of me, isn't it?

MARY. What a brute of a man.

JOHN. O, I suppose he was doing his silly duty. But it rankled.

MARY. He'd no right to do any such thing! He'd no right to touch you!

JOHN. O, well, never mind.

MARY. I should like to have been there. . . . I'd have . . .

JOHN. O, well, it can't be helped now; but I'd like to have caught it in sp . . . (*An idea seizes him.*)

MARY. What is it?

JOHN. Can't be helped, I said. *It's the very thing that can be helped.*

MARY. Can be helped, John? Whatever do you mean?

JOHN. I mean he'd no right to stop me catching that train. I've got the crystal, and I'll catch it yet!

MARY. O, John, that's what you said you wouldn't do.

JOHN. No. I said I'd do nothing to alter the past. And I won't. I'm too content, Mary. But this can't alter it. This is nothing.

MARY. What were you going to catch the train for, John?

JOHN. For London. I wasn't at the office then. It was a business appointment. There was a man who had promised to get me a job, and I was going up to . . .

MARY. John, it may alter your whole life!

JOHN. Now do listen, Mary, do listen. He never turned up. I got a letter from him apologising to me before I posted mine to him. It turned out he never meant to help me, mere meaningless affabilities. He never came to London that day at all. I should have taken the next train back. That can't affect the future.

MARY. N-no, John. Still, I don't like it.

JOHN. What difference could it make?

MARY. N-n-no.

JOHN. Think how we met. We met at Archie's wedding. I take it one has to go to one's brother's wedding. It would take a pretty big change to alter that. And you were her bridesmaid. We were bound to meet. And having once met, well, there you are. If we'd met by chance, in a train, or anything like that, well, then I admit some little change might alter it. But when we met at Archie's wedding and you were her bridesmaid, why, Mary, it's a cert. Besides, I believe in predestination. It was our fate; we couldn't have missed it.

MARY. No, I suppose not; still . . .

JOHN. Well, what?

MARY. I don't like it.

JOHN. O, Mary, I have so longed to catch that infernal train. Just think of it, annoyed on and off for ten years by the eight-fifteen.

MARY. I'd rather you didn't, John.

JOHN. But why?

MARY. O, John, suppose there's a railway accident? You might be killed, and we should never meet.

JOHN. There wasn't.

MARY. There wasn't, John? What do you mean?

JOHN. There wasn't an accident to the eight-fifteen. It got safely to London just ten years ago.

MARY. Why, nor there was.

JOHN. You see how groundless your fears are. I shall catch that train, and all the rest will happen the same as before. Just think, Mary, all those old days again. I wish I could take you with me. But you soon will be. But just think of the old days coming back again. Hampton Court again and Kew, and Richmond Park again with all the May. And that bun you bought, and the corked ginger-beer, and those birds singing and the 'bus past Isleworth. O, Mary, you wouldn't grudge me that?

MARY. Well, well then all right, John.

JOHN. And you will remember there wasn't an accident, won't you?

MARY (resignedly, sadly). O, yes, John. And you won't try to get rich or do anything silly, will you?

JOHN. No, Mary. I only want to catch that train. I'm content with the rest. The same things must happen, and they must lead me the same way, to you, Mary. Good night, now, dear.

MARY. Good night?

JOHN. I shall stay here on the sofa holding the crystal and thinking. Then I'll have a biscuit and start at seven.

MARY. Thinking, John? What about?

JOHN. Getting it clear in my mind what I want to do. That one thing and the rest the same. There must be no mistakes.

MARY (sadly). Good night, John.

JOHN. Have supper ready at eleven.

MARY. Very well, John. (Exit.)

JOHN (on the sofa, after a moment or two). I'll catch that infernal train in spite of him. (He takes the crystal and closes it up in the palm of his left hand.) I wish to go back ten years, two weeks and a day, at, at—8.10 a.m. to-morrow; 8.10 a.m. to-morrow, 8.10.

[Re-enter MARY in doorway.]

MARY. John! John! You are sure he *did* get his fifty pounds?

JOHN. Yes. Didn't he come to thank me for the money?

MARY. You are sure it wasn't ten shillings?

JOHN. Well, Cater paid him, I didn't.

MARY. Are you sure that Cater didn't give him ten shillings?

JOHN. It's the sort of silly thing Cater 10 *would* have done!

MARY. O, John!

JOHN. Hmm.

CURTAIN

SCENE 3

Scene: As in Act I, Scene 1.
Time. Ten years ago. 20

BERT. 'Ow goes it, Bill?

BILL. Goes it? 'Ow d'yer think it goes?

BERT. I don't know, Bill. 'Ow is it?

BILL. Bloody.

BERT. Why, what's wrong?

BILL. Wrong? Nothing ain't wrong.

BERT. What's up, then?

BILL. Nothing ain't right.

BERT. Why, wot's the worry?

BILL. Wot's the worry? They don't give you better wages nor a dog, and then they thinks they can talk at yer and talk at yer, and say wot they likes, like.

BERT. Why? You been on the carpet, Bill?

BILL. Ain't I! Proper.

BERT. Why? Wot about, Bill?

BILL. Wot about? I'll tell yer. Just coz I let a lidy get into a train. That's wot about. Said I ought to 'ave stopped 'er. Thought the train was moving. Thought it was dangerous. Thought I tried to murder 'er, I suppose.

BERT. Wot? The other day?

BILL. Yes.

BERT. Tuesday?

BILL. Yes.

BERT. Why? The one that dropped her bag?

BILL. Yes. Drops 'er bag. Writes to the company. They writes back she shouldn't 'ave got in. She writes back she should. Then they gets on to me. Any more of it and I'll . . .

BERT. I wouldn't, Bill; don't you.

BILL. I will.

BERT. Don't you, Bill. You've got your family to consider.

BILL. Well, anyway, I won't let any more of them passengers go jumping into trains any more, not when they're moving, I won't. When the train gets in, doors shut. That's the rule, and they'll have to abide by it.

[*Enter* JOHN BEAL.]

BILL (*touching his hat*). Good morning, sir.

[JOHN *does not answer, but walks to the door between them.*]

Carry your bag, sir?

JOHN. Go to hell! (*Exit through door.*)

30 BILL. Ullo.

BERT. Somebody's been getting at 'im.

BILL. Well, I never did. Why, I knows the young feller.

BERT. Pleasant spoken, ain't 'e, as a rule?

BILL. Never knew 'im like this.

BERT. You ain't bin sayin' nothing to 'im, 'ave yer?

40 BILL. Never in my life.

BERT. Well, I never.

BILL. 'Ad some trouble o' some kind.

BERT. Must 'ave. (*Train is heard.*)

BILL. Ah, 'ere she is. Well, as I was saying . . .

CURTAIN

SCENE 4

In a second-class railway carriage.

Time: Same morning as Act I, Scene 1.

Noise, and a scene drawn past the windows. The scene, showing a momentary glimpse of fair English hills, is almost entirely placards, "GIVE HER BOVRIL," "GIVE HER OXO," alternately, for ever.

Occupants, JOHN BEAL, *a girl, a man.*

All sit in stoical silence like the two images near Luxor. The man has the window seat, and therefore the right of control over the window.

MIRALDA CLEMENT. *Would* you mind having the window open?

THE MAN IN THE CORNER (*shrugging his shoulders in a shivery way*). Er—certainly. (*Meaning he does not mind. He opens the window.*)

MIRALDA CLEMENT. Thank you so much.

MAN IN THE CORNER. Not at all. (*He does not mean to contradict her. Stoical silence again.*)

MIRALDA CLEMENT. Would you mind having it shut now? I think it is rather cold.

MAN IN THE CORNER. Certainly. (*He shuts it. Silence again.*)

MIRALDA CLEMENT. I think I'd like the window open again now for a bit. It is rather stuffy, isn't it?

MAN IN THE CORNER. Well, I think it's very cold.

MIRALDA CLEMENT. O, do you? But would you mind opening it for me?

MAN IN THE CORNER. I'd much rather it was shut, if you don't mind.

[*She sighs, moves her hands slightly, and her pretty face expresses the resignation of the Christian martyr in the presence of lions. This for the benefit of John.*]

JOHN. Allow me, madam.

[*He leans across the window's rightful owner, a bigger man than he, and opens his window.* MAN IN THE CORNER *shrugs his shoulders and, quite sensibly, turns to his paper.*]

MIRALDA. O, thank you *so* much.

JOHN. Don't mention it. (*Silence again.*)

VOICES OF PORTERS (*off*). Fan Kar, Fan Kar.

[MAN IN THE CORNER *gets out.*]

MIRALDA. Could you tell me where this is?

JOHN. Yes, Elephant and Castle.

MIRALDA. Thank you so much. It *was* kind of you to protect me from that horrid man. He wanted to suffocate me.

JOHN. O, very glad to assist you, I'm sure. Very glad.

MIRALDA. I should have been afraid to have done it in spite of him. It was splendid of you.

JOHN. O, that was nothing.

MIRALDA. O, it was, really.

JOHN. Only too glad to help you in any little way.

MIRALDA. It *was* so kind of you.

JOHN. O, not at all. (*Silence for a bit.*)

MIRALDA. I've nobody to help me.

JOHN. Er, er, haven't you really?

MIRALDA. No, nobody.

JOHN. I'd be very glad to help you in any little way.

MIRALDA. I wonder if you could advise me.

JOHN. I—I'd do my best.

MIRALDA. You see, I have nobody to advise me.

JOHN. No, of course not.

MIRALDA. I live with my aunt, and she doesn't understand. I've no father or mother.

JOHN. O, er, er, really?

MIRALDA. No. And an uncle died and he left me a hundred thousand pounds.

JOHN. Really?

MIRALDA. Yes. He didn't like me. I think he did it out of contrariness as much as anything. He was always like that to me.

JOHN. Was he? Was he really?

MIRALDA. Yes. It was invested at twenty-five per cent. He never liked me. Thought I was too—I don't know what.

JOHN. No.

MIRALDA. That was five years ago, and I've never got a penny of it.

JOHN. Really. But, but that's not right.

MIRALDA (*sadly*). No.

JOHN. Where's it invested?

MIRALDA. In Al Shaldomir.

JOHN. Where's that?

MIRALDA. I don't quite know. I never was good at geography. I never quite knew where Persia ends.

JOHN. And what kind of an investment was it?

MIRALDA. There's a pass in some mountains that they can get camels over, and a huge toll is levied on everything that goes by; that is the custom of the tribe that lives there, and I believe the toll is regularly collected.

JOHN. And who gets it?

MIRALDA. The chief of the tribe. He is called Ben Hussein. But my uncle lent him all this money, and the toll on the camels was what they call the security. They always carry gold and turquoise, you know.

JOHN. Do they?

MIRALDA. Yes, they get it from the rivers.

JOHN. I see.

MIRALDA. It does seem a shame his not paying, doesn't it?

JOHN. A shame? I should think it is. An awful shame. Why, it's a crying shame. He ought to go to prison.

MIRALDA. Yes, he ought. But you see it's so hard to find him. It isn't as if it was this side of Persia. It's being on the other side that is such a pity. If only it was in a country like, like . . .

JOHN. I'd soon find him. I'd . . . Why, a man like that deserves anything.

MIRALDA. It is good of you to say that.

JOHN. Why, I'd . . . And you say you never got a penny?

MIRALDA. No.

JOHN. Well, that is a shame. I call that a downright shame.

MIRALDA. Now, what ought I to do?

JOHN. Do? Well, now, you know in business there's nothing like being on the spot. When you're on the spot you can—but then, of course, it's so far.

MIRALDA. It is, isn't it?

JOHN. Still, I think you should go if you could. If only I could offer to help you in any way, I would gladly, but of course . . .

MIRALDA. What would you do?

JOHN. I'd go and find that Hussein fellow; and then . . .

MIRALDA. Yes?

JOHN. Why, I'd tell him a bit about the law, and make him see that you didn't keep all that money that belonged to someone else.

MIRALDA. Would you really?

JOHN. Nothing would please me better.

MIRALDA. Would you really? Would you go all that way?

JOHN. It's just the sort of thing that I should like, apart from the crying shame. The man ought to be . . .

MIRALDA. We're getting into Holborn. Would you come and lunch somewhere with me and talk it over?

JOHN. Gladly. I'd be glad to help. I've got to see a man on business first. I've come up to see him. And then after that, after that, there was something I wanted to do after that. I can't think what it was. But something I wanted to do after that. O, heavens, what was it? (*Pause.*)

MIRALDA. Can't you think?

JOHN. No. O, well, it can't have been so

very important. And yet . . . Well,
where shall we lunch?

MIRALDA. Gratzenheim's.

JOHN. Right. What time?

MIRALDA. One-thirty. Would that suit?

JOHN. Perfectly. I'd like to get a man like

Hussein in prison. I'd like . . . O, I
beg your pardon. (*He hurries to open
the door. Exit* MIRALDA.) Now what was
it I wanted to do afterwards? (*Throws
hand to forehead.*) O, never mind.

CURTAIN

ACT II

JOHN'S *tent in Al Shaldomir. There are
two heaps of idols, left and right, lying upon
the ground inside the tent.* DAOUD *carries another idol in his arms.* JOHN *looks at its face.*
*Six months have elapsed since the scene in
the second-class railway carriage.*

JOHN BEAL. This god is holy. (*He points to
the left heap.* DAOUD *carries it there and
lays it on the heap.*)

DAOUD. Yes, great master.

JOHN BEAL. You are in no wise to call me
great master. Have not I said so? I am
not your master. I am helping you
people. I know better than you what
you ought to do, because I am English. But that's all. I'm not your master. See?

DAOUD. Yes, great master.

JOHN BEAL. O, go and get some more
idols. Hurry.

DAOUD. Great master, I go. (*Exit.*)

JOHN BEAL. I can't make these people out.

DAOUD (*returning*). I have three gods.

JOHN BEAL (*looking at their faces, pointing
to the two smaller idols first*). These two
are holy. This one is unholy.

DAOUD. Yes, great master.

JOHN BEAL. Put them on the heap.
(DAOUD *does so, two left, one right.*) Get
some more.

[DAOUD *salaams. Exit.*]

JOHN BEAL (*looking at right heap*). What a
—what a filthy people.

[*Enter* DAOUD *with two idols.*]

JOHN BEAL (*after scrutiny*). This god is
holy, this is unholy.

[*Enter* ARCHIE BEAL, *wearing a "Bowler"
hat.*]

JOHN BEAL. Why, Archie, this is splendid
of you! You've come! Why, that's
splendid! All that way!

ARCHIE BEAL. Yes, I've come. Whatever
are you doing?

JOHN BEAL. Archie, it's grand of you to
come! I never ought to have asked it
of you, only . . .

ARCHIE BEAL. O, that's all right. But
what in the world are you doing?

JOHN BEAL. Archie, it's splendid of you.

ARCHIE BEAL. O, cut it. That's all right.
But what's all this?

JOHN BEAL. O, this. Well, well they're
the very oddest people here. It's a
long story. But I wanted to tell you
first how enormously grateful I am to
you for coming.

ARCHIE BEAL. O, that's all right. But I
want to know what you're doing with
all these genuine antiques.

JOHN BEAL. Well, Archie, the fact of it is
they're a real odd lot of people here.
I've learnt their language, more or
less, but I don't think I quite understand them yet. A lot of them are Ma-
hommedans; they worship Mahom-
med, you know. He's dead. But a lot
of them worship these things, and . . .

ARCHIE BEAL. Well, what have you got
'em all in here for?

JOHN BEAL. Yes, that's just it. I hate interfering with them, but, well, I simply had to. You see there's two sorts of
idols here; they offer fruit and rats to

some of them; they lay them on their hands or their laps.

ARCHIE BEAL. Why do they offer them rats?

JOHN BEAL. O, I don't know. They don't know either. It's the right thing to do out here, it's been the right thing for hundreds of years; nobody exactly knows why. It's like the bows we have on evening shoes, or anything else. But it's all right.

ARCHIE BEAL. Well, what are you putting them in heaps for?

JOHN BEAL. Because there's the other kind, the ones with wide mouths and rust round them.

ARCHIE BEAL. Rust? Yes, so there is. What do they do?

JOHN BEAL. They offer blood to them, Archie. They pour it down their throats. Sometimes they kill people, sometimes they only bleed them. It depends how much blood the idol wants.

ARCHIE BEAL. How much blood it wants? Good Lord! How do they know?

JOHN BEAL. The priests tell them. Sometimes they fill them up to their necks —they're all hollow, you know. In spring it's awful.

ARCHIE BEAL. Why are they worse in spring?

JOHN BEAL. I don't know. The priests ask for more blood then. Much more. They say it always was so.

ARCHIE BEAL. And you're stopping it?

JOHN BEAL. Yes, I'm stopping these. One must. I'm letting them worship those. Of course, it's idolatry and all that kind of thing, but I don't like interfering short of actual murder.

ARCHIE BEAL. And they're obeying you?

JOHN BEAL. 'M, y-yes. I think so.

ARCHIE BEAL. You must have got a great hold over them.

JOHN BEAL. Well, I don't know about that. It's the pass that counts.

ARCHIE BEAL. The pass?

JOHN BEAL. Yes, that place you came over. It's the only way anyone can get here.

ARCHIE BEAL. Yes, I suppose it is. But how does the pass affect these idols?

JOHN BEAL. It affects everything here. If that pass were closed no living man would enter ever or leave, or even hear of, this country. It's absolutely cut off except for that one pass. Why, Archie, it isn't even on the map.

ARCHIE BEAL. Yes, I know.

JOHN BEAL. Well, whoever owns that pass is everybody. No one else counts.

ARCHIE BEAL. And who does own it?

JOHN BEAL. Well, it's actually owned by a fellow called Hussein, but Miss Clement's uncle, a man called Hinnard, a kind of lonely explorer, seems to have come this way; and I think he understood what this pass is worth. Anyhow, he lent Hussein a big sum of money and got an acknowledgment from Hussein. Old Hinnard must have been a wonderfully shrewd man. For that acknowledgment is no more legal than an I.O.U., and Hussein is simply a brigand.

ARCHIE BEAL. Not very good security.

JOHN BEAL. Well, you're wrong there. Hussein himself respects that piece of parchment he signed. There's the name of some god or other written on it that Hussein is frightened of. Now you see how things are. That pass is as holy as all the gods that there are in Al Shaldomir. Hussein possesses it. But he owes an enormous sum to Miss Miralda Clement, and I am here as her agent; and you've come to help me like a great sportsman.

ARCHIE BEAL. O, never mind that. Well, it all seems pretty simple.

JOHN BEAL. Well, I don't know, Archie. Hussein admits the debt, but . . .

ARCHIE BEAL. But what?

JOHN BEAL. I don't know what he'll do.

ARCHIE BEAL. Wants watching, does he?

JOHN BEAL. Yes. And meanwhile I feel sort of responsible for all these silly people. Somebody's got to look after them. Daoud!

DAOUD (off). Great master.   10

JOHN BEAL. Bring in some more gods.

DAOUD. Yes, great master.

JOHN BEAL. I can't get them to stop calling me absurd titles. They're so infernally Oriental.

[Enter DAOUD.]

ARCHIE BEAL. He's got two big ones this time.

JOHN BEAL (to ARCHIE). You see, there is rust about their mouths. (To DAOUD.) 20 They are both unholy. (He points to R. heap, and DAOUD puts them there. To DAOUD.) Bring in some more.

DAOUD. Great master, there are no more gods in Al Shaldomir.

JOHN BEAL. It is well.

DAOUD. What orders, great master.

JOHN BEAL. Listen. At night you shall come and take these gods away. These shall be worshipped again in their 30 own place, these you shall cast into the great river and tell no man where you cast them.

DAOUD. Yes, great master.

JOHN BEAL. You will do this, Daoud?

DAOUD. Even so, great master.

JOHN BEAL. I am sorry to make you do it. You are sad that you have to do it. Yet it must be done.

DAOUD. Yes, I am sad, great master.   40

JOHN BEAL. But why are you sad, Daoud?

DAOUD. Great master, in times you do not know these gods were holy. In times you have not guessed. In old centuries, master, perhaps before the pass. Men have prayed to them, sorrowed before them, given offerings to them. The light of old hearths has shone on them, flames from old battles. The shadow of the mountains has fallen on them, so many times, master, so many times. Dawn and sunset have shone on them, master, like firelight flickering; dawn and sunset, dawn and sunset, flicker, flicker, flicker for century after century. They have sat there watching the dawns like old men by the fire. They are so old, master, so old. And some day dawn and sunset will die away and shine on the world no more, and they would have still sat on in the cold. And now they go. . . . They are our history, master, they are our old times. Though they be bad times they are *our* times, master; and now they go. I am sad, master, when the old gods go.

JOHN BEAL. But they are bad gods, Daoud.

DAOUD. I am sad when the bad gods go.

JOHN BEAL. They must go, Daoud. See, there is no one watching. Take them now.

DAOUD. Even so, great master. (He takes up the largest of the gods with rust.) Come, Aho-oomlah, thou shalt not drink Nideesh.

JOHN BEAL. Was Nideesh to have been sacrificed?

DAOUD. He was to have been drunk by Aho-oomlah.

JOHN BEAL. Nideesh. Who is he?

DAOUD. He is my son. (Exit with Aho-oomlah.)

[JOHN BEAL almost gasps.]

ARCHIE BEAL (who has been looking round the tent). What has he been saying?

JOHN BEAL. They're—they're a strange people. I can't make them out.

ARCHIE BEAL. Is that the heap that oughtn't to be worshipped?

JOHN BEAL. Yes.

ARCHIE BEAL. Well, do you know, I'm going to chuck this hat there. It doesn't seem to me somehow to be any more right here than those idols would be at home. Odd isn't it? Here goes. (*He throws hat on right heap of idols.* JOHN BEAL *does not smile.*) Why, 10 what's the matter?

JOHN BEAL. I don't like to see a decent Christian hat among these filthy idols. They've all got rust on their mouths. I don't like to see it, Archie; it's sort of like what they call an omen. I don't like it.

ARCHIE BEAL. Do they keep malaria here?

JOHN BEAL. I don't think so. Why? 20

ARCHIE BEAL. Then what's the matter, Johnny? Your nerves are bad.

JOHN BEAL. You don't know these people, and I've brought you out here. I feel kind of responsible. If Hussein's lot turn nasty you don't know what he'd do, with all those idols and all.

ARCHIE BEAL. He'll give 'em a drink, you mean.

JOHN BEAL. Don't, Archie. There's no 30 saying. And I feel responsible for you.

ARCHIE BEAL. Well, they can have my hat. It looks silly, somehow. I don't know why. What are we going to do?

JOHN BEAL. Well, now that you've come we can go ahead.

ARCHIE BEAL. Righto. What at?

JOHN BEAL. We've got to see Hussein's accounts, and get everything clear in black and white, and see just what he 40 owes to Miss Miralda Clement.

ARCHIE BEAL. But they don't keep accounts here.

JOHN BEAL. How do you know?

ARCHIE BEAL. Why, of course they don't. One can see that.

JOHN BEAL. But they must.

ARCHIE BEAL. Well, you haven't changed a bit for your six months here.

JOHN BEAL. Haven't changed?

ARCHIE BEAL. No. Just quietly thinking of business. You'll be a great business man, Johnny.

JOHN BEAL. But we must do business; that's what I came here for.

ARCHIE BEAL. You'll never make these people do it.

JOHN BEAL. Well, what do you suggest?

ARCHIE BEAL. Let's have a look at old Hussein.

JOHN BEAL. Yes, that's what I have been waiting for. Daoud!

DAOUD (*off*). Master. (*Enters.*)

JOHN BEAL. Go to the palace of the Lord of the Pass and beat on the outer door. Say that I desire to see him. Pray him to come to my tent.

[DAOUD *bows and exit.*]

JOHN BEAL (*to* ARCHIE). I've sent him to the palace to ask Hussein to come.

ARCHIE BEAL. Lives in a palace, does he?

JOHN BEAL. Yes, it's a palace, it's a wonderful place. It's bigger than the Mansion House, much.

ARCHIE BEAL. And you're going to teach him to keep accounts.

JOHN BEAL. Well, I must. I hate doing it. It seems almost like being rude to the Lord Mayor. But there's two things I can't stand—cheating in business is one and murder's another. I've got to interfere. You see, if one happens to know the right from wrong as we do, we've simply got to tell people who don't. But it isn't pleasant. I almost wish I'd never come.

ARCHIE BEAL. Why, it's the greatest sport in the world. It's splendid.

JOHN BEAL. I don't see it that way. To me those idols are just horrid murder. And this man owes money to this girl with no one to look after her, and he's got to pay. But I hate being rude to a man in a place like the Mansion House, even if he is black. Why, good Lord, who am I? It seems such cheek.

ARCHIE BEAL. I say, Johnny, tell me about the lady. Is she pretty?

JOHN BEAL. What, Miss Miralda? Yes.

ARCHIE BEAL. But what I mean is— what's she like?

JOHN BEAL. Oh, I don't know. It's very hard to say. She's, she's tall and she's fair and she's got blue eyes.

ARCHIE BEAL. Yes, but I mean what kind of a person is she? How does she strike you?

JOHN BEAL. Well, she's pretty hard up until she gets this money, and she hasn't got any job that's any good, and no real prospects bar this, and nobody particular by birth, and doesn't know anybody who is, and lives in the least fashionable suburb and can only just afford a second-class fare and . . .

ARCHIE BEAL. Yes, yes, go on.

JOHN BEAL. And yet somehow she sort of seems like a—like a queen.

ARCHIE BEAL. Lord above us! And what kind of a queen?

JOHN BEAL. O, I don't know. Well, look here, Archie, it's only my impression. I don't know her well yet. It's only my impression. I only tell you in absolute confidence. You won't pass it on to anybody, of course.

ARCHIE BEAL. O, no. Go on.

JOHN BEAL. Well, I don't know, only she seemed more like—well, a kind of autocrat, you know, who'd stop at nothing. Well, no, I don't mean that, only . . .

ARCHIE BEAL. So you're not going to marry her?

JOHN BEAL. Marry her! Good Lord, no.

Why, you'd never dare ask her. She's not that sort. I tell you she's a sort of queen. And (good Lord!) she'd *be* a queen if it wasn't for Hussein, or something very like one. We can't go marrying queens. Anyhow, not one like her.

ARCHIE BEAL. Why not one like her?

JOHN BEAL. I tell you—she's a—well, a kind of goddess. You couldn't ask her if she loved you. It would be such, such . . .

ARCHIE BEAL. Such what?

JOHN BEAL. Such infernal cheek.

ARCHIE BEAL. I see. Well, I see you aren't in love with her. But it seems to me you'll be seeing a good deal of her some day if we pull this off. And then, my boy-o, you'll be going and getting in love with her.

JOHN BEAL. I tell you I daren't. I'd as soon propose to the Queen of Sheba.

ARCHIE BEAL. Well, Johnny, I'm going to protect you from her all I can.

JOHN BEAL. Protect me from her? Why?

ARCHIE BEAL. Why, because there's lots of other girls, and it seems to me you might be happier with some of them.

JOHN BEAL. But you haven't even seen her.

ARCHIE BEAL. Nor I have. Still, if I'm here to protect you I somehow think I will. And if I'm not . . .

JOHN BEAL. Well, and what then?

ARCHIE BEAL. What nonsense I'm talking. Fate does everything. I can't protect you.

JOHN BEAL. Yes, it's nonsense all right, Archie, but . . .

HUSSEIN (*off*). I am here.

JOHN BEAL. Be seen.

[HUSSEIN *enters. He is not unlike Bluebeard.*]

JOHN BEAL (*pointing to* ARCHIE). My brother.

[ARCHIE *shakes hands with* HUSSEIN. HUS- SEIN *looks at his hand when it is over in a puzzled way.* JOHN BEAL *and* HUSSEIN *then bow to each other.*]

HUSSEIN. You desired my presence.

JOHN BEAL. I am honoured.

HUSSEIN. And I.

JOHN BEAL. The white traveller, whom we call Hinnard, lent you one thousand greater gold pieces, which in our money is one hundred thousand pounds, as you acknowledge. (HUS-SEIN *nods his head.*) And every year you were to pay him for this two hundred and fifty of your greater gold pieces—as you acknowledge also.

HUSSEIN. Even so.

JOHN BEAL. And this you have not yet had chance to pay, but owe it still.

HUSSEIN. I do.

JOHN BEAL. And now Hinnard is dead.

HUSSEIN. Peace be with him.

JOHN BEAL. His heiress is Miss Miralda Clement, who instructs me to be her agent. What have you to say?

HUSSEIN. Peace be with Hinnard.

JOHN BEAL. You acknowledge your debt to this lady, Miss Miralda Clement?

HUSSEIN. I know her not.

JOHN BEAL. You will not pay your debt?

HUSSEIN. I will pay.

JOHN BEAL. If you bring the gold to my tent, my brother will take it to Miss Clement.

HUSSEIN. I do not pay to Miss Clement.

JOHN BEAL. To whom do you pay?

HUSSEIN. I pay to Hinnard.

JOHN BEAL. Hinnard is dead.

HUSSEIN. I pay to Hinnard.

JOHN BEAL. How will you pay to Hinnard?

HUSSEIN. If he be buried in the sea . . .

JOHN BEAL. He is not buried at sea.

HUSSEIN. If he be buried by any river I go to the god of rivers.

JOHN BEAL. He is buried on land near no river.

HUSSEIN. Therefore I will go to a bronze god of earth, very holy, having the soil in his care, and the things of earth. I will take unto him the greater pieces of gold due up to the year when the white traveller died, and will melt them in fire at his feet by night on the mountains, saying, "O, Lruru-onn (this is his name) take this by the way of earth to the grave of Hinnard." And so I shall be free of my debt before all gods.

JOHN BEAL. But not before me. I am English. And we are greater than gods.

ARCHIE BEAL. What's that, Johnny?

JOHN BEAL. He won't pay, but I told him we're English and that they're greater than all his bronze gods.

ARCHIE BEAL. That's right, Johnny.

[HUSSEIN *looks fiercely at* ARCHIE. *He sees* ARCHIE'S *hat lying before a big idol. He points at the hat and looks in the face of the idol.*]

HUSSEIN (*to the idol*). Drink! Drink! (*He bows. Exit.*)

ARCHIE BEAL. What's that he's saying?

JOHN BEAL (*meditatively*). O, nothing—nothing.

ARCHIE BEAL. He won't pay, eh?

JOHN BEAL. No, not to Miss Miralda.

ARCHIE BEAL. Who to?

JOHN BEAL. To one of his gods.

ARCHIE BEAL. That won't do.

JOHN BEAL. No.

ARCHIE BEAL. What'll we do?

JOHN BEAL. I don't quite know. It isn't as if we were in England.

ARCHIE BEAL. No, it isn't.

JOHN BEAL. If we were in England . . .

ARCHIE BEAL. I know; if we were in England you could call a policeman. I tell you what it is, Johnny.

JOHN BEAL. Yes?

ARCHIE BEAL. I tell you what; you want to see more of Miss Clement.

JOHN BEAL. Why?

ARCHIE BEAL. Why, because at the present moment our friend Hussein is a craftier fellow than you, and looks like getting the best of it.

JOHN BEAL. How will seeing more of Miss Miralda help us?

ARCHIE BEAL. Why, because you want to be a bit craftier than Hussein, and I fancy she might make you.

JOHN BEAL. She? How?

ARCHIE BEAL. We're mostly made what we are by some woman or other. We think it's our own cleverness, but we're wrong. As things are you're no match for Hussein, but if you altered . . .

JOHN BEAL. Why, Archie; where did you get all those ideas from?

ARCHIE BEAL. O, I don't know.

JOHN BEAL. You never used to talk like that.

ARCHIE BEAL. O, well.

JOHN BEAL. You haven't been getting in love, Archie, have you?

ARCHIE BEAL. What are we to do about Hussein?

JOHN BEAL. It's funny your mentioning Miss Miralda. I got a letter from her the same day I got yours.

ARCHIE BEAL. What does she say?

JOHN BEAL. I couldn't make it out.

ARCHIE BEAL. What were her words?

JOHN BEAL. She said she was going into it closer. She underlined closer. What could she mean by that? How could she get closer?

ARCHIE BEAL. Well, the same way as I did.

JOHN BEAL. How do you mean? I don't understand.

ARCHIE BEAL. By coming here.

JOHN BEAL. By coming here? But she can't come here.

ARCHIE BEAL. Why not?

JOHN BEAL. Because it's impossible. Absolutely impossible. Why—good Lord —she couldn't come here. Why, she'd want a chaperon and a house and—and—everything. Good Lord, she couldn't come here. It would be—well, it would be impossible—it couldn't be done.

ARCHIE BEAL. O, all right. Then I don't know what she meant.

JOHN BEAL. Archie! You don't really think she'd come here? You don't really think it, do you?

ARCHIE BEAL. Well, it's the sort of thing that that sort of girl might do, but of course I can't say . . .

JOHN BEAL. Good Lord, Archie! That would be awful.

ARCHIE BEAL. But why?

JOHN BEAL. Why? But what would I do? Where would she go? Where would her chaperon go? The chaperon would be some elderly lady. Why, it would kill her.

ARCHIE BEAL. Well, if it did you've never met her, so you needn't go into mourning for an elderly lady that you don't know; not *yet*, anyway.

JOHN BEAL. No, of course not. You're laughing at me, Archie. But for the moment I took you seriously. Of course, she won't come. One can go into a thing closely without doing it absolutely literally. But, good Lord, wouldn't it be an awful situation if she did.

ARCHIE BEAL. O, I don't know.

JOHN BEAL. All alone with me here? No, impossible. And the country isn't civilised.

ARCHIE BEAL. Women aren't civilised.

JOHN BEAL. Women aren't . . . ? Good Lord, Archie, what an awful remark. What *do* you mean?

ARCHIE BEAL. We're tame, they're wild. We like all the dull things and the quiet things, they like all the romantic things and the dangerous things.

JOHN BEAL. Why, Archie, it's just the other way about.

ARCHIE BEAL. O, yes; we *do* all the romantic things, and all the dangerous things. But why?

JOHN BEAL. Why? Because we like them, I suppose. I can't think of any other reason.

ARCHIE BEAL. I hate danger. Don't you?

JOHN BEAL. Er—well, yes, I suppose I do, really.

ARCHIE BEAL. Of course you do. We all do. It's the women that put us up to it. She's putting you up to this. And the more she puts you up to the more likely is Hussein to get it in his fat neck.

JOHN BEAL. But—but you don't mean you'd hurt Hussein? Not—not badly, I mean.

ARCHIE BEAL. We're under her orders, Johnny. See what she says.

JOHN BEAL. You, you don't really think she'll come here?

ARCHIE BEAL. Of course I do, and the best thing too. It's her show; she ought to come.

JOHN BEAL. But, but you don't understand. She's just a young girl. A girl like Miss Miralda couldn't come out here over the pass and down these mountains, she'd never stand it, and as for the chaperon . . . You've never met Miss Miralda.

ARCHIE BEAL. No, Johnny. But the girl that was able to get you to go from Bromley to this place can look after herself.

JOHN BEAL. I don't see what that's got to do with it. She was in trouble and I had to help her.

ARCHIE BEAL. Yes, and she'll be in trouble all the way here from Blackheath, and everyone will have to help her.

JOHN BEAL. What beats me is how you can have the very faintest inkling of what she's like without ever having seen her and without my having spoken of her to you for more than a minute.

ARCHIE BEAL. Well, Johnny, you're not a romantic bird, you're not a traveller by nature, barring your one trip to Eastbourne, and it was I that took you there. And contrariwise, as they say in a book you've never read, you're a level-headed business man and a hardworking respectable stay-at-home. You meet a girl in a train, and the next time I see you you're in a place that isn't marked on the map and telling it what gods it ought to worship and what gods it ought to have agnosticism about. Well, I say *some girl*.

JOHN BEAL. Well, I must say you make the most extraordinary deductions, but it was awfully good of you to come, and I ought to be grateful; and I am, too, I'm awfully grateful; and I ought to let you talk all the rot you like. Go ahead. You shall say what you like and do what you like. It isn't many brothers that would do what you've done.

ARCHIE BEAL. O, that's nothing. I like this country. I'm glad I came. And if I can help you with Hussein, why all the better.

JOHN BEAL. It's an awful country, Archie, but we've got to see this through.

ARCHIE BEAL. Does she know all about Hussein?

JOHN BEAL. Yes, everything. I've written fully.

OMAR (*off*). Al Shaldomir, Al Shaldomir, The nightingales that guard thy ways . . .

JOHN BEAL (*shouting*). O, go away, go away. (*To* ARCHIE.) I said it was an awful country. They sit down outside one's tent and do that kind of thing for no earthly reason.

ARCHIE BEAL. O, I'd let them sing.

JOHN BEAL. O, you can't have people doing that kind of thing.

OMAR (*in doorway*). Master, I go.

JOHN BEAL. But why do you come?

OMAR. I came to sing a joyous song to you, master.

JOHN BEAL. Why did you want to sing me a joyous song?

OMAR. Because a lady is riding out of the West. (*Exit.*)

JOHN BEAL. A lady out of . . . Good Lord!

ARCHIE BEAL. She's coming, Johnny.

JOHN BEAL. Coming? Good Lord, no, Archie. He said a lady; there'd be the chaperon too. There'd be two of them if it was Miss Miralda. But he said a lady. One lady. It can't be her. A girl like that alone in Al Shaldomir. Clean off the map. O, no, it isn't possible.

ARCHIE BEAL. I wouldn't worry.

JOHN BEAL. Wouldn't worry? But, good Lord, the situation's impossible. People would talk. Don't you see what people would say? And where could they go? Who would look after them? Do try and understand how awful it is. But it isn't. It's impossible. It can't be them. For heaven's sake run out and see if it is; and (good Lord!) I haven't brushed my hair all day, and, and—oh, look at me.

[*He rushes to camp mirror. Exit* ARCHIE. JOHN BEAL *tidies up desperately. Enter* ARCHIE.]

ARCHIE BEAL. It's what you call *them*.

JOHN BEAL. What I call *them?* Whatever do you mean?

ARCHIE BEAL. Well, it's her. She's just like what you said.

JOHN BEAL. But it can't be. She doesn't ride. She can never have been able to afford a horse.

ARCHIE BEAL. She's on a camel. She'll be here in a moment. (*He goes to door.*) Hurry up with that hair; she's dismounted.

JOHN BEAL. O, Lord! What's the chaperon like?

ARCHIE BEAL. O, she's attending to that herself.

JOHN BEAL. Attending to it herself? What do you mean?

ARCHIE BEAL. I expect she'll attend to most things.

[*Enter* HAFIZ EL ALCOLAHN *in doorway of tent, pulling back flap a little.*]

JOHN BEAL. Who are you?

HAFIZ. I show the gracious lady to your tent.

[*Enter* MIRALDA CLEMENT, *throwing a smile to* HAFIZ.]

MIRALDA. Hullo, Mr. Beal.

JOHN BEAL. Er—er—how do you do? (*She looks at* ARCHIE.) O, this is my brother—Miss Clement.

MIRALDA *and* ARCHIE BEAL. How do you do?

MIRALDA. I like this country.

JOHN BEAL. I'm afraid I hardly expected you.

MIRALDA. Didn't you?

JOHN BEAL. No. You see—er—it's such a long way. And wasn't it very expensive?

MIRALDA. Well, the captain of the ship was very kind to me.

JOHN BEAL. O! But what did you do when you landed?

MIRALDA. O, there were some Arabs coming this way in a caravan. They were really very good to me too.

JOHN BEAL. But the camel?

MIRALDA. O, there were some people the other side of the mountains. Everybody has been very kind about it. And then there was the man who showed me here. He's called Hafiz el Alcolahn. It's a nice name, don't you think?

JOHN BEAL. But, you know, this country, Miss Clement, I'm half afraid it's hardly—isn't it, Archie? Er—how long did you think of staying?

MIRALDA. O, a week or so.

JOHN BEAL. I don't know what you'll think of Al Shaldomir. I'm afraid you'll find it . . .

MIRALDA. O, I like it. Just that hollow in the mountains, and the one pass, 10 and no record of it anywhere. I like that. I think it's lovely.

JOHN BEAL. You see, I'm afraid—what I mean is I'm afraid the place isn't even on the map!

MIRALDA. O, that's lovely of it.

JOHN BEAL. All decent places are.

MIRALDA. You mean if a place is on the map we've got to behave accordingly. But if not, why . . . 20

JOHN BEAL. Hussein won't pay.

MIRALDA. Let's see Hussein.

JOHN BEAL. I'm afraid he's rather, he's rather a savage-looking brigand.

MIRALDA. Never mind.

[ARCHIE *is quietly listening and smiling sometimes. Enter* DAOUD. *He goes up to the unholy heap and takes away two large idols, one under each arm. Exit.*]

MIRALDA. What's that, Mr. Beal? 30

JOHN BEAL. O, that. I'm afraid it's rather horrible. I told you it was an awful country. They pray to these idols here, and some are all right, though of course it's terribly blasphemous, but *that* heap, well, I'm afraid, well *that* heap is very bad indeed.

MIRALDA. What do they do?

JOHN BEAL. They kill people.

MIRALDA. Do they? How? 40

JOHN BEAL. I'm afraid they pour their blood down those horrible throats.

MIRALDA. Do they? How do you know?

JOHN BEAL. I've seen them do it, and those mouths are all rusty. But it's all right now. It won't happen any more.

MIRALDA. Won't it? Why not?

JOHN BEAL. Well, I . . .

ARCHIE BEAL. He's stopped them, Miss Clement. They're all going to be thrown into the river.

MIRALDA. Have you?

JOHN BEAL. Well, yes. I had to. So it's all right now. They won't do it any more.

MIRALDA. H'm.

JOHN BEAL. What, what is it? I promise you that's all right. They won't do that any more.

MIRALDA. H'm. I've never known anyone that tried to govern a country or anything of that sort, but . . .

JOHN BEAL. Of course, I'm just doing what I can to put them right. . . . I'd be very glad of your advice. . . . Of course, I'm only here in your name.

MIRALDA. What I mean is that I'd always thought that the one thing you shouldn't do, if you don't mind my saying so . . .

JOHN BEAL. No, certainly.

MIRALDA. . . . was to interfere in people's religious beliefs.

JOHN BEAL. But, but I don't think you quite understand. The priests knife these people in the throat, boys and girls, and then acolytes lift them up and the blood runs down. I've seen them.

MIRALDA. I think it's best to leave religion to the priests. They understand that kind of thing.

[JOHN BEAL *opens his mouth in horror and looks at* ARCHIE. ARCHIE *returns the glance; there is very nearly a twinkle in* ARCHIE'S *eyes.*]

MIRALDA. Let's see Hussein.

JOHN BEAL. What do you think, Archie?

ARCHIE BEAL. Poor fellow. We'd better send for him.

MIRALDA. Why do you say "poor fellow"?

ARCHIE BEAL. Oh, because he's so much in debt. It's awful to be in debt. I'd sooner almost anything happened to me than to owe a lot of money.

MIRALDA. Your remark didn't sound very complimentary.

ARCHIE BEAL. O, I only meant that I'd hate to be in debt. And I should hate owing money to you, because . . .

MIRALDA. Why?

ARCHIE BEAL. Because I should so awfully want to pay it.

MIRALDA. I see.

ARCHIE BEAL. That's all I meant.

MIRALDA. Does Hussein awfully want to pay it?

ARCHIE BEAL. Well, no. But he hasn't seen you yet. He will then, of course.

[*Enter* DAOUD. *He goes to the unholy heap.*]

JOHN BEAL. Daoud, for the present these gods must stay. Aho-oomlah's gone, but the rest must stay for the present.

DAOUD. Even so, great master.

JOHN BEAL. Daoud, go once more to the palace of the Lord of the Pass and beat the outer door. Say that the great lady herself would see him. The great lady, Miss Clement, the white traveller's heiress.

DAOUD. Yes, master.

JOHN BEAL. Hasten. (*Exit* DAOUD.) I have sent him for Hussein.

MIRALDA. I don't know their language.

JOHN BEAL. You will see him, and I'll tell you what he says.

MIRALDA (*to* ARCHIE). Have you been here long?

ARCHIE BEAL. No. I think he wrote to me by the same mail as he wrote to you (if they have mails here). I came at once.

MIRALDA. So did I; but you weren't on the *Empress of Switzerland.*

ARCHIE BEAL. No, I came round more by land.

JOHN BEAL. You know, I hardly like bringing Hussein in here to see you. He's such a—he's rather a . . .

MIRALDA. What's the matter with him?

JOHN BEAL. Well, he's rather of the brigand type, and one doesn't know what he'll do.

MIRALDA. Well, we must see him first and hear what he has to say before we take any steps.

JOHN BEAL. But what do you propose to do?

MIRALDA. Why, if he pays me everything he owes, or gives up the security . . .

JOHN BEAL. The security is the pass.

MIRALDA. Yes. If he gives up that or pays . . .

JOHN BEAL. You know he's practically king of the whole country. It seems rather cheek almost my sending for him like this.

MIRALDA. He must come.

JOHN BEAL. But what are you going to do?

MIRALDA. If he gives up the pass . . .

JOHN BEAL. Why, if he gives up the pass you'd be—you'd be a kind of queen of it all.

MIRALDA. Well, if he does that, all right. . . .

JOHN BEAL. But what if he doesn't?

MIRALDA. Why, if he doesn't pay . . .

HUSSEIN (*off*). I am here.

JOHN BEAL. Be seen. (*Enter* HUSSEIN.)

HUSSEIN. Greeting once more.

JOHN BEAL. Again greeting. . . . The great lady, Miss Clement, is here. (HUSSEIN *and* MIRALDA *look at each other.*) You will pay to Miss Clement and not to your god of bronze. On the word of an Englishman, your god of bronze shall not have one gold piece that belongs to the great lady!

HUSSEIN (*looking contemptuous*). On the word of the Lord of the Pass, I only pay to Hinnard. (*He stands smiling while* MIRALDA *regards him. Exit.*)

ARCHIE BEAL. Well?

JOHN BEAL. He won't pay.

ARCHIE BEAL. What are we to do now?

JOHN BEAL (*to* MIRALDA). I'm afraid he's rather an ugly customer to introduce you to like that. I'm sorry he came now.

MIRALDA. O, I like him, I think he looks splendid.

ARCHIE BEAL. Well, what are we to do?

JOHN BEAL. Yes.

ARCHIE BEAL. What do you say, Miss Clement?

JOHN BEAL. Yes, what do you feel we ought to do?

MIRALDA. Well, perhaps I ought to leave all that to you.

ARCHIE BEAL. O, no.

JOHN BEAL. No, it's your money. What do you think we really ought to do?

MIRALDA. Well, of course, I think you ought to kill Hussein.

[JOHN BEAL *and* ARCHIE BEAL *look at each other a little startled.*]

JOHN BEAL. But wouldn't that—wouldn't that be—murder?

MIRALDA. O, yes, according to the English law.

JOHN BEAL. I see; you mean—you mean we're not—but we are English.

MIRALDA. I mean it wouldn't be murder —by your law, unless you made it so.

JOHN BEAL. By *my* law?

MIRALDA. Yes, if you can interfere with their religion like this, and none of them say a word, why—you can make any laws you like.

JOHN BEAL. But Hussein is king here; he is Lord of the Pass, and that's everything here. I'm nobody.

MIRALDA. O, if you like to be nobody, of course that's different.

ARCHIE BEAL. I think she means that if Hussein weren't there there'd be only you. Of course, I don't know. I've only just come.

JOHN BEAL. But we can't kill Hussein! (MIRALDA *begins to cry*.) O Lord! Good heavens! Please, Miss Clement! I'm awfully sorry if I've said anything you didn't like. I wouldn't do that for worlds. I'm awfully sorry. It's a beastly country, I know. I'm really sorry you came. I feel it's all my fault. I'm really awfully sorry. . . .

MIRALDA. Never mind. Never mind. I was so helpless, and I asked you to help me. I never ought to have done it. I oughtn't to have spoken to you at all in that train without being introduced; but I was so helpless. And now, and now, I haven't a penny in the world, and, O, I don't know what to do.

ARCHIE BEAL. We'll do anything for you, Miss Clement.

JOHN BEAL. Anything in the wide world. Please, please don't cry. We'll do anything.

MIRALDA. I . . . I only, I only wanted to—to kill Hussein. But never mind, it doesn't matter now.

JOHN BEAL. We'll do it, Miss Clement, won't we, Archie? Only don't cry. We'll do it. I—I suppose he deserves it, doesn't he?

ARCHIE BEAL. Yes, I suppose he does.

JOHN BEAL. Well, all right, Miss Clement, that's settled. My brother and I will talk it over.

MIRALDA (*still sniffling*). And—and—don't hang him or anything—he looks so fine. . . . I—I wouldn't like him treated like that. He has such a grand beard. He ought to die fighting.

JOHN BEAL. We'll see what we can do, Miss Clement.

MIRALDA. It is sweet of you. It's really sweet. It's sweet of both of you. I don't know what I'd have done without you. I seemed to know it that day the moment I saw you.

JOHN BEAL. O, it's nothing, Miss Clement, nothing at all.

ARCHIE BEAL. That's all right.

MIRALDA. Well, now I'll have to look for an hotel.

JOHN BEAL. Yes, that's the trouble, that really is the trouble. That's what I've been thinking of all the time.

MIRALDA. Why; isn't there . . .

JOHN BEAL. No, I'm afraid there isn't. What are we to do, Archie?

ARCHIE BEAL. I—I can't think. Perhaps Miss Clement would have a scheme.

MIRALDA (to JOHN BEAL). I rely on you, Mr. Beal.

JOHN BEAL. I—I; but what can I . . . You see, you're all alone. If you'd anyone with you, you could have . . .

MIRALDA. I did think of bringing a rather nice aunt. But on the whole I thought it better not to tell anyone.

JOHN BEAL. Not to tell . . .

MIRALDA. No, on the whole I didn't.

JOHN BEAL. I say, Archie, what are we to do?

ARCHIE BEAL. Here's Daoud.

　　　　　[Enter DAOUD.]

JOHN BEAL. The one man I trust in Al Shaldomir!

DAOUD. I have brought two watchers of the doorstep to guard the noble lady.

JOHN BEAL. He says he's brought two watchers of the doorstep to look after Miss Clement.

ARCHIE BEAL. Two chaperons! Splendid! She can go anywhere now.

JOHN BEAL. Well, really, that is better. Yes that will be all right. We can find a room for you now. The trouble was your being alone. I hope you'll like them. (To DAOUD.) Tell them to enter here.

DAOUD (beckoning in the doorway). Ho! Enter!

JOHN BEAL. That's all right, Archie, isn't it?

ARCHIE BEAL. Yes, that's all right. A chaperon's a chaperon, black or white.

JOHN BEAL. You won't mind their being black, will you, Miss Clement?

MIRALDA. No, I shan't mind. They can't be worse than white ones.

[Enter BAZZALOL and THOOTHOOBABA, two enormous Nubians, bearing peacock fans and wearing scimitars. All stare at them. They begin to fan slightly.]

DAOUD. The watchers of the doorstep.

JOHN BEAL. Idiot, Daoud! Fools! Dolts! Men may not guard a lady's door.

[BAZZALOL and THOOTHOOBABA smile ingratiatingly.]

BAZZALOL (bowing). We are not men.

　　　　　CURTAIN

ACT III

SCENE 1

Six and a half years later.
Al Shaldomir.
A room in the palace.
　MIRALDA *reclines on a heap of cushions.*
JOHN *beside her.*
　BAZZALOL *and* THOOTHOOBABA *fan them.*

OMAR (*declaiming to a zither*).

Al Shaldomir, Al Shaldomir,
　The nightingales that guard thy ways
Cease not to give thee, after God
　And after Paradise, all praise.
　Thou art the theme of all their lays.

Al Shaldomir, Al Shaldomir. . . .

MIRALDA. Go now, Omar.

OMAR. O lady, I depart. (*Exit.*)

MIRALDA (*languidly*). John, John. I wish you'd marry me.

JOHN. Miralda, you're thinking of those old customs again that we left behind us seven years ago. What's the good of it?

MIRALDA. I had a fancy that I wished you would.

JOHN. What's the good of it? You know you are my beloved. There are none of those clergymen within hundreds of miles. What's the good of it?

MIRALDA. We could find one, John.

JOHN. O, yes, I suppose we could, but . . .

MIRALDA. Why won't you?

JOHN. I told you why.

MIRALDA. O, yes, that instinct that you must not marry. That's not your reason, John.

JOHN. Yes, it is.

MIRALDA. It's a silly reason. It's a crazy reason. It's no reason at all. There's some other reason.

JOHN. No, there isn't. But I feel that in my bones. I don't know why. You know that I love none else but you. Besides, we're never going back, and it doesn't matter. This isn't Black-heath.

MIRALDA. So I must live as your slave.

JOHN. No, no, Miralda. My dear, you are not my slave. Did not the singer compare our love to the desire of the nightingale for the evening star? All know that you are my queen.

MIRALDA. They do not know at home.

JOHN. Home? Home? How could they know? What have we in common with home? Rows and rows of little houses; and if they hear a nightingale there they write to the papers. And— and if they saw this they'd think they were drunk. Miralda, don't be ab-surd. What has set you thinking of home?

MIRALDA. I want to be crowned queen.

JOHN. But I am not a king. I am only Shereef.

MIRALDA. You are all-powerful here, John, you can do what you please, if you wish to. You don't love me at all.

JOHN. Miralda, you know I love you. Didn't I kill Hussein for you?

MIRALDA. Yes, but you don't love me now.

JOHN. And Hussein's people killed Archie. That was for you too. I brought my brother out here to help you. He was engaged to be married, too.

MIRALDA. But you don't love me now.

JOHN. Yes, I do. I love you as the dawn loves the iris marshes. You know the song they sing.[1]

MIRALDA. Then why won't you marry me?

JOHN. I told you, I told you. I had a dream about the future. I forgot the dream, but I know I was not to marry. I will not wrong the future.

MIRALDA. Don't be crazy.

JOHN. I will have what fancies I please, crazy or sane. Am I not Shereef of

[1] THE SONG OF THE IRIS MARSHES

When morn is bright on the mountains olden
Till dawn is lost in the blaze of day,
When morn is bright and the marshes golden,
Where shall the lost lights fade away?
And where, my love, shall we dream to-day?

Dawn is fled to the marshy hollows
Where ghosts of stars in the dimness stray,
And the water is streaked with the flash of
swallows
And all through summer the iris sway.
But where, my love, shall we dream to-day?

When night is black in the iris marshes.

Shaldomir? Who dare stop me if I would be mad as Herod?

MIRALDA. I will be crowned queen.

JOHN. It is not my wish.

MIRALDA. I will, I will, I will.

JOHN. Drive me not to anger. If I have you cast into a well and take twenty of the fairest daughters of Al Shaldomir in your place, who can gainsay me? 10

MIRALDA. I will be crowned queen.

JOHN. O, do not be tiresome.

MIRALDA. Was it not my money that brought you here? Was it not I who said "Kill Hussein"? What power could you have had, had Hussein lived? What would you have been doing now, but for me?

JOHN. I don't know, Miralda.

MIRALDA. Catching some silly train to the 20 City. Working for some dull firm. Living in some small suburban house. It is I, *I*, that brought you from all that, and you won't make me a queen.

JOHN. Is it not enough that you are my beloved? You know there is none other but you. Is it not enough, Miralda?

MIRALDA. It is not enough. I will be 30 queen.

JOHN. Tchah! . . . Miralda, I know you are a wonderful woman, the most wonderful in the East; how you ever came to be in the West I don't know, and a train of all places; but, Miralda, you must not have petty whims, they don't become you.

MIRALDA. Is it a petty whim to wish to be a queen?

JOHN. Yes, when it is only the name you 40 want. You *are* a queen. You have all you wish for. Are you not my beloved? And have I not power here over all men? Could I not close the pass?

MIRALDA. I want to be queen.

JOHN. Oh-h! I will leave you. I have more to do than to sit and hear your whims. When I come back you will have some other whim. Miralda, you have too many whims. (*He rises.*)

MIRALDA. Will you be back soon?

JOHN. No.

MIRALDA. When will you come back, John? (*She is reclining, looking fair, fanning slightly.*)

JOHN. In half an hour.

MIRALDA. In half an hour?

JOHN. Yes. (*Exit.*)

MIRALDA. Half an hour. (*Her fan is laid down. She clutches it with sudden resolve. She goes to the wall, fanning herself slowly. She leans against it. She fans herself now with obvious deliberation. Three times the great fan goes flat against the window, and then again separately three times; and then she puts it against the window once with a smile of ecstasy. She has signalled. She returns to the cushions and reclines with beautiful care, fanning herself softly.*)

[*Enter the Vizier,* HAFIZ EL ALCOLAHN.]

HAFIZ. Lady! You bade me come.

MIRALDA. Did I, Hafiz?

HAFIZ. Lady, your fan.

MIRALDA. Ah, I was fanning myself.

HAFIZ. Seven times, lady.

MIRALDA. Ah, was it? Well, now you're here . . .

HAFIZ. Lady, O star of these times. O light over lonely marshes. (*He kneels by her and embraces her.*) Is the Shereef gone, lady?

MIRALDA. For half an hour, Hafiz.

HAFIZ. How know you for half an hour?

MIRALDA. He said so.

HAFIZ. He said so? Then is the time to fear, if a man say so.

MIRALDA. I know him.

HAFIZ. In our country who knows any man so much? None.

MIRALDA. He'll be away for half an hour.

HAFIZ. (*embracing*). O, exquisite lily of unattainable mountains.

MIRALDA. Ah, Hafiz, would you do a little thing for me?

HAFIZ. I would do all things, lady, O evening star.

MIRALDA. Would you make me a queen, Hafiz?

HAFIZ. If—if the Shereef were gathered?

MIRALDA. Even so, Hafiz.

HAFIZ. Lady, I would make you queen of all that lies west of the passes.

MIRALDA. You would make me queen?

HAFIZ. Indeed, before all my wives, before all women, over all Shaldomir, named the elect.

MIRALDA. O, well, Hafiz; then you may kiss me. (HAFIZ *does so ad lib*.) Hafiz, the Shereef has irked me.

HAFIZ. Lady, O singing star, to all men 20 is the hour.

MIRALDA. The appointed hour?

HAFIZ. Even the appointed hour, the last, leading to darkness.

MIRALDA. Is it written, think you, that the Shereef's hour is soon?

HAFIZ. Lady, O dawn's delight, let there be a banquet. Let the great ones of Shaldomir be bidden there.

MIRALDA. There shall be a banquet, 30 Hafiz.

HAFIZ. Soon, O lady. Let it be soon, sole lily of the garden.

MIRALDA. It shall be soon, Hafiz. (*More embraces*.)

HAFIZ. And above all, O lady, bid Daoud, the son of the baker.

MIRALDA. He shall be bidden, Hafiz.

HAFIZ. O lady, it is well.

MIRALDA. Go now, Hafiz. 40

HAFIZ. Lady, I go (*Giving a bag of gold to* BAZZALOL.) Silence. Silence. Silence.

BAZZALOL (*kneeling*). O, master!

HAFIZ. Let the tomb speak; let the stars cry out; but do you be silent.

BAZZALOL. Aye, master.

HAFIZ (*to* THOOTHOOBABA). And you. Though this one speak, yet be silent, or dread the shadow of Hafiz el Alcolahn. (*He drops a bag of gold.* THOOTHOOBABA *goes down and grabs at the gold; his eyes gloat over it.*)

THOOTHOOBABA. Master, I speak not. Oh-h-h.

[*Exit* HAFIZ.]

10 [MIRALDA *arranges herself on the cushions. She looks idly at each Nubian. The Nubians put each a finger over his lips and go on fanning with one hand.*]

MIRALDA. A queen. I shall look sweet as a queen.

[*Enter* JOHN. *She rises to greet him caressingly. Enter* DAOUD.]

MIRALDA. Oh, you have brought Daoud with you.

JOHN. Why not?

MIRALDA. You know that I don't like Daoud.

JOHN. I wish to speak with him.

[MIRALDA *looks straight at* JOHN *and moves away in silence. Exit L.*]

JOHN. Daoud.

DAOUD. Great master.

JOHN. Daoud, one day in spring, in the cemetery of those called Blessed, beyond the city's gates, you swore to me by the graves of both your parents . . .

DAOUD. Great master, even so I swore.

JOHN. . . . to be true to me always.

DAOUD. There is no Shereef but my master.

JOHN. Daoud, you have kept your word.

DAOUD. I have sought to, master.

JOHN. You have helped me often, Daoud, warned me and helped me often. Through you I knew those currents that run through the deeps of the market, in silence and all men feel them, but a ruler never. You told me of them, and when I knew—then I could look after myself, Daoud. They could do nothing against me then. Well, now I hold this people. I hold them at last, Daoud, and now——well, I can rest a little.

DAOUD. Not in the East, master.

JOHN. Not in the East, Daoud?

DAOUD. No, master.

JOHN. Why? What do you mean?

DAOUD. In Western countries, master, whose tales I have read, in a wonder- 10 ful book named the "Good Child's History of England," in the West a man hath power over a land, and lo! the power is his and descends to his son's son after him.

JOHN. Well, doesn't it in the East?

DAOUD. Not if he does not watch, master; in the night and the day, and in the twilight between the day and the night, and in the dawn between the 20 night and the day.

JOHN. I thought you had pretty long dynasties in these parts, and pretty lazy ones.

DAOUD. Master, he that was mightiest of those that were kings in Babylon had a secret door prepared in an inner chamber, which led to a little room, the smallest in the palace, whose back door opened secretly to the river, even 30 to great Euphrates, where a small boat waited all the days of his reign.

JOHN. Did he really now? Well, *he* was taking no chances. Did he have to use it?

DAOUD. No, master. Such boats are never used. Those that watch like that do not need to seek them, and the others, they would never be able to reach the river in time, even though 40 the boat were there.

JOHN. I shouldn't like to have to live like that. Why, a river runs by the back of this palace. I suppose palaces usually are on rivers. I'm glad I don't have to keep a boat there.

DAOUD. No, master.

JOHN. Well, what is it you are worrying about? Who is it you are afraid of?

DAOUD. Hafiz el Alcolahn.

JOHN. O, Hafiz. I have no fears of Hafiz. Lately I ordered my spies to watch him no longer. Why does he hate me?

DAOUD. Because, most excellent master, you slew Hussein.

JOHN. Slew Hussein? What is that to do with him? May I not slay whom I please?

DAOUD. Even so, master. Even so. But he was Hussein's enemy.

JOHN. His enemy, eh?

DAOUD. For years he had dreamed of the joy of killing Hussein.

JOHN. Well, he should have done it before I came. We don't hang over things and brood over them for years where I come from. If a thing's to be done, it's done.

DAOUD. Even so, master. Hafiz had laid his plans for years. He would have killed him and got his substance; and then, when the hour drew near, you came, and Hussein died, swiftly, not as Hafiz would have had him die; and lo! thou art the Lord of the Pass, and Hafiz is no more than a beetle that runs about in the dirt.

JOHN. Well, so you fear Hafiz?

DAOUD. Not for himself, master. Nay, I fear not Hafiz. But, master, hast thou seen when the thunder is coming, but no rumble is heard, and the sky is scarce yet black, how little winds run in the grass and sigh and die; and the flower beckons a moment with its head; all the world full of whispers, master, all saying nothing; then the lightning, master, and the anger of God; and men say it came without warning? (*Simply.*) I hear those things coming, master.

JOHN. Well?

DAOUD. Master, it is all silent in the market. Once, when the price of turquoises was high, men abused the Shereef. When the merchant men could not sell their pomegranates for silver they abused the Shereef. It is men's way, master, men's way. Now it is all silent in the market. It is like the grasses with the little winds, that whisper and sigh and die away; like the flowers beckoning to nothing. And so, master, and so . . . 10

JOHN. I see, you fear some danger.

DAOUD. I fear it, master.

JOHN. What danger, Daoud?

DAOUD. Master, I know not.

JOHN. From what quarter, Daoud?

DAOUD. O master, O sole Lord of Al Shaldomir, named the elect, from that quarter. 20

JOHN. That quarter? Why, that is the gracious lady's innermost chamber.

DAOUD. From that quarter, great master, O Lord of the Pass.

JOHN. Daoud, I have cast men into prison for saying less than this. Men have been flogged on the feet for less than 'this.

DAOUD. Slay me, master, but hear my words. 30

JOHN. I will not slay you. You are mistaken, Daoud. You have made a great mistake. The thing is absurd. Why the gracious lady has scarcely seen Hafiz. She knows nothing of the talk of the market. Who could tell her? No one comes here. It is absurd. Only the other day she said to me . . . But it is absurd, it is absurd, Daoud. 40 Besides, the people would never rebel against me. Do I not govern them well?

DAOUD. Even so, master.

JOHN. Why should they rebel, then?

DAOUD. They think of the old times, master.

JOHN. The old times? Why, their lives weren't safe. The robbers came down from the mountains and robbed the market whenever they had a mind.

DAOUD. Master, men were content in the old times.

JOHN. But were the merchants content?

DAOUD. Those that loved merchandise were content, master. Those that loved it not went into the mountains.

JOHN. But were they content when they were robbed?

DAOUD. They soon recovered their losses, master. Their prices were unjust and they loved usury.

JOHN. And were the people content with unjust prices?

DAOUD. Some were, master, as men have to be in all countries. The others went into the mountains and robbed the merchants.

JOHN. I see.

DAOUD. But now, master, a man robs a merchant and he is cast into prison. Now a man is slain in the market and his son, his own son, master, may not follow after the aggressor and slay him and burn his house. They are ill-content, master. No man robs the merchants, no man slays them, and the merchants' hearts are hardened and they oppress all men.

JOHN. I see. They don't like good government?

DAOUD. They sigh for the old times, master.

JOHN. I see; I see. In spite of all I have done for them, they want their old bad government back again.

DAOUD. It is the old way, master.

JOHN. Yes, yes. And so they would rebel. Well, we must watch. You have warned me once again, Daoud, and I am grateful. But you are wrong, Daoud, about the gracious lady. You are mistaken. It is impossible. You are mistaken, Daoud. I know it could not be.

DAOUD. I am mistaken, master. Indeed, I am mistaken. Yet, watch. Watch, master.

JOHN. Well, I will watch.

DAOUD. And, master, if ever I come to you bearing oars, then watch no longer, master, but follow me through the banquet chamber and through the room beyond it. Move as the wild deer move when there is danger, without pausing, without wondering, without turning round; for in that hour, master, in that hour . . .

JOHN. Through the room beyond the banquet chamber, Daoud?

DAOUD. Aye, master, following me.

JOHN. But there is no door beyond, Daoud.

DAOUD. Master, I have prepared a door.

JOHN. A door, Daoud?

DAOUD. A door none wots of, master.

JOHN. Whither does it lead?

DAOUD. To a room that you know not of, a little room; you must stoop, master.

JOHN. O, and then?

DAOUD. To the river, master.

JOHN. The river! But there's no boat there.

DAOUD. Under the golden willow, master.

JOHN. A boat?

DAOUD. Even so, under the branches.

JOHN. Is it come to that? . . . No, Daoud, all this is unnecessary. It can't come to that.

DAOUD. If ever I come before you bearing two oars, in that hour, master, it is necessary.

JOHN. But you will not come. It will never come to that.

DAOUD. No, master.

JOHN. A wise man can stop things before they get as far as that.

DAOUD. They that were kings in Babylon were wise men, master.

JOHN. Babylon! But that was thousands of years ago.

DAOUD. Man changes not, master.

JOHN. Well, Daoud, I will trust you, and if it ever comes to that . . .

[*Enter* MIRALDA.]

MIRALDA. I thought Daoud was gone.

DAOUD. Even now I go, gracious lady.

[*Exit* DAOUD. *Rather strained silence with* JOHN *and* MIRALDA *till he goes. She goes and makes herself comfortable on the cushions. He is not entirely at ease.*]

MIRALDA. You had a long talk with Daoud.

JOHN. Yes, he came and talked a good deal.

MIRALDA. What about?

JOHN. O, just talk; you know these Eastern people.

MIRALDA. I thought it was something you were discussing with him.

JOHN. O, no.

MIRALDA. Some important secret.

JOHN. No, not at all.

MIRALDA. You often talk with Daoud.

JOHN. Yes, he is useful to me. When he talks sense I listen, but to-day . . .

MIRALDA. What did he come for to-day?

JOHN. O, nothing.

MIRALDA. You have a secret with Daoud that you will not share with me.

JOHN. No, I have not.

MIRALDA. What was it he said?

JOHN. He said there was a king in Babylon who . . .

[DAOUD *slips into the room.*]

MIRALDA. In Babylon? What has that to do with us?

JOHN. Nothing. I told you he was not talking sense.

MIRALDA. Well, what did he say?

JOHN. He said that in Babylon . . .

DAOUD. Hist!

JOHN. O, well . . .

[MIRALDA *glares, but calms herself and says nothing. Exit* DAOUD.]

MIRALDA. What did Daoud say of Babylon?

JOHN. O, well, as you say, it had nothing to do with us.

MIRALDA. But I wish to hear it.

JOHN. I forget. (*For a moment there is silence.*)

MIRALDA. John, John. Will you do a little thing for me?

JOHN. What is it?

MIRALDA. Say you will do it, John. I should love to have one of my little wishes granted.

JOHN. What is it?

MIRALDA. Kill Daoud, John. I want you to kill Daoud.

JOHN. I will not.

[*He walks up and down in front of the two Nubians in silence. She plucks petulantly at a pillow. She suddenly calms herself. A light comes into her eyes. The Nubians go on fanning.* JOHN *goes on pacing.*]

MIRALDA. John, John, I have forgotten my foolish fancies.

JOHN. I am glad of it.

MIRALDA. I do not really wish you to kill Daoud.

JOHN (*same voice*). I'm glad you don't.

MIRALDA. I have only one fancy now, John.

JOHN. Well, what is it?

MIRALDA. Give a banquet, John. I want you to give a banquet.

JOHN. A banquet? Why?

MIRALDA. Is there any harm in my fancy?

JOHN. No.

MIRALDA. Then if I may not be a queen, and if you will not kill Daoud for me, give a banquet, John. There is no harm in a banquet.

JOHN. Very well. When do you want it?

MIRALDA. To-morrow, John. Bid all the great ones to it, all the illustrious ones in Al Shaldomir.

JOHN. Very well.

MIRALDA. And bid Daoud come.

JOHN. Daoud? You asked me to kill him.

MIRALDA. I do not wish that any longer, John.

JOHN. You have queer moods, Miralda.

MIRALDA. May I not change my moods, John?

JOHN. I don't know. I don't understand them.

MIRALDA. And ask Hafiz el Alcolahn, John.

JOHN. Hafiz? Why?

MIRALDA. I don't know, John. It was just my fancy.

JOHN. Your fancy, eh?

MIRALDA. That was all.

JOHN. Then I will ask him. Have you any other fancy?

MIRALDA. Not now, John.

JOHN. Then go, Miralda.

MIRALDA. Go?

JOHN. Yes.

MIRALDA. Why?

JOHN. Because I command it.

MIRALDA. Because you command it?

JOHN. Yes, I, the Shereef of Al Shaldomir.

MIRALDA. Very well. (*Exit L.*)

[*He walks to the door to see that she is really gone. He comes back to centre and stands with back to audience, pulling a cord quietly from his pocket and arranging it.*

[*He moves half left and comes up behind* BAZZALOL. *Suddenly he slips the cord over* BAZZALOL'S *head, and tightens it round his neck.* BAZZALOL *flops on his knees.* THOOTHOOBABA *goes on fanning.*]

JOHN. Speak!

[BAZZALOL *is silent.* JOHN *tightens it more.* THOOTHOOBABA *goes on quietly fanning.*]

BAZZALOL. I cannot.

JOHN. If you would speak, raise your left hand. If you raise your left hand and do not speak you shall die.

[BAZZALOL *is silent.* JOHN *tightens more.* BAZZALOL *raises his great flabby left*

hand high. JOHN *releases the cord.* BAZ-
ZALOL *blinks and moves his mouth.*]

BAZZALOL. Gracious Shereef, one visited
the great lady and gave us gold, saying, "Speak not."

JOHN. When?

BAZZALOL. Great master, one hour since.

JOHN (*a little viciously*). Who?

BAZZALOL. O heaven-sent, he was
Hafiz el Alcolahn.

JOHN. Give me the gold. (BAZZALOL
gives it.) (*To* THOOTHOOBABA.) Give
me the gold.

THOOTHOOBABA. Master, none gave me
gold.

[JOHN *touches his dagger, and looks like
using it.* THOOTHOOBABA *gives it.*]

JOHN. Take back your gold. Be silent
about this. You too. (*He throws gold
to* BAZZALOL.) Gold does not make
you silent, but there is a thing that
does. What is that thing? Speak.
What thing makes you silent?

BAZZALOL. O, great master, it is death.

JOHN. Death, eh? And how will you die
if you speak? You know how you will
die?

BAZZALOL. Yes, heaven-sent.

JOHN. Tell your comrade, then.

BAZZALOL. We shall be eaten, great
master.

JOHN. You know by what?

BAZZALOL. Small things, great master,
small things. Oh-h-h-h. Oh-h-h.

[THOOTHOOBABA'S *knees scarcely hold him.*]

JOHN. It is well.

CURTAIN

SCENE 2

A small street. Al Shaldomir.
Time: Next day.

[*Enter* L. *the* SHEIK OF THE BISHAREENS.
*He goes to an old green door, pointed of
course in the Arabic way.*]

SHEIK OF THE BISHAREENS. Ho, Bishareens!

[*The* BISHAREENS *run on.*]

SHEIK. It is the place and the hour.

BISHAREENS. Ah, ah!

SHEIK (*to* FIRST BISHAREEN). Watch.

[FIRST BISHAREEN *goes to right and watches
up sunny street.*]

FIRST BISHAREEN. He comes.

[*Enter* HAFIZ EL ALCOLAHN. *He goes
straight up to the* SHEIK *and whispers.*]

SHEIK (*turning*). Hear, O Bishareens.

[HAFIZ *places flute to his lips.*]

A BISHAREEN. And the gold, master?

SHEIK. Silence! It is the signal.

[HAFIZ *plays a weird, strange tune on his
flute.*]

HAFIZ. So.

SHEIK. Master, once more.

[HAFIZ *raises the flute again to his lips.*]

SHEIK. Hear, O Bishareens!

[HAFIZ *plays the brief tune again.*]

HAFIZ (*to* SHEIK). Like that.

SHEIK. We have heard, O master. (*He
walks away* L. *Hands move in the direction of knife-hilts.*)

THE BISHAREENS. Ah, ah!

[*Exit* HAFIZ. *He plays a merry little tune on
his flute as he walks away.*]

CURTAIN

SCENE 3

*The banqueting hall. A table along the
back.* JOHN *and* MIRALDA *seated with
notables of Al Shaldomir.*

JOHN *sits in the centre, with* MIRALDA *on
his right and, next to her,* HAFIZ EL ALCO-
LAHN.

MIRALDA (*to* JOHN). You bade Daoud be
present?

JOHN. Yes.

MIRALDA. He is not here.

JOHN. Daoud not here?

MIRALDA. No.

JOHN. Why?

MIRALDA. We all obey you, but not
Daoud.

JOHN. I do not understand it.

A NOTABLE. The Shereef has frowned.

[*Enter R. an* OFFICER-AT-ARMS. *He halts at once and salutes with his sword, then takes a side pace to his left, standing against the wall, sword at the carry.* JOHN *acknowledges salute by touching his forehead with the inner tips of his fingers.*]

OFFICER-AT-ARMS. Soldiers of Al Shaldomir; with the dance-step; march. 10

[*Enter R. some men in single file; uniform, pale green silks; swords at carry. They advance in single file, in a slightly serpentine way, deviating to their left a little out of the straight and returning to it, stepping neatly on the tips of their toes. Their march is fantastic and odd without being exactly funny.*

[*The* OFFICER-AT-ARMS *falls in on their left flank and marches about level with the* 20 *third or fourth man. When he reaches the centre he gives another word of command.*]

OFFICER-AT-ARMS. With reverence: Salute.

[*The actor who takes this part should have been an officer or N. C. O.* JOHN *stands up and acknowledges their salute by touching his forehead with the fingers of the right hand, palm turned inwards. Exeunt soldiers L.* JOHN *sits down.*] 30

A NOTABLE. He does not smile this evening.

A WOMAN. The Shereef?

A NOTABLE. He has not smiled.

[*Enter R.* ZABNOOL, *a* CONJURER, *with brass bowl. He bows. He walks to centre opposite* JOHN. *He exhibits his bowl.*]

ZABNOOL. Behold. The bowl is empty. (ZABNOOL *produces a snake.*)

ZABNOOL. Ah, little servant of Death. 40 (*He produces flowers.*) Flowers, master, flowers. All the way from Nowhere. (*He produces birds.*) Birds, master. Birds from Nowhere. Sing, sing to the Shereef. Sing the little empty songs of the land of Nowhere. (*He seats him-*

self on the ground facing JOHN. *He puts the bowl on the ground. He places a piece of silk, with queer designs on it, over the bowl. He partly draws the silk away with his left hand and puts in his right. He brings out a young crocodile and holds it by the neck.*) Behold O Shereef; O people, behold; a crocodile. (*He arises and bows to* JOHN *and wraps up the crocodile in some drapery and walks away. As he goes he addresses his crocodile.*) O eater of lambs, O troubler of the rivers, you sought to evade me in an empty bowl. O thief, O appetite, you sought to evade the Shereef. The Shereef has seen you, O vexer of swimmers, O pig in armour, O . . .

[SHABEESH, *another* CONJURER, *rushes on.*]

SHABEESH. Bad man, master; he very, very bad man. (*He pushes* ZABNOOL *away roughly, impetus of which carries* ZABNOOL *to the wings.*) Very, very bad man, master.

MIRALDA (*reprovingly*). Zabnool has amused us.

SHABEESH. He very, very bad man, lily lady. He get crocodile from devil. From devil Poolyana, lily lady. Very, very bad.

MIRALDA. He may call on devils if he amuse us, Shabeesh.

SHABEESH. But Poolyana, *my* devil. He call on *my* devil, lily lady. Very, very, very bad. My devil Poolyana.

MIRALDA. Call on him yourself, Shabeesh. Amuse us.

SHABEESH. Shall one devil serve two masters?

MIRALDA. Why not?

SHABEESH (*beginning to wave priestly conjurer's hands*). Very bad man go away. Go away, bad man: go away, bad man. Poolyana not want bad man: Poolyana only work for good man. He mighty fine devil. Poolyana,

Poolyana. Big, black, fine, furry devil. Poolyana, Poolyana, Poolyana. O fine, fat devil with big angry tail. Poolyana, Poolyana, Poolyana. Send me up fine young pig for the Shereef. Poolyana, Poolyana. Lil yellow pig with curly tail. (*Small pig appears.*) O Poolyana, great Poolyana. Fine black fur and grey fur underneath. Fine ferocious devil, you *my* devil, 10 Poolyana. O, Poolyana, Poolyana, Poolyana. Send me a big beast what chew bad man's crocodile. Big beast with big teeth, eat him like a worm. (*He has spread large silk handkerchief on floor and is edging back from it in alarm.*) Long nails in him toes, big like lion, Poolyana. Send great smelly big beast—eat up bad man's crocodile. (*At first stir of handkerchief* 20 SHABEESH *leaps in alarm.*) He come, he come. I see his teeth and horns. (*Enter small live rabbit from trapdoor under handkerchief.*) O, Poolyana, you big devil have your liddle joke. You laugh at poor conjuring man. You send him lil rabbit to eat big crocodile. Bad Poolyana. Bad Poolyana. (*Whacks ground with stick.*) You plenty bad devil, Poolyana. (*Whacking it* 30 *again. Handkerchief has been thrown on ground again. Handkerchief stirs slightly.*) No, no, Poolyana. You not bad devil. You not bad devil. You plenty good devil, Poolyana. No, no, no! Poor conjuring man quite happy on muddy earth. No, Poolyana, no! O, no, no, devil. O, no, no! Hell plenty nice place for devil. Master! He not my devil! He other man's devil! 40

JOHN. What's this noise? What's it about? What's the matter?

SHABEESH (*in utmost terror*). He coming, master! Coming!

ZABNOOL. Poolyana, Poolyana, Poolyana. Stay down, stay down, Pooly-

ana. Stay down in nice warm hell, Pollyana. The Shereef want no devil to-day.

[ZABNOOL *before speaking returns to centre and pats air over ground where handkerchief lies. Then* SHABEESH *and* ZABNOOL *come together side by side and bow and smile together toward the* SHEREEF. *Gold is thrown to them, which* ZABNOOL *gathers and hands to* SHABEESH, *who gives a share back to* ZABNOOL.]

A NOTABLE. The Shereef is silent.

[*Enter three women R. in single file, dancing, and carrying baskets full of pink rose-leaves. They dance across, throwing down rose-leaves, leaving a path of them behind them. Exeunt L.*]

A NOTABLE. Still he is silent.

MIRALDA. Why do you not speak?

JOHN. I do not wish to speak.

MIRALDA. Why?

[*Enter* OMAR *with his zither.*]

OMAR (*singing*).

Al Shaldomir, Al Shaldomir,
  Birds sing thy praises night and day;
The nightingale in every wood,
  Blackbirds in fields profound with may;
Birds sing of thee by every way.

Al Shaldomir, Al Shaldomir,
  My heart is ringing with thee still;
Though far away, O fairy fields,
  My soul flies low by every hill
And misses not one daffodil.

Al Shaldomir, Al Shaldomir,
  O mother of my roving dreams,
Blue is the night above thy spires,
  And blue by myriads of streams,
Paradise through thy gateway gleams.

MIRALDA. Why do you not wish to speak?

JOHN. You desire me to speak?

MIRALDA. No. They all wonder why you do not speak; that is all.

JOHN. I will speak. They shall hear me.

MIRALDA. O, there is no need to.

JOHN. There *is* a need. (*He rises.*) People of Shaldomir, behold I know your plottings. I know the murmurings that you murmur against me. When I sleep in my inner chamber my ear is in the market, while I sit at meat I hear men whisper far hence and know their innermost thoughts. Hope not to overcome me by your plans nor by any manner of craftiness. My gods are gods of brass; none have escaped them. They cannot be overthrown. Of all men they favour my people. Their hands reach out to the uttermost ends of the earth. Take heed, for my gods are terrible. I am the Shereef; if any dare withstand me I will call on my gods and they shall crush him utterly. They shall grind him into the earth and trample him under, as though he had not been. The uttermost parts have feared the gods of the English. They reach out, they destroy, there is no escape from them. Be warned; for I do not permit any to stand against me. The laws that I have given you, you shall keep; there shall be no other laws. Whoso murmurs shall know my wrath and the wrath of my gods. Take heed, I speak not twice. I spoke once to Hussein. Hussein heard not; and Hussein is dead; his ears are closed for ever. Hear, O people.

HAFIZ. O Shereef, we murmur not against you.

JOHN. I know thoughts and hear whispers. I need not instruction, Hafiz.

HAFIZ. You exalt yourself over us as none did aforetime.

JOHN. Yes. And I will exalt myself. I have been Shereef hitherto, but now I will be king. Al Shaldomir is less than I desire. I have ruled too long over a little country. I will be the equal of Persia. I will be king; I proclaim it. The pass is mine; the mountains shall be mine also. And he that rules the mountains has mastery over all the plains beyond. If the men of the plains will not own it let them make ready; for my wrath will fall on them in the hour when they think me afar, on a night when they think I dream. I proclaim myself king over . . .

[HAFIZ *pulls out his flute and plays the weird, strange tune.* JOHN *looks at him in horrified anger.*]

JOHN. The penalty is death! Death is punishment for what you do, Hafiz. You have dared while I spoke. Hafiz, your contempt is death. Go to Hussein. I, the king . . . say it.

[DAOUD *has entered R., bearing two oars.* DAOUD *walks across, not looking at* JOHN. *Exit by small door in L. near back.* JOHN *gives one look at the banqueters, then he follows* DAOUD. *Exit. All look astonished. Some rise and peer.* HAFIZ *draws his knife.*]

OMAR (*singing*).

Al Shaldomir, Al Shaldomir,
  The nightingales that guard thy ways
Cease not to give thee, after God
  And after Paradise, all praise,

CRIES (*off*). Kill the unbeliever. Kill the dog. Kill the Christian.

[*Enter the* SHEIK OF THE BISHAREENS, *followed by all his men.*]

SHEIK. We are the Bishareens, master.

[MIRALDA *standing up, right arm akimbo, left arm pointing perfectly straight out towards the small door, hand extended.*]

MIRALDA. He is there.

[*The* BISHAREENS *run off through the little door.*]

A NOTABLE. Not to interfere with old ways is wisest.

ANOTHER. Indeed, it would have been well for him.

[*The* BISHAREENS *begin to return looking all about them like disappointed hounds.*]

A BISHAREEN. He is not there, master.

HAFIZ. Not there? Not there? Why, there is no door beyond. He must needs be there, and his chief spy with him.

SHEIK (*off*). He is not here.   10

MIRALDA (*turning round and clawing the wall*). O, I was weary of him. I was weary of him.

HAFIZ. Be comforted, pearl of the morning; he is gone.

MIRALDA. When I am weary of a man he must die.

[*He embraces her knees.*]

ZAGBOOLA (*who has come on with a little crowd that followed the* BISHAREENS. *She is blind*). Lead me to Hafiz. I am the mother of Hafiz. Lead me to Hafiz. (*They lead her near.*) Hafiz! Hafiz! (*She finds his shoulder and tries to drag him away.*)

HAFIZ. Go! Go! I have found the sole pearl of the innermost deeps of the sea. (*He is kneeling and kissing* MIRALDA'S *hand.* ZAGBOOLA *wails.*)

CURTAIN

ACT IV

SCENE 1

Three years elapse.
Scene: The street outside the Acacias.
Time: Evening.
[ALI *leans on a pillar-box watching.* JOHN *shuffles on L. He is miserably dressed, an Englishman down on his luck. A nightingale sings far off.*]

JOHN. A nightingale here. Well, I never.

Al Shaldomir, Al Shaldomir,
   The nightingales that guard thy ways
Cease not to give thee, after God
   And after Paradise, all praise. . . .

The infernal place! I wish I had never seen it! Wonder what set me thinking of that? (*The nightingale sings another bar.* JOHN *turns to his left and walks down the little path that leads to the door of the Acacias.*) I mustn't come here. Mustn't come to a fine house like this. Mustn't. Mustn't. (*He draws near it reluctantly. He puts his hand to the bell and withdraws it. Then he rings and* 40 *snatches his hand away. He prepares to run away. Finally he rings it repeatedly, feverishly, violently.*)

[*Enter* LIZA, *opening the door.*]

LIZA. Ullo, 'Oo's this!

JOHN. I oughtn't to have rung, miss, I know. I oughtn't to have rung your   20 bell; but I've seen better days, and wondered if—I wondered . . .

LIZA. I oughtn't to 'ave opened the door, that's wot *I* oughtn't. Now I look at you, I oughtn't to 'ave opened it. Wot does you want?

JOHN. O, don't turn me away now, miss. I must come here. I must.

LIZA. Must? Why?

JOHN. I don't know.

30 LIZA. Wot do you want?

JOHN. Who lives here?

LIZA. Mr. and Mrs. Cater; firm of Briggs, Cater, and Johnstone. What do you want?

JOHN. Could I see Mr. Cater?

LIZA. He's out. Dining at the Mansion House.

JOHN. Oh.

LIZA. He is.

JOHN. Could I see Mrs. Cater?

LIZA. See Mrs. Cater? No, of course you couldn't. (*She prepares to shut the door.*)

JOHN. Miss! Miss! Don't go, miss. Don't

shut me out. If you knew what I'd suffered, if you knew what I'd suffered. Don't!

LIZA (*coming forward again*). Suffered? Why? Ain't you got enough to eat?

JOHN. No, I've had nothing all day.

LIZA. 'Aven't you really now?

JOHN. No. And I get little enough at any time.

LIZA (*kindly*). You ought to work.

JOHN. I . . . I can't. I can't bring myself . . . I . . . I've seen better times.

LIZA. Still, you could work.

JOHN. I—I can't grub for halfpennies when I've—when I've . . .

LIZA. When you've what?

JOHN. Lost millions.

LIZA. Millions?

JOHN. I've lost everything. 20

LIZA. 'Ow did you lose it?

JOHN. Through being blind. But never mind, never mind. It's all gone now, and I'm hungry.

LIZA. 'Ow long 'ave you been down on your luck?

JOHN. It's three years now.

LIZA. Couldn't get a regular job, like?

JOHN. Well, I suppose I might have. I suppose it's my fault, miss. But the 30 heart was out of me.

LIZA. Dear me, now.

JOHN. Miss.

LIZA. Yes?

JOHN. You've a kind face . . .

LIZA. 'Ave I?

JOHN. Yes. Would you do me a kind turn?

LIZA. Well, I dunno. I might, as yer so down on yer luck—I don't like to see 40 a man like you are, I must say.

JOHN. Would you let me come into the big house and speak to the missus a moment?

LIZA. She'd row me awful if I did. This house is very respectable.

JOHN. I feel, if you would, I feel, I feel my luck might change.

LIZA. But I don't know what she'd say if I did.

JOHN. Miss, I must.

LIZA. I don't know wot she'd say.

JOHN. I must come in, miss, I must.

LIZA. I don't know what she'll say.

JOHN. I must. I can't help myself.

LIZA. I don't know what she'll . . . 10

[JOHN *is in, door shuts.*]

[ALI *throws his head up and laughs, but quite silently.*]

CURTAIN

SCENE 2

The drawing-room at the Acacias.
A moment later.
The scene is the same as in Act I, except that the sofa which was red is now green, and the photograph of Aunt Martha is replaced by that of a frowning old colonel. The ages of the four children in the photographs are the same, but their sexes have changed.

[MARY *reading. Enter* LIZA.]

LIZA. There's a gentleman to see you, mum, which is, properly speaking, not a gentleman at all, but 'e would come in, mum.

MARY. Not a gentleman! Good gracious, Liza, whatever do you mean?

LIZA. 'E would come in, mum.

MARY. But what does he want?

LIZA (*over shoulder*). What does you want?

JOHN (*entering*). I am a beggar.

MARY. O, really? You've no right to be coming into houses like this, you know.

JOHN. I know that, madam, I know that. Yet somehow I couldn't help myself. I've been begging for nearly three years now, and I've never done this before, yet somehow to-night I felt impelled to come to this house. I beg your pardon, humbly. Hunger drove me to it.

MARY. Hunger?

JOHN. I'm very hungry, madam.

MARY. Unfortunately Mr. Cater has not yet returned, or perhaps he might . . .

JOHN. If you could give me a little to eat yourself, madam, a bit of stale bread, a crust, something that Mr. Cater would not want.

MARY. It's very unusual, coming into a house like this and at such an hour— it's past eleven o'clock—and Mr. Cater not yet returned. Are you really hungry?

JOHN. I'm very, very hungry.

MARY. Well, it's very unusual; but perhaps I might get you a little something. (*She picks up an empty plate from the supper table.*)

JOHN. Madam, I do not know how to thank you.

MARY. O, don't mention it.

JOHN. I have not met such kindness for three years. I . . . I'm starving. I've known better times.

MARY (*kindly*). I'll get you something. You've known better times, you say?

JOHN. I had been intended for work in the City. And then, then I travelled, and—and I got very much taken with foreign countries, and I thought— but it all went to pieces. I lost everything. Here I am, starving.

MARY (*as one might reply to the Mayoress who had lost her gloves*). O, I'm so sorry.
[JOHN *sighs deeply.*]

MARY. I'll get a nice bit of something to eat.

JOHN. A thousand thanks to you, madam.
[*Exit* MARY *with the plate.*]

LIZA (*who has been standing near the door all the time*). Well, she's going to get you something.

JOHN. Heaven reward her.

LIZA. Hungry as all that?

JOHN. I'm on my beam ends.

LIZA. Cheer up!

JOHN. That's all very well to say, living in a fine house, as you are, dry and warm and well-fed. But what have I to cheer up about?

LIZA. Isn't there anything you could pop?

JOHN. What?

LIZA. Nothing you can take to the pawn-shop? I've tided over times I wanted a bit of cash that way sometimes.

JOHN. What could I pawn?

LIZA. Well, well you've a watch-chain.

JOHN. A bit of old leather.

LIZA. But what about the watch?

JOHN. I've no watch.

LIZA. O, funny having a watch-chain then.

JOHN. O, that's only for this; it's a bit of crystal.

LIZA. Funny bit of a thing. What's it for?

JOHN. I don't know.

LIZA. Was it give to you?

JOHN. I don't know. I don't know how I got it.

LIZA. Don't know how you got it?

JOHN. No, I can't remember at all. But I've a feeling about it, I can't explain what I feel; but I don't part with it.

LIZA. Don't you? You might get something on it, likely, and have a square meal.

JOHN. I won't part with it.

LIZA. Why?

JOHN. I feel I won't. I never have.

LIZA. Feel you won't?

JOHN. Yes, I have that feeling very strongly. I've kept it always. Everything else is gone.

LIZA. Had it long?

JOHN. Yes, yes. About ten years. I found I had it one morning in a train. It's odd that I can't remember.

LIZA. But wot d'yer keep it for?

JOHN. Just for luck. (LIZA *breaks into laughter*.)

LIZA. Well, you are funny.

JOHN. I'm on my beam ends. I don't know if that is funny.

LIZA. You're as down in your luck as ever you can be, and you go keeping a thing like that for luck. Why, you 10 couldn't be funnier.

JOHN. Well, what would you do?

LIZA. Why, I 'ad a mascot once, all real gold; and I had rotten luck. Rotten luck I had. Rotten.

JOHN. And what did you do?

LIZA. Took it back to the shop.

JOHN. Yes?

LIZA. They was quite obliging about it. Gave me a wooden one instead, what 20 was guaranteed. Luck changed very soon altogether.

JOHN. Could luck like mine change?

LIZA. Course it could.

JOHN. Look at me.

LIZA. You'll be all right one of these days. Give me that mascot.

JOHN. I—I hardly like to. One has an awfully strong feeling with it.

LIZA. Give it to me. It's no good. 30

JOHN. I—I don't like to.

LIZA. You just give it to me. I tell you it's doing you no good. I know all about them mascots. Give it me.

JOHN. Well, well, I'll give it you. You're the first woman that's been kind to me since . . . I'm on my beam ends. (*Face in hands—tears.*)

LIZA. There, there. I'm going to smash it, I am. These mascots! One's better 40 without 'em. Your luck'll turn, never fear. And you've a nice supper coming.

[*She puts it in a corner of the mantelpiece and hammers it. It smashes. The photographs of the four children change slightly. The Colonel gives place to Aunt Martha. The green sofa turns red.* JOHN'S *clothes become neat and tidy. The hammer in* LIZA'S *hand turns to a feather duster. Nothing else changes.*]

A VOICE (*off, in agony*). Allah! Allah! Allah!

LIZA. Some foreign gentleman must have hurt himself.

JOHN. H'm. Sounds like it . . . Liza.

[LIZA, *dusting the photographs on the wall, just behind the corner of the mantelpiece.*]

LIZA. Funny. Thought I—thought I 'ad a hammer in my hand.

JOHN. Really, Liza, I often think you have. You really should be more careful. Only—only yesterday you broke the glass of Miss Jane's photograph.

LIZA. Thought it was a hammer.

JOHN. Really, I think it sometimes is. It's a mistake you make too often, Liza. You—you must be more careful.

LIZA. Very well, sir. Funny my thinking I 'ad an 'ammer in my 'and, though.

[*She goes to tidy the little supper table. Enter* MARY *with food on a plate.*]

MARY. I've brought you your supper, John.

JOHN. Thanks, Mary. I—I think I must have taken a nap.

MARY. Did you, dear? Thanks, Liza. Run along to bed now, Liza. Good gracious, it's half-past eleven. (MARY *makes final arrangements of supper table.*)

LIZA. Thank you, mum. (*Exit.*)

JOHN. Mary.

MARY. Yes, John.

JOHN. I—I thought I'd caught that train.

CURTAIN

MOTION PICTURE DRAMA

Liam O'Flaherty

THE MOTION PICTURE drama has established itself in recent years as an art form of major importance. It has become an integral part of the contemporary theatre, and as such it may no longer be lightly ignored as a trivial and popular type of mechanized entertainment for the ignorant masses. In its lowest form of course it is tawdry and ridiculous. So, we may remind ourselves, are many of the highly successful plays produced each year in the theatres of New York and London. But the last decade has seen marked advances in the number of important and meritorious motion pictures dealing honestly with their materials and achieving genuine artistic distinction in their peculiar medium. Films like *I Am A Fugitive* (1932), exhibiting the brutality and tyranny of a chain gang; the artistic triumph of *As You Desire Me* (1934) starring Greta Garbo; *Winterset*, adapted from Anderson's stage play; distinguished biographical plays such as *The Life of Louis Pasteur* (1936), *Emile Zola* (1937), and *Abe Lincoln in Illinois* (1940), and on down through a list of goodly length and thrilling memory—such motion picture dramas were as notable in their way as any comparable stage plays produced in the legitimate theatre. Yet because of perfectly natural reasons originating in the newness of the cinema and the peculiar mechanical circumstances under which motion picture plays are produced and exhibited, very little serious study has been given to this potent off-shoot of modern drama, which has far overshadowed its parent in the vastness of its appeal and its public.

The cinema play has been regarded as a cheap form of mass amusement with an existence no more permanent than the shadows that flit across the screen to create the momentary illusion. The films were projected a night or two and then disappeared, leaving no record except the deceptive one of an idle memory. Only in the last few years have alert organizations like the Museum of Modern Art in New York recognized the value of these perishable film documents and begun to collect them into a permanent library where they may be re-exhibited. The good pictures are now being revived from time to time, and in many universities these showings have become a significant part of the educational program. It is now physically possible at least to study the motion picture drama with some thoroughness, if not with the same ease and exhaustiveness as the printed play. The spectator has the advantage also of seeing the complete performance instead of merely the script core.

So many allied arts have gone into the making of this fragile strip of film illusion that its written scenario is almost universally ignored. In the old days of the silent picture, which told its story in pantomime with occasional subtitles, the scenario was only a blueprint to be thrown away when construction was ended. But the rapid perfecting of the talking picture has conferred greater dignity on the script and removed the final barrier to the cinema as an interesting form of drama. Some of the world's foremost talent has gone into the making of picture plays, though that talent has often enough been stultified by the network of censorship that has moved in upon the industry. Some of the cinema plays are true works of art in their dialogue as well as in their mechanical perfection. By the very nature of the cinema, however, the dialogue is as fleeting as the image and exists only as sound. Important though it is, it is only one small element in the production and seldom if ever may be seen in print, though a few outstanding scripts are beginning to find their way into book form. No human art ever before co-ordinated into a single effect so many allied arts, or levied so heavily upon the stupendous resources of modern science, or drafted into its service such a complicated battalion of technical experts. The rise of the cinema has made accessible to playwrights and producers resources of unimagined richness and mobility over and above the written word. In fact these resources for a time threatened to overwhelm and suffocate the poor weakling of a play which they had presumably come to aid and exalt.

The play is still the thing, however, even in motion picture drama. As the newness has worn off the gadgets, and directors have learned to subordinate their acts and sound effects to the central drive of the play, masterpieces in cinema form have been created. These masterpieces on film, of course, differ in many perfectly obvious ways from the traditional stage plays of Aeschylus and Ibsen. In the opinion of many, they can never displace, or even adequately substitute for, the living actor on the living stage. But we may well consider whether Aeschylus and Ibsen, as well as Shakespeare and Goethe, would not have been cheered to find at their service such vast resources for producing their *Midsummer Night's Dreams* and their *Fausts*. Certainly they would have rejoiced over having at hand so practicable a medium for reaching in a single evening's showing more people than have seen *King Lear* in all the years since it was "played before the King's Majestie at Whitehall upon S. Stephans night in Christmas Hollidays" in 1606. For under the best of circumstances comparatively few people ever attend legitimate theatres, and for millions, including many college students, the motion picture is the only available form of drama; many will see no other. In unprotesting recognition of these facts and of the phenomenon that leads each year to the announcement that Hollywood is taking over Broadway, we have chosen to add to this collection of plays the basic word-soul of one of the moving picture masterpieces of our time—*The Informer*, adapted by Dudley Nichols from Liam O'Flaherty's novel and directed by John Ford.

Liam O'Flaherty, the author of the story, was born in 1896 in the Aran Islands made famous in drama in the plays of Synge. Like most of the Islanders, his people were poor, but he was educated for the church at the Jesuit College and at University College, Dublin. He was caught up in the World War and was plunged out of a training for the priesthood into the trenches on the Western Front. He was shell-shocked and sent back to Ireland. There he not only saw, but took an active part in, the Irish uprisings during and following the War. The gripping verisimilitude of *The Informer* has its origin in personal experience and observation during those strife-torn years.

Not long after the War, O'Flaherty began his travels about the world, as recorded in his autobiographical fragment, *Two Years* (1930). He engaged in all sorts of jobs from Istanbul to South America and Canada, and gulped experiences and the spectacle of life in all its aspects. He was working in a tire factory in Hartford, Connecticut, when he first began to write short stories in the early 1920's. He quickly won success with his short stories and novels in America, England, and on the Continent. *The Informer*, published in 1925, had marked success in France, as well as in America and the British Empire. His home is nominally Dublin, or a cottage in the Aran Islands. He has continued to travel about the world as his impulse directs, and frequently disappears beyond communication. (It took months to locate him for permission to use *The Informer* in this collection. He was found in a Mexican village.) His extraordinarily vivid and virile novels are recreated out of the zestful experience and knowledge of the world which he has absorbed while living adventurously.

The masterful adaptation of *The Informer* by Dudley Nichols, and the imaginative direction of John Ford, maker of *The Lost Patrol*, *It Happened One Night*, and other quality films, transferred to the screen the full force of O'Flaherty's novel, if it did not actually enhance it. The film was shot within three weeks and at small cost, and was released with no fanfare and little publicity. To the surprise of the studio, which hardly knew that the picture had been made, it caught on by the appeal of its own merits. Audiences were enthusiastic about it, and critics were unanimous in acclaiming it the unrivalled triumph of 1935.

After much deliberation and experiment, we have decided to print the cutting continuity of *The Informer* and to leave it entirely unedited. As it stands it is a technical and, to a degree, a literary document of the highest interest. Not many people, and few students, have ever had opportunity to see or to study a work in this form. Among other sources of interest, it offers a stimulating exercise in imaginative reading and interpretation of a play. Its flash phrases of detailed direction indicate how the stunning effects of *The Informer* were achieved. A little practice in this form of creative reading will soon overcome the initial puzzlement the reader may feel on first meeting with this unfamiliar technical form of communication. This difficulty, if such it should prove, is confined chiefly to the first reel where there is almost no dialogue. It opens with a sharp atmospheric thrust of foreboding. The intense, premonitory scenes tighten as the psychological nature of the drama is unfolded. During most of the first reel, this is accomplished entirely in the unique pictorial terms of the cinema. No word is spoken until the drama is well under way. Hence the first reel as here printed is composed largely of technical description of the scenes, the movement of the characters, and the action of the camera in building the dramatic effects. In this regard alone, this continuity is a marvel of skill. The following reels progressively call more heavily upon dialogue.

A careful study of this unedited continuity will show better than a chapter of detailed analysis and exposition how a story is told and how dramatic effects are produced in terms of this new film art. Dialogue is used sparingly, and every sentence is stripped bare of verbiage, every phrase is laced taut with life, atmosphere, character, and story. The talk is heightened by the action and symbolism that fill the intervals. The entire build-up of Frankie's betrayal is enacted in Gypo's sluggish mind, but his mental processes are pictured in objective form through the swift-moving sequence of symbolic images of the poster, the £20 reward for Frankie, the swirl of fog and the sound of the street singing, the vision of the ship that could carry him and Kate to Canada, the wind blowing the poster against his legs as he walks through the fog, the tortured features of Frankie as fire curls up the poster and foreshadows both the betrayal and its motive. The somber mood is suggested by the drifting fog and the descending darkness of night. It is deepened by such devices as the ominous ticking of the clock as Gypo at police headquarters looks up at the hands showing five minutes after six, then six minutes after; the scene then dissolves to the clock in Frankie's home where the hands indicate sixteen minutes after six, the continuous ticking rhythmically tying together the two scenes physically and psychologically. We know that Gypo has informed on his friend, and that Frankie is doomed.

There are many examples in *The Informer* of such skillful use of the cinema's unique adaptability to symbolism. One of the best and most subtle is the opening scene of the third reel where Gypo takes his blood money and goes furtively into the street. He meets the blind man tapping his way through the fog with his cane. Gypo grabs him by the throat, backs away, passes his hand in front of the blind man's eyes, then looks about cautiously and runs while the tapping goes on behind him. Dudley Nichols himself explained that the blind man was introduced as a symbol of Gypo's conscience "slowly working up out of his unconscious mind." When Gypo comes upon him so unexpectedly it is "as if he has seen his own conscience. . . . I dare say nobody was aware that it was a symbol, but it very definitely was." And these are but a few of the many remarkable effects achieved in *The Informer* which may be studied at leisure in this scenario. As Lewis Jacobs points out concerning *The Informer* in his *The Rise of the American Film*, "every small item in the picture is used to intensify the moment; nothing appears that is not made significant. A richness resulting from economy is the paradoxical result." We believe that the study of this continuity will be found interesting for itself, that it will sharpen the appreciation of the superior film plays, and that it may deepen the understanding and heighten the reading pleasures of the more literary dramas.

Cutting Continuity on THE INFORMER

ABBREVIATIONS AND STUDIO TERMS

BG: Background

CS: Close shot, relatively nearer to the scene, but not so near as in the close-up

CU: Close-up, usually of head or small detail of the action

Cut-in: To insert a shot of poster, letter, etc., into the action

Cutting Continuity: Complete scenario as used by the film editor

Dissolve: Gradual disappearance of a scene, or fading from one scene into another

EXT: Exterior scene

Fade-in: Gradual emergence of a scene on the screen

Fade-out: Gradual disappearance of a scene on the screen

FG: Foreground

FS: Full shot, embracing all the characters in a scene

Insert: Same as cut-in

INT: Interior scene

Lap Dissolve: Gradual blending of one scene with another, usually by fading and overlapping a few feet of two different scenes to make a new negative

LS: Long shot, indicating an over-all view of the scene

MCS: Medium close shot

MCU: Medium close-up

MLS: Medium long shot

MS: Medium shot

Pan (from panorama): To move camera slowly from side to side, or up and down, to follow the action

REEL 1

1   [*Fade in – Title #1 – Title over letters MPPDA –*]

This picture approved by
The Production Code Administration
of The Motion Picture Producers
& Distributors of America.
Certificate No. 734

[*Fade out*]

2   [*Fade in – Title #2 – NRA Insignia –*]

NRA
Member
. (Eagle)
U. S.
We do our part.

[*Fade out*]

3   [*Fade in – Title #3 – Radio Broadcasting –*]
A Radio Picture

[*Fade out*]

The Informer. Copyright, 1935, by RKO Radio Pictures, Inc. A cutting continuity of the motion picture from the novel by Liam O'Flaherty, herein published with the kind permission of Mr. O'Flaherty and RKO Radio Pictures, Inc., *The Informer*, an RKO-Radio Picture, was released and copyrighted by RKO Radio Pictures, Inc., in 1935, with the following credits: A John Ford Production; Associate Producer, Cliff Reid; Screen Play by Dudley Nichols. Among its feature players were Victor McLaglen, Heather Angel, Preston Foster, Margot Grahame, Wallace Ford, and Una O'Connor.

4   [*Fade in – Title #4 – Animated 'Pictorial BG – Orchestra heard playing –*
      "Medley" –]

                         Radio Pictures Presents
                         A John Ford Production
                                 The
                               Informer
               Copyright MCMXXXV RKO Radio Pictures, Inc.
                           All Rights Reserved

                                                              [*Lap dissolve*]

5   [*Title #5 – Animated Pictorial BG – Orchestra heard –*]
                                 with
                  Victor McLaglen   Heather Angel
                  Preston Foster   Margot Grahame
                  Wallace Ford   Una O'Connor

                                                              [*Lap dissolve*]

6   [*Title #6 – Animated Pictorial BG – Orchestra heard –*]

                              Directed by
                              John Ford

                                                              [*Lap dissolve*]

7   [*Title #7 – Animated Pictorial BG – Orchestra heard –*]

                          Associate Producer
                             Cliff Reid

                                                              [*Lap dissolve*]

8   [*Title #8 – Animated Pictorial BG – Orchestra heard –*]

                           Screen Play by
                           Dudley Nichols

                          From The Story by
                          Liam O'Flaherty

                             Music by
                            Max Steiner

                                                              [*Lap dissolve*]

9   [*Title #9 – Animated Pictorial BG – Orchestra heard –*]
           Photographed by   Joseph H. August, A. S. C.
           Art Director   Van Nest Polglase
           Associate   Charles Kirk
           Costumes by   Walter Plunkett
           Recorded by   Hugh McDowell, Jr.
           Edited by   George Hively
                       Recorded by RCA Victor System

                                                              [*Lap dissolve*]

10   [*Title #10 – Animated Pictorial BG – Orchestra heard –*]

The Players

J. M. Kerrigan
Joseph Sauers
Neil Fitzgerald
Donald Meek
D'Arcy Corrigan
Leo McCabe
Gaylord Pendleton
Francis Ford
May Boley
Grizelda Harvey
Dennis O'Dea

[Fade out]

11   *[Fade in – Title #11 – Orchestra heard –]*

A Certain Night
In Strife-Torn
Dublin – 1922

[Lap dissolve]

12   *[Title #12 – Orchestra heard –]*

"Then Judas repented himself – and
cast down the thirty pieces of
silver – and departed."

[Fade out]

13   *[Fade in – Ext. wall MS – Shadow seen on wall – Music heard – GYPO comes on at left – Camera following him across to right – WOMAN comes on at right, crossing in front of him to left – Exits – He walks along to right – Camera following him – MAN comes on at right – Crosses in front of him to left – Exits – GYPO stops at corner of bldg – Looks at poster on wall –]*

14   *[Ext. wall CS – GYPO partly on at left FG – Back partly to camera – Looking at poster on wall – Music heard – Poster reads –]*

£20 Reward
Wanted For Murder
Frankie McPhillip

[GYPO exits as camera moves closer to poster – Fog drifting across in front of it – Superimposed over poster is CS of FRANKIE and GYPO at bar, singing –]
BOTH *(singing)*   . . sing a song of soldiers . .
[They laugh – Superimposed scene goes out –]

15   *[Ext. street CU – GYPO looking to right FG – Music heard – Fog drifting behind him – His lips move as he thinks –]*

16   *[Insert #1 – Printing on poster – Music heard – Poster reads –]*

Police Notice
£20 Reward
Wanted For Murder

17 [*Ext. bldg CS* – GYPO *looking at poster of* FRANKIE *on wall* – *Pats it affectionately* – *Music heard* – *Fog drifting about him* – *He looks around cautiously* – *Music stops* – *He rips poster from wall* – *Music heard* – *He throws poster down* – *Comes to right FG* – *Exits* –]

18 [*Ext. street MLS* – *Group on corner in BG standing around street* SINGER *and* VIOLINIST – *Fog drifting about* – GYPO *coming on at left FG* – *Looks about cautiously* – *Goes to BG* – SINGER *heard singing* – "*Rose of Tralee*" –]
SINGER (*singing*)   . . The pale moon was rising above the green mountain, the sun was declining . .
[*Poster blowing on after* GYPO *as he walks down street* –]

19 [*Ext. street MCU* – GYPO *coming on at right* – *Leans on seat of wagon* – *Singing and violin heard* –]
SINGER (*off*)   . . beneath the blue sea . .

20 [*Ext. street CU* – *Street* SINGER *singing* – *Fog drifting about him* – *Violin heard* –]
SINGER   . . when I strayed with my love to the pure crystal fountain . .

21 [*Ext. street MCU* – GYPO *leaning on seat of wagon listening* – *Fog drifting about him* – *Singing and violin heard* –]
SINGER (*off*)   . . that stands . .

22 [*Ext. street CS* – *Camera following poster as it is blown along walk to right* – *Singing and violin heard* –]
SINGER (*off*)   . . in the beautiful vale . .
[*Camera following crumpled poster to right reveals* GYPO *partly on at right* – *Poster blows against his leg* –]
SINGER (*off*)   . . of . .

23 [*Ext. street MCU* – GYPO *with back to camera, looking to BG* – *Group in BG around* SINGER *and* VIOLINIST – *Music heard* – *Fog drifting* – GYPO *turns* – *Looks down* –]
SINGER   . . Tralee . .

24 [*Ext. street CS* – GYPO *partly on, trying to kick poster away from feet* – *singing and violin heard* –]
SINGER (*off*)   . . she was lovely . .
[*Poster blows away to right* –]

25 [*Ext. street MCU* – GYPO *looking to left FG listening* – *Singing and violin heard* – *Fog drifting about him* –]
SINGER (*off*)   . . and fair as the rose . .

26 [*Ext. street MCS* – SINGER *singing* – *Others standing about listening* – GYPO *in BG leaning on cart* – *Watching* – *Fog drifting about them* –]
SINGER   . . of the summer yet 'twas not her beauty alone . .

27   [*Ext. street MCU – * GYPO *leaning on cart – Looking to left FG – Listening – Singing and violin heard – Fog drifting about – *]

SINGER (*off*)   . . that won me
                    Oh, no, 'twas . .

[GYPO *looks up to FG frightened – *]

SINGER (*off*)   . . the truth . .

28   [*Ext. street MS – * SINGER *leaning against post singing – * GYPO *in BG watching as soldiers come on in FG going to BG – Others standing about – Violin heard – Fog drifting – *]

SINGER   . . in her eye ever dawning . .

[*Cart comes to left FG – Exits as soldiers frisk * SINGER *– Others dispersing quickly – Exit – *]

SINGER   . . that made me love Marie . .

[SOLDIER *throws coin to * SINGER *– He catches it – *]

SINGER   . . The Rose of Tralee.

[*He leans against wall – Back to camera – Watching after soldiers – *]

                                        [*Lap dissolve*]

29   [*Ext. street CU – * KATIE *looking up to right FG – Fog drifting about – Music heard – Playing "Medley" – *]

30   [*Ext. street CS – * DANDY *standing by bldg – Watching to right FG – Fog about – Music heard – *]

31   [*Ext. street CU – * KATIE *looks down – Fog about her – Music heard – She looks up – Camera moves back as she puts shawl around shoulders – Camera moves back as she starts to FG – *]

32   [*Ext. street MS – * DANDY *standing at corner of bldg – Watching as * KATIE *comes on at left – Crosses in front of him – Music heard – He turns, watching after her – She stops at right – Leans against lamp post – He starts toward her – *]

33   [*Ext. street MCU – * KATIE *leaning against lamp post – Back partly to camera – Fog about her – Music heard – Hands come on at left – Strike match on post – * DANDY *comes on at left as he lights cigarette – *]

34   [*Ext. street MS – * GYPO *coming to FG – Fog about him – Wind blowing – Music heard – He stops – Looks off to right FG – Sees – *]

35   [*Ext. street MCU – * KATIE *leaning against post – Back partly to camera – * DANDY *partly on at left FG looking her over – Music heard – He blows smoke in her face – She looks at him – He smiles at her – She looks away – Fog about – *]

36   [*Ext. street MCU – * GYPO *watching to right FG jealously – Music heard – Fog about him – He comes to right FG – Exits – *]

37   [*Ext. street MS – * DANDY *and * KATIE *standing by lamp post – she turns away from him – Goes toward window at right – Music heard – * DANDY *watching after her – * GYPO *comes on at left – Picks up * DANDY *– Throws him off to left – * KATIE *turns quickly – Watching – *]

38   [*Ext. street MS – Camera shooting down at* DANDY *landing in middle of street –*
       Wind blowing papers about him – Music heard – He starts to rise –]

39   [*Ext. street MCU –* KATIE *coming to FG as she talks – Music heard – Fog drifting*
       about her –]

KATIE   Gypo!

40   [*Ext. street CU –* GYPO *turning to right FG – Fog about him – Music heard –*]

41   [*Ext. street MCU –* KATIE *looking to left FG – Drops eyelids slowly – Fog about*
       her – Music heard – She starts to look up –]

42   [*Ext. street CS –* KATIE *leaning against post – Looking up at* GYPO *as he comes to*
       left FG – Going to her – Music heard – Fog about them – She talks –]

KATIE   Ah, Gypo, what's the use? I'm hungry and I
can't pay my room rent . .

43   [*Ext. street CU –* KATIE *looking up at* GYPO *partly on at left FG – Back to camera –*
       Talking to him – Music heard –]

KATIE   . . have you the price of a flop on you? No. Oh,
what's the use?

44   [*Ext. street CU –* GYPO *looking down at* KATIE *partly on at left FG – Back to cam-*
       era – Talking – Music heard – Fog about them –]

KATIE   . . Oh, don't look at me like that, Gypo . .

45   [*Ext. street CU –* KATIE *looking up at* GYPO *partly on at left FG – Back to camera –*
       Talking to him – Music heard – Fog about them –]

KATIE   . . you're all I got. You're the only one, you
know that, but what chance have we to escape! . .
[*She turns – Starts to BG –*]

46   [*Ext. window MCU –* KATIE *coming on at left FG – Stops at window – Looking
up at printing on window – Music heard – Printing reads –*]

£10
To
America
Information
Within

[*She talks disgustedly –*]
KATIE   Money! Some people have all the luck. Look at
that thing! . .
[*Reflection of* GYPO *comes on in window –*]
KATIE   . . handing us the Ha-Ha. Ten pounds to Amer-
ica. Twenty pounds and the world is ours.
[GYPO *comes on at left – Grabs her as he talks furiously – Music stops –*]
GYPO   What are ye sayin' that for?
KATIE   Sayin' what . . twenty pounds?
GYPO   What are ye drivin' at?

KATIE   Oh, Gypo, what's the matter with you? Twenty
pounds! Might as well be a million.

GYPO   Go on, go on, go on! Get your twenty pounds
from that scut I threw in the gutter.

KATIE   Saint Gypo! Too good for me, Eh? Well, let me
tell you something. You're no better than any other man. You're all alike.

[*She crosses in front of him to left — He grabs her — Turns her toward him — Talks —
Music heard playing —*]

GYPO   Aw, Katie, I didn't mean that.

KATIE   Go along with you and your fine principles . .

47 [*Ext. street MS —* GYPO *and* KATIE *in front of window — Fog about them — Music
heard —* KATIE *talking —*]

KATIE   . . I can't afford 'em.

[*She goes to left — He exits as camera follows her —*]

GYPO (*off*)   Katie!

[*Camera pans to left as she goes to left BG —* GYPO *comes on at right watching after
her — She exits in fog in BG —*]

                                                         [*Lap dissolve*]

48 [*Ext. street CS — Camera following feet along to right — Music heard — Feet coming
on at right — Crossing to left — Exit — Camera following first feet along to right —
Poster blows on at right — Stops against feet — Hands coming on, pick up poster —
Camera panning up as poster is picked up — Reveals* FRANKIE *— He looks at
poster — Sees —*]

49 [*Ext. street CU — Camera shooting over* FRANKIE's *shoulder at poster in his hands —
Picture of himself — Wind blowing poster — Music heard —*]

50 [*Ext. street CU —* FRANKIE *looking down to right — Fog about him — Music heard —
He sees —*]

51 [*Ext. street CU —* FRANKIE *partly on at left looking at poster — Fog about him —
Music heard — Poster reads —*]

£20
Wanted

52 [*Ext. street CS —* FRANKIE *looking at poster — Fog about him — Music heard — He
crumbles poster — Throws it down angrily — Looks about — Sees —*]

53 [*Ext. street MLS — Squad of soldiers coming on at right BG — Fog about — Music
heard — Soldiers start to FG —*]

54 [*Ext. street CS —* FRANKIE *looking off to left — Turns quickly — Exits right — Fog
about — Music heard —*]

55 [*Ext. street MS — Soldiers coming to FG — Fog about — Music heard — Soldiers
nearly exiting left FG —*]

56 [*Ext. street MS —* FRANKIE *running on at left — Runs into archway — Stops at
right — Music heard — Fog in BG — Soldiers come on at left —* OFFICER *talks —*]

OFFICER   Throw a light in there, lads.

[*Men flash lights to FG as they march across to right —*]

57   [*Ext. street MCS – Light flashing on wall of bldg – Poster on wall –*]

58   [*Ext. bldg CS –* FRANKIE *standing stiffly against wall – Gun in hand –*]

59   [*Ext. street MCS – Soldiers looking in archway – Flashing lights about –* SOLDIER
     talks – Fog in BG –]

SOLDIER   I'll bet he's not out tonight, boys.
[*They march across to right – All exit except one – He flashes light to FG –*]

60   [*Ext. wall MCS – Light flashing on wall – Moves along posters – Stops on poster
     of* FRANKIE, *revealing –*]

£20 Reward
Wanted For Murder

[*Light moves down to picture of* FRANKIE *–*]

61   [*Ext. wall CS –* FRANKIE *standing stiffly against wall – Watching to left – Gun in
     hand –*]

62   [*Ext. street MCS*   SOLDIER *standing in archway – Flashing light to FG – Fog in
     BG –*]

63   [*Ext. street MS –* FRANKIE *standing tensely against wall at right FG –* SOLDIER *in
     BG in archway flashing light to FG – He flashes light to left – Turns it out –
     Exits right –*]

64   [*Ext. bldg CS –* FRANKIE *standing tensely against wall – Watching to left – Gun
     in hand – He relaxes – Relieved –*]

65   [*Ext. street MS –* FRANKIE *runs to BG – Exits in BG around corner of bldg – Fog
     about –*]

66   [*Ext. street MS –* FRANKIE *running on at right – Crossing street to left – Camera
     following him – He stops at left – Looks about cautiously – Comes to FG –
     Stops – Looks about – Looks up to left – Sees –*]

67   [*Ext. doorway MCS – Camera shooting up at window over doorway – Music heard
     playing "Medley" – Printing on window reads –*]

Dunboy
House

68   [*Ext. street MS –* FRANKIE *partly on in FG – Entrance of Dunboy House in BG –
     Music heard – He goes to entrance cautiously – opens door – Goes into bldg –
     Shadow seen through window – He exits as he opens second door of entrance –*]

69   [*Int. Dunboy House MCS – Camera shooting along line of stoves – Men on either
     side of stoves – Preparing meals – Music heard –*]

70   [*Int. Dunboy House CS –* GYPO *seated at table – Eating – Others in BG at tables –
     Music heard –* FRANKIE *comes on at left FG – Sits down – Back to camera –*
     GYPO *stares up at him – Surprised – Music stops –*]

71   [*Int. Dunboy House MCU –* FRANKIE *seated at table – Smiling – Looking to left
     FG –*]

REEL 2

1   [*Int. Dunboy House CU* – GYPO *seated at table* – *Looking to right FG* – *Mumbling heard* –]

2   [*Int. Dunboy House MCU* – FRANKIE *seated at table* – *Looking across to left FG* – *Talks* – *Mumbling heard* –]

   FRANKIE   Don't you know me, Gypo? Ah, I don't wonder that you stare. I'm lucky to be finding you here . .

3   [*Int. Dunboy House CU* – GYPO *seated* – *Looking to right FG* – *Mumbling heard* –]

4   [*Int. Dunboy House MCU* – FRANKIE *seated at table* – *Looking across to left FG* – *Mumbling heard* – *Superimposed over him is printing from poster reading* –]

£20 Reward

[FRANKIE *talks*]

   FRANKIE   . . Man, what is it? . .
[*Printing from poster dissolves out* – FRANKIE *sits back as he talks frightened* –]
   FRANKIE   . . What are you starin' at?

5   [*Int. Dunboy House MCU* – GYPO *seated* – *Looking across to right FG* – *Talks* –]
   GYPO   Nothin', Frankie. But you came up to me so sudden-like.

6   [*Int. Dunboy House CS* – GYPO *seated at left* – FRANKIE *seated at right* – *Talks* –]
   FRANKIE   I guess I'm gettin' jumpy. Findin' out there's a price on my head. Twenty pounds! Ah, so that's all I'm worth. Uh, six months is a long time, me boy, to be on the run . .

7   [*Int. Dunboy House MCU* – FRANKIE *seated* – *Looking across to left FG* – *Talking* – GYPO *partly on at left FG* –]
   FRANKIE   . . sleepin' out in the hills; freezin' to death; and no decent grub. So I says to meself, I'll sneak into town and see me mother and I'd duck right out again, and here I am . .

8   [*Int. Dunboy House MCU* – GYPO *seated at table* – *Staring at* FRANKIE *partly on at right FG* – *Back to camera* – FRANKIE *talking* –]
   FRANKIE   . . Did . . did you deliver any messages? And what did my mother say?
   GYPO   Oh, she blessed the Saints ye were alive. She followed me out cryin' and put half a quid in me hand to give ye. Well, I was that hungry meself that I spent it.

9   [*Int. Dunboy House MCU* – FRANKIE *seated* – *Talks to* GYPO *partly on at left FG* –]
   FRANKIE   Ah, you big lubber, that was her way of giving it to you. She likes you, Gypo, the Lord knows why . .

10 [*Int. Dunboy House MCU* − GYPO *seated* − *Staring at* FRANKIE − FRANKIE *looks at him* − *Talks* −]

FRANKIE   . . What's come over you? What are you gawkin' at? Is there something queer about me?

GYPO   No, Frankie. You see, I've been court-martialed.

11 [*Int. Dunboy House MCU* − FRANKIE *seated* − *Talks to* GYPO *partly on at left FG* − *Back to camera* −]

FRANKIE   Man . . what for?

12 [*Int. Dunboy House CS* − GYPO *seated at left of table* − FRANKIE *seated at right* − GYPO *talks* −]

GYPO   You remember the Tan that killed Quincannon? . .

[FRANKIE *nods* −]

GYPO   . . We drew lots for it an' I got the short match. Well, I took him out in a lorry and he begged for his life. I couldn't do it, Frankie, not in cold blood. Besides, he swore he'd desert if I let him go.

FRANKIE   And you believed him . . what did Commandant Gallagher say?

13 [*Int. Dunboy House MCU* − GYPO *seated* − *Shakes head* − *Talks to* FRANKIE *partly on at right FG* − *Back to camera* −]

GYPO   Oh, he near had me plugged when I went back to report. Then they threw me out of the organization, and now the British think I'm with the Irish, and the Irish think I'm with the British, and the long and short of it is I'm walkin' round starvin', without a dog to lick me trousers.

14 [*Int. Dunboy House MCU* − FRANKIE *seated* − *Talks to* GYPO *partly on at left FG* − *Back to camera* −]

FRANKIE   Ah, you poor fathead! Think of all the jobs we pulled off together, and the scrapes we come thru. Ahh, we were a great pair, Eh, Gypo . . with your muscles and my brains . .

15 [*Int. Dunboy House CS* − GYPO *seated at left of table* − FRANKIE *at right* − *Talking* −]

FRANKIE   . . When we'd get in a tight place, it was me that formed a plan, and thought a way out, remember? Ah, and I leave you alone for a minute and you're in trouble again. Man, alive, I'm your brain! . .

16 [*Int. Dunboy House MCU* − FRANKIE *seated at table* − GYPO *partly on at left FG* − *Back to camera* − FRANKIE *looks about cautiously* − *Talks* −]

FRANKIE   . . It's your help I'm needin' now. I've looked you up first thing to find out if the Tans are still watchin' my mother's house. Is there any guard on the house?

17 [*Int. Dunboy House MCS* − GYPO *and* FRANKIE *seated at table* − FRANKIE *with back partly to camera* − GYPO *talks* −]

GYPO   Not since Christmas.
[FRANKIE *rises as he talks – Music heard playing "Medley" –*]
FRANKIE   Well, I'm off. If I get a chance to see Gallagher,
I'll put in the word for you. Up the rebels!
[*He pats* GYPO *on back – Exits left –* GYPO *looks after him thoughtfully – Camera
moving closer to him – He looks up to right BG – Superimposed on wall appears
poster of* FRANKIE *– It dissolves out –*]

[*Lap dissolve*]

18 [*Ext. street MS – Window of shipping offices – Printing on window reads –*]

£10
to
America

[*Music heard –* GYPO *comes on at left slowly – Stops at window – Looking in –
Fog about –*]

19 [*Int. window MCU –* GYPO *outside looking through window to FG – Music heard –
Fog seen outside – He looks down thoughtfully – Rubs face with hands –*]

[*Lap dissolve*]

20 [*Ext. headquarters MS –* SENTRY *on steps of entrance – Watching to FG – Music
heard – Fog about –* GYPO *coming on slowly in FG – Raises arms –* SENTRY
talks –]
SENTRY   Carry on.
[*He goes to BG –*]

[*Lap dissolve*]

21 [*Int. headquarters MS –* MAJOR *seated at desk in FG – Writing –* OFFICER *standing
at desk – Others in BG – Music heard – Door at right BG opening –* SOLDIER
comes in, followed by GYPO *– He slams door shut after* GYPO *–* GYPO *turns
nervously – Looks about office –*]

22 [*Int. office MCS –* GYPO *standing at railing –* OFFICER *at right watching – Others
in BG – Music heard –* GYPO *glances about nervously –*]

23 [*Int. office MS –* MAJOR *seated at desk in FG writing –* OFFICER *standing at desk –*
GYPO *in BG at railing – Others about – Music heard –* OFFICER *motions to*
GYPO *– He comes through gate to* MAJOR'S *desk – Stops at desk – Music stops –*]

24 [*Int. office CS – Camera shooting down at* MAJOR *seated at desk – Writing –*
OFFICER *partly on at right by him –* GYPO *partly on in FG – Back to camera –*]

25 [*Int. office CU –* GYPO *looking down to left – Rubs face with cap –*]

26 [*Int. office CS – Camera shooting down at* MAJOR *seated at desk – Writing –*
OFFICER *partly on at right by him –* GYPO *partly on in FG – Back to camera –*
MAJOR *looks up – Bellows –*]
MAJOR   Yes.

27 [*Int. office CU –* GYPO *looking to BG – Turns quickly – Looks down to left –
Frightened –*]

28   [*Int. office MCS —* GYPO *standing at desk —* MAJOR *partly on at left seated at desk —*
      OFFICER *standing by him — Others in BG —* GYPO *talks nervously —*]
      GYPO   Well, I . . It was like this. I . .
      OFFICER   Well, speak up. What do you want to say?
      [GYPO *leans across desk as he talks to* MAJOR —]
      GYPO   I've come to claim the twenty pounds reward
      for Frankie McPhillip.
      [*Men in BG stand alert —*]
      MAJOR   Frankie McPhillip?

                                                                    [*Lap dissolve*]

29   [*Ext. headquarters MLS — Camera shooting down at soldiers getting into trucks —*
      Sound of motors heard — General indistinct talking — OFFICER *gives command*
      indistinctly — Trucks start to left —]

30   [*Int. office MS —* GYPO *seated in BG in front of desk — Head bowed —* MAJOR *and*
      OFFICER *in BG at windows — Sound of motors heard — Shadows seen through*
      windows in BG — Sound of motors die — MAJOR *and* OFFICER *turn — Look at*
      GYPO — *Look up to left — He looks up to left — Sees*]

31   [*Int. office MCS —* GYPO *partly on in FG — Back to camera — Looking up at clock*
      on wall — Hands indicating five minutes after six —]

32   [*Int. office CU —* GYPO *seated — Watching up to left —*]

33   [*Int. office MCS —* GYPO *partly on in FG — Back to camera — Looking up at clock*
      on wall — Hands indicating six minutes after six —]

                                                                    [*Lap dissolve*]

34   [*Int. kitchen CS — Camera shooting down at clock on wall by door — Hands indicating*
      sixteen minutes after six — Door opening slowly — FRANKIE *comes on listening —*]
      MOTHER (*off*)   Mary, the bread's that fresh I can't cut it . .

35   [*Int. kitchen MS —* MARY *and* MOTHER *standing at table in FG —* FRANKIE *by door*
      in BG — Looking at them happily — MOTHER *talking —*]
      MOTHER   . . look at the crumbs it makes . .
      [MARY *looks at BG — Sees* FRANKIE — *Drops silverware at table —* MOTHER *looks*
      up at her — Looks to BG — Sees FRANKIE — *He closes door as she runs to him —*
      Talking —]
      MOTHER   . . Oh, me boy, me boy!
      [*He takes her in his arms —* MARY *goes to them —*]
      FRANKIE   Mother . . Mary!
      MARY   Oh, Frankie!

36   [*Int. kitchen CS —* FRANKIE *with arms around* MARY *and* MOTHER — MOTHER
      laughing and sobbing — Talks —]
      MOTHER   Oh, praise be to God, you've come back to us.
      FRANKIE   Save yer praises for this fog that's upon us,
      Mother. It's the best friend I have this night, and me dodgin' down dark
      streets to get here. Ah, I was so homesick to see you, I'd have walked down
      the middle of O'Connell Street to get a glimpse of the two of you.

MOTHER   Ah, Muscha . . me son. Sure, you must be
starvin'.
[*She comes to right FG – Exits –* MARY *talks to* FRANKIE *as he removes coat –*]
MARY   Frankie, you shouldn't have come.
FRANKIE   Aw.
MARY   It's not safe.
FRANKIE   What a long face for a sister. I'm in with the fog
and I'm out with the fog, and nobody will be the wiser.

37   [*Int. kitchen MS – Table in FG –* MARY *and* FRANKIE *in BG – She talks wor-
      riedly –*]
      MARY   You're sure nobody's seen you?
      [*They come to table as he talks –*]
      FRANKIE   Just my old pal, Gypo Nolan. You see, I had to
      find out if the Tans had a guard on the house.
      [*He sits down at table –* MARY *exits left –* MOTHER *comes on at right – Talking –*]
      MOTHER   Have a nice cup of tea. You can do all your
      talking afterwards.

38   [*Ext. house MS – Two women standing near entrance of bldg – Motors heard –
      They look to BG – Run to right FG – Exit as trucks drive on at left BG – Stop
      in front of camera –* SERGEANT *comes on in FG talking –*]
      SERGEANT   Go on up there to the front door there. Get to
      the door there . .
      [*Soldiers run to entrance –* SERGEANT *talks to others –*]
      SERGEANT   . . machine gun . . machine gun . . get over
      there!
      [*Soldiers run across to right with machine gun –*]

39   [*Int. kitchen MCS –* FRANKIE *seated at table – Eating –* MARY *at left –* MOTHER
      at right – He rises as pounding is heard – They look to FG frightened –]

40   [*Ext. entrance MS – Soldiers pounding on door with guns – Talking indistinctly –*]

41   [*Int. kitchen MCS –* FRANKIE *standing at table –* MARY *at left by him –* MOTHER
      at right – All looking to BG – Pounding – Indistinct yelling heard – MOTHER
      and MARY *exit as camera follows* FRANKIE *across to left – He takes gun from coat
      pocket – Camera following him across to right reveals two standing at table –
      They try to stop him –*]
      MARY   No, no!
      [*All talking at once –* MOTHER *wailing –* FRANKIE *pushes them aside – Goes to
      door at right –* MOTHER *and* MARY *following him – They exit through door-
      way –*]

42   [*Int. hallway MS –* FRANKIE *running on at left FG – Runs to door in BG – Pound-
      ing and indistinct yelling heard –* MARY *and* MOTHER *coming on at left FG after*
      FRANKIE *– He yells at them –*]
      FRANKIE   Stay back! Mary, get back!
      [*All talking at once – Confusion –*]

FRANKIE   I can get away!

[*He starts upstairs at right —* MOTHER *looking after him — Screams —*]

MOTHER   Frankie . . don't!

43   [*Int. stairway MS —* FRANKIE *running upstairs to landing above — Pounding and indistinct yelling heard —*]

44   [*Ext. door CS — Two soldiers partly on — Beating door down with butts of guns — Noise of pounding heard —*]

45   [*Int. hallway MS —* MARY *and* MOTHER *at foot of stairs — Looking up to right FG — Pounding on door heard — They look to BG as sections of door splinter revealing soldiers outside —* SOLDIER *reaches through broken door — Unlocks it — Enters hall — Talking — Confusion —*]

OFFICER   Where's McPhillip?

46   [*Int. hallway MCU —* MARY *standing at foot of stairs — Talks defiantly — To soldier partly on at left FG —* MOTHER *heard screaming indistinctly —*]

MARY   He's not here. Get out!

47   [*Int. stairway MS — Camera shooting up stairs at* FRANKIE *above on landing — He fires gun —*]

48   [*Int. hallway MS — Soldiers in doorway — Much confusion as soldier pushes* MOTHER *to FG —* MOTHER *yelling —* MARY *standing at foot of stairs screaming — Soldiers trying to pull her away —*]

MARY   Oh, Frankie . . Frankie!

49   [*Int. stairway MCS — Camera shooting up at* FRANKIE *on landing — Looking down to FG — Confusion heard — He talks —*]

FRANKIE   Mary, get out of the way! Get out of the way and let me shoot.

50   [*Int. hallway MCS —* MARY *standing at foot of stairs — Fighting soldiers — Screaming at them indistinctly — Confusion —*]

51   [*Int. hallway MCS — Camera shooting up at* FRANKIE *on landing looking down to FG — Confusion heard — He talks —*]

FRANKIE   Mary, get out of the way . . go on!

52   [*Int. stairway MS — Camera shooting down stairway at soldiers below —* MARY *screaming as they drag her away — Two soldiers run upstairs to FG — Shots heard — Soldiers fall downstairs — Others below firing up to FG — Much confusion — Yelling heard —* MOTHER *heard wailing —*]

53   [*Int. doorway CS —* MOTHER *struggling with* SOLDIER *— Screaming — Shooting and confusion heard —*]

MOTHER (*off*)   Frankie!

54   [*Int. hallway CS — Camera shooting down at* FRANKIE *raising window — Confusion heard — He steps out of window onto ledge — Screaming heard —*]

MOTHER (*off*)   Frankie, don't . . stop!

[*Soldiers coming on below in BG — Fire machine gun up at* FRANKIE *— His hand slowly slips from window ledge — His nails drag across sill — Exits —*]

55 [*Int. hallway CS* − SOLDIER *and* MARY *standing in doorway* − *Looking up to right FG* − MARY *horrified* −]

56 [*Int. hallway CS* − MOTHER *and* SOLDIER *standing in doorway* − MOTHER *screams hysterically* − *Struggles with* SOLDIER − *He exits as camera follows her as she sinks to floor* − *Wailing* −]

REEL 3

1   [*Int. office CS* − GYPO *standing at table* − *Others about* − *Phone rings* − SENTRY *picks up phone* − *Talks* −]
SENTRY   Yes, yes. Right . .
[*He puts down phone* − *Talks to* MAJOR −]
SENTRY   . . McPhillip was killed trying to escape, Sir.
[MAJOR *takes bills from wallet* − *Tosses them on table* − *Music heard playing medley* (*"The Money" and "The Blind Man"*) − MAJOR *exits right* − OFFICER *pushes money to* GYPO *with cane* − *Talks* −]
OFFICER   Twenty pounds. You'd better count it. Show him out the back way.
[*He exits right* − GYPO *picks up money* − *Crosses to left* − *Exits* − SENTRY *following him* −]

2   [*Ext. headquarters MCS* − *Wires crossing in FG* − *Door opening* − GYPO *comes on through doorway* − *Music heard* − *He closes door* − *Looks about furtively* − *Puts money in pocket* − *Camera follows him across to right* − *Moves back as he comes to FG revealing* BLIND MAN *at left FG* − GYPO *lurches at him* − *Grabs his throat* −]
GYPO   Why, you . .

3   [*Ext. street MCU* − GYPO *looking at* BLIND MAN − *Hands on his throat* − *Music heard* − *He takes hands away from* MAN's *throat* − *Backs away* −]

4   [*Ext. street CU* − BLIND MAN *staring up to FG* − *Music heard* −]

5   [*Ext. street MCU* − GYPO *looking at* BLIND MAN *partly on at left FG* − *Music heard* − *He passes hand in front of* MAN's *eyes* −]

7   [*Ext. street CS* − GYPO *passing hand in front of* BLIND MAN's *eyes* − *Looking about cautiously* − *Music heard* − *He turns quickly* − *Runs to right* − *Exits* −]
[*Lap dissolve*]

8   [*Ext. street MS* − GYPO *coming on at left* − *Camera following him across to right* − *Fog about* − *Music heard* − *He stops by bldg* − *Looks about frightened* − *Walking heard* − *He looks off to left* − *Sees* −]

9   [*Ext. street MLS* − BLIND MAN *coming around corner at left FG* − *Tapping cane as he walks* − *Music heard* − *Fog about* − BLIND MAN *coming toward FG* −]

10 [*Ext. street MCS* − GYPO *watching off to left* − *Fog about* − *Music heard* − GYPO *turns to right* − *Stops as he sees bare wall* −]

11 [*Ext. street CS* − GYPO *looking at bare wall* − *Fog about* − *Music heard* − *Superimposed on wall is poster offering reward for* FRANKIE −]

12 [*Ext. street MCU –* GYPO *looking to right FG – Music heard – Fog about – He sees –*]

13 [*Ext. wall CU – Picture of* FRANKIE *on poster – Music heard –*]

14 [*Ext. street CS –* GYPO *looking at poster on wall – Poster dissolves out –* GYPO *looks about frightened – Starts to right – Music heard –*]

[*Lap dissolve*]

15 [*Int. pub MCS –* BARTENDER *at counter – Man standing at counter – Music heard – Door in BG opening –* GYPO *comes on through doorway – Comes to bar – Talks to* BARTENDER *–*]
GYPO   Whiskey.

16 [*Int. pub MCU –* BARTENDER *at counter – Looking to right FG – Laughs – Talks –*]
BARTENDER   Ah, ha, there's a lot of things I'd like if I could afford it.

17 [*Int. pub CU –* GYPO *looking to left – Camera follows him as he turns to right – Pans down revealing him taking bills from pocket cautiously – Music heard –*]

18 [*Int. pub MCU –* BARTENDER *watching to right – Music heard playing "Medley" –*]

19 [*Int. pub CU –* GYPO'S *hands taking bill from roll of bills – Camera pans up revealing his face as he turns to left – Music heard –*]

20 [*Int. pub MCU –* BARTENDER *behind bar – Takes bill – Looks at it suspiciously – Music heard – He glances up to right –*]

21 [*Int. pub CU –* GYPO *looking to left – Music heard –*]

22 [*Int. pub MCS –* GYPO *standing at bar – Waiting –* BARTENDER *turns from bar – Exits left –* MAN *standing at bar in BG – Music heard –* BARTENDER *comes on at left – Puts bottle on bar –* GYPO *pours drink – Drinks –*]

23 [*Int. pub CU –* GYPO *gulping drink down – Smacks lips – Music heard –*]

24 [*Int. pub MCS –* GYPO *standing at bar – Bottle and glass in hand –* BARTENDER *watching him –* MAN *standing at bar in BG – Music heard –* GYPO *turns to right – Goes to BG – Looks about –* MAN *talks as he goes to BG –*]
MAN   Good Night.
[*He exits through doorway –* GYPO *turning to bar – Puts bottle down –* BARTENDER *picks it up –* GYPO *reaches for it –*]

25 [*Int. pub MS –* GYPO *grabs bottle from* BARTENDER *– Music heard –* BARTENDER *exits as camera follows* GYPO *across to right – He goes to table at right BG –* MAN *seated at table at right – Rises – Crossing to left – Exits –* GYPO *sits down at table in BG – Watches out window – People seen crossing outside in BG – Two policemen coming on outside – Crossing in front of window –*]

26 [*Int. pub CS –* GYPO *seated at table – Turns face away from window as two policemen pass outside – Music heard – Policemen exit –* GYPO *whispers to self –*]

GYPO   I've got to have a plan! I've got to have a plan!
[*He looks up as he hears voice* —]
FRANKIE (*off*)   Ah, Gypo, I'm your brain. You can't think
without me. You're lost. You're lost.
[*He pours drink quickly* — *Gulps it down* —]

27   [*Ext. pub MCS* — GYPO *seen inside, seated at table* — *Drinking* — *Music heard* —
      Fog about — KATIE *comes on at left FG* — *Stops at window as she sees* GYPO *in-
      side* — *She crosses to right FG* — *Exits* —]

28   [*Int. pub CS* — GYPO *seated at table* — *Head bowed* — *Music heard* — KATIE *comes
      on at left* — *Puts hand on his shoulder* — *Music stops as he jumps back frightened* —
      Camera moves back as he looks up at her — *Talks* — *Nervously* —]
GYPO   What do you want to be, sneakin' up behind a
man like that for?
KATIE   I've been looking all over for you . .
[*Music heard playing* —]
KATIE   . . Oh, I'm so sorry . . I blew up on you like
that, out in the street, I mean. Ah, Gypo, you know that I love you.
You're the only one. You know that. Sometimes I get so crazy I don't
know what I'm doing.
GYPO   I got it. I did it for you.
KATIE   You did what?
[BARTENDER *comes partly on at left as he starts to put change on table* —]

29   [*Int. pub CU* — BARTENDER *partly on at left* — *Dropping coins on table* — KATIE
      and GYPO *partly on at right* — *Music heard* —]
BARTENDER (*off*)   Ye forgot yer change me boyo.
[KATIE *sits down at table* — *Looking at money* — *Talks* —]
KATIE   Gypo, where did you get that money? Look at
it . . and not a hour ago you hadn't a penny to warm your pocket. Did
somebody die and leave you a pot of gold?

30   [*Int. pub CS* — GYPO *seated* — *Talks angrily to* KATIE *partly on at left FG* — *Music
      heard* —]
GYPO   What are ye sayin' that for?
KATIE   Or did you rob a church, or what?
GYPO   That's it.

31   [*Int. pub CS* — KATIE *seated* — *Looking to right* — *Talks* — *Music heard* —]
KATIE   You . . you mean that you robbed a church?

32   [*Int. pub CS* — GYPO *seated* — *Looks sharply at* KATIE *partly on at left FG* — *Music
      heard* — *He talks* —]
GYPO   No, no, it wasn't a church . .

33   [*Int. pub CS* — KATIE *seated* — GYPO *leaning on at right* — *Talking to her* — *Music
      heard* —]
GYPO   . . it was a . . a sailor . . off an American ship.
KATIE   Ssssh, not so loud.

GYPO   I went through him at the back of Cassidy's Pub
on Jerome Street. He was drunk, but if ye say a word of it, you'll get me
into trouble.

KATIE   Who, me? . .

[GYPO *exits right as* KATIE *talks* –]

KATIE   . . What do you take me for? . .

34   [*Int. pub CS* – GYPO *seated at table* – KATIE *partly on at left FG* – *Talking* –
      Music heard –]

KATIE   . . An informer?

[*He rises angrily* – *Grabs her* – *Music stops* – *He talks* –]

GYPO   What are ye talkin' about informin' for?

KATIE   Gypo!

GYPO   Who's an informer?

KATIE   Gypo!

GYPO   Don't be sayin' things like that.

35   [*Int. pub MCS* – BARTENDER *behind counter* – *Looking to right FG* – *Talks* –]

BARTENDER   What's the matter here? . .

36   [*Int. pub MCS* – GYPO *and* KATIE *standing by table* – *Looking to left FG listen-
      ing* –]

BARTENDER (*off*)   . . What's the matter?

[GYPO *pours drink* – *Drinks as she talks* –]

KATIE   Oh, it's all right, Barney. Let him alone. He
didn't mean any harm. Oh, come on, let's get out of here . .

[*She picks up money from table*   *Talking* –]

KATIE   . . come on up to my room. There's a nice warm
fire there. Come on. Here's your money, Gypo. You'll be all right.

[*She takes him across to left* – *Nearly exiting* –]

37   [*Ext. pub MS* – GYPO *and* KATIE *coming on through doorway at left* – MAN *standing
      at right* – KATIE *talking indistinctly* – GYPO *drinks from bottle* – *She tries to
      take it from him as she talks* –]

KATIE   Oh, darling, you don't want any more of that.
Come on. Let's be gettin' in the car . .

[*She speaks to the cab driver*]

KATIE   . . all right, Jarvey . .

[*She talks to* GYPO *as they come to FG* – *Camera moving back* –]

KATIE   . . I'll take you back to . . Oh, no, Gypo! . .

[*He throws bottle down on street* – *Picks her up* – *Puts her in cab* –]

KATIE   . . Oh!

[*Music heard playing* – BLIND MAN *comes on in FG* – *Tapping cane* – GYPO
starts to get into cab – *Stops as he sees* BLIND MAN –]

38   [*Ext. street CS* – GYPO *looking up at* BLIND MAN *going to BG* – *Stops by him* –
      Music heard –]

39   [*Ext. street CS* – BLIND MAN *staring up to FG* – GYPO *partly on at left* – *Looking up at him* – *Music heard* – *He takes bill from pocket* – *Puts it in hand of* BLIND MAN – BLIND MAN *comes to right FG* – *Exits* – GYPO *looking after him* –]

40   [*Ext. street MCS* – KATIE *seated in cab* – GYPO *standing by her* – *Back to camera* – *Watching after* BLIND MAN *going to BG* – *Music heard* – KATIE *talks* –]

KATIE   Gypo, you gave him a pound note.

[*He turns to FG* – *Talks* – *Music stops* –]

GYPO   I forgot something. They'll be wondering why I'm not there already.

[*Music heard playing medley* ("*The Blind Man*" *and* "*The Minstrel Boy*") – *He comes to left FG* – *Exits* –]

41   [*Ext. street MS* – GYPO *walking rapidly to FG* – KATIE *seated in cab watching after him* – *Camera moving back as* GYPO *comes to FG* – *Music heard* – *He exits left FG* –]

                                                 [*Lap dissolve*]

42   [*Ext. house MS* – *People standing in front of entrance* – GYPO *coming to FG* – *Fog about* – *Singing heard* –]

SINGER (*off*)   The minstrel boy to the war has gone in the ranks. .

[GYPO *stops at right FG* –]

43   [*Ext. entrance CS* – SINGER *leaning against railing* – *Singing* – MAN *in FG* – *Back to camera* – *Playing violin* – SISTER *going up steps in BG to entrance* –]

SINGER   . . of death you'll find him . .

44   [*Int. room MS* – MOTHER *and others seated about at wake* – SISTERS *in BG by casket* – *Singing and violin heard* –]

SINGER (*off*)   . . his father's sword he has . .

45   [*Ext. street CS* – SINGER *leaning against railing* – *Singing* – MAN *in FG* – *Back to camera* – *Playing violin* – SISTER *entering house in BG* –]

SINGER (*off*)   . . girded on . .

46   [*Ext. street CU* – GYPO *looking to FG* – *Violin and singing heard* –]

SINGER (*off*)   . . and his wild harp slung behind him . .

47   [*Ext. street CS* – SINGER *leaning against railing* – *Singing* – MAN *in FG* – *Back to camera playing violin* – MAN *going up steps to entrance* –]

SINGER (*off*)   . . land of song, said the warrior . .

48   [*Ext. street CU* – GYPO *looking to left FG* – *Violin and* SINGER *heard* –]

SINGER (*off*)   . . bard

                          Though all the world betrays thee . .

[GYPO *comes to left FG* – *Exits* –]

49   [*Ext. street MLS* – *Group in front of entrance of house across street* – GYPO *coming on at right FG* – *Going toward them* – SINGER *and* VIOLINIST *in front of house* –]

SINGER   . . one sword at least they rights shall guard . .

[GYPO *goes up steps of entrance* –]

SINGER   . . one faithful harp shall . .

50   [*Ext. entrance MCS* — GYPO *coming up steps to FG* — *Others on steps* — *He stops in*
     FG — *Violin and* SINGER *heard* —]
     SINGER (*off*)   . . praise thee.
     [*He removes cap* — *Hears* —]
     MAN (*off*)   'Tis easy seen it was the work of an informer.
     2ND MAN (*off*)   'Tis sure . . 'tis the work of an informer.
     [*Gaelic chant heard indistinctly* — GYPO *comes to left FG* — *Nearly exits* —]

51   [*Int. room MS* — MOTHER *and others seated about sorrowfully* — SISTERS *and* PRIEST
     in BG by casket — *Chanting indistinctly in Gaelic* — GYPO *comes on at right BG*
     through doorway — *Looks about* —]

52   [*Int. room MCS* — BARTLEY *and* MAN *seated* — *Others in BG* — *Chanting heard*
     indistinctly — *They look up* —]

53   [*Int. room CS* — GYPO *with back to camera* — *Looking to BG* — SISTERS *and* PRIEST
     by casket — *Chanting indistinctly in Gaelic* —]

54   [*Int. Room MCS* — *Men partly on in FG* — *Two* SISTERS *standing by casket* —
     Chanting indistinctly in Gaelic —]

55   [*Int. room MCS* — MOTHER *seated* — MARY *seated at her feet* — *Chanting heard*
     indistinctly — MOTHER *wails* —]
     MOTHER   Oh, Frankie . .

56   [*Int. room CS* — GYPO *looking to BG* — *Back to camera* — SISTERS *in BG at casket* —
     Others around casket — *Chanting indistinctly* — GYPO *looks around to right FG*
     as he hears sobbing —]
     MOTHER (*off*)   . . Oh, Frankie!

57   [*Int. room MS* — MOTHER *and others seated about* — MOTHER *sobbing* — SISTERS
     and others in BG at casket chanting indistinctly in Gaelic — GYPO *starts toward*
     FG —]

58   [*Int. room MCS* — BARTLEY *and* MAN *watching to right FG* — *Others behind*
     them — *Indistinct chanting heard* —]

59   [*Int. room MS* — MOTHER *and others seated about* — SISTERS *and others in BG* — *At*
     casket — *Chanting indistinctly in Gaelic* — GYPO *crossing slowly to* MOTHER *at*
     right —]

60   [*Int. room MCS* — MOTHER *and* MARY *seated* — *Chanting heard indistinctly* —
     GYPO *coming on in FG* — *Sits down on floor* —]

61   [*Int. room MCS* — BARTLEY *and* MAN *seated* — *Watching to FG* — *Others in BG* —
     Chanting heard indistinctly — BARTLEY *whispers to man* —]

62   [*Int. room CS* — GYPO *seated on floor* — *Looking off to left sadly* — *Chanting heard*
     indistinctly — *He tries to talk* — *Blurts out loudly* —]
     GYPO   I'm sorry for yer trouble, Mrs. McPhillip.

63   [*Int. room MS* — MAN *seated at table* — *Others standing in doorway in BG* — *Turn*
     to FG shocked — BARTLEY *rises at left FG* — *Talks* —]
     BARTLEY   What are ye shoutin' for? Don't you know there's
     a wake goin' on?

64   [*Int. room CS — Camera shooting down at* MOTHER *and* MARY *seated —* MOTHER
     looks up to right FG — Talks —]

MOTHER   Ah, let him alone, Bartley. Sure he was a friend
of me dead boy.
[*She sobs —*]

REEL 4

1   [*Int. room MS —* MOTHER *and* MARY *seated —* GYPO *seated on floor —* BARTLEY
     standing at left — Looking down at him — Talks — Others in BG —]

BARTLEY   All the same, ye should show more respect for the
dead.
[GYPO *rises — Coins fall from hand —*]

2   [*Insert #1 — Coins on floor — Music heard playing medley (" The Money" and "The
     Informer")* —]

3   [*Int. room CU —* GYPO *looking down — Looks up slowly — Music heard —*]

4   [*Int. room MCS —* WOMAN *seated at table — Men standing behind her — All
     watching to FG — Music heard —*]

5   [*Insert #2 — Coins on floor — Music heard —*]

6   [*Int. room CS —* GYPO *looking to left FG — Looks about — Music heard —*]

7   [*Int. room CS —* BARTLEY *and* MAN *looking off to left — Others behind them —
     Music heard —*]

8   [*Int. room CS — Camera shooting down at* MOTHER *and* MARY *seated — Music
     heard — They look up to right —*]

9   [*Int. room CU —* GYPO *looking about furtively — Music heard —*]

10   [*Int. room CS —* MAN *seated at table — Looking down to FG — Others partly on in
     BG — Music heard —* MAN *starts to rise —*]

11   [*Int. room MS —* GYPO *standing at right FG —* MOTHER *and* MARY *seated — Others
     about room — Music heard —* MAN *rising — Starts to reach down for money —*]

12   [*Int. room CU —* GYPO *looking down — Bellows — Music heard —*]

GYPO   Leave 'em alone!

13   [*Int. room MCS —* MAN *straightens up — Others in BG — Music heard —* MAN
     backs away to table as he talks —]

MAN   Sure, I was only goin' to give them back to you,
Mr. Nolan.

14   [*Int. room MS —* GYPO *stoops to pick up coins —* BARTLEY *and* TOMMY *rising at
     left — Others about room — Music heard —* GYPO *starts to rise —*]

15   [*Int. room MCS —* BARTLEY *and* TOMMY *in FG — Backs to camera —* GYPO *rising — Facing them — Music heard — He looks about — Talks — Music stops —*]

GYPO   I swear by all that's holy, I warned him to keep
away from this house.

16   [*Int. room MCS –* BARTLEY *and* TOMMY *at left – Others in BG –* TOMMY *talks –*]
 TOMMY   Good heavens, man . . there's no one suspects
 you.

17   [*Int. room CS –* WOMAN *seated at table – Two* MEN *standing by her – Others in
 BG – Man talks –*]
 MAN   Sure, that's right, Gypo.
 [*Others mumbling indistinctly –*]

18   [*Int. room CU –* GYPO *looking to left FG –* MAN *heard talking – Others heard
 · mumbling indistinctly –*]
 MAN   No one suspects you.

19   [*Int. room MCS –* TOMMY *and* BARTLEY *at left FG – Backs to camera –* GYPO
 looking about – Music heard – GYPO *moves slowly to left –*]

20   [*Int. room MCS –* MARY *and* MOTHER *seated – Man partly on at right FG – Back
 to camera – Music heard –* GYPO *coming on at right – Stops by* MARY *–
 Talks –*]
 GYPO   You've been very good to me, Mrs. McPhillip,
 and I'm sorry for yer trouble.
 [*He drops coins in her lap – Camera follows him to right BG – He exits quickly –
 Through doorway –*]

21   [*Ext. entrance MLS – People standing about entrance – Music heard –* GYPO *comes
 out of entrance – Hurries across to left – Others exit as camera follows him –*]
 TOMMY (*off*)   Gypo, Gypo, Gypo! . .
 [GYPO *stops at corner –* TOMMY *comes on at right after him – Talking –*]
 TOMMY   . . Man alive, what are ye hurryin' for?

22   [*Ext. street MCS –* GYPO *standing near lamp post – Talking angrily –* TOMMY
 at right –]
 GYPO   Who's in a hurry? What makes you think I'm in
 a hurry?
 TOMMY   Ah, now don't be gettin' your rag out, me
 boyo . .

23   [*Ext. street MCU –* TOMMY *looking to left FG – Talking –*]
 TOMMY   . . 'tis a free country and a man can ask questions without all this gostherin' . . especially from an old pal . .

24   [*Ext. street MCU –* GYPO *standing by lamp post – Looks to right FG as he listens –*]
 TOMMY (*off*)   . . Are ye workin' now?
 GYPO   No!

25   [*Ext. street MCS –* GYPO *standing near lamp post –* TOMMY *at right – Talks –*]
 TOMMY   Don't be shoutin' at me like an aboriginal. Sure,
 ye can't blame Bartley and me for takin' a friendly interest in ye for old
 times' sake . . seein' as how you were one of us at one time . .

26   [*Ext. street MCU –* GYPO *standing by lamp post listening suspiciously –*]
 TOMMY (*off*)   . . Ye don't seem to be in any need of money
 tonight, Gypo.

27 [*Ext. street MCS* — GYPO *turns to* TOMMY — *Grabs him by throat* — *Confusion as they struggle* —]

TOMMY   Bartley!

[BARTLEY *runs on at right* — *Talking as he separates them* —]

BARTLEY   What's wrong, boys? What are ye up to?

GYPO   He suspects me.

BARTLEY   Suspects ye of what?

TOMMY   I didn't say anything, Bartley. I only asked him to . .

GYPO   You're a liar! You did, both of you and well, l know ye. Bartley Mulholland and Tommy Conner . . you're Commandant Gallagher's right-hand men, and I'll . .

[BARTLEY *stops him* —]

BARTLEY   Sssh, shut up, Gypo, are ye mad? Don't ye know there are people listenin'?

GYPO   Well, don't be accusin' me, then.

BARTLEY   Come on, then. Let's get outa here.

GYPO   No!

TOMMY   Commandant Gallagher wants to see ye.

GYPO   Well, I'm not goin'.

BARTLEY   Come on, man. He's not goin' to eat ye.

TOMMY   Is it afraid of the Commandant ye are?

[BARTLEY *exits right as* GYPO *pushes him away* — *Starts to remove coat as he talks* —]

GYPO   Afraid! I'm not afraid of the finest man that was ever whelped.

[BARTLEY *comes on at right* — *Talking* —]

BARTLEY   Come on, man, let's get out of here. Come on.

[BARTLEY *exits as* GYPO *pushes him away* — *Talking* —]

GYPO   Keep your hands off'n me. Come on.

[GYPO *crosses in front of* TOMMY *to left* — *Exits* — *Music heard playing medley* — BARTLEY *comes on at right* — *He and* TOMMY *cross to left* — *Exit* —]

28 [*Int. office CS* — DAN *seated on table* — *Looking at crumpled poster* — *Music heard* — *He looks off thoughtfully* —]

29 [*Int. office MS* — DAN *seated on edge of table* — *Looking off thoughtfully* — *Music heard* — *Knock heard* — *He rises* — *Puts poster down on chair* — *Puts gun in pocket* — *Goes to door at right* — *Opens peep-hole* —]

MAN (*off*)   Captain Mulholland, Sir.

[*He unlocks door* — *Opens it* — BARTLEY *comes on* — *Talks* —]

BARTLEY   Gypo Nolan.

[DAN *comes to left to table* — GYPO *comes on through doorway at right followed by* TOMMY — BARTLEY *closes door* — DAN *picks up crumpled poster* — *Looks at it* — *Starts to put it in fireplace* — TOMMY *sitting down at right of table* —]

30 [*Insert #3* — *Hand partly on at right putting crumpled poster on grate in fireplace* — *Music heard* — *Printing on poster reads* —]

£20 Reward

[*Poster starts to burn* –]

31 [*Int. office MCU* – GYPO *looking down to left* – *Reflection of fire on his face* – *Music heard* –]

32 [*Int. office CU* – DAN *looking down to left* – *Reflection of fire on his face* – *Music heard* – *He looks off to right* –]

33 [*Int. office CU* – BARTLEY *looking down to left* – *Reflection of fire on his face* – *Music heard* – *He looks to right* –]

34 [*Int. office CU* – TOMMY *seated at table* – *Reflection of fire on his face* – *Music heard* – *He looks up to left* –]

35 [*Int. office MCU* – GYPO *looking down to left* – *Reflection of fire on his face* – *Music heard* –]

36 [*Insert #4* – *Poster burning on grate in fireplace* – *Music heard* – *Poster consumed by fire* –]

37 [*Int. office MCU* – GYPO *watching down to left nervously* – *Music heard* – *Reflection of fire on his face* –]

38 [*Insert #5* – *Ashes of poster on grate in fireplace* – *Music heard* – *Flames carry ashes upward* – *They exit* –]

39 [*Int. office MCS* – TOMMY *seated at right* – GYPO *and* DAN *standing by table* – BARTLEY *behind them* – DAN *talks to* GYPO –]

DAN   Well, Gypo, you don't seem glad to see me. You've got a grudge against me; Why?

40 [*Int. office CS* – GYPO *standing by table* – *Removes cap as he talks* – *Throws it down* –]

GYPO   Ah, there isn't a thing I wouldn't do for ye, Dan Gallagher, and ye had me court-martialed and expelled from the organization.

41 [*Int. office MCU* – DAN *looking to right* – *Talks* –]

DAN   You disobeyed orders, endangered the organization. You had a fair trial, Gypo. Only for me you wouldn't have got away as easily as you did. There were others who wanted to give you this . .

[*He reaches in pocket* –]

42 [*Insert #6* – *Gun falling on table by glass* –]

43 [*Int. office CS* – GYPO *standing at table* – *Looking down* – *Looks up to left as he hears* –]

DAN (*off*)   Forget that . .

44 [*Int. office MCS* – TOMMY *seated at right of table* – GYPO *standing by him* – DAN *at left* – BARTLEY *in BG* – DAN *talking* –]

DAN   . . We've got something on hand now that is as much your business as ours. Frankie McPhillip was your pal, wasn't he? . .

[GYPO *picks up cap* − *Toys with it nervously* −]

DAN   . . I want your help, that's all . .

45   [*Int. office CS* − GYPO *standing by table* − *Listening nervously* −]

DAN (*off*)   . . This looks like the job of an informer, and we have to get that informer, you understand? . .

46   [*Int. office MCU* − DAN *looking off to right, talking* −]

DAN   . . All I can say is that if you don't help us, with this job, people might think . .

47   [*Int. office CS* − GYPO *standing by table* − *Looking to left* − *Talks* −]

GYPO   It isn't that . . it isn't that! Look here, Commandant, it's . . it's how . . Uh . . it's how . . Ah, I don't know what I'm doin'.

DAN (*off*)   What's the matter, Gypo?

GYPO   What's the matter! For the last six months I've been starvin', that's what's the matter.

48   [*Int. office MCU* − DAN *looking down* − *Listening* −]

GYPO (*off*)   . . I've been livin' from hand to mouth, on whatever I could borry from sailors and dockers . .

49   [*Int. office CS* − GYPO *standing by table, talking* −]

GYPO   . . I got no clothes; I got no money; I got nothin'!

[*He puts hands into pockets* − *Removes hand quickly* −]

50   [*Int. office MCS* − TOMMY *seated at right of table* − GYPO *standing by him* − DAN *at left* − BARTLEY *in BG* − DAN *talks to* GYPO −]

DAN   Look here, Gypo. I'm going to make a fair deal with you. Last October you put us all in a very dangerous position. We'll call that quits and reinstate you on one condition . .

51   [*Int. office CS* − DAN *partly on at left FG* − *Talking to* GYPO *at right* − BARTLEY *in BG* −]

DAN   . . that you find the man that informed on Frankie McPhillip.

GYPO   Do you mean that?

DAN   Indeed I do, Gypo.

GYPO   Put it there, Dan me boy . .

[*He shakes hand* − *Talking* −]

GYPO   . . put it there. What did I tell you? What did I tell you, Bartley? There isn't anything I wouldn't do for ye, Dan. There isn't anything I wouldn't do. Can we have a drink on that? . .

[DAN *picks up bottle* − *Hands it to him* − GYPO *laughing* − *Pours drink as he talks* −]

GYPO   . . Let's have a drink on that . .

[*He drinks* − *Looks around* − *Talking* − *Pouring drinks* −]

GYPO   . . Have a drink on the Commandant, Tommy. Bartley, me boy, here's a drink for you . .

[*He drinks –* TOMMY *and* BARTLEY *put drinks on table –* GYPO *smacks lips –
Talks –*]

GYPO   . . Ah, that's fine . .

[*He picks up* BARTLEY'S *drink – Drinks it – Turns to* BARTLEY *mumbling indistinctly – Finishes drink – Sighs – Puts glass on table – Picks up* TOMMY'S
drink – Talks –]

GYPO   . . Danny, there isn't anything I wouldn't do
for you, anything. Ah, it's nice to be friendly. I'd go through fire and
water for ye.

[*He drinks –*]

52   [*Int. room CU –* DAN *looking off to right – Talks –*]

DAN   Who informed on Frankie McPhillip?

53   [*Int. room CS –* GYPO *standing at table – Coughs – Spits –* DAN *partly on at left –*
BARTLEY *in BG –* TOMMY *seated at right of table –* GYPO *looks around at men –
Talks –*]

GYPO   I'll tell you. It was that rat Mulligan.
BARTLEY   Mulligan?
TOMMY   Mulligan the tailor?
GYPO   Sure as you're born.
DAN   How do you make that out?
GYPO   I'll tell you, Commandant. I didn't like to say it
meself . . a man can't be too sure about a thing like that . .

[BARTLEY *crossing to right behind* GYPO *–* GYPO *going to* DAN *at left – Talking –*
BARTLEY *exits right –*]

GYPO   . . but just as ye put it yourself, Commandant,
and the way ye put it . .

DAN   Hurry up, man . . make your statement.

[GYPO *drinks – Talks –*]

GYPO   Ah, that's fine stuff. How didn't I think of that
before.

DAN   Think of what?
GYPO   Well, it was the grudge.
DAN   What grudge?
GYPO   Why, the grudge . . that grudge that . . that
Mulligan had on Frankie.

DAN   About what?
GYPO   Oh, it's a long, long story. It's a long story.
There's another little drink in the bottle.

DAN   Take it.

[GYPO *pours drink –*]

TOMMY   Man alive, you've already killed the whole bottle.

[GYPO *mumbles indistinctly – Drinks –*]

DAN   Come on now, Gypo, out with it. What grudge
are you talking about?

[GYPO *puts glass down* − *Talks* −]

GYPO   You remember his sister Susie?

DAN   Whose sister?

GYPO   Why, Mulligan's.

DAN   What has she got to do with it?

GYPO   What has she got to do with it? Why shouldn't
she have something to do with it? Wasn't she in trouble and wasn't
Frankie . .

54   [*Int. room CU* − BARTLEY *looking to left listening* −]
GYPO (*off*)   . . the boyo that was named?

55   [*Int. room CU* − DAN *looking to right* − *Talks* −]
DAN   I never heard that.
[*He looks off to right* −]

56   [*Int. room CU* − BARTLEY *looking to left* − *Shakes head* −]

57   [*Int. room CS* − GYPO *standing at table* − *Talks to* DAN *partly on at left* − TOMMY
partly on at right seated at table −]

GYPO   Well, well, it's true anyway. Well, here, figure it
out. Figure it out for yourself. That's why Mulligan informed. That's why
Mulligan informed. I . . I saw him go into the Tan . . Tan's headquarters tonight.

DAN   What time?

GYPO   What time?

[*He looks around* − *Talks* −]

GYPO   . . Half past six . .

58   [*Int. room MCS* − DAN *and* GYPO *standing at table* − TOMMY *seated at right of
table* − BARTLEY *standing at right* − GYPO *talks* −]

GYPO   . . Well . .

[GYPO *picks up cap* − *Talks* −]

GYPO   . . are ye taking me back, Dan?

DAN   If your statement checks up, you'll get back.
There will be a court of inquiry tonight at half past one, at the ammunition
dump. Be there. You take him up. Arrange to meet him somewhere.

GYPO   All right, Bartley, me boy. You'll find me down
at Katie Madden's.

BARTLEY   Right.

[GYPO *salutes* DAN − BARTLEY *opens door at right* −]

GYPO   I'll see ye boys later. Bartley, me boy.

[GYPO *exits through doorway* − BARTLEY *looking after him* −]

BARTLEY   Show him out.

[*He closes door* −]

REEL 5

[*Int. room MCS* − BARTLEY *standing at door at right* − TOMMY *seated at left at
table* − *Camera following* BARTLEY *to left as he talks revealing* DAN *standing at*

left of table — Music heard playing medley ("The Informer" and "Wearing of the Green") —]

BARTLEY It's him, Dan. I'd stake me life on it. He's the one that did it.

DAN He's drunk.

[TOMMY *rises — Talking —]*

TOMMY Drunk! It's a wonder he can walk at all.

2 [*Int. room CS — DAN partly on at left FG — BARTLEY at end of table — TOMMY partly on at right — Music heard — DAN sits on edge of table — Talks —]*

DAN Tell me, how is Mary taking it?

TOMMY Her heart is dyin' inside of her, Commandant. But ye'd never know it. She's waitin' for ye, Dan. Look, t'would be God's own blessin' for you to go and see her.

DAN One thing is certain, we must destroy this informer. It may be Gypo, though I don't believe it. He was Frankie's friend, and he had no motive, or it may be Mulligan, though I doubt it again . .

[*He rises —]*

DAN . . Whoever it was, we've got to find him before this night is over. One traitor can destroy an army. It's his life against ours . . you understand, Bartley?

BARTLEY I do.

DAN Then get started. Keep at Gypo's heels like a pot of glue. Find out all you can. And bring him to the ammunition dump at half past one sharp.

TOMMY Right.

[*He starts to right —]*

3 [*Int. room MCS — DAN standing at left of table — TOMMY at right — BARTLEY crossing to right — Exits — DAN talks to TOMMY — Music heard —]*

DAN You, Tommy, find Captain Conlon. He's to mobilize his company and round up Mulligan. I'll attend to the rest. Get started.

TOMMY Right.

[TOMMY *exits right — DAN picks up gun — Puts it in pocket — Camera follows him across to right — He turns off light — Opens door — Exits through doorway —]*

[*Lap dissolve*]

4 [*Int. pub MCS — Laughter heard — Doors opening — OFFICER looks in — Calls —]*

POLICEMAN Time, Time! Come along, it's closing time.

[*He starts to close doors —]*

5 [*Ext. pub MS — Men seen inside at bar — General indistinct talking and laughter — POLICEMAN crosses in FG — Exits left — GYPO seen inside — Leaves bar — Going to doors at right — Camera panning to right — He comes through doorway — Stops in street — Yells — Others around him —]*

GYPO Gypo! . .

[*Others coming on out of pub – General indistinct talking –* GYPO *talks to short*
   MAN *–*]

GYPO   . . Stand up, man, stand up! . . Shake hands
   with Gallagher's right-hand. Come on.

[*He shakes hands with short* MAN *– Pulls cap down over* MAN'S *eyes – Looks to*
   FG *–*]

6   [*Ext. street MLS –* GYPO *and crowd in BG in front of pub –* MAN *partly on in*
    FG *– Back to camera –* GYPO *comes toward FG singing "Improvise" indis-*
    tinctly – Crowd following – He stops at left FG – Looks at man – Talks –]

GYPO   What are you lookin' at me for?

MAN   Ahh, I'm not lookin' at ye.

7   [*Ext. street CS –* MAN *partly on at right FG – Back to camera –* GYPO *glaring at*
    him – Comes toward him as he talks – Others partly on –]

GYPO   You're a liar . . you're a liar! . .

8   [*Ext. street MCU –* MAN *looking up at* GYPO *partly on at left FG – Back to cam-*
    era – Talking angrily – Others partly on –]

GYPO   . . Can't you know that I can see you lookin' at
   me?

MAN   Well, a cat can look at a king.

9   [*Ext. street MCU –* GYPO *talks to* MAN *partly on at right FG – Back to camera –*
    Others partly on –]

GYPO   What are you talking about kings for?

MAN   Here, here.

GYPO   Don't be talkin' about kings around here.

[MEN *all talking at once –*]

MEN   That's right, Gypo, you tell 'em, Gypo. That's
   right. That's the boy.

GYPO   You'll all be gettin' yourself into trouble.

MAN   Aw, you're drunk.

[MAN *punches* GYPO *on chin –* GYPO *looks around –*]

10   [*Ext. street MCU –* MAN *looking up at* GYPO *partly on at left BG – Back to cam-*
     era – Others partly on – GYPO *punches* MAN *on chin – Knocking him to BG –*
     Confusion –]

11   [*Ext. street MS –* MAN *falling down to pavement – Indistinct exclamations heard –*]

12   [*Ext. street MCS – Crowd around* GYPO *looking down to right – All talking at*
     once – Indistinctly – POLICEMAN *comes on at right – Talking –*]

POLICEMAN   Come on, break it up. Break it up. Hey, what do
   you think you're doing? I saw you hit that man. You got no business hitting men on the street like that. You'll have to come along to the station.

[GYPO *punches* POLICEMAN *on jaw – Knocking him off to right – Indistinct exclama-*
   tions from crowd –]

13   [*Ext. street MS –* MAN *lying on street –* POLICEMAN *falling down by him –*
     Indistinct exclamations heard –]

14 [*Ext. street MCU – Crowd looking down to right –* GYPO *coming on at left FG –*
    Looking down – Indistinct exclamations heard – TERRY *talks to* GYPO –]
    TERRY   What a boy, Gypo . . what a blow! . .

15 [*Ext. street CU –* TERRY *looking down to right talking – Others partly on behind*
    them –]
    TERRY   . . Ah, will you look at the two of them dyin'
    there, sweet and peaceful . .

16 [*Ext. street CS – Camera shooting down at* MAN *and* POLICEMAN *partly on – Lying*
    on street – Hand reaching into MAN'S *pocket –*]
    TERRY (*off*)   . . as the babes in the woods . .

17 [*Ext. street MCU –* GYPO *partly on at left FG –* TERRY *looking up at him – Holds*
    up his hand as he talks – Others partly on behind them –]
    TERRY   . . and gentlemen, there's the hand that rocked
    the cradle . .
    [*Crowd laughs –*]
    TERRY   . . me old Gypo!

18 [*Ext. street MS – Crowd standing around* GYPO *– All talking at once – Laughing –*
    WOMAN *laughing shrilly – Police whistle heard – Crowd talking indistinctly as*
    they start to disperse –]

19 [*Ext. street MS –* GYPO *standing at corner – Others hurrying away –* POLICEMAN
    coming on in FG – Going toward GYPO *– Whistle heard – They go to* MAN *and*
    POLICEMAN *lying in street –*]

20 [*Ext. street MS – Crowd partly on in BG –* POLICEMEN *stopping by* MAN *and*
    POLICEMAN *lying in street –* POLICEMAN *talking as they pick up two men –*]
    POLICEMAN   So you'll try to beat up a policeman, will you?
    MAN   Aw, let me go. I had nothing to do with it at
    all . .
    [POLICEMEN *bringing* MAN *and first* POLICEMAN *to left FG –* MAN *talking –*
    Protesting –]
    MAN   . . What's the matter with you? I want to get
    me . .

21 [*Ext. street MLS –* POLICEMEN *bringing* MAN *and* POLICEMAN *to FG –* MAN
    talking – Struggling with them – Crowd partly on in BG –]
    MAN   . . pipe and hat. I paid three shillings for that
    pipe. Will you let me get back there . .

22 [*Ext. street MS –* GYPO *standing in front of pub at left – Crowd in BG –* MAN
    heard talking – TERRY *runs to left FG – Watching – Off –*]
    MAN (*off*)   . . and get me pipe and me hat.
    [TERRY *goes to* GYPO *– Patting him – Talking proudly – Others coming on to*
    them –]
    TERRY   Ah, me old Gypo!
    [*People crowding around* GYPO *– All talking at once –*]

23   [*Ext. street MCS –* GYPO *leaning against bldg –* TERRY *by him – Talking –*
     Crowd around them – All talking at once – TERRY *trying to quiet them –*]

TERRY   Gentlemen!
MAN   Quiet, quiet!
TERRY   I have an announcement to make. With me own
    two eyes I saw Gypo knock the scrapper Maloney flying across the road
    like a man divin' off the bull wall.
[*All talking at once –*]
ALL   Who is he? Who is he?
TERRY   Who is he, who is he? . .

24   [*Ext. street MCU –* GYPO *leaning against bldg – Glances down to right FG –*]
TERRY (*off*)   . . He's Gypo Nolan, and he's stronger than any
    bull, Eh, Gypo? Am I right?
MAN (*off*)   Didn't ye never hear of him?
TERRY (*off*)   I tell you what this boy is. He's a king. That's
    what he is . . King Gypo. Am I right?

25   [*Ext. street MCU –* MAN *looking up to left FG – Others around him – He talks –*]
MAN   Usen't he be pals with Frankie McPhillip who
    was shot by the Black and Tans tonight?

26   [*Ext. street CS – Crowd partly on at right FG – Others at left – All talking at once*
     indistinctly – GYPO *at right BG leaning against bldg – He throws down ciga-*
     rette – Comes to MAN *– Crowd quiets –* GYPO *talks –*]
GYPO   Hey, when you mention the dead, ye might add
    "May the Lord have mercy on his soul."
[TERRY *comes on at right – Steps between them – Talking –*]
TERRY   Unity, boys, now unity. Did you hear what he
    said?
MAN   I did.
TERRY   Did you hear what he said?
MAN   I did.
TERRY   May the Lord have mercy on his soul. He died
    fightin' for Ireland to be free and every man here should do the same thing,
    and I'll do it when my time is called, and so will King Gypo. So will
    King Gypo. Am I right, Gypo, me lord?
GYPO   Right.
[*Crowd yells –* GYPO *quiets them –*]
GYPO   Silence . . quiet!
TERRY   Silence, there. Quiet, everybody, Gypo, you
    have the floor.

27   [*Ext. street MS – Crowd around* GYPO *–* GYPO *talks –*]
GYPO   I want ever— . . I want everybody to come
    and have some chips . . some fish and chips with King Gypo.
[*All laugh – Yell – Talk at once – Much confusion –*]

28 [*Int. shop MS* – OWNER and WOMAN *behind counter at right* – MAN *seated at counter* – *Crowd pouring in through doorway in BG* – *Yelling* – *Talking* – *Much confusion as they rush to counter* –]

29 [*Ext. street MCS* – GYPO *picking up* WOMAN – *Holds her on shoulders* – *Others around them* – *All laughing* – *Talking* – *Yelling at once* – *Confusion* – GYPO *starts into shop* –]

30 [*Int. shop MS* – OWNER and WOMAN *behind counter* – *Crowd at counter* – *All talking and yelling at once* – GYPO *coming on in BG carrying* WOMAN *on shoulders* – *Much confusion* – *He stops at counter* –]

31 [*Int. shop MCS* – GYPO *stands woman on counter* – *Others around them* – WOMAN *dances on counter* – *All yelling* – *Talking at once* – *Confusion* – WOMAN *exits right* – GYPO *sits on counter* – *Raises arms* – *Talks* –]
GYPO   Silence . . quiet!

32 [*Int. counter MCU* – MAN and TERRY *seated at counter* – *Others behind them* – TERRY *looking about* – *Talks* –]
TERRY   Silence . . quiet, he said! . .
[*He yells in* MAN'S *ear* –]
TERRY   . . Quiet! . .
[*He looks up to right talking* –]
TERRY   . . Proceed, Gypo.

33 [*Int. counter MCU* – GYPO *seated on counter* – *Others partly on behind him* – GYPO *talks* –]
GYPO   Come on, every man-jack and woman, too.
It's all on Gypo.

34 [*Int. counter MCU* – TERRY and MAN *seated at counter* – *Others behind them* – TERRY *talks* –]
TERRY   D'ye hear that? You're all guests of King Gypo.
Am I right, Gypo?

35 [*Int. counter MCU* – GYPO *seated on counter* – *Others partly on behind him* – GYPO *talks* –]
GYPO   Right, and before long I'm going to be Cock of
the Walk around here, me and Commandant Gallagher. It's a secret.

36 [*Int. counter MCU* – TERRY and MAN *seated at counter* – *Others partly on behind them* – TERRY *talks to* MAN –]
TERRY   Do you hear that? It's a secret.

37 [*Int. shop MCS* – GYPO *seated on counter* – *Others crowded at counter* – OWNER and WOMAN *behind counter* – GYPO *talks* –]
GYPO   Come on, chuck 'em out, come on . . every man-
jack, I'm payin' for the lot.
OWNER   Blimey, there's a lot of people, governor.
TERRY   Yes, but they're a lovely crowd . . a lovely
crowd . .

38   [*Int. counter MCU –* TERRY *and* MAN *seated at counter – Others partly on behind them –* TERRY *talks to* MAN *–*]

TERRY   . . and every Tom and Judy is a friend of Gypo's. Now, now, do you get that?

39   [*Int. shop MCS –* GYPO *seated on counter – Others crowded at counter –* OWNER *and* GIRL *at right behind counter – General indistinct talking –* GYPO *talks –*]

GYPO   Come on, you little scut, get busy. Now, come on here. This'll pay for the lot.

TERRY   Now, do you hear that? He's gonna pay.

[GYPO *takes rolls of notes from pocket – Crowds exclaim – Indistinctly –* GYPO *throws notes on counter –*]

40   [*Int. counter MCU –* OWNER *and* GIRL *behind counter – Pick up notes – Look at them amazed – Crowd heard exclaiming – Crowd partly on in BG –* OWNER *talks – Music heard playing medley –*]

OWNER   Blimey, two quid. Come on, let 'em have it. Come on.

[*They turn to stoves – Crowd exclaiming –*]

41   [*Int. counter MCS –* GYPO *seated – Others around him – General indistinct talking –* TERRY *talks – Music heard –*]

TERRY   Order, please. Ladies first, ladies first.

[OWNER *handing out chips –* TERRY *takes one –* GYPO *handing them on to others – Much confusion –*]

42   [*Int. shop MS –* GYPO *seated on counter – Others crowding around – All reaching for fish and chips – All talking at once – Confusion – Music heard –*]

43   [*Int. shop CU –* MAN *reaching to right – Comes to left FG – Exits – Others crowding behind him – Music heard – Much confusion – Crowd laughing – Talking – Camera panning to BG over heads of people – People exit – Camera panning to BG reveals* BARTLEY *standing outside at window – Watching in –*]

44   [*Int. shop CS –* GYPO *seated on counter – Crowd around him – All reaching for fish and chips – Confusion – Music heard –* GYPO *stands up on counter –*]

45   [*Int. counter MCU –* TERRY *and* MAN *seated at counter – People reaching over them – Crowding them – Music and confusion heard –*]

46   [*Ext. window CS –* BARTLEY *standing at right of window – Watching into shop – Music heard – People seen inside – Struggling for food –*]

47   [*Int. shop CS –* GYPO *on counter – Putting sauce on packages of fish and chips – People crowding around him – Music heard –*]

48   [*Int. shop MCU –* MAN *and* TERRY *seated at counter – Others reaching over them – Crowding them – Music heard –*]

49   [*Int. shop CS –* GYPO *on counter – Others crowding about him – He pushes* MAN *aside – Music heard –*]

50 [*Ext. shop MCS – Two* MEN *come on out of doorway at right – Look to FG, talk-ing – Music heard –*]

MAN　　　　　　　　　　Come on . . come on, gentlemen. Gypo's buyin' fish and chips. Don't cost a ha' penny. Get in there.

[*Men running on – Run into shop –* BARTLEY *coming on at right FG –*]

MAN　　　　　　　　　　. . Hey, come on, get some grub. Come on.

[*All talking at once as men urge* BARTLEY *to go into shop – Confusion –* BARTLEY *talks –*]

BARTLEY　　　　　　　　Leave me alone, let go.

MAN　　　　　　　　　　Come on in. It doesn't cost a hebe. Gypo's buyin' it.

[*Music stops as* BARTLEY *talks angrily –*]

BARTLEY　　　　　　　　Let go. I don't want any. Leave me alone. Get back or I'll smash ye.

MAN　　　　　　　　　　Oh, so it's a fight you're lookin' for, are ye?

MAN　　　　　　　　　　So that's what's the matter with ye, uh? It's a fight you're lookin' for.

MAN　　　　　　　　　　Hold me hat. Stand back.

[MAN *starts to fight* BARTLEY – BARTLEY *pushes him into shop – All talking at once – Confusion –* MAN *runs out of shop – Exits left –* GYPO *follows him out – Looks around – Talking –*]

GYPO　　　　　　　　　Hey, what's the trouble? What's the trouble . .

51 [*Ext. street MCU –* BARTLEY *looking up at* GYPO – MAN *in BG –* MAN *partly on at right FG –* GYPO *looks at* BARTLEY *– Talks – Noise from shop heard –*]

GYPO　　　　　　　　　. . Bartley, me boy? Let 'im alone. He's a friend of mine. Get inside there . .

[*Two men exit through doorway at right –*]

GYPO　　　　　　　　　. . Lay a hand on me friend! . .

[GYPO *turns to* BARTLEY – *Puts arm around him as he talks –*]

GYPO　　　　　　　　　. . Come on, man, come on. Have some grub.

[BARTLEY *pushes* GYPO *aside – Talks –*]

BARTLEY　　　　　　　　I'm in a hurry, Gypo, but I'll see ye at one o'clock. You know where I mean.

GYPO　　　　　　　　　Sure, me boy, sure. Ah, it's a fine night. It's the finest night of me life. Gypooo!

[*He laughs – Snaps fingers – Talks – Music heard playing "I Adore Him" –*]

GYPO　　　　　　　　　That reminds me, there's somebody waiting for me. You know what I mean.

[*He starts to right FG –*]

52 [*Ext. street MS –* BARTLEY *standing by door at left FG – Watching as* GYPO *goes to BG – Music heard – He picks up rock – Throws it through window – Crash heard – He talks – Music stops –*]

GYPO　　　　　　　　　Good night, all.

[TERRY *comes on through doorway at left – Talking – Goes after* GYPO –]

TERRY   Gypo, Gypo . . Gypo, wait for me, you darling.
Wait for me, wait for me!
[*They go to BG singing "He Is Me Darlin' O" –*]
BOTH (*singing*)   Oh, of all the men that wear the green
He is me Darlin' O
For in every fight he will be seen
For he is me Darlin' O . .
[*They exit left BG around corner of bldg –* BARTLEY *walking to BG slowly –*]

53   [*Ext. street MCS – Camera following* TERRY *and* GYPO *as they walk along to right –*
Singing –]
BOTH (*singing*)   . . me Darlin 'O . . me Darlin' O.
Me rattlin' Darlin' O.
Of all the boys that wear the green . .
[*They stop at right singing –*]
BOTH (*singing*)   . . He is me Darlin' O–O–O.
[TERRY *talks –*]
TERRY   Ah, Gypo, ye have a sweet voice, a sweet voice.
Shhh, listen . .
[GYPO *looks about listening –* TERRY *talks –*]
TERRY   . . even the birds are still.
[GYPO *looks about – Camera follows them as they walk to right – Revealing sign in
window – They stop at window .–* GYPO *looks in – Music heard – Playing
"I Adore Him" –*]

54   [*Int. window CS –* GYPO *and* TERRY *outside –* GYPO *looking in through window –*
TERRY *looking at him questioningly – Music heard –* GYPO *scratches head
thoughtfully –*]

55   [*Ext. window CS –* GYPO *and* TERRY *standing in front of window – Music heard –*
GYPO *talks –*]
GYPO   Where ye takin' me to, yuh little scut? Ain't we
after gettin' to Katie's yet?
TERRY   Aw, there ye go, there ye go. Talkin' about
Katie, and we havin' a fine little jamboree. Now don't worry about your
little Judy. She'll be always on the streets, never fear.
[GYPO *grabs* TERRY *by collar – Twisting it –* TERRY *struggles with him – Talk-
ing –*]
TERRY   Hey, what are . . what are ye . . ye big stiff!
Ye're drunk and bedazzled, that's what ye are. Ye're as drunk as a
fiddlers' dog . .
[*He frees* GYPO'*s hand –*]
TERRY   . . Hey, take your hands off me! Ye think ye're
a king, do ye? Why, ye're a big lump of beef, that's all ye are . .
[TERRY *turns to right – Exits –*]
TERRY (*off*)   . . a big lump of beef! . .

56   [*Ext. street MS –* TERRY *running on at left FG – Stops – Turns to FG – Talking –*]

TERRY   . . Ye're drunk and your last penny is spent, and I have no further use for ye, Mr. Gypo Nolan. Ipso Facto!
[*He walks to BG –*]

REEL 6

1   [*Ext. street MCU –* GYPO *feeling in pockets – Looking off to right –*]

2   [*Ext. street MS –* TERRY *going to BG – Stops – Turns to FG – Talking –*]
TERRY   And another . .
[*He comes to FG – Stops in FG – Sees –*]

3   [*Ext. street CS –* GYPO *taking roll of notes out of pocket – Music heard playing medley ("The Money" – "I Adore Him" – "Bridal Chorus") –*]

4   [*Ext. street CS –* TERRY *looking to FG amazed – Music heard – He comes to left FG – Exits –*]

5   [*Ext. street CS –* GYPO *counting roll of notes – Music heard –* TERRY *coming on at right – Stops by him – Watching –* TERRY *talks –*]

TERRY   Oh, by the holy, where did ye get it, Gypo? There's enough there to choke a horse. Ha, Ha, and me joking about it a few minutes ago. Ah, Gypo, me boy, ye are a king and a descendant of kings, and I'd fight for ye and I'd die for ye if the time comes, and there's me hand on it, Gypo. The hand of a man that's loyal and true. Am I right, Gypo?
[GYPO *ignores him – Turns to window – Camera follows him as he goes to window –* TERRY *reaches down – Picks up note – Puts it in pocket –*]

6   [*Int. window MCU –* GYPO *holding notes looking in window – Music heard – He looks down – Sees –*]

7   [*Ext. window CS – Model ship in window – Reflection of* GYPO *seen on glass – Looking at ship – Music heard – Trick shot – Superimposed over this is scene of* GYPO *and* KATIE *on ship deck – Camera moving closer to them –* KATIE *wearing bridal gown – Scene dissolves out –*]

8   [*Ext. street MS –* GYPO *turning from window – Comes to* TERRY *at right – Music heard –* GYPO *talks –*]
GYPO   Come on, ye little scut.
[*Music stops –*]
GYPO   I'm going to find Katie.
[*He starts to left – Camera following –* TERRY *going after him, talking –*]
TERRY   Yes, and I'm the boy to lead ye to her . .
[TERRY *turns him to right – Camera following as they cross to right –* TERRY *talking –*]
TERRY   . . Come on. She's a lovely girl, Gypo, a lovely girl. You should be proud of her. You should be proud of her . .
[*They exit right –*]

                                                              [*Lap dissolve*]

9   [*Ext. street MCS* – TERRY *coming on at left with* GYPO – TERRY *talking* –]
     TERRY   . . Come on, don't waste the whole night on her.
        Come on.
     [*They stop in front of bldg* – *Piano heard playing "My Man"* – GYPO *talks* –]
     GYPO   I tell ye it's not the place.
     TERRY   Will ye listen to the man. Are ye tryin' to insin-
        uate that I would lead ye astray? Lead King Gypo astray? Never! . .
     [TERRY *goes up steps to entrance as he talks* –]
     TERRY   . . Up the barricades first. Up the barricades
        and die like a man.
     GYPO   Ah, I don't know where I'm at.
     TERRY   Listen, ye're in front of Aunt Betty's, the finest
        shebeen in town, and your little Katie is inside. Don't ye hear her laughin'
        and singin', and them all playing the piana?
     [*He pounds on door with cane* –]

10   [*Ext. door CS* – TERRY *standing at door* – *Talks* – *Piano heard playing* –]
     TERRY   Open up . . open up, or I'll put me fist through
        the door.
     [*He pounds on door with knocker* –]
     MAN (*off*)   What do you want?
     TERRY   Open up and find out . .
     [*Door opens revealing man inside* –]
     TERRY   . . Open wider or I'll smash ye to a mollycule.

11   [*Ext. entrance MS* – MAN *and* TERRY *at doorway* – GYPO *going up steps as* MAN
        talks –]
     MAN   Oh, you will, will you?
     [TERRY *steps aside* – *Talking* –]
     TERRY   Gypo, Gypo! Show him he can't intimidate
        us! . .
     [GYPO *picks* MAN *up* – *Hurls him off to right* – TERRY *and* GYPO *exit as camera
        follows* MAN *as he falls into street* –]
     TERRY (*off*)   Up the rebels!

12   [*Int. hallway CS* – *Piano heard* – GYPO *coming on at left FG* – *Followed by*
        TERRY – *They open doors revealing crowd in room in BG* – *All talking at once* –
        Laughing – *Confusion* – *Piano stops* – *Woman laughs shrilly* –]

13   [*Int. doorway CS* – GYPO *and* TERRY *standing in doorway* – GYPO *looking to*
        FG –]

14   [*Int. room CS* – GYPO *and* TERRY *standing in doorway* – *Looking about* – AUNT
        BETTY *comes on at right* – *Talks* –]
     AUNT BETTY   What do you want?
     TERRY   What does he want? What does he want? Now,
        now, don't be disrespectin' to me friend, Gypo, or ye'll have me to settle
        with.

AUNT BETTY   Aw, shut your gob! . .
[*She talks to* GYPO —]
AUNT BETTY   . . And what d'ye mean breakin' in here?
[*He takes drink from tray* — *Talks* —]
GYPO   I'm lookin' for Katie Madden.
AUNT BETTY   Well, ye won't be findin' her here.
[*Loud laughter heard* — GYPO *looks about* — *Turns* — *Starts through doorway* —
AUNT BETTY *exits as camera follows him* — TERRY *stops him* — *Talks* —]
TERRY   Wait, Gypo . . come back, Gypo . .
[GYPO *stops in doorway* — AUNT BETTY *coming partly on at right* —]
TERRY   . . come on back and face 'em like a man.

15 [*Int. room MS* — GYPO *and* TERRY *standing in doorway in BG* — *Others partly on
    at right and left* — *Laugh loudly* — *General indistinct talking* — MAN *at bar at
    left talks* —]
MAN   Aw, get out, get out. Throw him out . . throw
him out.
[*General indistinct talking* — TERRY *and* GYPO *come toward bar* — MAN *talking* —]
MAN   Throw 'em out of here.
[*They stop by bar* — *Small* MAN *talks to* GYPO *drunkenly* —]
MAN   You're in the wrong place, my young man . .

16 [*Int. room MCU* — MAN *looking up at* GYPO — *Talking* — *Others partly on* —]
MAN   . . can't you see we're havin' a party. Now get
out. Get out before I throw you out.
[GYPO *looks about* — *Looks down at* MAN — *Laughs* — *Puts hand in his face* —
Pushing him down — MAN *exits* — *Exclamations heard* — GYPO *looks to right
FG* —]

17 [*Int. room MCS* — GIRL *seated at table* — GYPO *in FG* — *Going toward her* — *Back
    to camera* — *He stops at right of table* — *Looking down at her* —]

18 [*Int. room CS* — GIRL *seated at table* — *Looking up at* GYPO *partly on at right* — *He
    leans across table* — *Reaching for her hand* — *She rises frightened* — *Stands in
    corner* — *Music heard playing* "I Adore Him" —]

19 [*Int. room CU* — GYPO *looking to left FG* — *Music heard* —]

20 [*Int. room CU* — GIRL *standing in corner* — *Watching to right FG* — *Frightened* —
    Music heard —]

21 [*Int. room MCS* — GIRL *standing in corner looking at* GYPO *partly on at right FG* —
    Back to camera — *Figure of* GIRL *dissolves into* KATIE —]

22 [*Int. room CU* — GYPO *looking to left FG* — *Smiles* — *Music heard* — *He talks* —]
GYPO   Katie!

23 [*Int. room CU* — GIRL *standing in corner* — *Looking to right FG* — *Talks* — *Music
    heard* —]
GIRL   My name isn't Katie. What is it you want?

24 [*Int. room MCS* – GIRL *standing in corner* – GYPO *standing at right* – *Back partly to camera* – AUNT BETTY *coming on at left FG* – *Talking* – TERRY *following her on* –]

AUNT BETTY   That's what I'm askin'. What do you want?

TERRY   What do ye suppose he wants, ye old harridan? He wants a drink.

25 [*Int. room MCU* – AUNT BETTY *talks to* TERRY *at left* – GIRL *partly on in BG* –]

AUNT BETTY   You can get no drink here, you social climber. Why don't you go back to the gutter where you belong.

TERRY   Now, don't talk to Gypo and me like that. And don't be lookin' down your nose either, you ould squint . .

26 [*Int. room MCS* – TERRY *talking to* AUNT BETTY – GYPO *at right* – GIRL *in BG* –]

TERRY   . . I suppose ye think we have no money. Well, we have lashings of it. Am I right, Gypo, or am I wrong? . .

[GYPO *takes roll of notes from pocket* – AUNT BETTY *sees them* – TERRY *turns to FG* – *Talking* –]

TERRY   . . What did I tell ye? What did I tell ye? He's as rich as Craysus.

[GYPO *hands notes to* AUNT BETTY – *Talks* –]

GYPO   Give everybody a drink. I'm calling for drinks for the house.

AUNT BETTY   Glasses for everybody! Glasses for everybody!

[*She comes to FG* – *Talking* –]

TERRY   Glasses for everybody! . .

[AUNT BETTY *and* TERRY *exit left FG* – *Talking* –]

TERRY (*off*)   . . Glasses for everybody.

AUNT BETTY (*off*) Glasses for everybody!

GYPO   Gypo!

27 [*Int. room MS* – *People standing about* – AUNT BETTY *and* TERRY *going to bar at left* – *All talking at once* – *Confusion* – TERRY *talks* –]

TERRY   Music, music . .

[*He turns to* PIANO PLAYER *at left FG* – *Talking* –]

TERRY   . . music for me ould fren' and bussom companion. Music for King Gypo!

[TERRY *runs to BG* – *Stands on divan* – PIANO PLAYER *starts to play* "*Dardanelly*" –]

28 [*Int. room MCS* – TERRY *standing on divan* – *Others around him* – *Piano heard* – TERRY *talking* –]

TERRY   . . And if there's any man here thinks he's a match for us with his fists, will you kindly step up. Am I right, Gypo, or am I wrong?

[GYPO *comes on at right FG* – *Talking* –]

GYPO   You're right . . you're right.

[TERRY *exits as camera follows* GYPO *to left to bar* − GIRL *standing by bar holding tray of drinks* − GYPO *picks up glass* − *Drinks* − TERRY *coming on at right* − *Picks up glass* − *Drinks* − *General laughter and indistinct talking* − *Much confusion* − *Noise stops as* GYPO *talks* −]

GYPO   Silence, quiet . . silence! Go to the devil all of ye! There's more drink where this came from.

[*He takes roll of notes from pocket* − *Puts some on tray* −]

GYPO   D'ye hear that? There's more where this came from.

[TERRY *and* GIRL *exit left* − *All talking at once* −]

GYPO   Hey, get some more drinks. Gypooo!

[GYPO *picks up* AUNT BETTY − *Whirls her around* − *All laughing* − *Loudly* − *He puts her down* − *Picks up* GIRL *at right* − *Whirls her around* −]

29 [*Int. room MCS* − AUNT BETTY *shouting at* GYPO − GYPO *partly on in FG whirling* GIRL *around* − *Laughter and talking heard* − *Piano heard* −]

AUNT BETTY   Stop it, stop it . . stop it, stop it! Do ye want me to get picked up by the police?

30 [*Int. room MS* − GYPO *holding* GIRL − *Others about them* − *Piano heard* − *He drops* GIRL *to floor* − *Others gasp* −]

GIRL   Oww!

[AUNT BETTY *and* GIRL *help* GIRL *up* − GYPO *talks* −]

GYPO   Hey, hey, I'll keep order for ye. Hey . .

[*He grabs cane from* TERRY − *Pounds it on bar* − *Talking* −]

GYPO   . . who's makin' all the row? . .

31 [*Int. room MCS* − GYPO *standing in front of bar at left* − *Shaking cane at others* − *Talking* −]

GYPO   . . The first one that opens his mouth above a whisper . .

[*He cracks cane on bar* −]

GYPO   . . I'll crack his skull open.

32 [*Int. room MCU* − TERRY *leaning on bar* − *Looking to FG* − *Talks* −]

TERRY   And he'd enjoy doin' it.

33 [*Int. room MCS* − TERRY *partly on at left FG* − GYPO *standing in front of bar* − *Others in BG* − GYPO *looks around* − *Talks* −]

GYPO   Yeah. Gypooo! . .

[*He laughs* −]

GYPO   . . come on.

[*He goes to bar* − *Others rush at bar* − *All talking and laughing at once* − *Small* MAN *comes to* GYPO − *Pats him on back* − *Laughter and indistinct talking stops as man talks* −]

MAN   I'll teach you to behave like a gentleman an amongst ladies.

[*He slaps* GYPO'S *face* − *Knocking cap off* − GYPO *catches cap* − *Starts to FG* −]

GYPO   Hey . .

34 [*Int. room MS – Crowd watching* GYPO *– He pushes small* MAN *to* BG *–* MAN
    falls over divan – Crowd exclaims – GYPO *talks –* MAN *picking up small*
    MAN *–*]

GYPO   . . Hey, can you play "All . . Those Endearin'
Charms?"

35 [*Int. room CS –* TERRY *standing by* GYPO *looking to* FG *– Talks – Others in*
    BG *–*]

TERRY   "Believe Me If All Those Endearing Young
Charms."

GYPO   That's what I said.

TERRY   Do you hear? That's what he said. Now, that's
what he said.

36 [*Int. room MCS –* PIANIST *seated at piano –* WOMAN *standing by piano – Motions*
    to him – He plays "Improvise" –]

[*Lap dissolve*]

37 [*Int. room CS – Two* WOMEN *seated – Looking off to right sadly – Chanting in*
    Gaelic heard indistinctly – (Nothing distinct enough for translation) – Door at
    right BG opening – MAN *comes on – Removes hat – Stands in doorway –* MARY
    comes on at right FG – Goes to him – Exits through doorway – MAN *closes*
    door – Exits –]

38 [*Int. room MS –* DAN *standing at window in BG – Back to camera – Music heard*
    playing medley ("Mary" – "The Informer" – "Wearing of the Green" – "The
    Informer" – "Wearing of the Green" – "Mary") – Door at left opening –
    DAN *turns toward it as* MARY *comes on – Goes to him – Talking –*]

MARY   Oh, Dan!
[*He takes her in his arms – Talking –*]
DAN   Mary, darling!

39 [*Int. room CU –* MARY *and* DAN *standing in front of window – Embracing – Music*
    heard – MARY *talks –*]

MARY   Oh . . Oh, you shouldn't come here. What if the
Tans should come back.

DAN   It's all right, dear. My lads are outside. Poor
darling, I know how you feel and there is nothing I can do or say to help
you, except that . . well, I wish it could have been me instead of Frankie.

MARY   If I lost you I would only want to die. Poor
mother! Oh, Dan, when is this trouble going to end? This killing and more
killing.

DAN   It's hard on you women, I know. You're braver
than we are.

MARY   Oh, I'm sorry, dear.
DAN   I love you, Mary.
MARY   I love you, Dan.
[*They embrace –*]

40   [*Int. room MS – * DAN *and* MARY *standing in front of window in BG – Embracing –*
      *Music heard – He talks – *]

DAN   I must ask you some questions about Frankie.
      May I?

MARY   Of course.

[*They come to right FG – Camera following them to right – They stop in front of*
*fireplace – * DAN *talking – *]

DAN   There must have been an informer. You know
      that. The man who knew about Frankie knows enough to destroy us all . .
      and the moment he is frightened, he'll run to the Tans and tell everything,
      and they'll wipe us out with one sweep . .

41   [*Int. room CS – * DAN *and* MARY *standing in front of fireplace – * DAN *talking – Mu-*
      *sic heard – *]

DAN   . . Oh, I'm not thinking about myself. It's the
      organization. It's Ireland. You know that, don't you?

MARY   I know that, dear.

DAN   I have to find that informer. Tell me, did Frankie
      think he was followed when he came home tonight?

MARY   No, he was sure he wasn't.

DAN   Had he seen or spoken to anyone?

MARY   Nobody, only his friend Gypo Nolan. He said
      he had to find him first to see if there was a guard on the house.

DAN   Where?

MARY   Let me see . . at the Dunboy House, I think he
      said.

DAN   I see. Did he mention a man named Mulligan?

MARY   No, I'm sure not.

[*Camera follows them across to left – * DAN *talking – *]

DAN   We are holding a court of inquiry at one-thirty.
      Can you come? I need you.

MARY   If you need me, I will come.

DAN   I'll come back for you about one o'clock. Can
      you slip out the back way?

MARY   Oh, Dan . . Dan, what would I do if anything
      happened to you? Whatever happens to you, happens to my own heart.

[*She sobs – He holds her closely – Knock is heard – * DAN *looks off to left quickly – *]

42   [*Int. room CS – Door at left opening – * DONAHUE *comes on in doorway – Looking*
      *to FG – Talks – *]

DONAHUE   Commandant, there's a patrol of Tans in the
      neighborhood . .

43   [*Int. room MS – * DAN *and* MARY *standing by table – * DONAHUE *at left BG in door-*
      *way – Talking – *]

DONAHUE   . . You'd better hurry.

[DONAHUE *exits through doorway – * DAN *goes to door – Exits – Closing door – *
MARY *goes to window – Sobs – *]

REEL 7

1   [*Ext. house MS* – BARTLEY *and two* MEN *coming on in FG* – BARTLEY *runs up steps to entrance* – *Two* MEN *stopping in FG* – *Piano and singing heard* –]
TERRY & WOMAN (*off*)   . . like fairy gifts fading away . .

2   [*Int. room CS* – TERRY *standing by* GYPO – *Others in BG* – *Piano heard* – TERRY *singing* – WOMAN *heard singing* – GYPO *listening sadly* –]
TERRY & OTHERS (*singing*)   . . thou would . .
[TERRY & OTHERS *exit as camera follows* GYPO *across to right* –]
TERRY & OTHERS (*off*)   . . still be adored, as this moment thou art . .
[GYPO *leans on mantel* –]

3   [*Int. room MCU* – TERRY *singing* – *Others behind him singing* – *Piano heard* –]
TERRY & OTHERS (*singing*)   . . let thy loveliness fade as it will and around . .

4   [*Ext. entrance MCU* – BARTLEY *standing at door* – *Back to camera* – *Listening* – *Singing and piano heard* –]
TERRY & OTHERS (*off*)   . . the dear ruins . .
[BARTLEY *opens door* – *Looks into hallway* –]
TERRY & OTHERS (*off*)   . . each wish of my heart . . would . .

5   [*Int. room MCU* – GYPO *standing by mantel* – *Listening sadly* – *Singing and piano heard* –]
TERRY & OTHERS (*off*)   . . entwine itself verdently still.
[*Singing and piano stop* – GYPO *talks* –]
GYPO   I forgot something. I got to be goin'.
[*Camera following him across to left reveals others in BG* – *Watching him* – *He starts to BG to doorway* – AUNT BETTY *and* TERRY *coming on at left FG after him* – *Talking* –]
AUNT BETTY   Oh, Gypo . . Gypo . . Gypo!
[TERRY *and* AUNT BETTY *both talking at once indistinctly* –]

6   [*Int. hallway MCS* – GYPO *coming to doorway* – AUNT BETTY *and* TERRY *after him* – *Both talking at once* – *Others in BG watching* – AUNT BETTY *stops him* – *Talking* –]
AUNT BETTY   Ah, Gypo, come on back. Now come on and I'll give you a nice drink.
TERRY   Yes, and I'll sing ye another song. Come on.
[GIRL *comes on in BG* – *Talks* –]
GIRL   Oh, how contemptible you are. You only tolerate him because of his money.
AUNT BETTY   Watch out what y're sayin', my fine lady.
[GIRL *steps forward as she talks* –]
GIRL   Oh, I know you hate me . .

7   [*Int. room MCU* – GIRL *looking to right FG* – *Talking* – *Others partly on behind her* –]
GIRL   . . simply because I . . I'm not coarse. Simply because I'm . .

[AUNT BETTY *comes partly on at right FG – Back to camera – Talking –*]

AUNT BETTY It's nothing of the kind. I hate ye because ye're a stuck up, ignorant person who thinks ye're better than anybody else.

8 [*Int. doorway MCS –* GYPO *and* AUNT BETTY *standing in doorway –* GIRL *between them – Crowd behind her laugh hilariously –* WOMAN *talks –*]

WOMAN She does too.

GIRL I had no right to come in here. I should have gone to the police.

[GIRL *starts to right FG –* GYPO *stops her – Talking –*]

GYPO Police! Ah, none of that talk. Now keep away from the police. What d'ye want the police for?

GIRL I want to get back home.

9 [*Int. doorway CU –* GYPO *looking across to right – Talks –*]

GYPO Where's your home?

10 [*Int. doorway CU –* GIRL *looking up to left – Talks –*]

GIRL It's near London.

11 [*Int. doorway MCS –* GYPO *and* GIRL *standing in doorway –* AUNT BETTY *and others in BG –* GYPO *reaches into pocket –* TERRY *talks to him –*]

TERRY Now listen, Gypo, be very careful now . .

[GYPO *takes roll of notes from pocket –*]

TERRY . . don't do anything you'll regret, Gypo.

GYPO How much will it cost to get back there? . .

[*He puts notes in her hand as he talks –*]

GYPO . . There, there's your fare.

TERRY Five pounds. What are ye after doin', Gypo?

GYPO Now, don't be afraid now. Get outa here. And go home. Keep the money. Go on, but keep away from the police.

GIRL Oh, you're a good man . . a good man.

[*She kisses him quickly – Exits left FG –* GYPO *looking after her surprised – Others laughing –* TERRY *talks –*]

TERRY Five pounds, on me immortal soul. Gypo, do you know what . .

AUNT BETTY That's all right, dearie, but she owed me four pounds for board and lodging. Now who's goin' to pay me that?

GYPO Oh, shut yer gob and not another word.

[*He stuffs notes into her hands – Pushes her away –*]

TERRY Now, listen, Gypo, don't start this all over again. Now listen, Gypo Nolan, you know what . . you've ruined a lovely evening. Come on. There's a few drinks left. Come on, let's finish them.

12 [*Ext. door MCU –* BARTLEY *and two* MEN *standing at door listening – Music heard playing medley ("The Money" and "The Informer") –* BARTLEY *talks –*]

BARTLEY Two and five are seven, and four is eleven.

MAN Eleven pounds.

[BARTLEY *nods –*]

13 [*Int. room MCS − Women partly on at left − Laughing − General indistinct talking
heard − Music heard −* TERRY *coming on at left − Stops at right − Talks −*]

TERRY   Ladies and Gentlemen, ye have seen the wonder
of our generosity. Money scattered like snuff at a wake . .

14 [*Int. room CS −* GYPO *leaning on bar − Others partly on behind him − Music
heard −*]

TERRY (*off*)   . . Now I want ye to drink to the health of
King Gypo, as brave as a lamb and as strong as a bull . .

15 [*Int. room MCS − Camera shooting down at* TERRY *talking to others − Music
heard −*]

TERRY   . . I would go through fire and water for him
and he'd do the same for me . .

[*Door in BG opening −* BARTLEY *and two* MEN *come on in doorway −*]

TERRY   . . and from now on, from this night, whenever
ye see the one of us, ye'll see the other, or vice versa as the case may be . .

16 [*Int. room CS −* GYPO *leaning on bar − Others partly on behind him − Music
heard − He glances off to right − Listening −*]

TERRY (*off*)   . . Am I right or am I wrong, Gypo?

GYPO   Right.

17 [*Int. room MCS −* BARTLEY *and two* MEN *coming to FG slowly − Stop in FG −
Music heard −*]

TERRY (*off*)   So I ask you to drink to the undyin' friendship . .

BARTLEY   Shut up.

18 [*Int. room MCS −* TERRY *and others look to left quickly − Music heard −* TERRY
talks −]

TERRY   And who may I ask has the impertinence to tell
me and Gypo to shut up?

19 [*Int. room CS −* BARTLEY *and two* MEN *looking to right FG −* MAN *talks − Music
heard −*]

MAN   Quiet!

[*Music stops −* BARTLEY *comes to right FG as he talks −*]

BARTLEY   Make way there . .

[*He exits left FG −*]

20 [*Int. room MCS −* GYPO *standing at bar − Others stepping aside as* BARTLEY
comes through crowd toward GYPO *− Talking −*]

BARTLEY   . . make way.

[GYPO *talks delighted −*]

GYPO   Bartley, me boy. Come have a drink.

BARTLEY   Come along, Gypo. It's time to be going.

GYPO   Ha-Ha, be off with ye. Who are ye to be givin'
me orders?

[TERRY *comes on at right − Talking −*]

TERRY   Bash 'im, Gypo, bash 'im! Who does he think he is, givin' orders to us.

BARTLEY   I said shut up.

21   [*Int. room MCU* – BARTLEY *turning to* GYPO *at left* – *Talks* – *Others partly on in BG* –]

BARTLEY   They're not my orders. They're Gallagher's and you'd better be careful about disobeying them.

GYPO   You're right, Bartley. Is it one o'clock?

BARTLEY   It is.

[GYPO *picks up glass* –]

22   [*Int. room MCS* – GYPO *and* BARTLEY *standing at bar* – TERRY *at right* – *Others in BG* – GYPO *drinks* – *Throws glass off to right* – *It breaks* – GYPO *turns* – *Goes to BG* – BARTLEY *following him* – AUNT BETTY *comes on at left FG* – TERRY *turns* – *Talks to her* –]

TERRY   I know who they are. They're the Republican Army . .

[GYPO *and* BARTLEY *stop in doorway in BG* –]

TERRY   . . the Republican Army. I am no friend of Gypo's. He wormed his way into me heart. I'm a true son of Erin but I'll never lift me hand against the crown.

[AUNT BETTY *goes to* GYPO *at left BG* – *Talking* –]

AUNT BETTY   Crown or no crown, army or no army . .

23   [*Int. room MCS* – GYPO, BARTLEY *and two* MEN *standing in doorway* – AUNT BETTY *coming on at left FG* – *Going to them* – *Talking* –]

AUNT BETTY   . . who's going to pay me for that last round of drinks?

[GYPO *reaches into pocket* – BARTLEY *pushes him to left BG as he talks* –]

BARTLEY   Come on, Gypo, let's go.

DENNIS   You ought to be thrown into the Liffey, ye old hag . .

[BARTLEY *exits through doorway with* GYPO – MAN *following them* – DENNIS *talking to* AUNT BETTY *as he starts to close doors* –]

DENNIS   . . for servin' liquor after hours, and on the holy day of obligation.

[*He exits as doors nearly close* –]

24   [*Int. room MS* – TERRY *standing at bar at left* – AUNT BETTY *watching to BG as doors close* – *Others about* – TERRY *goes to BG* – AUNT BETTY *stops him* – *Talking* –]

AUNT BETTY   Not so fast, ye little snake . .

25   [*Int. room MCS* – AUNT BETTY *turning* TERRY *toward her* – *Talking to him* –]

AUNT BETTY   . . ye can pay for the drinks yourself.

TERRY   Aw, now, listen . . Aunt Betty, you're a lovely, quiet, little woman, and if you'll only give me until tomorrow, till I raise the wind . .

AUNT BETTY   Um . . tomorrow is it? . .
[*She steps in front of doors – Calls –*]
AUNT BETTY   . . Mickeen!

26 [*Int. room CS – Closed doors –*]
  AUNT BETTY (*off*)   Mickeen!
  [*Doors opening –* MICKEEN *looks out to FG – Billyclub in hand –*]

27 [*Int. room MCS –* AUNT BETTY *standing in front of doors –* TERRY *by her –*
  Looking off to right frightened – Talks –]
  TERRY   Oh, dear . . oh, dear . . I have a queer feeling
  there's going to be a strange face in heaven in the mornin'.

28 [*Ext. street MS –* DENNIS *coming on around corner from right – Music heard playing
  medley – He stops at corner – Looks about cautiously – Gestures – Comes to
  right FG – Exits –*]

29 [*Ext. corner MCS –* GYPO *coming on around corner – Followed by* BARTLEY *and*
  MAN *– Music heard –* GYPO *stops in FG as he hears –*]
  KATIE (*off*)   Gypo!
  [KATIE *runs on at left –* GYPO *talks –*]
  GYPO   Katie, Katie, I've been lookin' all over for ye!
  Where've ye been?
  KATIE   I was in my digs. I waited for you. Why didn't
  ye come? . .
  [*She looks at two* MEN *– Talks frightened –*]
  KATIE   . . What's wrong, Gypo? Where they takin'
  you?
  GYPO   Aw, Katie, it's all right. It's all right. Don't
  worry. Gallagher's takin' me back.
  BARTLEY   Aw, shut up, Gypo.
  MEN   Come on . . come along.
  [*All talking at once indistinctly –* GYPO *struggling with two* MEN *–*]
  GYPO   Will you stop it? Keep your hands off of me,
  will you! . .
  [*He turns to* KATIE *– Talking –*]
  GYPO   . . Say, do you remember the twenty pounds I
  was talkin' about?
  KATIE   Twenty pounds?
  [*Music stops –*]

30 [*Ext. street CU –* MAN *looks off to right suspiciously –* GYPO *heard laughing –*]

31 [*Ext. street CU –* BARTLEY *looking to left FG listening –*]
  GYPO (*off*)   Yes, I got it. I got it for you . .

32 [*Ext. street MCS –* KATIE *and* GYPO *standing on corner –* BARTLEY *and* MAN *by
  them –* GYPO *talking to her – Music heard playing medley –*]
  GYPO   . . I got it for you. Twenty pounds . .
  [*He laughs – Takes bills from pocket – Puts them in her hand –*]

33   [*Ext. street CU* – DENNIS *looking off to left wide-eyed* – *Music heard* – GYPO *heard laughing* –]

34   [*Ext. street MCS* – GYPO *putting notes into* KATIE's *hand* – *Laughing* – *Talking* – BARTLEY *and* MAN *by him* – *Music heard* –]
GYPO   . . twenty pounds.
[*They grab* GYPO – *Talking* –]
BARTLEY AND MAN   Come on, we've had enough of that talk. Come on, come on.
[*They exit right FG with* GYPO – KATIE *looking after them* –]

35   [*Ext. street MS* – BARTLEY *and* MAN *going to BG with* GYPO – *Music heard* – DENNIS *standing in doorway* – *Follows them* – *They nearly exit in BG in fog* –]

36   [*Ext. street MCS* – KATIE *watching to FG thoughtfully* – *Music heard* – *She looks at bills in hand* – *Lets them fall to street* – *Talks* –]
KATIE   Gypo!
                                        [*Lap dissolve*]

37   [*Ext. Bogey Hole MLS* – MAN *standing guard above in BG* – MAN *coming on in FG* – *Music heard* – MAN *stops at top of steps* – MAN *in BG* – *Drops flag down below* – *Runs down steps* – MAN *standing at head of stairs* – *Talks* – *Music stops* –]
KERRIGAN   It's all right, Sir.
[MAN *runs downstairs to BG* – MARY *coming on in FG as men exit below* – DAN *comes on after her* – *Music heard* – *Two* MEN *follow them on* – *Stop in FG* – DAN *and* MARY *nearly exit below in BG* –]

38   [*Int. Bogey Hole MS* – DAN *and* MARY *coming down steps* – *Music heard* –]
TOMMY (*off*)   Attention.
[*Camera moves back as they come down steps to FG* – *Revealing men standing about at attention* – TOMMY *coming on at right* – *Takes* MARY *across to right* – *Camera moving back as* DAN *comes to FG* – MULLIGAN *seated at left* – DAN *stops at table at right* – *Talks to two men seated at table* –]
DAN   Our case is prepared, Gentlemen.

39   [*Int. Bogey Hole CS* – MARY *seated at table* – *Looking to right FG* – *Music heard* –]

40   [*Int. Bogey Hole CS* – *Camera shooting down at feet on floor* – *Hands partly on, counting beads on rosary* – *Music heard* – *Camera pans up revealing* MULLIGAN –]

41   [*Int. Bogey Hole CS* – MARY *seated at table* – *Looking about frightened* – *Music heard* –]

42   [*Int. Bogey Hole MCU* – *Camera panning to left revealing line of young boys standing in front of wall* – *Watching to FG* – *Music heard* –]

43   [*Int. Bogey Hole CS* – MARY *seated at table* – *Looking about* – *Music heard* – *She looks off to right* – *Exits as camera pans to right revealing two* JUDGES *seated at table* – *One nods* –]

44 [*Int. Bogey Hole CS* — MARY *seated at table* — *Looking to right* — *Music heard* —
Commotion heard — *She looks to left as she hears* —]
GYPO (*off*)   Look out below!

45 [*Int. Bogey Hole MS* — *Men standing at foot of steps* — *Commotion heard* — GYPO
falls on down steps followed by BARTLEY *and* MAN — *Music heard* —]

46 [*Int. Bogey Hole CS* — *Two* JUDGES *seated at table* — *Looking off to left* — *Confusion
heard* — *Music heard* —]

47 [*Int. Bogey Hole MS* — DAN *standing at right FG watching as men pick up* GYPO —
Music heard — *They start to bring* GYPO *to FG* — *Music stops* — *He struggles
with men* — *Talks* —]
GYPO   Let me alone, will you . .
[*He pushes men away* —]
GYPO   . . Hello, boys, here I am, and I can fight the
best six men that walked the earth. Come on . .
[*He swings arms about wildly* — *Turns* — *Sees* DAN — *Salutes him* — *Talking* —]
GYPO   . . Danny . . Danny, me boy. You and me, we
can put 'em on the run, huh? Come on.
DAN   What's the matter with your eye, Bartley?
[GYPO *laughs loudly* — *Slaps* BARTLEY *on shoulder* — *Talks* —]
GYPO   He got in me way and I hit him with a hander . .
[*He swings arms about wildly* — *Men grab him* — *Push him to FG* —]
DAN   Sit down.
MAN   Come on.

48 [*Int. Bogey Hole MS* — *Men pushing* GYPO *to bench at left* — MULLIGAN *seated on
bench* — *Boys standing at attention behind bench* — DAN *comes to right* — *Puts
hat down on table* — GYPO *talking to boy at left* —]
GYPO   Give me my hat, will you? Where's my hat? . .
[*He finds hat* —]
GYPO   . . Bartley, me boy . .

49 [*Int. Bogey Hole CS* — MULLIGAN *and* GYPO *seated on bench* — GYPO *laughing* —
Others partly on behind them — GYPO *talks* —]
GYPO   . . Bartley, me boy.
[*He laughs* — *Puts on cap* — MULLIGAN *coughs* — GYPO *turns* — *Sees him* — *Music
heard playing* "*The Meek Tailor*" — GYPO *puts arm around him as he talks* —]
GYPO   Mulligan, what brings you here? Man alive,
you ought to be in bed. This is no hour for a sick man to be out . .
[*He looks up to right* —]
GYPO   . . Dan, I . .

REEL 8

1   [*Int. Bogey Hole MCU* — DAN *looking down to left FG* — *Music heard playing
medley* — *He exits left revealing* TOMMY *and* MARY *seated at table* — *Camera
moves closer to them* — TOMMY *nearly exits left as camera moves closer to* MARY —]

2   [*Int. Bogey Hole CU –* GYPO *looking off to right thoughtfully – Others partly on behind him – Music heard – He looks to right FG – Sees –*]

3   [*Int. Bogey Hole CS –* JUDGE *seated at table – Looking to FG – Music heard – Camera pans to right revealing other* JUDGE *–* FIRST JUDGE *exits –* SECOND JUDGE *exits as camera pans to right revealing* BLIND MAN *seated at end of table –*]

4   [*Int. Bogey Hole CU –* GYPO *looking to right FG – Open-mouthed – Others partly on behind him – Music heard –*]

5   [*Int. Bogey Hole MCU –* BLIND MAN *staring up at FG – Music heard –*]

6   [*Int. Bogey Hole CS –* GYPO *seated on bench – arm around* MULLIGAN *seated by him – Others behind him – Music heard –* GYPO *looks at* MULLIGAN *slowly – Leans away from him – Pointing finger at* MULLIGAN *– Nearly exits right as he rises –*]

7   [*Int. Bogey Hole MCS –* DAN *and* BARTLEY *watching as* GYPO *comes on at left – Pointing to left – Others in BG – Music heard –* GYPO *looks about – Talks –*]
GYPO   Listen, men, I had a drop taken before I came in and I don't know what I was sayin' . .
[*He pounds fists together – Music stops – He points off to left – Talking –*]
GYPO   . . but now I remember. That's the one that informed on Frankie McPhillip . .

8   [*Int. Bogey Hole CS –* MULLIGAN *seated on bench – Others standing behind him – He rises slowly – Listening –*]
GYPO   . . I saw him and he knows it.
[*Music heard playing as* MULLIGAN *talks –*]
MULLIGAN   It's a lie, it's a lie. I swear on me knees I never left the house except to go to the chapel to say me prayers.

9   [*Int. Bogey Hole MCS –* GYPO *looking off to left FG – Laughs – Talks –* BARTLEY *and* DAN *on either side of him – Watching – Others in BG – Music heard –*]
GYPO   Ha, Ha, Ha, me fine boyo. It's easy work for an informer to be swearin' oaths.
MULLIGAN (*off*)   It's a lie, it's a lie.
DAN   Sit down, Gypo . .
[GYPO *salutes* DAN *–*]
DAN   . . sit down. Peter Mulligan, do you recognize the authority of this court?
[GYPO *comes to left FG – Exits –*]

10   [*Int. Bogey Hole CS –* MULLIGAN *looking to right FG – Talks – Others partly on in BG –*]
MULLIGAN   I do, I do, Commandant. Heaven knows I do.

11   [*Int. Bogey Hole MS –* JUDGES *partly on in FG – Seated at table – Backs to camera –* DAN *talking to* MULLIGAN *– Others in BG –* GYPO *seated on bench –*]

DAN   Will you stand over here, please? Give the court an account of your whereabouts from noon today.

[MULLIGAN *comes toward* JUDGES *as he talks* –]

MULLIGAN   Gentlemen, could ye find no better man to arrest and carry off in the middle of the night than me, that's havin' to work me hands off at me trade, a-tailorin' and a-stitchin' in a basement so cold and damp that I've caught me death of cold?

DAN   I'm sorry, Mulligan, start at noon. Where were you?

12   [*Int. Bogey Hole CS* – MULLIGAN *standing at table* – JUDGES *partly on in FG* – *Backs to camera* – *Others in BG* – MULLIGAN *talks* –]

MULLIGAN   At noon today, I was lyin' in me bed. I had a bad pain in me right side from bronchitis all morning and I had to stay in me bed. Then at one o'clock about, the old woman give me a cup of tay and an egg. I remember I couldn't eat the egg . . a good egg, too, but good or bad, no matter. I had to get up then on account of a suit that had to be finished for Mick Foley the carter . .

13   [*Int. Bogey Hole MS* – MULLIGAN *standing at table at right talking* – JUDGES *and* BLIND MAN *seated at table* – DAN *standing at left BG* – MARY *and* TOMMY *seated at table* – *Others in BG* –]

MULLIGAN   . . It's got to be ready Friday, mind you, because his daughter is getting married next Monday . .

DAN   Never mind Foley's daughter. Tell us about yourself.

[JUDGES *and others exit as camera pans to left revealing* GYPO *rising* – *Talks to* DAN –]

GYPO   There you are, there you are. Hear what he says? Hear what he says? Come on, Mulligan, now. Make a clean breast of it.

MULLIGAN   It's not for me to condemn ye, Gypo. Maybe ye're not responsible.

14   [*Int. Bogey Hole CS* – GYPO *takes cap from head* – *Throws it down as he talks angrily* – *Others in BG watching him* –]

GYPO   Why, blast ye, what do you mean? What are ye drivin' at?

DAN (*off*)   Sit down, Gypo, and keep quiet.

GYPO   Do you think I'm going to . .

[BARTLEY *comes on at right* – *Pushes* GYPO *down onto bench as he talks* –]

BARTLEY   Sit down, sit down.

GYPO   Bartley, me boy.

BARTLEY   Shut up.

15   [*Int. Bogey Hole MCS* – MULLIGAN *standing at table* – *Back to camera* – JUDGES *partly on at right* – MARY *and* TOMMY *seated at table* – DAN *at left BG* – *Talks to* MULLIGAN – *Others in BG* –]

DAN   Continue, Mulligan.

[MULLIGAN *turns to* JUDGES *partly on at right – Talks –*]

MULLIGAN   Well, I worked until about half past three or
maybe a quarter to four it was . .

16   [*Int. Bogey Hole CS –* GYPO *seated on bench – Looking up to right FG – Listen-
        ing – Others partly on behind him –*]

MULLIGAN (*off*)   . . when Charlie Corrigan came in and says his
brother Dage was just out of prison after bein' on a hunger strike for
eighteen days, Where is he, says I . . He's upstairs, says he . .

17   [*Int. Bogey Hole CS –* MULLIGAN *standing at table talking – Two* JUDGES *seated
        at table – Listening –*]

MULLIGAN   . . Well, we went up there, and we talked over
a cup of tay until about six o'clock. Yes, it was six. I remember I heard the
An- . .

18   [*Int. Bogey Hole CS –* GYPO *seated on bench – Watching up to right FG – Listen-
        ing – Others partly on behind him – He glances up to right –*]

MULLIGAN (*off*)   . . -gelus beginnin' to strike, and me on me way
down the stairs because I remember I stopped to cross meself . .

19   [*Int. Bogey Hole MCS –* MULLIGAN *standing at table – Talking to two* JUDGES
        seated – BLIND MAN *partly on at right FG – Back to camera –* DAN *standing in
        BG –* MARY *and* TOMMY *seated – Others in BG –*]

MULLIGAN   . . then I ran down home and put on me overcoat, the same one it was . . second-handed it is . .

[DAN *crossing to right –*]

MULLIGAN   . . and I went out to the chapel to do . . you
see . . I'm makin' the stations of the cross.

DAN   How far is the chapel from your house?

MULLIGAN   Oh, maybe a hundred yards, maybe it's more.
If ye go around the corner by Kane's, it's less; if ye go the long way
round . .

DAN   Well, let us say it's one hundred yards. You arrived at the chapel about three minutes past six. How long . .

20   [*Int. Bogey Hole MCU –* GYPO *seated – Looking up to FG – Listening – Nerv-
        ously – Others partly on behind him –*]

DAN (*off*)   . . did you stay?

MULLIGAN (*off*)   I stayed there till about half past six, and then I
stayed outside the door talking to Father Conroy for about ten minutes.

DAN (*off*)   Did you talk to anyone else?

MULLIGAN (*off*)   I was coming to that . .

21   [*Int. Bogey Hole MCS –* MULLIGAN *standing at table – Talking to* JUDGES *–
        Partly on in FG –* DAN *standing at right –* MARY *and* TOMMY *seated at table –
        Others in BG –*]

MULLIGAN   . . then after I left Father Conroy, I . . I met
Barney Kerrigan . .

[DAN *exits as camera pans to left –* MULLIGAN *pointing to left – Talking –*]

MULLIGAN	. . There he is.
DAN (*off*)	Near the chapel?

[DAN *comes on at right as camera pans to right* –]

MULLIGAN	Yes, it must have been within fifty yards of it as ye're goin' by measurements.
DAN	Never mind that.
MULLIGAN	But we never . .
DAN	Then you couldn't have been near the Black and Tan's headquarters say about six o'clock?
MULLIGAN	Heaven forbid. I hope to die right here if I was.

[GYPO *seated in GB* – *Rises as he talks* –]

GYPO	You're lyin' . . you're lyin'!

[BARTLEY *pushes him back to bench* – *Talking* –]

BARTLEY	Shut up.
GYPO	He's lyin', Bartley.
BARTLEY	Shut up.
DAN	Tell us what you did after you left Kerrigan?
MULLIGAN	Well, I went back to the house and did a bit more until about eight o'clock then I felt the pains in me side again, and I went to me bed until three men, under Mister . .

22   [*Int. Bogey Hole CS* – TOMMY *and* MARY *seated at table* – TOMMY *writing* – *Glances up to FG* – *Listening* –]

MULLIGAN (*off*)	. . Tom Connor there, came in and bundled me into a . .

23   [*Int. Bogey Hole MCS* – MULLIGAN *standing at table* – *Talking* – JUDGES *partly on in FG* – *Backs to camera* – DAN *standing at right* – *Others in BG* –]

MULLIGAN	. . car without a by yer leave, as if I was a criminal.
DAN	One more question, did you bear anyone a grievance, about your sister, Susie, I mean.

[MULLIGAN *starts toward* DAN – *Talking* –]

MULLIGAN	My sister Susie it is . .

24   [*Int. Bogey Hole CS* – DAN *at right FG* – *Back partly to camera* – MULLIGAN *coming on at left* – *Talking* – *Others partly on in BG* – MULLIGAN *talks* –]

MULLIGAN	. . sure, my sister Susie's name is Mary Ellen, and for the past twenty-eight years she's been livin' in Boston, Massachusetts. She's the mother of eight children.
DAN	That's enough.
MULLIGAN	It is that.
DAN	Did you bear any man a grudge?
MULLIGAN	I bear no fellow-man a grudge, on me oath.
DAN	You had no grievance against Frankie McPhillip?
MULLIGAN	The Lord have mercy on his soul, what for? I hope his sorrows are over him . .

[DAN *exits right — Revealing* MARY *and* TOMMY *seated at table — Camera following*
MULLIGAN *as he leans down to* MARY *— Talking to her —*]

MULLIGAN   . . I swear on me immortal soul, Miss McPhillip, I bore no grudge against your brother.

25   [*Int. Bogey Hole MCS —* DAN *standing at right of table —* JUDGES *partly on in FG —
Backs to camera —* MULLIGAN *standing by* MARY *and* TOMMY *seated at table —
Others in BG —* DAN *looking off to left — Talks —*]

DAN   Kerrigan.
KERRIGAN (*off*)   Yes, Sir.

[KERRIGAN *comes on at left — Stops at table —* DAN *talks —*]

DAN   Kerrigan, did you meet Peter Mulligan at about
half past six this evening?

KERRIGAN   I did, Sir.
DAN   You're sure about the time?
KERRIGAN   I am certain about the time. It was just about
half past six I was after passin' the . .

DAN   As you were.
KERRIGAN   Yes, Sir.

[DAN *leans over to* JUDGES *— They whisper indistinctly —*]

26   [*Int. Bogey Hole CS —* GYPO *seated —* BARTLEY *standing by him — Others partly
on behind them —* GYPO *worried — Talks to* BARTLEY *—*]

GYPO   Bartley . . Bartley . . Bartley.

[*He puts hand on* BARTLEY'S *hand — Feels gun in* BARTLEY'S *pocket — Removes
hand — Looks up at* BARTLEY *— Wipes face nervously with cap —*]

27   [*Int. Bogey Hole MS —* BLIND MAN *partly on at right FG seated at table —* KERRIGAN
and MULLIGAN *standing at left of table —* JUDGES *seated at right —* DAN *by
them —* MARY *and others in BG —* DAN *folds paper — Talks to* MULLIGAN *—*]

DAN   You will be taken home in the car that brought
you here. I'm sorry this had to happen, Mulligan. For the present this
may help you . .

[*He hands note to* MULLIGAN *—*]

DAN   . . we'll see what can be done for you later.
Good night, Mulligan. Show him out, Kerrigan.

[KERRIGAN *removes cartridge belt — Puts it on table —* DAN *and others exit as camera
pans to left revealing* GYPO *seated —* KERRIGAN *going to BG — Followed by*
MULLIGAN *—* GYPO *rises — Talking —* BARTLEY *holding him back —*]

GYPO   Hey, hey, wait a minute . . wait a minute!

[DAN *comes on at right —*]

GYPO   . . Hey, hey, Dan . . hey!

28   [*Int. Bogey Hole CS — Two* JUDGES *seated at table —*]

DAN (*off*)   Now, Gypo, suppose you tell us what you did
with your time from six o'clock this evening until Mulholland picked you
up at one.

29 [*Int. Bogey Hole MCS* – DAN *and* BARTLEY *watching* GYPO *closely* – *Others partly on* – GYPO *looks about confused* – *Talks* –]

GYPO   What . . what's it to do with you where I was?

DAN   Don't you feel like telling us what you did after meeting Frankie McPhillip at the Dunboy House at six o'clock or thereabouts?

GYPO   It's a lie.

[GYPO *and* BARTLEY *nearly exit as camera follows* DAN *as he turns to right revealing* MARY *seated at right BG* – DAN *talks to her* –]

DAN   I'm sorry, Mary. Will you repeat what Frankie told you when he came home tonight?

[MARY *starts to rise* –]

30 [*Int. Bogey Hole CS* – DAN *partly on in FG* – *Back to camera* – MARY *rising* – *Talks* – *Others partly on in BG* –]

MARY   He said that he met him at the Dunboy House. He said he had to make sure that there was no guard on our home.

[DAN *turns to left* – *Nearly exits* –]

31 [*Int. Bogey Hole MCU* – DAN *coming on at right FG* – *Back to camera* – *Talks to* GYPO – BARTLEY *by him* – *Others in BG* –]

DAN   Is that true, Gypo? If not, why did you shout out at the wake tonight that you had warned him to stay away from the house?

GYPO   That's it, that's it. That's what I did. That's what I told him.

DAN   You did see him then. What did you mean by telling all those lies about Mulligan? Were you drunk or what?

[GYPO *looks about confused* – *Talks hesitatingly* –]

GYPO   Well, I . . I . . I had taken a little drop. I . . maybe two . . I . .

32 [*Int. Bogey Hole MCU* – GYPO *partly on at left FG* – DAN *looking at him* – *Talks* – *Others partly on in BG* –]

DAN   What did you do after leaving Frankie? Tell me.

33 [*Int. Bogey Hole MCU* – DAN *partly on at right FG* – *Back to camera* – GYPO *looking at him confused* – *Others partly on in BG* – GYPO *starts to talk* –]

GYPO   Well . .

DAN   What did you do after leaving Frankie?

[GYPO *looks about helplessly* – *Looks at* DAN – *Talks defiantly* –]

GYPO   Well, suppose I don't tell ye. What'll you do?

DAN   Suit yourself. If you don't want to tell me, Bartley Mulholland there can do it for you . .

[GYPO *looks at* BARTLEY *partly on at right* – *Nodding* –]

DAN   Come on, better tell us.

GYPO   I . . I . . I . . I'm all mixed up. I . . I . .

don't know what I'm doin'. I . . I . . well, I . . I . . I . . don't know what I'm doin'!

[He turns to BG mumbling incoherently – Exits left BG – DAN and BARTLEY following him –]

34 *[Int. Bogey Hole MCU – GYPO sitting down on bench – Confused – Others partly on behind him –]*

DAN *(off)*   Where did you get all that money you spent?

[He looks up at DAN and BARTLEY partly on at right – Talks – Music heard playing "Medley" –]

GYPO   I can't make out nothin', Dan. I tell you I'm drunk. I can't . .

DAN *(off)*   You broke your first pound in Ryan's. The blind man there said you gave him a pound.

35 *[Int. Bogey Hole MCU – BLIND MAN seated – Talks – Music heard –]*

BLIND MAN   He did, he did. The poor man . . a pound note he gave me.

36 *[Int. Bogey Hole MCU – GYPO seated – Looking up – Listening dazed – Music heard –]*

DAN *(off)*   Two pounds you spent in the fish and chips shop. Another two pounds went for drinks at the shebeen where Mulholland picked you up. Five pounds you gave to some woman. Four pounds you gave to another woman known as Aunt Betty. And finally you gave five pounds to Katie Madden. That makes just twenty pounds.

GYPO   Ah, me head is sore, Dan . .

37 *[Int. Bogey Hole MCU – DAN and BARTLEY looking down to left – Others partly on in BG – Music heard –]*

GYPO *(off)*   Me head is sore. I . . I'm drunk, I tell ye.

DAN   Where did you get that twenty pounds? Tell us.

38 *[Int. Bogey Hole MCU – GYPO seated – Talks confused – Others partly on behind him – Music heard –]*

GYPO   I can't remember. I can't remember, Dan. I . . I don't know nothin'.

DAN *(off)*   Confess, man, and ease your soul . .

39 *[Int. Bogey Hole MCU – DAN and BARTLEY looking down to left – Others partly on in BG – Music heard – DAN talking –]*

DAN   . . Who was the informer?

40 *[Int. Bogey Hole MCU – GYPO seated – Others partly on behind him – Music heard – GYPO looks down sadly – Rubs hand over face – Trapped – He looks up – Talking – Starts to rise –]*

GYPO   I didn't know what I was doin', Dan. I didn't know what I was . .

41 *[Int. Bogey Hole MCU – DAN partly on at right – GYPO rising at left – Talking confused – Music heard – BARTLEY partly on behind them –]*

GYPO   . . doin', Dan. I didn't know what I was doin'. You see what I mean? Bartley . . Bartley! . .

[*He looks about beggingly — Talking —*]

GYPO   . . isn't there a man here that can tell me why I did it? Oh, me head is sore. I can't tell him! . .

[*He exits as he sits down —*]

42   [*Int. Bogey Hole MCU —* GYPO *sitting down — Holding head — Talking confused — Others partly on behind him — Music heard —*]

GYPO   . . I . . I can't tell him. I can't tell him. I don't know why I did it. I don't know why I did it.

[BARTLEY's *hand comes partly on at right holding gun — Points it at* GYPO *— Music stops —*]

MARY (*off*)   Dan!

DAN (*off*)   No . .

[*Hand comes on — Pushing gun away —*]

DAN (*off*)   . . lock him up.

[DAN *crosses in FG to left of* GYPO — BARTLEY *coming on at right — Talks as they lift* GYPO *up —*]

BARTLEY   Come on, Gypo, come on.

GYPO   I didn't know why I did it.

BARTLEY   Come on.

[*Music heard playing — They exit right with* GYPO — GYPO *mumbling incoherently — Boys watching off to right —*]

43   [*Int. Bogey Hole MS —* MAN *standing at door at right BG — Others in BG —* MARY *and* TOMMY *in FG — Backs to camera — Watching as* BARTLEY *and* MAN *bring* GYPO *on at left —* GYPO *talking — Music heard —*]

GYPO   I don't know why I did it.

[GYPO *mumbling incoherently as men put him into cell at right — Exit —* DAN *comes on at left FG — Stops by* MARY *— Music stops as she talks —*]

MARY   Oh, Lord have mercy on him. The Lord have mercy on him.

DAN   Mary, I'm sorry you had to see this.

MARY   Why must we be killing one another? What good will it do? . .

[*She looks about —*]

44   [*Int. Bogey Hole MCU —* JUDGE *seated at table — Looks down as he hears —*]

MARY (*off*)   . . Oh, why can't we have peace? . .

45   [*Int. Bogey Hole CS —* MARY *talking —* DAN *at left by her — Others in BG —*]

MARY   . . Have mercy on us all.

DAN   It's all over now, dear. I'll take you home in just a moment. It's not a matter of revenge. You know that. When a man turns informer, it's his life or ours.

[*He looks to BG —*]

DAN   . . Bartley, carry on.

[DAN *exits left —*]

REEL 9

1   [*Int. Bogey cell MS — GYPO seated on floor — Light shining through cracks in door — GYPO mumbling incoherently — Music heard playing "Medley" — GYPO rises — Leans on wall at right —*]

2   [*Int. Bogey Hole CU — Hand coming on at left — Holding broken matches between fingers — Men partly on at right — Music heard —*]

BARTLEY (*off*)   You're next, Donahue.

[*Hand comes on at right — Hesitates — Pulls match from other hand — Holds up long match — Camera moves back as BARTLEY partly on at left steps to FG — MAN partly on at right —*]

BARTLEY (*off*)   Next.

TOMMY (*off*)   Come on, Dennis, draw.

[*Camera pans up revealing DALEY whispering to TOMMY —*]

DALEY   No, you go first.

TOMMY   I'm not afraid to draw the last.

BARTLEY (*off*)   What difference does it make? You're nearest . . draw.

DENNIS   Why should I?

TOMMY   Come on. It's your turn.

DALEY   How do you make that out, man? How do you make that out?

BARTLEY (*off*)   Come on, draw. Are ye afraid or what?

TOMMY   No.

[*TOMMY draws — Holds up long match — DALEY stares at it — Hand comes on at left — Holding last match —*]

BARTLEY (*off*)   It's your shot, Dennis.

[*Hand exits left — TOMMY exits right FG — MAN exits left BG — DENNIS looks about nervously — Trying to smile — Looks at door behind him —*]

3   [*Int. Bogey cell MCU — GYPO leaning against wall at right — Music heard — Water dripping down — He looks up — Lights match — Glances off to left — Holds match up — Exits as camera pans up revealing cracks in boards of ceiling —*]

4   [*Int. Bogey Hole MCS — DENNIS turning slowly toward door in BG — Music heard — He goes to door — Stops —*]

5   [*Int. Bogey cell MS — GYPO climbing up on ledge — Music heard — He pushes against ceiling board with back — Puffs as he pushes hard —*]

6   [*Int. Bogey Hole MS — DENNIS standing at door — Back to camera — Hesitating — Music heard — He removes bar from door —*]

7   [*Int. Bogey cell MCS — GYPO on ledge — Pushing against ceiling board — Puffing — Music heard —*]

8   [*Int. Bogey Hole MS — DENNIS standing at door — Takes gun from pocket — Opens door quickly — Starts into cell — Music heard —*]

9 [*Int. Bogey cell MCS — Hole seen in ceiling — Music heard — Crash heard as boards fall into cell — Camera pans down to left revealing* DENNIS *standing in doorway — He fires gun up to right — Shots heard — He turns to left — Yelling —*]

DENNIS Commandant . . Bartley! He's gone!

10 [*Ext. Bogey Hole MS —* KERRIGAN *standing guard at foot of steps — Music heard —* GYPO *comes on in FG —* MAN *steps in front of him — Talking —*]

KERRIGAN Halt, who's that?

11 [*Ext. Bogey Hole MLS — Camera shooting down steps —* GYPO *below punches* MAN *in jaw — Knocking him flat — Music heard —* GYPO *runs up steps to FG —* MAN *firing after him —* GYPO *exits right FG —*]

12 [*Int. Bogey Hole MS —* DAN *standing on steps — Men running up steps rapidly to BG —* DAN *shouting at them — Music heard —*]

DAN Hurry up . . hurry up.

13 [*Ext. Bogey Hole MLS — Camera shooting down steps —* MAN *lying below on steps — Others running out of Bogey Hole —* MAN *firing to FG — Music heard —* BARTLEY *shouts at men —*]

BARTLEY Take him down below, lads. Come on, all of you. Down below.
[*Men pick up* KERRIGAN *— Start to carry him down steps —*]

14 [*Int. Bogey Hole MS —* DAN *coming on at right FG —* BARTLEY *and men running on down steps to him — Music heard —* BARTLEY *talks —*]

BARTLEY He got away, Dan. The fog is so thick you can't see your hand.
[*All talking at once indistinctly —*]
TOMMY The man is a devil, I tell you.
[*Two men carry* KERRIGAN *down steps —* DAN *sees them — Talks —*]
DAN Who's that?
BARTLEY It's Kerrigan . .
[*Men exit right FG with* KERRIGAN *—*]
BARTLEY . . his jaw is smashed to a jelly.
TOMMY That Gypo is an inhuman monster.
DAN We've got to work fast, lads . .

15 [*Int. Bogey Hole MCS — Camera shooting down at* DAN *talking to* MEN *— Music heard —*]

DAN . . if he reaches the Tans before we get him, we're finished. The whole movement's finished, you understand?
MEN Yes, Sir.
DAN Tommy, you and Daley cover the Tan's head-quarters, front and rear.
DALEY & TOMMY Right. Foga Balah!
[DENNIS *and* TOMMY *run up steps to FG — Exit —* DAN *talks to* MULHOLLAND *—*]
DAN Mulholland, you take the rest with you in the van and try to head him off before he gets to the river at Butt Bridge . .

16 [*Int. Bogey Hole MS — DAN at right FG — Back to camera — Talking to SLAT-
TERY — SLATTERY and men standing on steps — Music heard — *]

DAN . . Slattery, get reinforcements for Mulholland.
Now, jump to it and remember, we're done for if he gets away. Out you
go.

[*Men run up steps — All talking at once — DAN turns to right FG — Exiting — *]

[*Lap dissolve*]

17 [*Ext. street MS — GYPO coming along bldg to FG — Glancing about frightened —
Music heard — He runs to FG — Stops at corner of bldg — Music stops — Sound
of marching heard — He leans back against bldg — Nearly exits — *]

18 [*Ext. street MS — Soldiers crossing in BG to left — Marching heard — *]

19 [*Ext. bldg CU — GYPO leaning against bldg — Perspiration running down his face —
Marching and drums heard — *]

20 [*Ext. street MS — Soldiers marching across to left — Drums and marching heard — *]

21 [*Int. bldg CU — GYPO leaning against bldg — Perspiration running down face —
Marching and drums heard — Sound of drums fades out — GYPO starts to turn to
left — *]

22 [*Ext. bldg CS — GYPO turning to left — Sees vacant spot on wall of bldg — Music
heard playing "Medley" — Poster of FRANKIE appears on wall — Poster disappears as GYPO clutches at wall — Calling hysterically — *]

GYPO Frankie!

[*He exits right — Frightened — *]

[*Lap dissolve*]

23 [*Ext. entrance MS — GYPO running on in FG — Runs up steps — Music heard —
He stops at door — Looks around frightened — Opens door — Goes into hallway —
Opens inside door — Exits through doorway — *]

24 [*Int. hallway MS — Camera shooting down at stairs — Music heard — GYPO comes
on below — Looks about furtively — Camera follows him up steps — He turns out
light at top of stairs — Runs to door at left — Opens it — Starts through doorway — *]

25 [*Int. room MCS — GYPO coming on through doorway — Music heard — *]

KATIE (*off*) Gypo!

[*He closes door — Camera following him to left as he talks — Reveals KATIE at left — *]

GYPO They're after me, Katie.

KATIE Ah, ye put the heart cross-wise in me. Where
have ye been?

GYPO They're after me, but they're not goin' to get me.
We'll get away, you and me.

KATIE Gypo . . Shhh!

[*Camera follows her across to right — She locks door — He talks to her as she crosses
in front to left — *]

GYPO Where's the twenty pounds I gave ye?

KATIE What are you talking about? What's wrong with
you?

26 [*Int. room MCU* − GYPO *looking to left FG* − *Talks* − *Music heard* −]
GYPO   I done it for you. That's what I couldn't tell Gallagher. They wouldn't understand. You understand.

27 [*Int. room CU* − KATIE *looking up to right* − *Talks* − *Music heard* −]
KATIE   You did what? What have you done?

28 [*Int. room CU* − GYPO *looking to left FG* − *Talks* − *Music heard* −]
GYPO   I informed on Frankie.

29 [*Int. room MCS* − KATIE *looking at* GYPO *horrified* − *Talks* − *Music heard* −]
KATIE   Ah, Gypo . .
[*She sits down* − *Talking* −]
KATIE   . . may God have mercy on your soul.
GYPO   Katie, we'll get away. They won't get me. That's how I love ye, darling. I . . I . . sold out me own pal for ye . .
[*Camera follows him as he crosses in front of her to left* − *Talking* − *Sits down by fire* −]
GYPO   . . Ah, that's a lovely fire, a lovely fire.

30 [*Int. room CS* − KATIE *seated* − *Looking down to left* − *Sadly* − *Music heard* − *She talks* −]
KATIE   Lie and rest yourself.

31 [*Int. room CS* − GYPO *sitting in front of fire* − KATIE'S *hand on his shoulder* − *Music heard* − *He talks* −]
GYPO   Ah, this is good . .
[*Her hand exits right* −]
GYPO   . . good, ye don't know what it is to be runnin' around in the fog on a night like this . .
[*He turns to right* − *Talking* −]
GYPO   . . Katie . . Katie, sit down beside me, darling . .

32 [*Int. room CS* − GYPO *seated in front of fire* − KATIE *sitting down by him* − *Music heard* − GYPO *talking* − *He rests head on her lap* −]
GYPO   . . Oh, darling . . darling, you're the only one I can trust now. Do you love me, Katie?
KATIE   Yes, I love you, Gypo. I'll love ye when I'm clay. Ye don't know what ye've done to me. Ye don't know what ye've done to me. I'd lay my life down for you. Ye poor old blind boy.
[*She looks down at him sadly* − *Kisses him* −]

                 [*Lap dissolve*]

33 [*Int. room MS* − DAN *seated at right in front of fireplace* − MARY *standing at window in BG* − *Music heard* − MARY *turns toward* DAN − *Talks* −]
MARY   What time is it, Dan?
DAN   Half past five.
[*Door heard closing* − DAN *looks off to left* − *Talks* −]
DAN   Who's that?

REEL 10

1   [*Int. room CS* – MARY *standing at window* – MOTHER *seen outside on street* –
Music heard playing "Medley" – MARY *looks to right FG* – *Talks* –]

MARY   It's mother, going to church next door . .

[MOTHER *waves up at* MARY – *Goes to BG* – MARY *crosses to left of window* –
MOTHER *exits at right BG* – MARY *comes to right FG* – *Nearly exits* –]

2   [*Int. room MCS* – DAN *seated in front of fireplace* – MARY *coming on at left BG* –
Stops by his chair – *Talks* – *Music heard* –]

MARY   . . Dan, what if you don't find him? I'd die if I
lost you, too. I couldn't stand it.

DAN   Oh, I'm not thinking about myself, darling.
It's all the others. The movement . . it's Ireland. That poor fool knows
so blasted much.

MARY   If there was only something I could do. It's this
horrible waiting . .

[*She starts to kneel by his chair* –].

3   [*Int. room CS* – DAN *seated* – MARY *kneeling by him* – *Talking* – *Music
heard* –]

MARY   . . Can't I do anything?

DAN   Sure . .

[*He puts arm around her* – *Talking* –]

DAN   . . tell me you love me again.

MARY   I love you, Dan. I'll always love you, no matter
what happens. There'll never be anyone else.

4   [*Int. room MS* – DAN *seated* – MARY *kneeling by him* – *Music heard* – *Door at
left BG opening* – DAN *and* MARY *rise quickly* – TOMMY *comes on through doorway* – *Talking* –]

TOMMY   Commandant.

DAN   Yes.

TOMMY   She wants to see you. She insists on seeing you.

DAN   Who . . who?

TOMMY   She won't talk to a soul of us.

[KATIE *comes on through doorway followed by* BARTLEY –]

5   [*Int. room MCS* – KATIE *and two men standing at door* – DAN *and* MARY *at right* –
Backs partly to camera – KATIE *talks* – *Music heard* –]

KATIE   I'm Katie Madden. I'm Gypo Nolan's girl.

DAN   Shut the door.

[BARTLEY *and* TOMMY *exit through doorway* – *Closing door* – KATIE *goes to* DAN
as she talks –]

KATIE   Commandant . .

6   [*Int. room MCU* – KATIE *at left looking up at* DAN – *Talking* – *Music heard* –]

KATIE   . . I've come to beg of you on my knees. He
didn't know what he was doing. Ah, ye can't hurt him, if you know how it
was.

DAN You know what he did? There is a dead boy lying across the hall.

KATIE Yes, and I know why he did it, though he didn't know what he was doing. For me . . for me, I tell you. Oh, Almighty Father, forgive me for saying the words I did in anger. Shamin' him for his poverty and blamin' him for mine and puttin' the idea into his head. Forgive him . . forgive him. He didn't know what he was doin' . . Leave him go, Commandant, he'll be punishin' himself for the rest of his days and I with him.

DAN You're askin' something that's not within my power.

KATIE He'll never harm you again.

MARY (off) Dan!

[DAN *looks to right FG – Talking –*]

DAN Do you think the Tans will let him alone now? . .

[*He talks to* KATIE *–*]

DAN . . They'll drag everything he knows out of him. His own fear will drive him to them and make him a weapon to destroy us all.

KATIE I'll take him away.

DAN Please, Katie.

KATIE I swear . .

DAN Please . .

[DAN *starts to BG –*]

KATIE By all that's holy I will . .

7 [*Int. room MCS –* MARY *standing at table – Back partly to camera –* DAN *going to BG –* KATIE *comes to* MARY *– Talking – Music heard –*]

KATIE . . Ah, you're the one that's been hurt . .

8 [*Int. room CS –* KATIE *standing at table – Talking to* MARY *partly on at right FG – Back to camera – Music heard –*]

KATIE . . I'm not the kind of girl you are. There was a time when I was . .

9 [*Int. room CS –* MARY *standing at table – Listening as* KATIE *partly on at left FG – Back to camera – Talks – Music heard –*]

KATIE . . and I love Gypo no less for being what I am . .

10 [*Int. room CS –* KATIE *talking to* MARY *partly on at right FG – Back to camera – Music heard –*]

KATIE . . I can see by your eyes that you love him, too. Suppose it was his life you were beggin' for . .

11 [*Int. room MCS –* DAN *turning from window – Comes to FG as he listens – Music heard –*]

KATIE (off) . . wouldn't you be wantin' mercy then? And won't ye be givin' it to me now . .

12   [*Int. room CS — MARY standing at table — Looking to left — KATIE partly on at left
      BG — Back to camera — Talking — Music heard —]*
KATIE   . . a sinner?
[*MARY nods —]*

13   [*Int. room MCU — DAN looking to right FG — Music heard — He looks to left FG —
      Talks —]*
DAN   Where is Gypo now?

14   [*Int. room CS — KATIE standing at table — MARY partly on at right FG — Back to
      camera — Music heard — KATIE talks —]*
KATIE   Poor lad . .

15   [*Int. hallway CS — BARTLEY standing at door — Listening — Talks to TOMMY
      watching door in BG — Music heard —]*
BARTLEY   Listen.

16   [*Int. room CS — KATIE standing by table — Talks — MARY partly on at right FG —
      Back to camera — Music heard —]*
KATIE   He's in my room. The other side of the church.

17   [*Int. room CS — DAN standing at table — Music heard — He looks off to left as door
      is heard closing — He picks up coat — Starts to left — Camera following him —]*
MARY (*off*)   Dan!
[*KATIE comes on in FG — Stops DAN — Talking —]*
KATIE   Oh, tell me you'll be giving him a chancc.
There's no harm in him. He didn't know what he was doin' . .
[*DAN exits as camera follows KATIE to right revealing MARY — KATIE talks to her
pleadingly —]*
KATIE   . . Miss McPhillip, for the sake of your own
love, won't you be askin' him to give my man a chance?
[*DAN comes on at left — Talking —]*
DAN   Katie, Katie, this is no time for sentiment. This is
war. I tell you I gave Gypo the benefit of every doubt . . every chance.
He confessed. I didn't pass sentence on him. The court did. Don't you see
how helpless I am?
KATIE   Suppose it was your life you were begging for?
DAN   Oh, it is mine and the lives of hundreds of other
men who are fighting for what they believe in. Can't you see what you're
asking?
[*DAN goes to left BG — Exits — MARY turns to right — Exits — KATIE looks to left
BG — Talks hysterically —]*
KATIE   You won't do it. I see you won't do it. You
won't . .

18   [*Int. room MS — MARY kneels at right FG — Music heard —]*

19   [*Int. room MS — GYPO lying in front of fireplace — Sleeping — Music heard —]*

20   [*Int. hallway MS — Camera shooting down at TOMMY, DENNIS and DONAHUE coming*

upstairs – Music heard – TOMMY *points to door at left – They go to door slowly –*]

21 [*Int. room MCS –* GYPO *lying on floor sleeping – Music heard – He moves restlessly – Awakens – Looks up –*]

22 [*Int. hallway CS –* DENNIS *and two* MEN *standing at door – Music heard –* TOMMY *with back to camera – Whispers to* DENNIS *–*]

TOMMY   Come on now, Dennis, 'twas you that drew the match. Don't be afraid.

DENNIS   I'm not afraid.

23 [*Int. room MCS –* GYPO *lying on floor – Rises – Music heard – He looks about trapped as he hears whispering –*]

DONAHUE (*off*)   Ah, sure, he's not afraid.

TOMMY (*off*)   The door is locked.

DONAHUE (*off*)   Shall we force it open?

TOMMY (*off*)   It's locked, I tell you.

[GYPO *looks about – Calls helplessly –*]

GYPO   Katie, Katie!

[GYPO *picks up stove poker –*]

24 [*Int. hallway CS –* TOMMY *trying to open door –* DENNIS *whispers nervously –* DONAHUE *by them – Music heard –*]

DENNIS   I . . I can blow the lock off.

DONAHUE   Yes.

DENNIS   Shall I?

TOMMY   Yes, Go on . .

[TOMMY *steps back –* DENNIS *shoots at lock – Screams as he opens door –*]

DENNIS   Mother of God!

[*He starts into room –*]

25 [*Int. room MS –* DENNIS *coming on through doorway followed by* DONAHUE *– Music heard –* GYPO *at left strikes* DENNIS *over head – Knocks him down –* DONAHUE *fires at* GYPO *– Confusion as they struggle –* GYPO *thrusts him out through doorway –*]

26 [*Int. hallway MS –* TOMMY *standing at door – Back to camera –* DONAHUE *falls out of door – Falls over banister – Crashing onto stairs below –* TOMMY *fires into room –* GYPO *comes out – They roll over landing onto stairs below – Much confusion –*]

27 [*Int. stairway MS –* TOMMY *and* GYPO *falling downstairs – Music and confusion heard – They exit below –* GYPO *rising on in FG – Exits left FG –*]

28 [*Ext. entrance MS – Door opening –* GYPO *comes on – Closing door – Stops – Looks to FG frightened – Music heard – He yells as* BARTLEY *comes on at right FG – Back to camera –*]

GYPO   Bartley!

29 [*Ext. street CS –* BARTLEY *looking to FG – Gun and hand in pocket – He fires to FG several times – Exits right –*]

30 [*Int. room MCS – * MARY *and* KATIE *kneeling –* DAN *in BG at window –* KATIE
    talks horrified –]
KATIE   Gypo . .
[*They rise – Run to BG –* KATIE *screaming –*]
KATIE   . . Gypo!
[DAN *draws shade in BG – Music heard –* MARY *takes* KATIE *in her arms –*]

31 [*Ext. church MS –* GYPO *staggering on in FG – Music heard – He goes to BG
    toward church –*]

32 [*Ext. church MCS – Camera shooting down at* GYPO *walking along fence to left –
    Looking up to FG – Music heard – He exits left –*]

33 [*Ext. church MCS –* GYPO *coming on at right – Turns to FG wide-eyed – Music
    heard – He stops – Looks up to FG smiling –*]

34 [*Ext. church MLS –* GYPO *standing at entrance of church – Back to camera –
    Music heard – He staggers toward church doors –*]

35 [*Ext. doors CS –* GYPO *coming on in FG – Crashes through doorway revealing
    interior church – Music heard – He falls to floor –*]

36 [*Int. church MCU –* MOTHER *seated – Music heard – She turns – Looks to
    FG –*]

37 [*Int. church MCU –* GYPO *lying on floor – Music heard – He rises slowly –
    Painfully – Clutching at pew – He looks to FG –*]

38 [*Int. church MS –* GYPO *rising slowly – Music heard –* MOTHER *seated in pew in
    BG – He staggers toward her – Falls at her feet –*]

39 [*Int. church CU –* GYPO *looks up to FG –*]

40 [*Int. church CU –* MOTHER *looking up to left FG –*]

41 [*Int. church CU –* GYPO *looking up to right FG – Beads of sweat on face – He
    talks –*]
GYPO   'Twas I informed on your son, Mrs. McPhillip.
Forgive me.

42 [*Int. church CU –* MOTHER *looking up to left FG – Nods – Talks quietly – Music
    heard –*]
MOTHER   Ah, Gypo, I forgive ye. You didn't know what
you were doing. You didn't know what you were doing.

43 [*Int. church CU –* GYPO *looking to right FG gratefully – Beads of sweat on face –
    Music heard – Tears in eyes –*]

44 [*Int. church MS –* MOTHER *seated –* GYPO *kneeling by her – Rises slowly –
    Music heard – Choir heard singing indistinctly –* GYPO *staggers toward FG –
    Talks –*]
GYPO   Frankie, Frankie! Your mother forgives us.
[*He clutches side in agony – Sinks to floor – Exits –* MOTHER *reaches out toward
him –*]

[*Fade out*]

45   *[Fade in – Title #1 – Music and chorus heard –]*

The End

                                                           [Lap dissolve]

46   *[Title #2 – Music and chorus heard –]*

Radio
Pictures
Reg. U. S. Pat. Off.

                                                           [Fade out]

The End

STUDENTS' BIBLIOGRAPHY OF MODERN DRAMA

THE number of books on modern drama has grown to huge proportions. The subject has had so many points of interest, and it has been so dynamic over a period of sixty years, that it has called forth hundreds of articles, studies, and books on every aspect of drama and the theatre. Many of these works served a useful purpose but were outmoded by the onrush of the movement. Others have been superseded by later, more complete treatises. The following list is a beginner's guide to the most helpful books on the drama, the playwrights, and the theatre.

BIBLIOGRAPHY

ANDERSON, MAXWELL. The Essence of Tragedy. Washington, 1939.

ANDREWS, CHARLTON. The Drama of Today. Philadelphia, 1913.

BAHR, HERMAN. Expressionism (trans. by R. F. Gribble). London, 1925; Munich, 1920.

BAILLY, A. Maeterlinck (trans. F. Rothwell). London, 1931.

BELL, A. F. G. Contemporary Spanish Literature. New York, 1925.

BITHELL, JETHRO. Life and Writings of Maurice Maeterlinck. London, 1930.

BLOCK, ANITA. The Changing World in Plays and Theatre. Boston, 1939.

BROWN, JOHN MASON. Broadway in Review, New York, 1940.

—— The Modern Theatre in Revolt. New York, 1929.

—— Two on the Aisle: Ten Years of the American Theatre in Performance. New York, 1938.

CARTER, HUNTLEY. The New Spirit in the Russian Theatre, 1917–1928. New York, 1929.

—— The New Spirit in the European Theatre, 1914–1924. New York, 1926.

CHANDLER, FRANK W. The Contemporary Drama of France. Boston, 1925.

—— Modern Continental Playwrights. (Excellent survey, with complete bibliographies.) New York, 1931.

CHARQUES. R. D. (ed.). Footnotes to the Theatre. London, 1938.

CLARK, BARRETT H. Eugene O'Neill, The Man and His Plays. New York, 1929 and 1936.

—— A Study of the Modern Drama (Revised ed.). New York, 1936.

COATS, R. H. John Galsworthy as a Dramatic Artist. New York, 1926.

CORDELL, RICHARD. W. Somerset Maugham. New York, 1937.

CUNLIFFE, JOHN W. Modern English Playwrights. New York, 1927.

DAHLSTRÖM, CARL E. W. L. Strindberg's Dramatic Expressionism. Ann Arbor, 1930.

DANA, H. W. L. Handbook on Soviet Drama. New York, 1938.

DICKINSON, THOMAS H. An Outline of Contemporary Drama. Boston, 1927.

—— The Contemporary Drama of England. Boston, 1931.

—— (ed.). The Theatre in a Changing Europe. New York, 1937.

DUHAMEL, GEORGES. Paul Claudel, le philosophe, le poète, l'ecrivain, le dramaturge. Paris, 1913.

—— Paul Claudel, suivi de propos critiques. Paris, 1919.

DUKES, ASHLEY. The Youngest Drama. Chicago, 1924.

ELOESSER, ARTHUR. Modern German Literature. New York, 1933.

FAY, W. G., and CARSWELL, CATHERINE. The Fays of the Abbey Theatre. New York, 1935.

FLANAGAN, HALLIE. Shifting Scenes of the Modern European Theatre. New York, 1928.

FLEXNER, ELEANOR. American Playwrights: 1918–1938. New York, 1938.

FYFE, H. H. Sir Arthur Wing Pinero's Plays and Players. London, 1930.

GASSNER, JOHN. Masters of the Drama. New York, 1940.

GERHARDI, WILLIAM. Anton Chekhov, A Critical Study. London, 1923.

GILDER, ROSAMOND. A Theatre Library. A Bibliography of One Hundred Books Relating to the Theatre. New York, 1932.

GOLDBERG, ISAAC. The Drama of Transition: Native and Exotic Playcraft. Cincinnati, 1922.

GORELIK, MORDECAI. New Theatres for Old. New York, 1941.

GOSSE, EDMUND. Life of Henrik Ibsen. New York, 1907.

GREGORY, LADY. Our Irish Theatre, A Chapter of Autobiography. New York, 1913.

HALASZ, GEORGE. Ferenc Molnar, the Man Behind the Monocle. New York, 1929.

HAMILTON, CLAYTON MEEKER. The Theory of the Theatre. (Consolidated ed.) New York, 1939.

HENDERSON, ARCHIBALD. European Dramatists. New York, 1926.

—— G. Bernard Shaw: His Life and Works. New York, 1932.

HOUGHTON, NORRIS. Moscow Rehearsals; an Account of Methods of Production in the Soviet Theatre. New York, 1936.

KAUN, ALEXANDER. Maxim Gorky and His Russia. New York, 1931.

KOHT, HALDAN. The Life of Ibsen. 2 vols. New York, 1931.

KOMMISARJEVSKY, THEODORE. Myself and the Theatre. New York, 1930.

KRUTCH, JOSEPH WOOD. The American Drama Since 1918. New York, 1939.

LEWISOHN, LUDWIG. The Modern Drama. An Essay in Interpretation. New York, 1915.

—— The Drama and the Stage. New York, 1922.

MCCLINTOCK, LANDER. The Contemporary Drama of Italy. Boston, 1920.

MCGILL, V. J. August Strindberg, the Bedevilled Viking. New York, 1930.

MALONE, ANDREW E. The Irish Drama. New York, 1929.

MANTLE, ROBERT BURNS. Contemporary American Playwrights. New York, 1939.

MARKOV, PAVEL. The Soviet Theatre. New York, 1935.

MARRIOTT, JAMES WILLIAM. Modern Drama. London, New York, 1934.

MARROT, H. V. The Life and Letters of John Galsworthy. New York, 1936.

MARSAN, JULES. Tendances: Théâtre d'hier et d'aujourd'hui. Paris, 1926.

MARTINO, P. Le Naturalisme Français (1870–1895). Paris, 1923.

—— Parnasse et Symbolisme (1850–1900). Paris, 1928.

MAUGHAM, W. SOMERSET. The Summing Up. New York, 1938.

MILLER, ANNA IRENE. The Independent Theatre in Europe, 1887 to the Present. New York, 1931.

MODERWELL, H. K. The Theatre of Today. New York, 1927.

MORGAN, A. E. Tendencies of Modern English Drama. New York, 1924.

NEMIROVITCH-DANTCHENKO, VLADIMIR. My Life in the Russian Theatre. Boston, 1936.

NICOLL, ALLARDYCE. British Drama. Revised ed. New York, 1933.

O'HARA, FRANK HURBURT. Today in American Drama. Chicago, 1939.

PALMER, JOHN. Studies in the Contemporary Theatre. Boston, 1927.

PERRIN, E. S-M. Introduction a l'oeuvre de Paul Claudel. Paris, 1926.

QUINN, ARTHUR HOBSON. A History of the American Drama from the Civil War to the Present Day. New York, 1936.

ROBINSON, LENNOX (ed.). The Irish Theatre: Lectures Delivered during the Abbey Theatre Festival held in Dublin in August, 1938. London, 1939.

SARGENT, DANIEL. Four Independents. New York, 1935. (Chapter on Claudel.)

SAYLER, OLIVER M. Our American Theatre. New York, 1923.

SCHNEIDER, M. Expressionism in Drama. Stuttgart, 1920.

SÉE, EDMOND. Le théâtre français contemporain. Paris, 1933.

SKINNER, RICHARD DANA. Eugene O'Neill, A Poet's Quest. New York, 1935.

SMITH, HUGH ALLISON. Main Currents of Modern French Drama. New York, 1925.

SOBEL, BERNARD. The Theatre Handbook and Digest of Plays. (Useful but contains high percentage of errors.) New York, 1940.

STARKIE, WALTER. Luigi Pirandello, 1867–1936. New York, 1937.

SUBERVILLE, JEAN. Edmond Rostand: Son Théâtre, Son Oeuvre Posthume. Paris, 1922.

SUTTON, GRAHAM. Some Contemporary Dramatists. London, 1924.

SYMONS, ARTHUR. The Symbolist Movement in Literature. New York, 1917.

TAYLOR, UNA. Maurice Maeterlinck, a Critical Study. London, 1914.

THOMPSON, VANCE. Strindberg and His Plays. New York, 1921.

TOLLER, ERNST. I Was a German. London, 1934.

TOUMANOVA, PRINCESS NINA ANDRONIKOVA. Anton Chekhov, The Voice of Twilight Russia. New York, 1937.

VERNON, FRANK. The Twentieth-Century Theatre. London, 1924.

VITTORINI, DOMENICO. The Drama of Luigi Pirandello. Philadelphia, 1935.

WARREN, L. A. Modern Spanish Literature. New York, 1929.

WAXMAN, SAMUEL MONTEFIORE. Antoine and the Théâtre Libre. Cambridge, 1926.

WEIGAND, HERMANN J. The Modern Ibsen. New York, 1925.

WIENER, LEO. The Contemporary Drama of Russia. Boston, 1924.

WILSON, NORMAN SCARLYN. European Drama. London, 1937.

WINTHER, SOPHUS KEITH. Eugene O'Neill, A Critical Study. New York, 1934.

ZUCHER, A. E. Ibsen, the Master-Builder. New York, 1929.

PLAYS BY BRITISH AND IRISH DRAMATISTS REPRE-SENTED IN THIS VOLUME

THERE is some unresolved confusion in the dating of plays. This arises from the fact that usually there is a date of composition, a date of production, and a date of publication. Much work is yet to be done before this ideal three column chronology can be accurately set down. This bibliography lists the earliest date of the play, unless there is some good reason for choosing a production date, as when the date of composition is doubtful, or when the production date is of landmark importance.

LORD DUNSANY

The Glittering Gate (1909)
King Argimenes and the Unknown Warrior (1911)
The Gods of the Mountain (1911)
The Golden Doom (1912)
The Lost Silk Hat (1913)
The Tents of the Arabs (1914)
A Night at an Inn (1916)
The Queen's Enemies (1916)
Fame and the Poet (1918)
The Prince of Stamboul (1918)
The Laughter of the Gods (1919)
The Murderers (1919)
A Good Bargain (1920)
If Shakespeare Lived Today (1920)
The Compromise of the King of the Golden Isles (1920)

If (1921)
The Flight of the Queen (1923)
Cheezo (1923)
Alexander (1925)
The Old King's Tale (1925)
The Evil Kettle (1925)
The Amusement of Khan Kharuda (1925)
Lord Adrian (1925)
Mr. Faithful (1927)
The Jest of Hahalaba (1927)
Atalanta in Wimbledon (1928)
The Raffle (1928)
The Journey of the Soul (1928)
In Holy Russia (1928)
His Sainted Grandmother (1928)
The Hopeless Passion of Mr. Bunyon (1928)
The Old Folk of the Centuries (1930)

JOHN GALSWORTHY

The Silver Box (1906)
Joy (1907)
Strife (1909)
Justice (1910)
The Little Dream (1911)
The Pigeon (1912)
The Eldest Son (1912)
The Fugitive (1913)
The Mob (1914)
Hall-Marked (1914)
A Bit o' Love (1915)
The Little Man (1915)
The Foundations (1917)
The Skin Game (1920)

Defeat (1920)
The First and the Last (1921)
Punch and Go (1921)
A Family Man (1921)
The Sun (1921)
Windows (1922)
Loyalties (1922)
The Forest (1924)
Old English (1924)
The Show (1925)
Escape (1926)
Exiled (1929)
The Roof (1929)

SOMERSET MAUGHAM

Schiffbrüchig (in German) (1902)
A Man of Honor (1903)
Mlle. Zampa (1904)

Lady Frederick (1907)
Jack Straw (1908)
Mrs. Dot (1908)

The Explorer (1908)
Penelope (1909)
The Noble Spaniard (from the French) (1909)
Smith (1909)
The Tenth Man (1910)
Grace (or Landed Gentry) (1910)
Loaves and Fishes (1911)
The Perfect Gentleman (from the French of Molière) (1913)
The Land of Promise (1914)
Caroline (produced as The Unattainable) (1916)
Our Betters (1917)

Love in a Cottage (1918)
Caesar's Wife (1919)
Home and Beauty (Too Many Husbands) (1919)
The Unknown (1920)
The Circle (1921)
East of Suez (1922)
The Camel's Back (1924)
The Letter (1927)
The Constant Wife (1927)
The Sacred Flame (1928)
The Breadwinner (1930)
For Services Rendered (1932)
Sheppey (1933)

ALLAN MONKHOUSE

Mary Broome (1912)
The Education of Mr. Surrage (1913)
Four tragedies (Resentment; Reaping the Whirlwind; The Hayling Family; The Stricklands) (1913)
War Plays (Shamed Life; Night Watches; The Choice) (1916)
The Conquering Hero (1923)
First Blood (1924)

The Grand Cham's Diamond (1924)
Sons & Fathers (1925)
O Death Where Is Thy Sting? (1926)
The King of Barvender (1927)
The Rag (1928)
Nothing Like Leather (1930)
Paul Felice (1930)
Cecilia (1932)

ARTHUR W. PINERO

£200 a Year (1877)
Two Can Play at That Game (1877)
The Comet (1878)
Daisy's Escape (1879)
Hester's Mystery (1880)
Bygones (1880)
The Money-Spinner (1880)
Imprudence (unpublished) (1881)
The Squire (1881)
Girls and Boys (unpublished) (1882)
The Rector (unpublished) (1883)
Lords and Commons (unpublished) (1883)
The Rocket (1883)
Low Water (unpublished) (1884)
In Chancery (1884)
The Magistrate (1885)
The Schoolmistress (1886)
The Hobby Horse (1886)
Dandy Dick (1887)
Sweet Lavender (1888)
The Weaker Sex (1888)
The Profligate (1889)
The Cabinet Minister (1890)
Lady Bountiful (1891)
The Times (1891)
The Amazons (1893)
The Second Mrs. Tanqueray (1893)

The Notorious Mrs. Ebbsmith (1895)
The Benefit of the Doubt (1895)
The Princess and the Butterfly (1897)
Trelawney of the Wells (1898)
The Gay Lord Quex (1899)
Iris (1901)
Letty (1903)
A Wife Without a Smile (1904)
His House in Order (1906)
The Thunderbolt (1908)
Mid-Channel (1909)
Preserving Mr. Panmure (1911)
The "Mind-the-Paint" Girl (1912)
The Widow of Wasdale Head (1912)
Playgoers (1913)
The Big Drum (1915)
Mr. Livermore's Dream (1917)
The Freaks (1917)
Monica's Blue Boy (a play without words, unpublished) (1918)
Quick Work (1919)
The Enchanted Cottage (1922)
A Seat in the Park (1922)
Dr. Harmer's Holidays (1924)
A Private Room (1926)
Child Man (1928)
A Cold June (1932)

JOHN MILLINGTON SYNGE

The Shadow of the Glen (1903)
Riders to the Sea (1904)
The Well of the Saints (1905)

The Playboy of the Western World (1907)
The Tinker's Wedding (1909)
Deirdre of the Sorrows (1910)